Criminal Justice

Contemporary Literature in Theory and Practice

Series Editors

Marilyn McShane

Frank P. Williams III

California State University – San Bernardino

Garland Publishing, Inc.

New York & London

1997

Contents of the Series

Drug Use and Drug Policy

Edited with introductions by
Marilyn McShane
Frank P. Williams III
California State University – San Bernardino

GARLAND PUBLISHING, INC.
New York & London
1997

Library of Congress Cataloging-in-Publication Data

Drug use and drug policy / edited with introductions by Marilyn
McShane, Frank P. Williams III.
p. cm. — (Criminal justice ; vol. 2)
Includes bibliographical references.
ISBN 0-8153-2511-8 (alk. paper)
1. Narcotics, Control of—United States. 2. Drug abuse and crime—
United States. 3. Drug abuse—United States—Prevention. 4. Drug
abuse—Treatment—Government policy—United States. I. McShane,
Marilyn D., 1956– . II. Williams, Franklin P. III. Series:
Criminal justice (New York, N.Y.) ; vol. 2.
HV5825.D77725 1997
363.4'5'0973—dc21 96-37307
CIP

Printed on acid-free, 250-year-life paper
Manufactured in the United States of America

Contents

Series Introduction

At the turn of the century the criminal justice system will be confronting many of the same demons, although the drugs of choice, the technology of crime fighting, and the tools and techniques of management have evolved. Despite the enhancements of twenty-first century technologies, funding, crowding, and public concerns about effectiveness continue to be discussed in "crisis" terminology, and criminal justice scholars remain somewhat cynical about the ability to reform the criminal justice system. This pessimistic attitude may be fueled, at least in part, by the drama of real-life crime that plays itself out in courtrooms, newspapers, and talk shows across America every day. The combination of emotional political maneuvering and campaigning on punitive rhetoric assures us of a steady stream of legislation designed to reflect a zero tolerance for crime.

Testing the constitutional limits of our times, we have devised even more ways of imposing severe punishments, seizing assets, reinstituting corporal punishment, and penalizing the parents of delinquents. We have also created new offenses, such as recruiting someone into a gang, transmitting "indecent" images on the Internet, and knowingly passing along a disease. Despite these politically popular solutions to crime, problems of enforcement, equity, and affordability remain. The public's preoccupation with "what works?" and quick fixes to crime problems have never been reconciled with the more realistic ideas of "what can we live with?" and long-range preventive solutions.

Ironically, despite public perceptions that crime has been getting worse, statistics seem to indicate that the rates for virtually all offenses are either no worse than they were in 1980 or are now lower. Drug-related arrests and the rates for most forms of adult crime (in particular, most violent crimes) have actually decreased. Against this general backdrop, the rate of violent juvenile crime appears to be the sole increasing trend, leading to a situation in which risks of victimization by violent crime have also increased for juveniles. The contrary public perception of a massive and growing crime problem has created a situation in which the number of cases of juveniles transferred to adult court has increased, as has the proportion of inmates facing life sentences, life in prison without parole, and death sentences. On the other hand the risk of incarceration also appears to have increased for minorities, directing attention to questions of racial and economic disparity in the quality of protection and justice available in this country today.

While all this has been happening over the past two decades, academia has rather quietly developed an entire discipline dedicated to the study of crime and the criminal justice system. Though crime policy is still dominated largely by political interests swayed by public opinion, crime scholars have begun to have an impact on how crime is viewed and what can be done about it. While this impact is not yet a major one, it continues to gain weight and shows promise of some day achieving the influence that economists have come to wield in the realm of public policy-making.

Simultaneously with this growing scholarship comes an irony: academic journals, the major repository of scholarly wisdom, are being discontinued by libraries. Access, although ostensibly available in an electronic form, is decreasing. In many academic libraries, only a few select, "major" journals are being retained. Clearly, there is so much being done that the few "top" journals cannot adequately represent current developments (even if these journals were not focused in particular directions). Thus, the knowledge of the field is being centralized and, at the same time, more difficult to obtain. The multitude of criminal justice and criminology degree programs now face an interesting dilemma: how do students and faculty access current information? Or put differently, how does the field distribute its hard-gained knowledge to both assure quality of education and pursue efforts to offset the often ill-informed myths of public opinion?

Electronic access would appear to be one possible answer to the problem, especially with libraries facing yet another squeeze, that of space. On-line and media-based (CD-ROM) services promise quick availability of periodical literature, but remain futuristic. The costs associated with downloading articles can approximate the cost of the journal subscriptions themselves and many libraries cannot afford to participate in on-line periodical services. In addition, there is the inconvenience of translating the electronic images into the user's still-preferred paper-based format. Moreover, the paper-based serendipitous value of "browsing" decreases as only specific articles appear on-line, without surrounding materials.

An alternative solution is to review the range of journals and collect the "best" of their articles for reprinting. This is the approach this criminal justice periodical series has taken. By combining both depth and scope in a series of reprints, the series can offer an attractive, cost-effective answer to the problem of creating access to scholarship. Moreover, such a compact format yields the added advantage that individuals searching for a specific topic are more likely to experience the serendipity of running across related articles. Each of the six volumes presents a comprehensive picture of the state of the art in criminal justice today and each contains articles focused on one of the major areas of criminal justice and criminology: Police, Drugs, Criminological Theory, Corrections, Courts, and Victimology. Each volume contains approximately twenty articles.

The Article Selection Process

The articles appearing in the series represent the choices of the editors and a board of experts in each area. These choices were based on four criteria: (1) that the articles were from the time period of 1991–1995, (2) that they represent excellent scholarship, (3) that collectively they constitute a fair representation of the knowledge of the period, and (4) that where there were multiple choices for representing a knowledge area, the articles appeared in journals that are less likely to be in today's academic library holdings. We believe the selection criteria and the board of experts were successful in compiling truly representative content in each topical area. In addition, the authors of the selected articles constitute a list of recognizable experts whose work is commonly cited.

Finally, there is one other advantage offered by the volumes in this series: the articles are reprinted as they originally appeared. Scholars using anthologized materials are commonly faced with having to cite secondary source pages because they do not have access to the original pagination and format. This is a difficulty because mistakes in reprinting have been known to alter the original context, thus making the use of secondary sources risky (and synonymous with sloppy scholarship). In order to overcome this problem, the series editors and the publisher made the joint decision to photoreproduce each article's original image, complete with pagination and format. Thus, each article retains its own unique typesetting and character. Citations may be made to pages in confidence that the reproduced version is identical in all respects with the original. In short, the journal article is being made available exactly as if the issue had been on a library shelf.

We believe this series will be of great utility to students, scholars, and others with interests in the literature of criminal justice and criminology. Moreover, the series saves the user time that would have otherwise been spent in locating quality articles during a typical literature search. Whether in an academic or personal library, the only alternative to this collection is having the journals themselves.

EDITORIAL ADVISORY BOARD

Volume Introduction

Beginning in 1984, with President Reagan's campaign to make drugs an issue for the nation, citizens have been bombarded with the evidence of America's "drug problem" and the war against drugs. The way our political leaders have responded to the drug problem is now infamous. To refer to our existing methods of controlling drug use as punitive runs the risk of making an understatement. Absolute prohibition, "zero tolerance" of drugs, and maximum penalties are the bywords of the day. Moreover, for those in the criminal justice system, drugs and drug offenders have become a mainstay of business. They have contributed to massive budgetary increases for law enforcement agencies, constitute a major portion of the workload for prosecutors, defense attorneys, and court systems, and have swelled incarcerated populations beyond all existing capacities. Indeed, more than 60 percent of federal inmates are currently incarcerated for drug offenses. The only question seems to be whether we can build prisons fast enough.

Public Opinion

While there are several reasons for the emergence of the drug war, it is relatively clear that the public was manipulated into viewing drugs as a major problem in America. Two of the articles in the volume treat this issue. Katherine Beckett's article analyzes the relationship between drugs, crime statistics, and public opinion. She argues that social and political actors interpret information for the media which then serves to construct public opinion on drug issues.

Philip Jenkins explores the social history of a drug "panic," that of crystal methamphetamine in 1989–90. He demonstrates that local political problems in Hawaii played an important role in creating public opinion which then spread to the national scene. Jenkins views the short life of the panic as largely the difficulty of supporting a local problem on a national level.

Law Enforcement

The war on drugs has been largely a law enforcement war. The political response of prohibition and enforcement has resulted in the lion's share of drug war resources being channeled into various law enforcement agencies. Such an overemphasis created latent problems for many agencies. Using his 25 years of experience as a DEA agent, Michael Levine critiques the actions of the Reagan/Bush administrations in the war on drugs. Scrutinizing the lenient treatment given to government figures in the Iran/Contra affair, he describes U. S. involvement in Costa Rican cocaine trafficking. Levine also questions the 1992 Supreme Court decision that gave law enforcement authorities the right to enter other countries and abduct violators of U.S. drug laws (the Iranian government immediately proclaimed a similar right for violators of Islamic law).

Asset forfeiture has been another controversial weapon in the war against drugs. Mitchell Miller and Lance Selva use a 12-month observational study to highlight the problem of case selection based on seizure policies. They note that the result is that police erroneously concentrate on cases with little social benefit and frequently without any serious criminal activity, primarily to generate forfeiture income.

Courts and Law

With the effort to control drug use, legislation was the name of the game and every legislator strove to have his or her name on a bill to demonstrate a politically advantageous "hard on crime" stance. As one might expect, hastily and ideologically constructed laws can have undesirable side effects. James Halsted discusses new anti-drug statutes and demonstrates that wrongful convictions and sentencing inequities have resulted. With the advent of new "trafficking" terminology, conviction is easier and trafficking is assumed through the quantity of drugs in a defendant's possession. In addition, those convicted of trafficking are mandatorily punished more severely than defendants convicted of equally serious non-drug felonies.

Corrections and Drug Treatment

When it comes to drug offenses, the public is in a punitive mood and demanding of prison time for drug users and traffickers. Alternatives have been discussed mostly on a superficial level. Annual federal drug-fighting budgets have been approximately 70 percent law-enforcement-related with the remainder split between prevention, treatment, and research. Todd Clear, Val Clear, and Anthony Braga suggest that the currently favored one-size-fits-all incarceration approach to drug offenders ignores years of drug treatment research and wastes resources in an era of prison overcrowding. They propose four different strategies to create more effective alternatives for drug offenders.

Susan Ennett, Nancy Tobler, Cristopher Ringwalt, and Robert Flewelling examine evaluations of the preeminent drug education program—DARE. They use meta-analysis to review eight of the more rigorous DARE evaluations for immediate effects. Not surprisingly, the authors find that DARE is not as successful as other programs emphasizing social and general competencies with interactive teaching methods for short-term prevention. They conclude that DARE's limited influence on behavior is in direct contrast to its popularity and prevalence.

While drug treatment has a long history and an extensive research literature, the same cannot be said of drug treatment within the criminal justice system. Gregory

Falkin, Michael Prendergast, and Douglas Anglin argue that a substantial portion of offenders in the system need drug treatment but also need a wide variety of comprehensive services as well, including assistance with housing, health care, jobs, and education. The authors contend that a number of initiatives, such as deferred prosecution and transitional programs, may insure offenders seek out and stay in the programs that will prevent recidivism.

Crime and Drugs

The relationship between drugs and crime is assumed by most of the public to be a given. For those who are familiar with the literature, though, the relationship is anything but simple. Duane McBride and Clyde McCoy provide an overview of the problems of establishing the existence of a drugs/crime relationship and suggest some research strategies that might improve our analyses and conclusions. While there is strong empirical evidence of a relationship, they conclude that the relationship is not a simple one and that each probably affects the other. Further, they note that there are theoretical reasons for believing that drugs and crime emerge from the same causal mechanisms. The literature seems to suggest that drug treatment should be more readily available and economic opportunities should be increased in order to affect the problem.

Jim Inciardi, Duane McBride, Clyde McCoy, and Dale Chitwood examine a sample of crack and cocaine users in Miami, asking about their criminal behavior. They found little support for a relationship between crime and crack use, except to show that most of the drug users and dealers were selling and distributing primarily to support their own habits.

A reading of the drug literature makes it seem as if the drug trade is a male occupation. Jeffrey Fagan interviews 311 females to dispel the male-only myth. He finds that they are involved extensively in both drug and non-drug crimes. Females tend to hold lower status positions in the cocaine and crack industry, but are less exploited than in the heroin trade of the 1960s.

The issue of sellers using their own drugs is explored by Dan Waldorf in a study of San Francisco gangs. Crack sellers normally did not use the drug, but gang members who sold marijuana, powdered cocaine, and heroin were likely to use those drugs. Waldorf's information also demonstrates that African-American gang members were less likely to use drugs than gang members of other racial categories.

Explaining Drug Use

Why people use drugs and why they involve themselves in illegal trafficking is no mystery in the ideology of many citizens: these people are simply bad, have poor family values, and have chosen to engage in such behaviors. Under these explanations, one simply makes a rational choice not to use or sell drugs—it's that simple. Of course, those who have studied drug use and abuse and criminal behavior know the answers are not that obvious; indeed, they are complex. Eloise Dunlap and Bruce Johnson review social conditions from 1960 to 1992 as a method of explaining the emergence of crack cocaine. They argue that major macro-level conditions—housing abandonment, ghettoization, economic decline, job loss, and homelessness—are to blame for creating inner-city problems and micro-level consequences for those living there. Generated by these macro-level factors, economic marginality and unstable households facilitate drug use and conflict.

In another article, Ralph Weisheit looks at a rarely explored phenomenon: rural drug use. His study of rural marijuana growers and law enforcement agencies suggests that there are major differences between rural and urban drug cultures. He concludes that research and theory need to be more sensitive to these differences, particularly local culture differences, in order to understand the drug problem.

Measurement Issues

Estimating the incidence and prevalence of drug use is a particularly thorny problem for drug researchers and policy-makers. Although there are various methodologies, by far the most common is self-reporting through surveys or interviews. Michael Fendrich and Yanchun Xu probe the validity of self-report information through comparison with urine test results among juvenile arrestees in a national study. They find that self-report validity varies by race and ethnicity, by type of drug, and by the time-frame implied by the question. Thus, self-reports of drug usage in criminal justice settings may be suspect.

Drug Policy

The dominant policy of the recent drug war has been to interdict drug supplies at their source. Other policies, and variations on the existing one, have been suggested but largely untried. Using the example of Colombian cartels, Robert Filippone demonstrates the difficulty of winning the drug war primarily through a supply-reduction strategy. He explains the Medellin cartel organization and operations, arguing that the degree of influence and pervasiveness of cocaine production in the lives of Colombian society make it unlikely that significant inroads will occur.

One potential drug policy that is often-mentioned and produces heated debates is decriminalization or legalization of certain drugs. A prominent advocate of decriminalization, Ethan Nadelmann, argues that the harm from current drug policies could not possibly be worse under various policy alternatives, including drug decriminalization. Reviewing the various arguments, Nadelmann explores the drug legalization debate and attempts to identify a middle-ground position that minimizes the threats and fears of legalization critics. Based on the concept of harm reduction, he proposes a restricted distribution system that would balance interests between the extremes of prohibitionists and supermarket models.

Taking a middle position in the argument over the drug control policy, Mark Kleiman argues not for a continuation of existing prohibition policies but for a policy in between prohibition and legalization. He explores society's grudging toleration of vice and drugs, the definition of vice, and the problems of attempting to control vice and drugs through policy. Discussing the alcohol regulation model and describing possibilities of taxation and restrictions on buyers and sellers, Kleiman proposes similar models for the grudging toleration of marijuana and cocaine.

Peter Reuter, in an overview article, documents the punitive nature of U. S. drug policy. He analyzes drug war strategies based on the ideological classifications of hawks, owls, and doves. He then discusses the difficulties of assessing the effectiveness of current drug policies, particularly measurement issues such as estimating prevalence and cost and operationalizing dependence.

* * * * * *

We would like to thank the board members of this volume who assisted us in the selection of articles. Because only a limited number of pieces could be selected for this volume, an expanded bibliography is included to provide additional materials. Articles marked with an asterisk (*) are included in this anthology.

Anglin, Douglas and Yih-Ing Hser (1991). Criminal justice and the drug abusing offender: Policy issues and coerced treatment. *Behavioral Sciences and the Law* 9: 243–67.

Ball, John (1991). The similarity of crime rates among male heroin addicts in New York City, Philadelphia and Baltimore. *Journal of Drug Issues* 21(2): 413–27.

*Beckett, Katherine (1994). Setting the public agenda: "Street crime" and drug use in American politics. *Social Problems* 41(3): 425–47.

Belenko, Steven, Jeffrey Fagan, and Ko-lin Chin (1991). Criminal justice responds to crack. *Journal of Research in Crime and Delinquency* 28: 55–74.

Boyum, David and Mark Kleiman (1995). Alcohol and other drugs. Chapter 13 of *Crime,* edited by James Wilson and Joan Petersilia. San Francisco: ICS Press.

Brown, Joel and Jordan Horowitz (1993). Deviance and deviants: Why adolescent substance use prevention programs do not work. *Evaluation Review* 17(5): 529–55.

Caulkins, Jonathan (1992). Thinking about displacement in drug markets: Why observing change of venue isn't enough. *Journal of Drug Issues* 22(1): 17–30.

*Clear, Todd, Val Clear, and Anthony Braga (1993). Correctional alternatives for drug offenders in an era of overcrowding. *Prison Journal* 73(2): 178–98.

Davey, Joseph (1994). The death of the Fourth Amendment under the Rehnquist court: Where is original intent when we need it? *Journal of Crime and Justice,* 17(1): 129–48.

Davis, Robert, Barbara Smith, and Arthur Lurigio (1994). Court strategies to cope with rising drug caseloads. *Justice System Journal* 17(1): 1–18.

*Dunlap, Eloise and Bruce Johnson (1992). The setting for the crack era: Macro forces, micro consequences (1960–92). *Journal of Psychoactive Drugs* 24: 307–21.

*Ennett, Susan, Nancy Tobler, Christopher Ringwalt, and Robert Flewelling (1994). How effective is drug abuse resistance education? A meta-analysis of project DARE outcome evaluations. *American Journal of Public Health* 84(9): 1394–1401.

*Fagan, Jeffrey (1994). Women and drugs revisited: Female participation in the cocaine economy. *Journal of Drug Issues* 24: 179–226.

Fagan, Jeffrey and Ko-lin Chin (1991). Social processes of initiation into crack. *Journal of Drug Issues* 21: 313–34.

*Falkin, Gregory, Michael Prendergast, and Douglas Anglin (1994). Drug treatment in the criminal justice system. *Federal Probation* 58(3): 31–36.

*Fendrich, Michael and Yanchun Xu (1994). The validity of drug use reports from juvenile arrestees. *International Journal of the Addictions* 29(8): 971–85.

*Filippone, Robert (1994). The Medellin cartel: Why we can't win the drug war. *Studies in Conflict and Terrorism* 17(4): 323–44.

French, Michael (1995). Economic evaluation of drug abuse treatment programs: Methodology and findings. *American Journal of Drug and Alcohol Abuse* 21(1): 111–35.

French, Michael and Gary Zarkin (1992). Effects of drug abuse treatment on legal and illegal earnings. *Contemporary Policy Issues* 10(2): 98–110.

Giglio, Ernest (1991). Drug testing: Constitutional and policy implications. *Criminal Justice Policy Review* 5(1): 1–16.

Goldkamp, John (1994). Miami's treatment drug court for felony defendants: Some implications of assessment findings. *Prison Journal* 74(2): 110–66.

Golub, Andrew and Bruce Johnson (1994). The shifting importance of alcohol and marijuana as gateway substances among serious drug users. *Journal of Alcohol Studies* 55: 607–14.

Golub, Andrew and Bruce Johnson (1994). Cohort differences in drug use pathways to crack among current crack abusers in New York City. *Criminal Justice and Behavior* 21(4): 403–22.

Guerra, Sandra (1992). Domestic drug interdiction operations: Finding the balance. *Journal of Criminal Law and Criminology* 82(4): 1109–61.

Haas, Kenneth (1993). Constitutional challenges to the compulsory HIV testing of prisoners and the mandatory segregation of HIV-positive prisoners. *The Prison Journal* 73 (3-4): 391–422.

*Halsted, James (1994). The anti-drug policies of the 1980s: Have they increased the likelihood for both wrongful convictions and sentencing disparities? *Criminal Justice Policy Review* 6(3): 207–28.

Hamid, Ansley (1992). The developmental cycle of a drug epidemic: The cocaine smoking epidemic of 1981–91. *Journal of Psychoactive Drugs* 24: 337–48.

*Inciardi, James, Duane McBride, Clyde McCoy, and Dale Chitwood (1994). Recent research on the crack/cocaine/crime connection. *Studies on Crime and Crime Prevention* 3: 63–82.

Jacobsen, Chanoch and Robert Hannemann (1992). Illegal drugs: Past, present, and possible futures. *Journal of Drug Issues* 22(1): 105–20.

Jamieson, Alison (1992). Recent narcotics and Mafia research. *Studies in Conflict and Terrorism* 15(1): 39–51.

Jenkins, Philip (1992). Narcotics trafficking and the American Mafia: The myth of internal prohibition. *Crime, Law and Social Change* 18(3): 303–18.

*Jenkins, Philip (1994). The "ice age" the social construction of a drug panic. *Justice Quarterly* 11(1): 7–31.

Johnson, Bruce, Eric Wish, James Schmeidler, and David Huizinga (1991). Concentration of delinquent offending: Serious drug involvement and high delinquency rates. *Journal of Drug Issues* 21(2): 205–29.

Johnson, Bruce, Andrew Golub, and Jeffrey Fagan (1995). Careers in crack, drug use, drug distribution, and nondrug criminality. *Crime and Delinquency* 41(3): 275–95.

Jones, Peter and John Goldkamp (1993). Implementing pretrial drug testing programs in two experimental sites: Some deterrence and jail bed implications. *Prison Journal* 73(2): 199–219.

Kasinsky, Renee (1994). Child neglect and "unfit" mothers: Child savers in the Progressive Era and today. *Women and Criminal Justice* 6(1): 97–129.

Kenlock, Timothy (1991). Does phencyclidine (PCP) increase violent crime? *Journal of Drug Issues* 21(4): 795–816.

Kingery, Paul, B. E. Pruitt, and Robert Hurley (1992). Violence and illegal drug use among adolescents: Evidence from the U. S. National Adolescent Student Health Survey. *International Journal of the Addictions* 27(12): 1445–64.

*Kleinman, Mark (1992). Neither prohibition nor legalization: Grudging toleration in drug control policy. *Daedalus* 121(3): 53–83.

Kraska, Peter, ed. (1992). *Altered states of mind: Critical observations of the drug war.* New York: Garland.

Kraska, Peter (1992). The processing of drug arrestees: Questioning the assumption of an ambivalent reaction. *Journal of Criminal Justice* 20(6): 517–25.

Krasnow, Diane-Michele (1992). To stop the scourge: The Supreme Court's approach to the war on drugs. *American Journal of Criminal Law* 19(2): 219–66.

Lengyel, Linda (1992). A new crime has been created: Ingestion of drugs during pregnancy. *Justice Professional* 7(1): 17–24.

*Levine, Michael (1993). "I volunteer to kidnap Oliver North." *Crime, Law and Social Change* 20(1): 1–12.

Lightfoot, Lynn and David Hodgins (1993). Characteristics of substance-abusing offenders: Implications for treatment programming. *International Journal of Offender Therapy and Comparative Criminology* 37(3): 239–50.

MacCoun, Robert, James Kahan, and James Gillespie (1993). A content analysis of the drug legalization debate. *Journal of Drug Issues* 23(4): 615–29.

Mason, Derek, Mark Lusk, and Michael Gintzler (1992). Beyond ideology in drug policy: The primary prevention model. *Journal of Drug Issues* 22(4): 959–76.

Matza, David and Patricia Morgan (1995). Controlling drug use: The great prohibition. Chapter 13 of *Punishment and Social Control,* edited by Thomas Blomberg and Stanley Cohen. New York: Aldine de Gruyter.

*McBride, Duane and Clyde McCoy (1993). The drugs-crime relationship: An analytical framework. *The Prison Journal* 73(3-4): 257–78.

*Miller, Mitchell, and Lance Selva (1994). Drug enforcement's double-edged sword: An assessment of asset forfeiture programs. *Justice Quarterly* 11(2): 313–35.

*Nadelmann, Ethan (1992). Thinking seriously about alternatives to drug prohibition. *Daedalus* 121(3): 85–132.

Orcutt, James and Blake Turner (1993). Shocking numbers and graphic accounts: Quantified images of drug problems in print media. *Social Problems* 40(2): 190–206.

Peak, Ken and Frankie Sue Del Papa (1993). Criminal justice enters the womb: Enforcing the "right" to be born drug free. *Journal of Criminal Justice* 21(3): 245–63.

Pollock, Joycelyn and Alida Merlo (1991). Against compulsory treatment: No "quick fix" for pregnant substance abusers. *Criminal Justice Policy Review* 5(2): 79–99.

Powers, Keiko, Dominique Hanssens and Yih-Ing Hser (1991). Measuring the long-term effects of public policy: The case of narcotics use and property crime. *Management Science* 37(6): 627–44.

*Reuter, Peter (1992). Hawks ascendant: The punitive trend of American drug policy. *Daedalus* 121(3): 15–52.

Ryan, Kevin (1994). Technicians and interpreters in moral crusades: The case of the drug courier profile. *Deviant Behavior* 15(3): 217–40.

Sheley, Joseph (1994). Drug activity and firearms possession and use by juveniles. *Journal of Drug Issues* 24(3): 363–82.

Skolnick, Jerome (1992). Rethinking the drug problem. *Daedalus* 121(3): 133–59.

Smith, George and Gloria Dabiri (1991). Prenatal drug exposure: The constitutional implications of three governmental approaches. *Seton Hall Law School Constitutional Law Journal* 2(1): 53–126.

Stephens, Richard and Thomas Feucht (1993). Reliability of self-reported drug use and urinalysis in the drug use forecasting system. *The Prison Journal* 73 (3-4): 279–89.

Sybille, Guy, Gene Smith, and P. M. Bentler (1994). The influence of adolescent substance use and socialization on deviant behavior in young adulthood. *Criminal Justice and Behavior* 21(2): 236–55.

Tobolowsky, Peggy (1992). Drugs and death: Congress authorizes the death penalty for certain drug related murders. *Journal of Contemporary Law* 18(1): 47–73.

*Waldorf, Dan (1993). Don't be your own best customer—drug use of San Francisco gang drug sellers. *Crime, Law and Social Change* 19(1): 1–15.

*Weisheit, Ralph (1993). Studying drugs in rural areas: Notes from the field. *Journal of Research in Crime and Delinquency* 30(2): 213–32.

White, Helene (1992). Early problem behavior and later drug problems. *Journal of Research in Crime and Delinquency* 29(4): 412–29.

Williams, Phil (1993). International drug trafficking: An industry analysis. *Low Intensity Conflict and Law Enforcement* 2(3): 397–420.

Winfree, L. Thomas, Christine Sellers, and Dennis Clason (1993). Social learning and adolescent deviance abstention: Toward understanding the reasons for initiating, quitting and avoiding drugs. *Journal of Quantitative Criminology* 9(1): 101–25.

Zimring, Franklin and Gordon Hawkins (1992). *The search for rational drug control.* New York: Cambridge University Press.

Setting the Public Agenda: "Street Crime" and Drug Use in American Politics*

KATHERINE BECKETT, *University of California, Los Angeles*

Social control issues such as "street crime" and drug use have received an extraordinary degree of political attention in the United States since 1964. In this article, I use OLS and other methods to identify which factors are associated with subsequent shifts in levels of public concern about crime and drugs. The results indicate that state claimsmaking activities, and to some extent, media initiative on these issues, are associated with public concern about "street crime" and drug use. This study provides support for "constructionist" accounts of the politicization of crime and drugs by demonstrating that it is the definitional activities of the state and the media, rather than the reported incidence of crime or drug use and abuse, that has shaped public concern regarding those issues.

Introduction

Crime and drug use have received unprecedented levels of political and public attention in recent decades. For example, the percentage of Americans identifying crime-related problems as the nation's most important increased from 5.6 percent in 1957 to 37.9 percent in 1971 (Stinchcombe et al. 1980). Similarly, the percentage reporting that drug abuse was the nation's most important problem jumped from 3 percent in 1986 to 64 percent in 1989 (Berke 1989). The increased visibility of these issues has had dramatic consequences, as the federal government and many state legislatures have adopted and implemented increasingly punitive crime and drug policies. As of 1989, the rate of incarceration in the United States was the highest in the world, and nearly half of those in federal prisons had been convicted of drug law violations (Mauer 1991).

How can the growth of public concern regarding these problems be explained? What accounts for the emergence of these issues on the political agenda? To many observers, the causal relationship between the increasing crime rate, growing public concern about crime, and the importance of "street crime" in national politics during the 1960s and early '70s seemed obvious (see Mayer 1992; Niemi, Mueller, and Smith 1989; Wilson 1975). In contrast, the reported incidence of drug use declined while the drug issue in national politics and public concern increased during the 1980s (see Jensen, Gerber, and Babcock 1991; Reinarman and Levine 1989). These two case studies therefore provide a unique opportunity to examine the relative impact of the reported incidence of crime and drug use and state and media initiative on public concern about crime and drugs. Was growing concern about crime in the 1960s and drugs in the 1980s a response to increases in the reported incidence of crime and drug use? Or were the claimsmaking activities of state actors and the media more important in setting the public agenda?

My focus, then, is on the process by which some members of the public came to define crime and drugs as the most important problems facing the nation. The data presented here,

* I would like to thank Bruce Weston, whose generosity, patience and expertise made this project possible. I am also grateful to Franklin Gilliam, Steve Herbert, William Roy, and Ivan Szelenyi for their instructive comments and suggestions. Correspondence to: Beckett, University of California Los Angeles, Department of Sociology, 405 Hilgard Ave., Los Angeles, CA 90024-1551.

derived primarily from OLS regression techniques, suggest that increased public concern around "street crime" and drug use cannot be explained in terms of the reported incidence of those phenomena. Instead, the definitional activities of state actors and the mass media have played a crucial role in generating public concern about "street crime" and drug use.

These findings are consistent with a substantial body of research that suggests that state elites and the mass media play a prominent role in the construction of social issues, and, as a result, in the generation and shaping of public concern around those issues (Bennett 1980; Edelman 1988; Hall et al. 1978; Iyengar and Kinder 1987; Jensen, Gerber, and Babcock 1991; Nelson 1984; Reinarman and Levine 1989). Social actors attempt to place issues on the public agenda by calling attention to them and defining them as subject to political action. Furthermore, as advocates of particular kinds of political arrangements and policies, state actors and others represent social issues in ways that imply the need for desired policy outcomes (Edelman 1988). As Lukes (1974) and others have pointed out, the ability to politicize issues in this way represents an important component of the exercise of power: the selection, omission, and framing of issues and events are crucial in shaping not only public opinion, but political debate and policy as well.

While other researchers have suggested that campaigns against crime and drug use are not explicable solely in terms of the incidence of those phenomena (Dickson 1968; Epstein 1973; Fishman 1978; Gordon 1990; Hall et al. 1978; Helmer 1975; Himmelstein 1973; Jensen, Gerber, and Babcock 1991; Klein 1983; Mark 1975; Morgan 1978; Reinarman and Levine 1989; Rosch 1985; Scheingold 1986, 1990), the importance of specifically state and media activity in shaping public concern has not been demonstrated using quantitative methods.[1] The findings presented here provide support for these "constructionist" arguments by demonstrating that public concern about "street crime" and drug use is not determined by the reported incidence of those phenomena. Furthermore, the results presented here suggest that public concern about crime and drugs is strongly associated with state initiative on those issues, and thus highlight the importance of the role of the state in the construction of social problems.

Historical Background

The control of crime, with the exception of a limited number of federal crimes (including most narcotics law violations), has been largely the responsibility of local law enforcement throughout U.S. history (Epstein 1977; McWilliams 1991). Bureaucratic efforts to create and enlarge the scope of the FBI during the 1920s and '30s played on widespread concern about crime and immigration, and the federal government's responsibility for crime increased somewhat during this period (Fogleson 1977; Walker 1977). After its initial appearance on the national political scene, however, the the salience of the crime issue attenuated. Crime did not re-emerge as a major political issue at the national level until the 1960s.

"Law and order" rhetoric first re-emerged in the South in the late 1950s as southern politicians called for a crackdown on "hoodlums" and "agitators" who challenged segregation and black disenfranchisement. The issue of crime was subsequently seized and given a place on the national political agenda by Barry Goldwater in his 1964 presidential campaign (Caplan 1973). Goldwater and other conservatives focused on "street crime" in particular and linked such crime to social unrest, permissive courts, and declining moral standards (Matusow 1974). "Street crime" is not a legal category, and as a result its precise meaning is ambiguous. This category was generally used to refer to crimes of violence committed by strangers. The discourse of "law and order" conflated political protest and ordinary crime, and

1. Jensen, Gerber, and Babcock (1991) use some quantitative measures (but not regression techniques) to support their argument that state actors provided the impetus for the institutionalization of drug use as a social problem.

resonated most with those most opposed to racial and social reform (Cohn, Barkan, and Halteman 1991; Corbett 1981; Furstenberg 1971; Stinchcombe et al. 1980). The emergence of the Watergate scandal in 1974 relegated the issue of "street crime" to the back pages, and public concern about crime subsequently dropped.

Conservative analyses of crime since the early 1970s have not deviated from Goldwater's early approach. The Reagan and Bush administrations' "get tough" agenda also focused on "street crime" rather than organized, white-collar or domestic crime. In addition, these administrations defined "street crime" as the consequence of declining moral standards (linked in turn to the expansion of the welfare state). But the Reagan administration gradually focused on drugs as the most important component and cause of "street crime." Indeed, drug use, a minor political issue in the late 1970s, was declared by President Bush to be "the most pressing problem facing the nation" by the late 1980s (Berke 1989). Later that same month a New York Times/CBS News Poll found that 64 percent of those polled identified drugs as the most significant problem in the United States. This percentage had risen from 3 percent in April of 1986, and was the highest recorded percentage since the poll began in 1976 (Berke 1989).

The Reagan and Bush administrations not only paid an unusual amount of attention to "the drug problem," but defined it in a particular way — as a criminal rather than a public health or social problem. This definition is important, as it implies that a certain kind of "solution" (increased law enforcement rather than job creation, drug treatment, or educational programs) is appropriate. The public, too, came to support increased law enforcement efforts, harsher sentences, and the contraction of civil rights for alleged drug offenders as the appropriate solution to the drug problem. For example, the percentage of Americans who felt that "testing workers in general" for drug use would be an unfair invasion of privacy declined from 44 percent in 1986 to 24 percent in 1989 (Berke 1989). Similarly, the percentage of Americans who felt that possession of small amounts of marijuana should be treated as a criminal offense increased from 43 percent in 1980 to 74 percent in 1988 (Gallup 1988).

How did the issues of "street crime" and drug use assume such a central place in the public agenda? What accounts for increased public concern regarding these issues? I outline two main theoretical approaches to this question below.

The Politicization of "Street Crime" and Drug Use: Two Contending Models

Two main explanations of the politicization of "street crime" can be identified in the existing literature. These models can also be applied to the more contemporary "War on Drugs."[2] Each approach specifies a different relationship between reported rates of crime/drug use, state and media initiative, and public concern about crime and drugs.

The Objectivist Model

According to the objectivist model, knowledge of objective conditions is a necessary and largely sufficient condition for the identification of a social problem: social problems are those phenomena which are problematic for social well-being (Manis 1974). While most objectivists recognize the definitional component of social problems (see, for example, Merton and

2. While many social scientists have attempted to account for the emergence of "drug scares" in U.S. history (see Dickson 1986; Epstein 1977; Helmer 1975; Himmelstein 1973; Mark 1975; Morgan 1978; Musto 1973), the Reagan/Bush "War on Drugs," because it is so recent, is relatively untheorized (some exceptions: Jensen, Gerber, and Babcock 1991; Reinarman and Levine 1989; Scheingold 1990).

Nisbet 1971), their emphasis is nonetheless on the nature and extent of those social conditions that are defined as problematic.

Specifically, objectivists argue that the increased incidence of "street crime" and drug use has led to increased public concern about those issues. In this view, the Nixon, Reagan, and Bush administrations' "get tough" approach to crime has been a response to public concern, itself a consequence of the increased incidence of crime. For example, one major analysis of trends in public opinion concludes that increased fear of crime and support for punitive measures "have been shaped largely by objective shifts in the level of criminal activity" (Niemi, Mueller, and Smith 1989:133). Similarly, Mayer (1992:274) claims that "rising crime rates led to growing public support for the death penalty and a tougher criminal justice system." The argument that there has been "an objective shift in criminal activity" is based on official crime statistics that suggest such a trend. Thus, while the theoretical premise of objectivism does not necessarily imply an acceptance of official statistics as an accurate reflection of the actual incidence of social phenomena, objectivists rely on such statistics for their information about social conditions. As a result, objectivists anticipate that these measures will be associated with public concern[3] (see Morganthau and Miller 1986; Niemi, Mueller, and Smith 1989).

Objectivist accounts of the crime and drug issues also tend to conflate objectivism with the pluralist assumption that state actors primarily react to, rather than attempt to shape, public opinion. For example, Wilson (1975:xvi) argues that "public opinion was well ahead of political opinion in calling attention to the rising problem of crime." This approach thus presumes that state initiative on the crime issue was a response to a prior increase in public concern about crime.

The following hypotheses can be derived from this model: first, the objectivist hypothesis (H1) anticipates a positive relationship between the reported incidence of crime/drug use and subsequent levels of public concern regarding these issues; second, the pluralist hypothesis (H2) predicts that shifts in the level of public concern *precede* corresponding shifts in the level of state anti-crime and anti-drug activity.

The Constructionist Model

The constructionist model emphasizes the social nature of assessments of those phenomena that are defined as social problems. For constructionists, reality is not known directly, but must be comprehended through "maps of meaning" or "frames" which select, order, and interpret that reality (Hall et al. 1978). These "frames" give meaning and coherence to events and phenomena (Gamson et al. 1992), including social problems. Because each issue frame has a different set of political implications, a variety of social actors may compete in sponsoring their preferred frames[4] (Edelman 1988; Gamson et al. 1992). In sum, constructionists emphasize the subjective, social and political dimension of social problems.

A constructionist account of the crime and drug issues anticipates that the public's assessment of the nature of those problems will be shaped by their popular representation. This approach therefore rejects the objectivist hypothesis (H1) that levels of public concern will necessarily correspond to the reported incidence of crime/drug use. Instead, the constructionist hypothesis (H3) anticipates a strong association between media and state claimsmaking activities on the one hand and levels of public concern on the other. However, there is some

3. I therefore use these statistics to test the objectivist hypothesis that the reported rate of crime/drug use shapes public concern around those issues.

4. The construction of meaning and the struggle to imbue public discourse around events and issues with this meaning is an ongoing political process. For this reason, media discourse may be fruitfully conceptualized as an independent rather than dependent variable (Gamson et al. 1992:385).

disagreement among constructionists about the nature of the relationship between public opinion and state initiative on social problems such as crime and drug use.

Cultural Versus Elite Constructionism

Culturalist constructionists argue that the tendency to focus on the most terrifying types of "predatory crime" and the desire for a "quick fix" to complex social problems lead the public to become concerned about crime and to embrace a punitive approach toward it (Rosch 1985; Scheingold 1986). This tendency is exacerbated by "amorphous stress" which intensifies in times of perceived social crisis. According to these theorists, "law and order" politics do not emanate from politicians or the media. Instead, such policies are a response to public concern and orientation: the implementation of punitive policies by the state primarily reflects the public's desire for scapegoats against whom "free-floating anger" and anxiety can be directed (Rosch 1985; Scheingold 1990). The politicization of crime and drugs, then, is largely the consequence of social, economic and political forces which cause insecurity among Americans.

In sum, culturalists reject the objectivist hypothesis (H1) that public concern about crime/drugs necessarily corresponds to the reported incidence of "street crime" or drug use (Gordon 1990; Rosch 1985; Scheingold 1986, 1990). However, like the objectivist model, culturalists anticipate that shifts in public concern will precede shifts in levels of state initiative (H2), as state initiative is assumed to be a response to public sentiments.[5]

Others working within the constructionist paradigm (e.g., Bennett 1980; Edelman 1988; Hall et al. 1978), however, reject this pluralist hypothesis. According to these theorists, public opinion is more accurately conceptualized as fluid and variegated than as fixed and monolithic (Bennett 1980; Edelman 1964). This fluidity of public opinion, combined with the "ambiguity of events" and the unequal distribution of motivation, organizational capacity, and resources, means that most public issues are brought into being by political elites (Bennett 1980). This inequality is exacerbated by the reliance of the media on "institutional" sources, which ensures that political elites enjoy a high degree of access to the media (Gans 1980; Hall et al. 1978; Hertsgaard 1988; Whitney et al. 1989). Thus, while the capacity of political elites to mobilize public opinion is not unlimited, "the general public is most often called on by interest groups and elites to participate in the debate about issues that have already been defined" (Bennett 1980:57).

The relationship between elite definitional activities and public concern is undoubtedly a reciprocal one; it is unlikely that state actors and other elites would persist in these activities if the public did not appear to be receptive to them. Public receptivity, however, is not the same thing as public initiative, and it may be possible to determine whether shifts in the level of public concern about crime or drugs precede or follow shifts in the level of state activity. Elite theorists' agenda-setting hypothesis (H4) predicts that shifts in the level of state initiative will precede shifts in the level of public concern.

In sum, two sets of competing hypotheses may be derived from these models. First, the objectivist hypothesis (H1) predicts that the reported incidence of crime/drug use will be strongly related to subsequent levels of public concern, while the constructionist hypothesis (H3) suggests that state initiative and media coverage shape public opinion. Second, the pluralist hypothesis (H2) anticipates that shifts in the degree of public concern precede corresponding shifts in levels of state activity, while the agenda-setting hypothesis (H4) predicts that state initiative drives public concern.

5. Mauss's (1975) argument that social problems may be conceptualized as a particular type of social movement is also based on this pluralist assumption.

Research Design

Data and Variables

Information regarding the crime rate was taken from the FBI's Uniform Crime Index (1964-1974) (victimization surveys were not administered nationally until 1972).[6] The rate of "violent crimes" (per 100,000 persons) as reported by the FBI was utilized as an indicator of the incidence of "street crime."

Data regarding the incidence of drug use were taken from the National Institute on Drug Abuse survey, "The Household Survey on Drug Abuse." The percentage of survey respondents age twelve and over reporting drug use in the past month was used as an indicator of the incidence of drug use. While DAWN (Drug Abuse Warning Network) data report the number of drug-related emergency room visits and therefore better capture the intensity of the drug problem (rather than the incidence of drug use), these data were not collected throughout the period studied here. In addition, methodological changes in NIDA's estimation procedures means that the DAWN data collected before and after 1990 are not comparable. These data will, however, be considered in the discussion.

The level of media initiative was derived from the Television News Index and Abstracts[7] for the drug case and the New York Times Index for the crime case.[8] The number of stories indexed under "crime in the U.S." for the crime case and "drug abuse" and "drug trafficking" for the case of drug use served as an indicator of the level of media initiative. Only those stories in which federal state actors were not quoted or cited as sources were included in this category. "Media initiative" thus includes the number of stories which did not cite state actors as their source of information.[9]

In contrast, the number of speeches, statements and other crime or drug related activities undertaken by federal state actors and reported in the mass media (*The New York Times* for the crime case; network television news for the drug case) was utilized as an indicator of state initiative.[10] The use of this indicator rests in part on the assumption that federal state actors have a relatively constant degree of access to the mass media, and that fluctuations in the reported level of state initiative therefore reflect variation in state rather than media practices. Empirical studies that demonstrate that the media tend to consistently rely on institutional sources provide support for this assumption (see Gans 1980; Hall et al. 1978;

6. The FBI Uniform Crime Index is based on the number of crimes reported to the police, and is therefore considered by some to be less reliable than the national victimization surveys. While the FBI's Uniform Crime Index indicated that the incidence of crime was increasing, evidence suggests that the increased reporting of crime accounts for at least a substantial portion of this increase (see O'Brien 1985; President's Commission on Law Enforcement and the Administration of Justice 1968). In addition, the degree of professionalization of police departments and political factors may influence police reporting to the FBI (O'Brien 1985). These data, then, probably overestimate the extent to which crime was increasing in the '60s and early '70s, and may reflect in part increased public awareness of crime. The fact that the crime rate may be endogenous to public concern about crime may upwardly bias statistical estimates of the association between the two.

7. To ensure consistency, I enumerated only those stories which appeared on the early weeknight broadcast of the network television news.

8. Because the Vandenderbilt Television News Abstracts began in 1968, it was not possible to analyze television news coverage of the crime issue.

9. Because I analyzed newspaper stories indexed under "crime in the U.S." and national television news broadcasts, less than 2 percent of the stories analyzed focused on the activities of the police and local state actors. These stories were therefore eliminated from the analysis.

10. Because indexing procedures may vary from year to year, indexes are an imperfect measure of media coverage. Furthermore, because the abstracts offered for each story are incomplete, it is possible that some stories which covered state initiatives were included in the category "media initiative." However, it is unlikely that the abstracts for items in which state initiative figured prominently failed to mention that state activitity. (To the extent that less prominent state initiatives were omitted in the indexing process, the association between state initiative and subsequent public concern may be underestimated).

Hertsgaard 1988; Whitney et al. 1989). Furthermore, I assume that in order for state definitional activities to have an impact on public opinion, they must be made public by the mass media.

This indicator of state initiative was the best available option for other more practical reasons. First, no alternative indicator which simultaneously reflects the activities of the various groups which comprise the federal state — administration officials, legislators, and bureaucrats — exists. Second, while budget outlays have been used as indicators of state activity in historical analysis (see Mann 1986), government expenditures generally increase or decrease annually. In contrast, dramatic shifts in public opinion frequently occured in less than a month. The association between shifts in annual expenditures and the more short-term fluctuations in public opinion, therefore, is weak. Last, legislative activity varies dramatically depending on whether it is an election year or not, and is therefore a less desirable indicator of state activity.

Information regarding the dependent variable — public concern — was derived from the Gallup Poll and the New York Times/CBS News Polls. Both of these are national public opinion polls which ask the open-ended question "What do you think is the most important problem facing the nation?" on a fairly regular basis. The percentage of respondents identifying "crime," "juvenile delinquency" or "the breakdown of law and order" in the crime case, and "drugs" or "drug use" in the drug case as the "most important problem facing the nation" served as the indicator of public concern.

In the drug case (1985-1992), there were 25 polls taken in which this question was asked (n=25). Twenty-nine such polls were taken in the crime case (1964-1974) (n=29). These polls were taken at three- to five-month intervals. The periodization of these case studies was designed to capture the rise and fall of public concern around each issue: these cases could not be extended without including lengthy periods in which the dependent variable (public concern) remained at or close to zero.

Analysis

To test the objectivist hypothesis (H1) that public opinion is associated with the reported incidence of crime/drug use, and the constructionist hypothesis (H3) that such concern is associated with state and media initiative, the effects of the explanatory variables were estimated using OLS regression techniques for each of the two cases.[11] These explanatory variables were measured in terms of their average rate in the three- to five-month period preceding the public opinion poll; the (non-lagged) regression results thus indicate the level of association between these variables and *subsequent* levels of public concern. I also estimated these regressions with a lag of 1 (6-10 months) and 2 (9-12 months) in order to assess the extent to which the explanatory variables were associated with delayed shifts in the level of public concern.[12] Given the uncertainty associated with small samples such as those analyzed here, I employed bootstrap resampling techniques and used the distribution of these bootstrap replications to determine the significance of the original coefficients.[13]

11. Although the data analyzed are longitudinal, the residuals are not serially correlated. Time series techniques are therefore unnecessary.

12. The single equation models used here assume a one-way causal relationship between the explanatory and dependent variables. It is likely, however, that the dependent variable also influences the independent variables. These models thus tend to overestimate the effects of the independent variable; the results should be interpreted with this upward bias in mind.

13. In regression models, the bootstrap technique involves resampling rows from a matrix of regression coefficients in order to assess the significance of these coefficients. This technique provides a means by which the uncertainty associated with statistical estimates may be assessed, and is particularly useful where the sampling distribution is not normal or sample sizes are small.

The time series of each of the variables are depicted in Figures 1-8 below, and indicate that short-term fluctuations in all the variables except crime/drug use were quite pronounced. Because I am primarily interested in identifying those factors associated with short-term fluctuations in public concern, the regression results presented here are based on an analysis of the differenced data. Differencing is a technique used to remove the linear trend from the data. With the linear trend removed, the regression coefficients estimate the association between short-term fluctuations in the explanatory and dependent variables.

Adjudication between the pluralist (H2) and agenda-setting (H4) hypotheses requires that the relationship between public concern and state initiative be more clearly discerned. The existence of simultaneity bias between these two variables indicates that their relationship is a reciprocal one: state initiative and public concern are largely mutually reinforcing. Statistical techniques designed to estimate the effects of reciprocal causal relationships make an elaborate set of assumptions about the data, and as a result may introduce significant specification errors. Furthermore, the statistical properties of the techniques which propose to estimate reciprocal causal effects in small samples are unknown. Given these difficulties, I utilize a more straightforward case study method to explore the relationship between shifts in the level of public opinion and state initiative over time.

Figure 1 • ***Public Concern About Crime***

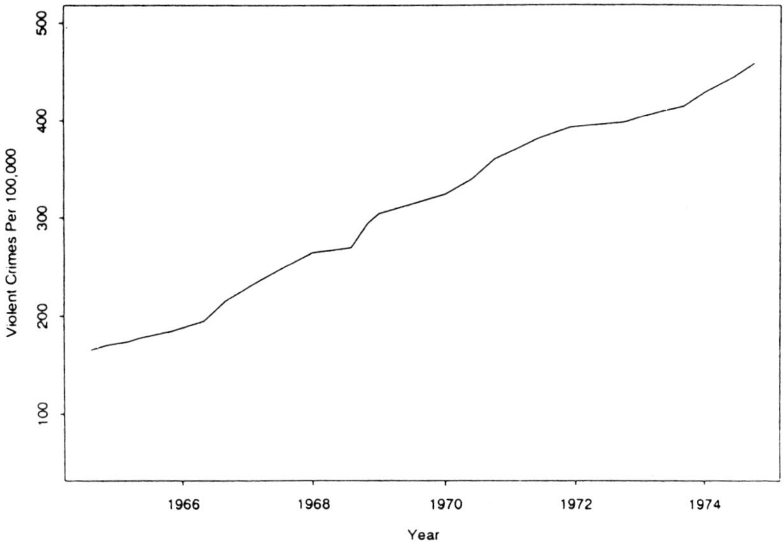

Figure 2 • ***Crime Rate***

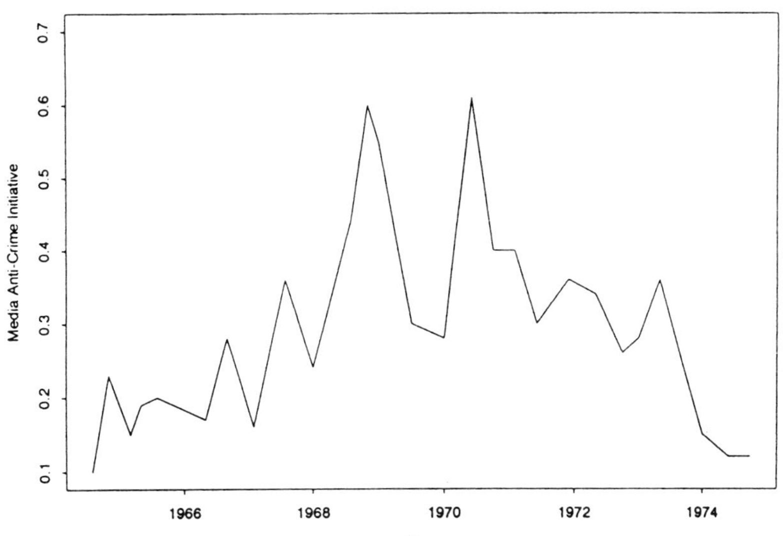

Figure 3 • ***Media Coverage of the Crime Issue***

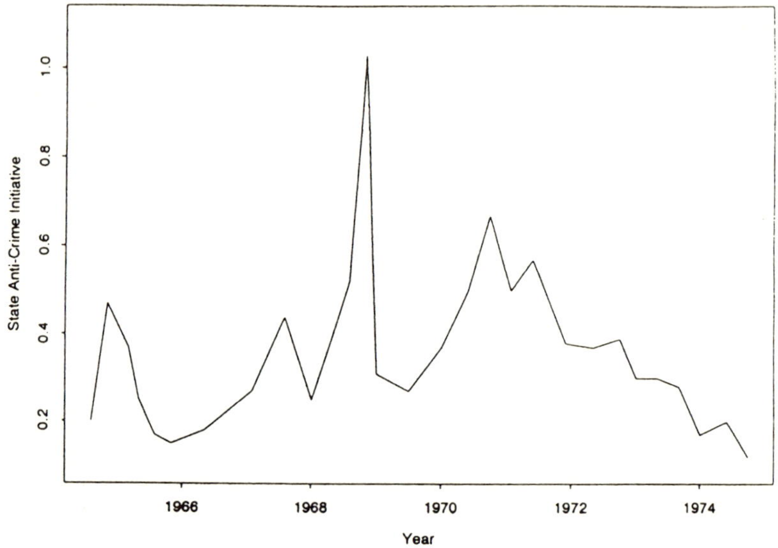

Figure 4 • *Anti-Crime Initiative*

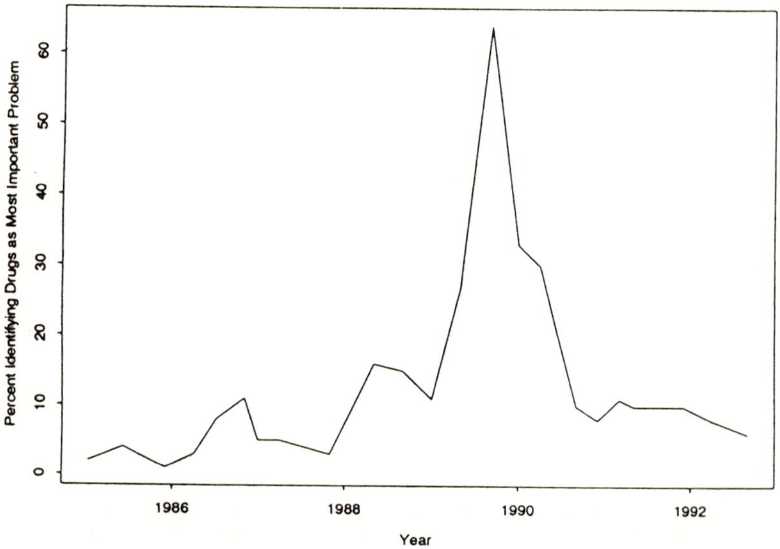

Figure 5 • *Public Concern About Drugs*

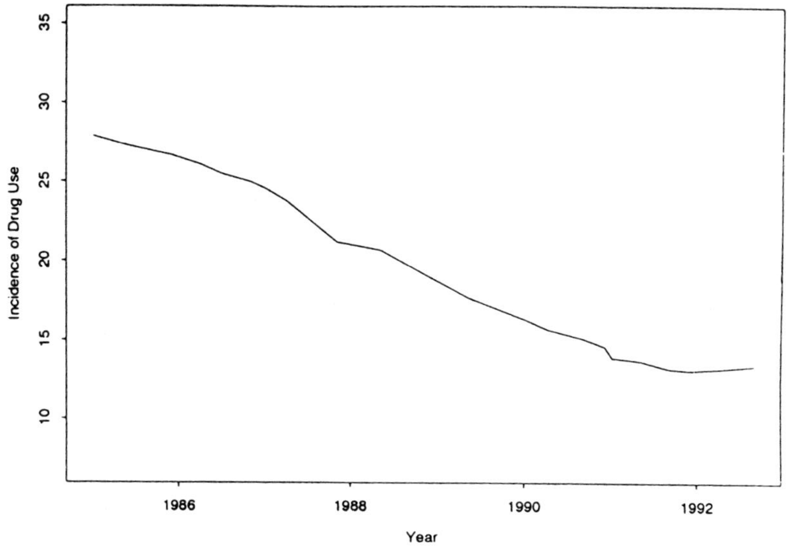

Figure 6 • ***Incidence of Drug Use***

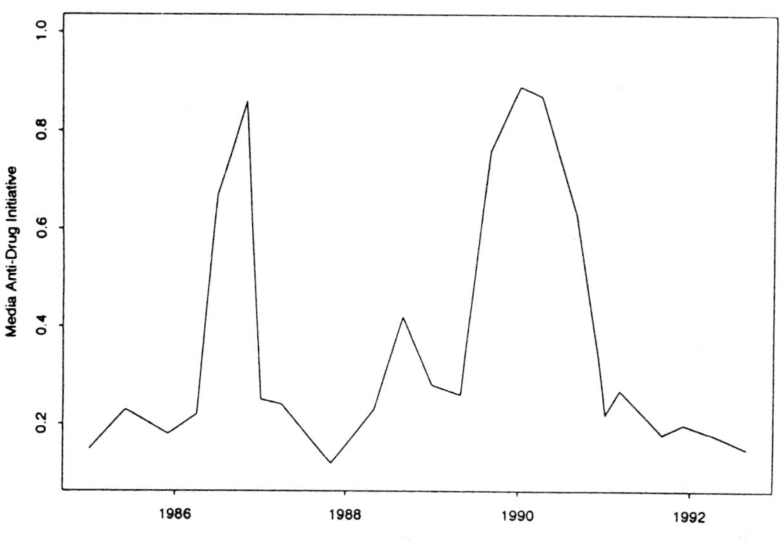

Figure 7 • ***Media Coverage of the Drug Issue***

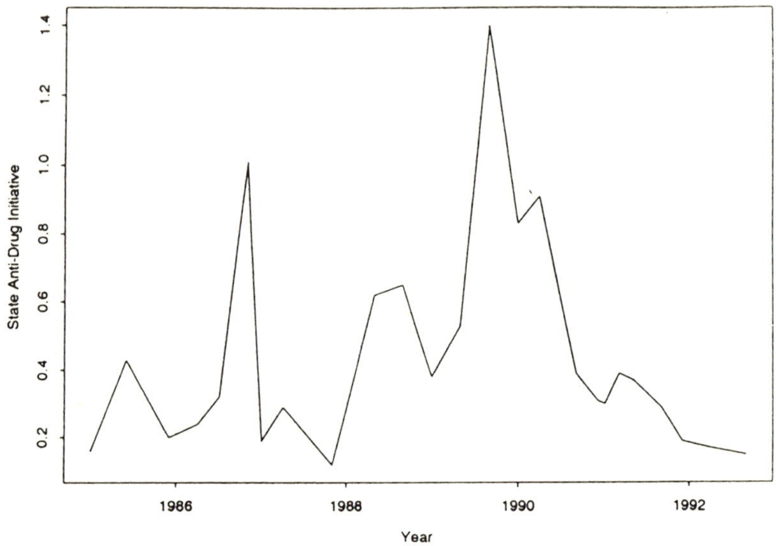

Figure 8 • ***State Anti-Drug Initiative***

Results

The regression results provide significant support for the constructionist hypothesis (H3). In the crime case, both state and media initiative are significantly associated with public concern about crime, while in the drug case only state initiative is significantly associated with public concern. The reported incidence of crime/drug use is not significantly associated with subsequent public concern about those phenomena. In addition, the analysis of the case studies indicates that shifts in the level of state initiative precede rather than follow corresponding shifts in public opinion, and thus provide support for the agenda-setting hypothesis (H4) rather than the pluralist hypothesis (H2). In general, the results provide support for the view that state and media definitional activities play a crucial role in shaping public opinion.

The Objectivist and Constructionist Hypotheses

The results of the OLS regressions are presented in Tables 1 and 2. The unstandardized coefficient for each variable is shown, and the standard error appears beneath it in parentheses.

The results of the OLS analysis of the crime case indicate that media and state initiative are associated with subsequent levels of public concern about crime. These relationships are consistent over time: state and media continue to be significantly and positively associated with public concern when an extended time period is analyzed.

The regression coefficients may be interpreted in the following manner. The coefficient for the crime rate (in Column 1) is –.0077: for every unit increase in the crime rate, the odds that a person would identify crime as the nation's most important problem would decrease $e^{-.0077}$ or 1.007 times. A unit increase in media and state initiative, according to the regression

Table 1 • *Crime Rate, Media and State Initiative, and Public Concern About Crime, 1964-1974*

Variables	*Lag=0 (3-5 months)*	*Lag=1 (6-10 months)*	*Lag=2 (9-15 months*
Intercept	−.1090	.111	.1079
	(.1322)	(.1301)	(.129)
Crime rate	−.0077	−.0067	−.005
	(.011)	(.013)	(.022)
Media initiative	1.2504*	1.3103**	1.2107*
	(.5547)	(.497)	(.5372)
State initiative	1.3711**	1.3511**	1.2721**
	(.3509)	(.3364)	(.3409)
Adjusted R^2	.5649	.5866	.5712

Notes:
* p < .05   ** p < .01   *** p < .001

Table 2 • *Rates of Drug Use, Media and State Initiative, and Public Concern About Drugs, 1985-1992*

Variables	*Lag=0 (3-5 months)*	*Lag=1 (6-10 months)*	*Lag=2 (9-15 months*
Intercept	.0541	.0622	.0619
	(.1736)	(.1811)	(.179)
Drug use	.0096	.0082	.014
	(.2178)	(.1917)	(.2077)
Media initiative	.0594	.0781	.0999
	(.7459)	(.699)	(.6781)
State initiative	1.8393***	1.762***	1.1221**
	(.4551)	(.446)	(.4997)
Adjusted R^2	.6337	.6291	.6009

Notes:
* p < .05   ** p < .01   *** p < .001

coefficients, means that respondents would be $e^{1.25}$ and $e^{1.37}$, or 3.49 and 3.94 (respectively) times more likely to identify crime as the nation's most important problem.

In the drug case, the results indicate that neither the incidence of drug use nor media initiative on the drug issue are significantly related to subsequent public concern about drug use. State initiative on this issue, however, is positively and significantly related to subsequent increases in public concern about drugs. The regression coefficients may be interpreted in the following manner. According to the results presented in Column 1, a single unit increase in the rate of drug use would lead to an increase of e^{0152} (1.015) in the odds that a respondent would identify drugs as the nation's most important problem. A unit increase in media and state initiative would increase the odds that a person would respond in this manner by e^{0295} and $e^{1.861}$ (1.29 and 6.43) times respectively.

Although diagnostics indicate that the residuals are normally distributed in both cases, the sample sizes are relatively small. In order to assess the uncertainty that may therefore be associated with these coefficients, I generated 500 bootstrap replications of these coefficients. Figures 9-11 and 12-15 depict the distribution of these replications for each case.

For the crime case, the state and media regression coefficients as predicted by the null hypothesis (0) fall outside the range of the 95 percent confidence interval, and the regression

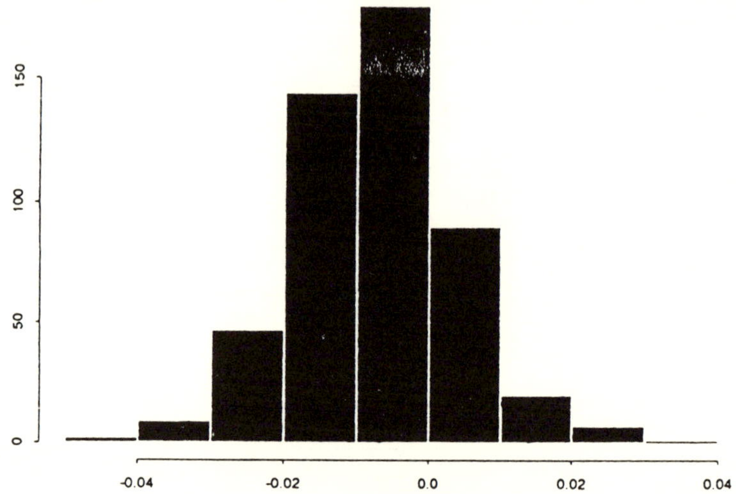

Figure 9 • ***Bootstrap Replications of Crime Rate Coefficient***

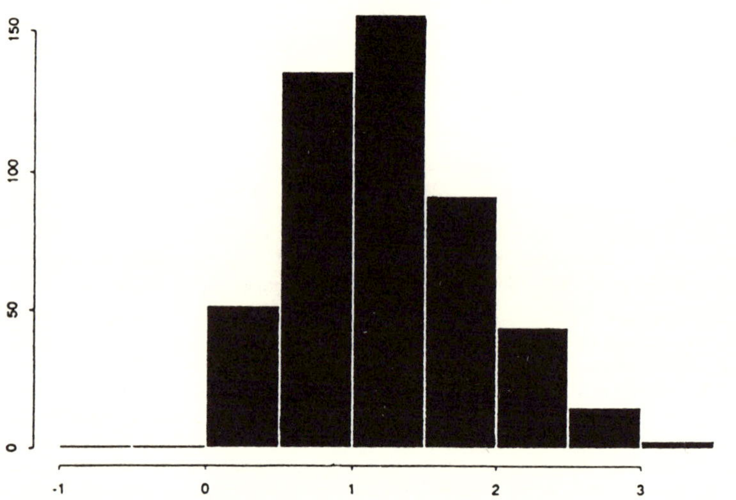

Figure 10 • ***Bootstrap Replications of Coefficient for Media Crime Coverage***

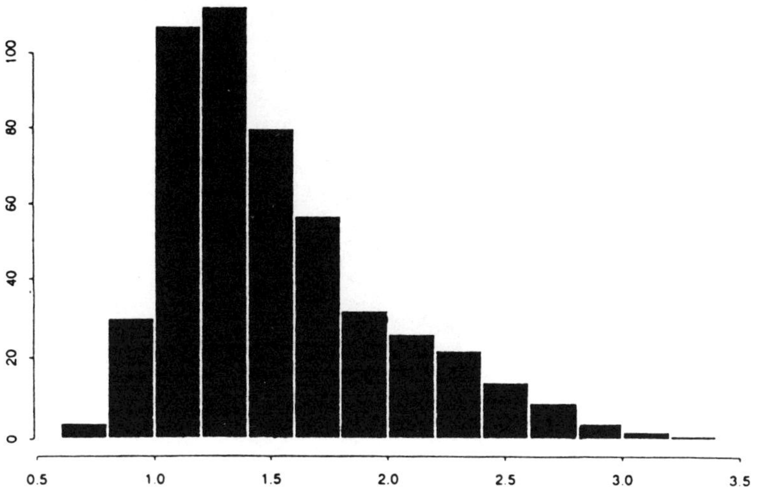

Figure 11 • ***Bootstrap Replications of Coefficient for State Anti-Crime Initiative***

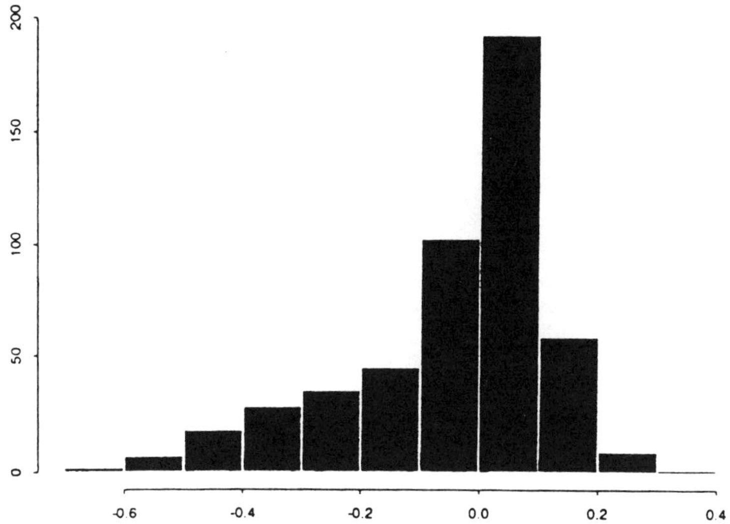

Figure 12 • ***Bootstrap Replications of Drug Use Coefficient***

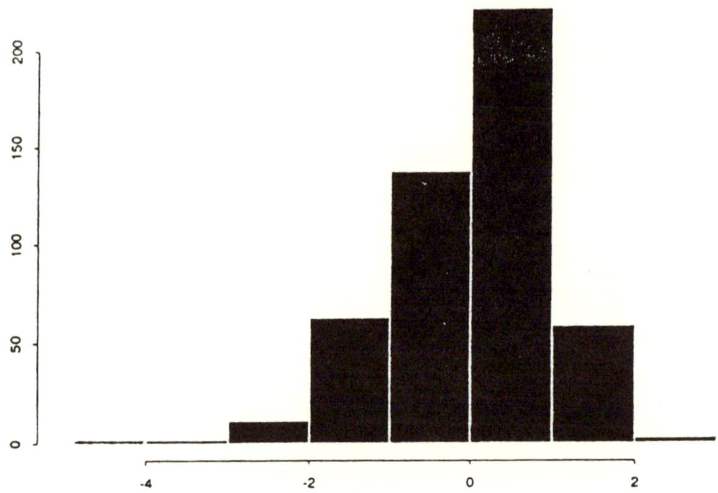

Figure 13 • ***Bootstrap Replications of Coefficient for Media Drug Coverage***

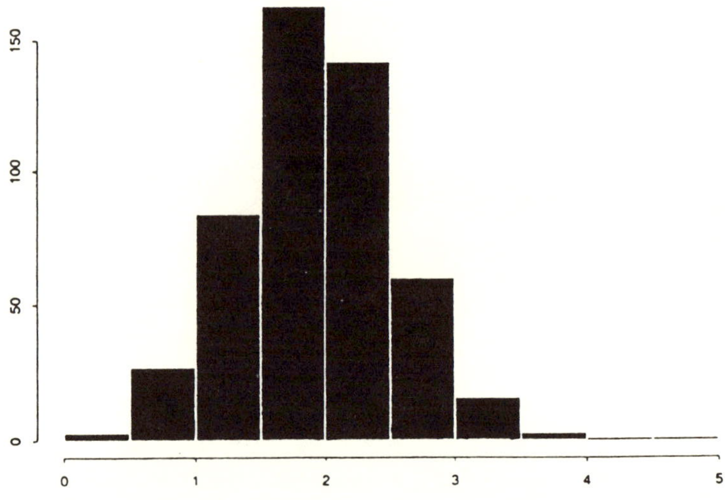

Figure 14 • ***Bootstrap Replications of Coefficient for State Anti-Drug Initiative***

coefficient can therefore be considered statistically significant. In contrast, the regression coefficient for the crime rate as predicted by the null hypothesis falls within the 95 percent confidence interval for the bootstrap replications, and therefore cannot be rejected. The bootstrap replications thus confirm the original results indicating that state and media initiative (but not the reported incidence of crime) are associated with subsequent levels of public concern about crime.

In the drug case, only the regression coefficient for state initiative predicted by the null hypotheses falls outside the 95 percent confidence interval and can therefore be considered statistically significant. The bootstrap results thus indicate that the uncertainty associated with the original regression model is minimal, and confirm that state and media initiative in the crime case and state initiative in the drug case are positively and significantly associated with subsequent public concern about crime and drugs.

The Pluralist and Agenda-Setting Hypotheses

Last, to evaluate the relationship between public concern and state initiative, I analyze several cases in which public opinion grew dramatically to determine whether shifts in state initiative followed or preceded changes in the level of public concern. While the existence of simultaneity bias in the regression results indicates that state initiative and public concern are mutually reinforcing, this case study method allows us to adjudicate between the pluralist hypothesis (H2), which predicts that the changing nature of public concern shapes the level of state activity, and the agenda-setting hypothesis (H4), which predicts that level of state activity shapes public concern. Four cases are presented in diagram form in Table 3.[14]

Table 3 • ***State Initiative and Public Concern About Crime and Drugs***

Case 1:	Public Concern and State Initiative on Crime, January 1968-January 1969								
State initiative		.25		.52		1.03		.31	
	1/68	-------------	>4/68	-------------	>7/68	-------------	>10/68	-------------	>1/69
Public concern	3%		4%		11%		17%		9%
Case 2:	Public Concern and State Initiative on Crime, May 1969-January 1971								
State initiative		.37		.50		.77		.50	
	5/69	-------------	>1/70	-------------	>5/70	-------------	>10/70	-------------	>1/71
Public concern	5%		6%		8%		13%		6%
Case 3:	Public Concern and State Initiative on Drugs, January 1986-January 1987								
State initiative		.24		.42		1.01		.19	
	1/86	-------------	>4/86	-------------	>7/86	-------------	>10/86	-------------	>1/87
Public concern	1%		3%		8%		11%		5%
Case 4:	Public Concern and State Initiative on Drugs, September 1988-December 1989								
State initiative		.38		.53		1.4		.83	
	9/88	-------------	>1/89	-------------	>5/89	-------------	> 9/89	-------------	>1/90
Public concern	15%		11%		27%		64%		33%

14. These cases were selected in the following manner. First, for each issue, I identified the poll in which the level of public concern reached its highest point. The three polls preceding and one following this poll represent a "case." The same procedure was used to identify a second case wherein public concern reached its second highest level. The number corresponding to "state initiative" indicates the average number of state initiatives per day in the period between the two polls.

In each of the cases, public concern and state initiative move largely in parallel directions. However, in each of the cases, a drop in the level of state initiative towards the end of the cycle is not explicable in terms of a preceding drop in public concern. For example, in Case 1, the level of state initiative drops from 1.03 to .31 initiatives per day, despite the fact that the most recent public opinion poll indicated that public concern about crime had increased. This drop in the level of state initiative is followed by a decline in the level of public concern about crime. The same pattern can be discerned in each of the four cases. Thus, while public concern and state initiative tend to move in parallel directions and are generally mutually reinforcing, dramatic drops in state initiative cannot be explained in terms of declining levels of public concern. These drops in state initiative are, however, *followed* by declining levels of public concern.

Discussion

The Objectivist and Constructionist Hypotheses

The results presented in Tables 1 and 2 lend greatest support to the constructionist hyopthesis (H3); very little is found for support for the objectivist hypothesis (H1). In particular, the results indicate that levels of public concern are not strongly correlated with the incidence of crime/drug use, but that media and especially state initiative play an important role in generating subsequent public concern. In the crime case, the regression results indicate that media and state initiative are positively associated with increased public concern about crime, while the crime rate does not appear to have had such an impact. These results thus provide support for the constructionist hypothesis (H3).

In the drug case, the regression results suggest that only state initiative is associated with concern about drugs. One possible explanation for the absence of significant association between drug use and concern about drugs is that it is not the reported incidence of drug *use* but the reported severity of drug *abuse* (and particularly abuse of cocaine and crack) which has contributed to the definition of drug use as the nation's most important problem. If this hypothesis were correct, we would expect the number of cocaine-related emergency room visits to correspond to rates of public concern about drugs. In fact, DAWN (Drug Abuse Warning Network) data indicate that the number of cocaine-related emergency room visits increased between 1986 and 1989, as did public concern (although the increase in concern was, again, much more uneven). After a brief drop in 1990, however, the number of cocaine (and heroin) related emergency room visits enumerated by DAWN began to increase. By 1992, the number of all drug emergency room visits, including those involving cocaine and heroin, had reached record levels (Treaster 1992, 1993). In contrast, public concern dropped dramatically between 1990 and 1992.

In sum, it does not appear that either the reported incidence of drug use or the severity of drug abuse is consistently related to levels of public concern about drugs. Instead, the significant positive effect of state initiative on public concern provides support for the constructionist hypothesis (H3), which predicts that the construction of the crime and drug issues is crucial in shaping public opinion. State actors appear to play a particularly important role in this process of signification.

The indeterminant nature of the relationship between the reported rate of crime/drug use and public concern around those issues found in this analysis does not apear to be unique to the two time periods selected for analysis. During the 1970s, reported rates of crime and drug use both increased dramatically: official statistics indicate that the crime rate peaked in 1981, while general drug use reached its zenith in 1979 and declined consistently thereafter (Federal Bureau of Investigation 1988; National Institute on Drug Abuse 1988). Despite this, the percentage of respondents indicating that crime/drugs were the nation's most important problem remained quite low (Gallup 1980). Thus, it does not appear that the public identifies crime/drugs as the nation's most important problem on the basis of the reported prevalence of those phenomena. Instead, the degree to which state actors and the mass media focus on those issues is crucial.

The Pluralist and Agenda-Setting Hypotheses

The results presented in Table 3 provide support for the agenda-setting (H4) rather than the pluralist (H2) hypothesis: while public concern and state initiative generally move in parallel directions and tend to be mutually reinforcing, drops in the level of state initiative are followed rather than preceded by declines in the level of public concern. In other words, state initiative on crime and drugs is not consistently explicable in terms of public concern around those issues, but plays a consistent role in shaping that opinion.

A more detailed examinination of these cases strengthens our confidence in these findings. Public concern about crime reached its zenith (17 percent) in October 1968, near the end of an election campaign in which "street crime" was a central issue. State initiative was at an all-time high of 1.03 initiatives per day in the period preceding this poll, while media initiative reached its peak at .6 stories per day. Post-election drops in state and media initiative on the crime issue were followed by corresponding drops in public concern (despite the ever-increasing crime rate).

Similarly, the percentage of poll respondents reporting that drugs were the most important problem facing the nation reached its peak at the end of a period characterized by unprecedented media and state anti-drug activity. In the first year after his election, President Bush increasingly focused on drugs as the central domestic issue. In late August and early September of that year, Bush made several special speeches on "the drug crisis" and unveiled his program for fighting drugs: the average number of state initiatives increased from .53 to 1.4 per day during this period. Media initiative also increased from .26 to .76 stories per day devoted to the drug issue. A subsequent public opinion poll indicated that 64 percent of the American public, the highest percentage ever recorded, felt that drugs were the most important problem facing the nation.

Furthermore, there is no evidence that state actors' initial involvement in the crime and drug issues was a response to public concern. For example, in 1964 when Goldwater declared that "crime is a major issue in this election — at least I'm going to make it one, because the responsibility has to start someplace," no public opinion research indicated that public concern about crime had increased. Similarly, when Reagan first declared a "national war on drugs" in 1982, and in 1986 when he called for a renewal of this "all-out effort," national opinion polls indicated that less than 3 percent of poll respondents were most concerned about drugs. In sum, it does not appear that either increases or decreases in the level of state initiative around crime and drugs are consistently explicable in terms of corresponding shifts in public concern.

Conclusion

The results of this analysis provide greatest support for the constructionist (H3) and agenda-setting (H4) hypotheses, and therefore for elite rather than cultural constructionism or objectivism. The elite constructionist approach emphasizes the social and political nature of the "street crime" and drug issues, as well as the role of the media and especially the state in shaping public concern around those issues.

Each of the contending models, however, makes an important contribution to our understanding of the politicization of crime and drug use and, more generally, the formation of the public agenda. The support found here for the constructionist hypothesis does not mean that "objective" factors and their indicators are irrelevant, but that their interpretation by social and political actors is crucial. For example, while the incidence of general drug use declined in the 1980s, and while only a very small proportion of the population has ever tried crack cocaine, it is true that heavy use of cocaine and its derivative, crack, appears to have increased throughout the 1980s (Goode 1989). The spread of crack, combined with its association with minorities, violent crime, and urban blight, undoubtedly facilitated the construction of drug use as "the gravest domestic challenge we've faced in decades" (Bush, quoted in Nelson 1989). As noted earlier, however, the reported increases in crack use have not been associated with high levels of public concern before 1986 or since 1990. Thus, it appears that the downward mobility of smokeable cocaine facilitated but did not determine the politicization of drug use in the 1980s.[15]

Similarly, it is true that public opinion plays an important role in the politicization of social problems. It does not follow from the agenda-setting hypothesis that the state's ability to influence public opinion is unlimited. State actors' success in mobilizing public concern around these particular issues was not inevitable, and must be explained in terms of the resonance of the construction of the crime and drug issues with particular themes in American political culture. Furthermore, claims about some types of issues may be more likely than others to generate high levels of public concern. For example, "valence issues" (see Nelson 1984) provoke a fairly uniform emotional response and, unlike "position issues," do not have supporters and opponents.[16] Similarly, the existence of a variety of interest groups making claims around a particular issue will likely diminish the capacity of a single group of claimsmakers to define that issue (Burstein 1991; May 1991). Thus, claimsmakers may be more successful in shaping public concern when there are fewer participants in the struggle to frame an issue, or when that issue provokes a fairly uniform emotional response. Further research is needed to assess the role of cultural and historical context and issue characteristics in shaping public receptivity to state and media claimsmaking activities.

In sum, the findings presented in this article suggest that the politicization of the crime and drug issues has been the result of their social construction by the mass media and especially state actors. While a complete explanation for the involvement of these actors is beyond the scope of this article, I suggest that state initiative on these issues may be seen as part of a "hegemonic project" (Omi 1987) aimed at rebuilding political consensus around opposition to the reform movements of the 1960s and to the subsequent expansion of the welfare state. Racially charged "social issues" such as "street crime" and drug use have played a central role in this project. The support found here for the constructionist and agenda-setting hypotheses are consistent with this interpretation and may serve as a useful starting point for further research.

15. This argument is consistent with Fishman's (1980) argument that reports of a "wave" of crime against the elderly in the 1970s did not require that there was an actual increase in such incidents. Instead, the occurence of this crime "wave" required only that some of these incidents occurred and that important news sources called attention to these incidents.

16. While there may be some debate about how to best respond to "valence issues" such as crime and child abuse, there is no "pro-crime" or "pro-child abuse" lobby.

References

Bennett, W. Lance
1980 Public Opinion in American Politics. New York: Harcourt Brace Jovanovich, Inc.

Berger, Peter, and Thomas Luckmann
1966 The Social Construction of Reality. New York: Doubleday.

Berke, Richard L.
1989 "Poll finds most in U.S. back Bush strategy on drugs." New York Times, September 12:B8.

Burstein, Paul.
1991 "Policy domains: Organization, culture and policy outcomes." Annual Review of Sociology 17:327-350.

Caplan, Gerald
1973 "Reflections on the nationalization of crime, 1964-8." Law and the Social Order 1973:583-638.

Cohn, Steven F., Steven E. Barkan, and William A. Halteman
1991 "Punitive attitudes toward criminals: Racial consensus or racial conflict?" Social Problems 38:287-296.

Corbett, Michael
1981 "Public support for 'law and order': Interrelationships with system affirmation and attitudes toward minorities." Criminology 19:328-343.

Department of Justice
1988 "Criminal victimization in the United States, 1988." Office of Justice Programs, Bureau of Justice Statistics Bulletin.

Dickson, Donald
1968 "Bureaucracy and morality: An organizational perspective on a moral crusade." Social Problems 16:143-157.

Edelman, Murray
1964 The Symbolic Uses of Politics. Chicago: University of Illinois Press.
1988 Constructing the Political Spectacle. Chicago: University of Chicago Press.

Epstein, Edward
1977 Agency of Fear: Opiates and Political Power in America. New York: Verso Press.

Federal Bureau of Investigation
1961-88 "The U.S. F.B.I. crime reports." Washington, D.C.: Department of Justice.

Fishman, Mark
1980 Manufacturing the News. Austin: University of Texas Press.

Fogelson, Robert
1977 Big City Police. Cambridge, Mass.: Harvard University Press.

Furstenberg, Frank
1971 "Public reaction to crime in the streets." The American Scholar 40:601-610.

Gallup, George
1964-90 The Gallup Poll. Wilmington, Del.: Scholarly Resources.

Gamson, William, David Croteau, William Hoynes, and Theodore Sasson
1992 "Media images and the social construction of reality." Annual Review of Sociology 18:373-393.

Gans, Herbert
1980 Deciding What's News. New York: Vintage Books.

Goode, Eric
1989 "The American drug panic of the 1980's: Social construction or objective threat?" Violence, Aggression and Terrorism 3:327-348.

Gordon, Diana R.
1990 The Justice Juggernaut: Fighting Street Crime, Controlling Citizens. New Brunswick: Rutgers University Press.

Hall, Stuart, Chas Critcher, Tony Jefferson, John Clarke, and Brian Roberts
1978 Policing the Crisis: Mugging, the State and Law and Order. London: Macmillan Press.
Helmer, John
1975 Drugs and Minority Oppression. New York: Seabury Press.
Hertsgaard, Mark
1988 On Bended Knee: The Press and the Reagan Presidency. New York: Schocken Books.
Himmlestein, Jerome
1973 "Drug politics theory: Analysis and critique." The Journal of Drug Issues 8:37-52.
Iyengar, Shanto, and Donald Kinder
1987 News That Matters. Chicago: University of Chicago Press.
Jensen, Eric L., Jurg Gerber, and Ginna M. Babcock
1991 "The new war on drugs: Grass-roots movement or political construction?" The Journal of Drug Issues 3:651-667.
Kitsuse, John, and Malcolm Spector
1987 Constructing Social Problems. New York: Aldine De Gruyter.
Klein, Dorie
1983 "Ill and aganst the law: The social and medical control of heroin users." Journal of Drug Issues 1983:31-54.
Lukes, Steven
1974 Power: A Radical View. London: Macmillan Press.
Manis, Jerome
1976 "The concept of social problems: Vox populi and sociological analysis." Social Problems 21:305-315.
Mann, Michael
1986 The Sources of Social Power. Oxford: Oxford University Press.
Mark, Gregory Yee
1975 "Racial, economic and political factors in the development of America's drug laws." Issues in Criminology 10:49-72.
Matusow, Allen J.
1984 The Unraveling of America: A History of Liberalism in the 1960's. New York: Harper Torchbooks.
Mauss, Armand L.
1975 Social Problems as Social Movements. New York: J.B. Lippincott Co.
Mauer, Marc
1991 "Americans behind bars: A comparison of international rates of incarceration." The Sentencing Project.
May, Peter J.
1991 "Reconsidering policy design: Policies and publics." Journal of Public Policy 11:187-206.
Mayer, William G.
1992 The Changing American Mind: How and Why American Public Opinion Changed Between 1960 and 1988. Ann Arbor: The University of Michigan Press.
McWilliams, John C.
1991 "Through the past darkly: The politics and policies of America's drug war." In Drug Control Policy: Essays in Historical and Comparative Perspective, ed. William O. Walker III, 5-41. State College: Pennsylvania State University.
Merton, Robert K., and Robert Nisbet
1971 Contemporary Social Problems. New York: Harcourt, Brace and World.
Morgan, Patricia
1978 "The legislation of drug laws: Economic crisis and social control." Journal of Drug Issues 8:53-62
Morganthau, Tom, and Mark Miller
1986 "Crack and crime." Newsweek, June 16:16-22.
Musto, David
1973 The American Disease: Origins of Narcotic Control. New York: Oxford University Press.
National Institute on Drug Abuse
1979-88 "National household survey on drug abuse: Main findings." Rockville, Md.: National Institute on Drug Abuse.

Nelson, Barbara J.
1984 Making an Issue of Child Abuse: Political Agenda Setting for Social Problems. Chicago: University of Chicago Press.

Nelson, Jack
1989 "Bush tells plan to combat drugs." New York Times, September 6:A1.

The New York Times/CBS News Polls
1989 August Survey:2-4. New York: New York Times Poll.

Niemi, Richard G., John Mueller, and Tom W. Smith
1989 Trends in Public Opinion: A Compendium of Survey Data. New York: Greenwood Press.

O'Brien, Robert M.
1985 Crime and Victimization Data. Law and Criminal Justice Series, Vol. 4. Beverly Hills: Sage Publications.

Office of the Federal Register
1981-91 Public Papers of the President. Washington, D.C.: U.S. Government Printing Office.

Omi, Michael Allen
1987 "We shall overturn: Race and the contemporary American right." Dissertation, University of California, Santa Cruz.

President's Commission on Law Enforcement and the Administration of Justice
1968 The Challenge of Crime in a Free Society. New York: Dutton Books.

Reinarman, Craig, and Harry Levine
1989 "Crack in context: Politics and media in the making of a drug scare." Contemporary Drug Problems 16:535-577.

Rosch, Joel
1985 "Crime as an issue in American politics." In The Politics of Crime and Criminal Justice, eds. E. Fairchild and E. Webb. Beverly Hills: Sage Publication.

Scheingold, Stuart
1986 The Politics of Law and Order: Street Crime and Public Policy. Philadelphia: Temple University Press.
1990 "The war on drugs in context: Crisis politics and social control." Paper presented at the 1990 Annual Meeting of the Law and Society Association, May.

Stinchcombe, Arthur L., Rebecca Adams, Carol A. Heimer, Kim Lane Scheppele, Tom W. Smith, and D. Garth Taylor
1980 Crime and Punishment in America: Changing Attitudes in America. San Francisco: Jossey-Bass Publishers.

Treaster, Joseph
1992 "Emergency room cocaine cases rise." The New York Times, October 24:A6.
1993 "Emergency hospital visits rise among drug abusers." New York Times, April 24:A8.

U.S. Office of the National Drug Control Policy
1989 National Drug Control Strategy. Washington, D.C.: Executive Office of the President.

Vandenderbilt Television News Archive
1980-90 The Television News Index and Abstracts. Nashville, Tenn.: Vandenderbilt Television News Archive.

Walker, Samuel
1977 A Critical History of Police Reform: The Emergence of Professionalism. Lexington, Mass.: Lexington Books.

Whitney, Charles, Marilyn Fritzler, Steven Jones, Sharon Mazzarella, and Lana Rakow
1989 "Source and geographic bias in television news 1982-4." Journal of Electronic Broadcasting and Electronic Media 33:159-174.

Wilson, William J.
1975 Thinking About Crime. New York: Basic Books, Inc.

CORRECTIONAL ALTERNATIVES FOR DRUG OFFENDERS IN AN ERA OF OVERCROWDING

TODD R. CLEAR
Rutgers University

VAL B. CLEAR
Madison County Unified Courts and Anderson College

ANTHONY A. BRAGA
Rutgers University

Given the severe overcrowding suffered by nearly all state and federal correctional systems, the antidrug movement in the United States faces extreme resource constraints. This article argues that patterns in the relationship between drug use and criminal behavior call for different correctional strategies. The utility of various nontraditional correctional alternatives for drug offenders is described based on the drug-crime relationship. Recent research on correctional strategies is applied to the special problems involved in the management of drug offenders.

The antidrug movement in the United States is running on a collision course with the problem of overcrowded prisons and jails. Regardless of the sincerity with which political leadership seeks to reduce certain types of drug use, the realities of the justice system are seriously strained resources at all levels of law enforcement, prosecution and adjudication, and correctional supervision and treatment. If there is hope for the so-called war on drugs, it must be based on a realistic assessment of affordable costs.

In corrections, this means that extensive use of alternatives to traditional corrections must occur. Stated bluntly, most corrections systems in the United States are so seriously overburdened in their traditional resources of jails,

---

This article is based on an earlier report of the Institute for Court Management under BJA Grant No. 87-DD-CX-002.

THE PRISON JOURNAL, Vol. 73 No. 2, June 1993 178-198

prisons, and probation, that small increases in demand will constitute major management problems.

Because of strained resources, many corrections systems have experimented with new types of alternatives to the traditional forms of corrections. The purpose of this article is to explore how the "new generation" alternatives to traditional corrections are relevant for the drug offender. The article begins with a description of the major types of correctional alternatives currently being used around the country, followed by a description of types of drug offenders and their suitability for different forms of alternatives. Drawing from research on alternatives, a set of principles in their application to offenders is then developed. The article concludes with suggested strategies for using alternative correctional forms for drug offenders.

MAJOR FORMS OF ALTERNATIVES TO TRADITIONAL CORRECTIONS

Nearly every jurisdiction has experimented with one form or another of corrections alternatives in recent years. This has resulted in a rich variety of programs for offenders falling between the prison and traditional probation. A description of prototypical programs is provided below, but the reader should be aware that many versions of each of these prototypes exist, and each extant program has unique characteristics that help it fit its jurisdiction.

SHOCK INCARCERATION

One of the newest forms of correctional alternatives involves a sentence to a "boot camp" type experience (Parent, 1989). Normally, the term is short (30 to 90 days), but the experience is intentionally harsh. Offenders are put through a regimen of long days of intense physical effort under strict discipline. In some respects, the new shock programs are a throwback to early forms of imprisonment that extolled the virtues of hard work and daily discipline. The idea of these programs is to "shock" offenders in two ways: first, by removing them from the community and, second, by subjecting them to harsh, unrelenting conditions of work.

Most shock programs target first offenders—many require no prior felony convictions—and most exclude violent or previously incarcerated offenders. In addition, most programs are limited to persons under a certain age, no older than early 20s, to have young, impressionable inmates in the programs.

RESIDENTIAL CENTERS

Because prisons are so expensive to build, many urban areas have renovated existing buildings, turning them into part-time or full-time residential facilities. In many ways, these programs resemble the traditional work release center or halfway house. Part-time programs are the most common, and they allow the offender to be away during work hours and for some social time, returning to sleep at night. Full-time programs usually restrict the offender's ability to be away from the facility to only special occasions.

Residential centers normally incorporate a treatment regime into their programs. Commonly, they use group-based approaches such as "guided group interaction" to help offenders confront their lifestyles. They also commonly restrict their populations to specific target groups: probation failures, substance abusers, persons owing restitution, and so forth. This enables the treatment programs to concentrate on a more homogeneous population. With drug-involved offenders, residential centers have often used "therapeutic community" methods. (DeLeon, 1987).

FINANCIAL PENALTIES

Financial penalties such as fines, restitution, and forfeitures have recently been advanced as an alternative approach to punishment. Advocates of financial penalties argue that they are particularly well suited to a capitalist society that places importance on monetary incentives and the accumulation of wealth. Not only can the fruits of crime be eliminated through monetary sanctions, but also substantial punishment can be inflicted on offenders by imposition of a financial penalty, all without the severe costs of incarceration (Hillsman & Greene, 1992).

The aim of fines and forfeitures is essentially punitive and deterrent, not reformative. The severity of a fine can even be adjusted to the seriousness of the offense and to the offender's financial circumstances taking into consideration the amount of the offender's income and assets (called the "day fine"). Some observers have argued that, potentially, fines are very different—and much fairer—than forfeitures, which can be arbitrary and disproportionate in impact.

COMMUNITY SERVICE

Community service—labor performed by the offender, generally for a public agency or nonprofit organization—has many attractive features: The person "pays back" to the offended community, all offenders are charged equally (in hours) regardless of their circumstances, and the cost is much less than prison (McDonald, 1992). Community service sanctioning programs have been successfully run in numerous jurisdictions around the United States.

One advantage of community service approaches has been that they provide a relatively efficient way to sanction repetitive minor offenders, such as misdemeanants. The cost of law enforcement for these offenders often outweighs the seriousness of their crimes, and community service can provide a vehicle for appropriate, inexpensive consequences for minor illegal activity.

CONVENTIONAL PROBATION

With caseloads often ranging from 100 to 300 offenders, most conventional probation systems do little more than monitor compliance and react to misbehavior of clients. Recently developed classification systems have allowed conventional probation supervision to focus attention on the most risky and needy clients within a caseload (Clear & Gallagher, 1983), and some research suggests that this approach can be promising with serious offenders (Markley & Eisenberg, 1987).

In many areas of the country, however, conventional probation remains a highly criticized form of correctional treatment. Some studies have shown that probationers exhibit high rates of rearrest while under supervision (Petersilia, Turner, Kahan, & Peterson, 1985), although this appears to be less true in some parts of the country than in others (Ficher, Hirschberg, & McGaha, 1987).

INTENSIVE SUPERVISION PROGRAMS (ISPs)

One of the most popular new approaches is to intensify the level of probation (or parole) supervision given to offenders. Instead of the common practice of one or two face-to-face contacts each month, these ISPs require a minimum of two or three per week, including unannounced evening visits to the home. They also typically employ "back-up" controls of electronic monitoring and/or urine testing (described below) to augment the level of surveillance (Byrne, 1990).

ISPs differ in their offender eligibility criteria and program philosophy. Many are designed to divert offenders from incarceration, and these typically will not consider offenders convicted of violent offenses. Other ISPs target the most difficult offenders already on probation or parole caseloads, and these ISPs normally do not use exclusionary criteria (Byrne, Lurigio, & Baird, 1989). Unlike their predecessors in the 1960s, most modern ISPs are unabashedly "tough" in their stance with offenders, although a handful advertise a treatment orientation.

ELECTRONIC MONITORING

The "hottest" of the new alternatives is not a program per se but, instead, a technique applied within a program. Made possible by recent technical advances in computers and telephones, electronic monitors are devices that emit a coded signal to a receiver. When these devices are attached to the body (usually the wrist or ankle) the signal can be used to indicate the offender's whereabouts—and especially to certify that the offender is home in accordance with a curfew or court order (Schmidt, 1989).

The use of monitors is in its technical and experiential infancy, and although the early results of these programs are intriguing, there is as yet no basis to say whether they succeed. Early experiments reported considerable technical problems, although many of these problems appear to have been eradicated in revised units. They are, however, expensive, running as much as $300 per month (although most units are considerably cheaper). Many programs therefore restrict themselves to offenders who are able to pay for the equipment, those who have telephones, and those whose offenses are nonviolent.

URINE TESTING

Like electronic monitoring, urine testing is not a program but a surveillance component that can be used in conjunction with any correctional program, even incarceration. These tests not only indicate whether a person has been using a substance, but they also indicate which substances. When urine testing is done with any population, a high proportion of "hits" (indicators of substance use) is found—but this is especially true for offender groups (Wish & Gropper, 1990).

Questions have been raised about the accuracy of urine tests, but research consistently shows that when recommended procedures are followed, the test results are highly reliable. For this reason, the high level of drug use in arrested offenders (ranging across the country from 50% to over 80%) is remarkable evidence about the extensiveness of drug involvement in this population.

ANTIDOTE DRUGS

A variety of drug use suppressants exist that either reduce the desire for drugs or counteract their effects. The oldest versions are methadone, a drug that replaces the heroin urge, and Antabuse, which causes unpleasant side effects when mixed with alcohol. Both drugs have been available for decades. More recently, new drugs have been used experimentally to combat the effects of cocaine and other sources of the "high" (Anglin & Hser, 1990).

Drug use suppression is controversial. All tests of the technique find that there are limits to the success experienced in eradication of substance use—often offenders under one drug suppression regimen simply change drugs of preference (Rosenbaum & Murphy, 1984). There is also a nagging conceptual problem with using drugs to fight drugs. Nonetheless, this approach is a frequently used tool in the arsenal of drug treatment agencies, once offenders have shown a motivation to quit.

TREATMENT

Although technically, all forms of intervention with drug offenders are *treatment*, the term usually denotes mental health approaches with the aim to change the offender's lifestyle. Treatment programs for drug offenders focus on the rationalizations, dependencies, and delusional thinking that feed the addictive lifestyle. They attempt, through therapeutic interaction with others, to convince the offender of the value of the wholesale lifestyle change needed to overcome drug abuse.

Treatment Alternatives to Street Crime (TASC) is a nationwide program that specializes in working with drug-abusing offenders. The program is eclectic, using numerous techniques, from direct, random urine testing to job training, counseling, and referral. Programs vary their approaches to fit local environments, but all serve as adjuncts to probation and parole operations using specially trained staff to work with drug users.

Narcotics Anonymous (NA) and Alcoholics Anonymous (AA) are well-established self-help programs that rely on reformed users (called *recovering*) to provide support for others interested in ending their drug use. Because the program is based on the desire of the clients to change, it is entirely voluntary (although courts will often violate this by ordering attendance). Members are aware of the games that drug users play, see through their manipulations, and challenge their co-users to sustain recovery.

In-patient drug treatment programs have become more common in recent years. These programs usually have highly structured environments in which the patient proceeds through a series of stages of treatment requiring 30 to 90 days to complete. Most programs accept nonoffenders, and all are expensive. Experts believe that follow-up treatment and support are necessary if drug abusers are to stay clean after release (Wexler & Lipton, 1985).

JAIL AND PRISON

Although these are not truly *alternatives* as the term is commonly used, short-term prison and jail stays are an important approach to be considered in lieu of longer penalties. When incapacitation is not a consideration, short prison stays are thought to provide an incentive for the offender to avoid repeat crimes. Although evidence for the usefulness of short-term prison sentences is inconclusive, many people argue that short prison sentences are as effective as long ones for most offenders, even drug offenders (Wexler & Williams, 1986).

Jail terms, by contrast, can play an important role in reinforcing compliance with alternative programs. Nearly all alternatives programs have strict rules, and when these are broken, it is often inadvisable to revoke the offender and impose the full, original sentence. Short stays in the local jail of 24 to 72 hours in length can serve to confirm the importance of the program's rules for offenders who are otherwise doing well in the community.

A DRUG-CRIME BEHAVIOR TYPOLOGY

The phrase "drug offender," when used to refer to all people who both use drugs and commit crimes, can be a misleading oversimplification. The high proportion of arrestees who have used drugs prior to their crimes is evidence that not all drug-crime relationships are the same (Fagan, 1990). The optimal use of correctional alternatives requires an understanding of the nature of drug-crime behaviors and their suitability for different types of programs. This suggests the need for a typology of offenders' drug-crime relationships. A typology would allow differential assignment of offenders to correctional programs, based on the nature of the program and the offender's crime-related drug problems.

In developing such a typology, an implicit assumption is made that the purpose of correctional intervention is to prevent or control the risk of criminal recidivism. Correctional programs are interested in the drug use of offenders only insofar as drug use relates to the potential for new criminal behavior. A typology is helpful if it identifies the different ways that drugs and crime can be related and classifies offenders according to those patterns.

Using such a typology requires caution, however. Although any correctional typology has the ultimate aim of informing action about offenders, the following typology is not about *people*, but about *events*. It posits that for drug-using offenders, their criminal events vary in the way they relate to drug use. Rather than classifying people, then, this typology attempts to classify drug use and criminal events into a logical framework.

The resulting behavior types are, in actuality, stereotypes—they fit more or less well to certain offenders. Although offenders vary in their drug-crime behavior pattern, the implication is that many offenders will exhibit a high concentration of one pattern. Stereotypes are not used merely to classify offenders but are developed to decide the kind of correctional programs that might be effective for an offender and why (Chaiken & Chaiken, 1984).

It is also important to note that a behavioral typology cannot result in static offender classifications. Offenders' behavior will sometimes change; especially, their drug-crime behavior may evolve. Correctional strategies should be designed to inhibit the continuation of this process. Interventions should aim to prevent the habituation of illicit drug involvement for the offender's current behavioral type.

TYPES OF DRUG-CRIME BEHAVIORS

The typology recognizes that drug use and criminal behavior are two different forms of deviance, and an offender might be more, or less, committed to either. Figure 1 shows the model.

For linguistic ease, the stereotypes will be described for persons whose drug-crime behavior is exclusively of that type. The reader should remember our caveats stated above. There are offenders for whom a "pure type" model is simplistic, and many (perhaps most) offenders will experience a change in the drug-crime pattern of their behavior over their lifetimes. Four types of drug-crime relationships are identified. *Users* are those who have little commitment to either drugs or crime. *Addicts* are committed to drugs but not to crime. *Sellers* are committed to crime but not to drugs. *Predators* are committed to both crime and drugs. A description of the four types follows.

Addicts. The Addict has become so attached to drug use that his or her lifestyle is built around the acquisition and consumption of drugs (Ball, Shaffer, & Nurco, 1983; Hanson, Beschner, Walters, & Bovelle, 1985). Because Addicts are physically and/or psychologically dependent on the drug, their problem is to break the addiction and learn a substance-free lifestyle.

Because many drugs are expensive, many Addicts must engage in criminal activity to obtain money to support their drug use. Studies show that

		Commitment to Crime	
		High	Low
Commitment to Drugs	High	Predator	Addict
	Low	Seller	User

Figure 1: A Model for Identifying Correctional Programs for Drug Offenders

criminal behavior remains high during periods of drug use (Speckart & Anglin, 1986). Common forms of such criminality are burglary, small item theft, and drug sales, although middle-class Addicts will choose other types of crime and alcoholics commit crimes by driving (Goldstein, 1981). For Addicts, however, the criminal activity is not an end but a means (Mieczkowski, 1986).

Addicts need correctional approaches that force them (or enable them) to confront the circumstances of their abuse of drugs. Many treatment programs are based on this model. They use various techniques to demonstrate to the offender the consequences of drug use, including direct education, confrontive counseling, drug therapy, and interventions from friends and family (Platt, 1986). When treatment is successful with this person, the results are significant: A drug user is reformed and criminal activity is prevented (Ball, Rosen, Flueck, & Nurco, 1982).

Sellers. The essential cog in the illicit drug machine is the Seller of drugs. Among Sellers there is a hierarchy, of course, with the street salespersons occupying the lowest rung and representing the most commonly arrested type. The drug-crime connection of many of those engaged in street sales is, in fact the Addict variety (Chaiken & Johnson, 1988).

True Sellers are involved with drugs solely (or primarily) as a way to make large amounts of money. Studies show that a small percentage of offenders arrested for drug sales or possession test negatively for drug usage—these are economically motivated drug offenders engaging in business (Goldkamp, 1989). Although the business risks are high—especially in terms of the violence inherent to the drug market—the potential reward is considerable (Reuter, Macoun, & Murphy, 1990). A street Seller can make hundreds of dollars in a day; a higher-level person even more. Frequently, juveniles are used in this role to avoid processing by the adult criminal justice system.

Because the Seller has no personal commitment to drugs but has accepted the risk of crime, little drug treatment is needed. Moreover, punishment is not likely to do much good, at least for crime control. A person who is willing to risk death is probably willing to risk prison—and while he or she is incarcerated, someone else will sell in his or her place.

Users. Unlike Addicts, Users have little commitment to drugs, and unlike Sellers, they are basically noncriminal in lifestyle. These offenders use drugs periodically because they like the high. Their lives are otherwise more or less normal, but they come to the attention of the criminal justice system as a result of an instance of their occasional drug use (Zinberg, 1984).

The Users' main problem is that they are now identified offenders. Treatment may help forestall movement toward greater drug abuse, and it may provide the offender with information, but it can do little to prevent crime, because there is little crime to prevent. For most Users, the issue is to avoid creating problems through correctional programming.

Predators. Some drug-using offenders are committed to a criminal lifestyle, a lifestyle of risk and excitement, and a part of that lifestyle is extensive use of drugs (Ball, 1986). Patterns of criminal behavior will include serious, violent crimes such as rape, armed robbery, assault, and burglary—drugs are often used to generate the "courage" to commit the offense (Chaiken & Chaiken, 1990; Johnson & Wish, 1987).

For the Predator, crime and drugs are linked (as they are for the addict), but crime is not just a means; it is also an end. These criminals enjoy the thrill and fruits of criminal acts as well as the thrill of drug use.

Correctional treatment can be useful for Predators but must be undertaken with the recognition that their drug use behavior is not the central cause of criminal behavior; instead, there is a criminal orientation that needs to be overcome. Treatment will need to address both the mood-changing aspects of drugs and the criminal thought patterns and desires of the offender (Andrews, Kessling, Robinson, & Mickus, 1986).

PRINCIPLES OF THE USE OF CORRECTIONAL ALTERNATIVES

Before concluding with a discussion of the strategies for using alternatives with drug offenders, it is important to summarize prior experiences with these alternatives when used on the larger body of offenders. These experiences form a framework for developing drug offender strategies.

ALTERNATIVES ARE SUSCEPTIBLE TO NET-WIDENING

The most pernicious aspect of alternatives to traditional corrections is that they frequently end up costing more tax dollars and interfering more with offenders than the programs they were designed to replace. Called *net-widening*, this means that the ultimate result of these programs is greater social control rather than reduced state involvement in cases (Austin & Krisberg, 1980). This is especially unfortunate, because these programs are normally based on the premise that they are less intrusive than traditional prison and more effective than traditional probation. Often sold as cost-effective alternatives to crowded prison systems, when these programs prove to be more expensive than the traditional system, serious questions are raised about their overall value.

There are two ways that programs widen the net. First, they may advertise that they are alternatives to prison, but instead they serve as alternatives to probation. In the typical case, judges are given authority to sentence directly to the program. Net-widening occurs when judges place borderline cases into the new programs, when most of the borderline cases otherwise would have gone to probation. The consequence is that the program is used to augment probation supervision, not to reduce reliance on incarceration. Because "new generation" programs are always more expensive than traditional probation, this means the programs fail to save tax dollars.

This problem happens in new programs when eligibility criteria are too conservative. For example, to restrict a program to nonviolent nonrecidivists, as so many of the new boot camps have done, is to invite net-widening, because these offenders seldom go to prison or jail anyway. To attain a diversion population, programs must be willing to accept offenders whose profiles and prior record make them likely prison candidates.

The second way that these programs can widen the net is by increasing the rate of imprisoned failures. Often, people who fail under a new program are charged an added "premium" for their failure. They receive a prison sentence of several years to make a point about the toughness of the alternative, even though their original sentence would have been much less had they not been given the alternative.

These two problems are particularly acute for drug offenders. Users seldom receive incarcerative terms. Admitting them to the alternatives is almost always going to widen the net. Addicts, on the other hand, go to prison or jail when their accompanying crimes are serious. They make good candidates for diversion, but their prognosis in these programs is problematic, although somewhat better than their prognosis in prison. Admitting them to these programs can accomplish goals of diversion and crime control, but it will guarantee a client group experiencing high levels of difficulty—dirty urines, unemployment, and so forth. Sellers and Predators are normally excluded from alternatives programs by virtue of their criminal history. In short, trying to reduce prison population through diverting drug offenders requires making difficult choices.

In addition, the experience of the alternative can actually be more intrusive than prison. Intensive supervision for 18 months, with surprise home visits, urine monitoring, a 7:00 p.m. curfew, electronic bracelets, and 120 hours of community service—many offenders might consider this worse than 6 months in a jail. And there is the very real question that such close control might draw a user into further difficulty with the system, even though adjustment is otherwise adequate.

The main point is that correctional alternatives are not a fail-safe way to reduce the pressure of prisons. If they are to work as true alternatives, they must be carefully designed, with eligibility criteria that are tightly drawn to guarantee true diversion from incarceration.

IT IS EASIER TO CONTAIN COSTS THAN TO REDUCE THEM

Much is made of the fact that alternatives are cheaper than traditional prison. When offenders assigned to alternatives are truly diverted from prison, they generally receive a less costly sentence. But this may not necessarily translate into cost savings. For one thing, the very best alternatives can approach the cost of prison. In-residence treatment and shock incarceration can be more expensive per day than traditional prison—they cost less only when the terms are shorter. ISPs, when truly intensive, can involve costs nearly half that of prison, and may be imposed for twice as long (McDonald, 1989).

A more difficult problem is that the total cost of running a prison is about the same when the prison is 90% full as when it is at capacity. The housing costs of a given prison (food and clothing) contribute insignificantly to the daily prison budget, but security needs, mostly in the form of personnel requirements, stay relatively stable within a range of capacity. (Conditions of extreme crowding will aggravate security costs, whereas closing unused units can eliminate some personnel needs.) No matter how extensively systems use their new alternatives, almost no states find they have vacant cells as a result.

Rather than reducing total systems costs, it is better to think in terms of cost containment, whereby expenditures on new facilities are avoided (or delayed) through the extensive use of less expensive alternatives. This strategy seems especially applicable to those drug offenders, in particular, addicts, who experience the system serially over their lifetimes (Ball et al., 1982). Costs of managing these offenders can be contained through careful use of layered alternatives, in which short treatment experiences are augmented by community control approaches (such as ISP). The long-term goal is desistance, which may require several years to achieve and may be accomplished through repeated use of alternatives that seem to fail in the short run. In this approach, program failure is accompanied by short-term consequences, including even short jail stays, followed by renewed attempts at treatment/control. If this seems an unappealing strategy, it is more desirable than longer prison stays, which cost much more and have little impact on desistance.

For Predators and Users, the concept of cost containment may not be so relevant. With Predators, their procriminal lifestyle is precisely the type on which correctional costs should be concentrated. For Users, the benefits of any system expenditures should be questioned. Sellers, on the other hand pose a dilemma. In today's atmosphere of toughness with "pushers," it is not easy to argue for cost containment. Yet research shows, first, that these offenders are quickly replaced by other sellers after their incarceration, and, second, that they have low failure rates after release. In other words, few crimes are prevented by their incarceration.

THE COSTS OF TOUGH ENFORCEMENT CAN BE CONSIDERABLE

All research on the new alternatives finds that they enforce program requirements stringently and thus have high program failure rates (Petersilia, Peterson, & Turner, 1992). This result should not surprise anyone. Offenders are not a compliant group to begin with. When they are made accountable for a large number of strict rules and then are closely monitored for compliance, they often fail. On the face of it, this seems both obvious and desirable. Closer analysis raises questions about the wisdom of a strategy of unrelenting enforcement.

The process of tough enforcement in these programs involves the imposition of costly consequences for behavior that is either noncriminal (failure to comply with curfew or failure to complete community service work) or of minor seriousness (marijuana in the urine). Imposition of an original prison term for such behavior may satisfy program directors that their requirements "have teeth," but it seems to miss the point that the program's ultimate responsibility is to prevent crime and change the offender's behavior patterns, not simply to run a tight ship. When program requirements are so strict that offenders are returned to prison for rules violations despite the absence of evidence of new criminality or impending criminal conduct, both the offender and the system lose.

This is especially likely to happen with drug offenders. Addicts will fail, and they will fail frequently. Any program built on a foundation of zero tolerance for failure will find the fully successful Addict to be in a small minority. By the same token, professionals who work with Addicts know that misbehavior must be met with consequences. The strategy is normally to impose sanctions of slowly ascending seriousness in the face of "slips" for persons thought otherwise to be noncriminal. Addicts can move up and down through phases of increased urine testing, curfews, loss of privileges (such as driving), and even short jail stays several times before they finally establish a period of sobriety that can form the foundation for recovery.

When prison is thought of as a last resort, programs take the approach of working with Addicts who exhibit motivation to stay clean, even in the face of occasional slips. The idea is to decrease the incidence and frequency of the slips and reward the offender in the process. But when reincarceration is thought of as the only consequence for misbehavior, none of this sequencing is possible, and addicts fail at very high rates.

This program is all the more difficult for Users, whose involvement in the criminal justice system is essentially a result of drug laws. To enforce packages of requirements on them in a nonnegotiable fashion is to invite failure where there would otherwise be success. For Predators and Sellers, the story is quite different. Misbehavior on the part of these offenders can be interpreted as predictive of a resumption of criminal activity. In these cases, rapid and serious consequences for noncompliance with program rules may prevent crime.

ALL ALTERNATIVES IMPOSE OPPORTUNITY COSTS

The popularity of alternatives to traditional corrections should not obscure the fact that the decision to invest in these programs ties up public dollars. It is the same for prisons—the decision to construct a prison means that dollars dedicated to that task cannot be spent on public health, schools, transportation, or other worthy public causes. The decision to develop alternatives may contain costs of traditional corrections, but that still means the devotion of tax dollars to that alternative.

From a broad perspective, the decision to expand alternatives for drug offenders may mean, for example, that noncorrectional treatment approaches receive less support. This certainly appears to have been the case since 1980, at least at the federal level of government. The appropriate public policy question is whether dollars put into correctional forms of treatment, traditional or nontraditional, pay off to the public more than dollars in noncustodial treatment or prevention. Insufficient information exists to answer this question, but it is certainly a question worth asking: If investing in prisons and special correctional programs means the decimation of mental health alternatives, is that a wise trade-off?

More narrowly, the problem of opportunity costs applies to the assignment of "spaces" to persons in alternatives programs. An ISP caseload, for example, has a capacity of 20 to 25 cases. Is it better to place a burglar or a drug offender under such close scrutiny? The question is not merely rhetorical, for as the system begins to devote more attention to the problem of drugs, other types of offenders take a backseat in its priorities.

The question of the wisdom of focusing alternatives on drug offenders instead of other offenders is probably dependent on the type of offender being considered. It would appear unwise, for example, to use up the scarce resources of an ISP program on mere Users when the traditional probation caseload contains burglars, assaulters, and others representing a much more significant risk to the general public. Regardless of the public relations value of zero tolerance, there may be serious detriment to focusing such resources on relatively minor problems (and problem makers). By contrast, when Predators are released from prison, it would seem wise to give them the closest control available (ISP with electronic and urine monitoring, for example) instead of traditional parole. Yet many of the alternative programs specifically exclude the latter and seek the former, advertising themselves as "fighting drugs." When this occurs, there are substantial opportunity costs in the misapplication of risk management resources in correction.

FOUR STRATEGIES FOR EFFECTIVE USE OF ALTERNATIVES WITH DRUG OFFENDERS

A clearer understanding of the types of alternative programs available and the types of offenders to be assigned to them helps put the usefulness of alternatives into perspective. The following discussion should not be taken as a recommendation for prison in cases where no other program seems to make sense. With the exception of some Predators, no consistent evidence can be found that prison is a preferable program placement to lesser alternatives for any drug offenders. Failure rates of drug offenders in most programs are high, but failure rates after prison are just as high and may be higher. Instead, the aim should be to put the use of alternatives into a perspective that both reflects evidence about their suitability and resists overreliance on them and unrealistic expectations of them.

DRUG OFFENDERS SHOULD BE ASSIGNED TO PROGRAMS THAT FIT THEIR DRUG-CRIME BEHAVIOR

Alternatives are not equally suitable for all drug offenders. Drug offenders vary in their manageability, their risk to the community, and their compunction to commit crimes. Using the typology described earlier, program recommendations can be made reflecting the fit between the program's ordinary

TABLE 1: Fitting Drug Offenders to Appropriate Correctional Alternatives

Type of Correctional Alternative	*Type of Offender*			
	Seller	*Addict*	*Predator*	*User*
Shock incarceration	–	–	–	0
Residential programs	0	+	+	0
Intensive supervision	+	+	+	–
Electronic monitoring	0	0	+	–
Urine testing	–	+	+	0
Drug suppression	–	+	0	–
Treatment programs	–	+	+	+

+ = Suggested as appropriate by research and theory.
0 = No research or theory to support this option.
– = Research or theory suggest this option is inappropriate.

capacity and the drug offender's needs. A summary of such suitability is presented in Table 1.

Predatory offenders appear well suited for several of these programs, especially intensive supervision and the close control inherent in residential programs and urine monitoring (Anglin & Hser, 1990). For the most part, however, Predators are not suitable subjects for diversion into these programs, for they are strong candidates for incarceration in the first place. After incarceration, Predators benefit (and the community can be protected) by the close supervision in these alternatives programs (Wexler, Lipton, & Johnson, 1988).

Addicts also fit intensive alternatives well, especially when control-oriented approaches are closely coupled with treatment interventions (Anglin, 1988). Conventional probation is seldom useful for long-term Addicts. Shock approaches also appear inadvisable, because the addict's drug use is not easily susceptible to deterrence through threats. The main aim of programs for Addicts is to lengthen the periods of drug-free street time. Total abstinence is usually seen as an unreasonable goal (Wexler & Lipton, 1985).

Users, by contrast, might benefit from treatment approaches, but the heavy control approaches are liable to be counterproductive by forcing the User deeper into the criminal justice system, should there be noncompliance with program rules (Petersilia, 1987; Petersilia & Turner, 1990). For many Users, fines, community service, and conventional probation are enough to deter.

Sellers can be managed in the context of intensive supervision but are not likely to do well in other strategies. Residential programs provide an audience of potential consumers; shock approaches are unlikely to deter, given the financial incentives of the drug business. Some have argued that fines and forfeiture help to remove the financial incentives for the drug business and thus are relevant to the Seller (Cole, Mahoney, Thornton, & Hanson, 1987).

These general strategies are suggested with caution. The research on program effectiveness with drug offenders is scanty at best, and few of the studies attempt to isolate the interaction effects proposed here. The type of research needed in this area is illustrated by a RAND study that attempted to classify offenders in an ISP experiment according to the model we have proposed. Overall, offenders did no better on ISP than on regular probation (in fact, evidence suggested they may have done worse under the ISP option). However, Users had a 50% higher (nonsignificant) arrest rate under ISP as compared to regular probation, consistent with the model (Deschenes, Turner, & Petersilia, 1992). (There was no difference for the other three types—a result perhaps due to small sample size, the pure control nature of the program, and the limited ability to classify offenders, post hoc.)

EXPECT HIGH RATES OF FAILURE; PREPARE PROGRAMMING OPTIONS

With the exception of users, drug offenders fail at high rates in any program placement, including prison (Wish & Johnson, 1986). Working with these offenders requires a large number of options and schedules of reinforcement, with the ability to intensify or reduce controls in small increments as justified by the offender's behavior.

One implication of this caution is that if these programs are working well, they will have lots of action in relation to offenders' conduct. Programs with low failure rates are probably either lax in enforcement or are drawing too heavily from user populations that would produce high success rates.

Because alternatives programs have high levels of enforcement action, they require a special type of staff and unusually consistent support from the courts. Staff need to be professionally trained and well experienced with drug users' special problems. Their expectations should be realistic, and their patience (grounded in firmness) should enable them to have credibility with the offenders they see. Courts need to encourage latitude in working with offenders, supporting approaches that maintain consistent programs of consequences. There is always a temptation to "do treatment" from the bench, but courts should resist the desire to innovate on an ad hoc basis because this usually undercuts the logic of a program.

The larger the number of alternatives, the better. It makes good public relations to present programs as "tough last stops before prison," but if this is the way the programs operate, they will be irrelevant to many drug users. Prison is a necessary option in the enforcement spectrum, especially for criminally active addicts, sellers, and predators, but its benefits are often overstated. Eventually, offenders are released, and drug programs have to begin with the progress made earlier on the street.

One way to view this system of approaches is to see traditional probation and prison as the "bookends" of a spectrum of available interventions. Strict enforcement requires that misbehaving drug users be moved off traditional probation relatively easily into nontraditional approaches but should encounter prison only as a last resort (except for Predators), and perhaps only for short periods. Offenders moving out of the courts (at sentencing) and out of prison (onto parole) should be placed initially in the approach that best fits their circumstances, not the one that has available space or is currently popular.

THERE ARE NO "PURE" TYPES AND NO "PERFECT" PROGRAMS

It goes without saying that complexity underlies any system of dealing with drug offenders, and so no perfect solution exists. In fact, many sellers are involved in other predatory crime (Spunt et al., 1987); many users stand on the brink of addiction and sell drugs to a small circle of friends (Biernacki, 1986). The drug offender types provide a heuristic device to analyze the problem, the program prototypes display general programs, but there is much overlap among them in practice (Chaiken & Johnson, 1988).

In the real world, the best program fit for an offender will not always be obvious, and all programs will have idiosyncratic strengths and weaknesses, often due to unique staff configurations. Predators will sometimes do quite well in response to an electronic monitoring program; users will occasionally fail miserably on traditional probation.

The term used to describe this situation is *technical uncertainty*—it means that the technologies for working with drug offenders are unpredictable in their outcomes. Because technical uncertainty produces frustrations for staff and system decision makers, there is a constant temptation to perceive alternatives to traditional corrections as ineffectual. The usual choice in the face of frustration is incarceration. Imprisonment has the advantage for decision makers of disengaging the decision from the feedback about its effectiveness. When drug offenders recidivate after imprisonment, it is unusual for the judge or the prosecutor to admit it was the wrong choice, even though they will be quick to do so after a similar failure under an alternative program.

If there is a secret in dealing with drug offenders, it is creative persistence with individually scripted strategies. Imprisonment has a role, but it will ultimately prove frustratingly ineffectual unless it is used appropriately in response to the right offenders and in the right situation.

FOCUS ON THE GOAL OF REDUCING THE PAINS OF DRUGS

In recent years, the American public has become increasingly sensitized to the harmful effects of drugs. There are many: Criminal networks, criminal acts, physical side effects, unsafe streets and lost lives are among them. These problems have fueled the war on drugs (Inciardi, 1992).

There are also harmful effects, just of the war itself. Sending people to prison seldom improves their life chances and is almost never intended to do so. When youngsters enter the criminal justice system, they face long odds of overcoming the negative impact of a record and the affiliations produced in processing their case. Removing men and women from their families can be permanently damaging to children and to their family units. Whole neighborhoods become dominated by definitions of deviance, lawbreaking, and avoiding "the man"—this changes the meaning of "growing up." In the pressure to respond to the problem of drugs, families are uprooted from public housing, draconian penalties are handed out, and irretrievable resources are committed to the problem. Almost no proposal is seen as too excessive. It is hard, sometimes, to know if the cure is more painful than the disease.

It is time to admit that a drug-free society is not now and never was a realistic aim. Whether or not it is good rhetoric, the desire for zero tolerance has fed a zealousness that overwhelms the realities of modern, urban America. A much more realistic and realizable goal must replace this unrealistic vision. The purpose of correctional intervention is to prevent crimes where possible, reduce harms to families and communities where feasible, and take reasonable steps to encourage and assist offenders to forgo drug use and related criminal activity. The aim is to reduce, in small measures, the pain experienced by all citizens, offenders and others alike, resulting from drugs in America.

REFERENCES

Andrews, D., Kessling, J., Robinson, D., & Mickus, S. (1986). The risk principle of case classification: An outcome evaluation with adult probationers. *Canadian Journal of Criminology, 28*, 377-396.

Anglin, D. (1988). The efficacy of civil commitment in treating narcotic addition. In C. Leukefeld & F. M. Tims (Eds.), *Compulsory treatment of drug abuse*. Rockville, MD: National Institute on Drug Abuse.

Anglin, D., & Hser, Y. (1990). Treatment of drug abuse. In M. Tonry & J. Q. Wilson (Eds.), *Drugs and crime*. Chicago: University of Chicago Press.

Austin, J., & Krisberg, B. (1980). *The unmet promise of alternatives to corrections*. San Francisco: National Council on Crime and Delinquency.

Ball, J. C. (1986). The hyper-criminal opiate addict. In B. D. Johnson & E. Wish (Eds.), *Crime rates among drug abusing offenders* (Final Report to the National Institute of Justice). New York: Narcotic and Drug Research, Inc.

Ball, J. C., Rosen, L., Flueck, J., & Nurco, D. (1982). Lifetime criminality of heroin addicts in the United States. *Journal of Drug Issues, 3*, 225-239.

Ball, J. C., Shaffer, J., & Nurco, D. (1983). The day-to-day criminality of heroin addicts in Baltimore: A study in the continuity of offense rates. *Drug and Alcohol Dependence, 12*, 119-142.

Biernacki, P. (1986). *Pathways to addiction*. Philadelphia: Temple University Press.

Byrne, J. (1990). The future of intensive probation supervision and the new intermediate sanctions. *Crime & Delinquency, 36*, 6-41.

Byrne, J., Lurigio, A., & Baird, C. S. (1989). *The effectiveness of the new intensive supervision programs* (Research in Corrections, No. 5). Washington, DC: National Institute of Corrections.

Chaiken, M., & Chaiken, J. (1984). Offender types and public policy. *Crime & Delinquency, 30*, 195-226.

Chaiken, J., & Chaiken, M. (1990). Drugs and predatory crime. In M. Tonry & J. Q. Wilson (Eds.), *Drugs and crime*. Chicago: University of Chicago Press.

Chaiken, M., & Johnson, B. (1988). *Characteristics of different types of drug involved offenders*. Washington, DC: National Institute of Justice.

Clear, T., & Gallagher, K. (1983). Screening devices in probation and parole: Management problems. *Evaluation Review, 7*, 217-234.

Cole, G. F., Mahoney, B., Thornton, M., & Hanson, R. (1987). *Attitudes and practices of trial court judges toward the use of fines*. Denver: Institute for Court Management.

DeLeon, G. (1987). Alcohol use among drug abusers: Treatment outcomes in a therapeutic community. *Alcoholism Clinical and Experimental Research, 11*, 430-436.

Deschenes, E., Turner, S., & Petersilia, J. (1992). *The effectiveness and costs of intensive supervision for drug offenders* (Working paper). Santa Monica, CA: RAND.

Fagan, J. (1990). Intoxication and aggression. In M. Tonry & J. Q. Wilson (Eds.), *Drugs and crime*. Chicago: University of Chicago Press.

Ficher, M., Hirschberg, P., & McGaha, J. (1987). Felony probation: A comparative analysis of public risk in two states. *Perspectives, 11*, 6-11.

Goldkamp, J. (1989, March). *The effectiveness of drug testing in the courts*. Paper presented to the Conference on Drugs and the Courts, Denver, CO.

Goldstein, P. (1981). Getting over: Economic alternatives to predatory crime among street drug users. In J. Inciardi (Ed.), *The drugs/crime connection*. Beverly Hills, CA: Sage.

Hanson, B., Beschner, G., Walters, J., & Bovelle, E. (1985). *Life with heroin: Voices from the inner city*. Lexington, MA: Lexington Books.

Hillsman, S., & Greene, J. (1992). The use of fines as an intermediate sanction. In J. Byrne, A. Lurigio, & J. Petersilia (Eds.), *Smart sentencing: The emergence of intermediate sanctions*. Newbury Park, CA: Sage.

Inciardi, J. (1992). *The war on drugs II*. Palo Alto, CA: Mayfield.

Johnson, B., & Wish, E. (1987). *Criminal events among seriously criminal drug abusers* (Final Report to the National Institute of Justice). New York: Narcotic and Drug Research, Inc.

Markley, G., & Eisenberg, M. (1987). *Evaluation of the Texas parole classification and case management system*. Austin: Texas Board of Pardons and Paroles.

McDonald, D. (1989). *The cost of corrections* (Research in Corrections, No. 4). Washington, DC: National Institute of Corrections.

McDonald, D. (1992). Punishing labor: Unpaid community service as a criminal sentence. In J. Byrne, A. Lurigio, & J. Petersilia (Eds.), *Smart sentencing: The emergence of intermediate sanctions*. Newbury Park, CA: Sage.

Mieczkowski, T. (1986). Geeking up and throwing down: Heroin street life in Detroit. *Criminology, 24*, 645-666.

Parent, D. (1989). *Shock incarceration: An overview of existing programs*. Washington, DC: National Institute of Justice.

Petersilia, J. (1987). *Expanding options for criminal sentencing*. Santa Monica, CA: RAND.

Petersilia, J., Peterson, J., & Turner, S. (1992). *Intensive probation and parole: Research findings and policy implications* (Working paper). Santa Monica, CA: RAND.

Petersilia, J., & Turner, S. (1990). Comparing intensive and regular supervision for high-risk probationers: Early results from an experiment in California. *Crime & Delinquency, 36*, 87-111.

Petersilia, J., Turner, S., Kahan, J., & Peterson, J. (1985). *Granting felons probation: Public risks and alternatives*, Santa Monica, CA: RAND.

Platt, J. (1986). *Heroin addiction: Theory, research and treatment* (2nd ed.). Malabar, FL: Krieger.

Reuter, P., Macoun, R., & Murphy, P. (1990). *Money from crime*. Santa Monica, CA: RAND.

Rosenbaum, M., & Murphy, S. (1984). Always a junkie? The arduous task of getting off methadone maintenance. *Journal of Drug Issues, 3*, 527-552.

Speckart, G., & Anglin, D. (1986). Narcotics use and crime: A causal modeling approach. *Journal of Quantitative Criminology, 2*, 3-28.

Schmidt, A. (1989). Electronic monitoring of offenders increases. *NIJ Reports, 212*, 2-5.

Spunt, B., Goldstein, P., Lipton, D., Bellucci, P., Miller, T., Cortez, N., Kahn, M., & Kale, A. (1987, November). *Systemic violence among street drug distributors*. Paper presented at the annual meetings of American Society of Criminology, Montreal, Canada.

Wexler, H., & Lipton, D. (1985, November). *Prison drug treatment: The critical ninety days of re-entry*. Paper presented at the annual meetings of the American Society of Criminology, San Diego, CA.

Wexler, H., Lipton, D., & Johnson, B. (1988). *A criminal justice strategy for treating drug offenders in custody*. Washington, DC: National Institute of Justice.

Wexler, H., & Williams, R. (1986). The Stay N' Out therapeutic community: Prison treatment for substance abusers. *Journal of Psychoactive Drugs, 18*, 221-230.

Wish, E., & Gropper, B. (1990). Drug testing by the criminal justice system: Methods, research, and applications. In M. Tonry & J. Q. Wilson (Eds.), *Drugs and crime*. Chicago: University of Chicago Press.

Wish, E., & Johnson, B. (1986). The impact of substance abuse on criminal career. In A. Blumstein, J. Cohen, J. A. Roth, & C. Visher (Eds.), *Criminal careers and "career criminals"* (Vol. 2). Washington, DC: National Academy Press.

Zinberg, N. (1984). *Drug, set and setting*. New Haven, CT: Yale University Press.

The Setting for the Crack Era: Macro Forces, Micro Consequences (1960-1992)†

Eloise Dunlap, Ph.D.* & Bruce D. Johnson, Ph.D.*

Abstract — This article provides an overview of the social history leading up to the crack era, especially 1960 to the present. The central theme holds that several major macro social forces (e.g., economic decline, job loss, ghettoization, housing abandonment, homelessness) have disproportionately impacted on the inner-city economy. These forces have created micro consequences that have impacted directly on many inner-city residents and have increased levels of distress experienced by households, families, and individuals. Economic marginality has generated high levels of alcohol and other drug abuse as well as criminality, which are exemplified in this article by one inner-city household having an extensive family history exhibiting the chronic impacts of these macro forces and their micro consequences.

Keywords — crack cocaine, inner-city household-family, macro social forces, micro social consequences.

This article examines the social history of the inner city from 1960 to 1992 in an effort to understand the social forces that provided support for the rapid and widespread adoption of crack cocaine after 1983–1984. The central argument is that several major *macro social forces* have disproportionately impacted on the inner-city economy and have increased levels of social distress. These forces have impacted directly on many inner-city residents and have increased levels of social distress experienced by households, families, and individuals, which in turn has generated alcohol and other drug abuse as well as criminality. The *micro consequences* are exemplified by one inner-city household (headed by Island and Ross) having an extensive family history paralleling these macro forces.

In addition, this article focuses on the continued socioeconomic decline in the inner city during the period 1960–1992, particularly in New York City. This 32-year period was chosen because virtually all evidence shows important declines in living standards among inner-city residents during that period (Jaynes & Williams 1989). New York City is a primary focus because its inner-city residents account for a disproportionate share of the nation's problem (Karsada 1992), and historically the city has had the nation's largest drug abuse problem. Additionally, most of the authors' prior research among inner-city drug abusers has been conducted in New York.

An important subtheme in this article is that the use, abuse, and sale or distribution of illegal drugs — especially heroin, cocaine, and crack — are both a consequence of the rising social distress in the inner city *and* an important contributor to the continuity and intensity of inner-city conditions, and the difficulty in alleviating them. Furthermore, all indicators currently suggest that social distress in the inner city is increasing, intensifying, and perhaps accelerating. Johnson and colleagues (1990) provided a more extended overview of the social history of crack abuse and macro level forces. The case history of Island and her household is more extensively documented in Dunlap (In press-a).

The American economy has historically been characterized by unequal resource allocation, particularly for mi-

†Supported by the Urban Institute's Urban Opportunities Program and presented at the Conference on Drugs, Crime, and Social Distress in Philadelphia, April 1991. This article also relies on much prior conceptualization and research by the authors on the Natural History of Crack Distribution, a project funded by the National Institute on Drug Abuse (1 R01 DA05126-04) as well as from other projects funded by NIDA (1 R01 DA01926-07, 5 T32 DA07233-08, 1 R01 DA06615-02), by the National Institute of Justice (80-IJ-CX-0049S2, 87-IJ-CX-0064, 91-IJ-CX-D014), and by support from Narcotic and Drug Research, Inc.

The opinions expressed do not necessarily represent official positions of the United States Government, National Development and Research Institutes, Inc. or the Urban Institute.

*National Development and Research Institutes, Inc. (formerly Narcotic and Drug Research, Inc.), 11 Beach Street, New York, New York 10013.

FIGURE 1
CONCEPTUAL MODEL OF SOCIAL DISTRESS AND DISTRESSED INNER-CITY HOUSEHOLDS

Macro Social Forces	National-Level Crisis Situation	Broader Conditions and Indicators	Distressed Inner-city Household-Family
Unequal resource allocations	Upper 20th percentile with 50% of wealth. Poverty for many minorities.	Economic stagnation/ decline for the majority. Declines in/less wealth.	Few possessions. Many economic problems. Have become relatively poorer.
Shifts in economic base	Manufacturing decline. Service jobs. Intellectual services. Few modest pay jobs. Few jobs for unskilled.	Unemployment; unskilled jobs. Part-time & low-wage pay. Unskilled not considered. Men unable to support family. Out of labor force.	No/fewer member(s) with legal income. Little/no employment income. Discouraged/do not seek jobs. Men leave/never form families. Multiple adults have no jobs.
Housing abandonment/ deterioration	Housing not available. Housing deteriorates. Housing costs high. Adults with no homes. Abandoned buildings.	Homeless persons/shelters. Substandard housing. Much income goes for shelter. Households double up.	Adults put out of household. Poor housing for all members. Removes money for food/ other expenses. Crowded, changing household composition. Family/kin cannot help.
Racial/ethnic discrimination	Poverty for many. Residential segregation increases.	Inadequate income for living. Less contact between races. Few contacts with informal job networks.	Adults cannot pay for food/shelter. Know few nonpoor persons. No access to networks for jobs in suburbs, other areas.
Health care declines	High costs, no or little health coverage.	Poor health, shortened life. Little/no preventive care.	Many acute illnesses, early death. Poor diet, chronic problems.
Advanced education needed	High HS dropout rate. Declining value of high school degree.	Low literacy, few skills. Higher human capital needed for low-wage job(s).	Cannot read, basic skills absent. HS graduates do not get jobs. HS dropouts excluded from jobs.
Family/kin instability	High rate of divorce, not married or common-law. Child rearing problems. Children do not live with mother.	Casual relationships. Children without two or even one natural parent. Grandparent/aunts/foster care rear children.	No/little birth control. No/little commitment to child rearing by parent(s). Caregiving forced on other adults, children semineglected.
Booming drug economy	Expanding illicit drug use/abuse/sales. Unstable, poor paying jobs in drug business.	Drug use and abuse. Alcohol abuse. Work in illegal markets. Use up economic returns.	Adults use/abuse drugs in household. Train children in abuse patterns. Most income from illegal work. No money for household.
Perceived rise in criminality	Modest change in nondrug criminality. Increases in drug crimes. Get-tough laws. Strong enforcement & lengthy punishments.	Homicide/robbery rate up somewhat. Expanding drug crime/arrests. New laws, more arrests/criminal justice system personnel/ longer sentences. Expand jail/prison cells.	Adult(s) arrested and imprisoned for nondrug crimes. Many members with drug arrests. Common behaviors criminalized. More arrests/time incarcerated. Longer time away from family.
Shifts in subcultures	Subculture of poverty. Subculture of violence. Subculture of refusal.	No expectation of work/legal income; value shifts. Use threats/violence to show love/resolve disputes. Denigrate square(s), legal work; oppose authority.	Confusion about seeking work. Contradictions in family. Constant arguments/fights, lack of household harmony. Avoid legal structure(s). Challenge legal order.

norities. While great racial and ethnic disparities existed in the early 1960s, Blacks who migrated from the South to northern cities, migrants from Puerto Rico to New York, and Hispanics to southwestern cities and Chicago made substantial gains economically. During the past three decades, however, American culture and the international economy shifted in emphasis from manufacturing to service sectors. This trend decreased the need for unskilled labor and increased the requirements for advanced education and technical skills. This transformation has generated several major crises, reallocated resources away from programs and services provided in the 1960s, and created numerous difficult conditions for those living in inner-city America.

Several eras of drug use, abuse, and sales have occurred in America since 1965 (Johnson & Manwar 1991) and dramatically transformed patterns of criminal behavior and social arrangements in inner cities. Numerous laws and efforts at controlling drug abusers have been politically popular but have had very repressive impacts on inner-city persons and households. Alcohol, heroin, cocaine, and, recently, crack abuse and distribution, combined with declining socioeconomic conditions, have severely disrupted many inner-city households and families across three and four generations. Such household-families with drug-abusing members serve as the primary vector in transmission across generations of drug abuse, drug sales and distribution, criminal behavior, and support for deviant behaviors.

Figure 1 summarizes key themes to be developed below. Macro social forces (e.g., shifting economic base, housing deterioration, drug economy expansion) have created nationwide crisis situations for those with low incomes, especially those living in American inner cities. In turn, such crises in the inner city have generated *conditions of social distress* that tend to be chronic and cumulative over years across generations. In sociological terms, crisis is a turning point, often brought about by a convergence of events that create new circumstances requiring new responses. The term "crisis" may be applied in a wide range of contexts, from macro to micro levels (Dunlap In press-a; Lyman 1975). Conditions are relatively objective circumstances that are measurable and can be used to document social distress across many persons.

These socioeconomic forces and conditions are intertwined in complex ways. They have their immediate and concrete impacts on households, families, and individuals. A key focus of this article is on what may be called the *severely distressed inner-city household-family* — those living in the inner cities of major urban centers in America, especially New York City. In Kasarda's (1992) study of the 95 most populated central cities in 1980, 15% of the most severely distressed Black households and 55% of the most severely distressed Hispanic households were in New York. Very similar problems and social distress (Kasarda 1992) are likely to emerge among poor households and families in many other parts of America outside of the inner cities (Jaynes & Williams 1989; Dembo 1988).

Many inner-city households and families manage to maintain continuity and relative stability for several years, and may not be classified as severely distressed. However, the focus here is on households that would meet (or exceed) all five distress criteria used by Kasarda (1992): low education (high-school dropout), single parenthood (household head with children under age 18), poor work history (worked less than half time in prior year), receipt of public assistance, and householder's family income from legal sources below the poverty line.

The present analysis focuses on the household-family because the usual census assumptions about family composition and household structure and processes are infrequently met among distressed inner-city households. Rather, the household-family has emerged as an adaptation that meets the survival needs of several persons in the kin network. The availability of a household is the determining factor. Many inner-city adults have great difficulty in acquiring and maintaining a place of residence. While a household head is usually present, the family composition of the household varies dramatically day by day (Dunlap In press-a, 1992) in response to conditions set in force by social and economic macro forces. Several blood relatives and fictive kin who are essentially homeless (and drug abusers) may claim a given household as their home. They may not usually live there, but may keep some clothes there and return periodically to wash and change their attire. They may also reside in the household for short periods of time.

One may speculate — noting that inadequate documentation currently exists — that a majority of these severely distressed inner-city household-families in 1992 probably have one or more adults (16 and older) who is a drug abuser, or drug seller, or who is criminally active. Such drug abusers and sellers may be present or absent from the household-family at any given time, but their appearances provide economic benefits as well as economic and social harms to household-family units. Moreover, drug abusers and sellers in such households act as role models, mentors, and employers (both positive and negative) for youths growing up — thus transmitting values, beliefs, and practices reflecting subcultures of drug abuse, drug sales, criminality, and violence (Dunlap In press-a, 1992). Indeed, such drug abusers and sellers routinely engage in behaviors that disrupt household harmony and stability.

The dynamic shifts and the intensity of problems in such severely depressed inner-city household-families confront researchers with formidable analytic problems and policymakers with complex issues to resolve. If policy could substantially alter the family interaction patterns among such severely depressed inner-city household-family units, policymakers could substantially reduce the magnitude of social distress, dramatically reduce drug abuse and sales, and greatly reduce other fundamental social problems in America. The continuing failure to address these problems — now well documented since the 1960s — is likely to lead to continuing expansion in generational transmission of drug abuse, continuing crises and social conditions, and continuing problems for society in the future.

AN OVERVIEW OF MACRO SOCIAL FORCES, CRISES, AND CONDITIONS 1960-1992

This section provides an overview of the broad socioeconomic forces and crises during the past 32 years, with special attention to contributions of drug abuse.

Before 1960

Before, during, and after World War II, thousands of Blacks left the South because few jobs were available, and higher paying jobs could be found in northern cities (even if pay was low relative to Whites employment). In the 1940s and 1950s, thousands of Puerto Ricans and individuals from the West Indies also migrated to New York. These immigrants settled in Harlem, East Harlem, the Lower East Side, and Brooklyn. Such immigrants and their families were severely impoverished in both the South and North. Nevertheless, expansion of the national economy decreased the proportion of Blacks living in poverty from 85% in 1944 to 55% in 1959 (Jaynes & Williams 1989). Like many postwar American families, these immigrants had children and contributed disproportionately to the baby-boom generation (born between 1946 and 1960). These minorities gained housing as thousands of White city dwellers moved to the mushrooming suburbs (Frey 1980).

The civil rights movement in the 1950s focused national attention on legal and civil inequalities and on the poverty and despair of Blacks and other minorities. Although (relative to Whites) housing discrimination, low incomes, and other problems beset minorities before 1960, most migrants were considerably better off economically in the cities than their relatives who had remained in the South or than their parents had been two decades earlier. A case study (see Dunlap In press-a, 1992) of one such household is interwoven with the following analysis to illustrate the interplay between the macro social forces and the micro consequences.

A Severely Distressed Inner-city Household-Family: Island, Ross, Sonya.

In 1990, Island and her household-family lived in a three-bedroom apartment in Central Harlem. Island is 60 years old and lives with her son, Ross (a 35-year-old active crack seller) and daughter, Sonya (a 37-year-old crack prostitute), as well as several other household members who circulate in and out. Island's story attests to the harsh reality confronting many inner-city families, and reflects the impact of larger social forces and conditions, especially the impact of alcohol and other drug abuse, and the drug economy on a severely distressed household across several years and generations. Despite its problems, it exemplifies the "least unstable households" (Dunlap 1992) affected by drug abuse.

1930 to 1947. In 1930, Island was born on a Caribbean Island and abandoned at birth by her natural mother; her father died when she was four. In 1935, Island was brought to New York, and raised by a stepmother as the youngest of six children. Their household was "doubled up" with the stepmother's sister and her five children. Island's childhood memories were of her stepmother working long hours as a domestic. From 1935 to 1948 Island lived in Harlem with her family and kin network. She therefore grew up in Harlem although her family were migrants. In twelfth grade, she dropped out of school to care for her stepmother who was very ill.

1948 to 1959. In 1947, Island met Joe who was about 25 years old and recently released from jail. He had come from South Carolina and found low-wage work as a coal deliverer. After they married in 1948, Island worked as a home attendant on and off until her first child, Sonya, was born in 1953; Ross was born in 1955. Island found her husband was a heavy alcohol abuser. In 1959 Island left her husband to protect herself and her children after Joe raped their six-year-old daughter. Two years later, her husband was hit by a car and killed.

The 1960s. The 1960s saw major changes in northern urban centers and the lives of minorities in those cities. The civil rights movement had its peak influence as the voting rights act and other legislation and federal enforcement efforts guaranteed the legal rights and equality of opportunity for Blacks and other minorities. The War on Poverty, launched in 1964,[1] promised better incomes and living standards for all the poor, but especially for Blacks. Several major books document the situation during this era.

In several volumes titled *Children of Crisis*, Robert Coles (1970, 1968) provided careful psychological case studies of the response to various crisis situations among persons living in poverty in a period of civil rights demonstrations, including sharecroppers and migrants from south to north. Oscar Lewis (1965) advanced the thesis of a culture of poverty (which he claimed is a subculture). The strengths and other characteristics of Black families were described by several authors (Hill 1971; Billingsley 1968). Wolfgang and Ferricutti (1967) described a subculture of violence and Cohen (1955) described a subculture of delinquency. Heroin abuse began to become a major issue (Brown 1965; Malcolm X & Haley 1965; Chein et al. 1964).

Relative to what was to transpire in the 1980s, these sources and many others document important elements of stability in the social and economic life of inner-city dwellers in the first half of the 1960s. Most inner-city families had one or more adults with some legal employment; Black men were almost as likely to be employed as White men, although at a lower wage rate (Jaynes & Williams 1989). Inner-city families could usually afford housing with about 30% of their income. If they doubled up with relatives, it was generally for less than a year. Almost no family or kin member was homeless or without a place to sleep. Minority couples either were married or maintained a common-law relationship for several years. Children in single-parent households were usually raised by their mothers, sometimes with a father or father substitute present. Occasionally children would be sent to a grandmother or female relative, but be returned to their mother. Grandmothers were seldom responsible for raising their grandchildren. While alcohol use and abuse were common, the use of illicit drugs (especially marijuana, heroin, cocaine) was rare. While there were common-law crimes (robbery, burglary, theft among men and theft or prostitution among women) among some low-income persons, the sale and distribution of illegal drugs was virtually unknown. Even among prostitutes, much income was expended to support their children and household.

In the last half of the 1960s, however, three major events sharply shifted national attention and resources away from poverty and civil rights. First, the Vietnam War (1965–1973) diverted public attention and many fiscal resources from antipoverty programs. Student and antiwar protests spread across American campuses and society; police riots against students generated further protests.

Second, civil disorders and riots in Black inner cities expressed Black rage and anger about the slow pace of economic progress (Grier & Cobbs 1963). These riots badly damaged the fragile infrastructure of Black inner-city communities, particularly in Newark, Detroit, and Los Angeles. The National Advisory Commission on Civil Disorders (1968:1-2) warned that America was headed toward "two societies, one black, one white — separate and unequal" and documented the rise of a Black ghetto "largely maintained by white institutions and condoned by white society" (see also Clark 1965).

Third, this decade marked the introduction of illicit drugs as a major recreational activity for millions of individuals of the baby-boom generation who were entering adolescence. Whites, Blacks, and Hispanics, from all class levels participated in this phenomenon. Three major "drug eras" (Johnson & Manwar 1991) began and overlapped. The marijuana era (1965–1979) began in 1965 when approximately 5% of college students in New York and California began using marijuana; the proportions of marijuana users and frequency of use increased steadily through the 1960s and 1970s. The psychedelic era (1967–1975) saw substantial but smaller increases in the use of LSD — such use occurred primarily among Whites from middle-class backgrounds; inner-city youths generally avoided psychedelics (Johnson 1973). The heroin era (1965–1973), however, occurred primarily among inner-city youths, especially in New York City (and somewhat later in other cities) (Hunt & Chambers 1976).

Despite these increases in social distress, the postwar economic boom continued relatively unabated and Blacks across the nation gained somewhat economically. In 1969, Black men were only 5% less likely than Whites to be employed, and they earned 62% as much as Whites (up from 53% in 1959). The proportion of Blacks in poverty dropped from over 50% to 30% during the 1960s, compared with a drop of 18% to 9% among Whites (Jaynes & Williams 1989). Poverty rates dropped from 51% in 1959 to 20% among Black families headed by men. Poverty rates among Black families headed by women increased from 70% in 1959 to 75% in 1964 but declined to about 60% in 1969 (Jaynes & Williams 1989). Island, her household, and kin network were impacted by alcoholism; they were one of many inner-city households bypassed by economic improvements and afflicted with the pressing problems of a severely distressed family.

1960 to 1969. Island left her husband and began to raise her children alone while supported by welfare. She soon became the caregiver for her kin network. All of Island's older siblings were alcoholics. Their offspring were taken to Island's house until the siblings could resume parental duties. For example, when Island's sister was imprisoned for killing a young woman while performing an abortion, Island took in her children until their mother returned from prison. While raising Ross and Sonya, Island also raised several nieces and nephews when parental acts resulted in jail or prison, or when alcohol consumption limited their ability to care for their children.

The 1970s and 1980s

The economic expansion and dramatic economic gains for Blacks came to an abrupt halt in the early 1970s (Jaynes & Williams 1989). Shifting social forces created a crisis, which impinged directly on inner-city household-families. Each of these larger structural forces has been magnified by the rise of the drug economy and drug abuse among household members.

Shifting Economic Base. Following the end of the Vietnam War in the early 1970s, the American and international economic base shifted substantially. The primary shift has been the decline of manufacturing jobs in the United States that rely on unskilled or semiskilled labor, offering a steady low-to-modest wage and creating goods for the consumer mass market. Foreign countries with lower wage rates and modern equipment now produce many consumer goods (e.g., automobiles, appliances, clothing) that were dominated by American manufacturers in the 1950s and 1960s. Many manufacturing plants located in central cities and employing thousands of inner-city minorities were closed in the 1970s and 1980s (Sullivan 1989). In New York City, over half a million manufacturing jobs plus 100,000 jobs in wholesale and retail trades were lost between 1967 and 1987 (Kasarda 1992). Most such jobs had been filled by blue-collar workers, many of whom faced unemployment or had to accept lower wage jobs. While many fast-food-type jobs were added during these two decades, these usually pay minimum wage or only slightly more; neither individuals nor families can afford housing with such low incomes.

A major shift rarely noted in the American economy was the explosive growth in the underground economy, especially the drug economy in the inner city. Many employed and unemployed persons (Ross and Sonya among them) were attracted by and had much better earnings from this illegal activity than were offered by minimum wage jobs or legal positions, a theme developed below.

Declining Labor Force Participation. By all measures of economic change, inner-city minority residents were literally left behind. For inner-city minority youths and for many adults, virtually no legal jobs were available in their communities or among their networks of associates (Sullivan 1989). Especially among out-of-school males ages 16 to 24, the percent not working (both unemployed and out of labor force) increased from 19% in 1968-1970 to 44% in 1986-1988 among central city residents in Boston, Newark, New York, Philadelphia, and Pittsburgh. The proportion of high-school dropouts ages 16 to 64 not working was over 50% among Black males in midwestern cities, including Cleveland, Chicago, Detroit, Milwaukee, and St. Louis (Kasarda 1992).

While unemployment has increased, nonparticipation in the labor force (not seeking work and not working) has also grown substantially. During a 45-year work career (from ages 20 to 65), Black men in 1970 could anticipate 36 years of work, two years unemployment, and eight years out of the labor force. In the following 15 years, both unemployment and nonparticipation grew substantially for Black men (but not Whites). By 1985, Black men were likely to work only 29 years, be unemployed for five years, and spend 11 years out of the labor force (Jaynes & Williams 1989).

Between 1972 and 1982 the number of unemployed Black persons increased by 1.3 million (140%, 900,000 in 1972 to 2.1 million in 1982). The unemployment rates for both Blacks and Whites in 1982 were the highest since World War II, but the Black unemployment rate was still double that of Whites. In 1982 the unemployment rate among Black teenagers reached 48%, 28 percentage points higher than that for White teenagers (20.4%).

Island had no legal job outside her house since the early 1950s, although she earned occasional money babysitting for neighbors. Her primary occupation was caregiver for her children and those of her siblings; Aid to Families with Dependent Children (AFDC) payments kept her household below the poverty line. In the early 1970s, Ross made a tentative entry into the legal labor force. He obtained a part-time job paying the minimum wage, but held it for only a year before losing it. He has not had a legal job since, nor has he sought legal employment; he has been out of the labor force for 15 years. Similar short job histories, followed by dropping out of the labor market, are common among Island's kin network. Only one distantly related nephew (whom Island did not help raise) has "gone good" by entering and having a career in the armed forces.

Although the mid-1980s were a time of economic expansion across the nation, few or no benefits "trickled down" to inner-city residents. Among high-school dropout minority males ages 16 to 64 living in inner-city neighborhoods in 1990, approximately half to three-quarters (depending on the city) lacked legal employment and many of these have not worked at all during the prior decade.

Advanced Education Needed for New Jobs. The American economy, however, has expanded considerably in the suburbs and in some southern and western cities. The major growth in the 1980s has occurred in service-sector jobs. The best jobs in the computer industry and financial services demand college and advanced degrees or special skills that can only be learned on the job. A quarter million such jobs were added to the New York City economy between 1977 and 1987, and a quarter million more were added in New York suburbs (Kasarda 1992). Yet the odds of a Black student entering college within a year of graduating from high school were less than one-half the odds for a White student. During the booming 1980s, however, out-of-school males 16 to 64 years of age who did not have a college degree and lived in major midwest and northeast cities experienced increasing rates of not working (both Blacks and Whites, center city and suburban residents). Especially in inner-city neighborhoods, high-school dropout rates approach 50% or higher and a high-school diploma from such schools was generally undervalued by employers (Jaynes & Williams 1989; Reed 1988). The vast majority of drug abusers are high-school dropouts, although high-school graduates are increasingly common as the value of education has declined. But during the 1970s and 1980s, school systems have kept most minorities in school so that declining proportions have not completed eighth grade.

Sonya left high school in the eleventh grade as a result of her heroin addiction. At age 16, Ross dropped out of high school to sell drugs, primarily PCP. Island did not encourage or support the children in her care to do homework and she ignored their poor attendance and grades. None did well or enjoyed school; they saw no point in completing it. Virtually all children raised by Island dropped out of high school, and none has entered, or seriously considered attending college. Advanced education was not even a distant possibility in Island's household.

Housing Abandonment and High Housing Costs. By 1960, many structurally sound housing units provided low-cost housing to working families living in the inner-city. During the past 30 years, large segments of the low-cost housing stock deteriorated or were abandoned, particularly in inner-city neighborhoods (Dolbeare 1983; Hartman 1983; Hartman, Keating & Le Gates 1982). In the 1980s, real estate values in most major metropolitan areas soared, so that affordable housing was beyond the economic means of much of the population (Tucker 1989).

Affordable housing was unreachable for nearly half of the nation's Black and Hispanic families; 42% of all Black and Hispanic households spent more on housing in 1985 than is considered affordable, compared to 27% among Whites. Among poor minority households, nearly four out of five pay more for housing than the affordable amount (Hartman 1983). Thus, about 40% of poor Hispanic and Black households spent at least 70% of their income on housing in 1985, leaving little money for food and other necessities.

Poor young adults frequently doubled up with parents or relatives, became couch people (i.e., sleeping on the couch or improvised bedding provided by a relative or friend) or slept in garages, cars or other locales (Ropers 1988). Sizable proportions, particularly alcoholics and other drug abusers, were without housing and unable to obtain couches or garages to sleep in (Johnson et al. 1990). Although the proportions vary, a sizable proportion of drug abusers are homeless, and sleep in abandoned buildings, crack houses, public shelters, and the streets (Johnson et al. 1990, 1988).

In 1975, however, Island acquired her present residence, a modest three-bedroom apartment with one bathroom, a kitchen, and a living room in a renovated building in Central Harlem. Even at the height of New York's fiscal crisis in 1976, Island was fortunate to find this apartment, which was then affordable with her low income. It is in one of the best buildings on a block in which most of the buildings were abandoned or in dire need of repair by the mid-1970s. The building is kept up fairly well, the halls are generally clean, even though many people hang out in the vestibule. Elevators constantly break down in this six-story building, but Island's apartment is on the first floor. Island's willingness to double up by accommodating numerous family and kin means that it is generally overcrowded; the household composition changes daily. Except for her older brothers and sisters (over age 60 in 1990), almost none of the adult family-kin members maintain their own households for more than short periods. Island also tolerates high levels of drug abuse and violence among persons in the household, so it is a favorite place for otherwise homeless drug-abusing family members to visit.

Funds for subsidized housing for poor and middle-income families were reduced by over 90% in the 1980s (Downs 1983; Sanjek 1982). In major cities, many low-cost hotels were closed or converted to luxury housing or condominiums (Blackburn 1986; National Bureau of Economic Research 1986). Thus, abandonment or demolition of low-cost housing, higher cost of existing housing, and the near disappearance of low-cost hotels led to a continuing housing crisis for low-income persons. Many families and individuals had to double up with relatives who had housing; young adults had to live with parents during their twenties and thirties. New shelter arrangements developed among the poor; many have been displaced and are essentially homeless (Hooper & Hamberg 1984; Hartman, Keating & Le Gates 1982).

Concentration of Social Distress. The growing literature on the underclass (Kasarda 1992; Jargowsky & Bane 1991; Jenck & Peterson 1991; Ricketts & Sawhill 1988; Hughes 1988; Wilson 1987; Glasgow 1981; Moynihan 1965; Myrdal 1962) documents clearly that social distress is increasingly concentrated in several areas of midwestern and northeastern cities. Based on comparisons between 1970 and 1980 (1990 census data not yet analyzed), studies show that (1) poor Blacks are more likely to live in census tracts that are insulated from those having any significant number of Whites (Hughes 1988), (2) the number of poverty census tracts increased (Jargowsky & Bane 1991), (3) the number of persons living in underclass areas grew by over 1.5 million between 1970 and 1980 — more than doubling (Ricketts & Sawhill 1988), and (4) two-thirds of the underclass census tracts were in New York, Chicago, Philadelphia, and Detroit. Among the nation's 95 largest cities, New York City contains 15% of Blacks and 55% of Hispanics who are severely distressed (Kasarda 1992). While inner-city citizens have the right to vote and participate in political life, they have become increasingly isolated socially and economically from the mainstream of American economic life. Economic forces and bureaucratic rules and practices effectively control most aspects of life for inner-city residents.

Island's block is located in Central Harlem, over two miles away from a predominantly White neighborhood, but a few blocks from Black middle-class housing. Whites are rarely observed on this block. Almost all Whites are police, teachers, social workers or other officials. Among the residents on the block, Ross and Island's household is among the more affluent; most families on the block live below the poverty line. Island, Ross, and Sonya rarely leave Harlem or meet nonpoor persons. They remain isolated from and limit contacts with Whites. Their contact with Whites is mainly through institutions of social control.

Family Composition. Important shifts also occurred in family structure, particularly among minorities. The proportion of Black children living in mother-only families increased from 30% to 51% between 1970 and 1985; almost 90% of Black children will experience poverty if they live in a household headed by a single woman under 30 (Gibbs 1988). Moreover, poor families headed by single women will likely be without adequate financial support for housing, so they must live with other relatives, in public shelters, or very deteriorated buildings (Smith 1988). Even when a household is maintained, several different family members, relatives, and unaffiliated persons may reside in it or be couch persons who contribute little to and consume much of the minimal fiscal resources provided by public transfers for the household head and children (Dunlap In press-a; Johnson et al. 1985).

A growing trend in child rearing is for neither the natural mother nor father to live with their child(ren); typically a relative (the child's grandparent or aunt) or the foster care system has primary responsibility for the care and nurturance of the child. (See Dunlap In press-a, 1992 for how drug and alcohol abuse contributes to this phenomenon.)

Island never remarried; she has maintained a sexual relationship with another woman of her age. Sonya has not had any children and is the only female in the family network who is childless. Ross married at 18 and had a son who died of crib death while Ross was in jail for selling angel dust (PCP); the marriage dissolved within two years. Ross also had three children by another woman who is raising the children. Ross occasionally buys presents for his children, and they can ask for help when they need it. Ross's children are being raised by their mother with support from AFDC, plus economic contributions from her brothers, also crack dealers. Except for a few years when he lived with his wife, Ross's primary residence has been Island's apartment. Over the years, Island has been awarded custody of several nieces and nephews (and their children), and has had substantial responsibility for raising almost 89 persons. She is unusual only in that she has not raised her own grandchildren (since Sonya had no children, and Ross's are raised by their mother).

Growth in Criminal Justice and Corrections Systems. The criminal justice system has expanded dramatically during the mid-1980s owing to convictions for drug sales (Mauer 1990; Austin & McVey 1989), primarily crack. At year end, prison populations grew from 196,007 in 1969 to 301,470 in 1979 (Cahalan & Parsons 1986), a 6% annual average increase, to 462,002 by 1984, a 10% annual average increase, to 710,054 by 1989 (Bureau of Justice Statistics 1990). The 1989 prisoner population represents a 10.1% average annual increase since 1984 or a 9% average annual increase during the 1980s. Near the end of 1991, one and a quarter million persons were behind bars (Bureau of Justice 1992a,b). The imprisonment rate has gone from one percent to about 4% of the adult population within 22 years. Much of the explosion since 1984 is directly traceable to increased length of sentence (Langan 1991), the explosion of crack abuse, and policy responses to it in the late 1980s.

From the ages of 18 to 24, Ross served jail time (but no prison terms) for various crimes, such as robbery, but mainly for drug-related arrests. Sonya robbed a store in which someone was killed and spent five years in prison in the 1970s. Both have managed to avoid incarceration in the 1980s, despite full-time involvement in crime. Ross's angel dust business was always lucrative and he was known for having large supplies of dust. During the 1980s, Ross was shot twice as a result of drug distribution. The first time, he was robbed and shot by drug abusers. The second time, he was shot while attempting to rob another dealer. Most of his heroin- and crack-abusing relatives had been (or continued to be) heroin addicts, have been in several rehabilitation institutions, or have served time in jail or prison for drugs or petty crimes. During 1990, four persons who had lived in Island's household for several days were arrested, convicted, and imprisoned for charges including drug sales, aggravated assault, and robbery.

Other Forces. In addition to the factors listed above, many others can be shown to impact on inner-city households. These include declines in preventive health care, hospital closings in inner-city areas, shortened life span, and acute and chronic illnesses. Contracting AIDS can be a direct outcome of heroin injection via dirty needles. The social welfare network has been undermined as welfare grants remained below poverty levels and lost purchasing power, family and child care services have been cut, yet cases become more complex and foster care and abuse and neglect cases have surged.

Island has been a court-appointed guardian for numerous children of her siblings; many of these children were born while their mothers used heroin or crack. In mid-1990, she had four children assigned to foster care in her household. When these children or other family members are hurt or ill, she spends long hours in emergency rooms. She provides few lessons in good health care or primary prevention. Almost no one in the entire family-kin network uses condoms, despite frequent participation in high-risk sex. Most of the heroin-abusing family members (like Sonya and other prostitutes) have not been tested (and avoid testing) for AIDS. When Ross was hospitalized in 1991, the doctor told him that he has AIDS. Ross refuses to believe he has AIDS and does not follow through on health practices that would extend his life. Many other family-kin members have died before age 50 as a result of illness, accident, killings, or disease.

Inner-city Reservations with Stressful Conditions. All of these forces combine into a multiplicity of stressful conditions that are even more concentrated in inner-city communities than the current quantitative evidence documents. In many census tracts of Central and East Harlem, the South Bronx, and several areas in Brooklyn and Queens, the ghettoization process is so nearly complete that near "reservations" have been created. Residents are socially isolated and cut off from mainstream American society and economy in many ways. From the viewpoint of many minority inner-city residents living in these communities, the social distance (if not physical distance) to the White middle class is almost as great as for Native Americans on geographically isolated reservations. Such inner-city minorities, especially males, rarely see (much less converse) with a White person (most Whites with whom they may occasionally converse are social control agents, such as police, social workers, and teachers). Nor do such residents have reasons, resources or desires to leave their communities, as they are likely to face rejection, avoidance, disrespect, and orders from others while rarely gaining resources they need and feel they deserve.

Among their family members and even neighbors, many inner-city residents are unlikely to know anyone who has a legal job, much less a job paying in excess of $25,000 a year. Almost all the stores at which they shop are owned and operated by Whites and Asians who live outside the community. Few or no factories or low-wage jobs are available within walking distance. Most friends and neighbors will have effectively been out of the labor market and impoverished for several years, have survived on welfare for years, and have been unable to maintain decent housing. Their neighbors will likely have dropped out of high school. Even if they completed high school or are literate or have some skills, the lack of networks with employed persons and the depressed economy mean that most will not be able to find jobs. Both men and women realize that the men cannot support families, so legal marriage may never occur among those who live together for years. Casual relationships may result in children who are reared by the mother or her relatives (and with no or meager assistance from the father). The mother's brother(s), other male family members and/or boyfriend(s) become father figures.

While females may receive AFDC grants (or relatives receive foster care funds), which support the rental of a deteriorated apartment, nonpayment of rent leads to frequent moves over the years. Households headed by someone like Island who can pay the rent regularly and maintain it have become the only stable location for several generations of family and kin who are essentially without residence. Such household-families are socially isolated and avoid so-called helping agencies except in acute emergencies. To this extensive social distress have been added drug abuse, drug sales and distribution, and dysfunctional household-family processes.

IMPACT OF DRUG ABUSE AND DISTRIBUTION ON INNER-CITY RESIDENTS

A variety of factors and impacts of drug abuse have been identified in prior analyses (Johnson et al. 1990, 1985) and will not be reiterated here. In the following, two primary vectors are identified as creating and maintaining the ghettoization process that has been underway in the 1970s and 1980s: the booming illicit drug economy and social processes in the household-family system (Dunlap In press-a, 1992).

The Booming Illicit Drug Economy

In many respects, the social forces and conditions leading to ghettoization set the conditions in which the illicit drug economy could grow and flourish. Especially important to its growth has been the effective exclusion of thousands of inner-city youths and young adults from legal jobs paying modest but sufficient income, such as those held by some of their parents a generation earlier. These youths generally did not remain entirely idle (although no good statistical evidence is available); some became active as criminals committing robbery, burglary, and theft.

What almost certainly occurred is that drug selling (legally defined as a crime for opiates and cocaine in 1914 and for marijuana in 1937) emerged sociologically as a new type of crime among inner-city (and middle-class) youths in the 1960s. Marijuana sales became a widespread phenomenon in the 1960s and 1970s. The illicit market exploded in economic importance during the crack era.

Before 1960, New York minorities had maintained prohibition-era practices in the form of after-hours clubs. These clubs operated when bars and liquor stores were closed, generally resold alcohol at higher prices to patrons, and had clientele who partied late at night. Frequently jazz musicians and other habitués would use the scarce and expensive heroin, cocaine, and marijuana; a few would sell it (Hamid 1992; Williams 1978; Malcolm X & Haley 1965).

Marijuana Sales

Marijuana use began to spread in 1965 in all segments of the American population. Inner-city youths began smoking it on a regular basis. An efficient but poorly documented distribution system emerged in Harlem and other inner-city locations in the late 1960s. As the proportion of youths using marijuana increased, and as the frequency and potency of the drug increased, a much more elaborate importation and distribution system emerged.[2] Marijuana distribution in the 1960s and 1970s was characterized by cultivation in the West Indies (Jamaica, Granada, and Colombia), importation of boatloads and tons into New York, and an efficient marketing system (Hamid 1990).

By the mid-1970s, almost every block in New York's inner-city neighborhoods had a smoke shop, a storefront from which marijuana was sold either as the only item or as one of several commodities. The proprietor of the store was usually a minority person (frequently from the West Indies) who made handsome profits and invested in his ethnic community (Hamid In press, 1990). In addition, thousands of minority inner-city youths would buy small wholesale amounts (an ounce or pound), roll it into marijuana cigarettes, and sell it on the streets and parks for about one dollar. Since competition among street sellers was vigorous, marijuana sellers rarely made substantial profits, but could generally smoke free and earn some cash ($20 to $50/day). By the late-1970s, virtually all passersby on a New York street would be offered marijuana (and other drugs); nonusers could not enter Union Square, Bryant Park or Washington Square (or walk down 42nd Street) without having to confront several persons attempting to sell them marijuana (or other drugs).

In 1970, almost 90% of college students using marijuana monthly or more often reported some cannabis sales; this was 21% of all students (Blacks and Whites were equally likely to use and sell (Carpenter et al. 1988; Johnson 1973) and the proportions of marijuana sellers was almost certainly as high or higher among inner-city marijuana users. Over half of the marijuana sellers also sold other illicit drugs they used. Those who sold three or more hard drugs were substantially more deviant on virtually all dimensions than persons who only sold or used marijuana (Johnson 1973). Indeed, the overall best indicator of a highly deviant lifestyle was the number of different drugs sold rather than the frequency of marijuana use (see also Carpenter et al. 1988).

In 1970, Ross began selling PCP, a little-known drug at the time. Although he occasionally sold marijuana, he specialized in PCP sales and did quite well through the 1970s. For the most part, marijuana was always a secondary drug of use and sale among Island's children, nephews, and nieces.

Heroin Sales

Heroin use was known among White ethnics and relatively small numbers of jazz musicians; its use began to grow among Harlem youths in 1955 (Preble & Casey 1969; Brown 1965; Malcolm X & Haley 1965) but remained less common than later in the 1960s. Among young men in Manhattan, onset of heroin use increased from 3% in 1963, peaked at 20% between 1970 and 1972, and began to decline as 13% used heroin in 1974 (Clayton & Voss 1981; Boyle & Brunswick 1980); the proportion initiating heroin probably declined further and remained low in the late 1970s. Thus, very low proportions of youths reaching adulthood after 1975 in Harlem and inner-city New York have initiated or become regular users of heroin. A definite norm against heroin use has become widespread among high-risk youths under age 20. Among those who initiated heroin injection during the heroin era, sizable proportions became addicted within two years. While less than half persist in their addiction for several years (Johnson 1978), this heroin-era cohort (estimated at 200,000 in New York City) constitutes the vast majority of heroin addicts who are in their thirties and forties in the 1990s (Frank 1986).

Moreover, almost all heroin abusers engaged in some form of heroin sales and other drug distribution activity, including direct sales, steering customers to sellers, touting a dealer's bag, copping drugs for customers who never meet, or performing a variety of other roles that protect or assist in the sale of heroin (Johnson, Hamid & Sanabria 1991; Johnson, Kaplan & Schmeidler 1990; Johnson et al. 1985). Heroin abusers occasionally also sold cocaine powder and marijuana, but these sales typically occurred on fewer days and generated less cash income than heroin; they frequently used these drugs while selling them.

The important point is that a large pool of heroin abusers had established patterns of irregular sales of heroin and cocaine, and received low to modest returns for several hours of dealing activity. Their sales were primarily designed to support their consumption of heroin, sometimes combined with cocaine. Perhaps some kilo-level suppliers were making sizable profits, but street heroin abusers were generally not making enough to keep themselves supplied with the heroin they needed; very few made substantial monetary returns or clear profits from such sales. This pattern of heroin sales with marginal returns to heroin abusers continued into the crack era and the 1990s.

Island's daughter reached age 17 in 1970, during the peak years for heroin initiation. Sonya began heroin use and rapidly became addicted. Various children of Island's siblings were also caught in the heroin epidemic of the 1970s. Sonya married a heroin addict and dealer who helped support her heroin addiction. While married, she prostituted and lived mostly in shooting galleries with her husband. While they have separated and he now lives in Florida, he returns for visits on occasions. By 1973 when he reached age 18, Ross claimed to have avoided heroin addiction. Ross and many other Harlem youths

(Brunswick 1988; Boyle & Brunswick 1980) observed what happened to virtually all his cousins and his sister and refused to consume heroin. He also tried to talk his cousins out of shooting heroin. In the 1970s, Ross felt so deeply about his sister's addiction that he "beat her bad enough" to discourage her from using it, but this treatment regime was not successful. In the late 1970s and early 1980s, Ross sold heroin, but avoided using it. He hated selling this drug, but "the money was good." Numerous kin were low-level heroin abusers and sellers. Most of these addicts spent intermittent periods in jail or prison.

Cocaine Powder Sales

While cocaine had been available before 1960, it was expensive and difficult to obtain. However, from 1975 to 1985 the use of cocaine powder grew steadily. Cocaine powder became the status drug for both rich and poor alike. Very substantial proportions of marijuana-using adolescents during the period from 1965 to 1979 became cocaine users as adults (Kandel, Murphy & Karus 1985; Kozel & Adams 1985). The greater and more frequent their cocaine use, the more likely they were to sell it.

The patterns of inner-city cocaine powder sales followed closely those of heroin, but with some important variations. In New York City, many cocaine habitués in the mid-1970s began attending after-hours clubs, which became a major socialization location for cocaine dealers who both used and dealt large amounts of cocaine. But patrons at after-hours clubs were expected to control their urges for cocaine and "be cool" (Hamid 1992; Williams 1978). Such cocaine sellers generally avoided heroin use and heroin abusers as customers, preferring to provide cocaine to those who wished to snort it. In the mid-1970s, cocaine users were probably three to five times more numerous than heroin users (Preble 1980). Cocaine powder dealers could usually earn enough cash to make a profit and support their own use, but not to supply their friends (Williams & Kornblum 1985). Between 1981 and 1984, cocaine free-basing began to confront cocaine sellers with a major problem. Sellers and persons who could base cocaine had a lively business, but smoking cocaine quickly ate up profits. Several major West Indian marijuana dealers quickly lost their profits and livelihood (Hamid In press, 1990).

While Sonya frequently injected cocaine with heroin (speedballing), she rarely used cocaine powder for snorting. Ross occasionally snorted cocaine during the 1970s but did not sell it. His main business was heroin and PCP sales.

Crack Sales

Between 1984 and 1985, crack use exploded in New York City (Golub, Lewis & Johnson 1991; Johnson, Hamid & Sanabria 1991). Prepared freebased cocaine was placed in small vials for retail sale at $3 to $10 per vial (price depended on size of vial and the street market). Virtually all crack abusers had prior experience with marijuana, cocaine powder or heroin; almost no drug-naive persons were recruited to crack use as their first drug (Fagan & Chin 1991; Fagan 1990). Unlike snorting cocaine, however, the rewards of the instant high and avoidance of dysphoria created many repeated episodes of use per day. While heroin users and cocaine snorters may consume their drug two to three times per day, many crack abusers consumed crack five to 15 times per day, limited primarily by their income. While relatively few new abusers emerged, among cocaine snorters or freebasers, crack consumption was usually added to preexisting drug abuse patterns, but they used crack two to three times as often as other drugs. In short, crack was used more intensively (higher frequencies and expenditures, especially among daily users) than was heroin or cocaine powder (Johnson, Elmoghazy & Dunlap 1990).

The primary means for supporting such crack consumption was crack selling. Because of the large number of purchases per day by most crack abusers, crack developed as an essentially new market. Even persons who limited their drug consumption to marijuana, cocaine powder or heroin, but who sold drugs, typically added crack to their sales activity (Fagan 1992). Crack sales generated higher cash incomes than the sale of heroin, cocaine powder or marijuana, or the commission of other crimes (e.g., robbery, burglary, thefts).

Overall, during the crack era, a significant expansion in the number of daily drug abusers seems to have occurred. In New York City, a substantial majority of an estimated 150,000 persistent heroin injectors appears to have added crack abuse and sale to their daily activities. A relatively small proportion (probably less than 20%) of recreational cocaine snorters (who avoid heroin) became crack abusers (Frank et al. 1988). But since recreational cocaine snorters were so numerous, substantial numbers became crack abusers. While precise figures are not available, the Senate Committee on the Judiciary estimated that in 1990 New York State had 434,000 cocaine or crack addicts; the same report estimated that nationally 2.2 million persons are cocaine addicts (Johnson, Dunlap & Hamid 1992; U.S. Senate 1990).

A study of Washington, D.C., probationers suggests that crack selling is very profitable. Many sellers sold crack for only short periods each week, but had earnings that were several times higher than the minimum wage or legal earnings (Fagan 1992; Reuter et al. 1990). Several studies suggest that some minorities engaged in crack sales but without using crack (Reuter et al. 1990), although noncrack-using crack sellers appear to be rare in New York City.

Sonya moved to crack rapidly when it became available. She was one of several heroin abusers who gave up heroin in favor of crack. She and three female relatives are crackheads, prostituting themselves daily for crack. As soon as they earn a few dollars from a trick, they immediately buy and smoke crack. Or they will exchange sex for crack without ever receiving money. Sonya never became a crack seller. Her brother sets aside hits for her. Her ex-husband will also supply her minimally when in New York. She finds it more beneficial to prostitute to support her habit because the money is steady and quick. She does not have to be responsible for the drug or money. In her view, prostitution leaves her carefree.

As crack began to become popular in the mid-1980s, Ross was once waiting in line with friends to buy freebase cocaine. He observed how many people were consuming crack and realized that he could make much more money selling crack than heroin or angel dust. He sought out those who knew how to cook up freebase. Once Ross became a competent cooker, he began to buy cocaine, in small amounts at first (e.g., $300 worth), cook it up, place it in vials, and sell it.

At first Ross gave out free samples to encourage users to return for purchase. He joined with other free-lance crack sellers and they took over a corner on a main avenue. Ross had long established himself as a dealer there and had his legitimate territory. While he snorts cocaine, Ross reports rarely smoking crack; he limits his consumption so that his business is maintained. When he cooks up crack for sales, he lets his crack-using relatives (including his sister) consume what he "leaves on the mirror"; this practice helps assure that they do not steal from him or set him up for a robbery.

At least during the expansion years between 1985 and 1988, crack selling was quite profitable for thousands of inner-city minorities, although many of these sellers became severely impoverished by their crack use. An interesting paradox arises: crack sales bring monetary wealth to some households in the subculture of poverty. That is, household-families that have been impoverished for generations will suddenly have some members with money in their pockets to buy what they want. In some cases, the illicit income provides sufficient money for the household. But these members have little or no access to the banking system, middle-class lifestyles, or ways of accumulating wealth (other than stashes of cash or jewelry).

The cash income from Ross's crack sales provides Island with much of the cash with which she pays the apartment's rent and purchases food for persons living in or visiting the household. Ross may earn $500 to $1000 when he has a good day; this may happen several times a year. Just before Christmas in 1990, for example, the family paid cash and installed an entire new living room set (e.g., couch, chairs, table, lamps). They have a large freezer stocked with food, everyone has several changes of clothing, and Ross and Island always have money in their pockets. Sonya and other kin in the household can never keep money (it is spent on crack), but they eat and sleep free and dress very well. In many respects, although no family member has a legal job or off-the-books legal income, the illicit income among the adults appears to be quite high. Certainly on days when they prostitute (which is most days), Sonya and other females earn more cash income in that day than a research fieldworker with a doctorate. Since all cash is immediately spent on crack, they remain impoverished. Ross can easily net over $100 a day when he works, but sometimes does not work. Because he is not a compulsive crack smoker, Ross earns enough to provide sufficient cash to keep the household solvent — even well-off by Harlem community standards.

But neither Ross nor Island has a bank account. They know little about income and expenses, they do not budget or plan expenditures, they have no plans to invest in a better apartment or car, and they know nothing about savings or financial instruments, such as stocks and bonds. So the household supports five to ten persons living there at one time. Family members "eat off the stove" (never at a sit-down meal). Ross is effectively subsidizing Sonya, Island, and other kin and friends who happen to be living in the household. Since the crack business is lucrative, and his younger male cousins (ages 17 to 25) were unable to find legal employment, Ross offered them work selling crack; most were quickly arrested and imprisoned for various offenses.

Most household members remain vigorous participants in the subcultures of violence, poverty, and drug abuse. Numerous squabbles and arguments break out on all subjects, but especially over drugs. For example, Ross and Sonya's cousin, Barbara (age 35) and her daughter, Susan (age 18), had both been raised by Island and frequently lived in Island's household in 1990. Barbara and Susan were crack prostitutes who routinely worked together. Barbara was temporarily living with an older john at his apartment. One evening in 1991, Susan came there while intoxicated and paranoid on crack and demanded money for crack. Barbara reported having no money so Susan beat her with a broom handle. When the john tried to stop her, Susan pulled out a knife and stabbed him repeatedly. Barbara was hospitalized and died shortly afterward. At her funeral, Susan was ostracized by all family and kin members; all drank heavily and used a variety of drugs during the wake.

Although Ross does not sell crack directly to his kin, a unique economic system appears to have evolved. The criminal gains from prostitution and other nondrug crimes by several crack abusers are rapidly spent on crack. These funds provide substantial income to crack sellers (like Ross) and/or his suppliers who are controlled (at least not compulsive crack) cocaine users. The net income from such crack sellers appears to provide the cash that supports household-families (like Island's) in which several crack abusers live (at least temporarily), eat, clean up, get clothing on occasion, and hang out. Of course, many crack abusers do not have such households that tolerate crack sellers or relatives who will subsidize them, so they live on the streets, in abandoned buildings or in shelters.

Stressed Household-Family Systems

A second major vector promoting ghettoization is the distressed inner-city household-family system described briefly above. Dunlap (In press-a, 1992) described the impact of crack on various households — from completely unstable to least unstable households.

Several important themes developed more fully elsewhere (Dunlap In press-a, 1992, 1991; Bourgois & Dunlap 1992) have important policy implications and represent a shift from the 1960s, especially when compared with the case materials provided in the culture of poverty (Lewis 1965). While important shifts in family composition have occurred since 1960 (e.g., higher proportion of single-family households), the critical shifts revolve around *social processes* and expectations among family members, both day by day and over the years:

1. An especially important shift across the generations is a decline in expectation that a young female will provide the primary care for children born to her. This trend has meant a rise in parenting by grandparents or older female relatives.
2. While most would like to have their own household, young adults quickly realize that they do not and will never have the income to afford their own household (e.g., to pay rent and maintain an apartment). They adjust to a permanent status of never having their own residence and to living with other family, relatives, temporary liaisons, or friends (if fortunate), or in shelters or streets (if not).
3. The option of a steady legal job appears so distant for inner-city high-school dropouts (and even graduates), that they cease job searches after a few attempts or experiences in low-wage jobs. Adult household members can rarely provide concrete assistance in finding jobs or help in accessing networks of employers. Such youths and young adults, with no hopes for legal work, are available for recruitment and work in illegal enterprises; drug sales loom largest among these opportunities.
4. Within the household-family, verbal aggressiveness and willingness to resort to physical violence appear to have increased as a means of both expressing love and settling disputes.

CONCLUSION

Numerous economic, sociological, and psychological studies have documented the decline of America's inner cities, and the worsening of chronic conditions therein. All of the macro social forces worsened during the 1970s and 1980s. These forces engendered numerous crisis situations, which converged in the mid-1980s to provide the setting for the crack era.

While the crack epidemic may be easing somewhat in 1991, severely impacted individuals — like Sonya, Barbara, Ross (Dunlap 1992) and household-families (like Island's) will continue to be negatively impacted by the behavior of crack abusers and problems with their children. They will also gain a few benefits if a household member can provide some income through crack sales.

Furthermore, the federal, New York State, and New York City budgets being debated at the time of writing are likely to extract an additional $1 billion to $5 billion in government services and goods that were previously provided to residents of New York's inner city. These cuts are in addition to the retreat from and absence of private investment and employment in the inner city. Even if youths reaching adulthood in the 1990s avoid crack and heroin completely, the absence of legal employment, declining value of welfare benefits, and many other forces will provide them with no or few options other than engaging in criminality or the drug business.

NOTES

1. Poverty among Blacks had declined to 30% by 1969, but has remained unchanged to 1984 (Jaynes & Williams 1989).

2. A parallel and vigorous market in marijuana existed among Whites and hippies of the marijuana era; this market relied on private sales generally in the customer's or seller's home, and avoided street sales and storefront sales (Carpenter et al. 1988).

ACKNOWLEDGEMENTS

The authors would like to thank Harry Sanabria, of the University of Pittsburgh, for his contributions to this paper and research.

REFERENCES

Austin, J. & McVey, A. 1989. The impact of the war on drugs. *Focus* (newsletter). San Francisco: National Council on Crime and Delinquency. December.

Billingsley. A. 1968. *White Families, Black Families*. Englewood Cliffs, New Jersey: Prentice-Hall.

Blackburn, A.J. 1986. *Single Room Occupancy in New York City*. New York: New York City Department of Housing Preservation and Development.

Boyle, J. & Brunswick, A.F. 1980. What happened in Harlem? Analysis of a decline in heroin use among a generation unit of urban black youth. *Journal of Drug Issues* 10(1):109-130.

Brown, C. 1965. *Manchild in the Promised Land*. New York: Signet Books.

Brunswick, A.F. 1988. Young black males and substance use. In: J.T. Gibbs (Ed.) *Young, Black, and Male in America: An Endangered Species*. Dover, Massachusetts: Auburn House.

Bureau of Justice Statistics. 1992a. *Jail Inmates 1991*. Washington, D.C.: Bureau of Justice Statistics. May.

Bureau of Justice Statistics. 1992b. *Prisoners in 1991*. Washington, D.C.: Bureau of Justice Statistics. May.

Bureau of Justice Statistics. 1990. *Prisoners in 1989*. Washington, D.C.: Bureau of Justice Statistics. May.

Carpenter, C.; Glassner, B.; Johnson, B.D. & Loughlin, J. 1988. *Kids, Drugs and Crime*. Lexington, Massachusetts: Lexington Books.

Cahalan, M.W. & Parsons, L.E. 1986. *Historical Corrections Statistics in the United States, 1850-1984*. Washington, D.C.: Bureau of Justice Statistics.

Chein, I.; Gerard, D.L.; Lee, R.S. & Rosenfeld, E. 1964. *The Road to H*. New York: Basic Books.

Clark, K. 1965. *Dark Ghetto*. New York: Harper & Row.

Clayton, R.R. & Voss, H.L. 1981. *Young Men and Drugs in Manhattan: A Causal Analysis*. Rockville, Maryland: National Institute on Drug Abuse.

Cohen, A.K. 1955. *Delinquent Boys*. Glencoe, Illinois: The Free Press.

Coles, R. 1970. *Children of Crisis III: The South Goes North*. Boston: Little, Brown.

Coles, R. 1968. *Children of Crisis II: Migrants, Sharecroppers, Mountaineers*. Boston: Little, Brown.

Dembo, R. 1988. Young black males and delinquency. In: J.T. Gibbs (Ed.) *Young, Black, and Male in America: An Endangered Species*. Dover, Massachusetts: Auburn House.

Dolbeare, C. 1983. The low income housing crisis. In: C. Hartman (Ed.) *America's Housing Crisis: What Is to Be Done?* Boston: Routledge & Degan Paul.

Downs, A. 1983. *Rental Housing in the 1980s*. Washington, D.C.: Brookings Institution.

Dunlap, E. In press-a. Inner-city crisis and crack dealing: Portrait of a drug dealer and his household. In: S. MacGregor (Ed.) *Crisis and Resistance: Social Relations and Economic Restructuring in the City*. London: Edinburgh Press.

Dunlap, E. 1992. Impact of drugs on family life and kin networks in the inner-city African-American single-parent household. In: A. Harrell & G. Peterson (Eds.) *Drugs, Crime, and Social Isolation: Barriers to Urban Opportunity*. Washington, D.C.: Urban Institute Press.

Dunlap, E. 1991. Rachael's place: Case study of a female crack distributor. Paper presented at the Meeting of the American Society of Criminology, San Francisco, November 21.

Fagan, J. 1992. Drug selling and licit income in distressed neighborhoods: The economic lives of street-level drug users and dealers. In: A. Harrell & G. Peterson (Eds.) *Drugs, Crime, and Social Isolation: Barriers to Urban Opportunity*. Washington, D.C.: Urban Institute Press.

Fagan, J. 1990. Special Issue on Crack Cocaine. *Contemporary Drug Problems* 16(4) & 17(1).

Fagan, J.A. & Chin, K. 1991. Social processes of initiation into crack. *Journal of Drug Issues* 21(2):313-344.

Frank, B. 1986. What is the future of the heroin problem in New York City. Paper presented at the Third Annual Northeast Regional Methadone Conference, Baltimore, Maryland. December 3.

Frank, B.; Morel, R.; Schmeidler, J. & Maranda, M. 1988. *Cocaine and Crack Use in New York State*. New York: Division of Substance Abuse Services.

Frey, W.H. 1980. Black in-migration, white flight, and the changing economic base of the central city. *American Journal of Sociology* 85(6):1396-1418.

Gibbs, J.T. (Ed.) 1988. *Young, Black, and Male in America: An Endangered species*. Dover, Massachusetts: Auburn House.

Glasgow, D. 1981. *The Black Underclass*. New York: Vintage Books.

Golub, A.; Lewis, C. & Johnson, B.D. 1991. Modeling the epidemic of onset to crack abuse. Unpublished manuscript.

Grier, W.H. & Cobbs, P.M. 1968. *Black Rage*. New York: Bantam.

Hamid, A. In press. *The Political Economy of Drugs: The Caribbean Connection*. New York: Plenum.

Hamid, A. 1992. The developmental cycle of a drug epidemic: The cocaine smoking epidemic of 1981-1991. *Journal of Psychoactive Drugs* 24(4).

Hamid, A. 1990. The political economy of crack-related violence. *Contemporary Drug Problems* 17(1):31-78.

Hartman, C. (Ed.) 1983. *America's Housing Crisis: What Is to Be Done?* Boston: Routledge & Degan Paul.

Hartman, C.; Keating, D. & Le Gates, R. 1982. *Displacement: How to Fight It*. Berkeley, California: National Housing Law Project.

Hill, R. 1971. *The Strengths of the Black Family*. New York: National Urban League.

Hooper, K. & Hamberg, J. 1984. *The Making of America's Homeless: From Skid Row to New Poor, 1945-1984*. New York: Community Service Society.

Hughes, M.A. 1988. *Concentrated Deviance or Isolated Deprivation?: The "Underclass" Idea Reconsidered*. Report prepared for the Rockefeller Foundation. Princeton, New Jersey: Princeton University Press, Princeton Urban and Regional Research Center.

Hunt, L.G. & Chambers, C.D. 1976. *The Heroin Epidemics: A Study of Heroin Use in the U.S., 1965-75. Part II*. Holliswood, New York: Spectrum.

Jargowsky, P.A. & Bane, M.J. 1991. Neighborhood poverty: Basic questions. In: C. Jencks & G. Peterson (Eds.) *The Urban Underclass*. Washington, D.C.: Brookings Institution.

Jaynes, G.D. & Williams, Jr., R.M. 1989. *A Common Destiny: Blacks and American Society*. Washington, D.C.: National Academy Press.

Jencks, C. & G. Peterson. 1991. (Eds.) *The Urban Underclass*. Washington, D.C.: Brookings Institution.

Johnson B.D. 1978. Once an addict, seldom an addict. *Contemporary Drug Problems* Spring:35-53.

Johnson, B.D. 1973. *Marijuana Users and Drug Subcultures*. New York: Wiley-Interscience.

Johnson, B.; Dunlap, E. & Hamid, A. 1992. Changes in New York's crack distribution scene. In: P.A. Vamos & P. Corriveau (Eds.) *Drugs and Society to the Year 2000*. Washington, D.C.: U.S. Information Agency.

Johnson, B.D.; Elmoghazy, E. & Dunlap, E. 1990. *Crack Abusers and Noncrack Drug Abusers: A Comparison of Drug Use, Drug Sales, and Nondrug Criminality*. New York: Narcotic and Drug Research, Inc.

Johnson, B.D.; Frank, B.; Morel, R.; Schmeidler, J.; Maranda, M. & Gillman, C. 1988. *Illicit Drug Use Among Transient Adults in New York State*. Albany, New York: Division of Substance Abuse

Services.

Johnson, B.D.; Goldstein, P.; Preble, E.; Schmeidler, J.; Lipton, D.; Spunt, B. & Miller, T. 1985. *Taking Care of Business: The Economics of Crime by Heroin Abusers*. Lexington, Massachusetts: Lexington Books.

Johnson, B.D.; Hamid, A. & Sanabria, H. 1991. Emerging models of crack distribution. In: T. Mieczkowksi (Ed.) *Drugs and Crime: A Reader*. Boston: Allyn-Bacon.

Johnson, B.D.; Kaplan, M.A. & Schmeidler, J. 1990. Days with drug distribution: Which drugs? How many transactions? With what returns? In: R.A. Weischeit (Ed.) *Drugs, Crime, and the Criminal Justice System*. Cincinnati, Ohio: Anderson.

Johnson, B.D.; Lipton, D.S. & Wish, E. 1986. *Facts About the Criminality of Heroin and Cocaine Abusers and Some New Alternatives to Incarceration*. New York: Narcotic and Drug Research, Inc.

Johnson, B.D. & Manwar, A. 1991. Towards A paradigm of drug eras: Previous drug eras help to model the crack epidemic in New York City during the 1990s. Paper presented at the Meeting of the American Society of Criminology, San Francisco, November 21.

Johnson, B.D. & Muffler, J. 1992. Sociocultural aspects of drug use and abuse in the 1990s. In: J. Lowinson; P. Ruiz; R. Millman & J. Langrod (Eds.) *Substance Abuse Treatment*. 2nd ed. Baltimore: Wilkins and Wilkins.

Johnson, B.D.; Williams, T.; Dei, K. & Sanabria, H. 1990. Drug abuse in the inner city: Impact on hard drug users and the community. In: M. Tonry & J.Q. Wilson (Eds.) *Drugs and Crime*. Crime and Justice Series. Vol. 13. Chicago: University of Chicago Press.

Kandel, D.B.; Murphy, D. & Karus, D. 1985. Cocaine use in young adulthood: Patterns of use and psychosocial correlates. In: N. Kozel & E.H. Adams (Eds.) *Cocaine Use in America: Epidemiologic and Clinical Perspectives*. Research Monograph Series 61. Rockville, Maryland: National Institute on Drug Abuse.

Kasarda, J.E. 1992. The severely distressed in economically transforming cities. In: A. Harrell & G. Peterson (Eds.) *Drugs, Crime, and Social Isolation: Barriers to Urban Opportunity*. Washington, D.C.: Urban Institute Press.

Kozel, N.J. & Adams, E.H. (Eds.) 1985. *Cocaine Use in America: Epidemiologic and Clinical Perspectives*. Research Monograph Series 61. Rockville, Maryland: National Institute on Drug Abuse.

Langan, P.A. 1991. America's soaring prison population. *Science* 251:1568-73.

Lewis, O. 1965. *La Vida*. New York: Basic Books.

Lyman, S. 1975. Legitimacy and consensus in Lipset's America: From Washington to Watergate. *Social Research* 42:729-757.

Malcolm X & Haley, A. 1965. *Autobiography of Malcolm X*. New York: Signet.

Mauer, M. 1990. *Young Black Men and The Criminal Justice System: A Growing National Problem*. Washington, D.C.: The Sentencing Project.

Moynihan. D.P. 1965. *The Black Family: The Case for National Action*. Washington, D.C.: U.S. Department of Labor, Office of Family Planning and Research.

Myrdal, G. 1962. *Challenges to Affluence*. New York: Pantheon.

National Advisory Commission on Civil Disorders. 1968. *U.S. Riot Commission Report*. New York: Bantam Books.

National Bureau of Economic Research, Inc. 1986. *Permanent Homelessness in America?* Washington, D.C.: U.S. GPO.

Phillipe, B. & Dunlap, E. In press. Exorcising sex-for-crack: An ethnographic perspective from Harlem. In: M. Ratner (Ed.) *Crack Pipe as Pimp: An Eight-City Study of the Sex-for-Crack Phenomenon*. New York: Lexington Books.

Preble, E.J. 1980. Personal Communication. New York: Narcotic and Drug Research, Inc.

Preble, E.J. & Casey, J.J. 1969. Taking care of business: The heroin user's life on the street. *International Journal of the Addictions* 4(1):1-24.

Reed, R.J. 1988. Education and achievement of young black males. In: J.T. Gibbs (Ed.) *Young, Black and Male in America: An Endangered Species*. Dover, Massachusetts: Auburn House.

Reuter, P.; MacCoun, R.; Murphy, P.; Abrahamse, A. & Simon, B. 1990. *Money from Crime: A Study of the Economics of Drug Dealing in Washington, D.C.* Santa Monica, California: Rand.

Ricketts, E. & Sawhill, I. 1988. Defining and measuring the underclass. *Journal of Policy Analysis and Management* 7(2):316-25.

Ropers, R.H. 1988. *The Invisible Homeless: A New Urban Ecology*. New York: Insight Books.

Sanjek, R. 1982. *Federal Housing Programs and Their Impact on Homelessness*. New York: National Coalition for the Homeless.

Smith, J.P. 1988. Poverty and the family. In: G.D. Sandefur & M. Tienda. *Divided Opportunities. Minorities, Poverty, and Social Policy*. New York: Plenum.

Sullivan, M. 1989. *Getting Paid*. New Brunswick, New Jersey: Rutgers University Press.

Tucker, W. 1989. *The Excluded Americans. Homelessness and Housing Politics*. San Francisco: Laissez Faire Books.

U.S. Senate Committee on the Judiciary. 1990. Hardcore cocaine addicts: Measuring—and fighting—the epidemic. A Staff Report. 101st Congress. Washington, D.C.: U.S. GPO.

Williams, T. 1989. *The Cocaine Kids*. New York: Addison-Wesley.

Williams, T. 1978. The Cocaine Culture in After-Hours Clubs. Ph.D. thesis. Graduate School and University Center, City University of New York.

Williams, T. & Kornblum, W. 1985. *Growing Up Poor*. Lexington, Massachusetts: Lexington Books.

Wilson, W.J. 1987. *The Truly Disadvantaged*. Chicago: University of Chicago Press.

Wolfgang, M.E. & Franco, F. 1967. *The Subculture of Violence*. London: Tavistock.

How Effective Is Drug Abuse Resistance Education? A Meta-Analysis of Project DARE Outcome Evaluations

ABSTRACT

Objectives. Project DARE (Drug Abuse Resistance Education) is the most widely used school-based drug use prevention program in the United States, but the findings of rigorous evaluations of its effectiveness have not been considered collectively.

Methods. We used meta-analytic techniques to review eight methodologically rigorous DARE evaluations. Weighted effect size means for several short-term outcomes also were compared with means reported for other drug use prevention programs.

Results. The DARE effect size for drug use behavior ranged from .00 to .11 across the eight studies; the weighted mean for drug use across studies was .06. For all outcomes considered, the DARE effect size means were substantially smaller than those of programs emphasizing social and general competencies and using interactive teaching strategies.

Conclusions. DARE's short-term effectiveness for reducing or preventing drug use behavior is small and is less than for interactive prevention programs. (*Am J Public Health.* 1994;84:1394–1401)

Susan T. Ennett, PhD, Nancy S. Tobler, MS, PhD, Christopher L. Ringwalt, DrPH, and Robert L. Flewelling, PhD

Introduction

School-based drug use prevention programs have been an integral part of the US antidrug campaign for the past two decades.[1,2] Although programs have proliferated, none is more prevalent than Project DARE (Drug Abuse Resistance Education).[3] Created in 1983 by the Los Angeles Police Department and the Los Angeles Unified School District, DARE uses specially trained law enforcement officers to teach a drug use prevention curriculum in elementary schools[4] and, more recently, in junior and senior high schools. Since its inception, DARE has been adopted by approximately 50% of local school districts nationwide, and it continues to spread rapidly.[3] DARE is the only drug use prevention program specifically named in the 1986 Drug-Free Schools and Communities Act. Some 10% of the Drug-Free Schools and Communities Act governors' funds, which are 30% of the funds available each fiscal year for state and local programs, are set aside for programs "such as Project Drug Abuse Resistance Education,"[5] amounting to much of the program's public funding.

Given its widespread use and the considerable investment of government dollars, school time, and law enforcement effort, it is important to know whether DARE is an effective drug use prevention program. That is, to what extent does DARE meet its curriculum objectives, most prominently "to keep kids off drugs"?

DARE's core curriculum, offered to pupils in the last grades of elementary school, is the heart of DARE's program and the focus of this study. We evaluate here the core curriculum's short-term effectiveness by using meta-analytic techniques to integrate the evaluation findings of several studies.[6,7] We searched for all DARE evaluations, both published and unpublished, conducted over the past 10 years and selected for further review those studies that met specified methodological criteria. We calculated effect sizes as a method for establishing a comparable effectiveness measure across studies.[7–9] In addition, to put DARE in the context of other school-based drug use prevention programs, we compared the average magnitude of the DARE effect sizes with those of other programs that target young people of a similar age.

DARE's Core Curriculum

The DARE core curriculum's 17 lessons, usually offered once a week for 45 to 60 minutes, focus on teaching pupils the skills needed to recognize and resist social pressures to use drugs.[4] In addition, lessons focus on providing information about drugs, teaching decision-making skills, building self-esteem, and choosing healthy alternatives to drug use.[4] DARE officers use teaching strategies, such as lectures, group discussions, question-and-

Susan T. Ennett, Christopher L. Ringwalt, and Robert L. Flewelling are with the Research Triangle Institute, Research Triangle Park, NC. Nancy S. Tobler is with the State University of New York, at Albany, NY.

Requests for reprints should be sent to Susan T. Ennett, PhD, Center for Social Research and Policy Analysis, Research Triangle Institute, PO Box 12194, Research Triangle Park, NC 27709-2194.

This paper was accepted February 15, 1994.

Note. The views expressed here are the authors' and do not necessarily represent the official position of the US Department of Justice or the US Department of Health and Human Services.

answer sessions, audiovisual material, workbook exercises, and role-playing.[4]

The training that DARE officers receive is substantial. They are required to undergo 80 training hours in classroom management, teaching strategies, communication skills, adolescent development, drug information, and curriculum instruction.[4] In addition, DARE officers with classroom experience can undergo further training to qualify as instructors/mentors.[4] These officers monitor the program delivery's integrity and consistency through periodic classroom visits.

Methods

Identification of Evaluations

We attempted to locate all quantitative evaluations of DARE's core curriculum through a survey of DARE's five Regional Training Centers, computerized searches of the published and unpublished literature, and telephone interviews with individuals known to be involved with DARE. Eighteen evaluations in 12 states and one province in Canada were identified. Several evaluations were reported in multiple reports or papers. (See Appendix A for a bibliography of the studies considered.)

Evaluation Selection Criteria

To be selected for this meta-analysis, an evaluation must have met the following criteria: (1) use of a control or comparison group; (2) pretest-posttest design or posttest only with random assignment; and (3) use of reliably operationalized quantitative outcome measures. Quasi-experimental studies were excluded if they did not control for preexisting differences on measured outcomes with either change scores or covariance-adjusted means.[10] In addition, to ensure comparability, we focused on results based only on immediate posttest. Because only four evaluation studies were long term (two of which were compromised by severe control group attrition or contamination), we were unable to adequately assess longer-term DARE effects.

We examined several other methodological features, such as the correspondence between the unit of assignment and analysis, the use of a panel design, matching of schools in the intervention and control conditions, and attrition rates. Although these factors were considered in assessing the studies' overall methodological rigor, we did not eliminate evaluations on the basis of these criteria.

Data Analysis

For each study, we calculated an effect size to quantify the magnitude of DARE's effectiveness with respect to each of six outcomes that reflect the DARE curriculum's aims. An effect size is defined as the difference between the intervention and the control group means for each outcome measure, standardized by dividing by the pooled standard deviation [effect size = $\text{mean}_I - \text{mean}_C/\text{SD}$].[7-9] If means and standard deviations were not available, we calculated effect sizes using formulas developed to convert other test statistics and percentages to effect sizes.[9] In all cases, we used statistics reflecting covariance-adjusted means, with pretest values as covariates rather than unadjusted means so that any differences between the comparison groups before the intervention would not be reflected in the effect sizes.[10]

The six outcome measure classes include knowledge about drugs, attitudes about drug use, social skills, self-esteem, attitude toward police, and drug use. Some studies did not include all six, and some outcomes were measured by more than one indicator. When multiple indicators were used (e.g., two measures of social skills), we calculated separate effect sizes and then averaged them.[6,10] This procedure yielded one effect size per study for each measured outcome type. In the one study that reported only that a measured outcome was not statistically significant (and did not provide any further statistics), we assigned a zero value to that effect size.[10] To calculate effect sizes for drug use, we considered only alcohol, tobacco, and marijuana use; we averaged effect sizes across these substances. In a supplementary analysis, we considered use of these substances separately. The prevalence of other drugs, such as cocaine, was too small to produce meaningful effects.

In addition to calculating one effect size per outcome per study, we calculated the weighted mean effect size and 95% confidence interval (CI) for each outcome type across programs. The weighted mean is computed by weighting each effect size by the inverse of its variance, which is a reflection of the sample size.[8,9] The effect size estimates from larger studies are generally more precise than those from smaller studies.[8] Hence, the weighted mean provides a less biased estimate than the simple, unweighted mean because estimates from larger samples are given more weight. The 95% CI indicates the estimated effect size's accuracy or reliability and is calculated by adding to or subtracting from the mean 1.96 multiplied by the square root of 1 divided by the sum of the study weights.[8]

TABLE 1—DARE Evaluation Studies Selected for Review

Location	References[a]
British Columbia (BC)	Walker 1990
Hawaii (HI)	Manos, Kameoka, and Tanji 1986
Illinois (IL)	Ennett et al. 1994 (in press)
Kentucky-A (KY-A)	Clayton et al. 1991a, 1991b
Kentucky-B (KY-B)	Faine and Bohlander 1988, 1989
Minnesota (MN)	McCormick and McCormick 1992
North Carolina (NC)	Ringwalt, Ennett, and Holt 1991
South Carolina (SC)	Harmon 1993

[a]See Appendix A for full references.

Comparison of DARE with Other Drug Use Prevention Programs

For comparison with DARE, we used the effect sizes reported in Tobler's meta-analysis of school-based drug use prevention programs.[10] To allow the most appropriate comparisons with DARE effect sizes, we obtained Tobler's results for only those programs (excluding DARE) aimed at upper elementary school pupils. These programs are a subset of 25 from the 114 programs in Tobler's meta-analysis, whose studies are referenced in Appendix B.

We selected this meta-analysis for comparison because of its greater similarity to ours than other meta-analyses of drug use prevention programs.[11-14] Tobler's studies met the same methodological standards that we used for the DARE studies. The only differences were that Tobler excluded studies that did not measure drug use and considered results from later posttests, whereas we considered only immediate posttest results. Neither of these differences, however, should seriously compromise the comparison.

The evaluation studies included in Tobler's meta-analysis are classified into

TABLE 2—Sample and Methodological Characteristics of the DARE Evaluations (n = 8)

Study	Schools, n	Subjects, n	Research Design	Matching	Unit of Analysis	Pretest Equivalency[a]	Scale Reliabilities	Attrition
BC	11	D = 287 C = 175	Quasi, cross-sectional	Yes	Individual	Yes	No	Not applicable
HI	26	D = 1574 C = 435	Quasi, panel	No	Individual	No	No	No
IL	36	D = 715 C = 608	Experimental/quasi, panel	Yes	School based	Yes	Yes	Yes[b]
KY-A	31	D = 1438 C = 487	Experimental, panel	No	Individual	Yes	Yes	Yes[b]
KY-B	16	D = 451 C = 332	Quasi, panel	Yes	Individual	Yes	Yes	No
MN	63	D = 453 C = 490	Quasi, panel	No	Individual	Yes	Yes	Yes[c]
NC	20	D = 685 C = 585	Experimental, panel	No	School based	Yes	Yes	Yes[b]
SC	11	D = 295 C = 307	Quasi, panel	Yes	Individual	Yes	Yes	Yes[c]

Note. See Table 1 for information on study locations and references. D = DARE; C = comparison.
[a]Pretest equivalency on demographic variables assessed and controlled if necessary.
[b]Attrition rates reported and differential attrition across experimental conditions analyzed.
[c]Attrition rates reported only.

TABLE 3—Unweighted Effect Sizes Associated with Eight DARE Evaluations

Study	Knowledge	Attitudes about Drugs	Social Skills	Self-Esteem	Attitude toward Police	Drug Use[a]
BC	.68	.00	...	...	...	.02
HI	...	.07	.34	...	...	...
IL	...	.03	.15	.15	.12	.05
KY-A	...	.11	.10	.07	...	.00
KY-B	.58	.19	.30	.14	.27	...
MN	.19	.06	.08	−.03	.05	...
NC	...	.19	.17	.00	...	.11
SC	...	.32	.19	.06	.08	.10

Note. See Table 1 for information on study locations and references.
[a]Limited to alcohol, tobacco, and marijuana.

two broad categories based on the programs' content and process. Process describes the teaching approach (how the content is delivered). Programs classified by Tobler as "noninteractive" emphasize intrapersonal factors, such as knowledge gain and affective growth, and are primarily delivered by an expert. "Interactive" programs emphasize interpersonal factors by focusing on social skills and general social competencies and by using interactive teaching strategies, particularly peer to peer. Consistent with other meta-analyses showing that programs emphasizing social skills tend to be the most successful,[11-13,15] interactive programs produced larger effect sizes than noninteractive programs. We compared DARE with both categories of programs.

Results

Characteristics of Evaluations

Of the original 18 studies, 8 met the criteria for inclusion. One additional study met the methodological criteria but did not administer the first posttest until 1 year after DARE implementation; therefore, it could not be included in our analysis of immediate effects.[16,17] The location and primary reference for each evaluation are shown in Table 1, and study characteristics are summarized in Table 2.

Each evaluation represents a state or local effort. The number of student subjects in all studies was large, each study comprising at least 10 schools with approximately 500 to 2000 students. Although demographic information was not given for three studies, the remaining five studies in the sample primarily consisted of White subjects.

Assignment of DARE to intervention and control groups was by school for all eight studies. In one study, DARE also was assigned by classroom in certain schools.[18] Because of potential contamination in this study of the control group classrooms by their close proximity to DARE classes, we eliminated these control classrooms; only control schools with no DARE classes were included. Two studies used a true experimental design in which schools were randomly assigned to DARE and control conditions; a third study used random assignment for two thirds of the schools. The remaining five evaluations used a nonequivalent control group quasi-experimental design.

Because there were relatively few sampling units across studies—ranging from 11 to 63 schools, with all except one study involving fewer than 40 schools—it is unlikely that equivalence between groups was obtained without prior matching or blocking of schools, even with randomization. Only half the studies matched comparison schools on selected demographic characteristics. Most studies (75%), however, assessed the equivalency of the comparison groups at pretest and made adjustments for pretest differences on demographic characteristics. All studies adjusted for pretest differences on outcome measures.

All but one study used a panel design that matched subjects from pretest to posttest with a unique identification code.

Outcome measures used in the DARE evaluations were based on responses to self-administered questionnaires. Seven studies used standardized scales or revised existing measures; six studies reported generally high scale reliabilities (usually Cronbach's alpha). Validity information, however, was rarely reported, and no study used either a biochemical indicator or "bogus pipeline" technique to validate drug use self-reports.[19]

Most studies (75%) did not use a data analysis strategy appropriate to the unit of assignment. Because schools, not students, were assigned to DARE and control conditions, it would have been appropriate to analyze the data by schools with subjects' data aggregated within each school or to use a hierarchical analysis strategy in which subjects are nested within schools.[20,21] Six studies ignored schools altogether and analyzed individual subjects' data, thereby violating the statistical assumption of independence of observations. Ignoring schools as a unit of analysis results in a positive bias toward finding statistically significant program effects.[21] This bias may be reflected in CIs reported for each outcome's weighted mean effect size.

Five studies reported generally small attrition rates. None of the three studies that analyzed attrition found that rates differed significantly across experimental and control conditions. In addition, subjects absent from the posttest were not more likely to be drug users or at risk for drug use. Although attrition usually is greater among drug users,[22] given the sample's young age (when school dropout is unlikely and drug use prevalence is low), these results are not surprising.

DARE Effect Sizes

Study effect sizes are shown in Table 3. In general, the largest effect sizes are for knowledge and social skills; the smallest are for drug use.

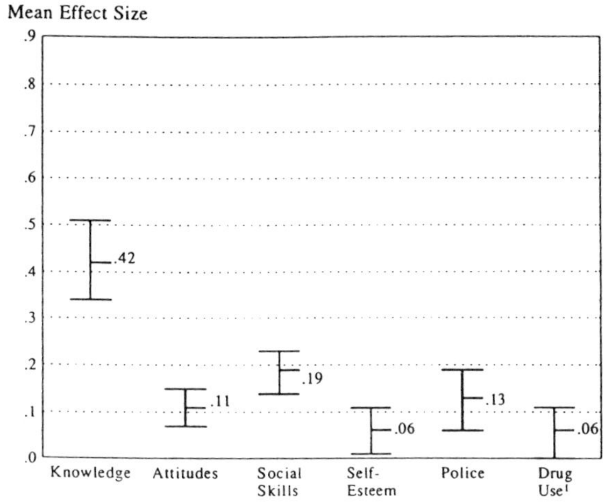

¹Drug use includes alcohol, tobacco, and marijuana.

FIGURE 1—Magnitude of DARE's weighted mean effect size (and 95% CI), by outcome measure.

Figure 1 shows the mean weighted effect size and 95% CI for each outcome based on the eight studies combined. The largest mean effect size is for knowledge (.42), followed by social skills (.19), attitude toward the police (.13), attitudes about drug use (.11), self-esteem (.06), and drug behavior (.06). The effect sizes for knowledge, social skills, attitude toward the police, attitudes about drug use, and self-esteem are statistically significant. The CI for the mean drug use effect size overlaps with zero (i.e., it is not significantly different from zero).

Because averaging alcohol, tobacco, and marijuana use for the drug use effect size could obscure substantial differences among the substances, we calculated DARE's mean weighted effect sizes separately for these substances. The weighted mean effect size for alcohol use is .06 (95% CI = .00, .12); for tobacco use, .08 (95% CI = .02, .14); and for marijuana use, −.01 (95% CI = −.09, .07). Only the mean for tobacco use is statistically significant.

Mean Effect Sizes for DARE vs Other Drug Use Prevention Programs

We compared by type of outcome the mean weighted DARE effect size with the mean weighted effect size for noninteractive (n = 9) and interactive (n = 16) programs; effect sizes for the comparison programs are derived from Tobler.[10] The comparison programs target youth of the same grade range targeted by DARE. The outcomes assessed by both DARE and the comparison programs are knowledge, attitudes, social skills, and drug use behavior.

Across the four outcome domains, DARE's effect sizes are smaller than those for interactive programs (Figure 2). Most notable are DARE's effect sizes for drug use and social skills; neither effect size (.06 and .19, respectively) is more than a third of the comparable effect sizes for interactive programs (.18 and .75, respectively). DARE's effect size for drug use is only slightly smaller than the noninteractive programs' effect size. DARE's effect sizes for knowledge, attitudes, and social skills, however, are larger than those for noninteractive programs.

Comparison of effect sizes separately for alcohol, tobacco, and marijuana use shows that DARE's effect sizes are smaller than those for interactive programs (Figure 3). Except for tobacco use,

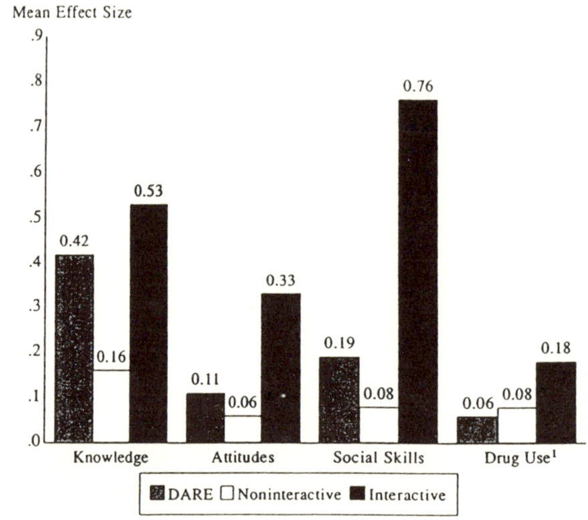

Note. Comparison programs selected from Tobler.[10]
[1]Drug use includes alcohol, tobacco, and marijuana.

FIGURE 2— Weighted mean effect size, by outcome, for DARE and other drug use prevention programs.

they also are smaller than those for noninteractive programs.

Discussion

The results of this meta-analysis suggest that DARE's core curriculum effect on drug use relative to whatever drug education (if any) was offered in the control schools is slight and, except for tobacco use, is not statistically significant. Across the studies, none of the average drug use effect sizes exceeded .11. Review of several meta-analyses of adolescent drug use prevention programs suggests that effect sizes of this magnitude are small.[10–14]

The small magnitude of DARE's effectiveness on drug use behavior may partially reflect the relatively low frequency of drug use by the elementary school pupils targeted by DARE's core curriculum. However, comparison of the DARE effect sizes with those of other school-based drug use prevention programs for same-age adolescents suggests that greater effectiveness is possible with early adolescents. Compared with the programs classified by Tobler as interactive, DARE's effect sizes for alcohol, tobacco, and marijuana use, both collectively and individually, are substantially less.[10] Except for tobacco use, they also are less than the drug use effect sizes for more traditional, noninteractive programs.

It has been suggested that DARE may have delayed effects on drug use behavior once pupils reach higher grades.[23,24] Longer-term follow-up studies are needed to test this possibility. Only four reviewed studies administered multiple posttests, and for two of these the results from some later posttests are uninterpretable. However, based on two experimental studies for which reliable information 1 and 2 years after implementation is available, there is no evidence that DARE's effects are activated when subjects are older.[25,26] Most long-term evaluations of drug use prevention programs have shown that curriculum effects decay rather than appear or increase with time.[27,28]

DARE's immediate effects on outcomes other than drug use were somewhat larger (especially for knowledge) and were statistically significant. These effect sizes, however, also were less than the comparable effect sizes for same-age interactive programs. That DARE's effect sizes for knowledge, attitudes, and skills were greater in magnitude than those of noninteractive programs may not be particularly meaningful because many of these types of programs, such as programs using "scare tactics" or emphasizing factual knowledge about drug use, have been discredited as unsuccessful.[29,30]

Comparison of DARE's core curriculum content with the interactive and noninteractive programs' curricula may partially explain the relative differences in effect sizes among these programs. Interactive programs tend to emphasize developing drug-specific social skills and more general social competencies, whereas noninteractive programs focus largely on intrapersonal factors. Because DARE has features of both interactive and noninteractive programs, it is perhaps not surprising that the effect sizes we reported should fall somewhere in between. Perhaps greater emphasis in the DARE core curriculum on social competencies and less emphasis on affective factors might result in effect sizes nearer to those reported for interactive programs. However, it is difficult to speculate on the effect of adding or subtracting particular lessons to or from DARE's curriculum. Most school-based prevention program evaluations have assessed the effectiveness of an overall program rather than various program components or combinations of components.

Who teaches DARE and how it is taught may provide other possible explanations for DARE's limited effectiveness. Despite the extensive DARE training received by law enforcement officers, they may not be as well equipped to lead the curriculum as teachers. No studies have been reported in which the DARE curriculum was offered by anyone other than a police officer; results from such a study might suggest whether teachers produce better (or worse) outcomes among pupils.

Regardless of curriculum leader, however, the generally more traditional teaching style used by DARE has not been shown to be as effective as an interactive teaching mode.[10,14] Although some activities encourage pupil interaction, the curriculum relies heavily on the officer as expert and makes frequent use of lectures and question-and-answer sessions between the officer and pupils. In fact, it is in teaching style, not curriculum content, that DARE most differs from the interactive programs examined by Tobler.

The DARE core curriculum recently was modified to introduce more participatory activities, which may lead to greater program effectiveness.

Several limitations should be considered in evaluating our findings. The number of evaluations reviewed (eight) is not large when compared with the vast number of sites where DARE has been implemented. The consistency of results across studies, however, suggests that the results are likely to be representative of DARE's core curriculum. Even so, we would have preferred a full set of eight effect sizes for each outcome.

It is possible that the effect sizes for the DARE studies may have been attenuated compared with the drug use prevention programs reviewed by Tobler because the control groups were not pure "no treatment" groups. As documented by Tobler, effect sizes are lower when the control group receives some sort of drug education.[10,14] The DARE evaluations generally lacked information on alternative treatments received by the control groups, but it is likely that most control groups received some drug education because the studies occurred after the 1986 Drug-Free Schools and Communities Act. However, approximately half (54%) of the programs reviewed by Tobler also were conducted between 1986 and 1990, suggesting that they may suffer from the same effect.[10]

Most of the drug use prevention programs evaluated by Tobler were university research-based evaluation studies, whereas DARE is a commercially available curriculum. Although the magnitude of the resources invested in DARE is considerable, the intensity of effort devoted to smaller-scale programs may be greater. Some diminished effectiveness is perhaps inevitable once programs are widely marketed.

Although we found limited immediate core curriculum effects, some features of DARE may be more effective, such as the middle school curriculum. In addition, DARE's cumulative effects may be greater in school districts where all DARE curricula for younger and older students are in place. Other DARE outcomes, such as its impact on community law enforcement relations, also may yield important benefits. However, due to the absence of evaluation studies, consideration of these features is beyond this study's scope.

DARE's limited influence on adolescent drug use behavior contrasts with the program's popularity and prevalence. An important implication is that DARE could be taking the place of other, more beneficial drug use curricula that adolescents could be receiving. At the same time, expectations concerning the effectiveness of any school-based curriculum, including DARE, in changing adolescent drug use behavior should not be overstated.[31] □

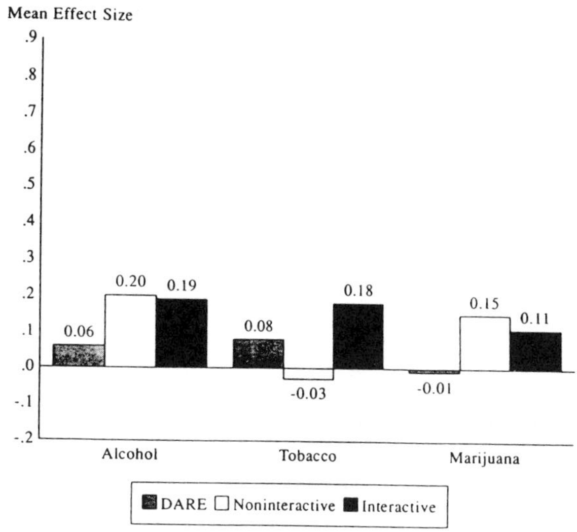

Note. Comparison programs selected from Tobler.[10]

FIGURE 3—Weighted mean effect size, by drug, for DARE and other drug use prevention programs.

Acknowledgments

This research was supported by awards from the National Institute of Justice, Office of Justice Programs, US Department of Justice (91-DD-CX-K053) and the National Institute on Drug Abuse, US Department of Health and Human Services (5 R01 DA07037).

We thank Susan L. Bailey, Karl E. Bauman, George H. Dunteman, Robert L. Hubbard, Ronald W. Johnson, and J. Valley Rachal for their thoughtful comments on an earlier draft of this paper. In addition, we acknowledge the support and assistance of Jody M. Greene on this project and the editorial assistance of Beryl C. Pittman, Linda B. Barker, and Richard S. Straw.

References

1. Glynn TJ. Essential elements of school-based smoking prevention program. *J Sch Health.* 1989;59:181–188.
2. *Healthy People 2000.* Washington, DC: US Dept of Health and Human Services; 1988. DHHS publication no. PHS 91-50212.
3. Ringwalt CL, Greene JM. Results of school districts' drug prevention coordinator's survey. Presented at the Alcohol, Tobacco, and Other Drugs Conference on Evaluating School-Linked Prevention Strategies; March 1993; San Diego, Calif.
4. *Implementing Project DARE: Drug Abuse Resistance Education.* Washington, DC: Bureau of Justice Assistance; 1988.
5. Drug-Free Schools and Community Act. Pub L No. 101-647, §5122(e)(1).
6. Bangert-Drowns RL. Review of developments in meta-analytic method. *Psychol Bull.* 1986;99:388–399.
7. Rosenthal R. *Meta-Analytic Procedures for Social Research.* Applied Social Research Methods Series. Vol 6. Newbury Park, Calif: Sage Publications; 1991.
8. Hedges LV, Olkin I. *Statistical Methods for Meta-Analysis.* New York, NY: Academic Press; 1985.
9. Perry PD, Tobler NS. Meta-analysis of adolescent drug prevention programs: final report. In: *Manual for Effect Size Calculation: Formula Used in the Meta-Analysis of Adolescent Drug Prevention Programs.* Rockville, Md: National Institute on Drug Abuse; 1992: appendix 3.
10. Tobler NS. *Meta-Analysis of Adolescent Drug Prevention Programs: Final Report.*

Rockville, Md: National Institute on Drug Abuse; 1992.
11. Bangert-Drowns RL. The effects of school-based substance abuse education: a meta-analysis. *J Drug Educ.* 1988;18:243–264.
12. Bruvold WH. A meta-analysis of adolescent smoking prevention programs. *Am J Public Health.* 1993;83:872–880.
13. Bruvold WH, Rundall TG. A meta-analysis and theoretical review of school-based tobacco and alcohol intervention programs. *Psychol Health.* 1988;2:53–78.
14. Tobler NS. Meta-analysis of 143 adolescent drug prevention programs: quantitative outcome results of program participants compared to a control or comparison group. *J Drug Issues.* 1986;16:537–567.
15. Hansen WB. School-based substance abuse prevention: a review of the state of the art in curriculum, 1980–1990. *Health Educ Res.* 1992;7:403–430.
16. Nyre GF, Rose C. *Drug Abuse Resistance Education (DARE) Longitudinal Evaluation Annual Report, January 1987.* Los Angeles, Calif: Evaluation and Training Institute; 1987. Unpublished report.
17. Nyre GF, Rose C, Bolus RE. *Drug Abuse Resistance Education (DARE) Longitudinal Evaluation Annual Report, August 1987.* Los Angeles, Calif: Evaluation and Training Institute; 1987. Unpublished report.
18. Manos MJ, Kameoka KY, Tanji JH. *Evaluation of Honolulu Police Department's Drug Abuse Resistance Education Program.* Honolulu, Hawaii: University of Hawaii-Manoa, School of Social Work, Youth Development and Research Center; 1986. Unpublished report.
19. Bauman KE, Dent CW. Influence of an objective measure on the self-reports of behavior. *J Appl Psychol.* 1982,67:623–628.
20. Moskowitz JM. Why reports of outcome evaluations are often biased or uninterpretable. *Eval Progr Plan.* 1993;16:1–9.
21. Murray DM, Hannan PJ. Planning for the appropriate analysis in school-based drug use prevention studies. *J Consult Clin Psychol.* 1990;58:458–468.
22. Biglan A, Ary DV. Methodological issues in research on smoking prevention. In: Bell CS, Battjes R, eds. *Prevention Research: Deterring Drug Abuse Among Children and Adolescents.* Rockville, Md: National Institute on Drug Abuse; 1985:170–195.
23. Clayton RR, Cattarello A, Day LE, Walden KP. Persuasive communication and drug abuse prevention: an evaluation of the DARE program. In: Donohew L, Sypher H, Bukoski W, eds. *Persuasive Communication and Drug Abuse Prevention.* Hillsdale, NJ: Lawrence Erlbaum Associates, Inc; 1991:295–313.
24. Ringwalt CL, Ennett ST, Holt KD. An outcome evaluation of Project DARE (Drug Abuse Resistance Education). *Health Educ Res.* 1991;6:327–337.
25. Clayton RR, Cattarello A, Walden KP. Sensation seeking as a potential mediating variable for school-based prevention intervention: a two-year follow-up of DARE. *Health Commun.* 1991;3:229–239.
26. Ennett ST, Rosenbaum DP, Flewelling RL, Bieler GS, Ringwalt CL, Bailey SL. Long-term evaluation of Drug Abuse Resistance Education. *Addict Behav.* 1994;19:113–125.
27. Ellickson PL, Bell RM, McGuigan K. Preventing adolescent drug use: long-term results of a junior high program. *Am J Public Health.* 1993;83:856–861.
28. Murray DM, Pirie P, Luepker RV, Pallonen U. Five- and six-year follow-up results from four seventh-grade smoking prevention strategies. *J Behav Med.* 1989;12:207–218.
29. Botvin GJ. Substance abuse prevention: theory, practice, and effectiveness. In: Tonry M, Wilson JQ, eds. *Drugs and Crime.* Chicago, Ill: University of Chicago Press; 1990:461–519.
30. Moskowitz J. Preventing adolescent substance abuse through education. In: Glynn T, Leukefeld CG, Ludford JP, eds. *Preventing Adolescent Drug Abuse: Intervention Strategies.* Rockville, Md: National Institute on Drug Abuse; 1983:233–249.
31. Dryfoo JG. Preventing substance abuse: rethinking strategies. *Am J Public Health.* 1993;83:793–795.

APPENDIX A—Bibliography of DARE Evaluations

Aniskiewicz RE, Wysong EE. *Project DARE Evaluation Report: Kokomo Schools Spring, 1987.* Kokomo, Ind: Indiana University–Kokomo; 1987. Unpublished report.

Aniskiewicz R, Wysong E. Evaluating DARE: drug education and the multiple meanings of success. *Policy Stud Rev.* 1990;9:727–747.

Anonymous. *Project DARE Evaluation, Spring, 1987.* Pittsburgh, Pa; 1987. Unpublished paper.

Becker HR, Agopian MW, Yeh S. Impact evaluation of Drug Abuse Resistance Education (DARE). *J Drug Educ.* 1990;22:283–291.

Clayton RR, Cattarello A, Day LE, Walden KP. Persuasive communication and drug abuse prevention: an evaluation of the DARE program. In: Donohew L, Sypher H, Bukoski W, eds. *Persuasive Communication and Drug Abuse Prevention.* Hillsdale, NJ: Lawrence Erlbaum Associates; 1991a:295–313.

Clayton RR, Cattarello A, Walden KP. Sensation seeking as a potential mediating variable for school-based prevention intervention: a two-year follow-up of DARE. *Health Commun.* 1991b;3:229–239.

DeJong W. A short-term evaluation of Project DARE (Drug Abuse Resistance Education): preliminary indicators of effectiveness. *J Drug Educ.* 1987;17:279–294.

Dukes R, Matthews S. *Evaluation of the Colorado Springs Citywide DARE Program.* Colorado Springs, Colo: University of Colorado, Center for Social Science Research; 1991. Unpublished report.

Earle RB, Garner J, Phillips N. *Evaluation of the Illinois State Police Pilot DARE Program.* Springfield, Ill: A.H. Training and Development Systems, Inc; 1987. Unpublished report.

Ennett ST, Rosenbaum DP, Flewelling RL, Bieler GS, Ringwalt CR, Bailey SL. Long-term evaluation of Drug Abuse Resistance Education. *Addict Behav.* 1994;19:113–125.

Evaluation and Training Institute. *DARE Evaluation Report for 1985–1989.* Los Angeles, Calif: Evaluation and Training Institute; 1990. Unpublished report.

Faine JR, Bohlander E. *Drug Abuse Resistance Education: An Assessment of the 1987–88 Kentucky State Police DARE Program.* Bowling Green, Ky: Western Kentucky University, Social Research Laboratory; 1988. Unpublished report.

Faine JR, Bohlander E. *DARE in Kentucky Schools 1988–89.* Bowling Green, Ky: Western Kentucky University, Social Research Laboratory; 1989. Unpublished report.

Harmon MA. Reducing the risk of drug involvement among early adolescents: an evaluation of Drug Abuse Resistance Education (DARE). *Eval Rev.* 1993;17:221–239.

Kethineni S, Leamy DA, Guyon L. *Evaluation of the Drug Abuse Resistance Education Program in Illinois: Preliminary Report.* Normal, Ill: Illinois State University, Department of Criminal Justice Sciences; 1991. Unpublished report.

McCormick, FC, McCormick ER. *An Evaluation of the Third Year Drug Abuse Resistance Education (DARE) Program in Saint Paul.* Saint Paul, Minn: Educational Operations Concepts, Inc; 1992. Unpublished report.

McDonald RM, Towberman DB, Hague JL. *Volume II: 1989 Impact Assessment of Drug Abuse Resistance Education in the Commonwealth of Virginia.* Richmond, Va: Virginia Commonwealth University, Institute for Research in Justice and Risk Administration; 1990. Unpublished report.

Manos MJ, Kameoka KY, Tanji JH. *Evaluation of Honolulu Police Department's Drug Abuse Resistance Education Program.* Honolulu, Hawaii: University of Hawaii–Manoa, School of Social Work, Youth Development and Research Center; 1986. Unpublished report.

APPENDIX A—Continued

Nyre GF, Rose C. *Drug Abuse Resistance Education (DARE) Longitudinal Evaluation Annual Report, January 1987.* Los Angeles, Calif: Evaluation and Training Institute; 1987. Unpublished report.

Nyre GF, Rose C, Bolus RE. *Drug Abuse Resistance Education (DARE) Longitudinal Evaluation Annual Report, August 1987.* Los Angeles, Calif: Evaluation and Training Institute; 1987. Unpublished report.

Ringwalt C, Ennett ST, Holt KD. An outcome evaluation of Project DARE (Drug Abuse Resistance Education). *Health Educ Res.* 1991;6:327–337.

Walker S. *The Victoria Police Department Drug Abuse Resistance Education Programme (D.A.R.E.) Programme Evaluation Report #2 (1990).* Victoria, British Columbia: The Ministry of the Solicitor-General, Federal Government of Canada; 1990. Unpublished report.

APPENDIX B—Bibliography of Comparison Program Evaluations

Allison K, Silver G. Dignam C. Effects on students of teacher training in use of a drug education curriculum. *J Drug Educ.* 1990;20:31–46.

Dielman T, Shope J, Butchart A, Campanelli, P. Prevention of adolescent alcohol misuse: an elementary school program. *J Pediatr Psychol.* 1986;11:259–281.

Dielman T, Shope J, Campanelli P, Butchart A. Elementary school-based prevention of adolescent alcohol misuse. *Pediatrician: Int J Child Adolesc Health.* 1987;14:70–76.

Dielman T, Shope J, Leech S, Butchart A. Differential effectiveness of an elementary school-based alcohol misuse prevention program. *J Sch Health.* 1989;59:255–262.

Dubois R, Hostelter M, Tosti-Vasey J, Swisher J. *Program Report and Evaluation: 1988–1989 School Year.* Philadelphia, Pa: Corporate Alliance for Drug Education; 1989. Unpublished report.

Flay B, Koepke D, Thomson S, Santi S, Best J, Brown S. Six-year follow-up of the first Waterloo school smoking prevention trial. *Am J Public Health.* 1989;79:1371–1376.

Flay B, Ryan K, Best J, et al. Cigarette smoking: why young people do it and ways of preventing it. In: McGrath P, Firestone P, eds. *Pediatric and Adolescent Behavioral Medicine.* New York, NY: Springer-Verlag, 1983:132–183.

Flay B, Ryan K, Best J, et al. Are social psychological smoking prevention programs effective? The Waterloo study. *J Behav Med.* 1985;8:37–59.

Gersick K, Grady K, Snow D. Social-cognitive development with sixth graders and its initial impact on substance use. *J Drug Educ.* 1988;18:55–70.

Gilchrist L, Schinke S, Trimble J, Cvetkovich G. Skills enhancement to prevent substance abuse among American Indian adolescents. *Int J Addict.* 1987;22:869–879.

Johnson C, Graham J, Hansen W, Flay B, McGuigan K, Gee M. *Project Smart After Three Years: An Assessment of Sixth-Grade and Multiple-Grade Implementations.* Pasadena, Calif: University of Southern California, Institute for Prevention Research; 1987. Unpublished report.

McAlister A. Approaches to primary prevention. Presented at the National Academy of Science National Research Council Conference on Alcohol and Public Policy; May 1983; Washington, DC.

Moskowitz J, Malvin J, Schaeffer G, Schaps E. Evaluation of an affective development teacher training program. *J Primary Prev.* 1984;4:150–162.

Sarvela P. Early adolescent substance use in rural northern Michigan and northeastern Wisconsin. In: *Dissertation Abstracts International.* 1984:46 01, 2000A. University Microfilms No. 84-22, 327.

Sarvela P. McClendon E. An impact evaluation of a rural youth drug education program. *J Drug Educ.* 1987; 17:213–231.

Schaeffer G, Moskowitz J, Malvin J, Schaps E. *The Effects of a Classroom Management Teacher Training Program on First-Grade Students: One Year Follow-Up.* Napa, Calif: The Napa Project, Pacific Institute for Research; 1981. Unpublished report.

Schaps E, Moskowitz J, Condon J, Malvin J. A process and outcome evaluation of an affective teacher training primary prevention program. *J Alcohol Drug Educ.* 1984;29:35–64.

Schinke S, Bebel M. Orlandi M, Botvin G. Prevention strategies for vulnerable pupils: school social work practices to prevent substance abuse. *Urban Educ.* 1988;22:510–519.

Schinke SP, Blythe BJ. Cognitive-behavioral prevention of children's smoking. *Child Behav Ther.* 1981;3:25–42.

Schinke S, Gilchrist L. Primary prevention of tobacco smoking. *J Sch Health.* 1983;53:416–419.

Schinke S, Gilchrist L, Schilling R, Snow W, Bobo J. Skills methods to prevent smoking. *Health Educ Q.* 1986;13:23–27.

Schinke S, Gilchrist L, Snow W. Skills interventions to prevent cigarette smoking among adolescents. *Am J Public Health.* 1985;75:665–667.

Schinke S, Gilchrist L, Snow W, Schilling R. Skills-building methods to prevent smoking by adolescents. *J. Adolesc Health Care.* 1985;6:439–444.

Shope J, Dielman T. Leech S. An elementary school-based alcohol misuse prevention program: two year follow-up evaluation. Presented at the American Public Health Association Annual Meeting; November 1988; Boston, Mass.

Drug Treatment in the Criminal Justice System

BY GREGORY P. FALKIN, PH.D., MICHAEL PRENDERGAST, PH.D., AND M. DOUGLAS ANGLIN, PH.D.*

RESEARCH CONDUCTED during the past decade has demonstrated a need to enhance treatment for drug-involved offenders at all stages of the criminal justice process. Data from the National Institute of Justice's Drug Use Forecasting (DUF) program show that as many as three-quarters of arrestees (men and women) test positive for one or more illicit drugs; many of these arrestees are dependent on drugs and in need of treatment (National Institute of Justice, 1992). Abundant evidence exists that crime rates are higher among drug-dependent offenders than among offenders who do not use drugs, and among addicts during periods of drug use compared with periods when drugs are not used (Ball et al., 1981; Hanlon et al., 1990; Speckart & Anglin, 1986). Fortunately, research has also shown that drug treatment can curb recidivism and relapse among drug-using offenders (Anglin & Hser, 1990; Falkin et al., 1992; Leukefeld & Tims, 1992).

To understand the current scope of the problem and the state-of-the-art in treating drug-abusing offenders, a number of questions related to needs assessment, program effectiveness, and the delivery of treatment services must be addressed. The main policy related questions discussed in this article are: How many offenders need drug treatment, and to what extent is this need being met? How effective are different types of drug treatment programs, particularly those that specialize in treating drug-dependent offenders, and what kinds of programs work best for different types of offenders? What is the state-of-the-art in criminal justice drug treatment, and what can be done to enhance treatment efforts?

A Substantial Proportion of Offenders Need Drug Treatment

There has been a huge influx of drug users in the criminal justice system since the early 1980's, and many of these individuals have problems serious enough to warrant treatment. In the mid-1970's, states began passing tougher laws to protect the public and to exact retribution for criminals. Law enforcement agencies stepped up campaigns against drug law violators, especially drug traffickers and neighborhood dealers (Coldren et al., 1990; Uchida et al., 1992). As a consequence, prosecutors and probation and parole officers were forced to struggle with unmanageable caseloads, court calendars became backlogged, and the Nation's jails and prisons became overcrowded (Belenko, 1990). (America's prison system grew three-fold in the last decade, becoming the largest in the free world—and at a staggering price [Morris, 1993].) A sizable proportion of offenders in each segment of the system are either there on drug charges, or they have a substance abuse problem, which is often related to their criminal involvement.

Perhaps the most widely cited indication of this problem is the DUF data, which have shown a generally high rate of drug prevalence among arrestees (National Institute of Justice, 1992). DUF data show that about 50 to 80 percent of arrestees in the 24 DUF cities tested positive for one or more drugs shortly after arrest. These prevalence figures have remained fairly constant over the last several years, while drug use in the general population has been declining. Rates of drug use are especially high for minorities and for women, and there are some indications that their rates of use (e.g., for cocaine) have been growing. Several other surveys corroborate these findings and show that drug use is prevalent among probationers, jail inmates, prisoners, and parolees (Prendergast et al., 1992).

It is possible that not all of these individuals need drug treatment. To learn more specifically how many offenders need treatment, the research team analyzed recent DUF data based on a few indications of need. The criteria for needing treatment are (a) offenders who test positive for drugs admitted using drugs regularly before being arrested (at least 10 times in the past month), (b) they were in treatment when they were arrested, or (c) they said that they wanted to be in treatment. According to this fairly conservative definition, the percentage of arrestees who are probably in need of treatment is about 45 percent for those who test positive for cocaine (in DUF cities), about 60 percent for those who test positive for opiates, and slightly more than 75 percent for those who inject cocaine, opiates, or amphetamines (Prendergast et al., 1992).

***Dr. Falkin is principal investigator, National Development and Research Institutes, Inc. Dr. Prendergast is assistant research historian and Dr. Anglin is director at the UCLA Drug Abuse Research Center.** **The research reported in this article was supported under grant 91-IJ-CX-K009 from the National Institute of Justice, Office of Justice Programs, U.S. Department of Justice. Points of view in this article are the authors' and do not necessarily represent the official position of the U.S. Department of Justice.**

The Need for Treatment Is Not Being Met

Although these figures demonstrate the extent of the aggregate need for treatment, they do not fully convey the magnitude of the problem. First, many arrestees who need treatment are not in treatment at the time they are arrested. In the DUF cities, the number of arrestees who need treatment, relative to the number enrolled in treatment, is about 16 to 1 for those who test positive for cocaine, 10 to 1 for those who test positive for opiates, and 12 to 1 for those who inject drugs (Prendergast et al., 1992). Second, less than one-third of the Nation's jails have a drug treatment program (most of these programs consist of drug education and group counseling rather than comprehensive services) (Peters et al., 1993). Third, although the number of prison inmates who receive treatment has increased dramatically since 1980 (Falkin et al., 1992; Harlow, 1992), the "majority of inmates with substance abuse problems still do not receive treatment while in prison" (Falkin et al., 1992). Ironically, Federal and state treatment capacity is under-utilized because some inmates who need treatment do not meet certain admission criteria (e.g., parole date is too far away), and others refuse to enter treatment (Harlow, 1992).

Finally, treatment is obviously needed because conventional criminal sanctions are not effective in reducing recidivism among drug-using offenders (Beck & Shipley, 1989; Farrington et al., 1986; Langan & Cunniff, 1992). Despite the efforts in the last several years to expand and enhance treatment programs for offenders (some of which are discussed below), indications are that treatment is not available to a large proportion of offenders who need it. A recent survey of over 2,000 criminal justice officials pointed out that "many survey respondents expressed concern that arrest and incarceration alone were insufficient to deter drug-dependent offenders from continuing their criminal behavior" and that "officials in all criminal justice professions reported needing affordable drug treatment programs" (National Institute of Justice, 1991). A more recent survey conducted specifically of judges and prosecutors found that they believe that treatment is more readily available in correctional settings and that the courts also need resources to intervene with offenders who have drug problems (Milkman et al., 1993).

Drug Treatment Is an Effective Government Response

A large body of literature has consistently shown that drug treatment is associated with significant reductions in criminality, drug use, and other lifestyle problems (Anglin & Hser, 1990; De Leon, 1985; Hubbard et al., 1989). Clients who are mandated to community-based treatment programs tend to remain in treatment longer than those who are admitted voluntarily, and length of stay is one of the best predictors of success after treatment (Anglin & Hser, 1990; Hubbard et al., 1988). A few intensive prison-based drug treatment programs have also been found to be effective in curbing recidivism (Falkin et al., 1992).

A careful review of 24 evaluation studies of drug treatment programs developed specifically for offenders (e.g., intensive supervision with treatment and prison- and jail-based programs), however, found mixed results in terms of treatment effectiveness (Falkin & Natarajan, 1993). Some studies showed favorable results in terms of lower recidivism, lower drug use, and lower rule violations, but others did not. The failure of some studies to demonstrate a positive treatment outcome may be due to one of two possibilities: either the treatment is not intensive enough to change behavior or weaknesses in the research methodologies result in inconclusive findings about treatment effects. Because there are a variety of limitations in the methodologies, it is difficult to make a definitive statement about the effectiveness of treatment programs geared specifically for offenders, and therefore additional and more methodologically sound research on these programs is needed. There are a number of national and local evaluation studies currently under way, but it will be a few years before the cumulative results can be appraised.

Offenders Have Various Needs, and Many Need Comprehensive Services

As criminal justice officials see firsthand, drug abuse is usually part of a disadvantaged and troubled lifestyle. Most drug-using arrestees have inadequate job skills, are uneducated (sometimes illiterate), without adequate housing, and in poor health, often as a direct result of drug use (e.g., hepatitis, tuberculosis, and AIDS). In addition, some suffer from mental illness. Research has shown that people with such complex difficulties can succeed in treatment, provided that it is intensive enough and that comprehensive services are delivered (Anglin & Hser, 1990; De Leon, 1985; Falkin et al., 1992). Thus, in matching offenders to appropriate treatments, it is crucial to consider the intensity and variety of services needed relative to the severity of offenders' problems.

Most criminal justice agencies, however, assign clients to treatment primarily on the basis of criminal charges and prior record, which do not necessarily reflect the severity of an individual's drug use and other psychosocial problems. The Offender Profile Index (OPI) was developed to counter this limitation (Inciardi et al., 1993). The OPI assigns clients to different levels of treatment (long-term residential, short-term residential, intensive outpatient, outpatient, and urine testing only) based on a number of aspects of their "stakes in conformity," which includes drug use and treatment histories, job situation, education, and housing, as well as criminal involvement. The OPI is currently being used in a number of jurisdictions; it is perhaps the most sophisticated method of matching offenders to treatment. Nonetheless, questions have been raised about the validity of this instrument; further research on matching offenders to appropriate treatments would certainly be valuable.

The Treatment System for Offenders Is Being Expanded and Enhanced

In the last several years, criminal justice authorities in many jurisdictions throughout the country have dramatically increased their efforts to engage drug-dependent offenders in treatment. These initiatives include deferred prosecution programs, supervised pretrial release with a condition of treatment, special drug courts, drug testing and evaluation programs, Treatment Alternatives to Street Crime (TASC), intensive supervision programs that require treatment, and jail- and prison-based treatment (e.g., therapeutic communities). Many of these criminal justice efforts are supported by agencies in the drug treatment system, such as the Center for Substance Abuse Treatment. Federal and state alcohol and drug treatment agencies have provided funding not only for community-based programs to which offenders are referred, but also for criminal justice-based programs. Treatment slots are being dedicated specifically for offenders, and treatment professionals are providing criminal justice personnel with training and technical assistance. Thus, the considerable expansion of, and improvements in, treatment for offenders that has occurred throughout the country in the last several years has come about through the joint efforts of criminal justice and drug treatment agencies.

The State-of-the-Art Is Based on Coordination

Various approaches to drug treatment have been developed, many facilitated by linkages between the criminal justice and drug treatment systems. Some of the recent developments include contracts between probation departments and community-based treatment programs, acupuncture as a component of diversion programs, day treatment programs for offenders, boot camps devoted to drug treatment, therapeutic communities in prisons and jails, and transitional release programs that extend services from institutions into the community. These programs are often developed and implemented jointly by criminal justice agencies and drug treatment providers. To clarify some of the different approaches, and to suggest some strategies for treating offenders, the following paragraphs describe case studies that were conducted in three state and local jurisdictions that have been developing a comprehensive array of treatment programs and a continuum of services for offenders. The sites are Multnomah County (Portland), Oregon; Jefferson County (Birmingham), Alabama; and Kings County (Brooklyn), New York. The main focus of the study concerned how linkages are involved in the development and implementation of the treatment system for offenders (for a full description, see Falkin, 1993).

Case Study Overview

In general, the main differences among the sites are as follows. Oregon's Community Corrections Act (CCA) requires criminal justice authorities to use the least restrictive sanctions possible, and it provides funding and an administrative infrastructure that fosters the use of drug treatment. Officials in the criminal justice and drug treatment systems participate in a number of state and local committees, task forces, and informal work groups to coordinate the development and implementation of treatment programs in community corrections and the prison system, including a program that provides transitional services for prisoners returning to the community. The state Department of Corrections administers the CCA, and the Office of Alcohol and Drug Abuse Programs supports correctional treatment efforts in a variety of ways (e.g., funding, training, technical assistance).

Jefferson County criminal justice authorities access treatment resources through TASC, which provides a continuum of services to offenders in each stage of the justice process. The Alabama Department of Corrections has dramatically expanded treatment in the prison system in the last several years, establishing an innovative "therapeutic prison" for 640 inmates; however, linkages with community-based treatment are not as well developed as they are in the other two states. In New York, the treatment system for offenders has undergone considerable changes in the last few years, but most of these developments are the result of agency initiatives (supported by the Mayor's Office, the state Office of Alcohol and Substance Abuse Services, and the state Anti-Drug Abuse Council). The system is much more decentralized than in the other two states, and change is accomplished more bureaucratically. Most of the criminal justice treatment efforts in the three sites are recent developments, and they are currently being evaluated.

Deferred Prosecution Programs

All three jurisdictions have a deferred prosecution program in which drug-using defendants are diverted to drug treatment. In Multnomah and Jefferson Counties, defendants charged for the first time for possession of small amounts of controlled substances (e.g., less than 5 grams of cocaine) are offered treatment as an alternative to prosecution. In Multnomah County, the program is a cooperative venture of the court, the District Attorney's Office, and the Public Defender's Office. There, clients are placed in an outpatient treatment program that contracts to provide acupuncture and counseling. In Jefferson County, clients are placed in TASC, which refers them to various community-based outpatient treatment programs with which it has formal agreements. The program in Kings County is much different in that it was developed by the District Attorney as an alternative to incarceration for prison-bound offenders. Only nonviolent second felony offenders arrested for drug dealing in buy-and-bust operations are eligible; if convicted, these offenders would receive mandatory minimum prison sentences. They are placed in one of two long-term residential treatment programs (therapeutic communities) with which the District Attorney's Office contracts for treatment services. The Drug Treatment Alternative-To-Prison (DTAP) program has a warrant enforcement team so that any client who leaves treatment is almost certain to be rearrested and sent to prison.

Treatment for Released and Jailed Defendants

Multnomah and Jefferson Counties also provide treatment to defendants whose abuse of drugs places them at risk of failing to appear in court if they are released from jail pending trial. Multnomah County's pretrial service agency operates a Pretrial Supervision Release Program (PSRP) in which staff refer defendants who need treatment to community-based treatment programs. The Public Defender's Office also has a treatment resource databank (with daily information on treatment availability), and attorneys refer clients to appropriate services. Although treatment in the jails is limited, there is a comprehensive program for women who are identified as pregnant drug users. The Alcohol and Drug Abuse Prenatal Treatment (ADAPT) program is coordinated by corrections, social service, and health care agencies, and is a model jail transition program, extending services into the community (Wellisch et al., 1993).

In Jefferson County, the pretrial service agency refers to TASC all drug using defendants who are released with contact conditions. (TASC eventually intervenes with all drug use cases that remain in the system.) Again, TASC assesses clients and refers them to an array of community-based treatment programs (based on the OPI); it also provides the criminal justice system with case management services. The jail does not operate a drug treatment program. In New York, the situation with respect to where and when agencies intervene during the pretrial stage is different. There is no formal pretrial supervision and treatment program, but the city's Department of Corrections operates a large drug treatment program at the Rikers Island jail. The Substance Abuse Intervention Division (SAID) provides short-term therapeutic community treatment (inmates are released within 45 days on average) to up to 1,600 inmates. Kings County has a TASC program that intervenes during the presentence stage, but it usually intervenes later in the process than Jefferson County TASC. Multnomah County also has a TASC program, but it serves mainly sentenced offenders.

Treatment for Probationers and Parolees

In Jefferson County, the state Board of Pardons and Paroles refers probationers and parolees who have drug problems to TASC. Thus, TASC provides a continuum of services, referring sentenced offenders to various treatment programs with which it has formal agreements and providing case management services for the state agency. A key feature of the linkage between the two systems is a coordinated response to behavioral problems (e.g., drug use, lack of compliance with program rules). This approach coordinates graduated sanctions with gradations in treatment intensity, with TASC moving clients to more or less intensive programs, depending on their behavior.

In New York and Oregon, the probation and parole agencies have developed various systematic approaches to linking clients with treatment. The main features of their approaches are: (1) contracts with drug treatment programs and (2) a centralized assessment and referral unit that places clients in contracting, and other, treatment programs. These approaches strengthen linkages between the community corrections and community-based drug treatment providers, and they assure a greater degree of client compliance with treatment than the traditional approach which leaves assessments, referrals, and monitoring to the discretion of line officers.

Treatment in the Prison System and Transitional Programs

All three states have expanded drug treatment in the prison system significantly in the last few years. They have created a comprehensive array of programs, including drug education and counseling, short-term inpatient programs, and long-term therapeutic communities, and, in Alabama, a total therapeutic institution that includes each of the previous components. Some of the therapeutic community programs have been evaluated and have been shown to be effective in reducing recidivism (Falkin et al., 1992).

In addition, New York and Oregon have developed transitional programs to continue offenders in treatment and to provide them with other services when they return to the community. There are two main aspects to Oregon's Transitional Release Program: in-prison services for inmates and formal linkages with community-based organizations. TASC of Oregon operates the Success Through Education and Planning (STEP) component, which provides inmates at a prerelease facility with drug education (including relapse prevention) and transitional planning, and staff from several counties visit the facility regularly to assist inmates who will be returning to their communities with services (drug treatment, housing, etc.) that they need to remain drug-free and crime-free. The Comprehensive Alcohol and Substance Abuse Treatment (CASAT) program in New York consists of three phases: treatment in a prison therapeutic community, treatment in a work release facility, and treatment in a community-based program when clients are paroled. CASAT is operated jointly by the Department of Correctional Services, the Division of Parole, and community-based treatment providers.

The Federal Government Can Foster System Developments

The idea of promoting formal cooperation between the criminal justice and drug treatment systems is not new (Wellisch et al., 1994). In the 1970's, there were a number of Federal efforts aimed at forging system linkages, including the development of TASC and regional workshops to facilitate cooperative planning between state criminal justice and treatment agencies. The possibility of improved cooperation and coordination, however, became the victim of the budget cuts and decentralization of the early 1980's. Since then, some Federal efforts to forge linkages between the two systems have continued. TASC survived this period and expanded its role under the sponsorship of the Bureau of Justice Assistance (BJA). From 1986 until 1992, about one dozen states enhanced their prison-based treatment programs as participants in two federally funded projects, REFORM and RECOVERY. These projects engaged drug treatment professionals to share their expertise with prison authorities and program staff both in a series of national conferences and at program sites. In a similar way, the American Probation and Parole Association and the National Association of State Alcohol and Substance Abuse Directors recently joined as partners in a national "Coordinated Interagency Drug Training and Technical Assistance" project (funded by BJA and the Center for Substance Abuse Treatment) that is linking community-based corrections and drug treatment.

Without Federal assistance provided through such discretionary grants and the formula grants, it is doubtful that the recent developments in state and local treatment systems for offenders would have been possible. Given the need for treatment, and the potential that treatment offers for reducing recidivism among drug-using offenders, it is important that such efforts continue. Part of any effort to develop treatment systems for offenders must include carefully designed research studies because much still needs to be learned about the effectiveness of various approaches.

References

Anglin, M.D., & Hser, Y.I. (1990). Treatment of drug abuse. In M. Tonry & J.Q. Wilson (Eds.), *Drugs and crime* (pp. 393-460). Chicago: University of Chicago Press.

Ball, J.C., Rosen, L., Flueck, J.A., & Nurco, D.N. (1981). The criminality of heroin addicts: When addicted and when off opiates. In J.A. Inciardi (Ed.), *The drugs-crime connection* (pp. 39-65). Beverly Hills, CA: Sage Publications.

Beck, A.J., & Shipley, B.E. (1989). *Recidivism of prisoners released in 1983.* Washington, DC: Bureau of Justice Statistics.

Belenko, S. (1990). The impact of drug offenders on the criminal justice system. In R. Weisheit (Ed.), *Drugs, crime and the criminal justice system* (pp. 27-78). Cincinnati: Anderson Publishing Co.

Coldren, J.R., Coyle, K.R., & Carr, S.D. (1990). *Multi-jurisdictional drug control task forces 1988: A key program of state drug control strategies.* Washington, DC: Bureau of Justice Assistance.

De Leon, G. (1985). The therapeutic community: Status and evolution. *International Journal of the Addictions, 20,* 823-844.

Falkin, G.P. (1993). *Coordinating drug treatment for offenders: A case study.* New York: National Development and Research Institutes, Inc.

Falkin, G.P., Lipton, D.S., & Wexler, H.K. (1992). Drug treatment in state prisons. In D.R. Gerstein & H.J. Harwood (Eds.), *Treating drug problems* (Vol. 2). Washington, DC: National Academy Press.

Falkin, G.P., & Natarajan, M. (1993). *Evaluations of treatment programs for drug-dependent offenders.* New York: National Development and Research Institutes, Inc.

Farrington, D.P., Ohlin, L.E., & Wilson, J.Q. (1986). *Understanding and controlling crime: Toward a new research strategy.* New York: Springer-Verlag.

Hanlon, T.E., Nurco, D.N., Kinlock, T.W., & Duszynski, K.R. (1990). Trends in criminal activity and drug use over an addiction career. *American Journal of Drug and Alcohol Abuse, 16*(3,4), 223-238.

Harlow, C.W. (1992). *Drug enforcement and treatment in prisons, 1990.* Washington, DC: Bureau of Justice Statistics.

Hubbard, R.L., Collins, J.J., Rachal, J.V., & Cavanaugh, E.R. (1988). The criminal justice client in drug abuse treatment. In C.G. Leukefeld & F.M. Tims (Eds.), *Compulsory treatment of drug abuse: Research and clinical practice* (NIDA Research Monograph 86). Rockville, MD: National Institute on Drug Abuse.

Hubbard, R.L., Marsden, M.E., Rachal, J.V., Harwood, H.J., Cavanaugh, E.R., & Ginzburg, H.M. (1989). *Drug abuse treatment: A national study of effectiveness.* Chapel Hill, NC: The University of North Carolina Press.

Inciardi, J.A., McBride, D.C., & Weinman, B.A. (1993). *The Offender Profile Index: A user's guide.* Washington, DC: National Association of State Alcohol and Drug Abuse Directors.

Langan, R.A., & Cunniff, M.A. (1992). *Recidivism of felons on probation, 1986-89.* Washington, DC: Bureau of Justice Statistics.

Leukefeld, C.G., & Tims, F.M. (Eds.) (1992). *Drug abuse treatment in prisons and jails* (NIDA Research Monograph 118). Rockville, MD: National Institute on Drug Abuse.

Milkman, R.H., Beaudin, B.D., Tarmann, K., & Landson, N. (1993). *Drug offenders and the courts.* McLean, VA: Lazar Institute.

Morris, N. (1993). *Intermediate sanctions: Between prison and probation*. Presented at the Third National Conference on Drugs and Crime, Austin, TX.

National Institute of Justice. (1991). *Assessing criminal justice needs*. Washington, DC: National Institute of Justice.

National Institute of Justice. (1992). *Drug use forecasting—1991*. Washington, DC: National Institute of Justice.

Peters, R.H., May, R.L., & Kearns, W.D. (1992). Drug treatment in jails: Results of a nationwide survey. *Journal of Criminal Justice, 20*, 283-295.

Phillips, M.D. (1992). Courts, jails, and drug treatment in a California county. In D.R. Gerstein & H.J. Harwood (Eds.), *Treating drug problems* (Vol.2). Washington, DC: National Academy Press.

Prendergast, M.L., Hser, Y.I., Chen, J., & Hsieh, J. (1992). *Drug treatment need among offender populations*. Paper presented at the annual meeting of the American Society of Criminology, New Orleans, LA, November 4-7, 1992.

Speckart, G.R., & Anglin, M.D. (1986). Narcotics use and crime: An overview of recent research advances. *Contemporary Drug Problems, 13*, 741-769.

Uchida, C.D., Forst, B., & Annan, S.O. (1992). *Controlling street-level drug trafficking: Evidence from Oakland and Birmingham*. Washington, DC: National Institute of Justice.

Wellisch, J., Prendergast, M.L., & Anglin, M.D. (1993). Jail: A found opportunity for intervening with drug-abusing pregnant women. UCLA Drug Abuse Research Center (submitted for publication).

Wellisch, J., Prendergast, M.L., & Anglin, M.D. (in press). Criminal justice and drug treatment system linkage: The Federal promotion of interagency collaboration in the 1970s. *Contemporary Drug Problems*.

The International Journal of the Addictions, 29(8), 971–985, 1994

The Validity of Drug Use Reports from Juvenile Arrestees

Michael Fendrich, Ph.D.,[1,*] and Yanchun Xu, M.S.[2]

[1]*Institute for Juvenile Research, University of Illinois at Chicago, M/C 747, 907 South Wolcott Avenue, Chicago, Illinois 60612*

[2]*School of Public Health, University of Illinois at Chicago, Chicago, Illinois*

ABSTRACT

Using urine test results as a gold standard, this report evaluates the validity of illicit drug use reports for five illicit substances provided in a multisite, national interview study of juvenile arrestees. Willingness to report substance use varied according to the type of substance, the time frame for substance use reports, and the characteristics of the juveniles asked to provide the reports. Youth were particularly reluctant to disclose recent use of cocaine and heroin. Race/ethnicity and willingness to disclose other substance use were the most important predictors of cocaine use disclosure among those testing positive for this drug. Race/ethnicity differences in validity were evaluated in the context of other recent epidemiological findings from surveys of drug use in the United States. Implications for the measurement of drug use in criminal justice samples are discussed.

INTRODUCTION

The accurate assessment of substance use among youth in contact with the criminal justice system has critical implications for the planning and allocation of treatment and prevention services. Such an assessment is contingent on the validity of reports provided by a group which may have little motivation to

*To whom correspondence should be addressed.

accurately disclose illicit behavior. How valid are reports of drug use provided by juvenile arrestees/detainees? How should information about drug use be obtained in order to enhance validity? Are some substances reported on more honestly than others? Are there particular characteristics of respondents which are associated with valid reporting? Using urine test results as a "gold standard," this report addresses key questions about the validity of illicit drug use reports provided in a multisite, national interview study of juvenile arrestees.

Prior research on drug use reporting validity is limited in at least two respects. First, it has mainly focused on samples of adults (usually clients in treatment). Second, it has tended to ignore correlates of underreporting (Maisto et al., 1990). With respect to this second limitation, the research by Magura et al. (1987) was an exception. Magura et al. reported on 14 studies (including their own) comparing urine tests to drug use reports in samples of adults in treatment. The variation in findings across studies suggested that urine test screening procedure influences results; these researchers suggested that the enzyme multiplied immunoassay technique (EMIT) is a considerably more sensitive criterion than thin-layer chromatography (TLC). Other variables affecting underreporting in the Magura et al. study were subject age (older clients were more likely to underreport than younger clients) and interviewer status (paraprofessional interviewers received more accurate responses than professional interviewers). Although they did not directly examine the effects of recall period, Magura et al. suggested that respondents were more likely to discuss drug use during more remote periods (such as the past month) than they were to discuss drug use during the days immediately preceding the interview.

Dembo et al. (1990) provided one of the few published studies specifically assessing the validity of self-reported drug use in a sample of juvenile arrestees. They report EMIT self-report comparisons over two waves of interviews for cocaine and marijuana use. Reanalysis of their findings using coefficient Kappa (Fleiss, 1981) suggests that reports of marijuana use are considerably more valid than reports of cocaine use. Kappas for 30-day marijuana use at the first and second interview were .51 and .48, respectively; Kappas for 3-day cocaine use at the first and second interview were .25 and .15, respectively. These findings corroborate an emergent literature focused on samples of adult arrestees suggesting that underreporting of cocaine use is a substantial problem (Rosenfeld and Decker, 1992).

METHODS

As part of a special project for the Drug Use Forecasting Program (DUF) beginning in 1990, the National Institute of Justice obtained research interviews from male juvenile arrestees ages 9 to 18 years held in booking facilities in 11 cities throughout the United States (see Tabie 1 for a list of the cities). For approximately 14 consecutive evenings every 3 months (each quarter), trained local staff obtained voluntary, anonymous interviews from a new sample of juvenile arrestees/detainees. Interviewers were nonuniformed personnel. Most worked for independent agencies who were contracted by the National Institute of Justice to provide the drug screening and interviewing service (see Note 1). Juveniles contacted for the study were asked if they were interested in answering questions about their "lifestyle." Once they agreed to participate, youth were given a questionnaire that inquired about educational status, employment, current living arrangements, drug treatment, as well as about lifetime and current illicit substance use (see Note 2). The drug use section of the survey employed a branching format that began by asking whether a youth "ever" used a substance; those who reported ever using a particular substance were then asked when they first tried that substance, whether they used that substance in the last 3 days, how many days during the last month they used that substance, whether they were ever dependent on that substance, and the age that they were first dependent on that substance. Immediately following the interview, interviewees were asked to voluntarily submit urine specimens for drug testing. All juveniles were tested (using the EMIT procedure) for 10 substances, including cocaine, opiates, marijuana, PCP, methadone, benzodiazepines, methaqualone, propoxyphene, barbiturates, and amphetamines (see National Institute of Justice, 1990, for details about the laboratory procedure for conducting EMIT tests).

Since this study focuses on methodological issues in drug use reporting, comparisons are limited to only the five substances with sufficient self-report and urinalysis prevalence rates to generate reliable estimates of validity, including marijuana, PCP, cocaine (including crack), amphetamines, and opiates (see Note 3). For each of these substances, urine tests are compared to self-reports provided with respect to three time periods, including 3-day use, 30-day use, and lifetime use. Additional summary indices are also constructed to measure self-reported use and urine test results from any of the five substances combined. In order to evaluate the validity of self-reports, we employ three statistics, including coefficient Kappa (Fleiss, 1991) conditional Kappa (Bishop et al., 1975), and interview report sensitivity. For some substances (amphetamines, cocaine, and opiates), urine tests may not be sensitive to periods of use exceeding 3 days prior to testing; for other substances (marijuana and PCP) the duration of detectability can exceed 1 week (Miller, 1991; Visher, 1991). Conditional Kappa statistics calculate chance corrected agreement conditional on a positive urine test; the coefficient does not reflect inconsistencies based on the results of honest disclosure of use during periods in which the test is unable to detect actual use. Sensitivity calculates the proportion of those with a positive urine test for any particular substance (true positives) who actually reported use of the substance (self-reported positives divided by urine test positives). Cross-tabulations are used to examine bivariate relationships between substance use underreporting and subject characteristics (age, race/ethnicity, living arrangement, and arrest charge). Follow-up analyses employ logistic regression to investigate correlates of underreporting in a multivariate context.

RESULTS

The total sample with complete data included 3,086 youths, ranging in age from 9 to 20 (the vast majority of youths in the study were under the age 18 at the time of the interview). The aggregate demographic characteristics including respondents from all 11 cities combined are presented on Table 1. Note that

Table 1.

Drug Use Forecasting Sample Description—1990. Age, Race, Ethnicity, and Site (N = 3,086)

	N	%
Age group (years):		
9–11	47	1.5
12–14	737	23.9
15–17	2,144	69.5
18+[a]	158	5.1
Total	3,086	100.0
Race/ethnicity:		
Black	1,722	55.8
Spanish-speaking	556	18.0
White	675	21.9
Other	75	2.4
Data not obtained	58	1.9
Total	3,086	100.0
Site:		
Birmingham, AL	187	6.1
Cleveland, OH	387	12.5
Indianapolis, IN	391	12.7
Kansas City, MO	139	4.5
Los Angeles, CA	388	12.6
Portland, OR	266	8.6
St. Louis, MO	280	9.1
San Antonio, TX	121	3.9
San Diego, CA	348	11.3
San Jose, CA	185	6.0
Washington, D.C.	394	12.8
Total	3,086	100.1

[a] Includes nine youths older than 18 years.

the majority of respondents were between 15 and 17 years old (69.5%). Close to one-fourth of all respondents were between 12 and 14 years old. Few respondents were younger than 11 or older than 17. The majority of respondents were Black (55%). Slightly over one in five respondents were White; Spanish-speaking participants also constituted about 20% of the sample. All of the cities were roughly similar in terms of age distribution. Although our analyses do not control for "city" effects, where appropriate, we do investigate the effects of race/ethnicity, the major variable which differentiates cities in terms of arrestee characteristics.

Table 2 indicates the prevalence rates for the six substance use measures considered in the analyses. In general, arrestees were reluctant to disclose recent (72-hour) use of all illicit substances except marijuana. Urine test positive prevalence exceeded 72-hour interview report prevalence for all substances except marijuana. Willingness to report use increased as the time frame for use expanded beyond the 72-hour period. Thirty-day interview report prevalence exceeded urine positive prevalence for all substances except cocaine and heroin. For every substance the lifetime interview report prevalence rate was at least three times the 72-hour interview report prevalence rate.

Table 3 contains a listing of the sensitivity of the interview reports, along with levels of interview report–urine test agreement, and levels of conditional agreement. The sensitivity statistics reflect the previously noted unwillingness of arrestees to report cocaine or heroin use. Only 16% of the cocaine positives disclosed 72-hour cocaine use, and only 5% of the heroin positives disclosed 72-hour heroin use. For amphetamines and PCP, underreporting of recent use was still evident but not as striking, with only 33% of the amphetamine positives disclosing 72-hour use and 29% of the PCP positives disclosing 72-hour use.

Table 2.

Interview Report and Urine Test Prevalence Rates by Substance, DUF 1990 (N = 3,086)

Substance	Urine positive prevalence % (N)	Interview report prevalence: 72-hour % (N)	30-day % (N)	Lifetime % (N)
Cocaine	8.0 (248)	2.2 (68)	4.9 (151)	14.8 (458)
Heroin	0.7 (21)	0.1 (4)	0.3 (10)	1.7 (52)
Amphetamines	1.8 (55)	1.2 (36)	3.2 (60)	11.5 (356)
PCP	1.3 (41)	0.8 (25)	1.8 (55)	6.3 (195)
Marijuana	12.4 (382)	15.3 (471)	29.3 (905)	51.1 (1,576)
Any of the above substances	20.3 (628)	16.8 (519)	30.9 (956)	52.5 (1,619)

Table 3.

Urine Test Interview Report Agreement by Substance and Time Frame, DUF 1990 Juvenile Data

Substance	Time frame	Interview report sensitivity	Kappa (95% CI)	Conditional Kappa (95% CI)
Cocaine	72-hour	0.16	0.23 (0.16, 0.29)	0.14 (0.10, 0.18)
	30-day	0.21	0.22 (0.16, 0.28)	0.17 (0.13, 0.22)
	Lifetime	0.32	0.13 (0.09, 0.18)	0.20 (0.16, 0.24)
Heroin	72-hour	0.05	0.08 (−0.07, 0.22)	0.05 (−0.04, 0.14)
	30-day	0.05	0.06 (−0.06, 0.18)	0.04 (−0.05, 0.13)
	Lifetime	0.10	0.05 (−0.03, 0.12)	0.08 (−0.04, 0.20)
Amphetamines	72-hour	0.33	0.39 (0.26, 0.52)	0.32 (0.20, 0.44)
	30-day	0.42	0.28 (0.19, 0.37)	0.40 (0.28, 0.52)
	Lifetime	0.62	0.14 (0.09, 0.18)	0.57 (0.47, 0.67)
PCP	72-hour	0.29	0.36 (0.21, 0.51)	0.29 (0.15, 0.42)
	30-day	0.44	0.37 (0.24, 0.49)	0.43 (0.28, 0.57)
	Lifetime	0.56	0.18 (0.11, 0.24)	0.53 (0.40, 0.66)
Marijuana	72-hour	0.58	0.45 (0.40, 0.49)	0.51 (0.48, 0.54)
	30-day	0.77	0.35 (0.31, 0.38)	0.68 (0.66, 0.70)
	Lifetime	0.88	0.18 (0.16, 0.20)	0.76 (0.76, 0.77)
Any of the above	72-hour	0.45	0.38 (0.34, 0.42)	0.34 (0.32, 0.37)
	30-day	0.62	0.33 (0.29, 0.36)	0.45 (0.44, 0.47)
	Lifetime	0.77	0.19 (0.17, 0.22)	0.51 (0.51, 0.52)

Sensitivity increased sharply with a 30-day and a lifetime time frame for reported use of amphetamines, PCP, and marijuana. Even though changes in time frame increase the willingness to disclose heroin and cocaine use, most youths who test positive for these substances continued to deny ever using them; less than one-third of all cocaine positives and 10% of all heroin positives reported that they ever used cocaine or heroin, respectively.

For the most part, agreement between 72-hour reported use and urine positive tests was poor. Most youths who tested positive for substances other than marijuana were not willing to disclose use in the period immediately preceding their arrest. Using the 72-hour reporting frame, only comparisons with respect to marijuana reached a level considered "fair to good" (i.e., Kappa of at least .40). The generally poor level of agreement between lifetime interview reports and urine test results reflects the fact that many who actually reported use did not use in the period immediately preceding their arrest; those reporting lifetime use were not the same group as those who actually tested positive.

Using the conditional agreement criteria, the findings parallel those obtained in the sensitivity analysis. For all substances except cocaine and heroin, agreement improved considerably as the time expanded beyond the 72-hour period. Fair to good levels of agreement were observed between reports of 30-day use and positive tests for amphetamines, PCP, and marijuana. Conditional agreement between reports of lifetime use of marijuana and positive marijuana tests approached a level generally considered indicative of excellent agreement. Agreement between positive tests for cocaine or heroin and 72-hour, 30-day, or lifetime use reports of these two substances was poor. Conditional Kappas of .14 and .05 for cocaine and heroin, respectively, suggested that there was almost no overlap between those testing positive and those reporting 72-hour use of either substance.

Using the urine test results as the standard, we evaluated several demographic background, arrest, and reporting variables in association with underreporting for the two most highly prevalent substances, marijuana and cocaine (see Table 4). Underreporting was defined as denying recent use (i.e., use in the last 72 hours) even though the EMIT test indicates a positive result. Overall rates of denial for recent cocaine use were high; about 84% of all youths testing positive denied that they recently used cocaine. Race/ethnicity, arrest charge, and reported recent use of any other drug besides cocaine (see Note 4) were all significantly associated with denial of cocaine use. Compared to White and Spanish-speaking arrestees, Black respondents overwhelmingly denied cocaine use when they tested positive for the substance. Ninety-three percent of the Black youths with positive tests denied use compared to 73% of the Spanish-speaking youths and 59% of the White/other youths. A nonsignificant trend suggested that youths who identified two parents at home were less likely to deny than other youths; 75% of those with a mother and father at home denied cocaine use when they tested positive compared to 88% of those who lived with either a mother or a father at the time of the arrest and 84% of those who lived with neither a mother or a father at the time of their arrest. Arrestees with violent and drug-related arrest charges were more likely to deny use of cocaine when they tested positive than youths with property offense charges; rates of denial were 75% for arrestees charged with property crimes compared to 90% for arrestees charged with violent offenses and 92% for arrestees charged with drug offenses (see Note 5). Even though a majority of those disclosing other recent drug use denied using cocaine when they tested positive for this substance, this subgroup was significantly less likely to deny use than other youths who tested positive. That is, 58% of those admitting other recent drug use who tested positive for cocaine denied recent cocaine use; the proportion denying was 92% for those not disclosing other recent drug use.

A majority of youths who tested positive for marijuana (58%) admitted to recent use. None of the sociodemographic or arrest charge variables were significantly associated with levels of denial for marijuana use. The only variable showing an association with denial was the indicator of other recent substance

Table 4.

Drug Use Denial by Sociodemographic Variables and Drug-Related Top Arrest Charge for Cocaine and Marijuana Positive Arrestees (72-hour report)

	Cocaine use			Marijuana use		
	Urine positive, N	Denial, N	%	Urine positive, N	Denial, N	%
A. Sociodemographic variables						
1. Age at arrest:						
9–11 years	0	0	0.0	1	0	0.0
12–14 years	22	17	77.2	32	13	40.6
15–17 years	197	168	85.2	313	129	41.2
18–20 years	29	23	79.3	36	17	47.2
	248	208	N.S.	382	159	N.S.
2. Race/ethnicity:						
Black	162	151	93.2	140	57	40.7
Spanish-speaking	55	40	72.7	101	42	41.6
White/other	27	14	51.9	133	57	42.9
	244	205	**	374	156	N.S.
3. School status:						
In school	156	133	85.3	240	102	42.5
Not in school	91	74	81.3	140	56	40.0
	247	207	N.S.	380	158	N.S.
4. Family living arrangement:						
Lives with:						
No parents	61	51	83.6	95	41	43.2
Mother or father	131	115	87.8	190	73	38.4
Mother and father	56	42	75.0	97	45	46.4
	248	208	N.S.	382	159	N.S.
B. Top arrest charge[a]						
Property crime	111	83	74.8	236	97	41.1
Person (violent) crime	40	36	90.0	74	32	43.2
Drug crime (possession and sales)	97	89	91.8	72	30	41.7
	248	208	*	382	159	N.S.
C. Other recent drug use, interview report[b]						
Reports 72 hour use other drugs	62	36	58.1	36	2	5.6
No 72 hour use of other drugs	186	172	92.5	346	157	45.4
	248	208	**	382	159	**

[a] See Note 5 for definition of crime categories.

[b] For cocaine use, other drugs include heroin, amphetamines, PCP, and marijuana; for marijuana use, other drugs include heroin, amphetamines, PCP, and cocaine.

*$p < .01$.

**$p < .001$.

use reporting (see Note 6). Only two of 36 youths (6%) admitting to other substance use denied recent use of marijuana; the proportion denying was 45% for youths admitting no other substance use.

A final set of analyses (see Table 5) includes most of the variables discussed in Table 4 using multiple logistic regression (school enrollment status was eliminated from the model since it showed no association with denial of use for either of the two substances). The model includes two dummy variables for race (one for Hispanics and one for Blacks) and for crime (one for violent arrest charges and one for drug-related arrest charges). Dummy variables for family living arrangement (the group of youth with both parents at home was contrasted with other youth) and for reports of other recent drug use are also included in the model along with a continuous variable assessing age at arrest. Exponentiated coefficients in logistic regression models approximate odds ratios when the outcome is rare (Hosmer and Lemeshow, 1989). We constructed models predicting admission of use among those testing positive for cocaine (the inverse of denial). Only two variables are significantly associated with rates of cocaine use admission: race and reports of other current drug use. Compared to White/other arrestees, Black arrestees had significantly reduced odds for admitting recent cocaine use when they tested positive for the substance. Those who admit to other recent drug use had significantly increased odds for admitting recent co-

Table 5.

Predictors of Cocaine Use Reports among Urine Positive Youth—Logistic Regression Coefficients and Odds Ratios, DUF Sample 1990 (N = 244)[a]

Variable	b	S.E.	Odds ratio	(95% CI)
Age at arrest	0.10	0.17	—	—
Race:				
Black (vs White)	−1.91	0.61*	0.15	(0.04, 0.49)
Spanish-speaking (vs White)	−0.87	0.58	0.42	(0.13, 1.31)
Family living arrangement:				
Mother and father (vs other)	0.55	0.47	1.73	(0.69, 4.35)
Top arrest charge[b]:				
Violent crime (vs property)	−1.17	0.67	0.31	(0.08, 1.15)
Drug crime (vs property)	−0.77	0.53	0.46	(0.16, 1.31)
Drug use reports:				
Other drug use[c] (vs none)	2.07	0.43**	7.92	(3.41, 18.41)

[a] Model $\chi^2 = 63.14$, $df = 7$, $p < .001$.
[b] See Note 5 for definition of crime categories.
[c] Includes interview 72-hour reports of heroin, amphetamines, PCP, or marijuana.
*$p < .01$.
**$p < .001$.

caine use when they tested positive for the substance. Taking into account differences in ethnic/racial composition associated with interview location, an additional regression model was estimated including 10 dummy variables representing interview site. Inclusion of these variables increased the significance of the coefficients for both of the dummy variables for race (suggesting that both Blacks and Spanish-speaking youths were significantly less likely to disclose recent use when they used). Nevertheless, none of these dummy variables were significant individually, and inclusion of these 10 dummy variables did not reflect an improvement over the original model presented on Table 5 (χ^2 increment = 15.2, df = 10; N.S.)

DISCUSSION

Even though this study focuses on a nonrandom sample of juvenile arrestees, an inspection of the 11 cities noted on Table 1 suggests that the DUF sampling strategy provided representation to most regions of the United States. Not all youths asked to participate in the study actually agreed to participate (see Note 1). We speculate that those who refused to participate would be less inclined to report about recent drug use. This implies that our analyses may underestimate the extent of underreporting of drug use among juvenile arrestees.

The assessment of recent drug use may be of critical importance in outpatient substance abuse treatment studies of adolescents and young adults. Our data provide some preliminary evidence that clinical outcome researchers should not rely on reports provided by youth in treatment; drug testing may serve a critical role in short-term outcome assessment. Nevertheless, our findings are based on samples of juvenile arrestees; they may have limited relevance to samples of youth who are questioned about substance use in a less threatening environment.

Another important methodological consideration is the relatively small numbers of cocaine users among White and Spanish-speaking arrestees compared to Black arrestees. Our comparisons with respect to cocaine underreporting were based on a sample of 27 White/other youths, 55 Spanish-speaking youths, and 162 Black youths who tested positive for cocaine use. The small numbers of cocaine users among White and Spanish-speaking youths limited our statistical power to evaluate differences in underreporting between groups; it also diminished the reliability of our estimates of underreporting within those subgroups. With limited power to detect differences, our finding that validity varies by race/ethnicity subgroups suggests a large effect size for this variable (see Cohen, 1988). Nevertheless, future studies attempting to confirm our findings might consider oversampling non-Black youths in order to obtain more reliable estimates of race/ethnicity differences in underreporting.

A potential limitation in our study concerns the use of EMIT as a "gold standard." Since our analyses focus on the subgroup of youths testing positive for each substance, the likelihood that EMIT may generate false positives is of particular concern. Comparing the accuracy of five different urinalysis drug-testing procedures, Visher (1991) suggested that immunoassay procedures such as EMIT generate few false positives; based on this previous study, we would estimate that only about 1 to 2% of all youth would falsely test positive for any of the substances that we investigated in this study. We have considerable confidence in comparative analyses conducted on substances with relatively high base rates for use in our sample; our findings with respect to marijuana and cocaine would not be substantially affected even if 2% of the youths in our sample falsely tested positively for these substances.

Marijuana and cocaine vary considerably with respect to possession and sales penalties and with respect to perceptions regarding acceptability and danger of use (Bachman et al., 1990). Juvenile arrestees are less reluctant to indicate use of the more acceptable substance (marijuana) than they are of the less acceptable substance (cocaine). This may suggest that special considerations are necessary in drug treatment screening (absent urine tests) for youth in criminal justice settings. Perhaps initial questions about marijuana use could be used as a preliminary means of identifying youths at risk for heavier substance use. Nevertheless, the findings with respect to the association between willingness to report other drug use and cocaine use admission are troubling. The youths who report other drug use (including marijuana use) are also those most willing to disclose cocaine use. Almost none of the youths who denied other recent drug use were willing to admit to recent use of cocaine. Thus, there appears to be a subgroup of youths who are consistently willing to disclose recent drug use, irrespective of the drug inquired about. Future research needs to identify more systematically the correlates of membership in this subgroup.

Differences in reporting that appeared to be associated with race/ethnicity in our own study may have resulted from differences in involvement in drug-related offenses. Compared to White youths, Black and Spanish-speaking arrestees were more likely to be arrested on drug-related charges (17% of all Black youths were arrested on drug-related charges compared to 8% of Spanish-speaking youth and just 3% of White youth). Youths arrested for drug-related charges may have more reluctance to disclose use, regardless of guarantees of confidentiality. Nevertheless, underreporting of cocaine use by Black youths persisted even after controlling for drug charge.

Other kinds of data pertaining to criminal record or previous criminal justice experiences (number of prior arrests) that were not collected could have revealed important differences between White and Black youths which may have influenced reactions and responses to interviewers in the detention/arraignment setting. Previous contact with the criminal justice system may affect the level of trust which minority youth have in any research enterprise occurring within the context of that system. Failure to disclose recent use of an illicit substance may also reflect a realistic perception of consequences for disclosure based on experience within the criminal justice system.

The race/ethnicity differences found in this study parallel observations drawn from research on drug use in high school seniors. Johnston et al. (1984) reported that compared to White respondents, Black respondents were much more likely to leave responses about drug use blank; additionally, in supplemental questions, Black respondents indicated that if they used drugs, they would not have been willing to report it. Recent work summarizing the trends in prevalence across race/ethnic groups suggests relatively low levels of cocaine use prevalence (based on a 1-year reporting frame) for non-White youths compared to White youths (Bachman et al., 1991). These differences were more striking for Black youths than for Hispanic youths. Our findings suggest the possibility that differences in prevalence may be due to differences in willingness to admit use. In general, Black youths may be more reluctant to disclose drug use than White youths; these differences may result from a lack of trust in the research process (Mensch and Kandel, 1988; Johnston et al., 1984).

Even though respondents were probably aware that the "truth" about their behavior could be detected, many provided inaccurate drug use reports (see Note 7). This suggests that attempts to "fool" respondents about the availability of objective measures of drug use (for example, through the use of the "bogus pipeline"; see Midanik, 1988) will not enhance the validity of substance use reports provided in criminal justice settings, especially when the substance inquired about is cocaine. Indeed, earlier research on a sample of college students suggested that reporting of illicit drug use may be influenced more by concerns about anonymity than by knowledge that the "truth" about use can be obtained by the interviewer (Hill et al., 1988).

This report suggests that more study of the issue of drug use disclosure is needed before we can continue to rely on survey reports of drug use, especially in criminal justice settings. In the meantime, concrete steps to identify and control for potential sources of reporting bias or nondisclosure in survey reports on drug use should be taken. Researchers should consider spending more time educating respondents about the research process, about their value as study participants, and about the potential benefits of participation in the study. Mechanisms for reassuring participants about the confidentiality of responses need to be given special emphasis. We underscore the finding that a change in the time frame for use to a "lifetime" basis dramatically increased the sensitivity levels of drug use reports for all drugs that we studied in this report. Those interested in drug use screening for organizing prevention and treatment efforts are advised to ask about lifetime patterns of use. Juvenile arrestees who are drug users are more likely to disclose use if questions are not focused on the immediate days preceding their arrest.

ACKNOWLEDGMENTS

This research was supported in part by a grant from the National Institute on Drug Abuse (Grant 5R29DA07995) and by a grant from the University of Illinois at Chicago. The authors would also like to acknowledge the assistance provided by Joyce O'Neil at the National Institute of Justice Drug Use Forecasting Program.

NOTES

1. Demographic characteristics of the 1990 interviewers were not available to the authors for analysis.
2. All arrestees/detainees were free to refuse to participate. The interview was anonymous and confidential and unrelated to the disposition of a youth's case. Although the precise numbers with respect to participation rates are not available, DUF program staff at the National Institute of Justice estimate that over 90% of all youth asked to participate actually agreed to participate. Copies of the questionnaire are available upon request from the first author.
3. The urine test detected opiates; self-report comparisons for this substance are based on reports of heroin use. For the sake of convenience, we use the word "heroin" to describe both urine test analyses of opiates and self-reports of heroin in the remainder of this paper.
4. This measure is based on interview reports of 72-hour heroin, amphetamine, PCP, or marijuana use.
5. The arrest charge categories were defined as follows: Violent crimes included assault, homicide or manslaughter, robbery, sex offenses and weapons charges. The property crimes category included all other non-drug related charges (including public order and status offenses); specifically, this category includes burglary, stolen property, larceny, pickpocketing, status offenses, and all other charges. The drug charge category included drug sales and possesion.
6. This measure is based on interview reports of 72-hour heroin, amphetamine, PCP, or cocaine use.
7. Although interviews were carried out prior to the urine test, interviewed subjects were sometimes made aware that urines were to be collected at the conclusion of the interview (through contact with other arrestees). Unfortunately, we do not have a precise estimate of the extent of this prior awareness in our sample.

REFERENCES

BACHMAN, J. G., JOHNSTON, L. D., and O'MALLEY, P. M. (1990). Explaining the recent decline in cocaine use among young adults: Further evidence that perceived risks and disapproval lead to reduced drug use. *J. Health Soc. Behav.* 31: 173–184.

BACHMAN, J. G., WALLACE, J. M., O'MALLEY, P. M., JOHNSTON, L. D., KURTH, C. L., and NEIGHBORS, H. W. (1991). Racial/ethnic differences in smoking, drinking, and illicit drug use among American high school seniors, 1976–89, *Am. J. Public Health* 81: 372–377.

BECK, A. J., KLINE, S. A., and GREENFELD, L. A. (1988). *Survey of Youth in Custody, 1987,* Bureau of Justice Statistics Special Report NCJ-113365.

BISHOP, Y. M., FEINBERG, S. E., and HOLLAND, P. W. (1975). *Discrete Multivariate Analysis: Theory and Practice.* Cambridge, Massachusetts: MIT Press.

COHEN, J. (1988). *Statistical Power Analysis for the Behavioral Sciences*. Hillsdale, New Jersey: Lawrence Erlbaum Associates.

DEMBO, R., WILLIAMS, L., WISH, E. D., and SCHMEIDLER, J. (1990). *Urine Testing of Detained Juveniles to Identify High Risk Youth*. Washington, D.C.: National Institute of Justice.

FLEISS, J. L. (1981). *Statistical Methods for Rates and Proportions*. New York: Wiley and Sons.

HILL, P. C., DILL, C. A., and DAVENPORT, E. C. (1988). A reexamination of the bogus pipeline. *Educ. Psychol. Meas.* 48: 587-601.

HOSMER, D. W., and LEMESHOW, S (1989). *Applied Logistic Regression*. New York: Wiley and Sons.

JOHNSTON, L. D., BACHMAN, J. G., and O'MALLEY, P. M. (1984). *Monitoring the Future. Questionnaire Responses from the Nation's High School Seniors, 1983*. Ann Arbor, Michigan: Institute for Social Research.

MAGURA, S., GOLDSMITH, D., CASRIEL, K., GOLDSTEIN, P. J., and LIPTON, D.S. (1987). The validity of methadone clients' self-reported drug use. *Int. J. Addict.* 22: 727-749.

MAISTO, S. A., McKAY, J. R., and CONNORS, G. J. (1990). Self-report issues in substance abuse: State of the art and future directions, *Behav. Assess.* 12: 117-134.

MENSCH, B. S., and KANDEL, D. B. (1988). Underreporting of substance use in a national longitudinal youth cohort: Individual and interviewer effects. *Public Opin. Q.* 52: 100-124.

MIDANIK, L. T. (1988). Validity of self-reported alcohol use: A literature review and assessment. *Br. J. Addict.* 83: 1019-1029.

MILLER, N. (1991). *The Pharmacology of Alcohol and Drugs of Abuse*. New York: Springer-Verlag.

NATIONAL INSTITUTE OF JUSTICE (1990). *Drug Use Forecasting Drugs and Crime 1990 Annual Report*. Washington, D.C.: National Institute of Justice.

ROSENFELD, R., and DECKER, S. (1992). Discrepant values, correlated measures: Cross-city and longitudinal comparisons of self reports and urine tests of cocaine use among arrestees. *J. Crim. Justice* 21: 223-230.

VISHER, C. (1986). The Rand inmate survey: A reanalysis. In A. Blumstein, J. Cohen, J. Roth, and C. A. Visher (Eds.), *Criminal Careers and "Career Criminals." Volume II*. Washington, D.C.: National Academy Press, pp. 161-211.

VISHER, C. (1991). *A Comparison of Urinalysis Technologies for Drug Testing in Criminal Justice*, Washington, D.C.: National Institute of Justice and the Bureau of Justice Assistance.

Studies in Conflict and Terrorism, Volume 17, pp. 323–344
Printed in the UK. All rights reserved.

1057-610X/94 $10.00 + .00

The Medellin Cartel: Why We Can't Win the Drug War

ROBERT FILIPPONE

The Fletcher School of Law and Diplomacy
Tufts University
Medford, MA, USA

This article details the reasons why the supply reduction strategies aimed at winning the drug war adopted by the Reagan, Bush, and Clinton administrations cannot work. Included in this article is a detailed examination of the organizational structure of the Medellin cartel. The cartel's operations extend well beyond the production and transportation of cocaine: The political, social, and cultural activities the cartel undertakes extend its influence well beyond those involved directly in the drug trade. In addition, the financial benefits of narcotics trafficking provide benefits to vast segments of Colombian society. The Cali cartel has learned from the mistakes of the Medellin cartel and is even more effective at putting drugs on American streets. The total failure of supply reduction programs is evidence of the strength of the cartels.

The Clinton administration recently announced a shift in its antidrug efforts that places greater emphasis on providing training and equipment to the countries that grow, refine, and export illegal drugs to the United States, primarily Colombia. The announcement followed an administration review of its drug policy that concluded that the interdiction efforts, the focus of the military's role in the drug war, had been largely ineffective. While this is certainly true, there is little reason to believe that additional efforts in the Andean nations will be any more effective. This policy demonstrates a lack of understanding of the strength of the cocaine cartels and their positions in their societies. The cartels are deeply rooted in Andean society, politically, economically, and socially. Even the death of a leader as powerful as Pablo Escobar will have little effect on the flow of drugs into the United States. A clear picture of the cartel organization reveals the folly of the current antidrug strategy.

The Colombian cartels have controlled the international cocaine trade since their formation over 10 years ago. They supply over 80% of all the cocaine smuggled into the United States each year. The most well-known and powerful of these cartels is based in the city of Medellin. Its somewhat more low-key rival is

Address correspondence to Robert Filippone, The Fletcher School of Law and Diplomacy, Tufts University, Medford, MA 02155.

based in the southern city of Cali. Through the power of the enormous profits that they derive from the cocaine trade, the cartels have created a huge, vertically integrated, multinational organization that in 1987 sold over $20 billion worth of cocaine in North America and Europe [1]. This translates into $2 to $4 billion per year in profits for the Colombians. They are not a cartel in the true sense of the word in that they do not control price or supply, yet their profits are astronomical.

The international nature of the Medellin cartel's operations was demonstrated by the Drug Enforcement Agency's [DEA's] special enforcement operation Bolivar, which targeted the cartel. Bolivar involved 15 countries, 51 separate DEA offices, and 201 separate investigations [2]. The Medellin cartel has remained at the center of attention because of its tactics, which are violent and conspicuous, and the fact that it has traditionally controlled at least 60% of the Colombian cocaine traffic. The organization that it has developed employs up to 120,000 people, including 2,000 to 3,000 in the United States [3]. This vast organization is controlled by a select few individuals, most notably the infamous Pablo Escobar, who continued to manage the cartel's operations even while incarcerated in his specially built prison in Envigado. The Medellin cartel has been the primary target of the U.S. government's war on drugs. In order to effectively attack the cartel, it is important to understand its organization, structure, ideology, and leadership. An organization with the level of resources, sophistication, and influence of the Medellin cartel cannot be destroyed by a limited strategy that does not learn from the failures of the past. Referring to the Medellin cartel, former Colombian president Belisario Betancur said in 1988, "We are up against an organization stronger than the state" [4].

The Medellin Cartel

While the Medellin cartel, as we know it today, is said to have been formed in 1982, the DEA, in congressional testimony, referred to the "Medellin trafficking syndicate" as early as 1977. The origins of the cocaine trade in Colombia go back to the 1950s, when the Colombians produced a small amount of cocaine and shipped it to the Cuban mafia. When the Cubans went to the United States in the 1960s, so did the cocaine. The primary method of smuggling cocaine into the United States was by using "mules," people who hide a relatively small amount of cocaine on their body or in their personal luggage and enter the United States through normal entry points. This all changed in 1976, when Carlos Lehder Rivas, a small-time car thief and marijuana smuggler serving time in a U.S. prison, conceptualized an important change in the cocaine-trafficking industry. Instead of using "mules," he would use small private aircraft to smuggle cocaine into the United States. This took advantage of the existing trafficking routes and distribution networks the Colombians had established for marijuana smuggling. The main differences were that the cocaine was easier to transport, required fewer people, and was far more profitable. On his first run after leaving jail, Lehder bought 550 pounds of cocaine and flew it into the United States, making $1 million profit [5]. Lehder's contribution to the cocaine trade prompted U.S. Attorney and Chief

Prosecutor Robert Merkle to say, "Lehder was to cocaine trafficking what Henry Ford was to automobiles" [6].

This rapid increase in profits led to the cocaine wars of 1978 and 1979 in south Florida. Over a period of 2 to 3 three years, the Colombians violently killed off the Cubans and took over the entire business, installing their own middlemen, increasing profits, and minimizing risk, since many of the Cubans had ties to the CIA. From this point on, the Colombians rapidly expanded their trafficking operations in response to the ferocious demand of the U.S. market. As the trafficking and profits increased, so did the associated criminal operations that accompany them.

There are several reasons why the Colombians have been the ones to control the cocaine trade in the United States. First, their geographic position has provided them with unique advantages. They are strategically positioned between the coca-growing countries of Bolivia and Peru and the sea and air access routes to the United States. In addition, their neighbor Panama has provided them with safe haven in times of crisis. Second, the terrain of the region is particularly favorable to their operations. The jungle and mountains afford them protection from the authorities as well as the ideal climate and soil for growing coca. Third, the Colombians have strong entrepreneurial skills that are well suited to the cocaine business. Fourth, the Colombians took full advantage of the existing network of middle-class distributors that had originally been put in place to serve the marijuana trade [7]. They also took advantage of the Mexican eradication programs in the mid- and late 1970s to increase their influence and establish their own labs.

The Medellin cartel was formed in early 1982 in response to the kidnapping of a member of the Ochoa family by the M-19 guerrillas. The traffickers realized that their wealth made them vulnerable to extortion of this type. The traffickers met, and each donated $7.5 million to the formation of a paramilitary organization, MAS, to fight the M-19. It was at this time that the drug lords began to work together in a more coordinated and cooperative fashion.

As with every successful organization, strong leadership is a critical ingredient. The cartel has had strong leaders. For most of the 1980s the organization was led by Pablo Escobar Gaviria, Jorge Luis Ochoa Vasquez, and Carlos Lehder Rivas, who were known as the "Big Three."

In 1977, at the time that Carlos Lehder was getting out of jail and starting his large-scale smuggling operation, Jorge Ochoa was running a small cocaine operation in Miami for his uncle, who worked out of Medellin. In a police sting operation Ochoa was nearly arrested, but slipped away. Frightened, he went back to Colombia and never returned to the United States again. He sent his younger brother Fabio to the United States to run the family's distribution networks in Florida, New York, and California [8]. Back in Medellin, Jorge Ochoa built the family business at the processing and distribution levels while his brother controlled the distribution side of the business.

The most famous of the Medellin leaders is Pablo Escobar. He began his criminal career stealing gravestones and cars before graduating to cocaine trafficking. Escobar spent some time in the United States in the 1960s and was impressed with the growing demand for drugs [9]. His early start in the cocaine business positioned him to take a leading role as the business took off in the late 1970s. His ruthlessness and boldness would prove to help, and hinder, him over the ensuing decade.

These cartel bosses did more than direct the processing and distribution of cocaine. They built the organization into a multinational entity that influenced events well beyond the scope of the international drug business. As their wealth and power grew, they expanded into politics, the media, private armies, real estate, and international banking. They espoused an ideology to legitimate and support their operations. It should be noted that they are motivated not by ideology but by greed and the phenomenal wealth of the drug trade.

Their ideology is centered on the fact that they are businessmen and their power is a function of their wealth, which is derived in a way that is considered illegal. Therefore their ideology seeks to protect them from prosecution, give legitimacy to their organization, and ensure the continued operation of their business. The ideology has three pillars: It is pro-Colombian, pro-status quo, and anti-United States.

The cartel bosses are pro-Colombian nationalists in that they portray themselves as defenders of national values, civic leaders, and fighters for progress. They argue that the narcotics industry is good for Colombia since it brings in such large amounts of money, aids development and progress, and helps keep down unemployment. There is some truth to this, although it ignores the overwhelming negative aspects of the cartels on Colombian society. As part of their argument that they are good for Colombia, the bosses are careful to point out that they are not involved in the sale of narcotics, specifically bazuco, a low-grade by-product of the cocaine manufacturing process, within Colombia. Bazuco is seen as a major public health problem in Colombia, though it is not important to the traffickers' profits. They have made public decrees denying any role in the bazuco or cocaine trade inside Colombia.

The bosses seek to maintain the status quo at all costs since it is the status quo that has allowed them to flourish and prosper. The free enterprise capitalist system is the basis of their business and their power. They are stridently against any left-wing guerilla movements. In 1984, Escobar wrote in a Medellin newspaper,

> I share with them [the guerrillas] a desire for a Colombia with more social equality for all, but I do not agree with their plans to obtain power by means of weapons, because to achieve power there exists a democratic system, faithfully watched over by our army, guardian of the constitution and of the laws of the Republic [10].

In a 1984 memorandum to then-Attorney General Jiminez Gomez from 100 leading drug lords, the cartel renounced any connection to guerrillas, stating, "Our activities have never been intended to replace the democratic and republican form of government" [11]. In fact, the cartels have sought to work within the democratic system to increase their power and prestige, as well as to advance the goals of their organization. They view themselves as pillars of the establishment and seek to become part of the upper crust of society.

The third pillar of their ideology is anti-U.S. sentiment. This is largely a result of the efforts made by the U.S. government to destroy the cartel and to extradite its leaders to the United States to face criminal charges. This would be the worst possible scenario for the cartel chiefs, who feel that their power and control will protect them as long as they are in Colombia but fear the fate they would meet if extradited to the United States. One manifestation of this is the claim that extradition is "anti-Latin" and another example of U.S. meddling in Latin American affairs. The traffickers look upon the traditional elite politicians who have agreed to extradition as unpatriotic sellouts to U.S. imperialism. Extradition is particularly hated by the traffickers because has it branded them as criminals, not as successful businessmen, as they view themselves [12]. The U.S. DEA is often singled out as being particularly anti-Latin. Carlos Lehder, who has always been more outlandish and crazy than the other cartel leaders, said one of his goals was to "flood the U.S. with cocaine and tear down the morality of the country." He went on to say that "cocaine is the atom bomb to be used against U.S. imperialism" [13]. These statements are important in that they are representative of the thoughts of one of the founders and leaders of the cartel. In general, there are many Colombians who are sympathetic to many aspects of this ideology.

The structure of the Medellin cartel is somewhat complex. The cartel is actually a conglomerate made up of the pooled resources of the individual groups. In addition to the large cocaine production, transportation, and distribution organizations, there are equally extensive and sophisticated organizations for political action, security and protection, and financial management. Each of these subordinate activities operates in slightly different ways, recruits from different segments of society, and performs unique, yet critical, functions in the overall scheme. Within each organization the division of labor is highly complex and organized. At the low and middle levels of these organizations, the managers are easily transferred but the positions remain constant [14]. Before exploring each area in detail, it is worthwhile to make some general statements regarding the relationships between the various functional organizations and the way the leadership directs the cartel's activities.

The Big Three control every aspect of the operation. Below them, the organization becomes more blurred and fluid. There are at least 17 distinct subordinate organizations that are controlled by the Big Three in a somewhat loosely structured and informal manner [15]. This allows for great flexibility in adapting to whatever means appear to be the most profitable at the time. The largest of these subordinate organizations are the Bogota and Atlantic Coast cartels. The Bogota cartel was headed by Jose Gonzalo Rodriguez Gacha, who took the place of Carlos Lehder as one of the Big Three after Lehder's arrest and extradition in 1987.

These subordinate units are generally family-based operations. The key figures are usually close relatives, childhood friends, or neighbors from hometowns in Colombia. This makes them very difficult to penetrate, since anyone who is not a family member or long-time friend will immediately arouse suspicion. The organization, like many underground organizations, is also rigidly compartmentalized in a cell-based structure, in order to minimize risk for security reasons [16]. Thus the loss or compromise of one branch of the organization will not put others at risk. This is particularly effective in insulating the bosses from prosecution. The extensive use of family-style units also means that by simply arresting the head of an organization one will not shut down its operations, since the group will most likely stay together and continue operating as long as the business is profitable. These family-based units have also permitted women to act as bosses of entire organizations, something that is very unusual in a Latin culture. For example, Veronica Rivera de Vargas and Griselda Blanco, once called the "Godmother," were not unassuming wives or mothers of cocaine bosses but cocaine bosses themselves.

The Medellin cartel requires strict discipline from its members, particularly regarding drug use. According to Diego Viafra Salinas, a former M-19 guerilla who penetrated one of the cartel's paramilitary groups, "One knows that using drugs means that you are cutting your own tombstone, you are calling for your own assassination. Within the organization, no drug abuse is allowed, nor is robbing or stealing permitted. You cannot steal any money, nor can you use drugs, nor can you get drunk" [17]. Viafra goes on to acknowledge that the leaders do occasionally use drugs, but in a very private way so that

> no one in the upper echelons of the power structure of the organization knows it. Because if they do, if it is Gacha using drugs, they would kill Gacha. If it is Fabio Ochoa Vasquez using drugs, they would kill him. But I personally know that some of them do use drugs [18].

The importance of discipline is reinforced by the motivational methods employed by the drug lords. Murder and torture have been traditional measures used by criminal organizations around the world, but the Colombian cartels have taken this to a new level. A violation of the cartel's rules or an attempt to double-cross them can bring an order to obliterate not just the violator, but his entire family—his wife, children, brothers, sisters, and parents [19].

Although the political, security, and financial aspects of the cartel may be the most interesting and least well known, an understanding of the portion of the organization that manufactures, transports, and distributes cocaine is fundamental to any study of the cartel. It is the profits derived from this business that enable the other activities to take place. The cocaine business incorporates more than one million people, from the peasant coca growers in Peru and Bolivia, to the chemists and processors in Colombia, to the distributors on the streets of America. This is the true base of the cartel and the primary source of its power and wealth.

The coca is grown primarily in the Andean nations of Peru and Bolivia. Approximately 55% of the world's cocaine is grown in Peru [20]. The soil and climate conditions in the Andean mountains in the Amazon River Basin are ideal for growing coca, and coincidentally quite poor for growing anything else. This business contributes upwards of $1 billion annually to the Peruvian economy. The Colombian traffickers control the majority of the coca production in Peru, with the Peruvian traffickers and the Sendero Luminoso guerrillas controlling much smaller portions. The severe economic problems in Peru have made it very easy for the Colombians to convince peasant farmers to grow coca. A farmer who cultivates a little over a hectare of coca leaf can earn the equivalent of several thousand dollars a year, at least 10 times more, and possibly 100 times more, than they could earn from any legal crop [21].

It is easy to see why the drug cartels have no trouble recruiting peasants to grow coca. Coca is a plant that has been grown for hundreds of years in these regions. It was traditionally chewed by the Inca kings of the region. This practice continues today among the Indians of the area as a means of fighting the effects of hunger, cold, and fatigue. Coca growing is woven into their culture and is not viewed in any negative context. In addition, there is a great attraction to the fast money and the things it can buy in these coca growing regions. Rensselaer W. Lee noted, "The town of Tochache in Peru's Upper Huallaga Valley has six banks, six Telex machines, several stereo dealerships, a discotheque, and one of the largest Nissan outlets in Peru. Tochache also has no paved streets, no drinking water, and no sewage system" [22]. For the peasant growers of coca there is no ideological motivation, simply an opportunity to survive by doing something they have done for centuries. It is particularly difficult to convince these people to stop growing coca just because the U.S. government says that it is bad for the United States.

The Peruvian government buys a small amount of coca leaf for legal purposes such as the production of Coca Cola and certain pharmaceutical products. The drug traffickers control the coca production, though, since they pay from 3 to 15 times the price on the legal market. They also pick up the leaves at the farm gate, saving the peasants the trouble of transporting their crops to the legal collection centers [23]. The cartels will also provide farmers who want to begin growing coca with financing, fertilizer, seed, and sometimes technical assistance. Once the farmer has begun planting coca, the traffickers can also provide protection from authorities in the form of bribes and intimidation. While the cartel does not cultivate much cocaine itself, the Gonzalo Rodriguez Gacha organization is believed to have grown its own coca inside Colombia as a means of protecting itself from interruptions in the Peruvian or Bolivian supply.

The coca leaves are purchased by cartel middlemen and transported to laboratories for processing into cocaine. The transporting of the leaves is labor intensive, with the leaves usually being carried on the backs of laborers, who use hidden jungle trails to avoid detection by the authorities. In the first step of the cocaine-making process, the leaves are mashed, then soaked in a solution of kerosene and sodium carbonate to precipitate out the alkaloid. The mashing is done by *pisadores*, literally tramplers, who crush the leaves before they are soaked, thereby expediting the process of extracting the cocaine. The *pisadores* usually work at night in what has become an almost ritualistic technique, according to sociologist Kevin Healy:

> Over the course of their twelve hours of nighttime work, the *pisadores* become animated as they "dance" on their leaves to the accompaniment of piped-in regional music. . . . To further arouse positive work spirits for their tedious routine, *pisadores* are encouraged to consume large quantities of chicha (corn beer) and coca paste, which are often mixed together in an unusual and potent concoction" [24].

The motivation for the *pisadores* is again financial. They can earn almost twice as much as a rural schoolteacher earns. The end-product of this operation is coca paste, a compound that is about 40% pure cocaine. The farmers, transporters, and *pisadores* all generally tend to be fairly closely linked, socially and geographically.

Whereas paste labs are numerous and widely dispersed around the coca-growing regions, the next steps in the process almost always take place in larger, more centralized processing laboratories. It is at this stage that the cartels take over the direct control and dominate the higher-value-added stages of production. Over 75% of the cocaine entering the United States is refined in Colombia [25]. Most Colombian labs are located far away from coca-growing regions. The most popular sites for labs have been on ranches in northeastern Colombia or in the jungles along the Brazilian and Peruvian borders. Labs are often moved, and there have been continual swings between the use of large lab complexes and smaller dispersed labs. The cartels are flexible and use whatever is most profitable at a given time.

The laboratories are the heart of the cartel's operations. Recent trends indicate that the cartel is moving more toward the use of smaller, more dispersed labs. The Colombian government reported that it destroyed 290 cocaine-processing labs in 1991 [26]. The size and scope of the Medellin cartel's production facilities first became known on March 10, 1984, when Colombian and U.S. authorities raided a laboratory in Caqueta Department on the banks of the Yari River. The police landed at a clandestine airstrip and were met with armed resistance. They eventually arrested 45 people and believe that five times that many managed to escape. The lab was processing coca base into cocaine HCL, and it is estimated that within the next few days more than 1,500 kilograms of cocaine would have been processed at the site. There was a dormitory for 60 people with a separate mess hall. There were six large electric generators and heavy tractors for clearing land. Next to the runway was a ramp for loading DC-6 size aircraft. Short- and long-range communications gear was also found. In the area police located five more clandestine airstrips and several more laboratories with an estimated total value of $4 to $5 million. Seized at the site were 8,530 kilos of cocaine HCL, 1,500 kilos of coca base, 10,800 barrels of processing chemicals, and seven aircraft. The street value of the cocaine seized was estimated at $2 billion [27]. Exactly 2 months later another similar complex was discovered at Vichada that included 12 buildings. This complex had been camouflaged by painting the roofs of the buildings green and surrounding them with trees. An additional 3,500 kilos of cocaine were seized here.

As part of the Bolivar operation in 1989, even more advanced processing laboratories were discovered. In one operation in August of that year in the Magdalena area of Colombia, five major laboratory complexes were seized and destroyed. The level of technology and capital investment being used had increased significantly since 1984. The labs contained equipment for the reprocessing of chemicals, including a distillation tower 40 feet high and very large chemical storage tanks, some of which were underground. In the drying operation they now used microwave ovens in place of heat lamps. There were three-story buildings with dormitories for a hundred people. There were aircraft hangers, a control tower, huge electrical generators, and extensive security facilities. Several labs of this nature were discovered in a 6-month period that included the seizure of over 4,500 kilos of cocaine and enough chemicals to produce over 125 metric tons of cocaine. It takes an enormous amount of money, time, and logistics to construct drug-processing complexes of this nature. In order to assemble a complex like this in such remote regions, heavy lift helicopters and river systems were used to bring materials to the sites [28]. These facilities were under the direct control of the bosses in Medellin.

The ability to undertake such large-scale projects is a result of the effective coordination of many different components and suborganizations. For ventures such as these, a wide array of highly educated professionals is required, including chemists, engineers, architects, and construction management personnel. These types of functions are generally performed by individuals working under contract to the cartel and not full-time members, though undoubtedly they know exactly what they are working on. In this way the cartel spreads its influence deep into Colombian society, using money to lure normally legitimate professionals into the drug-trafficking business.

Integral to the entire operation of the business is transportation. Airplanes are used to bring the coca paste from the growing regions to the processing laboratories and then to bring it into the United States, usually via an intermediate country that is used as a trans-shipment point. Airplanes and helicopters are also used to deliver supplies to remote laboratories and to ferry personnel around. The sizes of the planes varies from small single engine Cessnas to midsize cargo planes such as the DC-6. Supporting this air force of thousands of planes is an extensive network of thousands of clandestine airfields [29]. Some of these landing strips are equipped with infrared landing beacons or radio navigation equipment to guide planes to them at night [30]. They are well constructed and often have drainage ditches along the sides. To prevent unauthorized landings they spread empty metal drums with barbed wire across the surface of the runway. These are easily removed when friendly aircraft are expected [31].

Complementing the airplanes is a large armada of ships that are used to smuggle cocaine. Colombia's extensive Caribbean coast provides a multitude of secluded ports for loading cocaine and taking it up the heavily traveled shipping lanes. It is estimated that 40% of the Colombian cocaine leaves by sea, while the other 60% is flown north [32]. In both cases the great wealth of the traffickers affords them the ability to purchase the most modern equipment and electronic gear.

The pilots flying these planes, the captains driving these ships, and the electronics wizards who operate the sophisticated electronic equipment form a unique link in the cartel's structure. They form a layer of mid-level operatives that, to a large extent, is made up of Americans. They work with the cocaine bosses above them and the distributors below them. This is the only segment of the cartel that is not dominated by Colombians, who tend to be more loyal and feel more an integral part of the organization. Even the Colombians who work in the United States have family back in Colombia that serve as an emotional link to the cartel. The Americans that are used for the technical tasks do so only for the money and have no loyalty to the organization. In 1985 it was estimated that a pilot would get $3,500 for each kilo smuggled into the United States [33]. Hundreds of kilos can be loaded on even a small airplane.

The extensive network of airfields extends well beyond the borders of Colombia. Direct flights from Colombia to the United States are impossible for many aircraft and require so much fuel for others that the amount of cocaine that can be carried is minimal. To alleviate this problem the cartels have developed an elaborate network of trans-shipment points throughout the Caribbean, Mexico, and Central America. Some of the countries known to be used are Mexico, Guatemala, Belize, Honduras, Nicaragua, Costa Rica, Panama, the Bahamas, Turks, Caicos, Cuba, Haiti, and Jamaica. In all these countries the cartel takes advantage of poorly equipped and trained domestic police and armed forces. The expanse of remote regions that lie beyond the effective control of the local governments provides the cartels with ideal trans-shipment locations. Even when these are known, the cartel uses its conventional means of bribery and intimidation to ensure impunity. Social and economic conditions in most of these countries make them ripe for this type of activity. In some cases the government itself is directly involved in the drug trafficking business, as has been the case in Panama, Nicaragua, and Cuba.

The most notorious trans-shipment point may be the island of Norman's Cay in the Bahamas, which Carlos Lehder purchased in 1978. He used this as the main trans-shipment and distribution point for cocaine going into the United States. His facility included airplane hangars and refrigerated cocaine storage facilities operated by a full-time staff of 40 people. At a meeting in 1983 between then–Vice President George Bush and Bahamian Prime Minister Lynden Pindling, the vice president remarked to Pindling that the air traffic going in and out of Norman's Cay was "like O'Hare Airport." According to Admiral Daniel Murphy, former Chief of Staff to Bush, "At the meeting in Miami, we had evidence that we had accumulated to show the number of night flights going into the Bahamas. We took an E-2C and just tracked and plotted all those flights, and it was unbelievable the number of flights" [34]. Public exposure of this operation on the NBC "Nightly News" in September of 1983 led to Norman's Cay being shut down, yet the Bahamas remain a major trans-shipment point to this day [35].

The local political and military authorities are almost always involved in some way in permitting the cartel to operate out of their territory. The motivation for this is primarily financial, as was the case with Manuel Noriega in Panama.

There are some cases where the local authorities have more in mind than simply gaining financial wealth. Such is the case with Cuba, where Castro used the drug trade to further his own ideological interests. In the late 1970s, Castro saw a link between drug trafficking and revolution. He sought to use the power of drug trafficking and drug money to export revolution in Central America and to simultaneously ally himself with the traffickers and the regional military leaders, following the example set by General Noriega in Panama. Castro worked with the Medellin leaders as a mediator in their disputes with the guerrillas and with Noriega himself [36].

This connection led to the involvement of the Sandinista government of Nicaragua. The Sandinistas, as part of their support for revolutionary movements and their close ties to Fidel Castro, also assisted the Medellin cartel in using Nicaragua as a trans-shipment point and allowed them to set up some processing labs in Nicaragua [37].

The most ironic part of this is that at the same time the Nicaraguan resistance groups, or Contras, were also involved in drug trafficking. DEA Assistant Administrator David Westrate said of the Nicaraguan situation, "It is true that people on both sides of the equation were drug traffickers, and a couple of them were pretty significant" [38]. It was through the southern front of the Contra operations that the cartel was able to establish itself in Costa Rica. The same planes that carried cocaine north to the United States carried weapons to the Contras. The Contras used the drug-trafficking network to supply themselves with weapons. According to General Paul Gorman, former commander, U.S. Southern Command, "If you want to move arms or munitions in Latin America, the established networks are owned by the cartels. It has lent itself to the purposes of terrorists, of saboteurs, of spies, of insurgents and subversives" [39]. In this way the cartel further increased its wealth, power, and ability to conduct its business without fear of prosecution.

From the trans-shipment points the cartel flies the drugs into the United States and delivers them to its distributors. This is the most dangerous part of the operation due to the emphasis on interdiction by U.S. law enforcement agencies. For this reason the cocaine acquires most of its value here. Cocaine seized in Colombia has less than one tenth the value of cocaine seized in the United States. One way the cartel's subordinate organizations have worked together is in risk sharing on drug shipments. They avoid sending in half-full boats or planes and are able to insure themselves against loss in this way.

Once the cocaine is in the United States, it is taken to the market area and then stored, transported, and sold. Cartel operatives rent stash houses, vehicles, and the most advanced communications equipment as part of their business. The

Colombians who work in the United States are usually rotated back to Colombia every 6 months. This maintains their close ties to family and cartel members in Colombia and prevents the organization from being infiltrated by U.S. law enforcement agencies [40].

As part of a very advanced smuggling system, the traffickers carefully monitor law enforcement frequencies and route boats and planes away from any potential problems. In 1982 they set up a command post in Miami to handle these tasks [41]. The cartel's reliance on the most advanced electronics and communications technology is one of their trademarks and a key to much of their success.

Once the cocaine is sold, the money that is received is in the form of cash. The enormous profits derived from the drug trade leave the traffickers with very large sums of cash that cannot be hidden through consumption and business expenses. To retain these large sums of money in the form of cash is very expensive. Aside from the cost of secure storage and transportation, the opportunity costs in terms of lost earning power are tremendous. In order for this money to be invested, it must be laundered, or entered into the financial system in a way that does not betray its illicit origins. While originally most drug money was laundered in the United States, strict enforcement by the Reagan administration of the 1974 Bank Secrecy Act forced these activities offshore. Countries that had strict bank secrecy laws were the most obvious targets of the money launderers. The most prominent of these were the Cayman Islands, the Bahamas, and Panama.

The cash that is received by the distributors is usually collected by couriers and brought to safe houses located in major cities. Here it is counted, packaged in special boxes, palletized, and shipped to the country where it is to be laundered. The cartel set up its own courier company to handle this task. Ramon Milian Rodriguez was the cartel's principal money launderer from 1980 to 1983. He personally set up Consolidated Courier Services and says of its effectiveness,

> You have to admit, if you get a bunch of those boxes together and if all the trucks say Consolidated Courier, and the planes say Consolidated Courier, and the personnel has [sic] overalls with the logo on it, and the pilots all have the right uniforms, it looks like a very legitimate operation. I mean, people would actually ask us where we were shipping stuff so that they could use our service [42].

The cartel also owned people at the airport and the airline so that its boxes would always be allowed to be pulled off the planes immediately [43]. This prevented accidental loss or intentional theft.

In the first half of the 1980s Panama became the prime money launderer for the cartel. Panama was perfect because it used U.S. currency, and had favorable banking laws, a corrupt government, and an ideal location. Once the money reached Panama, it was deposited in various banks. There were more than 100 banks in Panama, and over 50 of them were owned by the Colombian traffickers [44]. These banks would send any excess cash to the Banco Nacional, which would then issue credit to the local banks and send the cash to major banks in the United States. The local banks would distribute funds from the credits into numerous different accounts. This compartmentalized the business so that individuals would be insulated and any leaks could be easily found and taken care of. The money would then be "clean." The Panamanian Defense Forces acted as guards and facilitators for the laundering operation. Rodriguez testified that he negotiated an agreement with Noriega under which Noriega received up to a 10% commission on all transactions that went through Panama [45].

Several other similar money-laundering schemes have been used by the cartels, most using multiple transfers, foreign banks, and phony companies. Cash-based businesses like the gold brokerage business have also been exploited for money-laundering purposes [46].

Once the money is clean, it is invested in legitimate businesses both in Colombia and abroad. These include newspapers, radio stations, television stations, soccer teams, land and forestry companies, construction, and auto agencies [47]. The traffickers have extensive real estate holdings in Colombia and the United States. In Colombia alone they have bought over 2.5 million acres of farmland [48]. The Ochoas' ranch outside of Medellin encompasses several towns within its borders. Pablo Escobar owns real estate that is worth an estimated $2 billion [49]. His famous Hacienda Napoles ranch in Puerto Triunfo includes a zoo, 24 artificial lakes, a guest house with room for 100, and a swimming pool flanked by statues and mortar emplacements. These ranches are basically self-sufficient entities, needing only occasional deliveries of fuel.

Of the approximately $1.5 billion that the Colombian drug lords make each year, it is estimated that one third to one half of the drug income is reinvested inside Colombia, with the rest invested primarily in the United States [50]. This investment can have a significant impact on the fragile economies of the Andean countries. The governments have even encouraged the absorption of the narco-dollars into the domestic economies. In Central and South America, the politics of the region, the fiscal policies of the countries, and drug dollars are inextricably linked [51]. The cocaine business may act as a buffer for the local economies during slow economic times, perhaps explaining why Colombia's economy grew every year in the 1980s and the country has never had to reschedule its debt [52].

The management of this international financial empire is left to a highly educated and experienced core of professionals. These include international financiers, accountants, investors, and legal experts. They almost always have advanced degrees, often from the most prestigious U.S. schools. Ramon Milian Rodriguez testified that his successor was a graduate of Harvard Law School [53]. The power and wealth of the cartel entice them into this business. Very few financial people anywhere manage the volume of money controlled by the cartel's financial team.

The drug bosses' unending lust for power and legitimacy induced them to seek political power. In addition to satisfying this drive for power, they used politics to espouse their ideology and to gain public support. The success of these efforts is demonstrated by the Cuban view of the situation, according to Jose

Blandon, a former crony of Noriega: "If you want to have influence on Colombia's political world, you have to have an influence on the drug trafficking world too" [54]. The drug bosses began by secretly funding political parties and organizations that they saw as compatible with their goals. This included direct contributions to political candidates, from village mayors to national officeholders. They later moved into direct political participation by running for and being elected to office, as well as forming their own political parties. This seemed to backfire, and they returned to behind-the-scenes support for candidates. They used their control of portions of the media to spread their message. Finally, they devoted substantial resources to philanthropic projects. This was particularly effective in elevating their status in the poorer zones of the country.

The first important attempt to gain political control with narco-donations occurred in the 1982 presidential elections in Colombia between Belisario Betancur and Alfonso Lopez Michelson. The *Wall Street Journal* reported that more than $1 million in narco-money was donated in that presidential election. According to the traffickers themselves, they donated over $3 million, split between both candidates [55].

The political participation escalated to direct involvement by 1982, when Pablo Escobar was elected to the Colombian House of Representatives as an alternate from Antioquia, running on the Liberal Party ticket. In 1986, Carlos Lehder ran for the Senate from Quindio although he was a fugitive from justice at the time. He was defeated. The publicity surrounding Escobar's election caused problems, and when Rodrigo Lara Bonilla, who had lost to Escobar, accused him of being one of Colombia's top drug lords on ABC television in 1983, things fell apart and he was forced to abandon his political career.

Lehder used money he had made from his drug-smuggling operations in the Bahamas to found his own political party, the Latin Nationalist Movement (MLN), in 1983. The essence of the party's platform was its strong antiextradition plank. This was its raison d'être. Though Lehder was a fugitive at the time, his party won 12% of the vote and several local seats in the 1984 regional elections. He used mass communications and money to gain support, often handing out 500 peso notes to everyone who came to his rallies and sometimes putting more money in the lunch boxes that he provided. His fleet of loudspeaker-equipped helicopters and airplanes dropped leaflets and spread his message across the countryside. The hollowness of his argument and his outlaw status brought on his rapid demise.

Direct political participation turned out to be a complete failure for the drug lords. Their status within society is one more of acceptance than of leadership. They learned that they are most successful when the level of their involvement is not widely known.

They began to use their influence in mayoral elections in the countryside. This gave them more low-level influence, which helped in protecting their laboratories and storage facilities that were spread around the rural regions. Their success with these tactics was noted by Diego Viafara Salinas, a cartel member for 6 years before defecting, who said of the 1985 elections,

> The drug traffickers in the Middle Magdalena invested money heavily in the election of mayors, and consequently mayors were elected in Puerto Parra, Cimitara, and La Dorda. The organization also sponsored the mayor of Pacho and the mayor of San Vicente del Caguan Monteria, Cordoba. These mayors were practically members of the organization [56].

The traffickers were also very smart in the way they sought to gain public support through the use of narco-philanthropy. They enacted a very deliberate campaign aimed at winning the hearts and minds of the people and convincing them that the drug business was good for Colombia. Pablo Escobar has been the leader in this regard. In 1982 he launched his "Medellin without Slums" project that planned to build 2,000 new housing units for poor families in Medellin. Although only 500 were eventually built, the housing development that bears his name remains as a symbol of the generosity and civic leadership of Escobar. He built and outfitted 80 illuminated sports arenas. He fixed sewage systems, illuminated poor neighborhoods, built and repaired schools and churches, and planted thousands of trees. His method was to send teams into the poor neighborhoods to consult with the residents and determine which projects they thought would be of most benefit to them. This endeared Escobar to the people, particularly the poor. Though the investment on the part of the cartel is relatively small, it has paid huge dividends.

The Catholic Church has even accepted charitable donations from the drug lords. The Bishop of Pereira stated in 1984 that "God's hands do not get dirty when they receive money from the cartel" [57].

To take full advantage of the good will these projects were developing, the traffickers used the media outlets they controlled to launch a public information campaign. The *Medellin Civico*, a newspaper that Escobar founded and owns, is the most popular forum for procartel, prodrug propaganda. This further propagated the image of Escobar as a legend and a folk hero, an image that he actively sought to create. This was very effective. To this day most Colombians refer to Escobar simply as "Pablo." He has a sort of godfather image among the general population, being looked upon as almost a part of their families. While the violence of the last few years has alienated many segments of society, this image is still very strong among the poor.

The final and possibly the most complex facet of the cartel structure is its security and intelligence organization. This covers a wide range of activities that can be broken down into three main categories.

The first and most common method of ensuring security is the use of bribes and payoffs. If this fails, the next step is to turn to violence. From assassination squads to small private armies, the Medellin cartel has become known for its penchant for ruthless violence. Finally, the cartel has an intricate intelligence network in place to give it advance warning of impending actions by the authorities.

The cartel's tremendous financial resources enable it to spend large sums of money on corrupting and coopting public officials and law enforcement personnel. It has used this technique extensively, both within Colombia and in foreign countries, including the United States. It especially targets the police, the military, judges, and politicians. The poor economic and social conditions, as well as certain cultural influences, make the Latin American and Caribbean countries where the cartel operates fertile ground for the use of bribery as an instrument of policy. The drug traffickers make it even easier for officials to cooperate with them and take their bribes by offering them the infamous choice between *plomo o plata*, lead or silver, death or money.

Within Colombia, the cartel has forged a close relationship with the army. This is in part due to their mutual efforts against communist insurgencies like the M-19, but also related to the financial benefits the military can receive for cooperating with the cartel. There is abundant evidence of army involvement in cartel business. In 1983, 59 army personnel, including 11 officers, were indicted for crimes associated with the cartel group MAS. These men were tried in military courts and found innocent. They were considered heros within the army, and the highest ranking officer was decorated. There were other examples of prolonged operations by army special forces units that involved protecting lab sites from guerrillas, and in one case moving a lab to a safer area in exchange for cash payments [58]. The army sees its main role as fighting the insurgents, not the drug traffickers. This has led to a situation in which the army is often at odds with the police.

The police are not beyond the corrupting influence of the narco-dollars either. In 1989, the national police force underwent a purge in which 2,000 officers were dismissed for collaborating with the cartel. By paying bribes to police officials, the cartel was able to use Medellin's main airport to make its drug shipments for a period of several months.

Judges were often paid off as well. When faced with the death threats of the cartel and their traditional low salary, they often allowed cases to go unprosecuted or simply discontinued investigations.

While the money and the threats are certainly the major factors in the corruption of all of these officials, it is likely that the cartel's political and propaganda efforts at portraying themselves as public benefactors and good for Colombia have also played a role.

The cartel also used bribes to secure the release of members who had been arrested. They reportedly paid $3 million in 1987 to secure the release of Jorge Ochoa from jail, and an additional $20 million to guarantee his entire escape route [59]. There are numerous other similar incidents that all point to the depth of penetration by the cartel into the state apparatus.

The cartel has also attempted to use bribery on a grandiose scale. In 1984, it offered to give $3 billion to the national economy in exchange for immunity from prosecution. This deal included the dismantling of its entire organization, but was rejected outright by the government. The cartel subsequently offered to pay off Colombia's entire national debt of $10 billion [60]. Since 1984 the Medellin cartel has taken four separate initiatives to negotiate with the government. Its primary goal has always been to avoid extradition to the United States.

The bribery that took place inside Colombia was overshadowed by the bribery that occurred in the other countries in which the cartel operated. Panama again is exemplary of this. At one point in 1984, Noriega took a payment of $5 million in return for protecting the cartel operations and providing safe haven for its members during a crackdown by the Colombian government [61].

This is fairly typical of the corruption in most of the Latin American countries involved in the drug trade. The lowest ranking officers to the highest ranking politicians and officers were all compromised by drug money. One popular method of gaining access to corrupt officials was for the traffickers to buy legitimate businesses in a country such as Haiti, thereby expanding their influence. Richard Gregorie, Chief Assistant U.S. Attorney for the Southern District of Florida testified in 1988 that

> you are able to get airfields, protection from police departments, information about where the law enforcement people will be, that is a regular chain of events in the Bahamas, in the Turks and Caicos, in Cuba, in Haiti, in Honduras. This is a regular set of events that are going on [62].

The extent of the ties between the Honduran military and the cartel was documented in a 1988 *New York Times* piece that said the cartel owns the Honduran military. A similar situation existed in Haiti, and in the Bahamas the trail goes back to the late 1970s and Carlos Lehder's Norman's Cay operation. It was revealed at his trial that Lehder paid Prime Minister Pindling $400,000 in 1978 as a bribe for protection from police interference. Though he was raided several times, each time he was given advance warning and was never arrested [63].

The allure of the drug money and the coercive influence of death threats appear to be almost irresistible, yet many principled and honest politicians, judges, police, and editors have stood up to the intimidation of the drug lords. Most of these people are now dead. The cartel uses assassination as a regular part of doing business. Jose Gacha, known as "El Mexicano," was responsible for lab security, debt collection, and assassination, as well as his production and distribution functions, until his death in a police shootout in 1989. Assassinations were carried out brutally, grotesquely, and often in public so as to maximize the psychological effect. Gacha personally oversaw these assassinations, often specifying the way someone was to be killed, such as being cut to pieces with a chain saw [64].

The killings were carried out by any one of several assassination gangs that the cartel hired. These gangs had names like Los Priscos, Smurfs, Nachos, and The Orphans. They always recruited their members from the south Medellin slums, where Pablo Escobar had invested a great deal of money to buy influence. These slums, where unemployment sometimes ran as high as 60%, were the primary recruiting ground for thousands of drug runners, enforcers, and hit men [65]. The usual pattern for the hit squads was to set up a headquarters in a local hotel and stalk their victim for days. They used motorcycles with following vans to carry out the hit.

The most infamous assassinations are well known, such as the 1984 murder of Justice Minister Rodrigo Lara Bonilla, the 1986 murder of Colonel Jaime Ramirez Gomez, a former head of Colombia's Anti-Narcotics Police, and the assassination of Guillermo Cano, editor and owner of the Bogota daily *El Espectador*, later that same year. These were all political statements that sought to prevent implementation of the 1979 extradition treaty with the United States. The cartel would pay more than $1 million for each of these hits, and there were many others too numerous to mention [66].

The assassinations were not confined to Colombia. The cartel had put out a $1 million contract on Manuel Noriega that required the intervention of Fidel Castro to have withdrawn. In 1988 Gacha hired three hit men to kill New York mayor Ed Koch and the DEA chief there, Robert Stutman [67]. In 1987 the cartel carried out an assassination attempt on a former Minister of Justice in Budapest, Hungary, demonstrating that their power knows no bounds.

In some cases assassination squads were not sufficient, so the cartel also built and financed private armies to carry out paramilitary operations of greater magnitude. These groups were well trained and supplied, often with the most advanced weapons and equipment. They operated under the direct control of the cartel bosses in missions that ranged from lab security to military attacks against left-wing groups.

The first group of this type was Muerte a Los Secuestradores (MAS), or Death to the Kidnappers. They raised a 2,000-man army that destroyed the M-19. They killed brutally, disembowelling and hanging the bodies from trees in order to discourage the population from cooperating with the M-19 [68].

In 1985 the paramilitary group was organized under the cover of a cattlemen's association named ACDEGAM. This group was trained in two camps Gacha had set up on large ranches in the Middle Magdalena Valley, one in Puerto Boyaca called "Escuela Almagher Cincuenta," and the other in Putamayo, named "Rescate" [69]. Advanced courses were set up by 1988 that employed British and Israeli mercenaries, as well as retired Colombian military and police instructors. They ran these schools like boot camps, training 150 men each year in combat patrol techniques, martial arts, weapons, intelligence, C-4 explosives and other subversive activities [70].

The Israeli trainers were led by Yair Klein, a former IDF colonel. This may account for the fact that the paramilitary group was able to get shipments of Israeli-made weapons. These included rockets, explosives, night vision goggles, and hundreds of Uzis and Galil assault rifles [71]. The cartel always has been able to procure advanced weapons, including surface-to-air missiles. In 1988 it planned to build a munitions factory, and it has weapons shops to fabricate special weapons. The cartel possesses capabilities at least equal to the state, according to Diego Viafra: "The combatants, the patrol people who work for the paramilitary narco organization, are more disciplined than any Army soldier in Colombia and they are smarter and they have more competent indoctrination than any Colombian soldier" [72].

The intelligence capabilities of the cartels rival those of most countries. The cartels have an extensive network of informers throughout their area of operations. They have state-of-the-art equipment, including satellite radios, digital encryption devices, and voice privacy mechanisms, that makes it difficult for even the U.S. armed forces to penetrate. General Gorman made this clear when he said, "I have seen equipment used on the aircraft that fly between the United States and Colombia, and I can assure you that it is more sophisticated and more facile than the equipment that I had on my aircraft of the U.S. Air Force in the U.S. Southern Command" [73]. He went on to say that the government's communication system is regularly intercepted by the traffickers and that traffickers can track the movements of armed forces units better than the respective commanders [74].

The cartel has infiltrated the Ministries of Justice and Foreign Affairs in Colombia [75]. It has informants inside the U.S. embassy in Bogota that give it access to cable traffic. It is able to do this because it pays its informants three times what the DEA pays. It reportedly had a list of all DEA agents and their code names that it circulated throughout South America [76]. It has also been able to receive information on AWACS monitoring and surveillance from the El Paso Information Center [77].

There has been a great deal made of the connection between the drug cartels and the left-wing guerrillas. In fact, there is no real alliance here. The traffickers have used the guerrillas at times when it was beneficial to them, to protect lab sites for instance, but they have also launched large-scale war against them. The guerrillas perform services for the cartel in exchange for weapons and money, which they desperately need. These two groups are ideologically diametrically opposed, and there is no real threat that they would band together, since their fundamental objectives do not coincide.

Conclusions

Recent developments show the strength and resilience of the Medellin cartel. Although its top leaders are either dead or in prison, and hundreds of lower level cadre are imprisoned as well, it continues to manufacture and export cocaine at levels only slightly below previous levels. The organization appears to remain flexible in finding the most profitable locations and methods for operating its business. The cartel has responded to efforts by the Bush administration to attack its processing operations by shifting operations into Ecuador and Brazil. There are large regions of these countries that are out of the control of the central government and therefore ripe for exploitation by drug traffickers, and this appears to be occurring [78]. Any slack in the operations of the Medellin cartel is taken up by the rival Cali cartel. There has been no decrease in the number of cocaine users in the United States, and the volume of cocaine produced continues to rise in response to increased interdiction. A strategy of measuring success in the drug war simply by the number of kilos seized, cadres jailed, or jungle labs raided may lead to the same types of mistakes that were made in Vietnam by failing to understand the nature and organization of the enemy.

It is obvious that the cartel has deeply embedded itself in the Colombian, and Andean, society. This has the effect of preventing a strictly military or law enforcement strategy from defeating it. The cartel must be attacked politically, economically, and psychologically in conjunction with military and law enforcement measures. The cartel has developed an extensive political following through the effective use of media and philanthropy to espouse its ideology. It has succeeded in convincing many, especially the poor, of its value to Colombian society. For those it cannot convince, it has a sophisticated security apparatus to make payoffs and, for those unwilling to take bribes, intimidate with violence.

Even for those not directly involved in the drug trade, there is a trickle-down effect that gives large sectors of the society a stake in its perpetuation. The billions of dollars of profit that are drained from the North American and European economies by way of the cartel are an important stimulus to the economies of the Andean countries. In this way the cartel indirectly incorporates business owners, real estate developers, farmers, and numerous others into its organization by linking their prosperity to that of the cartel.

The size, power, and wealth of the Medellin cartel extend well beyond the few big name traffickers we normally associate with it. It is this larger organization and all of its benefactors that must be analyzed, targeted, and attacked if we are to make true progress in the war on drugs.

Notes

1. "The Cocaine Economies," *Economist*, October 9, 1988, p. 21.
2. Congress, Senate, Committee on Governmental Affairs, *Structure of International Drug Trafficking Organizations: Hearings before the Permanent Subcommittee on Investigations of the Committee on Governmental Affairs*, 101st Cong., 1st Sess., Sept. 12 and 13, 1989, p. 31.
3. Agent Steven Moriale, U.S. Drug Enforcement Agency, interview by author, March 2, 1992, Boston.
4. Rensselaer Lee, *The White Labyrinth* (London: Transaction Publishers, 1990), p. 125.
5. "The Medellin Cartel," *Miami Herald*, November 29, 1987, p. A28.
6. "U.S. Weighs Pindling Indictment," *Washington Post*, June 25, 1988, p. A1.
7. Scott MacDonald, *Mountain High, White Avalanche* (New York: Praeger, 1989), p. 19.
8. Bruce Bagley, "Colombia and the War on Drugs," *Foreign Affairs*, vol. 67 (Fall 1988), p. 77.
9. MacDonald, *Mountain High*, p. 25.
10. "Escobar Gaviria refuta a Tambs," *Medellin Civico*, Mar. 1984, p. 3.
11. Rensselaer Lee, "Cocaine Mafia," *Society* (January 1990), p. 53.
12. Merrill Collett, *The Cocaine Connection* (New York: Foreign Policy Association, 1989), p. 29.
13. "Lehder Trial Begins Today," *St. Petersburg Times*, October 5, 1987, p. B1.
14. Congress, *Structure*, p. 169.
15. Ibid., p. 47.
16. President's Commission on Organized Crime, *America's Habit: Drug Abuse,*

Drug Trafficking and Organized Crime (Washington, D.C.: Government Printing Office, 1986), p. 79.

17. Congress, *Structure,* p. 85.
18. Ibid., p. 85.
19. Ibid., p. 164.
20. MacDonald, *Mountain High,* p. 59.
21. Ibid., p. 60.
22. Ibid.
23. Lee, *The White Labyrinth,* p. 25.
24. Ibid., p. 31.
25. Ibid., p. 32.
26. "Government Releases Drug Statistics," *Santa Fe de Bogota Radio,* Dec. 26, 1991, n.p.
27. Congress, House, Committee on Foreign Affairs, *Recent Developments in Colombian Narcotics Control: Hearings before the Committee on Foreign Affairs,* 98th Cong., 2nd Sess., May 24, 1984, p. 21.
28. Congress, *Structure,* p. 32.
29. Lee, *The White Labyrinth,* p. 103.
30. "The Medellin Cartel, part 2," *Miami Herald,* November 29, 1987, p. A28.
31. Interpol, "War on Drugs," *International Criminal Police Review,* (Jan. 1987), p. 26.
32. Moriale interview.
33. "The Medellin Cartel, part 1," *Miami Herald,* Nov. 29, 1987.
34. Congress, Senate, Committee on Foreign Relations, *Drugs, Law Enforcement, and Foreign Policy: The Cartel, Haiti, and Central America: Hearing before the Subcommittee on Terrorism, Narcotics, and International Operations of the Committee on Foreign Relations: Part 4,* 100th Cong., 2nd Sess., July 11, 12, and 14, 1988, p. 260.
35. Congress, Senate, Committee on Foreign Relations: *Drugs, Law Enforcement, and Foreign Policy,* Staff Report, Subcommittee on Terrorism, Narcotics, and International Operations (Washington, D.C.: Government Printing Office, 1988), p. 18.
36. Ibid., p. 65.
37. Ibid., p. 67.
38. Congress, *Drugs, Law Enforcement, Part 4,* p. 144.
39. Congress, Senate, Committee on Foreign Relations, *Drugs, Law Enforcement, and Foreign Policy: Panama: Hearings before the Subcommittee on Terrorism, Narcotics, and International Operations of the Committee on Foreign Relations: Part 2,* 100th Cong., 2nd Sess., Feb. 8, 9, 10, and 11, 1988, p. 44.
40. Congress, *Drugs, Law Enforcement, Part 2,* p. 160.
41. "The Medellin Cartel, part 2," *Miami Herald,* Nov. 29, 1987, p. A28.
42. Congress, Senate, Committee on Foreign Relations, *Drugs, Law Enforcement, and Foreign Policy: The Cartel, Haiti, and Central America: Hearings before the Subcommittee on Terrorism, Narcotics,and International Operations: Part 3,* 100th Cong., 2nd Sess., Apr. 4, 5, 6, and 7, 1988, p. 170.
43. Ibid., p. 171.
44. Congress, *Drugs, Law Enforcement, and Foreign Policy,* Staff Report, p. 116.
45. Ibid., p. 81.
46. Paula Dwyer, "Getting Banks to Just Say No," *Business Week,* Apr. 17, 1989, p. 17.
47. Congress, *Drugs, Law Enforcement, Part 3,* p. 176.

48. Collett, *The Cocaine Connection,* p. 15.
49. "The Cocaine Economies," p. 22.
50. Ibid., p. 21.
51. Congress, *Drugs, Law Enforcement, Part 3*, p. 179.
52. MacDonald, *Mountain High,* p. 53.
53. Congress, *Drugs, Law Enforcement, Part 3*, p. 176.
54. MacDonald, *Mountain High*, p. 33.
55. Lee, *The White Labyrinth*, p. 131.
56. Congress, *Structure*, p. 71.
57. Lee, *The White Labyrinth*, p. 133.
58. Ibid., p. 217.
59. MacDonald, *Mountain High*, p. 125.
60. Congress, *Drugs, Law Enforcement, and Foreign Policy*, Staff Report, p. 34.
61. Bagley, "Colombia," p. 82.
62. Congress, *Drugs, Law Enforcement, Part 4*, p. 160.
63. Congress, *Drugs, Law Enforcement, and Foreign Policy*, Staff Report, p. 17.
64. Congress, *Structure* p. 70.
65. "Vigilantes Retake Slums of Medellin," *Washington Post*, Dec. 7, 1991, p. A17.
66. "The Medellin Cartel, part 5", *Miami Herald*, Mar. 12, 1987, p. A20.
67. Poole, C., "Gonzalo Rodriguez Gacha: Gacha for Warlord," *Forbes*, July 24, 1989, p. 118.
68. Congress, *Drugs, Law Enforcement, and Foreign Policy*, Staff Report, p. 28.
69. Congress, *Structure*, p. 73.
70. Ibid.
71. Congress, House, Committee on Governmental Affairs, *Arms Trafficking, Mercenaries, and Drug Cartels: Hearings before the Permanent Subcommittee on Investigations of the Committee on Governmental Affairs*, 102nd Cong., 1st Sess., Feb. 27 and 28, 1991, p. 122.
72. Congress, *Structure*, p. 91.
73. Congress, *Drugs, Law Enforcement, Part 2*, p. 33.
74. Ibid.
75. Bagley, "Colombia," p. 58.
76. Lee, *The White Labyrinth*, p. 106.
77. Congress, *Drugs, Law Enforcement, Part 3*, p. 110.
78. Moriale interview.

CJPR, VOL. 6, NO. 3/92, pp. 207-228

The Anti-Drug Policies Of The 1980's: Have They Increased The Likelihood For Both Wrongful Convictions And Sentencing Disparities?

James B. Halsted
University of South Florida

Abstract

New statutory schemes enacted to support the "War on Drugs" policies of the 1980s are being enforced in a manner which is increasing the likelihood of a greater number of wrongful convictions. This study examines these new anti-drug statutes by analyzing how and when the American criminal justice system may be incarcerating marginally culpable and even innocent defendants due to the easier convictability of those prosecuted under the new statutes. One new crime created by these statutes is "trafficking in controlled substances." An accused can be convicted under this powerfully sanctioned crime whenever the prosecution proves that he or she is only in "constructive possession" of a statutorily designated amount of a controlled substance. The significant change embodied in the new crime of "trafficking" is that it has reduced the amount of proof which used to be necessary to convict an accused person of the old drug dealer's crime, "possession of drugs with the intent to distribute." In "trafficking" statutes, the seminal element of the older crime has been omitted. This omission has facilitated convictions. Additionally, this study uncovers statutorily built-in sentencing disparities among the punishments which judges are forced to impose on those convicted of "trafficking" versus the punishments which judges have the discretion to impose for other equally serious felonies.

Every American president since Richard Nixon has declared a "war on drugs." Each suggested that America's problem with illicit drugs is "epidemic." In every instance, one of the proposed solutions to America's drug problem has included an increase in the severity of criminal sanctions for drug offenders, especially for drug dealers.

Yet because of American prison overcrowding and the attendant federal court early release orders, past political solutions of the 1960s and the early 1970s to "lock up drug dealers for longer periods" proved to be unsuccessful during the late 1970s and the early 1980s. This policy failure was due in great part to the new "good time" and "gain time" correctional statutes enacted by state legislatures during this period.

This failure surfaced when the application of the "lock em up" policy resulted in an unintended situation after convicted drug dealers were sentenced and then behaved themselves in prison. They served but a minimal percentage of the time they were sentenced to by the trial judge; they were released early under the good time and gain time laws. As a consequence, convicted drug dealers were perceived by the general public to be serving unacceptably short lengths of time in prison.

This phenomenon has been labeled as the Department of Correction's "revolving door." In response, many state legislatures enacted new war on drugs laws during the 1980s. One of the most significant legislative responses to the "revolving door" problem was to replace the old crime of the 1960s and 1970s, "possession of drugs with the intent to distribute," with a new statutory crime called "trafficking in controlled drugs."

The new "trafficking" crime is different from the older crime it replaced in two significant ways: (1) the new offense has reduced the amount of evidence necessary to convict a suspected drug dealer for "dealing in drugs"; and (2) the sentences attached to the crime of "trafficking in drugs" often are "mandatory minimum" sentences. These special sentences result in greatly enhancing the length of the convicted drug dealer's sentence. Furthermore, this change has increased the actual time the defendants are required to serve in prison. Thus the political consequences of enacting these new "trafficking" crimes, in part, seem to have had their desired effects.

In spite of the apparent successes of this statutory change, an unintended problem has arisen. One consequence of these statutory changes is that convictions for "trafficking" are being obtained by the prosecution in some cases where the factual evidence suggests innocence.

The reason for the increase in wrongful convictions in these cases is embodied in the definitions of the elements of "trafficking." They are strict and narrow ones. Trial judges' instructions to juries on the definition of the crime of "trafficking" are rigid. Yet the definition is applied even if this strict interpretation is contrary to the will of the trial judge. Such a strict and narrow definition has had the effect of decreasing the amount of evidence necessary to prove "trafficking"; and this reduction may ultimately be responsible for an increase in the number of wrongful convictions on trafficking charges against certain marginally culpable or even innocent defendants.

An Overview Of The Problem Of Wrongful Convictions

Wrongful convictions are not a new catastrophe challenging the structures of the American criminal justice system. Over 160 years ago, a great American jurist opined that one nightmare of the principles which support the vision of the American criminal justice system is that defendants may be adjudicated wrongfully. Such a possibility, said Judge Learned Hand, has always caused those who seriously valued and esteemed their participation in our system to hold their collective breaths. Judge Hand said in 1923: "Our procedure has always been haunted by the ghost of an innocent man convicted. It is an unreal dream" (quoted in Silberman, 1978:262).

One of the more recent examples of this "unreal" specter came to the nation's attention through the press. It occurred with exposure of the facts which forced the Florida Governor to release Mr. James Richardson. Richardson was released from prison in 1989 because he had been wrongfully convicted. Newly uncovered facts clearly demonstrated that Mr. Richardson was the victim of an extreme injustice. He was wrongly convicted of murdering his seven children based on his alleged motive to receive a non-collectable $3,500 life insurance policy. The real murderer turned out to be the housekeeper who confessed two decades later while in a nursing home.

James Richardson's wrongful conviction renders a significant example supporting the protests of criminologists such as Huff, Rattner & Sagarin (1986). These authors passionately propose that few problems can pose a greater threat to free, democratic societies than a wrongful conviction. They define a "wrongful conviction" as the conviction of an innocent person. Also, they offer in their study two other separate definitions of a "wrongful conviction":

1. If there is some reasonable doubt as to their guilt (that is, if they have been convicted although the evidence does not demonstrate guilt beyond a reasonable doubt), then the verdict of guilt was wrong, and it can be said to be a *wrongful conviction*, from a strictly legal point of view. However, so long as guiltlessness has itself not been established, one cannot categorize such individuals as convicted innocents. (519)

and

2. Our operational definition of *wrongful conviction* includes only those cases in which a person is convicted of a felony but later is found to be innocent beyond a reasonable doubt, generally due to a confession by the actual offender, [or] evidence that had been available but was not sufficiently used at the time of conviction, [or] new evidence that was not previously available, and other factors (*sic*). (519)

In the same study, these two researchers also sought to discover the following essential information about wrongful convictions: Specifically, 1) how big is the problem?; 2) how does it happen?

The study concludes that no definitive answer exists regarding the frequency of wrongful convictions. Criminologists who have conducted serious research on this subject have derived their information mostly from the accumulation of case studies (Huff et al, 1986; Borchard, 1932; Gardner, 1952; Frank and Frank, 1957; Block, 1963; Radin, 1964; Bedau, 1967; MacNamara, 1969; Brandon and Davies, 1973; Loftus, 1979).

Huff's study does suggest an approximate number of wrongful convictions which occur each year in the United States:

> Therefore, although there is no known method of determining how many wrongful convictions occur each year, our literature review, our survey, our own primary database of nearly 500 wrongful conviction cases, and our analysis of the dynamics of wrongful conviction cause us to feel relatively confident in this conservative estimate of *less than 1%*. In other words, for every 200 persons convicted of felonies in the United States, we (and the great majority of our survey respondents) believe that 1 or 2 of them may well be innocent. The frequency of error may well be much higher in cases involving less serious felonies and misdemeanors (emphasis added). (523)

In attempting to answer their own question concerning the major causes of all these wrongful convictions, the authors proposed 17 empirical explanations.[1] Yet, nowhere in the analyses of Huff et al's. do these researchers recognize that the legislature, which passes statutes which reduce the amount of evidence necessary to convict, represent another significant but unrecognized cause for increasing the likelihood of wrongful convictions in the American courtroom. The present study initially will examine this particular phenomenon by presenting a case study demonstrating the possible wrongful conviction of Bill Neal.

None of Huff's 17 explanations of wrongful convictions explains Neal's wrongful conviction. Neal's case study, instead, demonstrates that in many of the state and federal legislative sessions, our lawmakers in their haste to fight and win the war on drugs have passed criminal statutes which decrease the quantity and quality of proof necessary to convict. Secondly, the case exposes the fact that these statutes were passed without the legislatures' anticipating some of the possible unjust consequences. Thirdly, the Neal case suggests that the implementations of these war-on-drugs statutes, although well intended, are potentially ripe for rendering wrongful convictions. Bill Neal is a possible victim of such a statute.

*The State Of Florida vs. Bill Neal **

Bill Neal is a 43-year-old business entrepreneur who owns his own company and two airplanes.[2] In 1989, his company experienced an extreme cash flow problem in its operating funds. As a result, Neal sought outside investors to pump money into his business. During this time, one of Bill Neal's former investors introduced him to Gregory Garrett.

Gregory Garrett is a 32-year-old businessman from Tennessee. Garrett and Neal hit it off instantly. In 1990, Neal was informed that Garrett had inherited a large sum of money and he persuaded Garrett to invest in his company. Subsequently, Neal's business began to turn around. Of even greater value to Neal was Garrett's network of wealthy associates because they also seemed to be interested in investing funds in Neal's company. To reward Garrett for obtaining new investors, Neal made Garrett a part-owner of his business.

* *The names used in this section are fictitious to protect the identities of all parties.*

Neal is a pilot, and from January through May of 1990, Neal and Garrett flew throughout Florida, Tennessee, and Arkansas to visit potential investors and to make sales pitches. These flights proved fruitful. The partners found new investors, and Neal's failing business seemed to be on the road to recovery. Then the door slammed shut.[3]

On May 15, 1990, after both men had returned from a business trip to Ft. Lauderdale, they parked Neal's airplane in a Tampa airstrip and drove a rental car back to Garrett's home. While at Garrett's house, Neal called his wife. She informed him that the airport had called and told her that his airplane was malfunctioning and that it would not be repaired for two days. Upon learning this, Neal asked Garrett if he could spend the night at his house until his plane was fixed. Garrett agreed.

Later that evening Garrett left the house to meet some friends. Alone in the home, having just taken a shower, Neal was in the kitchen drinking some fruit juice with a towel wrapped around him when the narcotics squad burst in and placed him under arrest. The squad searched Garrett's house and found a safe in the back bedroom. Before opening the safe, the officer in charge asked Neal if he knew the combination to the safe. Neal replied "Combination? I didn't even know Greg had a safe! If he does, I don't know where it is!" Subsequently, the squad broke open the safe and discovered over 400 grams of cocaine. They arrested Neal at the scene.

The next morning the State Attorney's office charged Neal with "trafficking in cocaine of over 400 grams" (the amount found in Garrett's safe). Even though Neal probably is innocent of the crime charged and even though he probably would have gained an acquittal if he had been charged with "possession of 400 grams of cocaine with the intent to distribute it," a substantial chance exists that Neal will be convicted for "trafficking." One of Neal's legal problems is the paucity of proof necessary for the prosecution to produce in order to successfully convict him or anyone else for "trafficking in cocaine."

Under Florida statutes (and under almost all other state statutes as well)[4] the only fact that the state need prove to convict a defendant for "trafficking" in 400 grams of cocaine is that the defendant was in "constructive possession" of this amount of the drugs.[5]

"Trafficking" Statutes Part Of An Arsenal Of New Weapons For The State's Assaults In The War On Drugs

The old statutes addressing drug violations often were categorized with respect to the severity of the sentences they imposed. For example, in the 1960s, the crime of "possession of drugs" carried a less severe penalty than did the "sale of drugs," the "distribution of drugs," or the "manufacture of drugs." However, during that time, states' legislators often were perplexed about what to do with those cases wherein a defendant was in mere possession of drugs at the time he or she was arrested but the substantial quantity of drugs in the defendant's control suggested that the defendant was more than just a substance abuser. The large quantity in fact implied that the defendant was a drug distributor or a "drug dealer." During the 1970s, the states responded to the problem by passing statutes which punished more severely those caught in possession of drugs with "the intent to distribute them" than they punished those who were in "simple possession" of contraband.

Under these 1970s statutes, if a defendant was charged with "possession of drugs with the intent to distribute," the state was required to prove an additional element beyond what it would be required to prove if he or she were charged with simple "possession of drugs." According to *United States v Brett* (1989:1370), "once a defendant is charged with possession of a particular controlled substance with the intent to distribute, *the government bears the burden of establishing sufficient proof of the possessor's 'specific intent' to distribute the contraband* and may do so either by direct or indirect circumstantial evidence" (emphasis added).

Thus, unless the state specifically proved that the defendant had the intention to distribute the drugs in his possession, he or she could not be convicted in the 1970s of the crime of "possession of drugs with the intent to distribute them." Yet under the newly adopted "trafficking" state and federal statutes of the 1980s and 1990s, the government's burden of proof has been significantly reduced. The state no longer is required to prove the defendant had an "intent to distribute" when the prosecution seeks to convict the defendant for "trafficking" in drugs. Therefore, in Neal's case, he can not require the state to prove the additional element of "possession with the intent to distribute" announced in *Brett* because the Florida statute under which Neal is charged has eliminated this particular *mens rea* in its definition of the crime of "trafficking."

In America's war on drugs, no single state has borne a greater burden than Florida. One study estimates that of all the illegal drugs manufactured in the world, 60 percent are consumed by Americans, and 80 percent of that amount enters the United States through Florida.[6] Responding to this volume of drugs flowing through the state, in the early 1980s the Florida Legislature passed statutes which required little proof of criminal activity or of criminal intent to convict drug dealers. Florida statute section 893.135, "trafficking... mandatory sentences,.." reads as follows:

> Any person who knowingly sells, purchases, manufactures, delivers, or brings into the state, or who is *in knowing or actual constructive possession of* 28 grams or more of cocaine...is guilty of a felony in the first degree, which felony shall be known as 'trafficking in cocaine'.
>
> If the quantity involved is *28 grams or more* but less than 200 grams such a person shall be sentenced to a mandatory minimum term in prison of *three calendar years* and to pay a fine of $50,000.
>
> If *200 grams or more but less than 400 grams* such person shall be sentenced to the mandatory minimum term in prison of *five calendar years* and to pay a fine of $100,000.

> If *400 grams or more* such a person shall be sentenced to a mandatory minimum term in prison of *fifteen calendar years* and to pay a fine of $250,000. (emphases added)

The initial polemic of this study is to examine how a potentially innocent person could be convicted of "trafficking in cocaine of over 400 grams" by suggesting that if he or she unwittingly is in a particular physical setting and in a certain physical proximity to the amount of contraband, these facts alone are legally interpreted to mean this person is in "constructive possession" of the 400 grams of cocaine. But of greater significance to this initial polemic is to expose how the 1980s legislative changes in the drug laws also mandate that this same unwitting person not only is legally in "constructive possession" but also is in legal possession of them. The third part of this study's first polemic demonstrates that this same person's physical proximity to these drugs also is interpreted to be the legal equivalent of guilt for "trafficking in 400 grams of cocaine."

Neal's First Jeopardy—"Trafficking In Drugs" Defined In The 1980s Merely As "Constructive Possession" Of Drugs—The Lowering Of The Amount Of Proof Necessary For Conviction

The legal definition of "possession" as it historically has related to crimes of possessing controlled substances has always been a controversial subject in American criminal law. At the core of this controversy is the courtroom application of the legal concept of "constructive possession." Under traditional standards in American criminal law, a person is in "constructive possession" of a drug when he or she has "dominion and control" over the drug, that is when the defendant is in the same location as the drug seized even though the drug is not on his or her person. Hence, in order for the prosecution to successfully prove that a defendant was in "possession of drugs" the state need only prove he or she had dominion and control of the drugs. Furthermore, in order for the state to prove a particular defendant was in "constructive possession of drugs" it is not necessary to prove either that the defendant owned the drugs nor that the drugs were found at his or her personal residence.

Recent federal case law has done little to change the interpretation of this broad definition. *United States v Caballeri* (1983) states that "constructive possession must be proved by ownership, dominion, control over the contraband itself or dominion and control over the premises or vehicle which the contraband is concealed" (129). In essence, according to *United States v Disla* (1986), "constructive possession" is the ability to reduce the object to actual possession. In the *Disla* case, the 9th Circuit emphasized that being in "constructive possession" of illegal drugs was not a legal fiction. Instead, the term reflects the common sense notion that one may possess a controlled substance "even though the substance is not on the person at the time of arrest" (1350).

Once the state proves that a defendant is in "constructive possession," this legally means he or she is deemed to be in legal "possession" of a certain large amount of drugs. Also, based on this proof alone, a defendant can be convicted of the serious offense of "trafficking" in the amount of the drugs discovered (See Florida Statute section 893.185, first clause, *supra*). Thus to get a trafficking conviction the state no longer needs to prove the defendant intended to distribute these drugs; the state need only prove the accused was in constructive possession of the drugs at the time of his or her arrest. Hence, the 1980s statutory definition of "trafficking" requires less proof to convict than was required previously when someone was caught in physical proximity to large quantities of drugs.

For Neal, this reduction of proof necessary to convict drug dealers increases his chances for a wrongful conviction. One of Neal's possible defenses in this case is that not only did he not know that the cocaine was in Garrett's safe (he didn't even know the combination to the safe), he also certainly did not intend to distribute that which he did not know existed. Yet this reduction in the amount of proof necessary to convict is a significant change that will affect the merit of Neal's two defenses. The significance of this change is demonstrated in the federal cases wherein drug dealers are still being prosecuted under the 1970's statutes criminalizing the "possession of a large quantity of drugs with the intent to distribute them." In order to successfully prosecute under previous statutes, federal prosecutors need to prove, in addition to the fact that the defendant was in possession of the drugs, that the defendant possessed the specific criminal intent (*mens rea*) to distribute the drugs he or she allegedly possessed.

Federal case law suggests that one way the government's evidence can prove "the intent to distribute" is through an inference created by the proof of any of the following facts: (1) a large quantity (*United States v LaGuardia* 1985); (2) the defendant was in possession of drug paraphernalia (*United States v Staten* 1978); (3) the drug had a high level of purity (*United States v Blake* 1973); (4) there was a presence of large sums of cash at the crime scene (*United States v Tramunti* 1975); (5) there was a presence of firearms at the crime scene (which is considered a tool of the narcotics dealers' trade) (*United States v Moses* 1973); or (6) the possessor was addicted to the same or a different drug (*United States v Ramirez Rodriguez* 1977).

In the case of Bill Neal, the only one of these six factors which possibly could be used to prove he had an intent to distribute the cocaine in the safe is the fact that a large quantity of cocaine was seized (over 400 grams) from the safe in Garrett's bedroom. Yet since Neal has evidence to prove that he was not aware of the safe's existence, let alone of its contraband contents, he probably could rebut successfully this inference (see quote below). In fact, the only reason Neal was in Garrett's house was that Neal's plane had broken down at the Tampa Airport. The fact of the matter was that Garrett had been duping Neal for months. Garrett, a drug dealer, had used Neal primarily for access to his airplane, telling Neal that the purpose of the plane trips was for Garrett to introduce Neal to other investors. In fact these trips were used by Garrett to travel by air to various locations in order to buy, sell, and distribute cocaine. Garrett admitted this to a state drug enforcement agent:

> I used Neal without his knowledge. Why should I pay someone as a 'mule' when I don't have to. If a pilot knew that narcotics were being transported on his plane, then I would have to pay them $2,000 to $3,000 for their services. If I brought anything aboard that aircraft Bill Neal could not have known about it...Furthermore Bill had no idea what was contained in my safe; he had no idea of the combination of the safe, let alone that the safe even existed.[7]

The Due Process Challenge To Prosecutions For The Various Crimes Which Substantively Restate The Crime Of "Constructive Possession"—The "Mere Presence" Defense—Neal's Slim Hope

Defendants and defense lawyers throughout the 1970s argued that if all the prosecutors could prove in a drug possession case was that a defendant was in "constructive possession" of drugs and nothing more, then a defendant's subsequent conviction based on this evidence alone violated the Due Process clause of the United States Constitution. It was in the 60s and 70s when these defense lawyers argued on their various appeals the same general proposition: Any law which convicts a citizen of possessing contraband only because it was discovered in a physical zone over which he or she had the potential to obtain dominion and control, but fails to require that the state prove that the defendant knew that the drugs were present, creates a fundamental unfairness. Eventually decisions emanating from the various state and federal appellate courts began to agree.

Subsequently, a substantial number of state and federal cases developed a defense doctrine in constructive possession cases known as the "mere presence defense." The meaning of the "mere presence defense" is clearly articulated in *United States v James* (1985). The D.C. circuit held that for the government to prove that the defendant was in constructive possession of the drugs, it must not only prove the defendant exercised dominion and control over the drugs, but also must offer evidence which proves beyond a reasonable doubt that the defendant's presence in the area was more than "mere presence" or an association with others who in fact owned, controlled, and possessed the illegal drugs. The court concluded that one's "mere presence" in an area in which drugs are found, by itself, will not automatically give rise to proof that the defendant was in constructive possession of the drugs.

Thus, for most prosecutorial agencies in the 1990s, the evidence necessary to prove a defendant to be in "constructive possession" of contraband must be such that the government also proves he or she "*knowingly* holds the power and the ability to exercise dominion and control over it" (*United States v Massey* 1982:1354). The practical consequences of this "mere presence" defense in the courtroom is as follows. Defendants who are charged with a crime the gravamen of which is "constructive possession" of drugs (which, as demonstrated, could also mean that the crime that the defendant is charged with is "trafficking") will be acquitted only if defense counsel can persuade a jury that the defendant did not know the drugs were there. But the defendant testifying to such may be insufficient.

A line of appellate court decisions have developed a set of legal inferences based on certain facts which can be used to rebut the new "mere presence defense." Based on certain facts, many types of these rebuttals exist. The first one is that if the prosecution can establish that the accused was involved in a joint venture with a person proved to have knowingly possessed the drugs, this joint venture creates a legal inference that the defendant knew the drugs were present. A second rebuttal is present whenever the state proves that a defendant has access to the location of the drugs (whether the drugs are found in a house, vehicle, boat, or plane). Proof of this access likewise creates an inference that the defendant knew the drugs were present in the location where they were found. A third rebuttal of the "mere presence" defense is effected when the prosecution proves the defendant had the power to dispose of the drug. The appellate courts have opined that proof of this power creates an inference that the defendant knew that the drugs were present in the area. This power to dispose can be demonstrated by the prosecution's proving the accused had the key to another's structure or that the owner gave the defendant permission to be present(*United States v Massey*, 1982; *United States v Brett*, 1989).

Some of these inferences may ruin Neal's mere presence defense. Garrett and Neal were in a "joint venture" in business together (Neal and Garrett certainly were doing business together). Also, the prosecution can easily prove that Neal had "access to the location" (since he was in Garrett's home alone). Hence, since the state can prove both "joint venture" and "access," these legal inferences stand a good chance of being used by the government to successfully rebut Neal's "mere presence defense."

Based on the above legal analysis, it is proposed that the state of Florida probably could successfully convict Neal of "trafficking in 400 grams of cocaine." The primary reason for this probable success is that it is no longer required to prove Neal intended to distribute the drugs. Thus, for the state, the new statutory elimination of a key element from the old drug dealer statute creates a greater likelihood of a wrongful conviction.

The possibility of being convicted of a crime he did not commit is not the only jeopardy which Bill Neal will face as he is processed through the Florida criminal justice system. Unlike many other defendants who have been wrongfully convicted, the possibility of injustice to Neal does not stop there. Subsequently Neal must begin a new, second phase of a triple jeopardy procedure which defendants like him must face whenever they are successfully prosecuted on drug dealer charges which have been streamlined by the changed state statutes.

After Neal's initial jeopardy of receiving a wrongful conviction, he must then encounter another jeopardy at the sentencing hearing. This jeopardy involves the nature of the sentencing disparities which are inherently and irrevocably received by those convicted under trafficking statutes. This sentencing disparity is blended into the sentencing structural procedures which dictate how the trial judge must determine the size of sentence to be imposed on those defendants (like Neal) who are convicted for trafficking in an excessive amount of cocaine.

Calculating "Time Sentenced" In Criminal Court Under Sentencing Guidelines

Like many other state criminal codes, Florida has adopted sentencing provisions similar to those suggested by the Model Penal Code. Instead of having a range of indeterminate sentences, Florida calls for sentencing based on the seriousness of felonies defined in terms of degrees. A "first degree felony," for example, yields a maximum authorized of 30 years in prison; a conviction for a "second degree felony" has as its maximum sentence 15 years imprisonment. A "third degree felony" has a maximum of five years in prison.

These sentences theoretically are the maximum sentences authorized by law for the conviction under each degree of felony. Yet, since Florida's (as well as a multitude of other states') adoption of sentencing guidelines, these maximum sentences have little if any practical relationship to the actual sentences imposed by trial judges. Instead, the sentences actually imposed in Florida, other states, and in federal courtrooms are the consequence of an impersonal calculation of the case on a tally sheet called the court's "sentencing guideline sheets."

For example, if, hypothetically, Bill Neal were charged with "attempted murder" on May 15, 1990 instead of with "trafficking in cocaine" on that same date, both criminal acts would cause him to be charged with a first degree felony. Hence, like "trafficking," attempted murder allegedly carries a maximum sentence of 30 years.

Before a felony court judge mechanically fills out the designated slots on the sentencing guideline sheets, the trial judge must consider certain circumstantial facts surrounding the defendant's offense and background. Included among these are the facts that Neal had no additional offenses at the time of his hypothetical attempted murder conviction, that he has no prior record, that he was not drunk during the crime's commission, and that he was not on restrictions at the time of the offense nor were there any physical injuries to the victim. Based on the absence of these factors, the only slot on the sentencing guideline sheet under which the trial judge could calculate points against Neal would be in the slot designated for the crime itself.

Because the judge is forced to sentence a defendant according to this sentencing guideline calculation alone, Neal's punishment for "attempted murder," assuming the trial judge adheres strictly to the dictates of the sentencing guidelines, would be ten years.

If, hypothetically, on the same day Neal had been charged and convicted of the crime of rape (or sexual battery in Florida), he would as in the other case have been convicted of a first degree felony. Yet instead of a possible 30 year sentence by the trial judge for rape, the actual sentence would be calculated mechanically according to the "plugged in" formula on the sentencing guideline sheet for rape. The resultant 216 points correspond to the sentencing cell on the back side of the sheet which renders a sentence of only four years.

Similarly, if Bill Neal hypothetically had chosen to have commit armed robbery on May 15, 1990, this crime is also a first degree felony in the state of Florida. In his sentencing phase, Neal would have been ordered by the trial judge to serve not thirty years but three years in the state penitentiary.

Finally, if, hypothetically, Neal had been charged and sentenced under the sentencing guidelines for "possessing 400 grams of cocaine with the intent to distribute it," this first degree felony would mean a four year term in the state penitentiary.

From the above, it becomes clear that whenever trial judges are mandated to impose punitive sentences in accordance with the state's sentencing guidelines procedures, the judges do not have much power either to be particularly lenient or to impose the legislative mandatory maximum sentence (30 years) on first time offenders.

Because Neal has not been charged with any of the first degree felonies examined above, his cause is not benefitted by the nature of his crime nor by his good character, nor by his clean record being mechanically filtered into the various slots in one of the eleven recognized Florida sentencing guidelines. Instead, Neal could be convicted of another kind of first degree felony called "trafficking in excess of 400 grams of cocaine." As a result, a whole new set of rules will determine which sentencing procedures will be used by Neal's future trial judge. The name of the sentencing procedure to be used on Neal is called "mandatory minimum sentencing." These mandatory minimum Florida statutes require that the trial judge's determination of the actual sentence be based on another set of sentencing procedures which are "outside" the normal sentencing guidelines.

Neal's Double Jeopardy—Calculating The "Time Sentenced" At Trial Under Mandatory Minimum Sentences

The sentencing procedure used for those convicted of "trafficking in cocaine" in Florida and other states involves a structure which is considered "outside" the normal calculations and procedures of traditional sentencing guidelines. In determining the sentence the trial judge should impose on anyone who hypothetically is convicted for trafficking in over 400 grams of cocaine, the trial judge must refer only to a set of "mandatory minimum sentencing" procedures.

If in the future Neal is convicted of "trafficking," the trial judge must impose on Neal a sentence calculated according to the mandatory minimum statute— a 15 year prison term for his conviction on this first degree felony.

Yet this result is a systematic sentencing disparity (See Table 1 *infra*) which constitutes a double jeopardy for Neal. His triple jeopardy comes after he is imprisoned.

In the case of the strict sentencing procedures which must be administered to those convicted on "trafficking" offenses, a trial judge's sense of powerlessness and frustration must reach a zenith when a harsher sentence must be imposed on a defendant than the judge so desires. For example, a judge might believe that this particular defendant is only marginally culpable of the crime; or the judge may believe the defendant has been wrongfully convicted by the jury. Yet regardless of the judge's personal doubts, a rigid set of statutory mandatory minimum sentencing rules forces the judge to impose this comparatively harsh sentence.

It appears that the whole purpose of mandatory minimum sentences structures is to ensure that trial judges have practically no discretion when determining the amount of punishment they will impose when sentencing a defendant convicted of a crime like trafficking. (The crimes of assaulting a police officer and selling drugs close to a school are examples of other crimes which carry mandatory minimum sentencing procedures. Habitual criminal enhancement statutes also follow the same sentencing procedures.) Thus, mandatory minimum statutes are written by legislatures in a way that makes the exercise of judicial leniency hardly possible even if it is deserved in a particular case.

The overall result of mandatory minimum sentencing structures seems to be a vulnerable one. It forfeits judicial discretion. Even if the sentence length goes directly against his or her own sense of justice, the judge has no other choice but to hammer the convicted defendant with an inflexibly stiff mandatory minimum sentence. If such is the case, then sentencing disparity occurs.

Calculating "Time Served" In Prison Under Sentencing Guidelines

As demonstrated above, hypothetically Bill Neal would have been sentenced by the trial judge, using sentencing guidelines, for a ten-year prison term for his hypothetical attempted murder conviction, for four years for his hypothetical rape conviction, for three years for a hypothetical armed robbery conviction, and for four years under the same guidelines for being convicted hypothetically of possessing cocaine with the intent to distribute it. Yet these sentences are not accurate reflections of the actual time Neal would serve in prison. The hypothetical time Neal would actually serve in prison would be significantly less than the amount of time which the trial judge would have imposed on him in a courtroom.

Like most other states, massive prison overcrowding in Florida has caused its legislature to pass five different and separate gain time provisions.[8] These gain time statutory provisions are what control the Department of Correction's decisions concerning when and under what circumstances the Department must release particular prisoners. This release time always (except in the case of severe misconduct by the prisoner) is significantly less than the time the prisoner is ordered to serve by the trial judge. Likewise, prison overcrowding has required Florida's Governor, from time to time, to order the Department of Corrections to give a large number of prisoners "early releases." This means that designated prisoners are often released many years before their credited gain time would have allowed. The Governor's early release programs are administered and referred to in the statutes as "provisional credits" to inmates. Often provisional credits target non-violent offenders.

A recent investigation performed by Florida's Department of Corrections has revealed that due to both the statutory gain time provisions and to the Governor's early release programs (provisional credits), the actual time served by inmates in Florida prisons is approximately 30 percent of the actual time they were sentenced to in prison by the trial judge.[9]

For Bill Neal this means another injustice because he is a hypothetical victim of a second sentencing disparity. If Neal had been sentenced by the trial judge for a term of ten years for attempted murder, he probably would have been released from prison after serving only three years of his sentence (30%) due to gain time and provisional credits. Likewise, although his hypothetical four-year term for rape or sexual battery conviction would have been reduced, due to credit for gain time (30%), to 14 and 1/2 months. Similarly, Neal's hypothetical three year sentence for armed robbery would have been reduced to only 10 months and 3 weeks. Finally, Neal's possible sentence if convicted of possession of cocaine with the intent to distribute it would likewise be radically reduced; if convicted of this drug dealer crime, the 4 year sentence he would receive at trial would be reduced to 14 and 1/2 months (30%). Yet the actual time Neal would serve for a "trafficking" conviction would be much greater than for these four other modified sentences.

Neal's Triple Jeopardy—Sentencing Disparity As Rendered By Calculating The Different Times Served Under The Sentencing Guidelines Versus Mandatory Minimum Sentencing Structures

When the Florida legislature passed its series of mandatory minimum sentences and attached them to the crime of "trafficking" in certain amounts of prohibited drugs, they dramatically affected two punitive outcomes. The change increased the length of sentence to be imposed by the judge as well as the actual amount of time the defendant is required to serve in prison.

Neal's hypothetical double jeopardy for a conviction for trafficking in excess of 400 grams of cocaine is due to the mandatory minimum sentencing structure which imposes a flat 15 years in prison. An analysis of how much of that 15 years Neal would be forced to serve in prison reveals Neal's triple jeopardy. This analysis also reveals a second significant sentencing disparity in Neal's case.

During the 1980s, state legislatures passed other provisions to fight the war on drugs. These govern the calculation of the amount of gain time which can be credited to those prisoners who are serving terms in prison imposed under mandatory minimum sentencing procedures.[10] Gain time and provisional credits afforded to other prisoners are not fully awarded to those who are serving mandatory minimum sentences. The practical consequences of this statutory restriction is that those convicted for trafficking in cocaine have far less gain time provisions available to them than have those prisoners sentenced under the ordinary sentencing guidelines.

An analysis of the release time of Florida prisoners serving mandatory minimum sentences reveals these prisoners usually are required to serve at least 60 percent of the sentence imposed on them by the trial judges (instead of serving 30% like those sentenced under the sentencing guidelines).[10]

These statutory changes, affecting the calculation of the release date only of those serving mandatory minimum sentences, represent an even greater instance of institutionalized sentencing disparity than the disparities manifest when a mandatory minimum sentence is imposed. In Neal's case, if he were convicted of "trafficking," he would probably have to serve at least 9 years (60%) of the 15 year sentence in prison regardless of his good behavior. This represents double and triple jeopardy in Neal's particular case.

Therefore, in addition to the demonstrated consequence that the new "war on drugs" statutes increase the likelihood of wrongful convictions, these new laws also produce possibly two other undesirable consequences: two major sentencing disparities. Significant examples of these two types of sentencing disparities are summarized in Table 1 below.

Clearly these significant sentencing variations represent classical sentencing disparities. Compounding the apparent injustice of this double sentencing disparity is the possibility at the outset of a wrongful conviction on a streamlined drug dealers statute.

William Bennett: USA's Drug Czar

> **"It's true under these new tough drug laws that some innocent defendants slip through the cracks."**

The intent of this study has been to demonstrate that the reduction of proof necessary for conviction in trafficking charges and the two brutal sentencing disparities that follow such a conviction have created a situation wherein most other citizens are now at a greater risk. There is a greater likelihood that they will be subjected to a trial and possibly receive a wrongful conviction. Then they will be sentenced to comparatively long punishments and serve comparatively lengthy prison terms for allegedly "trafficking in drugs" when in fact they are blameworthy of very little or of nothing at all.

Table 1
Sentencing Guidelines and Sentencing Disparities

Offense	Severity	Maximum Possible	Sentence imposed at Trial Under Sentencing Guidelines	Time Actually Served in Prison Due to Provisional Credits and 5 Gain Time Provisions
Attempted Murder	1st Degree Felony	30 Years	10 Years	(With 5 Gain Time Povisions) 3 Years
Rape (Sexual Battery)	1st Degree Felony	30 Years	4 Years	(With 5 Gain Time Provisions) 14 1/2 months
Armed Robbery	1st egree Felony	30 Years	3 Years	(With 5 Gain Time Provisions) 10 Months
Possession > 400 Grams of Cocaine With Intent to Distribute	1st Degree Feleony	30 Years	4 Years	(With 5 Gain Time Provisions) 14 1/2 months
Trafficking in Excess of 400 grams of Cocaine	1st Degree Felony	30 Years	(Mandatory Minimum Sententce) 15 Years	(With the Elimination of Some of the Gain Time Provisions and Provisionsl Credits) 9 Years

Yet when the former federal drug czar of the United States, William Bennett, was interviewed by NBC Nightly News and was made aware of this problem by being presented with real life case studies of those who first were wrongfully convicted of "trafficking" and then, to compound the initial error, were being forced to serve sentences under a mandatory minimum sentencing structure similar to that Bill Neal may face, his response was unsettling.

Mr. Bennett flippantly responded by stating that although these cases clearly were unjust, he believes that nothing should be done about them. His rationale: "When you are fighting a war, some people will slip through the cracks,"[11] Bennett then urged strict judicial conformity both to the standard of evidence of proof for convictions on "trafficking" laws and to the requirements that trial judges strictly adhere to the legislative sanctions of the mandatory minimum sentences. Hence, Bennett insisted the triple jeopardy of this situation should stay in place.

Proposed Policy Revisions To Fighting The War On Drugs: Allowing For Judicial Discretion To Both Reverse Wrongful Convictions And To Limit Sentencing Disparities.

Although probably not anticipated in their attempts to fight the war on drugs during the 1980s, some unintended victims have been created by both federal and state legislatures. By reducing the amount of proof necessary to convict defendants suspected to be in possession of a large amount of drugs, which traditionally had led to the charge of "possession of cocaine with the intent to distribute," the new statutory crime of "trafficking" has reduced significantly the traditional quantum of proof necessary to convict defendants charged with transactions involving drug dealing. Under this new reduced standard of proof, in order for the state to prove a defendant guilty of "trafficking," it need only prove that the defendant was in "constructive possession" of a certain amount of a controlled substance. Clearly many American citizens are unwittingly or technically negligent in their constructive possessions of contraband; should such citizens be considered so morally blameworthy as to deserve these drastic sentences and prison terms? Are they deserving of the exact same punishment which the government imposes on legitimate drug dealers for the crime of trafficking? As could be the case with Bill Neal, these new drug statutes have escalated the likelihood of increasing the number of wrongful convictions in American courtrooms. This risk is especially present for certain groups of ordinary citizens whose only error is that they happened to be in the wrong place at the wrong time with the wrong people. Potentially, a significant number of other law-abiding American citizens could find themselves in Bill Neal's situation and, like him, have to face the undeserved misfortune of triple jeopardy.

Convicting marginally culpable or innocent persons and then sentencing them to serious and woefully excessive punishments cannot be rationalized by comfortably regarding them as necessary exceptions who "slip through the cracks when you are fighting a war." Such cases always have been unacceptable in American jurisprudence.[12]

New policy revisions are needed in both state and federal criminal codes. These policy revisions should be enacted as amendments which would empower trial judges to practice personal discretion when determining whether or not to impose the full mandatory minimum sentences for those convicted of "trafficking." This discretion is especially important when the facts which support the conviction for trafficking are no greater or more inflammatory than facts which also would support a conviction of simple "constructive possession" of the contraband.[13]

Specifically, these amendments should allow the trial judge the discretionary power (1) to go outside the dictates of mandatory minimum sentencing structures and traditional sentencing guidelines and (2) to proclaim that the defendant will have the full benefit of gain time and provisional credits while serving his or her sentence; (3) this power should be reserved only for those cases wherein the judge concludes that the most just punishment would be one less severe than that allowed by the mandatory minimum sentencing structures attached to "trafficking." This renewed power of judicial discretion is especially needed for those citizens who technically are convicted of "trafficking" but whose moral blameworthiness is merely that of being (possibly unwittingly) in constructive possession of the contraband. (4) This amendment also should provide a safeguard for the prosecution. In those cases when a trial judges chooses to impose an unwarrantedly lenient sentence for a "trafficking" conviction, a procedure should be enacted which empowers the prosecution to appeal what the government perceives to be too lenient a sentence. This portion of the new policy amendments would act as a "check" by the appellate courts to ensure that overly lenient sentences imposed by the trial judge could be reversed if such a sentence violates the appellate courts' sense of justice.

Our Constitutional protection of due process has always been interpreted as a guarantee that no one, especially innocent persons, shall "slip through the cracks" without giving the criminal justice system a chance to reverse itself whenever it recognizes such an injustice. Our Constitutional protection of due process also demands that every statutory crime be drafted in a special way so as to ensure that a built-in safety net is always an integrated component of criminal procedure. At present, such protections do not exist in the arrest, prosecution, conviction, sentencing, and incarceration of those innocent or marginally culpable defendants charged with a violation of the drug "trafficking" statutes. Policy revisions must be made immediately to create fairness in the applications of these new drug laws, to ensure they will be not only powerful but just and humane as well.

Notes

1 Huff, Rattner, and Sagarin's seventeen reasons for wrongful convictions in the American criminal justice system can be summarized as follows: 1) eyewitness error; 2) community pressure for a conviction; 3) false accusations; 4) knowledge of an accused's criminal record; 6) judicial errors; 7) judicial bias; 8) judicial neglect of duty; 9) errors made by criminologists; 10) errors made by medical examiners; 11) errors made by forensic science experts; 12) errors in criminal record keeping; 13) errors in computerized informational systems; 14) voluntary false confessions; 15) deliberate false confessions; 16) the mental incompetency of the accused; and 17) incompetent defense counsel (pp. 324-333).

2 As of the date of this paper, Neal has yet to be tried for the crime. Bill Neal has given this author full permission to disclose all of the facts contained in this paper.

3 The author's knowledge of the facts of Neal's case derives from the author's initial representation of Bill Neal as his criminal defense attorney in the case. As demonstrated in the text, Neal subsequently was unable to accumulate the money necessary to retain private counsel due to the various civil measures taken against him.

4 All fifty state criminal codes were examined. Every state has enacted new kinds of drug dealer statutes (many called "trafficking," others not) during the 1980s. A significant majority of these statutes have either: 1)

reduced the amount of proof necessary to convict; 2) attached an enhancement statute as the flat time punishment for the crime; or 3) require the department of corrections to increase the time the defendant serves in prison - the triple jeopardy which Neal faces. Hence, these three changes are sufficiently wide spread and significantly similar in their applications to the processing of Florida's trafficking cases to allow this writer to conclude that the polemics addressed in this case study are applicable nationally.

5 Justice had a way of turning her head toward Bill Neal after all. In spite of the likelihood of a wrong conviction, Neal acting as his own counsel persisted in making discovery motions of the prosecution. The prosecution continued to withhold discovery. When the speedy trial time period was almost completely up, Neal still had not received the search warrant used to search Garrett's house. He asked for a continuance and asked the judge to attribute it to the prosecution. The judge agreed. This continuance would put Neal over the speedy trial limit. Thus, he would have had his case dismissed. However, the day before the limit manifested itself, the state prosecutors "nolle prossed," or dropped the charges without any reason. Subsequently, they sent the case to the federal government for processing. Two years have passed since the federal government received the case. Since the federal government investigates by grand jury, and the grand jury is secret, it is impossible to determine the present status of Neal's case.

6 Florida Department of Law Enforcement, "Drug Abuse in Florida," A Report prepared for the Governor and Cabinet of the State of Florida, February 17, 1987.

7 This statement was written by an unnamed state drug enforcement agent. The quotation was written by the agent after interviewing Garrett after he was in jail for only 5 days. At the time it seemed that Garrett had no reason to lie. Subsequently, however, Garrett has made a plea bargain with the State. Part of the bargain is to testify against Neal. Hence what his eventual testimony against Neal will be remains uncertain.

8 The following types of Gain Time are currently in effect in the Florida Department of Corrections:

> 1. *Basic Gain Time* - Florida Statute 944.27 (Repealed 1978), Florida Statute 944.273
>
> Basic gain time is not discretionary and is awarded at a fixed rate based on the term of the sentence, and the date of offense. Pursuant to the U.S. Supreme Court Decision in *Weaver v. Graham*, inmates serving sentences for offenses committed prior to 7-1-78, are awarded basic gain time at the rate of 5 days per month for the first and second years of the sentence imposed, 10 days per month for the third and fourth years of the sentence, and 15 days per month for the fifth and all succeeding years of the sentence. Inmates serving sentences for offenses committed on or after 7-1-78 are awarded basic gain time at the rate of 10 days per month for each month of each sentence imposed on them. Basic gain time is awarded as a means of encouraging satisfactory behavior.

2. *Incentive Gain Time* - Florida Statute 944.275(4)(b)

This gain time is awarded to inmates for above satisfactory work and adjustment. For most inmates, the maximum allowance for a month is 20 days. However, inmates serving sentences for offenses committed between July 1, 1978 through June 14, 1983 are eligible for up to one day of work gain time for each day worked and/or up to 6 days extra gain time per month in accordance with the Florida Supreme Court decision in *Waldrup v. Dugger.*

3. *Meritorious Gain Time* - Florida Statute 944.275(4)(c)

This type of gain time may be awarded to an inmate for an outstanding deed performed. The law allows for a maximum award of 60 days.

4. *Quick Construction/Meritorious Gain Time* - Florida Statute 944.598

This may be awarded for outstanding work performed on a quick construction project. Maximum award is *10 days* per month while the inmate is assigned to the project.

5. *Provisional Credits* - Florida Statute 944.277

Provisional credits were created to provide the Department of Corrections with a method of stabilizing the growth of the inmate population. The awarding of provisional credits allows the early release of certain inmates who are near the end of their sentences. *Inmate Information Manual*, Florida Department of Corrections, 1991.

9 This figure was given to this author by a high ranking administrator in the Florida Department of Corrections on this author's assurance his or her identity would remain confidential.

10 See note number 7.

11 *NBC Nightly News with Connie Chung*, "Interview with Drug Czar William Bennett," July 25, 1990.

12 A traditional principle of American jurisprudence announced by the Supreme Court in several opinions is that we "would rather let 100 guilty defendants go free than punish one innocent one." Also see the quote from Judge Learned Hand in the second section.

13 Three years after I wrote this polemic on the mandatory-minimum sentencing structures for the crimes of drug trafficking as an wasted effort on unjust sentencing disparity, the National Institute of Justice released the results of a two year study of the populations of American prisons. The study discovered that 1/3 of American prison beds were being filled by inmates convicted of trafficking offenses which really were for the most part minor drug possession charges. On February 5, 1994, they declared the current situation misguided and wrong. This is because the prison beds presently are occupied by these drug offenders; instead, they should be occupied by violent offenders. Due to prison overcrowding, violent offenders were receiving massive early releases from prison. The mandatory-minimum statutes, however, prohibited the early releases of the drub offenders. As a

result, according to this NIJ study, the violent offenders returned to their communities and committed additional crimes of violence. Then they received new prison sentences; they were re-released, recidivated again. All the while, the non-violent drug offenders served their strictly directed prison sentence. This situation acted to prohibit the old violent offenders and new ones from taking these drug offender's prison bed. Cauch on D. "Sentencing Study Treads Cautiously". *USA Today*, 7 February, 1994.

Cases Cited

United States v Blake 484 F.2d 50 (8th Cir. 1973)
United States v Brett 872 F.2d 1365 (8th Cir. 1989)
United States v Caballero 712 F.2d 126 (5th Cir. 1983)
United States v Disla 805 F.2d 1340 (9th Cir. 1986)
United States v James 764 F.2d 885 (D.C. Cir. 1985)
United States v La Guardia 774 F.2d 13417 (8th Cir. 1985)
United States v Martinez 588 F.2d 495 (5th Cir. 1979)
United States v Massey 687 F.2d 1348 (10th Cir. 1982)
United States v Moses 360 F.Supp. 301 (W.D.Ta. 1973)
United States v Ramirez-Rodriguez 552 F.2d 883 (9th Cir. 1977)
United States v Staten 581 F.2d 878 (D.C. Cir. 1978)
United States v Tramunti 513 F.2d 1087 (2d Cir. 1975)

Bibliography

Bedau, H.A.
1967 The Death Penalty In America. Garden City, NY: Anchor.

Blott, E.D.
1963 The Vindicators. New York: Doubleday.

Borchard, E.M.
1932 Convicting The Innocent: 65 Actual Airs Of Criminal Justice. Garden City, NY: Doubleday.

Brandon, R. and C. Davies
1973 Wrongful Imprisonment: Mistaken Convictions And Their Consequences. London: Allen & Unwin.

Chin, R and N. Grants
1989 Convicted of murdering one of his children, James Richardson hopes the truth will set him free. People, 6 March: 25-29.

Frank, J. and B. Frank
1957 Not Guilty. New York: Doubleday.

Gardner, E.S.
1952 Court Of Last Resort. New York: William Slone.

Huff, C., A. Rattner and E. Sagarin
1986 Guilty until proven innocent: Wrongful conviction and public policy. Crime And Delinquency 32:4 October: 518-544.

Loftus, E.F.
1979 Eyewitness Testimony. Cambridge, MA: Harvard Press.

MacMerma, D.E.J.
1969 Convicting the innocent. Crime and Delinquency 15:57-61.

Radin, E.D.
1964 The Innocents. New York: William Morrow.

Silverman, C.E.
1978 Criminal Violence, CriminalJustice. NewYork: Random House.

Recent Research on the Crack/Cocaine/Crime Connection

By James A. Inciardi, Duane C. McBride, H. Virginia McCoy and Dale D. Chitwood

Abstract

Research on the drugs/crime connection focuses on possible correlations between the two phenomena, and the nature and direction of the causality in the relationship. Many previous studies have documented that there is an economic component to the drugs/crime connection (users steal to obtain drugs), that illegal drug users come from backgrounds of illegal activity that predate drug use, and that drug use both sustains and intensifies criminal behavior. This paper reviews these issues, and presents recently collected drugs/crime data on a population of 699 criminally-involved crack and other cocaine users in Miami, Florida. In their last 90 days on the street, these users reportedly committed 1.76 million criminal acts. Over 90 % of the crimes were individual retail drug sales. The data reflect little relationship between crime and arrest. However, the primary statistical relationship between crime and crack use involves the retail sale and distribution of cocaine and crack by drug user/dealers who are attempting to support their drug habits. *(Studies on Crime and Crime Prevention Vol. 3 1994. National Council for Crime Prevention).*

Keywords: drugs-crime connection, early research, recent research, crack-addicts, criminal activity, generalizability.

BACKGROUND

The relationships between drug use and crime have occupied the attention of researchers and policy makers in the United States for almost a century. Interest has focused on a short series of questions. Is crime the result of circumstances brought about by the addiction to narcotics or other drugs? Or conversely, is addiction *per se* a deviant tendency characteristic of individuals already prone to offense behavior? Moreover, and assuming that criminality may indeed be a pre-addiction phenomenon, does the onset of chronic drug use bring about a change in the nature, intensity, and frequency of criminal acts? Does criminal involvement tend to increase or decrease subsequent to addiction? There have been related questions. What kinds of criminal offenses do addicts engage in? Do they tend toward violent acts of aggression? Are their crimes strictly profitoriented, geared toward theft, prostitution, and drug sales? Or do they include all of the above?

* This research was supported by HHS Grant "Crack Abuse Patterns and Crime Linkages," from the National Institute on Drug Abuse.

EARLY DRUGS/CRIME RESEARCH

As early as the 1920s, researchers were conducting studies seeking answers to these and related questions. Among the first were Edouard Sandoz (1922) of the Municipal Court of Boston and Lawrence Kolb (1925) of the United States Public Health Service. They examined the backgrounds of hundreds of heroin users, focusing on the drugs-crime relationship. Their conclusions were logical, but generally ignored. Basically, what they found within criminal justice and treatment populations were several different types of cases. Some drug users were habitual criminals, and probably always had been; others were simply violators of the newly passed drug laws, having been arrested for no more than the illegal possession of narcotics. Moreover, with both types a record of violent crimes was absent.

The analyses provided by Sandoz and Kolb offered a conceptual framework for several different points of view:

- Addicts ought to be the object of vigorous law-enforcement activity since the majority are members of a criminal element and drug addiction is simply one of the later phases of their deviant careers.
- Addicts are essentially law-abiding citizens who are forced to steal in order to support their drug habits.
- Addicts are predisposed to serious criminal transgressions and prey upon legitimate society because of the effects of drug use.
- Addicts are not necessarily criminals, but are forced to associate with an underworld element that tends to maintain control over the distribution of illicit drugs (Inciardi, 1974).

The notion that addicts ought to be the objects of vigorous police activity, a posture that might be called the *criminal model of drug abuse* was actively and relentlessly pursued by the United States Bureau of Narcotics (now known as the Drug Enforcement Administration, or DEA) and other law enforcement groups. Their argument was fixed on the notion of "criminality", for on the basis of their own observations the vast majority of narcotics users encountered were members of criminal groups. To support this view, the Bureau of Narcotics pointed to several studies which demonstrated that most addicts were already criminals before they began using heroin and other illegal drugs (U. S. Treasury Dept., 1940). Addicts, the Bureau emphasized, represented a destructive force confronting the people of America. Whatever the sources of their addiction might have been, they were members of a highly subversive and antisocial group. For the Bureau, this position did indeed have some basis in reality. Having been charged with the enforcement of laws that prohibited the possession, sale and distribution of narcotics, what Bureau agents were confronted with were *criminal* addicts, often under the most dangerous of circumstances. It was not uncommon for agents to be wounded or even killed in arrest situations, and analyses of the careers of many addicts demonstrated that their criminal records were lengthy. Moreover, there was the matter of "professional" underworld involvement with narcotics, a point that Bureau of Narcotics Commissioner Harry J. Anslinger commented on in 1951:

> It is well established that a larger proportion of the pickpocket artists, the shoplifters, the professional gamblers and card sharks, the confidence men operating fake horse race or fake stock sale schemes, the "short con" men such as the "shortchange artists" or the coin matchers, are addicted to the use of narcotic drugs (Anslinger, 1951).

Anslinger was referring to the world of *professional thieves*, and studies have demonstrated that predators of this kind were involved not only in the use of narcotics but in trafficking as well (Inciardi & Russe,

1977). However, Anslinger failed to consider that all heroin users were not alike. Studies of drug-using populations of his time have demonstrated the existence of numerous and alternative patterns of narcotic addiction. The professional thieves about which Anslinger spoke were a group of highly skilled yet essentially nonviolent criminals who made a regular business of stealing. Crime was their occupation and means of livelihood, and as such, they devoted their entire time and energy to stealing. They operated with proficiency; they had a body of skills and knowledge that was utilized in the execution and planning of their work; and they were graduates of an informal developmental process that included the acquisition of specialized skills, knowledge, attitudes, and experience. Finally, in identifying themselves with the world of crime, professional thieves were members of an exclusive fraternity that extended friendship, understanding, sympathy, security, safety, recognition, and respect (Sutherland, 1937; Inciardi, 1975). Their pattern of addiction revolved around the use of heroin or morphine by needle, or the smoking of opium. The spree use of drugs was also common, generally to reduce the boredom associated with incarceration, or as part of pleasure-seeking activities.

By contrast, during the years between 1900 and 1960, there was a pattern of addiction characteristic of a core of *middle-aged white Americans* from the southern regions of the United States. Identified through patient records at federal drug-treatment facilities, they were usually addicted to morphine or paregoric, and their drugs had been obtained from physicians through legal or quasi-legal means. As "patients" under treatment for some illness, these addicts were not members of any deviant subcultures and did not have contacts with other addicts (Ball, 1965; O'Donnell, 1967).

There were also groups of *hidden addicts* who, because of sufficient income and/or access to legitimate sources of drugs, had no need to make contacts with visibly criminal cultures to obtain drugs. Among these were musicians, physicians and members of other segments of the health professions (Winick, 1961a, 1961b; Ball & Chambers, 1970).

Finally, there was the stereotyped *heroin street addict* – the narcotics user of the American ghetto of whom the massmedia spoke. Heroin street addicts were typically from the socially and economically deprived segments of the urban population. They began their careers with drug experimentation as adolescents for the sake of excitement or thrills, to conform with peer-group activities and expectations, and/or to strike back at the authority structures which they opposed. The use of alcohol, marijuana, codeine or pills generally initiated them into substance abuse, and later drug intake focused primarily on heroin and cocaine. Their status of addiction was often said to have emerged as a result of an "addiction-prone personality," and they supported their habits through illegal means (see Gould et al., 1974; Hanson et al., 1985; Faupel, 1991; Stephens, 1991). Also among this group were *poly-drug users* – those who had multiple addictions and concurrently abused a variety of drugs.

Most law-enforcement agencies focused their attention and their commentaries on those who manifested the pattern of heroin street addiction. They argued that addiction was a criminal tendency, and that addicts should be pursued with the full force of the law enforcement community (Anslinger, 1951; Morgan, 1966).

The police were responding in their commentaries to the clinicians and social scientists of the 1930s who, up to the early 1960s, had put forth the notion of what might be called a "disease" or *medical model of addiction,* as opposed to the *criminal* view advocated by law enforcement. The medical model, which physicians first proposed in the late nineteenth century (see Terry & Pellens, 1928), held that addiction was a chronic and relapsing disease. The addict, it was argued, should be dealt with as any patient suffering from some physiological or medical disorder. At the same time, numerous proponents of the view sought to mitigate addict criminality by putting forth the "enslavement theory of addiction." The idea here was that the monopolistic controls over the heroin black market forced "sick" and otherwise law-abiding drug users into lives of crime to support their habits.

RECENT DRUGS/CRIME RESEARCH

In the mid-1970s, two U.S. federal research agencies – the National Institute on Drug Abuse (NIDA) and the National Institute of Justice (NIJ) – began funding studies in many parts of the nation for the purposes of developing a useful data base on the drugs-crime connection and addressing many of the unanswered questions. The research has been quite enlightening. On the basis of extensive follow-up studies of addict careers in Baltimore, Maryland, for example, John C. Ball and David N. Nurco found that there were high rates of criminality among heroin users during those periods when they were addicted, and markedly lower rates during times of non-addiction (Ball et al., 1981; Ball, Shaffer & Nurco, 1983). This finding was based on the concept of the "crime-days per year at risk." The "crime-day" was defined as a 24-hour period during which an individual committed one or more criminal offenses. Thus, "crime-days per year at risk" was a rate of crime commission that could vary anywhere from 0 to 365. Over the addiction careers of the Baltimore addicts studied, the average crime-days per year at risk was 230, suggesting that their rates of criminality were not only persistent on a day-to-day basis, but also tended to continue over an extended number of years and periods of addiction.

In a series of New York studies, the investigators operated from a store front. During their many projects, they conducted interviews with hundreds of criminally active drug users recruited from the streets of East and Central Harlem sections of Manhattan. The findings on drug-related criminality tended to confirm what was being learned elsewhere and provided insights as to how addicts functioned on the streets – how they purchased, sold, and used drugs; the roles that drugs played in their lives; and how the street-level drug business weaves structures (Johnson et al., 1985).

Studies conducted in Miami demonstrated that the amount of crime drug users committed was far greater than anyone had previously imagined, that drug-related crime could at times be exceedingly violent, and that the criminality of street drug users was far beyond the control of law enforcement (Inciardi, 1979; Inciardi & Pottieger, 1986; Pettiway, 1987). Research conducted elsewhere, furthermore, arrived at similar conclusions (Chaiken & Johnson, 1988; Wish et al., 1981; Speckart & Anglin, 1986; Anglin & Hser, 1987). And what the majority of the research findings seemed to be saying was that although the use of heroin and other drugs did not necessarily initiate criminal careers, it tended to intensify and perpetuate them. That is, street drugs were freezing users into patterns of criminality that are more acute, dynamic, unremitting, and enduring than those of other offenders.

Yet all of this research had been conducted, or at least initiated, before the arrival of *crack*-cocaine in America's inner cities. What was known about the relationship between drug use and crime related primarily to narcotics users, *not crack and other cocaine users*. Yet by contrast, since crack made its appearance on the streets of urban America during the mid-1980s, media attention has focused on how the high addiction liability of the drug instigates users to commit crimes to support their habits, and how rivalries in crack distribution networks have turned some inner city communities into urban "dead zones," where homicide rates are so high that police have written them off as anarchistic badlands.

CRACK-COCAINE AND CRIME

Crack is a variety of cocaine base, produced by "cooking" cocaine hydrochloride and baking soda in boiling water or a microwave oven. It has been called the "fast-food" variety of cocaine, and is popular in the United States because it is cheap, easy to conceal, it vaporizes with practically no odor, and the gratification is swift: a short-lived (up to five minutes) but nevertheless intense, almost sexual euphoria. Smoking cocaine as opposed to snorting it results in more immediate and direct absorption of the drug, producing a quicker and more compelling "high," greatly increasing the dependency potential. Moreover, there is increased risk of acute toxic reactions, including brain seizure, cardiac irregularities, respiratory paralysis, paranoid psychosis and pulmonary dysfunction (Wallace, 1991; Inciardi, 1987; Inciardi, 1992).

Users typically smoke for as long as they have crack or the means to purchase it – money, personal belongings, sexual services, stolen goods, or other drugs. It is rare that smokers have but a single "hit" of crack. More likely they spend $50 to $500 during what they call a "mission" – a three or four day binge, smoking almost constantly, 3 to 50 rocks per day. During these cycles, crack users rarely eat or sleep. And once crack is tried, for many users it is not long before it becomes a daily habit. The tendency to "binge" on crack for days at a time, neglecting food, sleep and basic hygiene, severely compromises physical health. Consequently, crack users appear emaciated most of the time. They lose interest in their physical appearance. Many have scabs on their faces, arms, and legs – the result of burns, and picking at the skin (to remove bugs and other insects believed to be crawling *under* the skin). Crack users tend to have burned facial hair from carelessly lighting their smoking paraphernalia; they have burned lips and tongues from the hot stems of their pipes; and many seem to cough constantly.

Much of the existing literature that discusses crack and crime has focused on the association between gang activity, especially violence, and crack use and sale. A major theme reported in both the professional and popular literature is one portraying young crack dealers as ruthless and brutal entrepreneurs, highly disciplined and coldly efficient in their business activities. Both Martinez (1992) and Skolnick et al. (1988), for example, concluded that gangs in California are heavily involved in the upper levels of crack distribution. A similar conclusion can be found in the "larger than life" cover story devoted to crack in the 19 August 1991 issue of *U. S. News & World Report* (Witkin, 1991).

The empirical evidence, however, suggests otherwise. Klein, Maxon and Cunningham (1988, 1991) found that gang participation in "rock" cocaine (crack) trafficking, although frequent, was no greater than non-gang participation. Moreover, their studies concluded that while growth in crack sales in Los Angeles was accompanied by major increases in street gang activity, most of the increases were in low-volume street sales and *not* at the higher levels of organized crack distribution. In New York, Fagan and Chin (1989) found that few adolescents participated in crack selling, and the occasional teenage participants worked in organizations that bore little resemblance to the youth gangs of Los

Angeles, Chicago, or other U. S. cities with long-standing gang activity (also see Belenko & Fagan, 1987; Fagan, 1990). This conclusion was supported by an ethnographic study in Detroit (Mieczkowski, 1990, 1992). Furthermore, a recent Miami-based street study of 611 serious delinquents heavily involved in drug use and crime found that few were involved in anything beyond street-level crack sales (Inciardi, Horowitz & Pottieger, 1993). In fact, only 11 (1.8) % of these hard-core adolescent offenders were gang members, and one of the conclusions of the study was:

> ... involvement in crack distribution does not necessarily mean *youth gang* involvement in crack distribution. The exploits of the "Crips," "Bloods," and other violent street gangs have become legend in Los Angeles and other parts of the United States, but gangs do not appear to be major participants in *every* active inner-city crack market (Inciardi, Horowitz & Pottieger, 1993:114).

Additional studies of the criminality of crack users are actually quite few in number, and focus almost exclusively on crack-related violence in New York City (Goldstein et al., 1989), or the prostitution associated with the bartering of sex-for-crack or for money to purchase crack (Ratner, 1993; Forney, Inciardi, & Lockwood, 1992; Bowser, 1989; Chaisson et al., 1991; Fullilove & Fullilove, 1989; Fullilove et al., 1990; Inciardi, 1989; Inciardi, 1991). By contrast, empirical studies of the full range of criminal activities engaged in by crack and other cocaine users are absent from the literature.

Within this context, and in an effort to generate a preliminary data base descriptive of the criminal activities associated with the use of crack and other forms of cocaine, this paper examines aspects of the drug-taking and drug-seeking careers of 699 cocaine and crack users.

METHODS AND SAMPLE

Patterns of cocaine initiation and use, and related criminality were among the interests of a study conducted between April 1988 and March 1990 in the Miami (Dade County), Florida, metropolitan area. A total of 699 cocaine users were interviewed, 349 sampled from residential drug treatment programs and 350 drawn from the street. Apart from demographic subsample criteria, discussed below, the only eligibility criterion was use of any form of cocaine – *crack*-cocaine, *powder*-cocaine, and *coca paste*[1] – during "the last 90 days on the street." For

1. For those unfamiliar with *coca paste,* also known as "basuco," "susuko," "pasta basica de cocaina" (in Spanishspeaking Latin America), "pasta de coca" (in Brazil), or just simply "pasta," it is an intermediate product in the transformation of coca leaves into cocaine. Coca paste is typically smoked straight, or in cigarettes mixed with tobacco or marijuana. The practice became popular in the coca growing regions of South America beginning in the early 1970s (Jeri, 1984). The drug was readily available, inexpensive, had a high cocaine content, and was absorbed rapidly when smoked. As the phenomenon was studied, it was quickly realized that the smoking of paste was likely far more dangerous than any other form of cocaine use. In addition to cocaine, coca paste contains traces of all the chemicals used to initially process the coca leaves – kerosene, sulfuric acid, methanol, benzoic acid, and the oxidized products of these solvents, plus any number of other alkaloids that are present in the coca leaf (Almeida, 1978). One analysis undertaken in Colombia in 1986 found, in addition to all of these chemicals, traces of various talcs, brick dust, ether, and leaded gasoline acid (Bogota *El Tiempo,* June 19, 1986, p. 2D).

the street sample, this was the 90 days prior to interview. For the treatment sample, it was the most recent continuous 90 days on the street prior to termination of a typical usage pattern because of entry into treatment (this includes their treatment event such as arrest or dosage reduction in anticipation of treatment entry). The 90-day period had to be within two years prior to interview. The total time period embraced by all respondents' "last 90 days on the street" was from November 1986 to December 1989.

The interviewers were highly experienced in talking to drug and crime-involved offenders. Moreover, they were intensively trained in administering the study's interview schedule, establishing rapport, and helping subjects with their problems of recall. Questions about drug use and criminal behavior were asked during an interview lasting from 30 to 60 minutes, and respondents were paid $10 for their time. Legal protection for subjects through assurances of anonymity (no names were collected or recorded) and a Certificate of Confidentiality from the National Institute on Drug Abuse were given. This certificate guarantees that project employees could not be compelled by any court or law enforcement agency in the United States to reveal information sources or questionnaire data. Treatment program clients were assured that nonparticipation in the study would not affect their program status and that their answers would not be seen by counsellors or other program personnel.

Selection of both street and treatment respondents was guided by subsample criteria for gender, age, and ethnicity in order to ensure a demographically diverse sample. In the treatment programs this generally meant returning repeatedly to interview every new client in the hard-to-fill subsamples (whites and Hispanics, and youths of all race/ethnic groups). On the street, it meant pushing the interview process into a variety of neighborhoods to get the required ethnic variety.

Street respondents were located through standard multiple-starting-point "snowball sampling" techniques in neighborhoods with high rates of cocaine use by street interviewers familiar with, and well known in, the target areas. The details of how this kind of street data collection is done are described elsewhere (Inciardi, 1986; Inciardi et al. 1993). Briefly, the peculiar life style, illegal drug-taking and drug-seeking activities, and mobility characteristics of active drug users, prevents any examination of this group through standard survey methodology. As such, samples were obtained through the use of a sociometrically oriented model.

Over the years the authors have developed and maintained extensive contacts within Miami's drug subcultures and drug user networks. These represented "started points" for interviewing. During and after each interview, at a time when the rapport between interviewer and respondent was considered to be at its highest level, each subject was requested to identify other current users with whom he or she was acquainted. These persons, in turn, were located and interviewed, and the process was repeated until the social network surrounding each respondent was exhausted. This method restricted the pool of users interviewed to those who were currently active in the street drug culture. In addition, it eliminated former users as well as those who were only peripheral to the mainstream of the street drug scene. Although this sampling method did not guarantee a totally unbiased sample, the use of several "starting points" within the same locale eliminated the problem of drawing all respondents from only one social network.

FINDINGS

As indicated in Table 1, the majority of the 699 crack and other cocaine users interviewed were males with a median age of 25.1 years. Virtually equal numbers were drawn from street and treatment settings, less than half had completed high school, and there were almost equal proportions of blacks and whites, while 20.2 % were Latinos. It should be noted here although almost half of the Dade County, Florida population is Latino, the fact that only 20.2 % of the sample are Latinos is a reflection of their limited numbers in the drug subcultures and treatment programs. Moreover, Hispanic women were not even sampled for this study because of their virtual invisibility in the Miami drug scene (see Inciardi et al., 1993: 62–63).

Important in Table 1, is the fact that almost three-quarters of the subjects were *primary crack users*. That is, for 71.4 % of the respondents, crack was the most widely used form of cocaine, representing at least 75% of all cocaine use during the last three months on the street. By contrast, 16.6 % preferred inhaling (snorting) *powder*-cocaine, 4.4 % were principally cocaine injectors (IV), and 7.6 % had mixed mechanisms of ingestion.

TABLE 1. *Sample description: 699 cocaine users interviewed in Miami, April 1988 – March 1990*

	Male (N=462)	Female (N=237)	Total (N=699)
Age at interview			
13–17	24.0 %	16.9 %	21.6 %
18–24	29.4 %	24.9 %	27.9 %
25–34	35.5 %	45.1 %	38.8 %
35–49	11.0 %	13.1 %	11.7 %
Mean	24.6	25.9	25.1
Ethnicity			
Black	33.8 %	54.4 %	40.8 %
White	35.7 %	45.6 %	39.1 %
Latino	30.5 %	0.0 %	20.2 %
High school graduate?			
No	55.2 %	55.7 %	55.4 %
Yes	44.8 %	44.3 %	44.6 %
Mean years of education	10.9	11.1	11.0
Sample			
Street	45.9 %	58.2 %	50.1 %
Treatment	54.1 %	41.8 %	49.9 %
Primary cocaine type (75 %+ of total last 3 mos)			
Crack	65.4 %	83.1 %	71.4 %
Snort	21.4 %	7.2 %	16.6 %
IV	3.9 %	5.5 %	4.4 %
Mixed	9.3 %	4.2 %	7.6 %

Drug use patterns

The crack and other cocaine users in this study had long histories of multiple involvement with clear sequential patterns of onset and progression. As indicated in Table 2, for example, virtually all of the respondents had used alcohol, marijuana, cocaine, and pills; almost half had some experience with hallucinogenic drugs and heroin; and almost a quarter (23.9 %) had a history of injecting drugs. Moreover, using *median age* as a measure, their drug using careers began with alcohol at age 11, followed by marijuana at age 14, and then more serious drug use. Their cocaine use had begun at age 16, followed by crack about four years later.

TABLE 2. *Earliest drug use: percentage ever and median age at first use*

	Male (N=462)	Female (N=237)	Total (N=699)
Percentage ever tried			
Alcohol	99.4 %	97.0 %	98.6 %
Marijuana	100.0 %	99.2 %	99.7 %
Hallucinogen/inhalant (any)	54.3 %	30.8 %	46.4 %
Pills (any)	84.2 %	84.4 %	84.3 %
Heroin (any)	48.3 %	48.9 %	48.5 %
IV drug (any)	24.9 %	21.9 %	23.9 %
Cocaine (any)	100.0 %	100.0 %	100.0 %
Snorting cocaine	97.0 %	84.8 %	92.8 %
IV cocaine	20.8 %	20.3 %	20.6 %
Crack	92.4 %	97.5 %	94.1 %
Median age first tried			
Alcohol	11.0	11.0	11.0
Marijuana	13.0	14.0	14.0
Hallucinogen/inhalant (any)	15.0	15.0	15.0
Pills (any)	15.0	15.0	15.0
Heroin (any)	17.0	17.0	17.0
IV drug (any)	18.0	18.0	18.0
Cocaine (any)	16.0	16.0	16.0
Snorting cocaine	16.0	16.0	16.0
IV cocaine	19.0	19.0	19.0
Crack	20.0	21.0	20.0

In terms of *current* drug use (use during the last 90 days on the street), five measures were calculated: "no use" (no use at all during the last 90 days); "infrequent use" (use 6 days or less in the last 90 days); "occasional use" (use at least 7 days but no more than 30 days in the last 90 days); "regular use" (use at least 3 or more times a week but less than daily in the last 90 days); and "daily use" (use every day during the last 90 days). As illustrated in Table 3, the majority of the respondents were at least occasional users of alcohol and marijuana, and just over 40% used these two drugs daily or several times a week. Considerably smaller proportions were current users of prescription (RX) depressants, and less than 10% had any use of street opiate drugs such as heroin or illegal methadone.

TABLE 3. *Current use frequency of drugs other than cocaine (days of use in the last 90 days)*

	Male (N=462)	Female (N=237)	Total (N=699)
Alcohol			
No use	18.2%	16.9%	17.7%
Infrequent	10.4%	11.8%	10.9%
Occasional	27.1%	38.0%	30.8%
Regular	28.1%	21.9%	26.0%
Daily	16.2%	11.4%	14.6%
Marijuana			
No use	15.6%	19.0%	16.7%
Infrequent	10.8%	10.5%	10.7%
Occasional	27.5%	33.8%	29.6%
Regular	32.5%	32.5%	32.5%
Daily	13.6%	4.2%	10.4%
RX depressants			
No use	60.8%	45.6%	55.7%
Infrequent	8.9%	18.1%	12.0%
Occasional	27.3%	32.5%	29.0%
Regular	1.7%	2.5%	2.0%
Daily	1.3%	1.3%	1.3%
Street opiates			
No use	92.9%	93.2%	93.0%
Infrequent	4.8%	3.4%	4.3%
Occasional	0.9%	1.7%	1.1%
Regular	0.9%	0.8%	0.9%
Daily	0.6%	0.8%	0.7%

No use = 0 days in last 90 days
Infrequent use = 1 to 6 days in last 90 days
Occasional use = 7 to 30 days in last 90 days
Regular use = 3 or more times a week but less tan daily use in last 90 days
Daily use = 90 of last 90 days

As indicated in Table 4, the overwhelming majority of these subjects were heavy users of cocaine, primarily *crack*-cocaine. More than three-quarters used crack either daily or several times a week, and about half of these crack smokers had taken the drug on at least 500 separate occasions during the last 90 days. By contrast, less than a fifth of the sample snorted *powder*-cocaine either daily or several times a week, and less than 10% were cocaine injectors. The smoking of either freebase cocaine or coca paste was uncommon.

TABLE 4. *Current cocaine use frequency (days of use in the last 90 Days)*

	Male (N=462)	Female (N=237	Total (N=699)
Crack			
No use	18.4%	9.3%	15.3%
Infrequent	3.5%	0.8%	2.6%
Occasional	5.4%	4.6%	5.2%
Regular	22.9%	16.5%	20.7%
Daily	49.8%	68.8%	56.2%
Snorted cocaine			
No use	56.7%	76.8%	63.5%
Infrequent	10.0%	6.3%	8.7%
Occasional	11.0%	8.4%	10.2%
Regular	11.5%	4.6%	9.2%
Daily	10.8%	3.8%	8.4%
IV cocaine			
No use	93.5%	92.0%	93.0%
Infrequent	1.7%	1.7%	1.7%
Occasional	0.2%	0.4%	0.3%
Regular	0.9%	1.3%	1.0%
Daily	3.7%	4.6%	4.0%
Freebase			
No use	96.1%	97.5%	96.6%
Infrequent	1.7%	0.4%	1.3%
Occasional	2.2%	1.3%	1.9%
Regular	0.0%	0.8%	0.3%
Coca paste			
No use	98.9%	99.6%	99.1%
Infrequent	0.4%	0.4%	0.4%
Occasional	0.4%	0.0%	0.3%
Regular	0.2%	0.0%	0.1%

No use = 0 days in last 90 days
Infrequent use = 1 to 6 days in last 90 days
Occasional use = 7 to 30 days in last 90 days
Regular use = 3 or more times a week but less tan daily use in last 90 days
Daily use = 90 of last 90 days

Criminal activity

Involvement in criminal activity was characteristic of virtually all of these crack and other cocaine users. As indicated in Table 5, for example, 91.9% reported histories of some form of crime, with their criminal careers beginning at a median age of 14 years. Almost all had engaged in drug sales and/or thefts, and 41.5% had participated in robberies. In addition, 5.6% of the men and 57.4% of the women reported histories of prostitution.

TABLE 5. *Crime history: percentage ever and median age at initial occurences*

	Male (N=462)	Female (N=237)	Total (N=699)
Percentage ever			
First crime (any type)	98.7%	96.2%	97.9%
First drug sale	90.7%	88.6%	90.0%
First theft	90.5%	86.1%	89.0%
First robbery	45.0%	34.6%	41.5%
First prostitution	5.6%	57.4%	23.2%
Median age at			
First crime (any type)	14.0	14.0	14.0
First drug sale	15.0	15.0	15.0
First theft	15.0	16.0	15.0
First robbery	16.0	16.0	16.0
First prostitution	18.0	19.0	19.0

The data displayed in Table 6 document how extensively involved in crime these crack and other cocaine users were. During the last 90 days on the street, they reportedly engaged in a total of 1,766,630 criminal acts. With 640 (91.6%) of the sample (N=699) participating in these crimes, the mean number of illegal acts per subject was 2,760. Although these numbers may appear extraordinary and impossible at first sight, a closer analysis suggests some logical and reasonable explanations. Of the more than 1.76 million offenses, practically all (92.8%) involved individual retail drug sales. By contrast, less than 2% of the crimes involved violence, less than two-tenths of 1% were burglaries or vehicle thefts, while another 1% accounted for other types of theft. In addition, 115 of the women in this sample reported engaging in 14,197 acts of prostitution during their last 90 days on the street. Although this number may appear large, it averages only 1.4 per person/per day.

It would appear that the majority of the subjects in this sample were crack and cocaine user/dealers. In fact, for their last 90-day period on the street, 74.8% reported involvement in some form of drug business activity, 64.7% reported selling crack, 21.0% reported selling other forms of cocaine, and 15.9% reported selling marijuana. As such, 523 subjects participated in 1,658,477 drug offenses in the 90-day period, and 506 subjects effected 1,639,428 retail drug sales, an average of 3,240 per subject.

Perhaps most interesting in these data is the finding that the criminal behavior of these 699 crack and other cocaine users was generally beyond the control of law enforcement. Of the more than 1.76 million criminal events, only 174, or less than one-tenth of 1%, resulted in arrest. Of these 174 arrests, the majority (54.6%) were for the most serious crimes (robbery, assault, weapons violations, burglary, and motor vehicle theft).

TABLE 6. *Criminal activity of 699 cocaine users during their last 90 days on the street in Miami, Florida*

Crime	Number of offenses	Percentage of total offenses	Percentage of sample involved	Percentage of offenses resulting in arrest
Robbery	3,223	0.2	9.7	0.7 (*n*=23)
Assault	1,499	0.1	11.6	0.3 (*n*= 5)
Weapons (show/use)	23,714	1.3	23.7	<0.1 (*n*= 8)
Burglary	2,128	0.1	16.9	1.8 (*n*=38)
Motor vehicle theft	1,110	0.1	8.6	1.9 (*n*=21)
Shoplifting	7,970	0.5	41.8	0.3 (*n*=23)
Theft from vehicle	4,257	0.2	26.0	0.1 (*n*= 6)
Pickpocketing	32	<0.1	1.1	0.0 (*n*= 0)
Prostitute's theft	873	<0.1	8.2	0.0 (*n*= 0)
Drug theft	1,730	0.1	7.7	0.0 (*n*= 0)
Sneak theft	3,203	0.2	12.6	<0.1 (*n*= 2)
Con games	12,425	0.7	16.0	0.0 (*n*= 0)
Bad checks, credit cards, etc.	3,534	0.2	34.3	0.2 (*n*= 6)
Sell/trade stolen goods	15,746	0.9	37.1	0.1 (*n*=14)
Wholesale drug business	16,670	0.9	9.3	<0.1 (*n*= 1)
Make/smuggle drugs	2,379	0.1	6.4	<0.1 (*n*= 1)
Retail drug business	1,639,428	92.8	72.4	<0.1 (*n*=22)
Prostitution	15,803	0.9	17.7	<0.1 (*n*= 4)
Procuring	10,600	0.6	14.9	0.0 (*n*= 0)
Professional gambling	306	<0.1	0.3	0.0 (*n*= 0)
Totals	1,766,630	100.0	91.6	<0.1 (n=174)

Criminal justice history

Although the data in Table 6 suggest that the criminal activity of these crack and other cocaine users rarely comes to the attention of law enforcement agencies, this should not suggest that these drug offenders always escape arrest and prosecution. Quite the contrary. As illustrated in Table 7, for example, almost all (89.8%) had been arrested at least once; the first arrest came at a median age of 16 years, and the mean number of lifetime arrests was 4.4. In addition, 67.1% had been convicted of a crime and the majority (52.6%) had served time in jail or prison.

TABLE 7. *Criminal justice history*

	Male (N=462)	Female (N=237)	Total (N=699)
Ever..? (% YES)			
Ever Arrested	92.9%	84.0%	89.8%
Ever Convicted	71.0%	59.5%	67.1%
Ever Incarcerated	54.1%	49.8%	52.6%
Median age at first arrest	16.0	15.0	16.0
Incarcerated in last 5 years?			
No	62.1%	69.2%	64.5%
Yes	37.9%	30.8%	35.5%
If incarcerated last 5 years	(N=175)	(N=72)	(N=274)
mean number of months incarcerated	8.2	6.7	7.8
If incarcerated prior to that, mean number of	(N=120)	(N=66)	(N=186)
months incarcerated	25.9	16.0	22.4
If ever arrested,	(N=429)	(N=198)	(N=627)
charge on first arrest			
Drug charge	47.1%	57.6%	50.4%
Property crime	37.1%	31.8%	35.4%
Robbery or assault	10.3%	4.5%	8.5%
Prostitution	0.0%	3.5%	1.1%
Other	5.6%	2.5%	4.6%
Mean number of arrests (Total sample)			
Major felony	2.4	1.6	2.3
Petty property	1.5	1.9	1.7
Drug offenses	2.3	1.9	2.1
Vice offenses	1.0	2.6	2.6
Total, all arrests	4.4	4.5	4.4

Street versus treatment subjects

An interesting finding in this study was the differences between the street and treatment samples along a variety of dimensions. Although there were no significant differences in their socio-demographic characteristics, the variations in criminal involvement were major. The street sample committed far more crimes, but seemed to focus almost exclusively on drug sales. In contrast, although drug sale offenses were also characteristic of the treatment sample, there was also a focus on petty property and vice offenses. Notable, as well, was the fact that the street-males were the most prone to violence.

One could argue that the street sample studied here was actually a "user-dealer" sample, and that the treatment sample was more characteristic of the general population of crack users. There is evidence to suggest that this might indeed be the case. On the one hand, *all* of the male and almost all of the female street subjects were indeed user-dealers. The women users who did not sell crack were primarily prostitutes who frequented the drug markets and crack houses and bazaars to exchange sex for drugs or for money to buy drugs. By contrast, an overview of other data in this study supports the contention that the treatment sample might be more representative of a wider crack-using population – one that has gotten into trouble as the result of crack use. For example, users drawn from the street tended to begin their drug use careers earlier in life, they used a wider variety of substances, and virtually none had prior treatment experiences. The treatment sample, on the other hand, began using drugs 4 to 5 median years later, but progressed from alcohol quite rapidly. Almost 50% had had treatment experience prior to study inclusion. Controlling for sample type, there were no significant differences between the drug use patterns of the men and women.

DISCUSSION

The findings of this study are consistent with other recent research on the drugs/crime relationship. The crack/crime connection is persistent; a vast number of crimes are committed by crack addicts; crack use appears to itensify and perpetuate criminal activity; some of the crimes are violent, but most are not. The focus is almost exclusively on retail drug sales and prostitution.

In retrospect, the data in this research point to the numerous changes in the route of administration of cocaine which have occurred during the past ten years in the United States. When the cocaine users in this study were interviewed, the majority *smoked* crack, and smoking constituted their primary if not their exclusive method of ingestion. However, their first use had been intranasal ingestion (at a median age of 16), and most had started crack use much more recently (at a median age of 20). Very few of these users reported injecting cocaine. This contrasts sharply with an earlier study of cocaine use that was conducted in Miami in 1980 and 1981 (Chitwood, 1985). Most of the users in that study also had started cocaine use by the intranasal route (snorting), but only about one-third had ever smoked cocaine (freebase, coca paste, or crack), while only two reported smoking as their primary means of administration. Among those users, the injection of cocaine was far more likely to be reported than was smoking (Chitwood, 1980; Martinez, 1980).

The phenomenon of crack smoking has extensively altered the nature of cocaine use in a relatively short time span, and additional changes are probable. Whereas intranasal ingestion was the first route of administration for most cocaine users during much of the 1980s, it is likely that crack smoking will become the initial means of ingestion for an increasing proposition of new cocaine users, because crack has become an established force in the set and setting of cocaine users. If this does indeed occur, there is every reason to expect that the age of first crack use will decrease, and new users will become involved in criminal behavior at an early age and will be at least as likely as existing users to engage in numerous criminal acts.

The high frequency with which nearly every crack user in this study participates in the sale of crack demonstrates that in many instances it is not possible to separate use from distribution. Most crack users sell crack or otherwise participate in the crack economy (e.g. by delivering crack to customers or bartering sex for crack) in order to obtain crack for personal use. This is not the stereotype picture of the dealer who sells crack for income only and never sells to facilitate his or her own drug use. Rather, it is a fluid image of a person who frequently is a user of crack and who just as frequently participates in the crack distribution system in order to acquire crack for personal consumption.

Finally, some comment seems warranted on both the accuracy and the generalizability of the data presented. On the first issue, were the subjects reporting their activities correctly? And further, is it even possible for 699 crack and other cocaine users to engage in so much criminal activity in such a short period of time? Is it possible to average literally thousands of drug sales in a three-month period?

In connection with this issue, questions are often raised about the validity of the data gathered in studies of this type. Do drug users tend to distort or cover up the less desirable aspects of their lives on the street? The answer is generally "no". A variety of controlled studies have been undertaken on this question over the years. Addict self-reports of arrests have been compared with official records; information on drug use has been compared with urinanalysis results; and intra-questionnaire safeguards and interview-reinterview procedures have been tested (Ball, 1967; Stephens, 1972; Bonito, Nurco & Shaffer, 1976; Cox & Longwell, 1974; Amsel et al., 1976). In all instances, it would appear that drug users tend to tell the truth to the best of their ability when they do not feel threatened. By contrast, when drug users are interviewed while they are in jail or are awaiting trial, their answers are less truthful (Wish & Gropper, 1990). In this study, all of the subjects were interviewed while on the street or in treatment programs, anonymity was guaranteed, and names were not collected.

Going further on this matter, problems of recall are always apparent in self-report studies, particularly when the subjects are heavily involved in both drug use and criminal activity. To mitigate this difficulty, interviewers were trained in assisting respondents to estimate the average number of drug sales per day, the number of days per week they sold drugs, and the number of "typical" weeks during the prior 90-day period. In addition, for the more active respondents, interviewers used calendars to "walk them through" the prior 90-day period, eliminating those days from the estimations that might have been spent in hospital emergency rooms (as the result of drug overdoses), off the street and in hiding, or out of circulation for some other reason.

In response to the other queries, thousands of drug sales per user/dealer in 90 days is by no means impossible, or even unusual. First, many of these subjects were sampled from Miami's open air drug markets and crack houses where drug sales occur continuously, day and night. Second, consider some of the characteristics of *crack*-cocaine mentioned earlier in this paper. The gratification engendered by the drug is exceedingly swift, yielding an intense, powerful, and almost sexual euphoria. The immediate and direct absorption of the drug combined with its quite compelling yet short-lived "high" greatly increases its dependency potential. It is for these reasons that many users will smoke crack for as long as a supply of it or the means to purchase more, money, sex, crime or other drugs, remain. As such, individual retail sales of crack are extremely numerous. As a 22-year-old crack user/dealer from one of Miami's street drug markets reported in 1989:

> I gets here every night, about 10. That's when the traffic gets heavy. The people keep comin' by – in cars, on foot, even on bikes and skate boards. On good nights *everybody* is buyin' the cracks, a rock here a rock there. Some nights I sell 50, 60, 70, 100 rocks, and a lot of *kibbles and bits* [small slivers of crack]. Friday an' Saturday nights things can be even heavier.

Similarly, a crack house drug dealer stated in 1990:

> I sell rocks around the clock. Some come in, pay $3 to use the house, and another $5 for a rock, smoke for a while, then leave. There are lots like that – maybe 100 a day, but a lot of the time it's the same ones comin' back, in and out, over an' over. They go out an' *score* ten bucks, then back in. Other people stay here all day an' night, buyin' rock after rock... That *rock hound* [crack addict] over there, the light-skinned one there in the red shorts, she just about lives here every weekend anymore. She'll give a *blow job* [oral sex] for $2, an' then comes to me for a small piece [of crack], and she crawls up over there to smoke, an' then she does it again. I've sold her as many as 25 small rocks in one night.

It should be emphasized, however, that the crack user/dealers contacted in this study were not necessarily representative of *all* crack users. The subjects sampled from the streets of Miami were drawn from those neighborhoods where crack use rates were highest and most visible, and the networks of users which were penetrated were those that were heavily involved in crack. As such, it is likely that this study gained access to the most serious users.

With respect to the generalizability of the data, one could argue that given Miami's position along international cocaine trafficking routes and its history as a major cocaine center (see Gugliotta & Leen, 1989; Eddy, 1988; Allman, 1987, 1990; Inciardi, 1992), cocaine-related crime would logically be more intense. Since there are no comparative and comprehensive empirical data on the criminal involvement of crack and other cocaine users in other cities, this matter can be addressed only indirectly, and there are a few indicators which suggest that the Miami crack/crime scene is *not* unique.

- *First,* patterns of crack use seem to be no different in Miami than those observed in other cities (Fagan & Chin, 1989; Bourgois, 1989; Waldorf, Reinarman & Murphy, 1991).
- *Second,* mechanisms of crack sale and distribution have many similarities from one locale to the next (DEA, 1989).
- *Third,* urban "crack houses" where the drug is used, sold, and exchanged for money, sex, or other drugs seem to have the same structure, functions, and characteristics regardless of the city in which they are located (Hamid, 1990; Mieczkowski, 1990, 1992; Riley, 1990; Ratner, 1993).
- *Fourth,* and finally, a recent ethnographic study of the sex-for-drugs exchanges that have become a characteristic feature of the U.S. crack scene found striking similarities in the eight cities studied (Ratner, 1993).

Given all of these comparative similarities, it is not unreasonable to conclude that even other aspects of the Miami crack scene are parallel to those elsewhere.

References

Allman, T. D. (1987). *Miami: City of the future.* New York: Atlantic Monthly Press.

Almeida, M. (1978). Contrabucion al estudio de la historia natural de la dependencia a la pasta basica de cocaina. *Revista de Neuro-Psiquiatria* 41: 44–45.

Amsel, Z., Mandell, W., Matthias, L., Mason, C. & Hocherman, I. (1976). Reliability and validity of self-reported illegal activities and drug use collected from narcotic addicts. *International Journal of the Addictions* 11: 325–336.

Anglin, M. D. & Hser, Y. (1987). Addicted women and crime. *Criminology* 25: 359–397.

Anslinger, H. J. (1951). Relationship between addiction to narcotic drugs and crime. *Bulletin on Narcotics* 3: 1–3.

Ball, J. C. (1965). Two patterns of narcotic addiction in the United States. *Journal of Criminal Law, Criminology and Police Science* 52: 203–211.

Ball, J. C. (1967). Reliability and validity of interview data obtained from 59 narcotic drug addicts. *American Journal of Sociology* 72: 650–654.

Ball, J. C. & Chambers, C. D. (1970). *The epidemiology of opiate addiction in the United States.* Springfield: Charles C. Thomas.

Ball, J. C., Rosen, L., Flueck, J. A. & Nurco, D. N. (1981). The criminality of heroin addicts: When addicted and when off opiates. In: Inciardi, J. A., ed. *The drugs-crime connection.* Beverly Hills: Sage.

Ball, J. C., Shaffer, J. W. & Nurco, D. N. (1983). The day-to-day criminality of heroin addicts in Baltimore: A study in the continuity of offense rates. *Drug and Alcohol Dependence* 12: 119–142.

Belenko, S. & Fagan, J. (1987). *Crack and the criminal justice system.* New York: New York City Criminal Justice Agency.

Bonito, A. J., Nurco, D. N. & Shaffer, J. W. (1976). The veridicality of addicts' self-reports in social research. *International Journal of the Addictions* 11: 719–724.

Bourgois, P. (1989). In search of Horatio Alger: Culture and ideology in the crack economy. *Contemporary Drug Problems* 16: 619–649.

Bourgois, P. & Dunlap, E. (1991). *Sex-for-crack in Harlem, New York.* Annual Meeting of the Society for Applied Anthropology, Charleston, South Carolina, March 13–17.

Bowser, B. P. (1989). Crack and AIDS: An ethnographic impression. *Journal of the National Medical Association* 81: 538–540.

Carr, P. (1990) *Sunshine states: Wild times and extraordinary lives in the land of gators, guns, and grapefruit.* New York: Doubleday.

Chaisson, M. A., Stoneburner, R. L., Hildebrandt, D. S., Ewing, W. E., Telsak, E. E. & Jaffe, H. W. (1991). Heterosexual transmission of HIV-1 associated with the use of smokable freebase cocaine (crack). *AIDS* 5: 1121–1126.

Chaiken, M. R. & Johnson, B. D. (1988). *Characteristics of different types of drug-involved offenders.* Washington, DC: National Institute of Justice.

Chitwood, D. D. (1980). Patterns of cocaine use: Preliminary observations. In: *Local drug abuse: Trends, patterns and observations.* Rockville, MD: National Institute on Drug Abuse.

Chitwood, D. D. (1985). Patterns and consequences of cocaine use. In: Kozel, N. J. & Adams, E. H., eds. *Cocaine use in America: Epidemiologic and clinical perspectives.* Rockville, MD: National Institute on Drug Abuse.

Cox, T. J. & Longwell, B. (1974). Reliability of interview data concerning current heroin use from heroin addicts on methadone. *International Journal of the Addictions* 9: 161–165.

Drug Enforcement Administration. (1989). Crack cocaine. Washington, DC: U. S. Department of Justice.

Eddy, P. (1989). *The cocaine wars.* New York: W. W. Norton.

Fagan, J. (1990). Social processes of delinquency and drug use among urban gangs. In: Huff, C. R., ed. *Gangs in America.* Newbury Park: Sage Publications.

Fagan, J. & Chin, K. (1989). Initiation into crack and cocaine: A tale of two epidemics. *Contemporary Drug Problems* 17: 579–617.

Faupel, C. E. (1991). *Shooting dope: Career patterns of hard-core heroin addicts.* Gainesville: University of Florida Press.

Forney, M. A., Inciardi, J. A. & Lockwood, D. (1992). Exchanging sex for crack-cocaine: A comparison of rural and urban communities. *Journal of Community Health* 17: 73–85.

Fullilove, M. T. & Fullilove, R. E. (1989). Intersecting epidemics: Black teen crack use and sexually transmitted disease. *Journal of the American Women's Medical Association* 44: 146–153.

Fullilove, R. E., Fullilove, M. T., Bowser, B. P. & Gross, S. A. (1990). Risk of sexually transmitted disease among black adolescent crack users in Oakland and San Francisco, California. *Journal of the American Medical Association* 263: 851–855.

Goldstein, P. J., Brownstein, H. H., Ryan, P. J. & Bellucci, P. A. (1989). Crack and Homicide in New York City, 1988: A conceptually based event analysis. *Contemporary Drug Problems* 16: 651–687.

Gould, L. C., Walker, A. L., Crane, L. E. & Lidz, C. W. (1974). *Connections: Notes from the heroin world.* New Haven: Yale University Press.

Gugliotta, G. & Leen, J. (1989). *Kings of cocaine.* New York: Simon and Schuster.

Hamid, A. (1990). The political economy of crack-related violence. *Contemporary Drug Problems* 17: 31–78.

Hanson, B., Beschner, G., Walters, J. M. & Bovelle. E. (1985). *Life with heroin: Notes from the inner city.* Lexington: D. C. Heath.

Inciardi, J. A. (1974). The vilification of euphoria: Some perspectives on an elusive issue. *Adductive Diseases: An International Journal* 1: 245.

Inciardi, J. A. (1975). *Careers in Crime.* Chicago: Rand McNally.

Inciardi, J. A. (1979). Heroin use and street crime. *Crime and Delinquency* 25: 335–346.

Inciardi, J. A. (1986). *The war on drugs: Heroin, cocaine, crime, and public policy.* Palo Alto: Mayfield.

Inciardi, J. A. (1987). Beyond cocaine: Basuco, crack, and other coca products. *Contemporary Drug Problems* 14: 461–492.

Inciardi, J. A. (1989). Trading sex for crack among juvenile drug users: A research note. *Contemporary Drug Problems* 16: 689–700.

Inciardi, J. A. (1991). *Kingrats, chicken heads, slow necks, freaks, and blood suckers: A glimpse at the Miami sex for crack market.* Annual Meeting of the Society for Applied Anthropology, Charleston, South Carolina, March 13–17.

Inciardi, J. A. (1992). *The war on drugs II: The continuing epic of heroin, cocaine, crack, crime. AIDS, and public policy.* Mountain View: Mayfield.

Inciardi, J. A. & Russe, B. R. (1977). Professional thieves and drugs. *International Journal of the Addictions* 12: 1087–1095.

Inciardi, J. A. & Pottieger, A. E. (1986). Drug use and crime among two cohorts of women narcotics users: An empirical assessment. *Journal of Drug Issues* 16: 91–106.

Inciardi, J. A. & Pottieger, A. E. (1991). Kids, crack, and crime. *Journal of Drug Issues* 21: 257–270.

Inciardi, J. A., Horowitz, R. & Pottieger, A. E. (1993). *Street kids, street drugs, street crime: An examination of drug use and serious delinquency in Miami.* Belmont: Wadsworth.

Inciardi, J. A., Lockwood, D. & Pottieger, A. E. (1993). *Women and crack-cocaine.* New York: Macmillan.

Jeri, F. R. (1984). Coca-paste smoking in some Latin American countries: A severe and unabated form of addiction. *Bulletin on Narcotics* April-June: 15–31.

Johnson, B. D., Goldstein, P. J., Preble, E., Schmeidler, J., Lipton. D. S., Spunt, B. & Miller, T. (1985). *Taking care of business: The economics of crime by heroin abusers.* Lexington: Lexington Books.

Klein, M., Maxson, C. L. & Cunningham, L. C. (1988). *Gang involvement in cocaine "rock" trafficking.* Los Angeles: University of Southern California. Social Science Research Institute.

Klein, M., Maxson, C. L. & Cunningham, L. C. (1991). Crack, street gangs, and violence. *Criminology* 29: 623–650.

Kolb, L. (1925). Drug addiction and its relation to crime. *Mental Hygiene* 9: 74–89.

Martinez, F. B. (1992). Impact of gangs and drugs in the community. In: Cervantes, R. C., ed. *Substance abuse and gang violence.* Newbury Park: Sage Publications.

Martinez, R. (1980). Freebase cocaine. In: *Local drug abuse: Trends, patterns and issues.* Rockville: National Institute on Drug Abuse.

Mieczkowski, T. (1990). Crack distribution in Detroit. *Contemporary Drug Problems* 17: 9–30.

Mieczkowski, T. (1992). Crack dealing on the street: Crew system and the crack house. *Justice Quarterly* 9: 151–163.

Morgan, J. P. (1966). Drug addiction: Criminal or medical problem. *Police* July-August: 6–9.

O'Donnell, J. A. (1967). The rise and decline of a subculture. *Social Problems* 15: 73–84.

Pettiway, L. (1987). Participation in crime partnerships by female drug users: The effects of domestic arrangements, drug use, and criminal involvement. *Criminology* 25: 741–766.

Ratner, M. S. (1993). *Crack pipe as pimp: An ethnographic investigation of sex-for-crack exchanges.* New York: Lexington Books.

Riley, R. (1990). Annapolis to evict drug users, dealers from public housing. *Washington Post,* November 21: 12.

Sandoz, E. C. (1992). Report on morphinism to the municipal court of Boston. *Journal of Criminal Law and Criminology* 13: 10–55.

Speckart, G. & Anglin, M. D. (1987). Narcotics use and crime: An overview of recent research advances. *Contemporary Drug Problems* 13: 741–769.

Skolnick, J. H., Correl, T., Navarro, E. & Rabb R. (1988). *The social structure of street drug dealing.* Sacramento: Office of the Attorney General.

Stephens, R. C. (1972). The truthfulness of addict respondents in research projects. *International Journal of the Addictions* 7: 549–558.

Stephens, R. C. (1991). *The street addict role: A theory of heroin addiction.* Albany: State University of New York Press.

Sutherland, E. H. (1937). *The Professional Thief.* Chicago: University of Chicago Press.

Terry, C. E. & Pellens, M. (1928) *The opium problem.* New York: Bureau of Social Hygiene.

Treaster, J. B. (1991). Inside a crack house: How drug use is changing. *New York Times,* April 6: 1, 10.

U. S. Treasury Department, Bureau of Narcotics (1940). *Traffic in opium and dangerous drugs for the year ended December 31, 1939.* Washington, DC: U. S. government Printing Office.

Waldorf, D., Reinarman, C. & Murphy, S. (1991) *Cocaine changes: the experience of using and quitting.* Philadelphia: Temple University Press.

Wallace, B. C. (1991). *Crack cocaine: A practical treatment approach for the chemically dependent.* New York: Brunner/Mazel.

Winick, C. (1961a). Physician narcotic addicts. *Social Problems* 11: 174–186.

Winick, C. (1961b). The use of drugs by jazz musicians. *Social Problems* 11: 240–253.

Wish, E. D. & Gropper, B. A. (1990). Drug testing by the criminal justice system: Methods, research, and applications. In: Tonry, M. & Wilson, J. Q., eds. *Drugs and crime.* Chicago: University of Chicago Press.

Witkin, G. (1991). The men who created crack. U. S. *News & World Report,* August 19: 44–53.

Received March 1993

James A. Inciardi
University of Delaware
77 East Main Street
Newark Delaware 19716–2582
USA

Duane C. McBride
Andrews University
Behavioral Sciences Department
123 Nethery Hall
Berrien Springs, Michigan 49104
USA

H. Virginia McCoy
Florida International University
North Miami Campus
North Miami, Florida 33181
USA

Dale D. Chitwood
Comprehensive Drug Research Center
University of Miami School of Medicine
1400 N. W. 10th Avenue
Miami, Florida 33136
USA

"THE ICE AGE" THE SOCIAL CONSTRUCTION OF A DRUG PANIC

PHILIP JENKINS
Pennsylvania State University

In 1989 and 1990 there was much media and political concern about use of the drug "ice," or smokable crystal methamphetamine, which was believed to pose a social threat potentially as great as that of crack cocaine. This concern was not sustained, however, and references to the topic diminished sharply within a few months. The incident thus offers a valuable opportunity to trace the history of a drug panic from its origins to its eclipse. Particular emphasis is placed on the role of domestic political divisions, especially in Hawaii, in citing the panic. It is suggested that this incident illustrates both the manner in which local problems come to be projected on the national political arena and the limitations inherent in such a process. The paper explores the rhetorical devices used to create a sense of impending menace around the supposed danger, and the reasons why such an apparently plausible danger failed to gain more public attention or credence.

Research in illicit drugs has often emphasized the disparity between the perceived threat of a substance and the actual social harm involved. A distinguished literature deals with successive drug "panics," which have focused on marijuana in the 1930s, amphetamines in the 1950s, glue sniffing in the 1960s, and crack cocaine in the last decade (Brecher 1972; Musto 1973; Reinarman and Levine 1989; Goode 1984; 310-34). This is not to argue that any of these substances is harmless or (necessarily) socially acceptable, but in each case, the extravagant claims permit us to employ the term *panic*.

Drug scares generally follow broadly similar patterns in which it is suggested, for example, that the drug in question is currently enjoying an explosive growth in popularity; that it is extremely addictive, and that even occasional use can cause severe physical addiction; and that it is destructive to the user or to others, threatening health or encouraging bizarre and violent behavior. Such claims are buttressed in a number of ways, including the use of exemplary cases and the parading of what appear to be objective statistics and scientific studies; the latter often turn out to be rather questionable on further examination. In addition, claims makers usually demonstrate a certain historical amnesia, often

JUSTICE QUARTERLY, Vol. 11 No. 1, March 1994

rediscovering problems which in fact are well-established while failing to note how thoroughly earlier panics were discredited.

Social scientists have explained such periodic waves of concern in various ways. Many emphasize the role of political or bureaucratic interest groups seeking to enhance their claims on resources and status. Others stress the role of factors in the broader society, such as ethnic or generational tension and hostility, which come to be symbolized by the drug in question. In this sense it is almost irrelevant whether the claims presented by the rhetoric of a "panic" are well-founded or wholly spurious: the panic itself is valuable in itself for what it suggests about the perceptions of a society as a whole, and specifically of policy makers and legislators. The incident thus has great significance for understanding the social construction of crime and deviance.

Some claims are widely accepted and have the effect of remolding law and public policy: the crack issue has done so in the last decade (Reinarman and Levine 1989). Other issues, however, are more ephemeral, and the claims appear to enjoy far less success. In recent years we have witnessed a dramatic example of such a short-lived panic in the public reaction to the alleged boom in the use of the drug "ice," or smokable methamphetamine. During 1989 and early 1990, it was widely claimed that this substance was becoming enormously popular in certain regions, and that it had the potential to "sweep the nation" in a few months or years. Dramatic statistics were offered to support these claims; it was suggested that ice was uniquely dangerous in combining extremely addictive qualities with the advantages of cheapness, easy access, and domestic manufacture. The media panic about ice found its focus in Congressional hearings during October 1989 and January 1990. The stage seemed to be set for a repetition of the crack "explosion" of 1986.

This concern about ice was not sustained, however, and media references to the topic diminished sharply within a few months. Outside a few cities and regions, the issue either has ceased to exist or is dormant. The incident thus offers an unusual opportunity to trace the creation of a drug panic from its inception to its eclipse. In understanding the phenomenon, we must emphasize that "ice" originated as a very localized event, confined largely to Hawaii, and that the words *epidemic* and *explosion* arose from partisan and bureaucratic rivalries within that state. The projection of this local concern onto the national stage was made possible by a number of factors, including the existence of specialized agencies and investigative bodies focusing on drug issues, and the intensification of public expectations and fears following the crack scare. I suggest that all these elements still exist and are likely to lead in future to other ephemeral drug panics. The "ice" incident is likely to be repeated in various forms.

THE METHAMPHETAMINE INDUSTRY

Methamphetamine is a stimulant of the central nervous system which, as a street drug, is often known as "speed" or "crank" (Graham 1976; Grinspoon 1975; *Methamphetamine Abuse* 1989; Miller and Kozel 1991). The illegal manufacture of methamphetamines began in the early 1960s, and networks of clandestine laboratories emerged to produce several synthetic drugs. During the 1970s, such laboratories tended increasingly to shift their production towards methamphetamine and away from other synthetics such as PCP (Jenkins 1992b). Between 1981 and 1984, methamphetamine producers represented half of all laboratory seizures; by 1988 they exceeded 80 percent (*U.S. Congress: Laboratories* 1980; *U.S. Congress: Re-emergence* 1990:25, 90-91).

The attractions of the industry were obvious. The manufacturing process required little expertise; several cheap "hands-on" manuals were available to provide detailed instruction. A laboratory could make as much as five to 10 pounds of methamphetamine in a week, and the pure substance usually was "cut" repeatedly for street sale. The annual production of a laboratory thus might be worth several million dollars (Jenkins 1992b). In 1989 a Dallas police officer remarked, "We think the profit is much greater when we look at methamphetamine production, as compared to heroin or cocaine. We know that an investment of $3000 to $4000 in chemicals, in glassware, can turn a profit of $25,000 to $30,000." (*U.S. Congress: Re-Emergence* 1990:39).

One appeal of methamphetamine was that the substance was manufactured in the United States and did not need the sophisticated importation and distribution networks required for heroin or cocaine. Laboratories needed no elaborate facilities or natural resources beyond an ample supply of electricity, and distribution demanded little more than convenient access to the interstate highway network (Skeers 1992; Weingarten 1989; Witkin 1989).

During the 1980s, methamphetamine manufacture tended to become strongly regionalized. In the late 1970s and early 1980s, the Philadelphia area was said to be "the speed capital of the world," with networks of hundreds of laboratories in the southern and eastern parts of the state (Jenkins 1992b; *U.S. Congress: Profile* 1983). By the mid-1980s, the city of Eugene, Oregon was believed to enjoy a similar role in manufacturing; other law enforcement sources emphasized the importance of San Diego and the San Francisco Bay area (*Organized Crime in California*

1989:55; Wiedrich 1987). In 1987 and 1988 more than 300 methamphetamine laboratories were seized in the San Diego area alone. Centers of methamphetamine use included Denver, Portland (Oregon), Dallas, and Phoenix; some problems also were observed in Los Angeles, San Francisco, and Seattle (*Arrestee Drug Use* 1990:6; *U.S. Congress: Re-Emergence* 1990:37, 46). Though it is hard to assess the extent of methamphetamine use, there appears to be substantial demand in many parts of the nation (Isikoff 1989; Miller and Kozel 1991; Morgan 1992; *Methamphetamine* 1989).

THE EMERGENCE OF ICE

Like other drugs, methamphetamine can be taken in various ways: either injected, smoked, or ingested orally. The dominant mode of use tends to reflect the tastes and traditions of local subcultures. In view of the highly regional nature of manufacture and distribution, suppliers do not find it difficult to accommodate these local tastes, and it is natural to find wide disparities in patterns of use. Fashions that emerge in one city or region can become dominant in that area without making much impact elsewhere. In short, there is no such thing as a national market in methamphetamines.

During the 1980s, a vogue for smokable crystal methamphetamine developed in Hawaii and some western states under the common nickname *ice* (Cho 1990; Pennell 1990). A similar, though somewhat less pure, product called *glass* also made its appearance in California. The manufacturing process has been described as follows:

> Two basic methods are used to produce crystal meth. The first and most common method is the reaction of phenyl-2-propanone (P2P or phenylacetone) and methylamine. The second method uses ephedrine as a precursor. The second method uses a simple formula and does not require the use of controlled precursors. It is known as the ephedrine/red phosphorus method and requires the use of a hydrogenator. It takes two to four days to make a batch of ice . . . .
>
> In Honolulu, crystal meth is most commonly smoked with a glass pipe, the bowl of which becomes coated with a milky white, brownish or black residue, depending on the form of crystal meth used. A gram of ice sells for $250 to $400 in Honolulu right now, with a 1/10 gram paper going for $50 to $75. It is inexpensive to produce, so the profit margin is tremendous. (*U.S. Congress: Re-Emergence* 1990:74-75).

The drug itself had long been known and used in this crystal form, but apparently the specific process used to make the extremely pure ice was not yet in use in the United States itself. Instead the substance, like the fashion for its use, had been imported from the Pacific Rim. Amphetamines, specifically methamphetamines, had long been popular in Japan and other east Asian countries. In that region, illicit markets were supplied by sizable narcotic networks with roots in organized crime among both Chinese triads and Japanese *yakuza* (Delfs 1991). During the 1970s and 1980s, such networks had collaborated in a variety of activities, including product counterfeiting and trafficking in guns and prostitutes in addition to narcotics; we have much evidence of cooperative endeavors, based (for example) in Taiwan or South Korea (Buruma and McBeth 1984-85; Posner 1988). For methamphetamines, the *yakuza* had developed manufacturing facilities in South Korea; these supplied much of east Asia, though the triads also were active in Hong Kong (Kaplan and Dubro 1986:198-200; *U.S. Congress: Re-Emergence* 1990:11, 99). Entrepreneurs and distributors might be nationals of any of a dozen Asian countries.

Though illegal, the amphetamine drug "family" was stigmatized far less severely than opiates, cocaine, or even marijuana. Most estimates place the number of regular amphetamine (*shabu*) users in Japan at more than half a million. In the 1980s, smokable methamphetamine became the drug of choice among upwardly mobile urban dwellers in several Pacific Rim nations, especially Taiwan, South Korea, and the Philippines (Delfs 1991; McBeth 1989; Savadove 1991).

Therefore it is not surprising to find a similar habit developing in Hawaii, which has so many cultural and economic affinities with the Pacific Rim, and in which Japanese organized crime had developed a strong foothold. In fact, Kaplan and Dubro's (1986) study of the *yakuza* calls Hawaii the "forty-eighth Prefecture," an annex to the 47 administrative units of the Japanese home islands. *Yakuza*-supplied amphetamines were identified in the state during the 1970s, and Korean-manufactured methamphetamines appeared in the following decade (Shoenberger 1989). Beginning in 1987, island authorities had described an "ice problem," linked in part to Filipino youth gangs and Korean groups (*U.S. Congress: Re-Emergence* 1990:5).

DISCOVERING A PROBLEM

By 1989, law enforcement agencies were finding evidence of localized use of smokable methamphetamine, originally in Hawaii and subsequently in and around San Diego. The perceived "wave" of new activity was epitomized by a series of federal drug raids on 20 laboratories in southern California during March, and by a series of smaller raids over the next year (Ford 1990; Reza 1989). Concern about the drug in Hawaii was given a new focus in March 1989 by the arrest of a substantial ice-importation ring headed by one Paciano Guerrero (*U.S. Congress: Drug Crisis* 1990:74-75; *U.S. Congress: Re-Emergence* 1990: 70-72).

It might be thought that the perceived boom in the smokable drug reflected strictly local conditions, unlikely to be replicated in other areas. Even in Hawaii, the problem was confined largely to Oahu (*U.S. Congress: Drug Crisis* 1990:56, 205, 215). Now, however, there began a media campaign to emphasize the perils of the "new" drug, and the danger that this would soon be reflected across the nation. A headline in the *Los Angeles Times*, for example, read "Potent Form of Speed Could Be Drug of 90s" (Corwin 1989). The *Economist* noted that ice could make crack seem almost benign ("Drugs: Ice Overdose" 1989). Rep. Charles Rangel coined the alliterative description "the narcotics nemesis of the nineties" (*U.S. Congress: Re-Emergence* 1990:59).

The theme was taken up by all the major regional newspapers and national newsmagazines, as well as more specialized publications serving the medical and pharmaceutical communities (Cho 1990; "Illicit Methamphetamine" 1991; Zurer 1989). Between September and December 1989, major stories appeared in the *New York Times* (Bishop 1989), *The Washington Post* (Thompson 1989), *The Atlanta Constitution* (Curriden 1989), *The Economist* ("Drugs; Ice Overdose" 1989), *The Boston Globe* (Howe 1989; Tabor 1989), *The Chicago Tribune* (Weingarten 1989), *The Christian Science Monitor* (Larmer 1989), and *Newsweek* (Lerner 1989). The tone of the coverage was epitomized by the *New York Times* headline "Fear Grows Over Effects of a New Smokable Drug" (Bishop 1989). This story was printed on the front page; equal prominence was given to ice related stories on the front pages of the *Los Angeles Times* (Corwin 1989) and *The Chicago Tribune* (Weingarten 1989). In October the *Los Angeles Times* presented a series of four stories on ice within a nine-day period (Corwin 1989; Essoyan 1989; Shoenberger 1989; Zamichow 1989). Clearly, pronouncements about the new drug were finding a ready and enthusiastic market in the mass media.

The jeremiads about ice were heard most frequently in the last quarter of 1989, though a few stories appeared in early 1990, and television news shows such as *60 Minutes* sustained the focus on methamphetamines in general for a few months more ("Meth" 1990). The height of the panic, however, can be identified clearly between about September 1989 and February 1990 (See Table 1 for a chronology of media accounts).

The peak of public concern can be associated with Congressional hearings on this topic; Rep. Rangel's Subcommittee on Narcotics Abuse and Control held a session titled "The Re-Emergence of Methamphetamine" in October. A follow-up session, the "Drug Crisis in Hawaii," was held in Honolulu the following January (*U.S. Congress: Re-Emergence* 1990; *U.S. Congress: Drug Crisis* 1990. For criticisms of the latter session as a Congressional junket, see Anderson and Van Atta 1990). Taken together with the media accounts, the hearings became the chief vehicle for the burgeoning panic about ice. Here it will be useful to analyze the language and rhetoric employed to present the new phenomenon as a major problem.

THE RHETORIC OF ICE

Certain themes and expressions recur with striking regularity. Ice was new, potent, and dangerous, and had acquired high prestige as the new "in" drug. Taken together, these features meant that the use of ice apparently was about to expand rapidly and to create a national menace at least comparable to crack cocaine.

The experience of Hawaii was recounted often, as in a *Boston Globe* story titled "Ice in an Island Paradise" (Tabor 1989). The use of ice, in the words of a Congressional report, "has escalated in such leaps and bounds that we have not been able to keep pace" (*U.S. Congress: Re-Emergence* 1990:2). Generally such accounts suggested that what such areas were experiencing today would be the fate of the whole country in a few months or years. Honolulu police chief Douglas Gibb told the story of a New York City Korean gang that had flown some members to Honolulu to attack some local Samoans. "The whole purpose . . . was to come into town to establish a connection for ice, a line for ice to take back to New York" (*U.S. Congress: Re-Emergence* 1990:8). "It is probably only a matter of time until other parts of the country start to see crystal meth and its attendant problems . . . we fully expect the Ice Age to spread east from Hawaii" (p.77).

The idea that ice was gradually penetrating areas of the mainland gave a local angle to media reporting of the drug in cities such as Atlanta (Curriden 1989), Boston (Howe 1989), and Philadelphia (Durso 1992). In the Congressional hearings, this was a frequent theme. One subcommittee member noted, "We have got ice in Virginia . . . it is for sure coming our way and we had better get ready for it" (*U.S. Congress: Re-Emergence* 1990:19). Another member stated, "Reports are already filtering in of ice use in New York and

Table 1. Chronology of Media Accounts, 1989-1991

	1989	
September		
First ice related stories in mainland newspapers		
Sept. 16	*New York Times*	(Bishop 1989)
October		
Oct. 1	*Boston Globe*	(Howe 1989)
Oct. 8	*Los Angeles Times*	(Shoenberger 1989)
Oct. 14	*Los Angeles Times*	(Essoyan 1989)
Oct. 16	*Los Angeles Times*	(Essoyan 1989)
Oct. 16	*Los Angeles Times*	(Zamichow 1989)
Oct. 24	Congressional hearings, *The Re-Emergence of Methamphetamine*	
November		
Nov. 6	*Chemical and Engineering News*	(Zurer 1989)
Nov. 21	*Washington Post*	(Thompson 1989)
Nov. 27	*Newsweek*	(Lerner 1989)
Nov. 30	*Atlanta Constitution*	(Curriden 1989)
December		
Dec. 2	*The Economist*	("Drugs: Ice Overdose" 1989)
Dec. 8	*Boston Globe*	(Tabor 1989)
Dec. 8	*Christian Science Monitor*	(Larmer 1989)
Dec. 18	*Jet*	(Carthane 1989)
	1990	
January		
Jan. 13	Congressional hearings, on *The Drug Crisis in Hawaii*	
February		
Feb. 8	*Rolling Stone*	(Sager 1990)
February	*Good Housekeeping*	(Holland 1990)
April		
April 22	CBS news program *60 Minutes* broadcasts story on methamphetamine trafficking ("Meth" 1990).	
May		
May 23	*Journal of the American Medical Association*	(Cotton 1989)
August		
Aug. 10	*Science*	(Cho 1990)
	1991	
March		
March 6	*Journal of the American Medical Association*	(Hong, Matsuyama, and Nur 1991)
May		
May 9	*Washington Post*	Holley, Venant, and Essoyan 1991)
June		
June 30	*Emergency Medicine*	("Illicit Methamphetamine" 1991)

Washington DC" (*U.S. Congress: Drug Crisis* 1990:3). A lengthy investigative account in *Rolling Stone* quoted law enforcement officials, who believed that the Hawaii "epidemic" soon would sweep the mainland and that the drug would surpass both heroin and cocaine, marking a new and still more deadly era in drug abuse (Sager 1990).

One paradox was that ice, by its nature, negated some of the obvious advantages of methamphetamine: as an imported drug for example, it encountered the obstacles and expense involved in crossing national borders. The witnesses at the hearings, however, emphasized repeatedly that it would only be a matter of time before domestic manufacturers learned to reproduce Asian techniques; at that point, ice would begin to conquer the American "speed" market. In the words of a Dallas police official, "We have cooks, we have numerous cooks scattered throughout the country, literally thousands of persons who are qualified to make methamphetamine. So, we have the processes in place to make ice. I think we also have a ready consumer market out there, individuals who want the drug. I have no doubt that ice will come to the United States" (*U.S. Congress: Re-Emergence* 1990:39-40).

Particularly evocative was the word *epidemic* which was employed in most of the accounts, with its implications of plague, disease, and uncontrollable spread (compare Reinarman and Levine 1989). During the Congressional hearings, U.S. Attorney Daniel Bent described Hawaii ice use as already an "epidemic" (*U.S. Congress: Re-Emergence* 1990:5). When a DEA spokesman was quoted as having denied the validity of the "epidemic," he was taken to task by members of the committee, especially Florida Rep. Tom Lewis, who described the opinion as "irresponsible" and "lackadaisical" (p.17). "Epidemic" was a politically valuable concept that would not be abandoned easily.

Other significant terms included *deluge*, *plague*, and *crisis*. Congressman Rangel remarked that Honolulu police were "deluged" by ice (*U.S. Congress: Re-Emergence* 1990:1). Sociologist Elliott Currie spoke of "this hidden methamphetamine plague" (p.44). The word *crisis* was much used, generally in the context of an "emerging" crisis, to suggest that what had gone before was trivial compared to what would come in future (p.61). As has been noted, the January hearings of the Narcotics Subcommittee were devoted explicitly to the drug crisis in Hawaii.

The term *ice* offered great potential for writers, suggesting as it did the phrase *ice age* and thus implying that the drug somehow could dominate American society so strongly that it could give its name to an era. The phrase *The Ice Age* was employed both by Douglas Gibb and Hawaii Rep. Daniel Akaka in the Congressional hearings (*U.S. Congress: Re-Emergence* 1990:3, 77). It was used subsequently for major investigative accounts in *Rolling Stone* in

1990 and in the *Washington Post* in 1991 (Holley, Venant, and Essayan 1991; Sager 1990; compare LaBianca 1992). "Ice" also suggested "chilling" in the metaphorical sense of "extremely frightening;" it was used in this sense by several journalists. In late 1989, for example, the *Atlanta Constitution* carried the headline "Police Chilled By New In-Drug: Ice" (Curriden 1989). Within two weeks, the *Christian Science Monitor* warned similarly, "Ice Chills US AntiDrug Officials" (Larmer 1989).

In addition, these arguments were stated by individuals and agencies with great expertise in the field. Every news story was buttressed by the opinions of prominent and credible law enforcement officials, police, and prosecutors from California and Hawaii, together with academics and other experts. In the Congressional hearings, major witnesses included Daniel Bent, the U.S. Attorney for Hawaii; Douglas Gibb, the police chief of Honolulu; and David Westrate of the DEA; all were prestigious and experienced officials. Other presentations were made by reputable doctors and academics. The potential "ice epidemic" thus appeared both plausible and threatening.

ICE AND COCAINE

One potent element of the attack on ice involved the analogy with cocaine. In seeking to portray a new problem as serious or dangerous, one well-known rhetorical device is to stimatize that problem by associating it with another, already familiar issue, thus placing into an existing context. Problem construction is a cumulative or incremental process in which each issue is built, to some extent, on its predecessors. As Best remarks.

> As an acknowledged subject for concern, a well established social problem becomes a resource, a foundation upon which other claims may be built. Rather than struggling to bring recognition to a new problem, claimants may find it easier to expand an existing problem's domain. These new claims take the form (new problem) X is really a type of (established problem) Y (1990:65-66).

Issue (X) therefore demands the array of responses and reactions that already have been judged appropriate for Problems (Y). This is the process described by Hall et al. (1978:223) as "convergence:"

> [C]onvergence occurs when two or more activities are linked in the process of signification so as to implicitly or explicitly draw parallels between them. Thus the image of "student hooliganism" links student protest to the separate problem of hooliganism—whose stereotypical characteristics are already part of socially available knowledge. . . . In both cases, the net effect is amplification, not in the real

events being described but in their threat potential for society (1978:223).

By 1989 cocaine, especially crack cocaine, had been invested with an enormous amount of "threat potential," suggested, for example, by the "drug war" rhetoric, which was then at its height. President Bush had made the "drug war" a major part of his domestic policy; his commitment to drug eradication was symbolized by the appointment of William Bennett as "drug czar." During 1989, American activism against international drug traffickers contributed to the near-civil war in Colombia, beginning in August, and to the invasion of Panama in December. Media coverage in the latter part of the year featured almost daily news of violence and conflict associated with these incidents. In September, President Bush made a nationally televised address on drug control strategy, in which he stated, "All of us agree that the gravest domestic threat facing our nation today is drugs . . . our most serious problem today is cocaine and in particular crack." Producing a sample of crack, which he said had been purchased close to the White House, the president continued, "It's as innocent looking as candy, but it is turning our cities into battle zones, and it is murdering our children. Let there be no mistake, this stuff is poison" ("Text" 1989). President Bush argued that the drug control budget for the coming year should be raised by more than one-third from the 1989 figure, to $8 billion.

If crack was indeed "the gravest domestic threat," then it was a highly effective strategy to suggest that ice was associated somehow with the better-known drug. Superficial parallels also existed. It could be suggested, for example, that crack was an especially virulent and addictive form of powder cocaine, while ice bore a similar relationship to "regular" methamphetamine. Also, the two substances were similar in general appearance and means of ingestion. The ice threat was amplified by its association with crack, an association pursued most vigorously on the Narcotics Subcommittee by Rep. Akaka. From the viewpoint of the media, the analogy with crack made ice an attractive subject because its dangers and thus its social significance could be comprehended easily; thus the drug would be likely to excite public concern and fear.

Ice was said to cause as much social damage as cocaine, in terms of overdoses and emergency room admissions (Gross 1988; "Illicit Methamphetamine" 1991). Rep. Akaka stated that in Hawaii, ice contributed to the problems that elsewhere were linked to crack: "ice-addicted babies, gang activities, turf battles and hospital emergency cases of overdoses . . . this drug has the capacity to drag our country even deeper into the dark abyss created by crack"

(*U.S. Congress: Re-Emergence* 1990:3). "It doesn't make any difference whether it is ice, crack, crank, cocaine. We are losing kids. We are corrupting our police departments. We are corrupting our political arena. We are breaking up families" (p.17).

U.S. Attorney Daniel Bent stated that ice was "in presenting the same problems to Hawaii as crack cocaine has in areas of the Continental United States in terms of its popularity, availability, addiction potential and destructiveness" (*U.S. Congress: Re-Emergence* 1990:64). It was alleged to stimulate violent behavior even more sharply than did crack; Hawaii, it was said, was seeing the birth of a generation of "crystal meth babies" (*U.S. Congress: Drug Crisis* 1990:2, 226-33; *U.S. Congress: Re-Emergence* 1990:66, 76; for the idea of the "crack baby," however, see Jacobs 1991). Such remarks made the two drugs appear all but indistinguishable; in fact, Rep. Akaka even asked a witness, "Can you explain to me the differences between crack, crank, ice and croak . . . ?" (*U.S. Congress: Re-Emergence* 1990:54).

In some ways, ice could be made to appear even more dangerous than crack. First, it was superior to crack because of its lower cost and its longer-lasting high. The effects were reported to last from four to 14 hours, as opposed to a few minutes for crack (Carthane 1989; Holley et al. 1991). Also, ice did not necessarily have to be imported from overseas (though it was imported currently); therefore it did not encounter the stringent restrictions imposed by Customs and the Coast Guard as part of the current "war on drugs." In addition, ice lacked the features that might safeguard individuals from experimenting with other substances. It did not require injection, as did heroin, and did not yet have the destructive associations of crack cocaine. By 1989, crack had acquired undesirable connotations that deterred many people from using it: it was associated with cultures of violence and extreme urban poverty, and was linked especially with racial minorities.

In contrast, methamphetamine generally was linked to hard work. Insofar as it had any racial overtones, it tended to be favored by white users (*Methamphetamine* 1989; Miller and Kozel 1991). Nationally, said the congressional account, "the typical methamphetamine user is a white male 22 to 26 years of age, who is employed in a blue-collar job. The most frequently cited occupations are in construction trades and the trucking industry" (*U.S. Congress: Re-Emergence* 1990:87). In the San Diego region, "abusing populations are predominantly white, lower middle income, high school educated, young adults ranging in age from 18-35 years" (p.111). A Texas police officer stated, "The persons who we most often encounter in Dallas, the users we most often encounter are primarily Caucasian, primarily lower income" (p.39).

Ice users tended to fit a similar profile. In Hawaii, ice was "'popular in the workplace, particularly among blue collar workers, people who do mechanical tasks, and it has also spread into office workplaces as well . . . (it is) the drug of choice for on the job use in Honolulu. . . . It is generally in the blue collar community and the service community" (*U.S. Congress: Re-Emergence* 1990:6-7-9). In short, ice could appeal to white or Asian middle-class people; teenagers especially were at risk. The title of a *Good Housekeeping* article described ice as "a New Drug Nice Kids Can Get Hooked On" (Holland 1990). Women also were believed to be particularly vulnerable: "In Honolulu, most ice users range in age from the late teens to the early thirties. The drug is popular with young women, perhaps because users tend to lose weight" (*U.S. Congress: Re-Emergence* 1990:75).

It was suggested that ice might able to wreak havoc in all sections of society, not merely in the inner cities. Rep. Rangel thus was tapping into potent fears when he write, "[W]e shudder to think of what would happen in this country if the devastation of the crack crisis were doubled or even tripled by adding on a whole new layer of illicit drug abuse" (*U.S. Congress: Re-Emergence* 1990:59). This rhetoric was even more powerful in the context of current developments in the "drug war" at home and overseas.

WHATEVER BECAME OF ICE?

"Ice" thus was attracting quite fervent interest. One might suggest that it had the potential to attract the same kind of fear as crack. The recent precedent of crack cocaine provided a set of stereotyped images and rhetoric on which ice could build readily, with the added "bonus" that ice threatened to reproduce these disturbing images outside the African-American urban community. Ice (it appeared) could cause the same kind of havoc as crack in geographical, social, and ethnic settings still untouched by ice or any other "hard" drug. It would not be difficult to imagine that the new problem could thrive through the use of ethnic and xenophobic stereotypes: the substance was imported from Asia, and had Japanese connotations. *Yakuza* drug dealers might easily acquire the stigma that had adhered earlier to gangsters from immigrant ethnic groups such as Jews and Italians.

In addition, it has been argued that intense media attention to a particular drug might tend to incite interest in the substance, and to lead to experimentation. Prophecies of an "epidemic" thus might be self-fulfilling in that they could unwittingly generate the problem that activists were seeking to avoid (MacDonald and Estep 1985; compare Young 1971). In the 1960s this kind of imitation caused glue sniffing to spread at "incredible speed . . . the enemies of glue-sniffing popularized the custom all by themselves" (Brecher 1972:326, 332). In the 1980s it was suggested that media portrayals of the effects of crack cocaine might have excited interest among users of powdered cocaine. With these precedents in mind, observers of ice warned that ice was being "beautifully advertised by the media" to cocaine users (Cotton 1990). The *Journal of the American Medical Association* warned, "News articles describing (ice) as like 'ten orgasms pronto' are working like paid ads. . . . If the media says it's an epidemic, drug adventurers say everybody's using it so I've got to try it" (Cotton, 1990).

The ice danger, however, did not materialize as a national crisis, and the prospective "plague" faded rapidly in early 1990. Media accounts became far less frequent from February onwards, and virtually none appeared between August 1990 and spring 1991 (see Table 1). In part this silence reflected the new concern of the media with political affairs in Iraq and the Persian Gulf, but the ice panic had been declining sharply for several months before the August invasion of Kuwait. The rather sudden eclipse of the ice problem requires explanation.

Some observers had been skeptical even during the height of the panic, and witnesses at the October hearings faced criticism for their use of the term *epidemic*. The evidence presented also contained clear contradictions— for example, in the damage caused by ice. Early reports of the testimony quoted Chief Gibb's statements that "since 1985, there have been 32 deaths in Honolulu attributed to ice," including eight homicides and seven suicides. (*U.S. Congress: Re-Emergence* 1990:76). Gibb, however, also stated that "32 people were confirmed to have crystal methamphetamine in their system at the time of deaths," which does not necessarily establish a causal link between the drug and the fatality (pp. 7-8). Hawaii's Governor Waihee placed the number of deaths at 36, of whom "three died as a direct result, and 32 had traces of the drug in their systems" (p. 80). It was embarrassing when Gibb was publicly challenged on his statistics; as a result, the early claims about the impact of the drug, even in Hawaii, were reduced substantially. Thus it was even more difficult to claim that ice presented a potential national menace.

During the October hearings, one DEA spokesman commented, "I can confirm there is a drug out there called ice, which is certainly bad news. But D.E.A. agents are not looking for it yet . . . . It will take a while for ice to proliferate. When we get reports from police departments that ice has gotten to be at the epidemic state, such as crack did in 1985, then we will move in" (*U.S. Congress: Re-Emergence* 1990:17). Such a drug "explosion" seemed remote, however. In early 1990, testing of arrestees confirmed considerable amphetamine use in San Diego, Portland, Phoenix, and San Jose, but the figures did not appear to be growing.

Moreover, ice as such had made few inroads among the arrestees, though a substantial majority knew the substance by reputation: the media were cited overwhelmingly as the main source. Even in San Diego, almost 70 percent of those who knew about ice based their knowledge on media accounts rather than on information provided by friends or dealers. Nationwide the proportion who admitted ever having used ice nowhere exceeded 3 percent (though no community in Hawaii was included in the survey) (*Arrestee Drug Use* 1990:6; Pennell 1990). This picture was confirmed by other survey data. Among male hustlers and sex workers in San Francisco, for example, ice had made very limited inroads, even among heavy users of methamphetamine. Moreover, the number of habitual ice users in such groups remained negligible (Lauderback and Waldorf 1992).

Largely on the basis of such data and of the reexamination of the drug's impact in Hawaii itself, law enforcement and DEA officials soon were saying that the danger of ice had been substantially overstated. Media rhetoric subsided within a few months of the Congressional hearings. Ice continues to be popular in some regions, but the language of epidemic no longer seems realistic—if it ever did.

THE CONSTRUCTION OF THE ICE DANGER

In retrospect it seems certain that the menace of ice was considerably overstated, and we might well ask how such a misperception could emerge. A considerable literature exists on the origins of such scares and perceived social problems; some of the explanations suggested by that literature seem relevant here. Many researchers, for example, follow some form of what is generally known as the "moral entrepreneur" theory. The classic discussion of this term comes from Becker, who emphasized the role of a particular individual in the formulation of American narcotics policy in the 1930s:

> Wherever rules are created and applied we should be alive to the possible presence of an enterprising individual or group. Their activities can properly be called "moral enterprise" for what they are enterprising about is the creation of a new fragment of the moral constitution of society, its code of right and wrong (1963:145).

Such entrepreneurs might have diverse motives. In the case of a drug panic, for example, we might find activism by an interest group or a bureaucratic agency that was seeking to portray a serious social danger in order to focus public attention on issues falling within its scope of activity. This effort would permit the agency to expand its influence and resources, and might allow local authorities and law enforcement agencies to justify and request for federal funding and other support. In such circumstances, we often find a cyclical pattern in which greater concern causes more resources to be devoted to a problem; the result is more detection and more vigorous prosecution of the activity in question. This process in turn generates statistical evidence that can be used to intensify public concern, and thus to argue for still more resources. "Epidemics" thus can be self-sustaining.

Such bureaucratic concerns may have played some role in the case of ice. One recurrent theme of the hearings was the need to strengthen still further the numbers and resources of the DEA (*U.S. Congress: Re-Emergence* 1990:8-9). This agency had grown in numbers from 1,900 in 1980 to 2,900 in 1989. Currently it was requesting 160 new agents, chiefly for international enforcement in Latin America and the Pacific Rim (34-35). An ice panic therefore served the interests of the DEA, but it certainly cannot serve as a full explanation. As we have seen, the DEA was strongly critical of the exaggerated claims made for ice, and during 1990 was instrumental in damping down the nascent panic. In January, for example, the head of the Honolulu office wrote that ice was still confined largely to Hawaii and "very limited West Coast areas;" otherwise, he reported, "we know of no ice samples (having) been analyzed elsewhere in the United States" (*U.S. Congress: Drug Crisis* 1990:76).

Instead of examining national groups and controversies, it would be more profitable to consider the needs of the political and bureaucratic interests in Hawaii that sponsored most of the extravagant claims about ice and first identified an "epidemic." For example, the major claims makers heard by the Congressional committees included two of the leading figures in the state's law enforcement bureaucracy, police chief Douglas Gibb and U.S. Attorney Daniel Bent. The evidence offered by these two witnesses accounted for more than one-third of the total testimony presented during the October hearings, and both men emphasized the "epidemic" quality of the ice threat. As in the case of the DEA, an ice panic would enhance the reputation of local police agencies as well as increasing their access to resources. In addition, the powerful office of U.S. Attorney often provides any incumbent with the opportunity to win prestige and visibility that can be translated subsequently into a wider political career. This is not to suggest that either individual was insincere in his claims about the ice problem, but both had clear bureaucratic interests in formulating the issue in a particular way.

Electoral politics also played a role in shaping official claims and statements. At the opening of the 1989 hearings, which did so much to put ice on the map of American social problems, Congressman Rangel emphasized that the impetus for concern came chiefly from the Hawaii Congressional delegation of Representatives Daniel Akaka and Patricia Saiki. Both in fact had a strong vested interest in appearing to be active and interested in drug issues, and in adopting hard-line antidrug stances. Therefore they stood to benefit from making ice seem as perilous and as threatening as possible; both can be viewed as classical moral entrepreneurs.

This political context can be observed if we describe recent developments in Hawaii, traditionally one of the most loyally Democratic states in the nation (Smith and Pratt 1992). In the 1980s, for example, both of the Democratic U.S. senators could count regularly on receiving 70 to 80 percent of the votes cast, and the powerful governor's office remained firmly in Democratic hands throughout these years (Benenson 1991). Republicans were placed extremely poorly; they won offices chiefly when Democratic factions were split, as when Republican Patricia Saiki won the First Congressional District. By 1989 she had retained this position in two elections, but with progressively slimmer majorities. Democrat Daniel Akaka had remained firmly in control of the Second District in every contest since 1976.

Saiki's presence as a Republican representative therefore might appear anomalous, but the Republicans had one major point of potential strength, namely in the general area of law and order. Throughout the decade, Democratic authorities had been involved in a series of scandals; these had exposed alleged links between organized crime and the labor unions, which play so crucial a role in Hawaii Democratic politics. These incidents reached a climax in 1984 with the investigation by Charles F. Marsland, the Republican Honolulu city/county prosecutor, into a series of gangland murders that included the killing of Marsland's own son. Marsland targeted a prominent political ally of Democratic Governor George Ariyoshi as the alleged "godfather" of organized crime in the state (Turner 1984a, 1984b). The ensuing scandals and lawsuits did not destroy Democratic power. In fact, the next governor, elected in 1986, was a close associate of Ariyoshi, but the incident suggested one area in which Democrats were politically vulnerable: Daniel Akaka himself had been an Ariyoshi protegé. In addition, he is of native Hawaiian descent, and thus could potentially be associated with Larry Mehau, the ethnically Hawaiian "godfather."

In the following years, Saiki and Akaka emerged as powerful figures in Hawaii politics, and they clashed on crime-related issues. In the U.S. Congress, Saiki voted for a measure to extend the death penalty to major drug dealers, which Akaka opposed. The rivalry between the two was especially significant in 1989, when it became increasingly likely that soon they would be vying for a U.S. Senate seat in Hawaii. The junior senator's position currently was held by Spark Matsunaga, a very popular figure first elected in 1972, but a series of health crises beginning in 1984 made it unlikely that Matsunaga would run again in 1990, even if he completed his current term.

Therefore it was likely that within a year, Saiki would challenge Akaka for the hitherto solidly Democratic Senate seat, but the balance in this apparently unequal match could be tipped in a number of ways. One would be the ethnic factor. As noted above, Akaka is a native Hawaiian. The strongest faction in his Democratic party, however, is Japanese-American, a group to which Saiki could be expected to appeal. In addition, it would be natural to portray the relatively liberal Akaka as soft on crime and drugs, and possibly not sufficiently vigorous in the war on local organized crime. As a result, it was important for Akaka to rebut such charges; his membership on the House Subcommittee on Narcotic Abuse provided an ideal opportunity.

Both representatives therefore needed to appear strong on drug issues, and ideally both needed national media credentials as antidrug crusaders. Local ethnic and partisan alignments, however, circumscribed the kinds of rhetoric that would be appropriate in such a campaign. Although organized crime in general could be denounced, it is significant that none of the ice rhetoric focused on the specifically Japanese component of drug manufacture and distribution or on the role of the *yakuza* described so frequently by other law enforcement agencies and investigators. One might suggest that the nature of the forthcoming Hawaii elections made such accusations too sensitive to be presented at that time, for fear of perpetrating ethnic slurs against one of the most influential communities in the islands.

In fact, both Akaka and Saiki succeeded in gaining significant political capital from the ice issue. Saiki earned credit for having brought the problem to national attention and for requesting increased resources, but Akaka also shared the credit, and was not portrayed as soft on the crime issue in any sense. Akaka first used the term *ice age* in the hearings, and drew some of the starkest analogies between ice and crack. Both confirmed their role as standard-bearers of their respective parties. When Senator Matsunaga died a few months later, in April 1990, Akaka was the natural choice to fill the unexpired portion of his term. Both he and Saiki easily won their parties' nominations or the November election ("Hawaiian Politics" 1990). That contest normally would have been a Democratic walkover, but Saiki had established her prestige so firmly that she made it a close race, and lost only narrowly to Akaka. He thereby became the first native Hawaiian to be represented in the U.S. Senate (Saiki went on to head the federal Small Business Administration) (Reinhold 1990; Richburg 1990).

Domestic politics in Hawaii thus made it likely that the state representatives would seek to focus on a crime or drug problem of local significance. It was by no means apparent, however, that these issues would come to wider attention, especially when conditions and controversies in Hawaii so rarely attract the attention of the national media. The opportunity was provided by Akaka's service on the House Narcotics Subcommittee, where he was aided by another representative with a strong record in drug issues and a long career as a "moral entrepreneur." This was a Pennsylvania representative named Lawrence Coughlin, from the thirteenth district in suburban Montgomery County, outside Philadelphia. Coughlin, the ranking Republican on the Narcotics Subcommittee, was instrumental in bringing Akaka's views to Rangel's attention. His advocacy was significant in showing that ice was causing concern far outside Hawaii, and legitimately could be presented as a national issue.

Other agendas, however, may have been at work here as well. Coughlin's interest in methamphetamine issues dated back at least to the late 1970s, when he had been one of the most active supporters of the theory that Philadelphia was the "speed capital of the world" (Jenkins 1992a, b). To illustrate this questionable assertion, Coughlin had publicized stories from local Montgomery County newspapers as if they represented conditions throughout the state or the nation, and in effect had generated a mythology about the prevalence of speed in southeastern Pennsylvania. In 1980, largely at Coughlin's behest, the Narcotics Select Committee had been persuaded to hold special hearings in Philadelphia, where local issues and investigations received national attention (*U.S. Congress: Laboratories* 1980). The campaign to link Philadelphia with speed was so successful that it became the focus of the popular 1985 film *Witness*, whose plot concerns a huge shipment of the precursor chemical P2P. Coughlin thus emerges as a long-standing protagonist of a "speed menace." As a result, it is scarcely surprising to see the limited experience of Hawaii extrapolated to the entire nation in the 1989-1990 hearings, just as had happened with conditions in Philadelphia in 1980.

TRANSFORMING LOCAL ISSUES INTO NATIONAL PROBLEMS

In studying social problems, one critical theme is the relationship between local and national perceptions, and the way in which some (but by no means all) local phenomena come to be regarded as issues of far wider significance. The panic about ice serves to remind us that drug problems are extremely localized, and that in crime, as in so much else, it is difficult to generalize about the American experience. Drug problems rarely strike the nation in a regular or homogeneous way. Much has been written about the "crack epidemic" that swept the United States in the mid-1980s, but we must always remember that this phenomenon was highly localized. The "epidemic" initially was centered in the major cities of the east and west coasts, but scarcely penetrated large sections of the midwest until the early 1990s. This situation has many possible explanations—the strength of local traditions and subcultures, patterns of law enforcement vagaries of manufacture and supply, the interests of criminal groups—but the point is that a "panic" might be well under way in one area years before it is felt elsewhere, and it is by no means inevitable that it ever will move beyond the original region (for the localized nature of drug cultures, see, for example, Weisheit 1992).

On the other hand, certain extraneous factors demand that a local problem should be viewed in a national context, and that policy responses should be developed accordingly. One important element in this regard is the mass media, which had come, during the 1980s, to treat drug-related stories as events of major significance. newspapers assigned journalists to cover such stories as their sole or major responsibility; thus the papers had a vested interest in the constant generation of newsworthy items in this area.[1] One way to achieve this goal was to focus on local concerns or incidents, but to project them as if they were of wider, even national significance. A

[1] I am indebted to one of the anonymous reviewers for raising this point when I originally submitted this article to *Justice Quarterly*.

notorious example appeared in 1986 in the CBS television documentary *48 Hours on Crack Street*. This program presented the (then) essentially New York City problem of crack cocaine as if it were already a national epidemic, with vials littering the streets and parks of virtually every community across the country (Reinarman and Levine 1989). Though largely spurious, this account had enormous influence in generating fears of a national crack epidemic.

In the early 1980s, before the advent of crack, the media often presented the localized PCP problem in Washington, DC in such a way as to suggest that it soon would become a national crisis. (Such "extrapolations" are not confined to drug issues: witness the suggestions, at about that time, that Los Angeles's distinctive gang problems were spreading to cities throughout the nation.) Once the media present a problem in this way, Congressional hearings permit the issue to be discussed in another national forum, with the certainty that national news coverage will reinforce perceptions of a widespread crisis.

This process of "nationalization" gives rich opportunities to local activists, moral entrepreneurs, or claims makers who wish to draw attention to a particular issue, and who do so by presenting it as more dangerous or more important than it may be in fact. One natural way to do this is to suggest that a local issue either is national in scope or has a strong potential to become so in the very near future: in short, that it is about to "sweep the nation." This process enhances the importance of local campaigns; it also offers the local moral entrepreneurs the opportunity to acquire the status of national leaders and experts, should their analysis be accepted. This enhancement, in turn, can reinforce the position of local figures in their home areas.

The panic about ice is a model example of this process. The use of the drug was a local phenomenon; the national concern about the drug in 1989 derived chiefly from Hawaii's elected officials and law enforcement agencies with a definite political agenda. For two specific reasons, they were relatively successful in projecting their concerns. First, the recent experience of crack made it easy for them to represent ice, in effect, as part of the same problem; this process is known by the rhetorical term *convergence*. The ice phenomenon occurred at precisely the right time, when the rhetoric about crack was still fresh in the public mind and when the "drug war" was reaching a crescendo. It is difficult to imagine that the ice issue would have arisen at all if public expectations had not been conditioned by these recent precedents.

Second, the intense public focus on drug issues during the 1980s had created bureaucracies and political frameworks able to publicize information and opinion about drugs. These groups, such as the DEA, the NIDA, and the Narcotics Subcommittee itself, had excellent media ties and could be relied on to provide newsworthy stories about crime and drug abuse. In the case of the Congressional committee, it is inevitable that members of any political organization charged with investigating drug problems will attempt to attract as much publicity as possible by presenting themselves as concerned, active, well-informed guardians of the public good. There are few better opportunities to do so than by recognizing a problem at an early stage to prevent it reaching crisis proportions. The case of Hawaii offered the committee members the chance to investigate and combat a drug problem in a proactive, farsighted way.

No significant risk was involved in this strategy. If an "ice epidemic" occurred, the committee earned credit for having predicted it and for urging preemptive action; if it faded away, the committee could claim that its forethought had prevented a drug crisis. Conversely, there was much to be lost by cautious or skeptical reactions to an incipient crisis. If the predicted menace actually materialized, an agency or an administration stood to attract most of the blame for the ensuing problems.

None of the factors that produced the ice panic has changed significantly since 1989, or is likely to change significantly in the near future. Therefore it is probable that local drug fads will be presented once again as potential crises, likely to spread rapidly across the entire country. Social scientists must recognize and publicize the social and political factors that generate such misleading expectations.

REFERENCES

Anderson, J. and D. Van Atta (1990) "Big Plane Junket for Hill Spouses." *Washington Post*, January 10, p. 3.

Arrestee Drug Use (1990) National Institute of Justice, Research in Action. Washington, DC: U.S. Government Printing Office.

Becker, H. (1963) *Outsiders*. New York: Free Press.

Benenson, B. (1991) "Democrats Reassert Primacy in Hawaii Politics." *Congressional Quarterly*, October 12.

Best, J. (1990) *Threatened Children*. Chicago: University of Chicago Press.

Bishop, K. (1989) "Fear Grows over Effects of a New Smokable Drug." *New York Times*, September 16, p. 4A.

Brecher, E.M. (1972) *Licit and Illicit Drugs*. Boston: Little, Brown.

Buruma, I. and J. McBeth (1984-85) "An East Side Story . . . ." *Far Eastern Economic Review*, 27 December/3 January, pp. 15.

Carthane, A. (1989) "Will New Drug 'Ice" Freeze Hope in Black Communities?" *Jet*, December 18.
Cho, A.K. (1990) "Ice: A New Dosage Form of an Old Drug." *Science* (249): 631-34.
Corwin, M. (1989), "Potent Form of Speed Could Be Drug of 90s." *Los Angeles Times*, October 8, pp. 1A.
Cotton, P. (1990) "Medium Isn't Accurate Ice Age Message." *Journal of the American Medical Association* (263):2717.
Curriden, M. (1989) "Police Chilled by New In Drug: Ice." *Atlanta Constitution*, November 30, p. 1.
Delfs, R. (1991) "Cocaine Surge." *Far Eastern Economic Review*, November 21, pp. 7.
"Drugs: Ice Overdose" (1989), *Economist*, December 2, pp. 29-30.
Durso, C. (1992) "Powerful Drug 'Ice' Is Found at Lab" *Philadelphia Inquirer*, August 14, p. 1B.
Essoyan, S. (1989) "Use of Highly Addictive 'Ice' Growing in Hawaii." *Los Angeles Times*, October 16, p. 3A.
Ford, A. (1990) "Federal, Local Police Raid House in San Diego." *Los Angeles Times*, July 26, p. 7A.
Goode, E. (1984) *Drugs in American Society*. 2nd ed. New York: Knopf.
Graham, J.M. (1976) "Amphetamine Politics on Capital Hill." In W.J. Chambliss and M. Mankoff (eds.), *Whose Law? What Order?*, pp. 107-22. New York: Wiley.
Grinspoon, L. (1975) *The Speed Culture: Amphetamine Use and Abuse in America*. Cambridge, MA: Harvard University Press.
Gross, J. (1988) "Speed's Gain in Use Could Rival Crack." *New York Times*, November 27, p. A9.
Hall, S., Critcher, C., Jefferson, T., Clarke, J. and Roberts, B. (1978) *Policing the Crisis*. London: Macmillan.
"Hawaiian Politics: Ethnic Pineapple Salad" (1990) *Economist*, October 20, pp. 32.
Holland, L. (1990) "All about Ice: New Drug Nice Kids Can Get Hooked On." *Good Housekeeping*, February, pp. 215-16.
Holley, D., E. Vernant, and S. Essoyan (1991) "The Ice Age." *Washington Post*, May 9, pp. 1A.
Hong, R., E. Matsuyama, and K. Nur (1991) "Cardiomyopathy Associated with the Smoking of Crystal Methamphetamine." *Journal of the American Medical Association* (265):1152-54.
Howe, P.J. (1989) "Ice Worse Than Crack, Officials Warn." *Boston Globe*, October 1, p. 2.
"Illicit Methamphetamine: Street Drug on the Rise" (1991) *Emergency Medicine*, June 30, pp. 13-17.
Isikoff, M. (1989) "Rural Drug Users Spur Comeback of Crank." *Washington Post*, February 20, p. 3A.
Jacobs, J. (1991) "Debunking the Crack Baby Myths." *Centre Daily Times*, State College, Pa, August 11, p. 6A.
Jenkins, Philip (1992a) "Narcotics Trafficking and the American Mafia: the Myth of Internal Prohibition." *Crime, Law and Social Change* 18: 303-318.
Jenkins, Philip (1992b) "The Speed Capital of the World: Organizing the Methamphetamine Industry in Philadelphia 1970-1990." *Criminal Justice Policy Review* 6(1): 17-39.
Kaplan, D.E. and A. Dubro (1986) *Yakuza*. Reading, MA: Addison-Wesley.
LaBianca, D.A. (1992) "The Drug Scene's New Ice Age." *USA Today*, January, pp. 54-56.
Larmer, B. (1989) "Ice Chills US Anti-Drug Officials." *Christian Science Monitor*, December 8, p. 7.
Lauderback, D. and D. Waldorf (1992) "Whatever Happened to Ice?" Paper presented at meetings of the American Society of Criminology, New Orleans.
Lerner, M.L. (1989) "The Fire of Ice." *Newsweek*, November 27, p. 26.
MacDonald, P.T. and R. Estep (1985) "Prime Time Drug Depictions." *Contemporary Drug Problems* 12(3):419-38.
McBeth, J. (1989) "The Junkie Culture: Supercharged Speed is Scourge of Manila's Smart Set." *Far Eastern Economic Review*, November 23, pp. 23-25.
"Meth" (1990) Report broadcast on *60 Minutes*, April 22.
Methamphetamine Abuse in the United States. (1989) Rockville, MD: U.S. Department of Health and Human Services.

Miller, M.A. and N.J. Kozel (1991) *Methamphetamine Abuse: Epidemiological Issues and Implications*. Rockville, MD: U.S. Department of Health and Human Services.

Morgan, J.P. (1992) "Amphetamine and Methamphetamine during the 1990s." *Pediatrics in Review* 13(9):330-336.

Musto, D. (1973) *The American Disease: Origins of Narcotic Control*. New Haven: Yale University Press.

Organized Crime in California: Annual Report to the California Legislature. (1989) State of California: Department of Justice.

Pennell, S. (1990) "Ice: DUF Interview Results from San Diego." *NIJ Reports* 221:12-13.

Posner, G.L. (1988) *Warlords of Crime*. New York: McGraw-Hill.

Reinarman, C. and H.G. Levine (1989) "The Crack Attack: Politics and Media in America's Latest Drug Scare." In Joel Best (ed.), *Images of Issues*, pp. 115-37. Hawthorne, NY: Aldine.

Reinhold, R. (1990) "Hawaii Race Tests Democratic Hold." *New York Times*. November 1, pp. 9B.

Reza, H.G. (1989) "Raids Shut 23 Drug Labs." *Los Angeles Times*, March 20.

Richburg, K.B. (1990) "For Hawaii Democrats, Anxiety Over Safe Seats." *Washington Post*, November 1, p. 7A.

Sager, M. (1990) "The Ice Age." *Rolling Stone*, February 8, pp. 53-57.

Savadove, B. (1991) "High Society: Growing Drug Abuse Reflects Economic Changes." *Far Eastern Economic Review*, September 12, pp. 45-46.

Shoenberger, K. (1989) "South Korea Seen as Major Source of Ice Narcotic." *Los Angeles Times*, October 14, pp. 9A.

Skeers, V.M. (1992) "Illegal Methamphetamine Drug Laboratories." *Journal of Environmental Health* 55(3):6-9.

Smith, Z.A. and R.C. Pratt, eds. (1992) *Politics and Public Policy in Hawaii*. Albany: SUNY Press.

Tabor, M. (1989) "Ice in an Island Paradise." *Boston Globe*, December 8, p. 7.

"Text of President's Speech on Drug Control Strategy" (1989) *New York Times*, September 6, p. 4A.

Thompson, L. (1989) "Ice: New Smokable Form of Speed." *Washington Post*, November 21, p. 2.

Turner, W. (1984a) "Hawaii Criminal's Pledge to Talk Seen as Door to Underworld." *New York Times*, July 24, p. 11A.

____ (1984b) "Inquiry on Murders in Hawaii Brings Governor and Prosecutor into Conflict." *New York Times*, August 28, pp. 7A.

U.S. Congress: Drug Crisis (1990) *Drug Crisis in Hawaii: Hearing before the Select Committee on Narcotics Abuse and Control House of Representatives 101st Congress, Second Session, January 13, 1990*. Washington, DC: U.S. Government Printing Office.

U.S. Congress: Laboratories (1980) *Illicit Methamphetamine Laboratories in the Pennsylvania/New Jersey/Delaware Area: Hearing before the Select Committee on Narcotics Abuse and Control, U.S. House of Representatives, 96th Congress, Second Session, July 7, 1980*. Washington, DC: U.S. Government Printing Office.

U.S. Congress: Profile (1983) *Profile of Organized Crime: Mid-Atlantic Region: Hearings before the Permanent Subcommittee on Investigations of the Committee on Governmental Affairs, United States Senate, 98th Congress, First Session, February 15, 23, and 24, 1983*. Washington, DC: U.S. Government Printing Office.

U.S. Congress: Re-Emergence (1990) *The Re-Emergence of Methamphetamine: Hearings before the Subcommittee on Narcotics Abuse and Control, U.S. House of Representatives, 101st Congress, First Session, October 24, 1989*. Washington, DC: U.S. Government Printing Office.

U.S. Congress: Small Business (1988). *Impact of Clandestine Drug Laboratories on Small Business: Hearings before the Subcommittee on Regulation and Business Opportunities of the Committee on Small Business, U.S. House of Representatives, 100th Congress, Second Session. Eugene, Oregon, May 13, 1988*. Washington, DC: U.S. Government Printing Office.

Weingarten, P. (1989) "Profits, Perils, Higher for Today's Bootleggers." *Chicago Tribune*, September 14, p. 16.

Weisheit, R.A. (1992) *Domestic Marijuana: A Neglected Industry*. Westport, CT: Greenwood.

Wiedrich, B. (1987) "San Diego Has Become National Center for Manufacture of Methamphetamine." *Chicago Tribune*, April 20, pp. 11.

Witkin, G. (1989) "The New Midnight Dumpers." *U.S. News and World Report*, January 9, p. 23.

Young, J. (1971) "Drugs and the Media." *Drugs and Society* 2(1):14-18.

Zamichow, N. (1989) "Navy Hopes Drug Test Will Detect, Deter Meth Users." *Los Angeles Times*, October 16, p. 6A.

Zurer, P.S. (1989) "Federal Officials Plot Strategy to Stop Methamphetamine Spread." *Chemical and Engineering News*, November 6, pp. 13-16.

Mark A.R. Kleiman

Neither Prohibition Nor Legalization: Grudging Toleration in Drug Control Policy[1]

IN THE DEBATE OVER THE LEGALIZATION OF DRUGS, each side can cite horrible examples of the failure of the other's policies. Advocates of legalization can point to the role of forbidden heroin and forbidden needles in spreading AIDS and to the violence incident to the traffic in illicit cocaine.[2] Advocates of prohibition can point with equal justice to the colossal price in death and disease exacted by licit tobacco and to the massive damage done by licit alcohol to drinkers, their families, and the victims of alcohol-induced crimes and accidents.[3]

Even if we restrict our gaze to alcohol, we can see both a failed prohibition and a disastrously inadequate attempt at control by regulation and taxation.[4] Not only did Prohibition generate crime and corruption, it also deprived millions of nonproblem drinkers of a harmless (to them) source of pleasure and comfort. To judge whether that collection of harms was, in the aggregate, greater or smaller than the harms done by alcoholism, binge drinking, fetal alcohol syndrome, drunken driving, drunken assault, and drunken accidents ranging from fires to pregnancies would require a truly heroic feat of imagined measurement.

It seems, then, that the nature of (some) chemicals, the human nervous system, and American society are such that either complete prohibition or virtually free legal commerce on the model of alcohol and nicotine is likely to carry heavy costs. That being so, we can

Mark A.R. Kleiman is Associate Professor of Public Policy at the John F. Kennedy School of Government, Harvard University.

either debate which set of costs is likely to be smaller for any given drug or we can try to invent a third course, some control regime between prohibition and legalization that would moderate the disadvantages of either extreme.

Indeed, it would be strange if one could not devise a set of laws and programs much tighter than the light taxes and poorly-enforced age restrictions now applied to alcohol, yet much looser than the virtually total prohibition now applied to marijuana. It would be almost equally strange if one could find no drug too dangerous for the current alcohol regime yet not dangerous enough to need the current marijuana regime. Perhaps alcohol and marijuana might both belong in that middle category, treated neither as legitimate articles of commerce nor as contraband, but as grudgingly tolerated vices.

THE CONCEPT OF VICE

What is a vice? We are not concerned here with the "vice" that is the antonym of "virtue," but the "vice" in the phrase, "vice squad": not, that is, with cruelty, hypocrisy, arrogance, cowardice, and laziness, but with drug-taking, gambling, and commercial sex. Some capsule scenarios may illustrate the characteristics of drugs that make them potentially vicious (in the etymological rather than the current meaning of that word) and thereby constitute a reason (whether or not a good enough reason) to institute special public policies, beyond those applied to most goods and services, to control them:

1) A man beats his wife in a drunken rage.

2) A chronic heavy cigarette smoker fails on her fifth attempt to quit, and her hacking cough gets worse.

3) A pregnant woman continues to take cocaine despite warnings about possible fetal damage.

4) A high-school junior with previously good grades spends most of the year under the influence of marijuana, and doesn't learn much.

5) A heroin user steals a television set to support his habit.

6) Two sixteen-year-olds share a few wine coolers and then have their first experience of coitus, unplanned and unprotected.

7) Under the influence of alcohol, an old man falls asleep with a lit cigarette, causing a fatal house fire.

These scenarios do not, of course, prove that all drug use is vicious or that all bad behavior comes from drug abuse. Knowing that a man beats his wife while drunk does not imply that he would never beat her if he were always sober. Nor do they separate drug-taking from other activities. Item 4 would make equally good sense with "in front of the television set" substituted for "under the influence of marijuana;" item 2 could be about overeating and obesity rather than smoking and coughing. But insofar as they represent plausible stories, and stories that are more plausible about drugs than about breakfast cereals, these scenarios help indicate why drug-taking might reasonably be a topic of special legislation.

A vice, in this sense, may be defined as an activity voluntarily engaged in that risks damage and threatens self-command.[5] It is a special kind of hazardous consumer product, in which some of the hazards are behavioral: that is, where part of what some consumers are in danger from is their own faulty decision making about whether, how often, when, where, and how much to consume, and how to behave afterwards.

The damage done by a vice may be purely behavioral, or it may be physical as well. The behavioral ill effects may last only as long as the pleasure, or they may through chronic use become part of the participant's character. The behavioral risk may be limited to consumption of the vice itself (as with a person unable to stop smoking) or it may extend to other behavior (as with a drunken assailant). We may distinguish these as "addictive" and "intoxicating" vices, respectively.

In the case of the addictive vices, the vice consumer will often be the only person at direct risk, although even in that case insurance or other risk-spreading mechanisms are likely to spread the costs around. Intoxicating vices are more likely to involve other immediate victims.

WHAT MAKES A VICE?

Potential vices are as varied as the kinks in the human psyche. Anything that is desired obsessively can generate behavior that seems irrational not only to outside observers but to the actor himself or herself in dispassionate moments. Gems, sports cars, paintings, rare books, postage stamps, coins, wealth, and power are all vices for some of those who collect them.

Still, it is possible to isolate characteristics of activities that will tend to make them vices of either the addictive or the intoxicating sort.

Anything will be an intoxicating vice to the extent that it reduces the capacity for rational self-direction. To be rationally self-directed, one must be able to correctly perceive what one is doing, to imagine its consequences, to evaluate those consequences, and to shape one's behavior in light of that evaluation.

The capacity to postpone gratification, and in particular to accept a moderate amount of immediate unpleasantness to avoid a large amount of deferred unpleasantness, is a hard-won and often incomplete victory of the process of growing up. It is also fragile, as anyone who has been very ill, or in battle, or drunk can testify.

As intoxicants, drugs stand out from other potential vices because of their direct and mechanical effect on the nervous system. This is less true of addictive vices. The physiological dependency most characteristic of the opiates gives some cases of drug addiction a physical substrate absent from addiction to soap operas, but most drug addiction—more broadly, most compulsive drug-taking—depends on faults in human decision making that make themselves felt in a wide range of activities.[6] Physiological dependency, or drug addiction proper, is the most spectacular but not the most important source of irrational drug-taking behavior.[7]

Any activity in which the reward and punishment pattern poorly represents the actual costs and benefits will be a frequent locus of behavioral departures from rationality. If the rewards are immediate, certain, powerful, and clearly linked to the activity, while the punishments are delayed, uncertain, diffuse, and hard to trace, then the practice will be behaviorally reinforced even though its costs exceed its benefits as valued by the participant. Thus an addictive vice is simply a potential bad habit.

Note that this account makes vices different only in degree from many commodities and activities. A vice has in abundance characteristics that many commodities have more or less: the tendency to induce error (especially excess) and a threat to self-command.

SHOULD WE HAVE VICE POLICIES?

Assume for the moment that drug-taking has the characteristics of a vice: that it is more prone than the typical activity both to escape control by its participants' voluntary self-restraint and to damage their capacity to exercise such self-restraint in other areas, in their own interest and in consideration for others. So what? If they damage themselves, why does that concern the state? If they damage others, do we not have criminal and civil laws to restrain them, and nonlegal institutions ranging from families to markets as well? Did not John Stuart Mill demonstrate that the greatest good of the greatest number is served by leaving "self-regarding actions," including private consumption choices, in the hands of individuals?

There are at least four questions entangled here, one normative and three more or less empirical.

1) If there are topics about which individuals systematically make such bad choices for themselves that their welfare, as they measure it, can be improved by state interference in their private affairs, is such interference justified?

2) Are there such topics, and can they be identified?

3) To what extent will damage to individual capacities for self-regulation spill over and damage other persons?

4) Given the imperfections in the processes of legislation and enforcement, will actual vice laws (assuming there are any) make matters better or worse for potential vice consumers and others? In particular, will vice laws tend to excessive meddling with harmless pleasures, and vice enforcement to excessive intrusiveness?

A utilitarian such as Mill, or any other proponent of a welfarist theory of the good, is forced to concede that an intervention that makes those subjected to it better off is justified. Those who value personal autonomy over personal well-being will tend to disagree.[8] I have no hope of settling that question here, only to pry the question free from the notion that Mill has already settled it in the negative.

The real force of the argument for absolute noninterference stems from the notion that no person will choose to damage himself. The rationally self-directed individual is assumed in so much economic, legal, and philosophical discourse that it is worth reminding ourselves that perfect self-command is no more to be met with in nature than is a perfect vacuum. Self-command is an achievement, not a given; even the wily Odysseus preferred to face temptation with the aid of physical restraint.

There is more basis for doubting that political institutions are well-designed to identify vices and to erect appropriate control regimes. Not only is the identification of vice likely to engage the most virulent social prejudice, but vice control seems to share with vice itself a tendency to excess. This line of argument is enough to support a rebuttable presumption against vice legislation, but the absolute presumption claimed by the strict libertarians seems harder to justify.

Nor is it plausible that, in a society based largely on self-direction, the costs of widespread failures of self-control will fall entirely on those individuals who suffer from them. A liberal society counts on its (adult, healthy) members both to manage their own affairs in their own interest and to restrict their behavior within the bounds of civil conduct and the rights of others, as embodied in laws and customs. No one does either of these tasks perfectly, and in any social group some will do them less well than others. But the less capable of self- management the members of any society are, the more formal social control they will require and the less happy that society will be under a liberal regime. "Whoever does not rule himself will be ruled by another."

Liberal institutions, including the market and the criminal law, rely on individuals' capacities to manage their own affairs in their own interest both to restrain their behavior in deference to the rights of others and to secure their cooperation for private and public purposes. Direct coercion (for example, imprisonment) is extremely rare, because it is extremely expensive, compared with incentives, including coercive threats.[9] Anything that makes individuals more present-oriented and less self-controlled will require an increase in external controls to achieve the same level of security for others.

Moreover, anything that makes someone a less competent steward of his own welfare is likely to make him also a less desirable coworker, neighbor, or fellow citizen by reducing his capacity and willingness to engage in the myriad forms of voluntary cooperation that characterize the workplace, the neighborhood, and the polity.

Thus the regime of liberty is not indifferent to the character of its members, and, paradoxically, liberal societies may need more restrictive policies about vice than regimes that rely more on coercion.

This becomes less paradoxical when it is remembered that the individuals who constitute a free society occupy the supreme office of citizen and voter. Under a democratic regime, the character of the populace is the character of the ruling class, and thus self-evidently a matter of political, and not merely private, concern. As Machiavelli warned, a corrupt people will not long retain its freedom.[10]

But will not this line of reasoning lead to regulating everybody's breakfast? That will indeed be the case if policymakers and citizens lack the virtue of moderation. Surely the range of possibly damaging activities is far broader than the range that could be usefully regulated.

One key piece of evidence that some practice may be so vicious that it needs to be coercively interfered with is that many of its participants regret their initial choice to adopt it. If the vice is an addictive one, there will be further evidence in the form of repeated and imperfectly successful attempts to quit and demand for external, professional help in doing so. If the vice is an intoxicating one, the regret will be centered less on the activity itself—its frequency and quantity—than on the resulting behavior.

Simply by treating their own behavior as a problem, participants in any activity provide evidence that it fits the model of rational self-control only imperfectly. To be sure, those who develop bad habits will not be the only ones to complain. Other sufferers—families, coworkers, neighbors, the victims of crimes and accidents—will add their voices to the chorus. But it is the testimony of those who find their own behavior slipping out of their control that is the most persuasive in overcoming the presumption that some particular activity is well-regulated by unconstrained individual choice.

ELEMENTS OF VICE POLICY

What can we do about vices, in the interest of their consumers and others? Conceptually, the list is short:

1) We can try to develop in the population at large better personal decision skills, better impulse control, and more awareness of self-command as a problem in general and the specific threats to it represented by particular potential bad habits.

2) We can create conditions that discourage the use, and especially inappropriate or excessive use, of vicious goods and services, by making them expensive or hard to obtain, and by restricting the distribution of promotional messages and fostering the distribution of antipromotional messages.

3) We can attempt to temper the bad results of vice consumption by making the world a safer place in which to be intoxicated (or by creating spaces for safe intoxication), by helping those who have become habituated, and now wish to stop, in the process of quitting, and by coercing those whose vice consumption is a problem for others either to moderate or cease their vice consumption or to reduce the behavior that causes external damage.

In the instance of alcohol consumption, the range of possible policies would then include: promoting the ideal and skills of moderation and self-command; spreading information about the risks of drunken behavior and alcohol habituation; taxing alcoholic beverages; restricting when, where, how, to whom, and in what quantities they may lawfully be advertised and sold; enforcing those restrictions against buyers and sellers; improving general highway safety to reduce the frequency of fatal injury from drunken driving; suspending the driving licenses of those who drive drunk; and requiring those who drive drunk, or commit drunken assaults, to abstain from alcohol. The requirement of abstinence could be enforced either directly on identified problem users or indirectly, via (licensed) alcohol sellers.

A different conceptual map would divide vice control regimes into laws and programs. Laws include taxes and regulations. (Prohibition can be conceived as the extreme of either taxation or regulation.) Programs enforce the laws, educate and persuade, or offer help to, and impose control on, identified problem users.

WHAT IS GRUDGING TOLERATION?

The analysis above suggests that free legal availability of all psychoactives is unlikely to be the best policy. But prohibition has equally obvious costs. Can we construct a middle course that will, for some drugs, outperform either of the extremes?

One way to think about doing so is to start with the current alcohol control regime. Of all the drugs not completely banned for nonmedical use, alcohol is the most tightly regulated; most of the possible forms of restriction are now present, if only in embryo. Still, a point-by-point examination of alcohol policy suggests how much room there is for further tightening, short of prohibition. For each proposed step there are one or more objections, disadvantages, design problems, and questions of enforceability. But for now it suffices to show how broad the possibilities are for discouraging drug abuse without forbidding all drug consumption.

Taxation

Alcohol is subject to special taxation (or the equivalent in monopoly pricing) at both the federal and the state level. The tax burden on the average drink is about ten cents, roughly one-tenth of its total price.

Yet the external costs of alcohol use (the costs imposed on nonusers via health insurance, accidents, etc.) are at least three times that high, even without reckoning the costs of crimes committed under the influence.[11] A good case can be made for alcohol taxes at the level of a dollar per drink.[12] The effect on drinking, especially heavy drinking and drinking by adolescents, would be substantial.[13]

Promotion

Advertising for distilled spirits is banned from television by broadcast industry practice, and federal regulation forbids advertisements that stress the potency of competing brands. Packages, but not advertisements, are required to carry health warnings. There are some attempts through "public service" messages to discourage drunken driving and underage drinking and promote moderation, but there is no mass-media campaign against drinking, or even drunkenness, as such. (The media outlets and advertising agencies that contribute talent and advertising space to the Media Partnership for a Drug-Free America derive much of their revenue from alcoholic-beverage advertising.) School-based antidrug programs cover alcohol as well as the illicit drugs, but the movement for controls on alcohol advertising aimed at the young is opposed on free-speech grounds.

These restrictions on promotion and efforts at "antipromotion" are quite modest by comparison with the potential. Advertising could be banned entirely (with the useful side effect of removing an important incentive for media self-censorship with respect to the alcohol problem) or its content could be restricted to facts about the various products, their prices, and where they can be obtained, after the fashion of the "tombstone" ads to which securities underwriters are limited. A serious campaign of negative advertising, like the one currently mounted against illicit drug use by the Media Partnership for a Drug-Free America, could be supported with public funds. Since alcohol is now more socially acceptable and less feared than the illicit drugs are or were, and since there is in fact considerable bad news about alcohol to disseminate, the effect of such a campaign might be quite substantial, as the antismoking campaign since 1964 has been.

Restrictions on Sellers

Sellers of alcoholic beverages, whether for on-premises consumption or for carry-out, are forbidden to sell to anyone visibly intoxicated. They have no responsibility not to provide the means of chronic alcohol abuse, even if they are aware of it. Tavernkeepers but not package-goods sellers may be held responsible for drunken misbehavior, including automobile accidents, by persons they have served. Tavernkeepers are also required to maintain orderly premises. Times of sale are restricted by law, and licenses to sell are kept in short supply and are subject to revocation for seller misbehavior. (In some states, package sales are a state monopoly.) Sellers are responsible for ensuring that customers are of legal age to drink.

There is little evidence that tighter time-and-place restrictions, or a reduction in the number of licenses, could noticeably reduce alcohol abuse, but such policies might bring benefits to the neighborhoods now inconvenienced by the presence of bars and liquor stores. A more drastic step would be to impose more liability on alcoholic beverage sellers for the behavior and welfare of the drinkers they serve: to require them, as stockbrokers are required, to "know their customer" and to act in a quasi-fiduciary capacity. This would mean training sales personnel to recognize the stigmata of chronic alcohol abuse, or even requiring buyers to establish relationships with a limited number of sellers who could then monitor consumption levels. It could also mean requiring tavernkeepers to provide a safe and comfortable space in which to enjoy the effects of the drug, and to allow or even require their customers to remain within it as long as the influence lasts.

Restrictions on Buyers

Drug users are heterogeneous; a substance harmless to one person can wreck the life of another and turn a third into a social menace. That is the great objection to blanket prohibition and blanket legalization alike; either one makes fewer discriminations than the topic demands.

Possible restrictions on buyers include limits on who can buy, limits on quantity (as a way of addressing the harms done to and by heavy users), and limits on behavior under the influence. Of these, only the last is usually enforced against the buyers directly; the others are enforced against the sellers, who then bear the responsibility for making the restriction felt by the buyers.

Of the possible range of possible criteria about who may buy alcohol, current US law makes use of only one: age. In effect, every American who turns twenty-one is given an unconditional and irrevocable license to drink. If even this restriction could be strictly enforced, the alcohol problem would shrink considerably; about four in ten male high-school seniors report having had five or more drinks at a single sitting within the previous two weeks.[14] Obviously, alcohol leaks through the age barrier by the gallon, primarily, it appears, through the simple expedient of having those who are of age buy for those who are not.[15]

Other possible criteria for a "drinker's license" might include knowledge of facts and safety rules about drinking, as demonstrated on a test like a written driving test or by completion of a training program like driver's education course; call this "positive licensure." The alternative is "negative licensure": every adult has a license unless it is lifted for a history of misbehavior such as drunken driving, drunken assault, or distribution of alcohol to unlicensed persons. (Why should drunken drivers lose their right to drive but keep their right to drink?) Under either system, a drinker could voluntarily cede his license, either as an aid to self-control or to secure the economic benefits, such as discounts on automobile, life, and health insurance, likely to be offered to nondrinkers.

In either case, eligibility to drink would need to be signified by a document, which could either be a new document, patterned after a driver's license, or the driver's license itself, with additional markings. This would allow the seller to verify the buyer's eligibility, as is currently done with proof of age. Such a system of licensure would also allow the enforcement of personal quantity limits for alcohol purchase, an idea which has in the past been tried in Oregon and some parts of Scandinavia but ran aground on administrative problems.

A less drastic, but also less effective, way to deal with the tendency of some problem drinkers to commit crimes and cause accidents would be to impose the order not to drink on them directly, rather than on the industry. Enforcing such an order would require either the compulsory administration of a drug to counteract the effects of alcohol (as naloxone blocks the effects of heroin) or to make them unpleasant (as Antabuse does for alcohol) or the development and administration of chemical tests for past alcohol use, like the chemical tests now available for past use of illicit drugs.

This list of possible components of a policy of grudging toleration toward alcohol is not quite comprehensive enough to serve for all possible drugs. It reflects the fact that alcohol is a relatively mild intoxicant at low doses, widely and frequently used. For drugs with much more profound effects, which most users take very infrequently, and which are not integrated into existing social rituals—for example, the psychedelics, including LSD, mescaline, psilocybin, ketamine, and MDMA—one could imagine a control regime based on a small number of licensed places of administration, employing licensed personnel, who would have the responsibility and the authority to exercise custodianship over drug-takers during their period of intoxication and recovery and would be liable to their customers and to third parties in the case of bad outcomes. Ideal control regimes might be nearly as various as drugs themselves; surely they are not as bipolar as the current control regimes.

GRUDGING TOLERATION IN ACTION: THREE EXAMPLES

Without specifics, grudging toleration is no more than a slogan. But specifics must involve specific drugs; I have chosen alcohol, marijuana, and cocaine as illustrations. (What forms grudging toleration might appropriately take for other vices is a topic for another day.) The actual details of any control regime would require volumes to describe; no more than a sketch is possible here. Even if fully-detailed plans could be presented, they would be of limited value. Actual essays in grudging toleration would quickly reveal problems and possibilities that no one had guessed at in advance. This is a topic on which an ounce of experience is worth a pound of speculation.

Alcohol illustrates how far laws about the currently licit drugs could be tightened without resorting to all-out prohibition, and how many difficult issues are raised when one attempts to interfere with a practice so deeply ingrained in personal habit and social ritual.

The design of a regime embodying the grudging toleration of alcohol also suggests the potential shape of grudging toleration for the second-most-popular intoxicant, marijuana. The potential gains are substantial, but the potential losses are not to be overlooked.

Cocaine illustrates the limits of grudging toleration as a policy approach, and in particular its dependence on a very widespread willingness among the partakers of the vice in question to maintain their consumption within some bounds. I am compelled to admit failure in the attempt to design a program of regulation short of prohibition that would adequately contain the nation's cocaine consumption, and I am skeptical that others will enjoy any better success unless they can invent genuinely new features for regulatory schemes rather than merely rearranging the elements discussed here. The result for heroin and the other opiates and opioids would likely be broadly similar.

Alcohol

The outlines of a system of grudging toleration for alcohol have already been sketched: heavy taxation, strict limits on promotion, a large dose of "negative advertising," a personal license to buy and use alcohol revocable for misconduct, and vigorous enforcement efforts to suppress noncommercial as well as commercial distribution to minors and other unlicensed persons. The likely results, for good and ill, are easy to imagine. On the plus side, there would be a large increase at least in the short run in the revenue from the alcohol tax, (in the range of tens of billions of dollars per year); less drinking by some current problem drinkers, and consequently less intoxicated crime and fewer intoxicated accidents; and a reduced (but how greatly reduced?) rate of initiation to drinking, and especially to heavy drinking, among adolescents. On the minus side, we would face the impoverishment of some heavy drinkers who cannot or will not cut back their drinking in the face of higher taxes; the lost benefits of whatever nonproblem drinking is suppressed by higher taxes and tighter controls; the substitution of other mind-altering substances for more-expensive and harder-to-get alcohol; administrative expense and inconvenience and the costs (to the state and to the individuals involved) of punishments imposed on those who violate the rules; and a substantial black market in untaxed alcohol and in alcohol for the unlicensed.

The precise mix of good and bad effects would depend in part on facts about the world (for example, the price-elasticity of demand for drink, the rate of substitution of marijuana for alcohol) and in part on the details of the regulatory regime. The level of taxation is an obvious control variable; less obvious, but not less important, is how aggressive to be in suspending or revoking drinking licenses. The potential customer base for a new bootlegging-and-speakeasy industry depends on the number of involuntarily unlicensed drinkers. The larger the customer base, the larger the enforcement effort required to keep unlicensed dram shops under control. This ought to, but might not, restrain judges or licensing authorities from going overboard in suspending drinking privileges. The place to start is with a relatively small number of repeated drunken drivers and drunken assailants, rather than with the chronic inhabitants of police station "drunk tanks."

In principle, the budget for enforcing the new drinking laws ought to be related to the need for enforcement arising from how tight they are; in practice, there will be a tendency toward a symbolic draconianism, with strong laws undermined by weak enforcement. This is likely to prove the worst possible combination. There is a case to be made for tightening regulations slowly, to avoid setting off a sudden rush of illicit activity that might explode beyond the capacity of the enforcement system to deal with it.

Another design question is whether to impose a quantity limit on monthly alcohol purchases, and if so how tight to make it. Quantity limits would help directly in controlling drinking by heavy drinkers, and indirectly by reducing the problem of leakage to unlicensed drinkers. Enforcing such a limit, virtually impossible in the precomputer era, would be no more technically difficult now than enforcing the purchase limits on credit cards. In addition to the obvious problems of privacy, governmental regulation of lifestyle choices in such detail would raise hackles.

In fixing a specific limit, policymakers would confront a tradeoff between tightness and enforceability; as a practical matter, no more than a few percent of the population should find the quantity limit constraining. This suggests what would seem a very loose limit, perhaps four drinks per day (three ounces of absolute alcohol) averaged over a month: about a case and a half of beer a week. After all, the question is about a legally enforced upper limit, not a guideline for moderation. Individuals could also be allowed to select lower limits for themselves, either as protection against their own impulses or to be able to certify their moderation to others, including spouses, employers, and insurers.

A relatively loose top limit would allow for routine hospitality without the need for special exemptions for party-givers. (An alternative would be the creation of a social norm of "bring your own bottle.") More difficult to deal with would be the responsibility of hosts, as opposed to tavernkeepers, to verify that they serve liquor only to licensed individuals. Compliance with this rule would be imperfect, and any vigorous enforcement measures would clearly run into problems of intrusiveness.

The same may well be true of the problem of drinking during pregnancy. Despite the great attention recently lavished on "crack babies," the largest group of profoundly drug-damaged newborns in the United States are the victims of their mothers' alcohol consumption. The problem goes well beyond clinically diagnosed fetal alcohol syndrome to a variety of less obvious developmental deficits.[16] But it is not obvious that coercion is a good way to deal with the issue; privacy, efficacy, and perverse incentives are all problems.

Grudging toleration of alcohol can produce some of the benefits of prohibition with only some of its costs. It cannot put an end to problem drinking, and it will create expense and inconvenience for millions of Americans whose drinking is not a problem to themselves or to anyone else. Alcohol is both a source of pleasure and comfort, sanctioned by long tradition, and a viciously dangerous intoxicant with a substantial risk of addiction; any policy will find itself caught between those two realities. Reflecting on the magnitude of the current alcohol problem—90,000 deaths and millions of crimes per year—will help create appropriately modest performance criteria for a new approach. It would take a remarkably poor set of regulations based on grudging toleration to do worse than we have done with virtually unconstrained legal availability.

Marijuana

Marijuana is easily the most widely used of the currently illicit psychoactives. While it clearly generates excessive and even compulsive consumption habits in some proportion of its users,[17] carries some health risks (at least those of repeatedly inhaling hot gasses, particulates, carbon monoxide, and "coal tars"), and produces an intoxication dangerous for driving or operating heavy machinery, the vast majority of those who have consumed it have done so without apparent ill effects.[18]

The costs of the current prohibition, including several hundred thousand arrests per year and the creation of an illicit market with approximately ten billion dollars in annual revenue, are very large. Concerns that marijuana may serve as a "gateway" to other psychoactive use are at least partially balanced out by accumulating evidence that, at least in the short run, it and alcohol substitute for one another; if that is true, some of the additional marijuana consumption will replace alcohol consumption, which is at least equally dangerous on average. If any controlled substance is a candidate for grudging toleration, marijuana is.[19] (I leave aside the question of marijuana's medical utility, for nausea control, appetite enhancement, and the control of spasticity and pain. The medical question ought to be resolved independently of the question of licit availability for nonmedical, "recreational" use.)[20]

Since grudging toleration of alcohol would represent a tightening of current controls, while any toleration, however grudging, of marijuana would represent a substantial loosening, the effect of instituting such policies in the two cases would be in opposite directions. Grudging toleration would reduce somewhat the current problem of alcohol abuse, while aggravating the problems associated with its control; by contrast, the severity of the marijuana abuse problem would increase, but the costs of control, especially law-enforcement costs, the damage done to users by enforcement action and punishment, and the corruption and violence associated with the illicit market would all diminish to some extent.

Marijuana, along with alcohol and nicotine, forms the entering wedge of drug experience for American adolescents.[21] One argument for changing the current laws is that they have signally failed in making marijuana unavailable to high-school and even junior-high-school students.[22] Worse, marijuana introduces some of them to the opportunities of black-market retailing, which opens up both access to more dangerous substances[23] and to undesirable career patterns. Removing adult marijuana demand from the illicit market will have some beneficial effects in this regard, although it is also to be expected that some juveniles now earning money dealing marijuana will begin to deal something worse, or to engage in theft, as the next-best way of deriving illicit income.

It remains the case that alcohol, which is licit for adults, is much more widely used and abused among adolescents than is marijuana. This suggests that loosening marijuana controls for adults might increase the (already substantial) ease of availability among teenagers (although it also means that substitution away from alcohol would be significant among this group). Thus preventing increased use among adolescents should be one goal in the design of a regime of grudging toleration for marijuana. Presumably, this would mean an age restriction like that now applied to alcohol; the problem would be to make the age restriction for marijuana actually restrict, as the current age restriction for alcohol so signally fails to do.

If all laws regarding marijuana were repealed at once and not replaced, three distinct effects would occur in the conditions of marijuana availability and use: it would be cheaper, it would be easier to obtain, and the enforcement risk associated with using it, and especially using it in public, would disappear. Each of these effects would be expected to result, other things equal, in increased consumption, which is to say an increased number of hours spent intoxicated. Since marijuana already contributes substantially to the nation's experience of intoxication,[24] and especially since most of these hours are accounted for by persons for whom marijuana intoxication is a more-or-less constant state, preventing a major upsurge in consumption, and in particular a substantial increase in the number of chronic heavy marijuana users, is a second design criterion.

Other goals would include encouraging those whose use has escaped their voluntary control to quit, if necessary with either professional help or assistance from one of the self-help groups, keeping the incidence of highway and workplace marijuana intoxication down, avoiding a problem with public marijuana intoxication, and reducing the health damage associated with smoking the drug.

The price effect of a complete abolition would be quite substantial. The current black-market price of marijuana (about $300 per ounce for high-potency "sinsemilla") works out to approximately ten cents per milligram of delta-9 tetrahydrocannabinol (THC), the main psychoactive agent. Roughly speaking, ten milligrams of THC produces one person-hour of intoxication, so the current price of a stoned hour is about a dollar. At a guess, the licit price might be one-tenth of that. Since marijuana intoxication is already substantially cheaper per hour than alcohol intoxication, there seems to be no good reason to let the price fall from its current level; anyone for whom the price of getting stoned represents an important economic burden is probably smoking too much.

If the price of licit marijuana were no higher than the price on the black market, the vast majority of users would probably prefer the legal product, which would be of known potency, free of adulterants, and so on. If the licit price were above the illicit price, moonshining would likely pose a more serious problem. Since the remaining illicit marijuana industry would also serve the juvenile market, keeping it small would be essential to the goal of protecting adolescents. Thus the current black-market price seems to be about the right target for tax policy. At that level, governments would be reaping several billions of dollars per year in marijuana tax revenues, money that had previously been going to criminals: not a trivial advantage to set off against the risks of grudging toleration.

High taxes would help reduce very heavy marijuana use, especially since heavy marijuana users would be less able to finance their habits with production or sales in the illicit market. Still, it seems unlikely that the current population of a few million chronic zonkers would shrink; if the total number of users grows once the barriers posed by prohibition are removed, it is probable that some of the additional users will become potheads. In addition, since the legal consequences of public marijuana intoxication would be less, we should expect its frequency, and perhaps the rate of disorderly or otherwise noxious behavior, to rise; one consequence of making a substance illegal is to encourage its consumers to behave discreetly to avoid the attention of the police. As we have found with alcohol, disorderly behavior is hard to separate from public intoxication; laws against disorderly conduct are simply too difficult to enforce.

The obvious approach to reducing heavy individual consumption would be to impose a personal quantity limit, as proposed above for alcohol. Administration of such a limit would be easier if purchase were limited to mail-order only. That would also make it possible to administer a system of user licensing (with revocation for intoxicated misconduct or distribution to minors or other unlicensed users) without creating a physical document representing the right to buy marijuana. Again as with alcohol, a quantity limit would reduce consumption by heavy users and at the same time limit leakage from adults to minors, since any one adult would be able to supply only a limited number of teenagers.

The entire system could be administered publicly, or the sellers could be licensees subject to regulation and audit. The shameless promotion of compulsive gambling by state lottery authorities suggests that it may be easier to control a regulated private industry than a public one. In either case, advertising and other promotion should be under strict limits, as securities advertising now is: sellers should be restricted to neutral factual statements about product characteristics, price, and the mechanics of purchase.

Since marijuana is an unprocessed plant material that can be grown indoors or outdoors without any special equipment or skill, a possible alternative to a regulated industry or public monopoly would be to forbid commercial transactions entirely, and simply give adults permission to grow their own. Alaska, where a state court decision effectively decriminalized domestic marijuana growing for personal use, experienced no obvious disaster in the period before a referendum restored full prohibition. Such a system would eliminate the problems of administration, and pressure from an agency or industry to allow promotion, at the sacrifice of tax revenue and of the any control over very heavy personal consumption.

The transition from prohibition to grudging toleration could not be made without risk. Consumption, and consumption-related damage of all kinds, might suddenly soar, or it might rise slowly but inexorably over a generation, as alcohol abuse did after repeal. In either case, reversing the process of change and returning to prohibition would be formidably hard, since the costs of enforcing a prohibition are directly related to the frequency of the practice to be prohibited. In the very circumstance in which reprohibition would seem most desirable—a huge increase in consumption—it would be least feasible. Our failure to erect a regime of grudging toleration for alcohol, and the huge toll of death and suffering associated with that failure, stand as a warning.

In my view, the costs of maintaining prohibition are sufficiently high, and the damage likely to be done by increased consumption sufficiently modest, to justify accepting the risk. Of course, given the climate of opinion in the United States today, such a proposal has no current prospect of enactment; the mood in parts of Europe may be different.

Cocaine

Cocaine also gives grudging toleration an easy mark to shoot at; the current situation under prohibition is so bad that even a quite poor result could still count as a change for the better. Cocaine-dealing violence is wrecking the inner cities and cocaine law enforcement is bankrupting the criminal justice system, leaving it without the resources to punish violators of other laws. Cocaine dealing plays a substantial role in the shockingly high rate of arrests and convictions among young African-American men.[25] Still, it is worth remembering that any situation, however bad, could get worse.

As the advocates of the repeal or modification of drug prohibitions never tire of reminding us, the measurable health damage done to Americans by cocaine is of trivial size compared to that done by alcohol.[26] This is so, not because cocaine is less physiologically damaging than alcohol, but because it is far less widely used: there appear to be about two million more-or-less frequent cocaine users (weekly or more), and another several million occasional users, in the United States.[27] By contrast, there appear to be more than ten million Americans who fit one definition or another of "problem drinking" (heavy daily drinking or repeated binge drinking) out of a population of more than one hundred million who use alcohol at least occasionally.[28]

Cocaine is less widely used than alcohol for many reasons, including tradition and reputation, that might change only slowly if cocaine's legal status were to change. But prohibition has also made cocaine very expensive and at least somewhat inconvenient and risky to obtain. Even after the collapse of cocaine prices during the 1980s, when a flood of cocaine swamped the capacity of the enforcement system, black-market cocaine retails for approximately $100 per pure gram, roughly twenty times the pharmaceutical price. In a genuinely free market in cocaine, a rock of crack would cost about twenty-five cents, as opposed to the current five dollars. Cocaine buyers must also face all the inconveniences of trading in illicit markets: lack of information, the risk of robbery or fraud, uncertainty about product quality, difficulty in locating a seller (more pronounced for inexperienced users and nonresidents of neighborhoods with open drug markets), and the risk of arrest.

Thus the bland assertion of some advocates of cocaine legalization that cocaine consumption might not change if all regulations were removed[29] seems difficult to square with ordinary theories and experience of consumer behavior. When a good gets much cheaper and much safer and easier to obtain, we ordinarily expect that consumers will demand more of it. Thus even if legal availability were accompanied by a complete ban on advertising and other forms of promotion, the expected result would be an upsurge in cocaine consumption.

What regulations, short of prohibition, could be put in place to limit the increase in the population of heavy cocaine users? How successful could one expect them to be?

Cocaine comes in several forms and is taken in several different ways. Traditional use in the Andes involves chewing the coca leaves themselves. The cocaine leaches out of the leaves so slowly that no marked intoxication is experienced. The leaves can also be infused with hot water to make "tea," or *mate de coca*. Again, the subjective effects are far from dramatic. Around the turn of the century, when cocaine was available almost without restriction in the United States, it was consumed most widely in a variety of dilute oral dosage forms, including a wide range of patent medicines, an alcohol-and-cocaine preparation called *Vin Mariani*, and a combination of cocaine, sugar, and carbonated water called Coca-Cola. In each case, the dose of actual cocaine is low, and the oral route of administration delivers it to the brain slowly, over a period of several minutes, thus creating a much less dramatic experience than smoking, injecting, or even snorting the pure active ingredient. If all cocaine-taking involved low-dosage oral forms of the drug, cocaine might be no more controversial than its chemical relative, caffeine. It is the administration of the purified chemical, either as a powdery hydrochloride salt, which can be snorted or injected, or as an anhydrous base (freebase or crack) which can be vaporized and inhaled, that has twice given cocaine an evil reputation.[30]

Thus an obvious regulatory approach would be to restrict cocaine to dilute forms designed to be swallowed rather than pure forms to be snorted, injected, or smoked. Even restriction to the hydrochloride powder would represent some progress, since snorting is less prone to generate a powerful habit than smoking,[31] and injection has remained relatively rare. Unfortunately, neither the extraction of pure cocaine from solutions in water nor the conversion of the hydrochloride to the base demand much in the way of equipment, reagents, or chemical knowledge. Thus there is no way to expand availability of the safer forms without making the more hazardous ones easier to get at the same time.

Even if supply regulation could be made effective (for example, by requiring that cocaine preparations include some chemical that would make extraction difficult), the mere existence of a licit market in some forms of cocaine would not by itself eliminate the illicit market in other forms. The regulated cocaine trade could be in addition to, rather than instead of, the illicit one. In that case, there might be social gain in the form of consumers' surplus from the newly-legalized products, but the problem of illicit-market violence that made cocaine legalization a plausible alternative in the first place would remain.

For some users, dilute oral cocaine would substitute for snorting, smoking, or injecting the pure drug. Almost certainly, a large proportion of the customers in any legal cocaine market would be drinking cocaine tea or cocaine tonics. This demand-side effect, substitution, is distinct from the intended supply-side effect of restricting availability to safer forms alone. However, the substitution effect would not be the only one present. Other users, who are now afraid to try pure cocaine because of its reputation, deterred by illegality and inconvenience, or simply priced out of the market by illicit-industry markups, would probably try dilute, legal, inexpensive cocaine beverages. Some of them would like the effect enough, or generate a sufficient tolerance for low doses, to want to "graduate" to more powerful forms of cocaine-taking.

Even if slow, low-dose forms gained *relative* market position at the expense of sudden, high-dose forms, the *absolute* number of snorters, smokers, and injectors could nonetheless rise substantially from its current level. It all depends on the relative magnitudes of two opposite effects: the expansion of the total size of the market, and the substitution of weak for strong forms. In any case, given the ease of purification and conversion, the effect will depend primarily on consumers' preferences rather than on official regulations.

That leaves a relatively small vocabulary of possible regulatory measures (taking for granted restrictions on promotion and some sort of official campaign to discourage use or at least to encourage moderation, and assuming that places-and-hours regulations quickly reach the limit of their effectiveness). We could try to manage the price (via taxation or its equivalent in government-monopoly pricing), restrict the quantity available for purchase by any one purchaser, or make the permission to purchase a licensed status.

As with any drug, the decision about price involves a trade-off. Higher prices discourage consumption, but tend to make those who do become heavy users worse off financially. The greater the cash drain on heavy users, the harder on their health and the welfare of their families, and the more of them who will be induced to turn to theft or prostitution as income sources. Lower prices make users better off and reduce their criminal activity, but increase their numbers and, perhaps, the proportion of them who go on to chronic heavy use or repeated binge use.

The current black-market price puts a practical upper limit on the price that could be charged in the newly licit market; otherwise, the promised benefits of the system in eliminating illicit dealing will not materialize.

If the tax level left cocaine near its current black-market price while changes in the laws made it more conveniently available, there appears to be no reason to expect crime by cocaine users (as opposed to dealers) to decrease. On the contrary, not only will any increase in the heavy-user population or the quantity per heavy user (due to increased availability and decreased fear of arrest) tend to boost the rates of property crime, but the current population of user/dealers, deprived of the easiest source of illicit income, will begin to look for others. While this loss of dealing income would help reduce the demand for cocaine, it would also tend to increase the rate of theft. Insofar as user/dealers are well armed, at least some of this theft will take the violent form of robbery, either street mugging or store hold-ups. Thus legalization at high prices would substitute robbery for the competitive violence of the current cocaine industry, while increasing other forms of property crime. The magnitudes of the various shifts are difficult to guess.

Even at high prices, the total number of heavy users would tend to grow. That effect would be magnified if taxes were set at levels that created licit prices below the current black-market level. No one has ever produced a persuasive estimate of the price-elasticity of demand for cocaine; the effect of quantity on price (via reduced per-unit costs generated by enforcement) confounds any measurement of the effect of price on quantity.[32] But price is surely an important factor in determining the quantity consumers buy; over the 1980s, as the retail price of cocaine fell from about $800 per pure gram to about $100 per pure gram, the physical quantity consumed rose from about 20 metric tons to about 250 metric tons. Thus a decrease to the pharmaceutical level, which would occur if the newly licit cocaine were untaxed or taxed only as heavily as alcohol now is, could easily give consumption another huge boost; a fivefold increase in consumption is not at all implausible as the consequence of a 95 percent decrease in price. The effect of the introduction of cheap gin into England in the early eighteenth century ought to be a warning.

Thus high taxes to maintain prices would have bad effects on crime, while low taxes would have bad effects on consumption levels. If I had to choose, I would be inclined to favor high taxes, but it isn't an attractive choice to face.

Alternatively, one could let prices fall and rely on a system of quantity restrictions to prevent growth in the chronic or binge-user population. But just as higher-than-current prices would defeat the objective of shrinking the black market, so too would quantity restrictions. Given the extremes of behavior which cocaine-seeking can create, it would require great optimism to assume that making a little cocaine available licitly would discourage people from buying more illicitly. On the contrary, the licit market could serve as a promotional mechanism for the illicit one, as some of the users introduced to cocaine under legal conditions found their habits growing beyond legal bounds.

To be enforceable, the quantity limit would have to be set high enough so that most of the current illicit demand could be supplied. But the roughly two million heavy users already account for about 80 percent of the illicit market. Thus a quantity limit so low as to exclude them would leave the black market problem largely unimproved, while a quantity limit high enough to embrace them would allow the new users to develop into problems for themselves, their families, and (at high prices) potential crime victims.

The same problem would apply to licensing cocaine use, as I propose to license drinking. Threatening to withhold cocaine buying privileges from those convicted of property crimes would help prevent a situation in which the revenue collector replaced the illicit cocaine dealer as the final recipient of the proceeds of theft, but carrying out that threat in a sufficient number of cases would help regenerate the black market that would arise to serve unlicensed and over-limit users as well as minors.

Again, if I had to choose, I would impose along with high taxes some sort of quantity limit, but make it generous enough to encompass 95 percent of all users. This would mean supporting a large number of very bad habits, and selling a substantial number of people enough cocaine to kill them. I would also use some sort of licensure to pluck off a few percent of the users who engaged in the most frequent and serious property crime to buy cocaine or assault under its influence. That would leave a significant black market, but probably smaller than the one we now have, and a substantial increase in the number of cocaine users and the health damage due to cocaine, but certainly less than under full unrestricted availability.

The opposite direction would be to "license" use *only* by identified problem users, on the condition that they subject themselves to some form of management by treatment providers, on the model of methadone provision for heroin users. (In Great Britain, where some heroin addicts are maintained on heroin rather than methadone, some cocaine addicts are also offered legal maintenance doses of cocaine.) It is possible that such a cocaine-maintenance strategy could be developed for use under US conditions, with some of the same advantages and disadvantages as methadone has, complicated by the extremely short action of cocaine and the frequent dosage that consequently characterizes its use. Such a strategy might help drain off users from the illicit market; if it were made sufficiently inconvenient and humiliating, it might do so without expanding the population of heavy cocaine users. Still, such a treatment option is a far stretch from regulated availability of the drug for use by the general population.

All the choices seem to me bad ones. The combination of cocaine's tendency to induce a strong compulsion to repeated binge use in a substantial proportion of its users with the physical and emotional damage such heavy use can produce makes it an unattractive drug for a regime of grudging toleration. As bad as our current cocaine prohibition is, I cannot invent a version of legal availability for cocaine that wouldn't be worse.

Other Drugs

Examples could be multiplied; the ideal control regimes are nearly as diverse as the categories of drugs to which they might apply. The psychedelics, for example, might best be controlled by requiring that use take place under trained (not necessarily medical) supervision and in physical settings designed to minimize the risk and physical consequences of "bad trips." A design for the regulated availability of substances designed to improve short-term intellectual performance would demand careful consideration of the strategic interactions among academic and professional competitors. Nicotine regulation might appropriately involve the prohibition of cigarettes, except for maintenance supplies for current addicts.[33] But the above probably contains as much speculation as can profitably be offered in advance of more experience.

THE POLITICS OF GRUDGING TOLERATION

Having, I hope, established that there is a vast territory of potential regulatory schemes between prohibition and the very loose controls we now place on alcohol and tobacco, we can now ask why that should be so. What forces drug policy toward the two extremes and away from what might be a sensible center? Alcohol, for example, has gone from being permitted, to being prohibited, to being permitted again, without ever being tightly regulated as proposed here.

Part of the answer may be technological; the information-processing demands of, for example, a quantity-regulation system were simply too great to make such a system feasible before recent advances in computers and telecommunications. But most of it must be ideological and organizational.

To regard a drug as at once safe (for most people under most circumstances) and dangerous (in the wrong hands or at the wrong times and places) puts a strain on individual and collective tolerances for cognitive dissonance. Nor is it comfortable for citizens and officials to think about the dangers of their own habits; it is far easier to locate the "drug problem" entirely in the other person's (or class's, or generation's) drugs. That is what creates controversy around what ought to be obvious propositions, such as "alcohol is a drug" or "nicotine is highly addictive."

Moreover, the strain between drug prohibition and ideological opposition to state interference in private choices can be relieved by asserting that any use of the banned drugs is harmful in itself, and that therefore no valuable liberty is denied by their prohibition. Such a claim would be much harder to square with a program of grudging toleration. In particular, any system of personal licensing and quantity limitation would require "bureaucracy" and "red tape." By contrast, a strict prohibition, though far more restrictive, does not require citizens to apply to officialdom for permissions of various kinds and generates no lists of those who engage in lawful but potentially embarrassing activity.

Any regulatory regime creates either a public monopoly or a regulated industry. The employees of either one will not be happy regarding themselves as purveyors of a vice, and as servants of either taxpayers or stockholders they will have every incentive to increase revenues by increasing the volume of consumption. Thus a program of strict regulation short of prohibition may not be stable over time. The state lotteries, with their relentless promotion, serve as a bad example.[34]

Finally, I must emphasize that grudging toleration does not hold out the prospect of a "solution" to the drug problem. Even for those substances to which it could be successfully applied, it would leave us with a mix of abuse costs and control costs. While one could hope that those costs would be, in sum, smaller than those we face under either prohibition or unrestricted legalization, they will not be close to zero. The potential for drug abuse appears to be a fundamental characteristic of the interaction of various chemicals with the human mind and body, and no combination of laws and programs will make it go away.

Nor is grudging toleration the best regime for all drugs. If it is not possible to create a control system sufficiently tight to avoid massive abuse but sufficiently loose that the vast majority of participants can be induced to observe it, grudging toleration fails. This, I have argued, is likely to be the case for cocaine under current conditions in the United States. Since cocaine is by any reasonable measure the most important among the nation's current illicit drug problems, the inapplicability of grudging toleration to the cocaine situation makes the concept less important than it would otherwise be. If I am right about this, then the legal and enforcement machinery of drug prohibition must remain in place even if we decide to cease applying them to some of the currently illicit drugs. Grudging toleration may be a good idea; a panacea it is not.

But that does not mean that our current policies toward cocaine are the ideal ones, or that improvements within the ambit of current laws are impossible. On the contrary, it is easy to list several major reforms within the enforcement sphere alone: shifting resources from high-level to retail-level enforcement, with an emphasis on low-arrest strategies; the abolition of long mandatory minimum sentences except for true "kingpins" and those who engage in violence in connection with dealing; and a program of coerced abstinence, backed by random testing and sanctions, for cocaine and heroin users who are also drug dealers, muggers, burglars, or assailants.[35]

It is regrettable that criticism of the excesses of the war on drugs has become identified with proposals for some form of legalization. This allows the drug warriors and their critics alike to duck the tough practical issues. The abolition of drug abuse, and of the drug laws, are alike utopian dreams. It is time to wake up.

ENDNOTES

[1]Many of the ideas in this essay were developed in collaboration with Aaron Saiger. See Kleiman and Saiger, "Drug Legalization: The Importance of Asking the Right

Question," *Hofstra Law Review* 18 (3) (Spring 1990): 527–65. Credit is also due to Lowry Heussler, who greatly improved the prose, and David Osborne, who found the references.

[2]For heroin and AIDS, see Charles F. Turner, Heather G. Miller, and Lincoln E. Moses, *AIDS: Sexual Behavior and Intravenous Drug Use* (Washington, D.C.: National Academy Press, 1989); Mark A.R. Kleiman and Richard A. Mockler, "AIDS and Heroin: Strategies for Control" (Washington, D.C.: Urban Institute, 1988); Gerry Stimpson, et al., "Preventing the Spread of HIV in Injecting Drug Users—The Experience of Syringe-Exchange Schemes in England and Scotland," in *Problems of Drug Dependence - 1988,* NIDA Research Monograph 90 (Rockville, Md.: National Institute on Drug Abuse, 1988), 302–11. For violence and illicit cocaine, see Ethan A. Nadelmann, "The Case for Legalization," in *The Public Interest* 92 (Summer 1988): 3–31; Milton Friedman, "An Open Letter to Bill Bennett," *Wall Street Journal,* 7 September 1989.

[3]Office on Smoking and Health, *Nicotine Addiction: The Health Consequences of Smoking* (Rockville, Md.: Department of Health and Human Services, 1988); Mark H. Moore and Dean R. Gerstein, eds., *Alcohol and Public Policy: Beyond the Shadow of Prohibition* (Washington, D.C.: National Academy Press, 1981); Willard G. Manning, Emmett B. Keeler, Joseph P. Newhouse, Elizabeth M. Sloss, and Jeffrey Wasserman, "The Taxes of Sin: Do Smokers and Drinkers Pay Their Way?" *Journal of the American Medical Association* 261 (11) (17 March 1989): 1604–609.

[4]Paul Aaron and David Musto, "Temperance and Prohibition in America: A Historical Overview," in Mark H. Moore and Dean R. Gerstein, *Alcohol and Public Policy: Beyond the Shadow of Prohibition* (Washington, D.C.: National Academy Press, 1981), 127–81; John P. Morgan, "Prohibition Is Perverse Policy: What Was True in 1933 Is True Now," in Melvyn B. Krauss and Edward P. Lazear, eds., *Searching for Alternatives: Drug-Control Policy in the United States* (Stanford, Calif.: Hoover Institution Press, 1991), 405–23.

[5]Thomas C. Schelling, "The Intimate Contest for Self-Command," and "Law, Ethics, and the Contest for Self-Command," in *Choice and Consequence* (Cambridge, Mass.: Harvard University Press, 1984).

[6]Peter K. Levison, Dean R. Gerstein, and Deborah R. Maloff, eds., *Commonalities in Substance Abuse and Habitual Behavior* (Lexington, Mass.: D.C. Heath and Company, 1983).

[7]John Kaplan, *The Hardest Drug: Heroin and Public Policy* (Chicago: The University of Chicago Press, 1983), 16–18.

[8]See Thomas Szasz, *Our Right to Drugs* (New Haven, Conn.: Praeger, 1992).

[9]Michael O'Hare, "A Typology of Governmental Action," *Journal of Policy Analysis and Management* 8 (4) (1989): 610–72; Charles L. Schultze, *The Public Use of Private Interest* (Washington, D.C.: Brookings Institute, 1977).

[10]Niccolo Machiavelli, *The Discourses on Livy,* Bernard Crick, ed. (Baltimore, Md.: Penguin Books, Inc., 1976), Book I, Discourse 17, 157–60.

[11]Manning, et al., "The Taxes of Sin: Do Smokers and Drinkers Pay Their Way?"

[12]Mark A.R. Kleiman, *Against Excess: Drug Policy for Results* (New York: Basic Books, 1992), 244–49.

[13]Phillip Cook and George Tauchen, "The Effect of Liquor Taxes on Heavy Drinking," *Bell Journal of Economics* 13 (1982).

[14]Preliminary data from Lloyd D. Johnston, Jerald G. Bachman, and Patrick M. O'Malley, *Monitoring the Future 1990* (Ann Arbor, Mich.: Institute for Social Research, 1991), Table 9.

[15]Kleiman, *Against Excess,* 211–12.

[16]Ruth E. Little, R.L. Asler, Paul D. Sampson, and J.H. Renwick, "Fetal Growth and Moderate Drinking in Early Pregnancy," *American Journal of Epidemiology* 123 (1986): 270–78; Ann P. Streissguth, Helen M. Barr, et al., "Attention, Distraction, and Reaction Time at Age Seven Years and Prenatal Alcohol Exposure," *Neurobehavioral Toxicology and Teratology* 8 (1986): 717–25; Daniel Coleman, "Lasting Costs for Children Are Found From a Few Early Drinks," *New York Times,* 10 March 1991.

[17]Kleiman, *Against Excess,* 258–59.

[18]Mark A.R. Kleiman, *Marijuana: Costs of Abuse, Costs of Control* (New Haven, Conn.: Greenwood Press, 1989), 3–22; Kleiman, *Against Excess,* 253; Institute of Medicine, *Marijuana and Health* (Washington, D.C.: National Academy Press, 1982).

[19]Kleiman, *Against Excess,* 277–80.

[20]"Cross-Eyed and Painless," *The Economist* (6 July 1991): 89; Richard E. Doblin and Mark A.R. Kleiman, "Marijuana as Antiemetic Medicine: A Survey of Oncologists' Experiences and Attitudes," *Journal of Clinical Oncology* 9 (7) (July 1991): 1314–19; Terry F. Plasse, "Correspondence: Clinical Use of Dronabinol," *Journal of Clinical Oncology* (November 1991): 2079–80; Mark A.R. Kleiman and Richard Doblin, "Correspondence: Reply," *Journal of Clinical Oncology* (November 1991): 2080.

[21]Denise B. Kandel and J.A. Logan, "Patterns of Drug Use From Adolescence to Young Adulthood: Periods of Risk for Initiation, Continued Use, and Discontinuation," *American Journal of Public Health* 74 (7) (1984): 660–66; Lloyd D. Johnston, Patrick M. O'Malley, and Jerald G. Bachman, *National Trends in Drug Use and Related Factors Among American High School Students and Young Adults, 1975–1986* (Washington, D.C.: Department of Health and Human Services, National Institute on Drug Abuse, 1987).

[22]More than four in five high school seniors report that marijuana is "easily available" to them if they want it. See Lloyd D. Johnston, Patrick M. O'Malley, and Jerald G. Bachman, *Illicit Drug Use, Smoking, and Drinking By America's High School Students, College Students, and Young Adults: 1975–1987* (Rockville, Md.: National Institute on Drug Abuse, 1989), 289–94.

[23]Richard R. Clayton and Harwin L. Voss, *Young Men and Drugs in Manhattan: A Causal Analysis,* Research Monograph No. 39 (Rockville, Md.: Department of Health and Human Services, 1981).

[24]Kleiman, *Against Excess,* 254.

[25]Marc Mauer, "Young Black Men and the Criminal Justice System: A Growing National Problem," (Washington, D.C.: The Sentencing Project, 1990); Peter Reuter, et al., *Money from Crime: A Study of the Economics of Drug Dealing in Washington, D.C.* (Santa Monica, Calif.: RAND Corporation, 1990); Jerome G. Miller, *Hobbling a Generation: You African American Males in D.C.'s Criminal Justice System* (Alexandria, Va.: National Center on Institution and Alternative, 1992).

[26]National Institute on Alcohol Abuse and Alcoholism, Sixth Special Report to the US Congress on Alcohol and Health (Rockville, Md.: Department of Health and Human Services, 1987), Table Y, p. 6; Kleiman, *Against Excess,* 290–91.

[27]US Senate, Committee on the Judiciary, "Hard-Core Cocaine Addicts: Measuring-And Fighting - the Epidemic," *Staff Report,* 10 May 1990; US Senate, Committee on the Judiciary, "Drug Use in America: Is the Epidemic Really Over?" *Staff Report,* 19 December 1990; National Institute on Drug Abuse, Overview of the National Household Survey on Drug Abuse (Washington, D.C.: Department of Health and Human Services, 1990); Office of National Drug Control Policy, *What American Users Spend on Illegal Drugs* (Washington, D.C.: Office of National Drug Control Policy, 1991).

[28]*Current Population Reports: Population Estimates and Projections* (Washington, D.C.: Department of Commerce, 1990); J.D. Miller et al., National Survey on Drug Abuse: Main Findings (Rockville, Md.: National Institute on Drug Abuse, 1985); N.S. Miller and M.S. Gold, *Alcohol* (New York: Plenum Press, 1991), 13.

[29]Friedman writes, ". . . if currently illicit drugs were decriminalized and handled exactly the way alcohol is now handled, there is no reason to suppose that there would be a vast increase in the number of addicts." See Milton Friedman, "The War We Are Losing," in Krauss and Lazear, *Searching for Alternatives,* 61; Nadelmann, "The Case for Legalization," 29.

[30]James B. Bakalar and Lester Grinspoon, *Cocaine: A Drug and Its Social Evolution* (New York: Simon and Schuster, 1985); David Musto, "Lessons of the First Cocaine Epidemic," *Wall Street Journal,* 11 June 1986.

[31]Frank Gawin and Everett Ellinwood, "Cocaine and Other Stimulants: Actions, Abuse and Treatment," *New England Journal of Medicine* 318 (18) (5 May 1988): 1173–83.

[32]Mark A.R. Kleiman, "Overview," in *Modelling Drug Markets* (Cambridge, Mass.: Program in Criminal Justice Policy and Management, Kennedy School of Government, Harvard University, 1991); Kleiman, *Against Excess,* 104–26; Mark A.R. Kleiman, "Enforcement Swamping: A Positive-Feedback Mechanism in Rates of Illicit Activity," *Mathematical and Computer Modelling* (forthcoming).

[33]Kleiman, *Against Excess,* 354–58.

[34]Charles T. Clotfelter and Philip J. Cook, *Selling Hope: State Lotteries in America* (Cambridge, Mass.: Harvard University Press, 1989).

[35]For these and other practical suggestions, see Kleiman, *Against Excess.*

Crime, Law and Social Change **20**: 1–12, 1993.

I volunteer to kidnap Oliver North

MICHAEL LEVINE

Abstract. "I Volunteer to Kidnap Ollie North," is an exercise in following our government's sometimes criminal, often bizarre and always hypocritical actions in the war on drugs during the Reagan-Bush years to their logical conclusion. The Supreme Court has indicated in its June, 1992 decision in U.S. v Machain, that American law enforcement officers can now enter the sovereign territories of other nations to legally abduct violators of U.S. drug laws. Iran immediately proclaimed that they had the same right for violations of Islamic law. What might happen if kidnapping becomes a recognized "tool" of international law enforcement? What prominent Americans might wake up in South American jails with bags over their heads?

Two years ago a maverick group of DEA agents (Drug Enforcement Administration), feeling enraged, frustrated and betrayed decided to take the law into their own hands. The U.S. government, including high ranking DEA officials, had joined the Mexican government in trying to sweep the "bothersome" matter of the torture death of Enrique "Kiki" Camarena – one of their fellow agents murdered by Mexican police working for drug traffickers – under a rug of political and bureaucratic maneuvering, where it would not disturb oil, trade banking and secret political agreements. Even the C.I.A. was implicated in protecting Camarena's murderers, which was no surprise to the DEA agents.[1] Working without the knowledge or approval of most of the top DEA bosses, whom they mistrusted, the agents arranged to have Dr. Humberto Alvarez Machain, a Mexican citizen alleged to have participated in Kiki's murder, abducted at gunpoint in Guadalajara Mexico and brought to Los Angeles to stand trial.[2]

On June 16, 1992, the United States Supreme Court ruled the actions of those agents "legal." The ruling said in no uncertain terms that U.S. law enforcement authorities could literally and figuratively kidnap violators of American drug law in whatever country they found them and drag them physically and against their will to the U.S. to stand trial. Immediately thereafter the Ayatollahs declared that they too could rove the world and kidnap violators of Islamic law and drag them back to Iran to stand trial. Kidnapping has now become an accepted tool of law enforcement throughout the world.

Resorting to all sorts of wild extremes to bring drug traffickers to justice is nothing new for the U.S. government. At various times during my career as a DEA agent I was assigned to some pretty unorthodox operations – nothing quite as radical as invading Panama and killing a few hundred innocents to capture Manny Noriega – but I was once part of a group of undercover agents posing as a travelling soccer team. We landed in Argentina in a chartered jet during the wee hours of the morning, where the Argentine Federal Police had three international drug dealers – two of whom had never in their lives set foot in the United States – waiting for us trussed up in straight-jackets with horse feed-bags over their heads, each beaten to a pulpy, toothless mess. In those years we used to call it a "controlled expulsion."[3] I think I like the honesty of kidnapping a little better.

And now, since the democratic and staunchly anti-drug nation of Costa Rica has publicly accused Oliver North and some other high-level U.S. officials, of running drugs from their sovereignty to the United States, and appears close to officially charging them with the crime, I find myself, duty-bound to make the following offer to Costa Rica, or any other nation that might have need of my services.[4]

I Michael Levine, twenty-five year veteran undercover agent for the Drug Enforcement Administration, given the mandate of the Supreme Court's Machain Decision and in fulfillment of my oath to the U.S. government and its taxpayers to arrest and seize all those individuals who would smuggle or cause illegal drugs to be smuggled into the United States or who would aid and abet drug smugglers, do hereby volunteer my services to any sovereign, democratic nation who files legal Drug Trafficking charges against Colonel Oliver North and any of his cohorts; to do everything in my power including kidnapping him, seizing his paper shredder, reading him his constitutional rights and dragging his butt to wherever that sovereignty might be, (with or without horse feed-bag); to once-and-for-all stand trial for the horrific damages caused to my country, my fellow law enforcement officers, and to my family.

Before I pack my horse feed-bags and chains, of course, my offer is based on the fulfillment of two additional requirements. First, an examination of that country's evidence to determine – utilizing my quarter century of court-recognized expertise, my almost perfect record of convictions in more than 3,000 cases and the expertise of some of my angry, disenchanted, frustrated, albeit frightened-for-their-jobs, fellow agenst whom share my feelings – that there would be a high likelihood of conviction, should Oliver North be brought to trial in the U.S.. Second, that it appear unlikely that U.S. authorities would ever conduct a proper narcotic conspiracy investigation – as opposed to a Senate hearing, which is like comparing a toothpick to a pneumatic drill – into the mountain of evidence indicating the systematic and massive violations of U.S. drug laws by Colonel Ollie and other high ranking U.S. government officials whom, as the evidence seems to indicate, aided, abetted and empowered him, and then covered up for him.

Now unless you're a dedicated drug war fan whose been following this three decade, hundred-billion dollar fiasco closely, you've got to be wondering what kind of evidence there could possibly be that this "American hero" who hid in a motel john to write his memoirs, violated United States drug laws?[5]

It will surprise many to know – since the mainstream media gave this important event very little coverage – that the Nobel prize winning President of Costa Rica, Oscar Arias – as a result of an indepth investigation by the Costa Rican Congressional Commission on Narcotics that found "virtually all [U.S. supported] contra factions involved in drug trafficking" – banned Oliver North, U.S. Ambassador Lewis Tambs, National Security Advisor Admiral John Poindexter, Presidential Advisor Richard Secord and C.I.A. station chief José Fernandez, by Executive order, from ever entering Costa Rica – for their roles in utilizing Costa Rican territory for cocaine trafficking.[6]

Costa Rica is not some third-world banana republic; it's considered one of the most enlightened, educated and truly democratic societies in the Americas – a nation without an army, secret police or a C.I.A.. And the really ironic part of their accusations against North and the others is that all of the many tons of cocaine involved were destined to the United States.

In my twenty-five years experience with DEA which includes running some of their highest level international drug trafficking investigations, I have never seen an instance of comparable allegations where DEA did not set up a multi-agency task force size operation to conduct an in-depth conspiracy investigation. Yet in the case of Colonel North and the other American officials, no investigation whatsoever has been initiated by DEA or any other investigative agency.

When President Bush said, "All those who look the other way are as guilty as the drug dealers," he was not only talking about a moral guilt, but a legal one as well. Thus, if any U.S. official knew of North and the contra's drug activities and did not take proper action, or covered up for it, he is "guilty" of a whole series of crimes that you go to jail for; crimes that carry a minimum jail term; crimes like Aiding and Abetting, Conspiracy, Misprision of a Felony, Perjury, and about a dozen other violations of law related to misuse and malfeasance of public office. If the Costa Rican charges, along with the growing mountain of evidence right here in the U.S.A. are ever fully investigated, I'm afraid we'll have a new jail overcrowding problem.

I'm not talking about some sort of shadow conspiracy here. As a veteran, criminal investigator I don't deal in speculation. I document facts and evidence and then work like hell to corroborate my claims so that I can send people to jail.

What I am talking about is "Probable Cause" – a legal principle that every junior agent and cop is taught before he hits the street. It mandates that an arrest and/or criminal indictment must occur when there exists specific, facts, circumstances and evidence that would give any "reasonable thinking person" grounds to believe, that anyone – U.S. government officials included – had violated the federal narcotic laws. Any U.S. government law enforcement officer or elected official who fails to take appropriate action when Probable Cause exists, is in violation of his oath as well as federal law; and under that law it takes surprisingly little evidence to show enough Probable Cause for an arrest and conviction.

As an example, early in my career (1971), I arrested a man named John Clements, a twenty-two year old, baby-faced guitar player, who happened to be present at the transfer of three kilos of heroin – an amount that doesn't measure up to a tiny percentage of the many tons of cocaine that North and his contras have been accused of pouring onto our streets. Clements was a silent observer in a trailer parked in the middle of a Gainesville, Florida swamp, while a smuggler – whom I had arrested hours earlier in New York City and "flipped" (convinced to inform for me) – turned the heroin over to the financier of the operation. Poor John Clements, a friend of both men, just happened to be there. There were no recorded incriminating conversations of Clements' voice; he wrote no prof notes; he didn't shred any documents; he did not lie to anyone; there were no millions in unaccounted funds at his disposal. He only had about $3 and change in his pocket. In fact, we couldn't prove that John Clements earned a nickel from the deal. He was just there. Yet under the law I had more than enough Probable Cause to arrest him – which I did.

Poor, young Mr. Clements couldn't claim "national security," or that he was under "political attack;" nor did he have elected officials clamoring for me to drop my investigation so that he could get on with the "more important" business of trying to govern his foundering live. And so it was, after a full jury trial – which is my ultimate goal for Colonel Ollie and his gang – the federal judge in Gainesville, Florida, sentenced him to thirty years in prison, where he remains to this day, for Possession and Conspiracy. Clements was present during the transaction therefore, it was presumed, that he had to have knowledge, and that was enough to prove Possession and Conspiracy to a jury of American citizens.[7]

Criminality in drug trafficking cases is lot easier than proving whether or not someone lied to Congress and is certainly a lot less "heroic." Statements like "I don't remember," "I didn't know," and "No one told me," or "I sought approval from my superior for every one of my actions,"[8] are only accepted as valid defences by Congressmen and Senators with difficulties balancing check books – not American jurors trying drug cases.

But before we can get to a trial there must first be an investigation. And if the American people demand and finally get that investigation – which would make my kidnapping mission unnecessary – it must have as its goal the answer to some very specific questions, of which the following are only a small sampling:

My first question to Colonel North – under oath – would be: Why did you campaign to obtain the release of Honduran army general, José Bueso-Rosa from a federal prison, after his arrest for smuggling 763 pounds of cocaine and murder?[9] Bueso-Rosa's partner in the venture was international arms dealer Felix Latchinian, who in turn was an ex-business partner of C.I.A. agent Felix Rodriguez, who, in turn, was in charge of the contra's supply network in El Salvador. If this sounds complicated just remember that all this drug trafficking activity was paid for by U.S. taxpayer dollars.

In North's efforts to spring the drug dealing general, whose case the Justice Department described as "the worst case of narco-trafficking in history," he asked for President Reagan's support, and got it – I would want to know, why?"[10]

North, when he wasn't shredding was not too good at covering his tracks. He wrote several damning prof notes to National Security Advisor, Admiral John Poindexter that wound up in the hands of Senate investigators. In one such note he wrote that if Bueso-Rosa was not made happy he could "sing songs that nobody wants to hear."[11] North's actions and the notes prompted former Ambassador to Costa Rica, Francis McNeil to state, "What were those songs? Were they about narcotics or possibly something else?"[12] If this were my drug case I'd begin a real narcotic conspiracy investigation that wouldn't end until I knew every note and every verse of every song Bueso-Rosa had to sing.

Colonel North appeared on a radio show – Michael Jackson KABC, Los Angeles California, 11/11/91 – to promote his book. I was telephoned at home in New York City and asked to participate in the discussion. I listened while Colonel Ollie lied on the air by claiming General Bueso-Rosa had been arrested for "some political reasons." When I confronted him and asked him about those "songs' he referred to, and Ambassador McNeil's comments, he indicated that the answer to my question would be a violation of national security.[13]

How in God's name in a nation with a drug-related homicide rate comparable to war-time casualty statistics, can the protection of any drug dealer be in the interests of national security? I have worked undercover all over the world, from Bangkok to Buenos Aires, on the highest level drug trafficking cases, and for the life of me have never seen the validity of such a claim.

Since there is no way that it can be proved that the ounces and grams of cocaine that DEA agents and police officers like Everett Hatcher, Eddie Byrnes and Chris Hoban died trying to take off the streets, was not part of the 763 pounds that North's friend, Bueso-Rosa, smuggled into the country or the many tons North's contras bombarded us with, I would insist that North, President Reagan and all those U.S. officials who feared that Bueso-Rosa might sing his "songs," explain – in a court of law – how the release of this drug smuggler was necessary for our national security. President Nixon tried to hide behind "national security" and we know what happened to him.

And what of Colonel North's 500 handwritten pages of personal notes devoted to drug trafficking, including mention of specific drug transactions and references to known, major drug traffickers like Carlos Escobar and Manuel Noriega, whom North was known to work closely with in the resupply of the contras? Why has not, every single page and notation been thoroughly investigated as would be done in any drug trafficking case? These hand-written notes also document North's numerous contact with high-level DEA officials throughout the time period covered in his memoirs, yet the only mention of drugs in his entire, allegedly factual, book, is a page-and-a-half disclaimer stating that the Special Prosecutor spent "tens of thousands of dollars" investigating the drug-smuggling allegations against him and the contras and that if any of it was true "it surely would have come out."[14] If only books were written under oath, I wouldn't have to kidnap Ollie.

Potentially the most damning physical evidence against North – his five-hundred pages of diary notes referencing drugs – were never even received by the Iran-contra investigators.[15] What kind of an investigation could they have possibly conducted? If poor John Clements had the Kerry committee investigating him, he'd be playing his guitar in some bar now, instead of serving his twenty-second year in prison.

The total "public" investigation into the drug allegations by the Senate was falsely summed up in the statement of a staffer, on the House select committee, Robert A. Bermingham who notified Chairman Hamilton on July 23, 1987, that after interviewing "hundreds" of people his investigation had not developed any corroboration of "media-exploited allegations that the U.S. government condoned drug trafficking by contra leaders ... or that contra leaders or organizations did in fact take part in such activity." Every government official accused of aiding and covering up for the contra drug connection, Colonel Ollie included, then hung his hat on this statement, claiming they had been 'cleared."

The only trouble was that investigative journalists, Leslie and Andrew Cockburn – after interviewing many of the chief witnesses whose testimony implicated North and the contras in drug trafficking, including several whose testimony was later found credible enough to be used to convict Manuel Noriega – could find not one who had been interviewed by Bermingham or his staff. In fact, the two journalists seem to have caught Bermingham red-handed in what can only be described, at best, as a gross misrepresentation of fact, when he (Bermingham) quoted the chief counsel of a House Judiciary subcommittee, Hayden Gregory as dismissing the drug evidence and calling it "street talk." Gregory told the Cockburns that the "street talk" comment was taken out of context; that he had not even met Bermingham until July 22 (two days before Bermingham wrote the report) and that he had in fact told Bermingham that there were "serious allegations against almost every contra leader."[16]

To any DEA agent with experience working high-level, international investigations that threaten "special interest" operations, even the half-baked ones like Colonel North's, all this has a familiar stench to it – the rot of high-level cover-up of official crimes and misconduct. A stench too many of us have had to live with in fear and silence throughout our careers. Senator John Kerry put the situation quite succinctly when he said that, as he saw it, the covert network [set up by North and aided by the C.I.A.] "became a further exploitation of the American people by violation of the narcotic laws, and it became a channel for the perversion of our own judicial process and enforcement process."[17]

During the Iran/Contra hearings, virtually all testimony implicating U.S. officials in drug trafficking was given in secret session, prompting senior investigator Jack Blum to state, "I am sick to death of the truths I cannot tell."[18] A sample of the kind of testimony heard in private was that of C.I.A. station chief in Costa Rica, José Fernandex who testified that as part of his C.I.A. duties he had to protect drug dealers.[19] Felix Milian Rodriguez, Medellin Cartel accountant and money-launderer – and C.I.A. asset – testified in a closed-door session, from which the public and press were barred, about the cartel's $180,000 contribution to the Reagan Presidential campaign. He also testified about a $10 million "contribution" the drug cartel made to the contras – at the C.I.A.'s request.[20]

Yet, with all the official rhetoric not a single United States indictment charging any U.S. official with narcotic law violations has been forthcoming. How ironic that the only official accusation would come from Costa Rica.

During my long career as an agent, I never lost a drug case anywhere in the world, (including far-flung places like Bangkok, Frankfort and Buenos Aires). My employer, the Drug Enforcement Administration, in fact, called me one of their top experts – a record and reputation I used to be proud of.[21] I would relish my own country giving me the opportunity to conduct a real conspiracy investigation into these allegations. But if they don't, to kidnap Ollie North for Costa Rica seems like the least I can do for the American people.

Now, you might ask, since there is so much evidence and information indicating wide-spread and high-level, "official" U.S. government involvement in drug trafficking, why focus on Ollie North?

I've been extremely successful throughout my career, picking out the weakest link of a conspiracy chain, the link in the most damaging position, the one most likely collapse and testify against the whole chain. I used to teach and lecture on Informant Development and Handling as part of my duties for DEA. A good sign of which criminal will make the most promising informant is often what I call the Stool Pigeon Profile. The best 'stools' are usually morally weak, not-too-bright and given to petty thievery. They are cowardly people whom – when it comes to saving their own skin – are capable of unlimited treachery.

Most top-level criminals, for example, don't make good informants; they are oddly "moral" people who tend to adhere closely to their own criminal code – preferring to do time in jail to "turning rat." The biggest drug dealers place a high value on their word and reputation; they will do multi-million dollar drug deals on nothing more than a handshake or a phone call. They usually have a powerful aversion to petty thievery recognizing that those associates who show themselves to be petty thieves are the least likely to be "stand up guys" if arrested – the most likely to turn rat.

Colonel North clearly comes under the category of Petty Thief. His conviction for illegally accepting a $10,000 security system, considering the many millions of unaccounted dollars that went through his hand, amounted to nothing more than the pettiest of thievery. The conviction was overturned by the Supreme Court for technical reasons, not for reasons of fact. And there were other petty theft allegations for which he was never tried. His safe, for instance, usually contained thousands of dollars in traveler's checks he claimed were "given" him by contra leader, Adolfo Calero; checks that he used for groceries, clothing (Park Lane Hosiery) and snow tires – a misuse of funds that would have gotten a DEA or FBI agent, fired from his job and indicted for Larceny.[22]

Add to this how easily Colonel North turned on the man who called him "an American hero," when he blew the whistle on President Reagan, while he was conveniently not under oath and on a book tour, making headlines with his "opinion" that the President "probably knew" of all his activities; and the fact that many of North's personal notes referencing drugs are coincidental with notations indicating phone calls to Cap Weinberger and Claire George (already under indictment for lying to Congress and Perjury) and Dewey Claridge (already convicted of perjury and lying to Congress). Retired Major General John Singlaub, himself deeply implicated in the Iran/contra scandal said of North: "To people all over the world, Ollie North was a hero. But I knew better. There was a wide gap between the media image .... and the sordid reality of his true character and performance .... Ollie, like other cowards, had faced a hard choice and made his decision."[23]

Colonel North also clearly comes under the "not-too-bright" category of potential informants. I mean it boggles my narc's imagination that after he was allowed to spend countless hours at the shredding machine he left all those incriminating pages untouched. This is precisely the kind of presence of mind I look for in a stool pigeon.

With the heat of a mandatory jail sentence under North I doubt that it will take much convincing before he tells an American Grand Jury the words to those "songs." His personal notes might then corroborate hundreds of overt acts – the best possible evidence you could have for a conspiracy investigation. North's diary might then be compared to the already incriminating diaries of Cap Weinberger and Claire George.[24] Who knows where it will all end. Potentially Colonel "Shredder" North could be the greatest snitch in Organized Government Crime since Deep Throat of Watergate infamy; the weakest and most corroded link in a chain linking together the Titanic of criminal Government Conspiracies. It would be the kind of investigation to make the mouth of a professional narcotic conspiracy investigators water; easier than locking up a high school marijuana ring – if the politicians let us do our job.

There is little chance that this evidence and information will ever be investigated in this country, since the very people who would be implicated as North's co-conspirators are the foxes who run this well-pillaged hen house; the critters who have already displayed their propensity to lie and destroy evidence and their power to hide behind "national security." Apparently the only chance I'll get to fulfill my oath to the American people will be if Costa Rica does the job for us. Unfortunately the Costa Rican authorities have found that the biggest enemy in their drug war are the American politicians and bureaucrats who are desperate to look the other way.

In fact, when Costa Rica began its investigation into the drug trafficking allegations against North and his smarmy little group, and naively thought that the U.S. would gladly lend a hand in efforts to fight drugs, they received a rude awakening about the realities of America's war on drugs as opposed to its "this-scourge-well-end" rhetoric.

After five witnesses testified before the U.S. Senate, confirming that John Hull – a C.I.A. operative and the lynch-pine of North's contra resupply operation – had been actively running drugs from Costa Rica to the U.S. "under the direction of the C.I.A.." Costa Rican authorities arrested him.[25] Hull then quickly jumped bail and fled to the U.S. – according to my sources – with the help of DEA, putting the drug fighting agency in the schizoid business of both kidnapping accused drug dealers and helping them escape; although the Supreme Court has not legalized the latter … yet.[26]

The then President of Costa Rica, Oscar Arias was stunned when he received letters from nineteen U.S. Congressman – including Lee Hamilton of Indiana, the Democrat who headed the Iran-contra committee – warning him "to avoid situations … that could aversely affect our relations."[27]

Arias, who won the Nobel prize for ending the contra war, stated that he was shocked that "relations between [the United States] and my country could deteriorate because [the Costa Rican] legal system is fighting against drug trafficking."[28]

He didn't know the half of it.

Costa Rica petitioned the United States for Hull's extradition. At present, Costa Rican public prosecutor, Jorge Chavarria has expressed his desire, "at minimum" to question North as a "materiel witness."[29] Evidence and testimony has been presented to the Kerry Committee about North's direct supervision of John Hull, including the fact that throughout the period Hull is charged with his crimes, North was paying him $10,000 a month. Therefore, it is a foregone conclusion by all of us with experience in the techniques of international narcotic prosecutions, that if Hull is extradited and convicted in Costa Rica, North and the rest of his crew will logically follow.[30]

Unfortunately the State Department has since rejected the Costa Rican petition for Hull's extradition, sending it back, for reasons of form (technical deficiencies) effectively delaying it. The newly elected President of Costa Rica – President Calderon, a known supporter of Colonel Ollie's contras – is not too anxious to re-file the extradition request – at least not while President Bush was in power. In fact, as my sources have told me, the Costa Rican government has already been threatened with losing U.S. aid if the charges against Hall don't "disappear."[31]

Under George, "I didn't know Manuel Noriega was a drug dealer" Bush, it would have been a cold day in hell before those U.S. authorities, willing to make our nation the most hypocritical on the face of the earth by invading other countries, murdering innocent civilians and violating international law, allegedly to capture drug dealers, will adhere to Costa Rica's extradition request for accused drug trafficker John Hull. Why? Because Hull is another man who fits squarely into the Stool Pigeon Profile. If he gets heavy jail time – not Community Service, the sentence given to most of the already-convicted Iran-contra crooks – and "flips," he is liable to sing the same kinds of "songs" we might have heard from General Bueso-Rosa; songs about all those he was working for – North? Poindexter? Reagan? Bush? God only knows where the songs will end once we get people singing. And without a federal judge of the caliber of a John Sirica or a House of Representatives with the courage and integrity to challenge the immense powers that be, the longest running, costliest and deadliest fraud against the American people in our history – by any measure – would undoubtedly go unpunished.

Now I do see some some indications that under the administration of President William Clinton things might change. I pray that this is so. However, as a retired narcotic agent who cannot distinguish between the ounces and grams of white powder found on almost any street corner of every inner city in our nation – killing innocent children and the law enforcement officers trying to stop the madness, now including my own son – from the many tons of the stuff that Colonel North and his cohorts are accused of spilling onto our streets, I have lost all confidence in leaving our system of justice in the hands of politicians. I say "If they're guilty, they gotta go! They've all gotta go to jail, no matter who they are!" If they don't, I'll have a hard time living with myself and the memory of the thousands I've put in cages for the same crimes they're getting away with.

So if my government refuses to cooperate with another country who is willing to put these alleged drug traffickers on trial; and all that's needed is a little kidnapping; I've got the horse feed-bags and handcuffs ready, and I'm willing to travel.

I volunteer.

Notes

1. The Boston Glone, 6/22/90, "DEA Witness says Mexicans thought US Supported Them" by Bill Girdner.
2. Associated Press news report 8/11/90, Linda Deutsch Associated Press Writer.
3. I took part in what was euphemistically called an "expulsion" in 1974, and was sued for kidnapping. U.S. v Yolanda Sarmiento, Francoise Chiappi and Miguel Russo, among other incidents. I have the documentation of the events.
4. I am in possession of original investigative documents of Costa Rican Congressional investigators. The accusation is also covered in *Unreliable Sources* by Martin Lee, Lyle Stewart Publications.
5. See *Under Fire* by Oliver North.
6. I am in possession of copies of original Costa Rican investigative documents. The incident is also covered in Unreliable *Sources,* Martin Lee, Lyle Stewart Publications, whose source was Robert Parry, an Associated Press reporter who first covered the story and *The San Juan Star* (Puerto Rico), the newspaper that first printed it.
7. This case is covered in *Undercover* by Donald Goddard, Times Books, October, 1989.
8. Oliver North, Iran-contra hearings.
9. Ibid, and *Cocaine Politics,* by Peter Dale Scott and Jonathan Marshall, University of California Press, 1992.
10. *Cocaine Politics,* by Peter Dale Scott and Jonathan Marshall, University of California Press, 1991.
11. *Vanity Fair,* March, 1990, "Hidden Agendas, by Mort Rosenblum.
12. Kerry Hearings, III, 48; also, *Cocaine Politics,* by Peter Dale Scott and Jonathan Marshall, University of California Press, 1991.
13. *Michael Jackson Show,* KABC, Los Angeles, November 11, 1991.
14. North's 2600 pages of notes are in the possession of the National Security Archives, Washington, D.C., where Kate Doyle is copying and cataloguing the approximately 500 pages devoted to drug trafficking. I am in possession of some 100 pages covering one year of North's involvement with drugs. Some of the specific notes describing drug transactions were also written about in *Out of Control* by Leslie Cockburn.
15. *Vanity Fair*, March, 1990, "Hidden Agendas, by Mort Rosenblum.
16. *Out of Control,* Leslie Cockburn, Atlantic Monthly Press.
17. Iran-contra hearings.
18. *Drug Wars,* by Jonathan Marshall, Cohan & Cohen Publishers, 1991.
19. Iran-contra hearings.
20. Ibid, P 154–155.
21. *New York Times,* "Acting on a Deadly Stage," by Peter Kerr, June 16, 1986; also *Undercover*, by Donald Goddard, Random House/Times Books, 1989.
22. *Out of Control,* Leslie Cockburn, Atlantic Monthly Press.
23. *The Unclassified,* newsletter, published by the National Security Alumni-Vol.3, No. 6; December-January 1992, page 23.
24. *Village Voice,* "Dear Diaries," by Frank Snepp, August 11, 1992.
25. *Boston Globe,* "A Call To Justice," by Jerry Meldon, May 6, 1991.
26. I have documentation of DEA's role in Hull's bail-jumping, through two independent confidential sources.

27. *Boston Globe,* "A Call To Justice," by Jerry Meldon, May 6, 1991.
28. Ibid.
29. I am in possession of full documentation, including testimony of investigators who have spoken to Chavarria.
30. *Out of Control,* Leslie Cockburn, Atlantic Monthly Press, 1987.
31. Former Christic Institute investigator Douglas Vaughan, is in possession of a signed statement from one of the staff of Costa Rican investigators, attesting to the details of this threat.

THE DRUGS-CRIME RELATIONSHIP: AN ANALYTICAL FRAMEWORK

DUANE C. McBRIDE
Andrews University

CLYDE B. McCOY
University of Miami

The relationship between drug use and criminal behavior has been of primary interest to researchers and practitioners for most of this century. As such, it is the purpose of this article to examine the historical underpinnings of current perceptions and to suggest an organizational paradigm for interpreting current drugs-crime literature. An overview of the literature and issues suggests that there is strong empirical evidence of the statistical overlap between drug using and criminal behavior. Further, drug use is seen as increasing and sustaining criminal behavior. However, a wide body of research suggests that drug use and crime have a complex recursive nature to their relationship, and that drug use, in spite of a long history of public perceptions, cannot be viewed as a direct and simple cause of crime. A review of subcultural, role, and ecological theory suggests that drug use and crime may emerge from the same etiological variables and become an integral part of a street-drug-using lifestyle and subculture. Radical theory argues that the drugs/crime relationship is created by social policy that makes drugs illegal. It is argued that this perspective fails to recognize the complexity of the drugs/crime relationship. The existing research suggests the need for increasing treatment availability and increasing economic opportunities within the framework of a careful review of drug policy and enforcement.

The relationship between drug using and criminal behavior has been a primary concern of researchers, policymakers and the general public for most of this century (see McBride & McCoy, 1982). Both the scientific and popular media have tended to view the existence of the drugs-crime relationship as the basis of the public concern about drug use, as well as of national and international drug policy and the current infrastructure of drug law enforcement, treatment, and research. Although in the public mind, the relationship between drugs and crime is often seen as fairly straightforeword—with drug use being viewed as directly causing criminal behavior—critical research analysis has indicated that the relationship is

THE PRISON JOURNAL, Vol. 73 Nos. 3 & 4, September/December 1993 257-278 conceptually and empirically quite complex. Given this, it is the purpose of this article to suggest an organizational paradigm for examining the literature on the drugs-crime relationship, to use that paradigm to review relevant literature and to examine the policy implications of recent research on the drugs-crime relationship.

AN ORGANIZATIONAL PARADIGM

Although the phrase "drugs-crime relationship" is commonly used, it often masks the variety of substances that are included under the concept of *drugs,* and the specific types of violations of the criminal law that is encompassed by the term *crime.* In addition, the phrase does not elucidate issues of the etiology of the relationship. It might be helpful if an analysis of the relationship between drug using and criminal behavior were organized within the following framework:

1. the historical underpinnings of current perspectives
2. types of drugs and types of criminal behavior
3. the statistical relationship: the extent and type of criminal behavior among various types of drug users and the extent and type of drug use among various types of criminals
4. the etiological nature of the relationship, including such issues as causality and interaction
5. theoretical interpretations of the relationship
6. the policy implications of research conclusions

HISTORICAL UNDERPINNINGS OF CURRENT PERSPECTIVES

THE 19th-CENTURY NATIONAL DRUG CULTURE

During the late 19th century, American society had a fairly laissez faire attitude toward what were called "patent medicines." These medicines, often containing opium, were touted as cure-alls for whatever ailed a person, from general aches and pains to sexual dysfunctions. They were available through a variety of means, including private physicians, the Sears catalog, and the traveling medicine show. The claims of one patent medicine, Hamlin's Wizard Oil, well illustrate the exaggerated assertions. The advertisement for the Hamlin product claimed that "there is no sore it will not heal, no pain it will not subdue." The oil was "Pleasant to take and magical in its effects" (Inciardi, 1992, p. 4). The makers and distributors of patent medicines were effective entrepreneurs organizing themselves as the Proprietary Medicine Manufactures Association in 1881. For over two decades they successfully prevented any attempt to limit their enterprise. They effectively marketed their products in most of the mass and professional media and catalogs of the era. The development of the hypodermic needle in the middle of the 19th century and advances in chemistry resulted in the development of more potent drugs that could be delivered in the most efficacious manner. As David Musto (1973) observed, "Opiates and cocaine became popular—if unrecognized—items in the everyday life of Americans" (p. 3). Although exact figures on the consumption of opium during this time period are not available, the U.S. Public Health Service estimated that between 1859 and 1899, 7,000 tons of crude opium and 800 tons of smoking opium were imported in the United States (Kolb & Du Mez, 1924).

The turn of the century seemed to initiate a broad-based social reform movement in a wide variety of areas of American culture. The developing American Medical Association (AMA) began questioning the effectiveness claims of the patent medicines. As a result of the failure to scientifically verify the claims, the AMA removed advertisements for patent medicines from their journals. By this means, the professional physicians began to disassociate themselves from the medicine show. Perhaps as a result of these professional critiques of patent medicines, journalists also began to focus on the industry. One of the most noted series of articles was in the national weekly magazine *Collier's*. For about a 4-month period during 1905 and 1906, a *Collier's* reporter, Samuel Adams, chronicled the fraudulent claims of the patent medicine sellers, the toxic ingredients they contained (often high dosages of opium and cocaine), and the consequences of their use. Adams claimed that the use of these medicines made criminals of young men and harlots of young women (see Young, 1967, p. 31).

Although the *Collier's* articles on the patent medicine industry did cause a great deal of discussion in the popular press, it was the impact of Upton Sinclair's *The Jungle* on legal policy that most effected the patent medicine industry. As a result of the documented filthy conditions in the American meat-packing industry, Congress passed the Pure Food and Drug Act in 1906. Although this act did not outlaw patent medicines, it did require that the ingredients and their proportions be listed on each bottle. This, coupled with persistent media focus on the horrors of opium and other drug use, appeared to prepare the public and the Congress for further restrictions on the industry. Within the next few years, many states severely restricted the distribution of narcotics through physicians and pharmacists or over the counter (see Musto, 1973, p. 18). The distribution was further restricted by the Harrison Act of 1914. In spite of what is popularly thought, this act did not make the manufacture, distribution, or use of opium, cocaine, or marijuana illegal. What it did was require that individuals and companies that manufactured or distributed these substances register with the Treasury Department and pay special taxes. The Treasury Department's interpretation of the Harrison Act and subsequent Supreme Court decisions served to make a wide variety of narcotics and other drugs illegal to manufacture, distribute, or even prescribe.

PERCEPTIONS OF DRUGS AND CRIME IN THE EARLY 20th CENTURY

Some critics have argued that the Harrison Act turned law-abiding users of patent medicines into criminals (King, 1974). Although this is probably an oversimplification, the Harrison Act did culminate and strongly support a popular social reform movement that increasingly defined drug use as criminal and often the cause of violent, bizarre behavior.

The medical literature of the early 20th century, by contrast, viewed the opiate user as lethargic and less likely to engage in violent crime. Whatever criminal behavior resulted from drug use was seen as occurring to obtain money to buy drugs. Shoplifting and other forms of petty theft were seen as the primary types of criminal behavior. Many observers noted that debauchery, laziness, and prostitution were the primary deviant behavioral consequences of opiate use—not violent predatory crime (see Kolb, 1925; Lichtenstein, 1914; Terry & Pellens, 1928). Overall, the medical and psychiatric literature of the early 20th century viewed opiate use as debilitating and a cause of petty property crimes or prostitution, but not as a cause of violent crime.

Some medical practitioners did consider cocaine to be different from opiates in its behavioral consequences (Kolb, 1925). Kolb's observation was that cocaine tended to make individuals more paranoid and that consequently, a cocaine user might strike out violently at an imagined pursuer. Although cocaine was used in many patent medicines and was included in the Harrison Act, the official government position seemed to conclude that cocaine use, although potentially a cause of crime, was relatively small and therefore of insignificant consequence (U.S. Treasury Department, 1939).

Although the medical literature did not see opiate use as a prime cause of violent street crime or crime in general, there were many popular lecturers who did. Perhaps the most prolific and popular antinarcotic lecturer was Richmond P. Hobson. He founded a number of anti-narcotics-use organizations and both published and lectured extensively on the violent crimogenic nature of narcotics use. Throughout the 1920s, Mr. Hobson argued that most property and violent crimes were committed by heroin and other types of drug addicts. He further argued that the continuity of civilization itself depended on the elimination of narcotics use (Hobson, 1928). With his frequent radio broadcasts, he played a significant role in creating a national perception of the direct link between all types of drug use and all types of crime.

Somewhat surprisingly, the primary drugs-crime connection portrayed in popular and government media involved marijuana use. On July 6, 1927, the *New York Times* reported that a family in Mexico City had become hopelessly insane by eating marijuana leaves. The epitome of the marijuana-causes-crime perspective was probably the Hollywood production of the film *Reefer Madness*. This film was strongly influenced by the Commissioner of the Treasury Department's Bureau of Narcotics, Harry J. Anslinger. *Reefer Madness* portrayed marijuana as the great destroyer of American youth. Marijuana, it was shown in the film, not only caused young people to become sexually promiscuous but also violently criminal and prone to suicide. Marijuana was viewed as the most dangerous substance in America and one that, unless stopped, would lead to the violent downfall of Western civilization. It was not only in the movies that marijuana was portrayed as causing violence. Anslinger and his colleagues at the Bureau of Narcotics published a number of books focusing on the direct violent criminal behavior caused by narcotics, particularly by marijuana use, and on the involvement of criminal gangs in the distribution of illegal drugs (Anslinger & Oursler, 1961; Anslinger & Tompkins, 1953). In all of his work, Anslinger listed cannabis as a narcotic and always described its consequences as the most violent and dangerous. For example, in the *The Murders*, he claimed that "All varieties (of Cannabis) may lead to acts of violence, extremes, madness, homicide" (p. 304). In this book, Anslinger provided many examples of the criminal horrors committed by those who had smoked even one reefer. The most gruesome illustration was the case of a 17-month-old White female raped and murdered by a cotton picker who had smoked one marijuana cigarette (Anslinger & Tompkins, 1953, p. 24). The popular book entitled *Dope* argued that "when you have once chosen marijuana, you have selected murder and torture and hideous cruelty to your bosom friends" (Black, 1928, p. 28). Popular periodicals such as *American Magazine* also told in lurid detail about ax-murdering marijuana-intoxicated youths on rampages (Sloman, 1979, p. 63).

A crucial implicit and often explicit aspect of the portrayal of the relationship between drugs and crime was the strong antiforeign feelings and racism of the 1920s and 1930s. Many of the horror stories that focused on the violence and degradation of narcotics users centered on African Americans, Mexicans, and Chinese. All of the illegal drugs were portrayed as foreign imports brought in by dark- or yellow-skinned outsiders wanting to corrupt White youth, seduce White women, and/or overthrow Northern European ascendancy. The drugs-crime relationship was thus an important aspect of a popular racial and national isolationist perspective (see Inciardi, 1992; Musto, 1973).

During the 1930s and 1940s, and even into the 1950s, the American government and the popular media seemed to work closely in continuing to create the image of the "dope fiend" as a violent, out-of-control sexual predator who accounted for a large proportion of America's heinous crimes. By the late 1950s, this image had been strongly challenged by a wide variety of academic and other critics. However, these formative images of the bizarre, violent dope fiend continue to provide at least a background schemata that affects cultural perceptions of the drugs-crime relationship.

THE INTERSECTION OF TYPOLOGIES

Although the historical and current discussions of the drugs-crime relationship often assume a particular intersection between specific types of drugs and specific types of crime, that intersection is generally not explicit or examined in a logical, sequential manner. As McGlothlin (1979) noted almost 15 years ago, if the drugs-crime relationship is to be examined logically, it is important to use typologies of both types of behaviors and proceed to review how each type of drug use relates to each type of crime. Drug abuse and crime are complex issues that include a multitude of specific behaviors.

TYPES OF DRUGS

At the turn of the century almost all drugs were called narcotics—including opium, marijuana, and cocaine. However, as is apparent, each of these substances has a very different chemical structure and a different psychopharmacological effect. Thus each potentially has a very different relationship to various types of criminal behavior. During the 1960s and 1970s, the term *drug abuse* primarily seemed to mean heroin use and, to a lesser extent, LSD use. Today, the term probably conjures up images of cocaine use. Regardless of what specific drug the term may be most associated with, an analysis of the drugs-crime relationship must conceptually use the major specific categories of drugs.

Generally, it has been recognized that the various types of illegal drugs have different possible relationships to criminal behavior, based on their chemical structure, subculture of use, cost, or differential patterns of control.

Over the last decade, major national surveys on illegal drug use have tended to develop a list of drug types that are routinely included in questionnaires (for example, see Clayton et al., 1988; Johnston, O'Malley, & Bachman, 1993; Liska, 1990). These are

1. narcotic analgesics: including heroin, Demoral, Percodan, and Dilaudid
2. stimulants: including cocaine in all of its forms and amphetamines
3. hallucinogens: for example, LSD, PCP, and MDA
4. inhalants: including gasoline, paint thinner, glue, other volatile hydrocarbons and amyl/butyl nitrites
5. sedatives: for example, barbiturates and methaqualone
6. major and minor tranquilizers
7. marijuana (although the effects of this drug combine some aspects of sedatives, tranquilizers, and hallucinogens, it is usually placed in its own sperate classification)
8. steroids and other types of hormonal substances designed to build muscle or increase aggressiveness.

In some research projects, these categories might need to be expanded to include more specific drugs within each category. However, these are the general categories used in drug research.

TYPES OF CRIME

Types of criminal behavior also need to be constructed in drugs-crime research and conceptual understandings. For the last two decades, researchers have explicitly argued that drugs-crime research needs to work within common parameter definitions of categories of criminal behavior (see Inciardi & McBride, 1976). Traditionally, criminologists have had a major focus on the construction of criminal behavior typologies. The aim has been to construct mutually exclusive homogeneous categories (see Hood & Sparks, 1970). Typically, typological constructions in criminology have been based on legal categories, such as the Uniform Crime Reports (UCR) (1993), the public's perception of the severity ranking of specific criminal behaviors (Rossi, Waite, Bose, & Berk, 1974), the social psychology and behavioral characteristics of offenders (Duncan, Ohlin, Reis, & Stanton, 1953), or combinations of all of the preceding (Clinard & Quinney, 1967). Recent criminology and criminal justice texts have tended to use the categorization of the UCR, which includes a sense of public and official views of seriousness plus elements of social psychological characteristics (see Inciardi, 1993).

The following categories of crimes are commonly used in criminal justice research:

1. crime against persons: including homicide, manslaughter, rape of all types, aggravated assault, assault and battery, and child molestation
2. armed robbery
3. property crimes: including breaking and entering, larceny, auto theft, arson, forgery, counterfeiting, passing worthless checks, buying, concealing, and receiving stolen property, vandalism
4. income-producing victimless crimes: including prostitution, commercialized vice, and gambling
5. violation of drug laws: including the possession or sale of dangerous drugs or the implements for their use
6. other offenses: for example, disorderly conduct, vagrancy, loitering, and resisting arrest.

Sequentially examining each of the specific intersections between each type of drug and each type of crime could help build a systematic body of knowledge about the totality of the drugs-crime relationship.

THE STATISTICAL OVERLAP

Historically, and currently, one of the major arguments for the existence of a drugs-crime relationship is the high level of drug use among populations of criminals and the frequent involvement in criminal activities of street-drug users. About 40 years ago Anslinger and Tompkins (1953), as a part of their argument that drug use was a component of a criminal culture, claimed that a large proportion of federal prisoners were users of illegal drugs. During the late 1960s and early 1970s, many epidemiologists, and certainly the popular culture, believed that the United States was undergoing a drug epidemic. The evidence for the epidemic was large increases in drug overdosages, drug-related arrests and drug treatment admissions (see O'Donnell, Voss, Clayton, Slatin, & Room, 1976). One of the major perceived consequences of increased drug use was the perception of an associated increase in street crime. This apparent epidemic stimulated the development or reinvigoration of a vast drug treatment, enforcement, and research endeavor culminating in the establishment of the National Institute on Drug Abuse (NIDA) in 1974. In 1971, during an address to Congress on June 17, President Richard M. Nixon called the drug epidemic a national emergency. The Federal Strategy Report of 1975 noted that the crime associated with drug use was a major reason for the national attention focused on drug abuse in that era.

DRUG USE IN POPULATIONS OF CRIMINALS

One of the tasks of the newly created NIDA and the National Institute of Justice was a series of studies and symposiums on the drugs-crime relationship (see Inciardi & McBride, 1976; Gandossy, Williams, Cohen, & Harwood, 1980). As these study groups documented, many research projects conducted in a variety of urban areas during the early 1970s found that somewhere between 15% and 40% of arrestees and prisoners were users of illegal drugs—mostly marijuana and heroin (see Eckerman, Bates, Rachal, & Poole, 1971; Ford, Hauser, & Jackson, 1975; McBride, 1976). These finding were seen, at the time, as dramatic evidence of the existence of the drug/crime connection and the need to integrate the criminal justice system with the drug treatment system. One of the outcomes of these types of studies was the establishment of the Treatment Alternatives to Street Crime (TASC) program, which attempted to identify drug users in populations of offenders, assess their treatment needs, and refer them to appropriate treatment facilities (see Inciardi & McBride, 1991).

Recent research has shown an even more extensive use of drugs in a variety of criminally involved populations. In a study of nonincarcerated delinquents in Miami, Florida, Inciardi, Horowitz, and Pottieger (1993) found that some three fourths of male and female delinquents used cocaine at least weekly. Further, the Drug Use Forecasting (DUF) program collects and analyzes urine from arrestees in 24 major cities across the United States. In most, over 60% of the male and female arrestees are positive for illegal drugs. The lowest rates for males were in Omaha and San Antonio, where only 48% were positive for an illegal drug. The lowest rate for females was 47% in New Orleans. The highest for females was 81% in Manhattan, and the highest rate for males was 80% in Philadelphia. In almost all of the cities in the study, cocaine was the most common drug found through urinalysis followed by marijuana and opiates (see DUF, 1993; Wish, 1987).

Surveys of incarcerated populations show a similarly high rate of illegal drug use just prior to incarceration. In 1990, for example, the Bureau of Justice Statistics found that over 40% of state prison inmates reported the daily use of illegal drugs in the month prior to the offense that resulted in their incarceration. A comparison of these data to that of criminally involved populations in the 1970s shows a much higher rate of illegal drug use in the current criminal justice population and a dramatic shift from heroin and marijuana to primarily cocaine and marijuana. These data also suggest a virtual saturation of the criminal justice system by illegal drug users who mostly consume cocaine in some form.

There is also a body of research that indicates a high level of drug use among incarcerated individuals. In a study of Delaware prison inmates, Inciardi, Lockwood, and Quinlan (1993) found that 60% of the respondents reported the use of drugs, mostly marijuana, while in prison. However, urinalysis found only about a 1% positivity rate. A random sample of urine collected in Wisconsin discovered a rate of 25% positive, mostly marijuana (Vigdal & Stadler, 1989). There is also some ethnographic evidence that drugs are integrated in the prison culture as a part of control, management, and reward systems (see Hawkins & Alpert, 1989; Inciardi, Horowitz, & Pottieger, 1993). Although there is no evidence that drug use is rampant in jails and prisons, the high use rates in the population prior to incarceration as well as the level of continuing use while in prison have stimulated the development of drug treatment services in prisons throughout the United States (Hayes & Schimmel, 1993).

CRIMINAL BEHAVIOR IN POPULATIONS OF DRUG USERS

Examinations of drug-using populations for the last few decades have found similarly high rates of criminal behavior. Surveys of populations of illegal drug users in the late 1960s and early 1970s generally found that a large majority had extensive criminal histories (see Defleur, Ball, & Snarr, 1969; Voss & Stephens, 1973). Recent local and national research has confirmed these early findings. In a population of over 400 street-injection-drug users in Miami, Florida, for example, McBride and Inciardi (1990) found that over 80% had been in jail in the last 5 years and about 45% had been incarcerated within the last 6 months. An analysis of over 25,000 street-injection-drug users from 63 cities found that some two thirds were in jail in the last 5 years, with over one third currently on probation or parole or awaiting trial (Inciardi, McBride, Platt, & Baxter, 1993). Consistently, examinations of populations of nonincarcerated drug users clearly show a high level of current involvement with criminal behavior and with the criminal justice system.

THE STATISTICAL OVERLAP IN THE GENERAL POPULATION

General-population surveys also show the overlap between drug using and criminal behaviors. In 1991, the National Household Survey of drug use conducted by the NIDA included questions on criminal behavior. Analysis of that data showed a correlation between drug use and engaging in criminal, particularly violent, behavior. Less than 5% of those who drank alcohol only or who consumed no substance engaged in a violent or property crime during the last year. About 25% of those who had used marijuana and cocaine in addition to alcohol admitted to the commission of a violent and/or property crime in the last year (Harrison & Gfroerer, 1992).

Analyses of data from the National Youth Survey also show a strong correlation between serious drug use and serious delinquent behavior. The National Youth Survey is a longitudinal study initiated in the late 1970s and was designed to survey a variety of behaviors, including substance use and crime (see Huizinga, 1978, for a description of the survey and its methodology). In an analysis of these data, Johnson, Wish, Schmeidler, and Huizinga (1993) found that only 3% of nondelinquents used cocaine, whereas 23% of those with multiple delinquency index crimes were current cocaine users. Examining the data from the perspective of drug-using behavior, they found that only 2% of those who used alcohol only had multiple index offenses compared to 28% of the cocaine users. Overall, these researchers found a correlation of .53 between the delinquency and drug use scales.

Although the complexity and causal nature of the drugs-crime relationship is open to considerable debate, there is little contention about the statistical correlation between drug use and crime. For a number of decades, the existence of the empirical relationship has been documented by researchers as well as by criminal justice practitioners and drug treatment professionals. The size of the relationship between using drugs and criminal behavior is a daily reality in criminal justice systems and drug treatment programs throughout the United States. This reality has stimulated a wide variety of critical thinking and research projects designed to sort out the nature of the drugs-crime relationship and policies that could be used to reduce the extent of the relationship.

THE ETIOLOGICAL NATURE OF THE DRUGS-CRIME RELATIONSHIP

WHICH CAME FIRST?

The issue of behavioral and causal priority in the drugs-crime relationship has been a primary research focus of numerous investigators. For the past 20 years, researchers have consistently found that individuals who frequently use illegal drugs such as cocaine, heroin, or marijuana have engaged in criminal behavior prior to or concurrent with the initiation of any stable illegal drug use pattern (see Anglin & Speckart, 1988; Huizinga, Menard, & Elliot, 1989; Inciardi, Lockwood, & Quinlan, 1993; O'Donnell et al., 1976; Stephens & McBride, 1976). Rather than innocents seduced or propelled into criminal activity by their drug use, existing data and research indicate that drug abuse and criminal activity are a part of a broader set of integrated deviant behaviors involving crime, drug use, and, often, high-risk sex. Although a variety of empirical data indicate that drug use does not appear to initiate a criminal career, a large volume of research clearly indicates that frequency of drug use has a strong impact on the extent, direction, and duration of that career.

THE IMPACT OF DRUG USE ON FREQUENCY OF CRIMINAL BEHAVIOR

A wide body of research indicates that although criminal behavior may be initiated prior to or concomitant with the genesis of illegal drug use, once illegal drug use is initiated it has a dramatic effect on the amount of criminal activity (Anglin & Hser, 1987; Anglin & Speckart, 1988; Ball, Rosen, Flueck, & Nurco, 1981; Chambers, Cuskey, & Moffett, 1970; Chaiken & Chaiken, 1990; Stephens & McBride, 1976). Particularly the work of Ball and his colleagues (1981), using longitudinal data, and Anglin and his colleagues (Anglin & Hser, 1987; Anglin & Speckart, 1988), using a life history method, clearly indicate the effect of narcotics use on rates of criminal behavior. These researchers found sharp decreases in criminal activity during periods of abstinence from heroin and large increases in criminal activity during periods of increased heroin use (see Anglin & Speckart, 1988; Ball et al., 1981; Ball, Shaffer, & Nurco, 1983).

The expense of cocaine and heroin use and the fact that most frequent users of these drugs are unemployed result in a high level of criminal activity in user populations. Inciardi, McBride, McCoy, and Chitwood (in press) describe what they call an amazing amount of criminal activity involving over 100,000 criminal acts (excluding drug law violations) committed by some 700 cocaine users in the 90 days prior to being interviewed. Johnson and his colleagues (1985) reported that over 40% of the total income of a population of street-drug users was generated from illegal activity. Using a variety of methodologies, including life histories, surveys, and longitudinal data, the existing research literature suggests that the frequent use of illegal drugs is clearly a part of the motivation for an increase in criminal activities that are designed to obtain funds for drugs or as a part of other activities designed to access, possess, and use drugs. In addition, the available data suggest that, rather than a simple linear relationship between drugs and crime, both may emerge at a similar time period and that the two behaviors may have a recursive element to their relationship. That is, drug use may be involved in increasing criminal behavior, but the initiation of criminal behavior may also result in subcultural participation and individual-risk decision making that involves taking high-risk drugs (see Clayton & Tuchfeld, 1982).

THE IMPACT OF DRUG USE ON SUSTAINED CRIMINAL BEHAVIOR

There is some evidence that frequent hard-drug use may be involved with a sustained criminal career. Longitudinal research indicates that most delinquents cease their illegal activity by late adolescence or early adulthood (e.g., see Kandel, Simcha-Fagan, & Davies, 1986). Traditionally, getting a steady job, getting married, and having children was viewed as a sign of maturation and as increasing an individual's stakes in conformity and therefore decreasing rates of illegal behavior. The UCR indicates a sharp drop in arrest rates for populations over 25 years of age. A wide variety of research data indicates that frequent drug use may severely interfere with that maturation process and consequent reduction in crime. National (Elliott & Huizinga, 1985) and local studies (Dembo et al., 1987) have indicated that chronic serious delinquent offenders are more likely to become involved with hard-drug use, which, in turn, relates to continued participation in a criminal subculture and high rates of criminal behavior. Life history research (Faupel & Klockars, 1987) also documents the recursive relationship of using drugs and criminal behavior.

The recursive nature of the drugs-crime relationship appears to act to reinforce continued drug use and crime. Ethnographers have described this as "taking care of business" (Hanson, Beschner, Walters, & Bovelle, 1985). Essentially, the argument is that the subcultural values that emerge in street-drug-using cultures encompass crime as a means to obtain drugs and as a cultural value itself in opposition to the straight world of legitimate low-paying jobs. Using drugs and criminal behavior become well integrated within the cultural/social role of the street-drug user (see Stephens, 1991). From this perspective, drug use does not directly cause crime, but, rather, is an integral part of the street-drug subculture. To focus only on drug-using behavior as a primary means to reduce crime misses the intertwined complexity of the drugs-crime relationship.

DRUG USE AND TYPE OF CRIME

Probably as a result of images created by decades of government and media messages about the violent dope fiend, the public has been concerned about the types of crime in which drug users engage. The particular concern has been that the use of many types of drugs causes extreme violence. As noted earlier in this article, many years ago, Kolb (1925) argued against the prevailing popular view of the crazed dope fiend. From a psychopharmacological perspective, he contended that the biochemical effect of opiate use was to make a user lethargic and less likely to engage in violent crime at least while under the influence of the drug. This original perspective continued to find empirical support for decades. For example, Finestone (1957) claimed that heroin users were much more likely to engage in petty property crime to support their use than in noneconomically productive violent crime. In fact, he observed that as street groups initiated and increased heroin use, the rate of violent crime decreased and their rate of property crime increased. These types of research findings continued through most of the next two decades. Basically, heroin users were found to be overrepresented among property criminals and underrepresented among those charged with crimes of violence (see Inciardi & Chambers, 1972; Kozel & DuPont, 1977; McBride, 1976).

In the late 1970s, researchers began to report an increase in violence in the street-heroin-using subculture, particularly among younger cohorts of users (Stephens & Ellis, 1975; Zahn & Bencivengo, 1974). During the 1980s, epidemiological data indicated a rapid increase in cocaine use. As has been noted, DUF (1993) data indicate a virtual saturation of cocaine use in arrested populations. This rapid rise in cocaine use and in rates of violent behavior has stimulated a variety of speculation and research about the impact of cocaine on criminal behavior and on the world of the street-drug user. For most of the last decade, researchers have been reporting that increased cocaine use was related to violent confrontational crime for men and women (Datesman, 1981; Goldstein, 1989; Simonds & Kashani, 1980; Spunt, Goldstein, Bellucci, & Miller, 1990). Research has also indicated that cocaine use may be related not only to being a violent offender but also to being a victim of violent crime. McBride, Burgman-Habermehl, Alpert, and Chitwood (1986), in an analysis of homicides in Miami, Florida, found that after alcohol, cocaine was the most common drug found in the bodies of homicide victims. Almost 10% of homicide victims had cocaine in their bodies at the time of death. This was more than 8 times the rate of any other illegal drug. Goldstein, Bellucci, Spunt, and Miller (1993), in a study in New York City, found that increased cocaine use was associated with being a victim of violent crime for women.

Paul Goldstein (1989) has proposed a very useable framework for interpreting the relationship between drugs and violence that seems particularly appropriate to interpreting the relationship between cocaine and violence. He calls this paradigm "a tripartite scheme." Goldstein sees this scheme as involving psychopharmacological, economically compulsive, and systemic aspects. Essentially, a part of the violent behavior of cocaine users may relate to the psychopharmacological consequences of cocaine use. This effect includes a strong stimulant impact, long periods without sleep, and increased paranoia. All of these effects could result in an increased willingness on the part of those using cocaine (and other stimulants, such as amphetamines) to engage in aggressive behavior or to put themselves into situations where aggressive behavior is more likely to occur. The economic demands involve the cost of heavy cocaine or crack use that may result in violent predatory behavior designed to obtain the most money. The systemic aspect of the model involves violent subcultural behavior patterns that are integral to being a street-drug user and those violent behavior patterns that are a part of the street distribution of cocaine. Other researchers (McBride & Swartz, 1990) have suggested that the drugs-violence and cocaine-violence relationship is also occurring within the framework of a rapid increase of heavy armaments in general society. That is, our whole society has undergone an increase in the availability and distribution of powerful automatic weapons. This general availability of weapons has also become a part of the street-drug-using culture. Rather than drug use being a direct cause of violence, it might be important to recognize that the drug culture has adapted the weaponry of the general culture and has used it for its own purposes. Regardless of the exact nature of the relationship, the existing data suggest that, increasingly, drug use, particularly cocaine use, has become integrated with a high level of international, national, and local street violence. The extent of cocaine use among felony offenders and the perceived relationship between cocaine and violence has played a major role in the reinvigoration of the debate about national drug policy and the issue of the decriminalization of drug use.

SOME THEORETICAL PERSPECTIVES ON THE DRUGS-CRIME RELATIONSHIP

From every conceivable methodological perspective, data consistently show that there is a strong correlation between drug use and criminal behavior and that increases in drug use are related to increases in crime. However, the theoretical analysis of the relationship has not been as extensive. Some perspectives argue that the interpretation of the empirical relationship might be very different from what the data initially suggest.

SUBCULTURAL, ROLE THEORY, AND ECOLOGICAL PERSPECTIVES

Ethnographic and role theory analyses have tended to view the crime and drug relationship as associated with subcultural roles that include what general society would call extreme deviant behavior (Hanson et al., 1985; Stephens, 1991). High frequencies of drug use, high rates of crime, and extensive high-risk sexual behavior are seen from this perspective as "taking care of business" or an integral part of the social role of the street-drug user. This type of conceptual analysis suggests that the drugs-crime relationship may not be directly linear in cause, but, rather, drug use and crime exist as a part of an intertwined mutually reinforcing subculturally contexted set of behaviors.

Ecological theoretical analysis has suggested that the drugs-crime relationship appears to be related because both types of behavior are caused by similar environmental conditions, such as poverty and lack of social control and economic opportunity. In that sense, some observers have concluded that drug use is spuriously related to crime. That is, there is the appearance of a statistical causal relationship, but that relationship may be an artifact of common etiology (Fagan, Weis, & Cheng, 1990; McBride & McCoy, 1981). Drugs and crime occur together because they share a similar set of causal variables and they are a part of the same subcultural value and role system. From these ecological and subcultural theoretical perspectives, the drugs-crime relationship is not so much affected by attempts to stop or reduce drug use but, rather, by attempts to address the common underlying initiating and sustaining causes of both behaviors.

A RADICAL INTERPRETATION OF THE DRUGS-CRIME RELATIONSHIP

Another major theoretical critique of the apparent drugs-crime relationship comes from radical theory. This perspective maintains that the drugs-crime relationship is an artifact of legal policy since 1914. From this viewpoint, the existence of a drugs-crime relationship simply resulted from laws that effectively criminalized a variety of drug-using behaviors. As the result of the Harrison Act and subsequent law, American society created a criminal subculture where none existed; drove up the cost of drugs, thereby providing an economic motivation for drug-related crime; and left the distribution of drugs to organized criminal networks. These, in turn, grew immensely wealthy and powerful through the distribution of the much-in-demand and now-expensive illegal drugs. The current violence, corruption, and civil rights issues associated with drug use and drug law enforcement are seen, from this perspective, as the inevitable result of the social construction of deviance. Radical theorists argue that the drugs-crime relationship can best be disentangled by decriminalizing drugs and treating drug abuse and addiction as mental and public health problems that are best addressed through psychological counseling and social work case management. The drug policy of the Netherlands is often advocated as an example of an enlightened, less criminogenic strategy (see Lindesmith, 1965; Nadelmann, 1989; Trebach & Inciardi, 1993).

There is considerable evidence that much of the crime committed by drug users involves only violations of drug laws involving possession and distribution of illegal drugs. For example, Inciardi et al. (in press) found that during the 90 days prior to being interviewed, their sample of some 700 cocaine users had committed over 1.7 million criminal acts with well over 95% of them involving violations of drug laws. Further evidence exists in examinations of the current operation of drug courts. Originally, these courts were designed to focus on the increasing number of drug-involved cases coming before the court. However, these courts may be increasing the focus on drug users who are involved only in drug law violations and not implicated in other types of crime and thereby furthering the appearance of a relationship between drug use and crime, particularly among African Americans in the inner city (Klofas, 1993).

The radical perspective does provide a valuable insight into how society may create by law that which it is attempting to avoid by law, and there may be some applicability to the interpretation of the drugs-crime relationship. The perspective is, however, often built on the notion that somehow the relationship between drug use and crime would virtually disappear if drugs were just decriminalized, that there would be no or minimal increase in drug use, and that any increase would have virtually no impact on violence or crime. Such a view would seem to ignore psychopharmacological aspects of the relationship, the fact that criminal behavior generally precedes drug use, and the findings that both behaviors arise from similar etiological variables and act in a mutually reinforcing manner.

In a recent analysis of the drugs-crime relationship in Amsterdam by Grapendaal, Leuw, and Nelen (1992), it was shown that 53% of a sample of 148 polydrug users engaged in acquisitive crime during an average month, and those 79 individuals netted almost $66,000 per month from their property crimes to buy drugs. Further, it was found that property crime accounted for 24% of total income in the sample. This was the second highest percentage of total income after welfare payments. During 1991, the city of Zurich, Switzerland experimented with the decriminalization of drugs and experienced an increase in property and violent crimes. Public pressure forced a reversal of Swiss policy (see the *New York Times*, February 11, 1992, A10). Although, as Grapendaal and his colleagues (1992) noted, the extent of drug-related crime in the Netherlands may not be as extensive as in New York or other American cities, there is a significant relationship even in a highly tolerant city. These researchers also noted that the policy of tolerance has created a permanent underclass whose crime may only be lessened by a generous welfare system but not eliminated. Just as the perspective arguing that drug use seduced innocent youth into a life of crime has been shown to be simplistic, so the perspective that drug laws throw otherwise peaceful citizens into a life of criminal violence that can be eliminated if drugs are just decriminalized may also be more simplistic than is warranted by the facts (for perspectives against decriminalization see Inciardi & McBride, 1989; Wilson, 1993).

POLICY IMPLICATIONS OF THE DRUGS-CRIME DATA

Although the drugs-crime data and conceptual understandings may be complex and even contradictory, there appear to be three major common implications from current knowledge.

1. There is a strong need for treatment services for drug-using, criminally involved populations. This would include both those who are incarcerated as well as those on probation or in a diversion program. Regardless of the complexity of the data, there is a clear indication that levels of drug use relate to levels of criminal activity. Reducing drug demand through treatment has a strong possibility for reducing levels of crime. Increasing treatment resources at all levels of the criminal justice system to eliminate waiting lists, as well as increasing recruitment outreach in criminal populations, has a significant potential to reduce the level of crime in a community.

2. The ecological and subcultural perspectives remind our society that the drugs-crime relationship is at least in part the result of a history of differential social, political, and economic opportunity. The development of oppositional subcultures in which drug use and crime are an integrated part will be addressed only by major efforts to provide educational and economic-development opportunities. Social and economic progress in communities with high rates of drug use and crime must be a local and national priority.

3. The radical perspective reminds us that in any application of drug policy, civil rights must be protected, that there are severe limits to the effectiveness of law enforcement, and enforcement practices can increase the appearance of the drugs-crime relationship well beyond the framework of psychopharmacology, economic demand, and subcultural roles. Drug laws and policy should focus on demand reduction at least equal to supply reduction. Drug law enforcement must never be an excuse for a retreat on hard-won legal and civil rights, and drug law and policy must rest on a strong public support base.

REFERENCES

Anglin, M. D., & Hser, Y. (1987). Addicted women and crime. *Criminology, 25*, 359-397.

Anglin, M. D., & Speckart, F. (1988). Narcotics use and crime: A multi sample, multi method analysis. *Criminology, 26*, 197-233.

Anslinger, H. J., & Ourlser, W. (1961). *The murderers*. New York: Farrar, Straus & Cudahy.

Anslinger, H. J., & Tompkins, W. F. (1953). *The traffic in narcotics*. New York: Funk & Wagnalls.

Ball, J. C., Rosen, L., Flueck, J. A., & Nurco, D. N. (1981). The criminality of heroin addicts: When addicted and when off opiates. In J. A. Inciardi (Ed.), The drugs-crime connection (pp. 39-65). Beverly Hills, CA: Sage.

Ball, J. C., Shaffer, J. W., & Nurco, D. N. (1983). The day-to-day criminality of heroin addicts in Baltimore: A study in the continuity of offense rates. *Drug and Alcohol Dependence, 12*, 119-142.

Black, W. (1928). *Dope: The story of the living dead*. New York: Star & Co.

Bureau of Justice Statistics. (1990). *Drugs and crime facts, 1989*. Washington, DC: Author.

Chaiken, J. M., & Chaiken, M. R. (1990). Drugs and predatory crime. In M. Tonry & J. Q. Wilson (Eds.), *Drugs and crime* (pp. 203-239). Chicago: University of Chicago Press.

Chambers, C. D., Cuskey, W. R., & Moffett, A. D. (1970). Demographic factors associated with opiate addiction among Mexican Americans. *Public Health Reports, 85*, 523-531.

Clayton, R. R., & Tuchfeld, B. S. (1982). The drug-crime debate: Obstacles to understanding the relationship. *Journal of Drug Issues, 12*, 153-166.

Clayton, R. R., Voss, H. L., Loscuito, L., Martin, S. S., Skinner, W. F., Robbins, C., & Santos, R. L. (1988). *National household survey on drug abuse: Main findings, 1985*. Washington DC: U.S. Department of Health & Human Services.

Clinard, M. B., & Quinney, R. (1967). Criminal behavior systems. New York: Rinehart & Winston.

Datesman, S. (1981). Women, crime, and drugs. In J. A. Inciardi (Ed.), The drugs/crime connection (pp. 85-104). Beverly Hills, CA: Sage.

Defleur, L. B., Ball, J. C., & Snarr, R. W. (1969). The long-term social correlates of opiate abuse. *Social Problems, 17*, 225-234.

Dembo, R., Washburn, M., Wish, E. D., Yeung, H., Getreu, A., Berry, E., & Blount, W. R. (1987). Heavy marijuana use and crime among youths entering a juvenile detention center. *Journal of Psychoactive Drugs, 19*,47-56.

Drug use forecasting. (1993, May). Washington, DC: National Institute of Justice.

Duncan, O. D., Ohlin, L. E., Reis A. J., & Stanton, H. E. (1953). Formal devises for making selection decisions. *American Journal of Sociology, 58*, 537-584.

Eckerman, W. C., Bates, J.J.D., Rachal, J. V., & Poole, W. K. (1971). *Drug usage and arrest charges*. Washington DC: Drug Enforcement Administration.

Elliott, D. S., & Huizinga, D. (1985). The relationship between delinqent behavior and ADM problems. *Proceedings of the Prevention Research Conference on Juvenile Offenders with Serious Drug, Alcohol and Mental Health Problems*. Washington, DC: Alcohol, Drug Abuse and Mental Health Administration, Office of Juvenile Justice and Delinquency.

Fagan, J., Weis, J. G., & Cheng, Y. T. (1990). Delinquency and substance use among inner-city students. *Journal of Drug Issues, 20*, 351-402.

Faupel, C. E., & Klockars, C. B. (1987). Drugs-crime connections: Elaborations from the life histories of hard-core heroin addicts. *Social Problems, 34*, 54-68.

Federal strategy for drug abuse and drug traffic prevention. (1975). Washington DC: U.S. Government Printing Office.

Finestone, H. (1957). Narcotics and criminality. *Law and Contemporary Problems, 9*, 69-85.

Ford, A., Hauser, H., & Jackson, E. (1975). Use of drugs among persons admitted to a county jail. *Public Health Reports, 90*, 504-508.

Gandossy, R. P., Williams, J. R., Cohen, J., & Harwood, H. J. (1980). *Drugs and crime: A survey and analysis of the literature* (National Institute of Justice). Washington, DC: U.S. Government Printing Office.

Goldstein, P. J. (1989). Drugs and violent crime. In N. A. Wiener & M. E. Wolfgang (Eds.), *Pathways to criminal violence* (pp. 16-48) Newbury Park, CA: Sage.

Goldstein, P. J., Bellucci, P. A., Spunt, B. J., & Miller, T. (1993). Volume of cocaine use and violence: A comparison between men and women. In R. Dembo (Ed.), *Drugs and crime* (pp. 141-177). New York: University Press of America.

Grapendaal, M., Leuw, E., & Nelen, H. (1992, Summer). Drugs and crime in an accommodating social context: The situation in Amsterdam. *Contemporary Drug Problems*, pp. 303-326.

Hanson, B., Beschner, G., Walters, J. M., & Bovelle, E. (1985). *Life with heroin: Voices from the inner city.* Lexington, MA. Lexington Books.

Harrison, L., & Gfroerer, J. (1992). The intersection of drug use and criminal behavior: Results from the national household survey on drug abuse. *Crime & Delinquency, 38*, 422-443.

Hawkins, R., & Alpert, G. P. (1989). *American prison systems: Punishment and justice.* Englewood Cliffs, NJ: Prentice-Hall.

Hayes, T. J., & Schimmel, D. J. (1993). Residential drug abuse treatment in the Federal Bureau of Prisons. *Journal of Drug Issues, 28*, 61-73.

Hobson, R. P. (1928). The struggle of mankind against its deadliest foe. *Narcotic Education, 1*, 51-54.

Hood, R., & Sparks, R. (1970). *Key issues in criminology.* New York: McGraw-Hill.

Huizinga, D. H. (1978). *Sample design of the National Youth Survey.* Boulder CO: Behavioral Research Institute.

Huizinga, D. H., Menard, S., & Elliot, D. S. (1989). Delinquency and drug use: Temporal and developmental patterns. *Justice Quarterly, 6*, 419-455.

Inciardi, J. A. (1992). *The war on drugs II.* Palo Alto, CA: Mayfield.

Inciardi, J. A. (1993). *Criminal justice.* Fort Worth, TX: Harcourt Brace Jovanovich.

Inciardi, J. A., & Chambers, C. D. (1972). Unreported criminal involvement of narcotic addicts. *Journal of Drug Issues, 2*, 57-64.

Inciardi, J. A., Horowitz, R., & Pottieger, A. E. (1993). *Street kids, street drugs, street crime.* Belmont, CA: Wadsworth.

Inciardi, J. A., Lockwood, D., & Quinlan, J. A. (1993). Drug use in prison: Patterns, processes, and implications for treatment. *Journal of Drug Issues, 23*, 119-129.

Inciardi, J. A., & McBride, D. C. (1976). Considerations in the definition of criminality for the assessment of the relationship between drug use and crime. In Research Triangle Institute (Ed.), *Crime and drugs* (pp. 123-137). Springfield, VA: National Technical Information Service.

Inciardi, J. A., & McBride, D. C. (1989). Legalization: A high risk alternative in the war on drugs. *American Behavioral Scientist, 32*, 259-289.

Inciardi, J. A., & McBride, D. C. (1991). *Treatment alternatives to street crime (TASC): History, experiences, and issues.* Rockville, MD: National Institute on Drug Abuse.

Inciardi, J. A., McBride, D. C., Platt, J. J., & Baxter, S. (1993). Injecting drug users, incarceration, and HIV: Some legal and social service delivery issues. In *The national AIDS demonstration research program.* Westport, CT: Greenwood.

Inciardi, J. A., McBride, D. C., McCoy, H. V., & Chitwood, D. D. (in press). Recent research on the crack-cocaine/crime connection. *Studies on crime and crime prevention.*

Johnson, B. D., Goldstein, P. J., Preble, E., Schmeidler, J., Lipton, D. S., & Miller, T. (1985). *Taking care of business: The economics of crime by heroin abusers*. Lexington, MA: Lexington Books.

Johnson, B. D., Wish, E. D., Schmeidler, J., & Huizinga, D. (1993). Concentration of delinquent offending: Serious drug involvement and high delinquency rates. In R. Dembo (Ed.), *Drugs and crime* (pp. 1-25). Lanham, MD: University Press of America.

Johnston, L. D., O'Malley, P. M., & Bachman, J. G. (1993). *Drug use among high school seniors, college students and young adults, 1975-1990* (NIH Publication No. 93-3597). Washington, DC: U.S. Department of Health and Human Services.

Kandel, D. B., Simcha-Fagan, O., & Davies, M. (1986). Risk factors for delinquency and illicit drug use from adolescence to young adulthood. *Journal of Drug Issues, 16*, 67-90.

Klofas, J. M. (1993). Drugs and justice: The impact of drugs on criminal justice in a metropolitan community. *Crime & Delinquency, 39*, 204-224.

Kolb, L. (1925, January). Drug addiction in its relation to crime. *Journal of Mental Hygiene*, pp. 74-89.

Kolb, L., & Du Mez, A. G. (1924, May 23). The prevalence and trend of drug addiction in the United States and factors influencing it. *Public Health Reports*.

Kozel, N. J., & DuPont, R. L. (1977). *Criminal charges and drug use patterns of arrestees in the District of Columbia*. Washington, DC: U.S. Government Printing Office.

King, R. (1974). The American system: Legal sanctions to repress drug abuse. In J. A. Inciardi & C. D. Chambers (Eds.), *Drugs and the criminal justice system* (pp. 17-37). Beverly Hills, CA: Sage.

Lichtenstein, P. M. (1914, November 14). Narcotic addiction. *New York Medical Journal*, pp. 962-966.

Lindesmith, A. R. (1965). *The addict and the law*. Bloomington, IN: Indiana University Press.

Liska, K. (1990). *Drugs and the human body*. New York: Macmillan.

McBride, D. C. (1976). The relationship between type of drug use and arrest charge in an arrested population. In Research Triangle Institute (Ed.), *Drug use and crime* (pp. 409-418). Springfield, VA: National Technical Information Service.

McBride D. C., Burgman-Habermehl, C., Alpert, J., & Chitwood, D. D. (1986). Drugs and homicide. *Bulletin of the New York Academy of Medicine, 62*, 497-508.

McBride, D. C., & Inciardi, J. A. (1990). AIDS and the IV drug user in the criminal justice system. *Journal of Drug Issues, 20*, 267-280.

McBride, D. C., & McCoy, C. B. (1981). Crime and drug using behavior: An areal analysis. *Criminology, 19*, 281-302.

McBride, D. C., & McCoy, C. B. (1982). Crime and drugs: The issues and literature. *Journal of Drug Issues, 12*, 137-151.

McBride D. C., & Swartz, J. (1990). Drugs and violence in the age of crack cocaine. In R. A. Weisheit (Ed.), *Drugs, crime and the criminal justice system* (American Academy of Criminal Justice Series, pp. 141-169). Cincinnati, OH: Anderson.

McGlothlin, W. (1979). Drugs and crime. In R. L. DuPont, A. Goldstein, & J. A. O'Donnell (Eds.), *Handbook on drug abuse* (pp. 357-364). Washington, DC: National Institute on Drug Abuse, Office of Drug Abuse Policy.

Musto, D. F. (1973). *The American disease*. New Haven, CT: Yale University Press.

Nadelmann, E. A. (1989, September). Drug prohibition in the United States, costs, consequences, and alternatives. *Science*, pp. 939-947.

O'Donnell, J. A., Voss, H. L., Clayton, R. R., Slatin, G. T., & Room, R.G.W. (1976). *Young men and drugs—A national survey* (National Institute on Drug Abuse Research Monograph 5). Washington, DC: U.S. Government Printing Office.

Rossi, P. H., Waite, E., Bose, C. E., & Berk, R. E. (1974). The seriousness of crimes: Normative structure and individual differences. *American Sociological Review, 31*, 324-337.

Simonds, J. F. & Kashani, J. (1980). Specific drug use and violence in delinquent boys. *American Journal of Drug and Alcohol Abuse, 7*, 305-322.

Sloman, L. (1979). *Reefer madness: A history of marijuana in America.* Indianapolis: Bobbs-Merrill.

Spunt, B. J., P. J. Goldstein, Bellucci, P. A., & Miller, T. (1990). Race/ethnic and gender differences in the drugs-violence relationship. *Journal of Psychoactive Drugs, 22*, 293-303.

Stephens, R. C. (1991). *The street addict role.* New York: State University of New York Press.

Stephens, R. C., & Ellis, R. D. (1975). Narcotic addicts and crime: An analysis of recent trends. *Criminology, 12*, 474-488.

Stephens, R. C., & McBride, D. C. (1976). Becoming a street addict. *Human Organization, 35*, 87-93.

Terry, C. E., & Pellens, M. (1928). *The opium problem.* New York: Bureau of Social Hygiene.

Trebach, A. S., & Inciardi, J. A. (1993). *Legalize it? Debating American drug policy.* Washington, DC: American University Press.

U.S. Department of Justice, Federal Bureau of Investigation. (1993). *Uniform crime reports.* Washington DC: U.S. Government Printing Office.

U.S. Treasury Department, Bureau of Narcotics. (1939). *Traffic in opium and other dangerous drugs.* Washington, DC: U.S. Government Printing Office.

Vigdal, G. L., & Stadler, D. W. (1989, June). Controlling inmate drug use: Cut consumption by reducing demand. *Corrections Today*, pp. 96-97.

Voss, H. L., & Stephens, R. C. (1973). Criminal history of narcotic addicts. *Drug Forum, 2*, 191-202.

Young, J. H. (1967). *The medical messiahs: A social history of health quackery in twentieth-century America.* Princeton, NJ: Princeton University Press.

Wilson, J. Q. (1993). Against the legalization of drugs. In R. Goldberg (Ed.), *Taking sides* (p. 25). Guildford, CT: Dushkin.

Wish, E. D. (1987). *Drug use forecasting: New York 1984-1986.* Washington, DC: U.S. Department of Justice.

Zahn, M. A. & Bencivengo, M. (1974). Violent death: A comparison between drug users and non drug users. *Addictive Diseases, 1*, 293-298.

DRUG ENFORCEMENT'S DOUBLE-EDGED SWORD: AN ASSESSMENT OF ASSET FORFEITURE PROGRAMS*

J. MITCHELL MILLER
University of Tennessee

LANCE H. SELVA
Middle Tennessee State University

This paper presents the first ethnographic examination of asset forfeiture during the drug war era. The study is based on 12 months of covert participant observation, in which one of the authors assumed the role of confidential informant in undercover narcotics operations in a southern state. Contemporary methods of narcotics policing are assessed at two vital points: case selection and police conduct. Findings suggest that asset forfeiture is a dysfunctional policy which, in implementation, has strayed from its original intent and has incurred unintended consequences. Although forfeiture programs generate income, they also cause drug enforcement to serve functions that are inherently contradictory and often at odds with the demands of justice.

In his 1989 inaugural address, President George Bush solemnly promised the country that the drug scourge would be eliminated. Despite the President's optimism and the pumping of $9.5 billion into the federal anti-drug effort in 1990, it is apparent that widespread drug abuse persists. Early indications suggest that the 1990s will witness a drug catastrophe even greater than in the past (Currie 1993; "Drug War Victory" 1991; Zimring and Hawkins 1992).

Many observers have characterized the current anti-drug effort, known familiarly as the "war on drugs," as a failed public policy (Bugliosi 1991; Elsasser 1990; Kleiman 1992; Trebach 1987; Wistosky 1990; Zimring and Hawkins 1992). Officially declared by the Reagan Administration in 1982, this publicly supported crusade

* An earlier version of this paper was presented at the 1993 meetings of the Academy of Criminal Justice Sciences, held in Kansas City. The authors appreciate the constructive comments of Professor Michael Benson and anonymous reviewers. Please address correspondence to Mitch Miller, 901 McClung Tower, University of Tennessee, Knoxville, TN 37996-0490.

JUSTICE QUARTERLY, Vol. 11 No. 2, June 1994

against drug abuse and narcotics trafficking was supposed to succeed where the supply reduction-oriented policies of the 1970s had failed. The war on drugs initially featured a pluralistic approach, incorporating an unprecedented amount of resources for enforcement, education concentrating on prevention of use, and treatment. Eradication of both foreign and domestic drug crops and interdiction of illicit substances at U.S. borders were added quickly to the enforcement strategy (Kleiman 1989). These methods, however, seemed to be futile; they called into question the efficacy of the present policy (Reuter and Kleiman 1986). Indeed, many measurable indicators of illicit drug activity demonstrate the ineffectiveness of this drug war strategy. Street-level prices of cocaine, for example, either have dropped or have remained relatively constant over the past decade, suggesting a consistent supply (Drug Enforcement Administration [DEA] 1992). More telling is the estimated prevalence of drug use issued by the Bureau of Justice Statistics: in spite of efforts to reduce demand, it reports, the American appetite for mood-altering substances remains insatiable (Bureau of Justice Statistics 1991).

Persistent public concern about the lack of success prompted policy makers to consider alternative strategies (Walker 1992). In attempts to find a magic bullet for drug control policy, suggestions ranged from the legalization of marijuana, cocaine, and even heroin to the death penalty for traffickers and solicitors (Inciardi 1991). After a long and heated debate in Congress, compromise overcame controversy to produce the 1988 Anti-Drug Abuse Bill, which largely continues to direct and shape the present drug enforcement strategy.

The 1988 Anti-Drug Abuse Bill created new legal tools to handle the special enforcement problems presented by crack cocaine, gang-related violence, and domestic marijuana production, all of which appeared to be increasing steadily (Weisheit 1991). The bill provided for additional allocation of resources for equipment and manpower, as well as stiffer legal penalties for drug law offenders. It also created an Asset Forfeiture Fund. This fund is modeled after the Racketeer-Influenced and Corrupt Organizations (RICO) and the Continuing Criminal Enterprise statutes as well as the Federal Criminal Forfeiture Act of 1984, which legalized seizing the fruits of criminal activities (Moore 1988).

The Asset Forfeiture Fund is much more than a depository for income generated by liquidating seized assets, whether cash, automobiles, jewelry, art, or real estate. It is the central component in a reciprocal relationship between law enforcement agencies and federal and state treasury departments, from which the attorney general may authorize

> payment of any expenses necessary to seize, detail/inventory, safeguard, maintain, advertise or sell property under seizure or detention pursuant to any law enforced . . . . Payments from the fund can be used for awards for information or assistance related to violation of criminal drug laws . . . . Deposits to the fund will be from the forfeiture of property under any law enforced or administered (Lawrence 1988:2).

The Asset Forfeiture Fund was created with the intention of helping law enforcement agencies to combat drug lords whose wealth gave them refuge from traditional enforcement tactics. Proponents were optimistic that seizing assets would limit the amount of working capital available to drug dealers, thereby reducing their ability to facilitate criminal activity (Drug Policy Foundation 1992; Fried 1988).

The fund calls on federal agencies to form special units for conducting operations to make seizures. Most state law enforcement agencies and several metropolitan police departments soon noted the monetary benefits of the fund and copied the federal approach, making asset seizure and forfeiture a sweeping narcotics policing strategy (United States Department of Justice 1988). Like any legal innovation, however, it had the potential for unintended consequences.

Critics contend that seizing assets and money has become a primary concern of vice divisions in smaller enforcement agencies, to the exclusion of traditional enforcement goals of deterrence and punishment (Stuart 1990; Trebach 1987). The routinization of seizure and forfeiture, others allege, has prompted enforcement agencies to develop new strategies of narcotics policing that are directed more toward asset hunting than toward reducing illegal drug use (Miller 1991; Trebach and Zeese 1990). Furthermore, this new policing strategy appears to be increasingly intrusive. A number of journalistic accounts describe civil liberties violations related directly to asset forfeiture enforcement (Jacobs 1992; Morganthau and Katel 1990). A series published by the Pittsburgh Press, titled *Presumed Guilty: The Law's Victims in the War on Drugs* (Schneider and Flaherty 1991), portrays the frequent, severe victimization of ordinary citizens through forfeiture. These excellent reports, based on reviews of 25,000 DEA seizures and 510 court cases, reveal that "enormous collateral damage to the innocent" is the effect of a new standard of presumed guilt. Other information on asset forfeiture comes from legal critiques dissecting the language of the

1988 Anti-Drug Abuse Act and surveying its feasibility as an effective drug enforcement initiative (Goldstein and Kalant 1990; Krauss and Laezear 1991). No grounded studies have been conducted, however, to examine asset forfeiture in the field and to assess whether it is fair practice or foul play.

This study is an empirical examination of asset forfeiture as a tool of drug enforcement policy. It differs from previous work in this area in that it examines the implementation of the laws from within forfeiture programs, explaining experientially rather than speculatively why and how one aspect of the drug war has gone astray. We begin with a survey of the literature, focusing on the legal basis of forfeiture policy and describing the extent of its use. This section also highlights major criticisms regarding problematic aspects of asset forfeiture programs. This discussion is followed by an explanation of the study. Next, we present observations. We conclude with an assessment of asset forfeiture.

BACKGROUND

An initial assessment of the 1988 Anti-Drug Abuse Bill might suggest that it is little more than an intensification of preexisting laws and enforcement programs. Most of the provisions are either replicas or renovations of previous initiatives, but closer examination of the component establishing the Asset Forfeiture Fund reveals new developments. A brief survey of the use of forfeiture in the United States provides a framework for examining these recent changes.

The seizing of assets, both as an enforcement tactic and as a sanction, was practiced long before the creation of the 1988 Anti-Drug Abuse Bill. Historically a felony was defined as a crime for which a person could be required to forfeit all property (Reid 1991). The power of forfeiture was recognized and approved by the American colonies and was used by the First Congress of the United States to confiscate smuggling, pirate, and slave ships (Greek 1992; Myers and Brzostowski 1982). Hundreds of forfeiture laws have been created and are now enforced by both state and federal governments.

The strategy of asset forfeiture was first used against drug dealers in 1970, when persons operating a trafficking organization were required to forfeit illegally acquired profits and assets according to the Comprehensive Drug Abuse Prevention and Control Act of 1970 (*United States Code* V.21). Subsequently Congress authorized federal attorneys to file *in rem* actions, civil lawsuits staking the government's claim to property and money related to the illicit drug industry. This step potentially enabled the government to obtain legal possession of property and currency even despite dismissal of criminal charges based on a legal technicality such as a faulty search warrant or a *Miranda* rights violation. In addition, prosecutors enjoyed the reduced burden of proof required under civil law; a simple preponderance of the evidence, as opposed to the "beyond a reasonable doubt" standard recognized in criminal courts.

The consequences were considerable. During 1979, the first full year of implementation, the DEA seized close to $10 million in assets; this figure reached $54.4 million in 1981 (Myers and Brzostowski 1982). In 1983 more than $100 million in cash and property was forfeited to the government (Stellwagen 1985); an astronomical $460 million was forfeited in 1990 (Bureau of Justice Statistics 1991). Despite these impressive statistics, advocates of asset forfeiture considered the power to be seriously underutilized.

In the early 1980s all states were seizing illicit substances during routine narcotics operations, but few were following the federal example of seizing drug profits. In 1982, to encourage states that had yet to pass laws attacking the profits of drug trafficking, the DEA developed a Model Forfeiture of Drug Profits Act and published a training manual titled "Drug Agents' Guide to Forfeiture of Assets" (Myers and Brzostowski 1982). The federal agency suggested that states adopting the Act, or a similar provision, allocate revenue generated through seizure and forfeiture to drug enforcement. By 1985, 47 states had passed legislation resembling the 1982 DEA Act (Stellwagen 1985). Federal policy recommendations, formulated in a 1985 U.S. Department of Justice study of 50 prosecutors, including extending statutes to condemn additional types of property and hiring staff for financial investigations and asset management (U.S. Department of Justice 1988). The practice of returning seized money to drug enforcers was incorporated in the 1988 Anti-Drug Abuse Bill and is the heart of the controversy surrounding asset forfeiture and its offspring, a seizure-based style of narcotics policing.

The importance of the Asset Forfeiture Fund, and the element that makes it more than a mere intensification of previous seizure laws, centers on the redirection of the income produced by asset forfeiture (Osborne 1991). Before provision was made for an Asset Forfeiture Fund, income raised by liquidating assets was generally channeled into treasury departments for redistribution into the national or state budgets. Under the present provision, however, a percentage of the funds generated by asset seizures is returned from treasury departments to law enforcement agencies to supplement their budgets. In 1988, in fact, the United States Justice Department shared $24.4 million with state and local law enforcement agencies that participated in investigations and arrests producing forfeitures (Burden 1988:29). A cycle was created, which allowed narcotics operations to make seizures that could be used to finance other operations in which yet more assets might be seized.

Proponents of asset seizure claim that it is necessary for enforcing the law and could turn the tide in the war on drugs. Substantial cash seizures, they argue, cripple large drug trafficking operations. The Los Angeles County Sheriff's Department, for example, seized more than $26 million in drug money in 1987 and another $33 million in 1988 (Stuart 1990). Forfeitures have included a Chevrolet dealership, a recording studio, a thousand-acre plantation, and numerous luxury homes, cars, boats, and planes (Wrobleski and Hess 1990:429). The distribution of the proceeds varies among federal agencies and from state to state. Under Louisiana's Drug Racketeering and Related Organizations law, all property associated with illegal drug activity is subject to forfeiture. Division of the spoils in Louisiana are 50 percent to the state, 25 percent to the district attorney's office, and 25 percent to the narcotics division of the seizing law enforcement agency. The Illinois Narcotics Profit Forfeiture Act allocates 50 percent for local drug policing, 25 percent for narcotics prosecution, and 25 percent to the State Drug Traffic Prevention Fund (U.S. Department of Justice 1988).

Problems

Success in drug work traditionally has been measured by the protection it provides society through ferreting out drugs and drug dealers, eradicating the substances, and apprehending offenders (Carter 1990; Moore 1977). The goal has been to diminish drug use and trafficking. Despite a problematic history, narcotics policing has employed strategies and tactics that at least appeared to be consistent with policy objectives (Carter and Stephens 1988; Klockars 1983; Manning and Redlinger 1977; Wilson 1961). Many of the traditional problems of drug control, such as exposure to pressures and invitations to corruption (Carter 1990; Chambliss 1988; Wilson 1978), still must be addressed, but new problems have developed since the implementation of asset forfeiture programs.

Journalistic accounts suggest that seizing assets has become a high-priority objective in drug enforcement (Dortch 1992; Shaw

1990; Willson 1990). According to Dan Garner, an undercover narcotics agent in southern California, drug enforcement success is measured by the amount of money seized:

> You see that there's big money out there, you want to seize the big money for your department. For our unit, the sign of whether you were doing good or poorly was how much money you seized, and the kind of cases you did. And my supervisor made it extremely clear that big money cases were a lot more favorable for your overall evaluation than big dope cases (Stuart 1990).

Garner and some of his fellow agents were accused of stealing dug profits during seizure operations. Their story has called attention to a growing problem, as have other highly publicized drug-related police scandals such as the Miami River murders of drug dealers by officers who stole their profits, and the arrest of more than half of the Sea Girt, New Jersey Police Department by the DEA on drug trafficking charges (Dombrink 1988).

Asset forfeiture was designed to be used against major dealers involved heavily in criminal activity. In practice, however, suspects not associated significantly with criminal activity often become the targets of operations because they have valuable assets. Under forfeiture laws, the potential value of assets strongly affects the priority of cases, thus determining who the suspects will be. The goal of raising revenue encourages selection of cases according to the suspect's resources. Targets of police surveillance thus are chosen for their resources rather than for their criminal activity, giving credence to frequent insinuations that the police facilitate crime (Block 1993; Braithwaite, Fisse, and Geis 1987; Marx 1988).

Observers argue that when narcotics officers become revenue producers, the system itself becomes corrupt (Carter 1990; McAlary 1987; Trebach 1987). As one critic points out,

> Once you focus on cash as the goal for the officers, they accept that and they forget about the ultimate goal of eliminating dope dealers. Seizure operations are simply revenue raising devices for departments, and divert officers' attention from the real goal, stopping dope (Stuart 1990).

According to one study, police in both Los Angeles and Miami routinely took assets from dealers but did not arrest them. Officers seized money from individuals and asked them to sign a disclaimer form before release. The disclaimer form stated that the suspect was not the owner of the seized money, had no knowledge of where it came from, and would not attempt to claim it. Such forms were used in investigations where money was seized but no drugs were found. The purpose, according to agency memos, "was to assist the department in gaining legal possession of the money" (Stuart 1990).

Examination of the forfeiture process from seizure to revenue highlights the steps involved in liquidating assets. Seized currency moves through the system more rapidly than do assets such as automobiles and real estate, which must be warehoused (when appropriate), advertised, and auctioned. By seizing cash, law enforcement agencies obtain their percentage of the revenue produced much sooner than by seizing property. For this reason, narcotics operations employ strategies designed to generate cash.

The "reverse sting" (Miller 1991) has emerged as the predominant choice of narcotics divisions. This type of operation features undercover agents as the sellers of drugs, rather than as buyers who seek out illicit substances. This controversial method involves negotiation, frequently through confidential informants, aimed at arranging a time and place at which undercover agents posing as drug dealers will provide felonious resale quantities of an illicit substance for a predetermined price. After the transaction has been completed, a "take-down" team of agents arrests the suspect and seizes any assets than can be associated with the deal (frequently an automobile) as well as any cash involved. The reverse sting is the preferred approach because agents can control and calculate the amount of money a deal will involve before they commit time and resources.

Traditional tactics, such as executing search warrants, often may produce arrests and confiscation of illegal substances, but no certain cash seizure. Narcotics enforcement is becoming a business, in which officers and equipment are allocated so as to maximize profits rather than to control or eradicate drugs. Efficiency is measured by the amount of money seized rather than by the impact on drug trafficking. In achieving efficiency, however, law enforcement has so misused the power of seizure that the Supreme Court recently has limited the scope of forfeiture laws.

In *Austin v. United States* (1993) the high court examined whether the Excessive Fines Clause of the Eighth Amendment applies to forfeitures of property. Although the court declined an invitation to establish a multifactor test for determining whether a forfeiture is excessive, it held that the principle of proportionality serves as a basis by which lower courts may decide individual cases. Thus the court determined that the government exacted too high a penalty (forfeiture of a home, $4,500, and an auto body shop) for the offense (sale of two grams of cocaine). Also, in *U.S. v. A Parcel of Land* (1993), some protection was provided to innocent owners of property related to the drug industry. Although these cases may slow the momentum of future asset-gathering operations, they address only a few of the real and potential dangers presented by forfeiture laws. Observations of undercover reverse sting operations point out these dangers and evidence the contradictions of such an approach.

THE STUDY: A YEAR UNDER COVER

The data for this study come from the observations and experiences of one of the authors, who assumed the role of confidential informant in undercover narcotics operations in a southern state. This position provided a rare opportunity to examine, through covert participant observation, the clandestine work of narcotics operations units and to observe undercover narcotics agents, typically an inaccessible subject group.

While the researcher was a graduate student in a criminal justice program, he became friendly with fellow students who were drug enforcement agents. They invited him to participate in narcotics cases as a confidential informant. Although these fellow graduate students enabled his initial entry, the researcher then interacted with drug agents who did not know him and who had no knowledge of his research objectives. The label *confidential informant* should not be misconstrued; the position typically involves undercover work more often than the revealing of privileged knowledge to narcotics agents. The primary functions of a confidential informant are negotiating with and manipulating suspects so as to involve them in reverse sting operations.

The sense of police fraternity (Wilson 1961) is intensified in narcotics units, making them neither open nor receptive to research. As a confidential informant, the researcher was not accepted fully in the group. Nevertheless, his position allowed him to penetrate the hidden activities of narcotics operations and provided an excellent vantage point for conducting a study of drug enforcement. Informants interact with agent and criminal alike, often serving as a communication link between the two. This position allows proximity to the thoughts, feelings, motives, and strategies of both agents and suspects, thus permitting an investigation of asset forfeiture as implemented at the street level.

The researcher remained in this position for one year; he participated in 28 narcotics cases with agents and officers from very small city police departments, larger county sheriff's departments, urban and metropolitan forces, and two state law enforcement agencies. Here a case is defined operationally as a series of events that culminated in arrest, seizure of assets, or both. Cases often overlapped because they ranged in duration from a few days to several months. The events of each case were recorded upon leaving the various field settings, maintained in seperate files, and updated as each case progressed.

As a "complete-member-researcher" (Adler and Adler 1987), the author conducted "opportunistic research" (Ronai and Ellis 1989) by studying phenomena in a setting in which he participated as a full member. This method also has been called "disguised observation" (Erikson 1967). Its distinguishing feature is that the research objectives are not made known to others in the field setting. The use of disguised or covert observational techniques often has been regarded as ethically controversial, as evidenced by the "deception debate" (Bulmer 1980; Galliher 1973; Humphreys 1970; Roth 1962). Participants in the debate tend to assume one of two polarized positions: moralistic condemnation or responsive justification. Opponents of this method hold that covert strategies should be banned from social science research (Erikson 1967). Their major objection is that these techniques often violate basic ethical principles such as informed consent, invasion of privacy, and the obligation to avoid causing harm to subjects. Specifically, the critics allege that misrepresentation can cause irreparable damage to subjects, to the researcher, and to science by evoking negative public scrutiny and by making subject populations wary of future researchers (Galliher 1973; Polsky 1967).

Justifications for the use of covert techniques have been presented on both practical and philosophical levels. One practical argument is that persons engaged in illegal or unconventional behavior, such as drug dealers and users, simply will not submit to or participate in study by overt methods. Similarly, those in powerful and authoritative positions, such as drug enforcement agents, have been considered secretive and difficult to observe openly (Shils 1975). From a philosophic perspective, Denzin (1968) argues, following Goffman (1959), that all researchers wear masks and ethical propriety thus depends on the context. Denzin suggests that

> the sociologist has the right to make observations on anyone in any setting to the extent that he does so with scientific intents and purposes in mind (1968:50).

The basis for disguise in this study, however, is "the end and the means" position stated first by Roth (1962) and later by Homan (1980). That the end may justify the means also is acknowledged by the British Sociological Association, which allows the covert approach "where it is not possible to use other methods to obtain essential data" (1973:3); such is the case in the present situation. We believe that the benefits of investigating and reporting on this expensive and dysfunctional drug enforcement strategy outweigh its potential costs. Failure to study how this strategy is implemented on the street would condemn other citizens to the misfortunes and abuses we describe below. In addition, scarce resources in the war on drugs would continue to be misused.

Drug enforcers' use of asset forfeiture has been questioned by the press and media so frequently and with such intensity that scholarly examination is warranted. The very nature of the allegations, however, has prompted the police fraternity to close ranks, thus making disguised entry a necessity. To rule out study of covert behavior, whether by the powerful or by the powerless, simply because it cannot be studied openly imposes artificial limits on science and prevents study of what may be important and consequential activities in society. The propriety and the importance of research activities always must be judged case by case. In this particular case, abandoning the study because it could not be conducted with overt techniques would cause the potential misconduct and betrayal of public trust by government officials to remain unexposed. We hope others will agree not only that the end justifies the means in the context of this research, but that it takes ethical precedence.

OBSERVATIONS: SOME TYPICAL CASES

The following examples of cases involve acts and decisions by narcotics agents that illustrate several troubling aspects of asset forfeiture. These concern the impact of forfeiture on both the type of cases selected for undercover operations and the function of covert policing in society.

The researcher first came to understand how cases were assigned priority while he was working with the police department of a medium-sized city in 1989. Still unaware of the profit-seeking nature of narcotics divisions, he began undercover work by "feeling out" possible deals and meeting with an undercover agent to discuss potential cases. The researcher mistakenly believed that a large quantity of drugs or a "known" dealer made a case desirable, and accordingly proposed two possible deals. The first deal involved 2 1/2 pounds of marijuana that a dealer was willing to sell to the researcher's buyer (the agent). The second involved a factory worker who was shopping for a half-pound of marijuana to resell to friends and co-workers. The agent asked the researcher to note the license plate numbers of the suspects' vehicles. The researcher believed the plate numbers were to be used for gathering information such as the suspects' ages, addresses, and arrest records. The primary purpose, however, was to learn whether the suspect owned the vehicle or whether a lien holder was involved. This information enabled the agent to determine the amount of equity in a suspect's vehicle.

The equity in a vehicle represented potential profit that officers could expect to receive if the vehicle was seized. If a person whose car had been seized had a clear title, he or she was likely to lose the car. It would be sold later at auction, and the seizing agency would receive a percentage of the money. If a person was still making payments, the situation was more complex. Normally the defendant was given the option of making a "contribution" to the arresting department's drug fund, equal to the level of equity, in exchange for the seized vehicle.

The agent in charge of this case compared the two proposed deals in order to assess which one would generate more income. The first case involved five times as much marijuana as the second. Also, by working the first deal, officers would take 2 1/2 pounds of marijuana out of circulation because the dealer would be selling. The seller was a full-time drug dealer with two prior drug-related convictions, and was on probation at the time of this case. The suspect in the second deal had no arrest record and appeared to be a relatively small-time user who hoped to make a modest profit by selling quarter-ounce bags of marijuana. Although the first deal seemed more serious, the second would guarantee seizure of at least $700 when the suspect purchased drugs from the agent. In addition, the latter suspect owned a truck, whereas the professional dealer had only a little equity in a late-model sports car. The officer explained that the first deal simply was not profitable and would not be pursued.

The researcher was instructed to arrange for the latter suspect to meet the "seller." When he expressed concern that the officer was encouraging the suspect to commit a crime, the officer justified the operation by contending that the suspect would secure marijuana elsewhere and eventually would become a major dealer. In this way, according to the officer, the problem would be "nipped in the bud" because the suspect would be deterred from future criminal activity. The purchase was consummated with the agent, the suspect was arrested, and his cash and vehicle were seized.

This case provided the agent's department with a small profit. The buyer may or may not have been deterred from future criminal behavior. On the other hand, no drugs were taken out of circulation, and the buyer might never have acted on his intentions to purchase a felonious quantity of drugs if the researcher and the agent had not presented him with such an opportunity.

The strategy involved in this case was termed a "reverse" sting because the visual undercover function of buying narcotics was the opposite of this arrangement: here, officers became sellers. This strategy was preferred by every agency and department with which the researcher was associated because it allowed agents to gauge potential profit before investing a great deal of time and effort. Reverses occurred so regularly that the term *reverse* became synonymous with the word *deal*.

This case was not an isolated incident; it was one of many such cases in which the operational goal was profit rather than the incapacitation of drug dealers. The pursuit of profit clearly influenced policies on case selection.

The researcher was told that only exchanges involving a certain amount of money or narcotics would be acceptable. It was apparent that these guidelines came from supervisors who did not want squads to work comparatively small cases or those of low monetary value, when more profitable options existed. These standards proved to be contrary to the notion of taking distributors off the street.

The drug trade, an illicit market, is similar to licit markets in several ways. One likeness is natural price regulation through the mechanics of supply and demand (Manning and Redlinger 1977). Upon seeing a large bust, supervisors tended mistakenly to believe that the drug markets in their jurisdictions were flooded with a particular substance. Consequently they imposed limits for agents and informants. Ironically, the arrest that prompted the decision was often an isolated incident that did not accurately reflect local drug-trading activity.

These limits were a constant source of annoyance for both the researcher and the officers with whom he worked. One case, in which the researcher and an agent had spent a week preparing a suspect for a deal, provides a revealing example.

The researcher had established a relationship with the suspect, having bought marijuana from him on one occasion and cocaine on another. The suspect was informed that he could discuss business with the researcher's connection, who could supply quantities of marijuana at a low price. Having gained the suspect's confidence and whetted his appetite for a substantial bargain, the researcher arranged a conference between his supplier (an undercover agent) and the suspect. A deal was struck whereby the agent would sell two pounds of marijuana to the suspect for $2,500. The deal was canceled before the transaction, however, because the agent's supervisor decided that only reverses of five pounds or more would be worked. The researcher was told to give the suspect a reason why the deal could not take place.

After two unproductive weeks, the supervisor realized that he had been unrealistic in setting a five-pound limit. He lowered the limit to the previous level of one pound and then ordered the agent to try to recover the deal he had canceled two weeks earlier. The deal could not be saved, however, because the suspect no longer trusted the researcher. The undercover work and the money spent on compensating the researcher had been wasted. In addition, the suspect, a recidivist with criminal intent, remained free to solicit illicit substances.

Another case that was lost because of imposed limits involved a well-known suspect whom an agent had kept under surveillance for more than a year. The suspect, a college student, dealt primarily in "ECSTASY", a hallucinogenic drug in tablet form. The agent told the researcher that previously he had served a search warrant at the suspect's apartment, but had found nothing to warrant an arrest. The student had abused the agent verbally and threatened to sue his department for harassment. Later the researcher learned when and where this suspect was to deliver a quantity of ECTASY and marijuana. Although the agent wanted to arrest this suspect, largely for revenge, his supervisor was reluctant to pursue the case because it was not regarded as profitable.

Episodes such as these not only involved nonenforcement of narcotics laws, but also promoted cynicism among officers, a troublesome aspect of police work (Carter 1990; Manning 1980). The ever-changing limits on deals magnified this problem as some officers began to question the nature and the true purpose of their occupation.

Other drug agents, however, demonstrated acceptance of asset forfeiture operations. When asked why a search warrant would not be served on a suspect known to have resale quantities of marijuana in his apartment, one officer replied: "Because that would just give us a bunch of dope and the hassle of having to book him (the suspect). We've got all the dope we need in the property room. Just stick to rounding up cases with big money and stay away from warrants."

Selecting cases on the basis of potential gain creates another problem, one that not only causes neglect of obligatory police functions but also tampers with civil rights. To raise revenue, asset-gathering operations must focus on suspects with money and other resources. Large-scale dealers could not have achieved their status without connections and suppliers. Their ties and their discretion make them largely inaccessible to seizure operations because they are not easily "reversible." Many of these dealers value safety more than profit, and work by selling drugs on credit in an operation known as "fronting." They recognize the legal advantage of keeping cash separate from illegal drugs. The big dealers do not make natural suspects for seizure strategies, nor are they easy prey. Consequently agents take the suspects they can get, namely lower-level dealers and ordinary users who fall victim to enterprising informants.

Another incident involved a 19-year-old male college sophomore, who came under surveillance while making routine deliveries of various drugs in a certain county jurisdiction. To obtain information, the researcher arranged and made an authorized purchase of two ounces of marijuana from the suspect. This individual turned out to be a "mule," a person who transports drugs but usually does not make buys or negotiate deals. The regular procedure in situations such as this was to arrest the suspect and then coerce him into cooperating with law enforcement by setting up the bigger dealer with whom he was working.

The researcher was surprised when the agent requested that a meeting be arranged with the suspect. A few days later, the researcher brought the suspect to a bar where the agent was waiting. The agent, having gained the suspect's confidence through conversation and by paying for drinks, persuaded him to secure a personal loan from a bank by using his vehicle as collateral so that he might purchase five pounds of marijuana. The ploy was successful and the suspect was arrested a few days later. This student was not searching for a large quantity of drugs, nor did he view himself as a dealer until the agent showed him how to become one. Thus, at times, undercover policing actually may promote crime by manipulating individuals who are naive, suggestible, or corruptible. Such activity not only victimizes ordinary people but also affects the conduct of police and their function in society.

THE IMPACT OF FORFEITURE ON POLICE CONDUCT

The following example demonstrates how the seizure motive can undermine police interest of service to the community. The suspect, one of the larger "players" whom the researcher encountered, dealt in marijuana, barbiturates, cocaine, and stolen property. The researcher had conducted two "buy-walks" with the suspect in order to establish a relationship. A buy-walk occurs when officers or their assistants purchase illegal substances, but officers do not make an arrest so that they may observe a situation and determine whether it will lead them higher in a drug ring's hierarchy.

The state agent wanted to reverse the suspect, but realized that a reverse strategy was impractical for this situation. The alternative was to serve a search warrant that ideally would occur when the suspect possessed a large amount of cash that could be seized. As a result, the researcher was required to stay in close contact with the suspect for two days; during that time the dealer received a quarter-kilogram of cocaine, a large shipment. This shipment was worth about $7,000 in bulk and as much as $13,000 on the street. The researcher relayed this information to the agent in charge of the operation.

In this case the researcher felt that the only decision to be made was when the warrant should be served. He believed that the narcotics division of the involved state agency would wish to intervene before the drugs could be resold. Proper police procedure does not mandate that agents act immediately on information which makes an arrest possible. If that were so, valuable periods of surveillance could not be conducted. The researcher, however, was surprised when he was instructed to observe the suspect's transactions to determine the rate at which the cocaine was being resold. Less drugs meant more cash, and the agent's objective was to seize currency rather than cocaine. The case was successful as to proceeds, but perhaps not in view of the quantity of cocaine that officers knowingly permitted to reach consumers. This incident illustrates that a focus on revenue requires police to compromise law enforcement in a manner that may harm rather than protect society.

The pressure created by a demand for productivity created competition among agents from nearby jurisdictions. This was magnified in rural county agencies that also had a city or town police force. Agents consequently became "turf conscious," regarding negatively the arrests of mutual suspects by agents from other agencies because those agents had taken away potential profit and had nullified the time and effort invested in surveillance. Thus operations often disintegrated because of a general lack of interagency cooperation, and numerous suspects were left at large.

One large case collapsed for this reason. A well-known drug dealer, who traded crack and cocaine in a small rural town, had been frequenting a neighboring jurisdiction to visit a woman with whom the researcher became acquainted. The suspect had been delivering drugs on weekly visits and was said to always have a large supply on his person. A city narcotics agent arranged for the researcher and a second undercover informant, a female posing as the researcher's date, to meet with the suspect for a small party at a residence approximately two miles from the city limit, the agent's jurisdictional boundary. The researcher notified the agent when the suspect was coming and described the route he would take.

The researcher and his associate noticed that the suspect possessed a kilogram of cocaine and had an unknown amount of cash in a gallon-sized plastic freezer bag. They attempted to manipulate the dealer into entering the city police department's jurisdiction by suggesting various bars that the group might patronize. The suspect refused to go, and the deal stalled.

Other agents learned what was happening by monitoring surveillance equipment, hidden wires fixed to each informant, but they were powerless to act because of the jurisdictional dilemma. Nothing prevented them, however, from contacting the county sheriff's department or notifying the state agency, who might have conducted a vehicle stop. Even so, the agents took no action, and the suspect slipped away with his bag of money and cocaine.

Even in cases involving children's welfare, officers sometimes failed to notify other agencies. In one such case, officers of a state agency monitored the daily activities of a marijuana and cocaine dealer for a long period because he was a vital link in an interstate drug ring. On one occasion, while the researcher was waiting with the suspect late at night for a phone call regarding a shipment of cocaine, he saw the suspect overdose; he had been injecting cocaine repeatedly for two hours. The man came staggering from a bathroom and muttered something unintelligible as he walked toward a patio. He forgot to open a sliding glass door and rammed his body through the glass, cutting his face and arms badly. His wife called for an ambulance and then revealed that he had overdosed twice before.

Less than a week later, the researcher was invited to a party to celebrate the suspect's release from the hospital. The party was disrupted when a friend of the suspect brought warning of a possible raid, thus prompting the suspect to retreat to a motel room with his wife and her 12-year-old son from a previous marriage. Suffering from intense paranoia, they remained there for eight days where the researcher visited them twice.

The boy in this family had failed three grades in school and was permitted to smoke pot and drink beer. The case was unfolding in late September, when he should have been attending school. This issue was raised by the suspect's wife, who had received warnings of legal action due to the boy's excessive absences. Furthermore, during this period, the suspect traveled with his wife to a bordering state to secure drugs, leaving the youth alone in the motel room for two days.

The researcher relayed the details of this situation to the agents working the case, who listened with indifference. The researcher recommended that the agents contact the Department of Human Services (DHS), but was told that such action would only disrupt the case; DHS would be notified after an arrest was made.

This case dragged on for another month before the suspect was arrested in a marijuana field in another county. When the researcher inquired about the boy, two agents explained that the time required to contact a social worker and complete the paperwork associated with that step could be better spent in making another case.

During the summer of 1990, the researcher spent several weeks concentrating on locating marijuana patches. This task was difficult because of the secretive nature of marijuana farming and the suspicion among farmers who previously had lost crops to thieves. To induce growers to reveal the location of their crops, the researcher joined suspects in planting other patches, thus becoming a "partner." This act fostered a common bond, which often produced the information that agents desired. The researcher observed that marijuana growers took a great deal of pride in their work and often bragged about their botanical abilities. When he expressed doubt about the truthfulness of growers' claims, occasionally they showed him a patch as proof of their cultivation skills.

One eradication case demonstrated how the objective of raising revenue undermined the police functions of apprehending criminals and enforcing narcotics laws. The researcher traveled with a suspect to a rural county, while six state agents in three vehicles tailed the suspect's truck to the site where the researcher had visited twice. Another group of state agents, the "take-down" team, waited in the woods at the edge of a marijuana field. This was the researcher's largest case in terms of the number of agents involved, the amount of marijuana (approximately 50 pounds), and the potential value of the plants. The marijuana grew in three loosely connected rectangular patches, each containing approximately 30 plants 12 to 16 feet high.

The researcher and the suspect arrived at the location and hiked two miles to reach the patches. This period was very suspenseful because armed, camouflaged agents were filming every move. The suspect was armed with a semi-automatic shotgun and a nine-millimeter pistol; the researcher carried a rifle. The possibility of gunfire and the size of the deal created a great deal of anxiety.

The suspect had come to the patches on this occasion to fertilize the plants with a liquid nitrogen solution. After he and the researcher had tended to about half of the plants, agents emerged from the brush, pointing automatic weapons. Both the suspect and the researcher were ordered to lie on the ground, and were handcuffed. To protect the researcher's identify, the agents subjected him to everything that was done to the suspect, such as frisking and interrogating. The agents cut down the plants, seized the suspect's firearms, took approximately $300 in cash, which was in his wallet, and another $200 from the glove box in his truck. A quick records check on the truck showed that the grower did not own it; thus seizure of this vehicle was an unattractive option.

After taking everything of value, the agents ordered the grower to enter his truck and leave, without formally arresting him for cultivating marijuana. In effect they appeared to rob the suspect. When the researcher inquired about this questionable use of discretion, an agent replied that the grower was subject to being indicted at a later date. The suspect had not been charged formally when this study was concluded.

In several cases that the researcher observed, members of the law enforcement community compromised legitimate police functions to secure profits. This last case is significant because the pursuit of higher goals was completely abandoned. Usually the objectives of seizure operations were disguised and mixed with traditional activities, including arrests, but in this case the taking of assets was displayed boldly as the foremost concern.

AN ASSESSMENT OF ASSET FORFEITURE

Before asset forfeiture policies were established, narcotics cases were assigned priority by the amount of drugs involved and the level of threat to society posed by suspects. The observations made here, however, show that asset seizure has become the primary objective of drug enforcement. The problematic nature of asset forfeiture policy became apparent when the development of specific narcotics cases was observed. Before the procedural stage of the observed cases, the fundamental function of narcotics divisions was made clear to officers and agents through supervisors' decisions as to which cases would be pursued.

Selection of cases on the basis of seizure policy creates two basic problems. First, the process of raising revenue through asset forfeiture often requires police to concentrate on cases that offer little or no direct social benefit. Second, the suspects involved in these cases often are not engaged in serious criminal activity. Their personal profiles differ greatly from those of the drug lords, for whom asset forfeiture strategies were designed.

Equally disturbing is the effect of asset-hunting operations on police conduct; they elevate both the image and the reality of the private soldier over those of the public servant. Too often the tactics required to generate regular seizures conflict with the ideals of protecting and serving the public. A situation has developed, which allows narcotics supervisors to choose justifiably between strategies that produce revenue and those which acknowledge the demands of justice.

The recent Supreme Court decisions have done little to alter the present approach of forfeiture programs. Both *Austin v. United States* (1993) and *U.S. v. A Parcel of Land* (1993) set limits on forfeiture, thus protecting citizens' civil liberties. These restrictions, however, will not necessarily limit the scope of victimization and intrusion; they may even worsen the present condition. The principle of proportionality, for example, confines law enforcers to less property per seizure, but may invite more frequent application of the tactic so as to maintain revenue levels already fixed in agency budgets.

In certain cases, asset forfeiture has proved to be a valuable enforcement tool. This potential benefit, however, must be weighed against unfavorable consequences. This study addresses what recently has been considered a primary question concerning forfeiture laws: "What impact will asset forfeiture have on police operations and management?" (Holden 1993:1). It is apparent that asset forfeiture is already being institutionalized within law enforcement; this process is influencing its disposition. Although the narcotics units observed in this study were confined to one general locale, the mid-south, neither empirical studies nor journalistic accounts suggest that seizure-based policing tactics differ elsewhere. Certainly, further examinations of asset forfeiture programs should be pursued. Interrelated topics to be addressed include comparative analysis of the levels of assets seized by federal and state agencies, by regions of the country; the relationship of forfeiture to the fiscal autonomy of the police (Miller and Bryant Forthcoming); the soundness of conceptualizing forfeiture as legitimized police deviance; and selective targeting by race and class.

The redirection of narcotics enforcement is manifested theoretically in broader implications for the entire interaction of law enforcement with society at large. The inherent contradictions of asset seizure practices have surfaced as highly controversial civil liberties violations which increasingly have eroded our sense of fairness and have caused drug enforcers to subordinate justice to profit.

This insidious redirection is rooted in and propelled by American values of success, specifically profit. Societal and governmental opposition rarely succeeds in deterring means of income generation. The enforcers' inability to combat the pervasive illicit drug market does not justify legal mechanisms whereby law enforcement agencies share the wealth of drug trafficking under the guise of "service" to society.

Asset forfeiture has given drug enforcers a powerful incentive to maintain and manage economic mechanisms that allow the illegal drug market to continue. In this market, the drug enforcers and the drug traffickers become symbiotic beneficiaries of the "War on Drugs." Ironically, in its failure to reduce the marketing of illegal drugs, drug enforcement has succeeded in profiteering. Unfortunately, continued "success" in this area portends further and more widespread subversion of our ideals of fairness and justice.

REFERENCES

Adler, P. A. and P. Adler (1987) "The Past and Future of Ethnography." *Journal of Contemporary Ethnography* 16:4-24.

Block, A. (1993) "Issues and Theories on Covert Policing." *Crime, Law and Social Change: An International Journal* (special issue) 18:35-60.

Braithwaite, J. B. Fisse, and G. Geis (1987) "Covert Facilitation and Crime: Restoring Balance to the Entrapment Debate." *Journal of Social Issues* 43:5-42.

British Sociological Association (1973) *Statement of Ethical Principles and Their Application to Sociological Practice.*

Bugliosi, V. T. (1991) *Drugs in America: The Case for Victory.* New York: Knightsbridge.

Bulmer, M. (1980) "Comment on the Ethics of Covert Methods." *British Journal of Sociology* 31:59-65.

Burden, O.P. (1988) "Finding Light at the End of the Drug War Tunnel." *Law Enforcement News*, December 15, pp. 8.

Bureau of Justice Statistics (1991) *Sourcebook of Criminal Justice Statistics.* Washington, DC: National Institute of Justice.

Carter, D.L. (1990) "Drug Related Corruption of Police Officers: A Contemporary Typology." *Journal of Criminal Justice* 18:85-98.

Carter, D.L. and D.W. Stephens (1988) *Drug Abuse by Police Officers: An Analysis of Policy Issues.* Springfield, IL: Thomas.

Chambliss, W. (1988) *On the Take: From Petty Crooks to Presidents.* Bloomington: Indiana University Press.

Currie, E. (1993) *Reckoning: Drugs, the Cities, and the American Future.* New York: Hill and Wang.

Denzin, N. (1968) "On the Ethics of Disguised Observation." *Social Problems* 115:502-504.

Dombrink, J. (1988) "The Touchables: Vice and Police Corruption in the 1980's." *Law and Contemporary Problems* 51:201-32.

Dortch, S. (1992) "356 Marijuana Plants, House, Weapons Seized." *Knoxville News-Sentinel*, August 29, pp. 1.

Drug Enforcement Administration (1992) *Illegal Drug Price/Purity Report.* Washington, DC: Drug Enforcement Administration.

Drug Policy Foundation (1992) "Asset Forfeiture: Fair Practice or Foul Play?" (Film) *Drug Forum*, Date Not Available

Elsasser, G. (1990) "A Just Cause: Washington Group Wages War on the War on Drugs." *Chicago Tribune*, May 24, pp. 13.

Erikson, K. T. (1967) "Disguised Observation in Sociology." *Social Problems* 14:366-72.

Fried, D.J. (1988) "Rationalizing Criminal Forfeiture." *Journal of Criminal Law and Criminology* 79:328-36.

Galliher, J.F. (1973) "The Protection of Human Subjects: A Reexamination of the Professional Code of Ethics." *The American Sociologist* 8:93-100.

Goffman, E. (1959) *The Presentation of Self in Everyday Life*. New York: Doubleday.

Goldstein, A. and H. Kalant (1990) "Drug Policy: Striking the Right Balance." *Science*, September 28, pp. 9-13.

Greek, C. (1992) "Drug Control and Asset Seizures: A Review of the History of Forfeiture in England and Colonial America." In Thomas Mieczkowski (eds.), *Drugs, Crime, and Social Policy*, pp. 4-32 Boston: Allyn & Bacon.

Holden, R.N. (1993) "Police and the Profit-Motive: A New Look at Asset Forfeiture." *ACJS Today* 12:2.

Homan, R. (1980) "The Ethics of Covert Methods." *British Journal of Sociology* 3146-59.

Humphreys, L. (1970) *Tearoom Trade: Impersonal Sex in Public Places*. New York: Aldine.

Inciardi, J.A. (1991) *The Drug Legalization Debate*. 2nd ed. Newbury Park, CA: Sage.

Jacobs, D. (1992) "Police Take $700 from Man, Calling It Drug Money." *Knoxville News-Sentinel*, February 23, pp. 1.

Kleiman, M.A.R. (1989) *Marijuana: Costs of Abuse, Costs of Control*. New York: Greenwood.

(1992) *Against Excess: Drug Policy for Results*. New York: Basic Books.

Klockars, C. (1983) *Thinking about Police*. New York: McGraw-Hill.

Krauss, M.B. and E.P. Laezear, eds. (1991) *Searching for Alternatives: Drug-Control Policy in the United States*. Stanford, CA: Hoover Institution Press.

Lawrence, C.C. (1988) "Congress Clears Anti-Drug Bills." *Congressional Quarterly Weekly Report*, October 29, pp. 3145.

Manning, P.K. (1980) *The Narc's Game: Organizational and Informational Limits on Drug Enforcement*. Cambridge, MA: MIT Press.

Manning, P.K. and L.J. Redlinger (1977) "Invitational Edges of Corruption: Some Consequences of Narcotic Law Enforcement." In P. Rock (ed.), *Drugs and Politics*, pp. 279-310. Rutgers, NJ: Transaction Books.

Marx, G. (1988) *Undercover: Police Surveillance in America*. Los Angeles: Twentieth Century Fund Books

McAlary, M. (1987) *Buddy Boys: When Cops Turn Bad*. New York: Putnam's.

Miller, J.M. (1991) "Inside Narcotics Policing Operations." Master's thesis, Middle Tennessee State University.

Miller, J.M. and K. Bryant (Forthcoming) "Predicting Police Behavior: Ecology, Class, and Autonomy." *American Journal of Criminal Justice*.

Moore, M. (1977) *Buy and Bust: The Effective Regulation of an Illicit Market in Heroin*. Lexington, MA: Lexington Books.

(1988) "Drug Trafficking." In *Crime File*, pp. 1-4. Washington National Institute of Justice.

Morganthau, T. and P. Katel (1990) "Uncivil Liberties? Debating Whether Drug-War Tactics Are Eroding Constitutional Rights." *Newsweek*, April 29, pp. 18-21.

Myers, H.L. and J. Brzostowski (1982) "Dealers, Dollars, and Drugs: Drug Law Enforcement's Promising New Program." *Drug Enforcement* (Summer): 7-10.

Osborne, J. (1991) *The Spectre of Forfeiture*. Frazier Park, CA: Access Unlimited.

Polsky, N. (1967) *Hustlers, Beats, and Others*. New York: Anchor.

Reid, S.T. (1991) *Crime and Criminology*. San Francisco: Holt, Rinehart, and Winston.

Reuter, P. and M. A. R. Kleiman (1986) "Risks and prices." In M. Tonry and N. Morris (eds.), *Crime and Justice: An Annual Review of Research*, pp. 289-340. Chicago: University of Chicago Press.

Ronai, C.R. and C. Ellis (1989) "Turn-Ons for Money: Interactional Strategies of the Table Dancer." *Journal of Contemporary Ethnography* 18:271-98.

Roth, J.A. (1962) "Comments on Secret Observation." *Social Problems* 9:283-84.

Schneider, A. and M.P. Flaherty (1991) "Presumed Guilty: The Law's Victims in the War on Drugs." *Pittsburgh Press*, August 11-16.

Shaw, B. (1990) "Fifth Amendment Failures and RICO Forfeitures." *American Business Law Journal* 28:169-200.

Shils, E.A. (1975) In *Center and Periphery: Essays in Macrosociology*, Chicago: University of Chicago Press.
Stellwagen, L.D. (1985) "Use of Forfeiture Sanctions in Drug Cases." *Research in brief* (July): —.
Stuart, C. (1990) "When Cops Go Bad." (Film) *Frontline*, July 18.
Trebach, A.S. (1987) *The Great Drug War*. Washington, DC: Drug Policy Foundation.
Trebach, A.S. and K.B. Zeese (1990) *Drug Prohibition and the Conscience of Nations*. Washington, DC: Drug Policy Foundation.
United States Department of Justice (1988) *Research Brief*. Washington, DC: National Institute of Justice.
Walker, W.O. (1992) *Drug Control Policy: Essays in Historical and Comparative Perspective*. University Park: Pennsylvania State University Press.
Weisheit, R.A. (1991) "Drug Use among Domestic Marijuana Growers." *Contemporary Drug Problems* 17:191-217.
Willson, E. (1990) "Did a Drug Dealer Own Your Home? (Criminal assets may be seized)." *Florida Trend*, February, pp. 6-9.
Wilson, J.Q. (1961) *Varieties of Police Behavior*. Cambridge, MA: Harvard university Press.
(1978) *The Investigators: Managing the F.B.I. and the Drug Enforcement Administration*. New York: Basic Books.
Wistosky, S. (1990) *Beyond the War on Drugs: Overcoming a Failed Public Policy*. Buffalo: Prometheus Books.
Wrobleski, H.M. and K.M. Hess (1990) *Introduction to Law Enforcement and Criminal Justice*. St. Paul: West.
Zimring, F.E. and G. Hawkins (1992) *The Search for Rational Drug Control*. New York: Cambridge University Press.

Cases Cited

Austin v. United States 113 S. Ct. 2801 (1993)
U.S. v. A Parcel of Land 113 S. Ct. 1126 (1993)

Ethan A. Nadelmann

Thinking Seriously About Alternatives to Drug Prohibition

FOUR YEARS AFTER THE NOTION of drug legalization reemerged into public view, the time has come to step back and evaluate what it is all about and where it should be headed.[1] I cannot help but write as one who has become closely identified with the notion, but I also write as one who has tried to step back from the debate over drug legalization and analyze critically its contributions, missteps, and potential to beneficially redirect drug control policies. My principal interest lies not in the debate itself but in the future of psychoactive drug use and drug control policies in the United States and abroad. This article is thus not a response to the many critics of drug legalization, nor even a dispute with those who have favored the notion with somewhat different arguments and suppositions. It generally refrains from repeating the well documented costs of drug prohibition or the reasons why we need to consider alternative approaches.[2] And it pays scant attention to the political context of the debate or the political future of drug control policy. Its objective, rather, is to create and advance a more informed and sophisticated public discourse about alternatives to drug prohibition—one that breaks free from the intellectual and moralistic confines of contemporary prohibitionist norms.[3]

My specific objectives are fourfold. The first is to identify and examine the essential differences that separate those in the reasonable middle ground of the debate. The second is to offer new ways of thinking about radical alternatives to current drug prohibition policies, to identify the sorts of questions that must be asked, and to

Ethan A. Nadelmann is Assistant Professor of Politics and Public Affairs at the Woodrow Wilson School of Public and International Affairs, Princeton University.

suggest how they might be addressed. The third is to provide evidence in support of the proposition that even a radical decriminalization of drug prohibition will not result in the sorts of dramatic increases in substance abuse that self-identified critics of drug legalization fear. And the fourth is to propose a drug regulatory model that eliminates many of the worst consequences of drug prohibition without reproducing the unfortunate consequences of our alcohol and tobacco control policies.

Many of the ideas and arguments presented in this paper were proposed and developed in meetings of the Princeton Working Group on the Future of Drug Use and Alternatives to Drug Prohibition. This group, composed of eighteen scholars representing more than a dozen disciplines, is currently pursuing each of these four objectives. This article should thus be read as a synopsis of a collaborative work-in-progress, the final version of which will be completed in late 1993. I anticipate that many of the ideas advanced below will be revised and refined as the working group proceeds.

THE "LEGALIZATION" LABEL

To legalize or not to legalize? That, as two pairs of drug policy skeptics have recently written, is not really the right question.[4] The appropriate question is much broader, and it is one that incorporates the "legalize or not" question with respect to particular psychoactive drug products: What, simply stated, are the best means to regulate the production, distribution, and consumption of the great variety of psychoactive substances available today and in the foreseeable future? For a variety of reasons, the efforts of myself and others to answer that highly complex question have been captured by the label of "legalization." The term itself proved immensely successful in drawing the attention of tens of millions in the United States and elsewhere to what was at once a radical sounding but quite sensible critique of American drug control policies. But it exacted a stiff price with its implication that the only alternative to current policies was something resembling current US policies with respect to alcohol and tobacco. Few of those publicly associated with legalization in fact advocated such an alternative, but the misimpression has stuck in the public mind.

Legalization has always meant different things to different people. From my perspective, it has been first and foremost a critique of American drug prohibitionist policies which stresses the extent to which most of what Americans commonly identify as part and parcel of "the drug problem" are in fact the results of those policies. The failure of most Americans to perceive the extent and content of this causal relationship, and to distinguish between the problems that stem from the misuse of drugs per se and those that stem from drug prohibitionist policies, remains the single greatest obstacle to any significant change in American drug control policies. The recognition of this causal relationship does not, it should be stressed, lead automatically to a public policy recommendation that all of drug prohibition be abandoned. But it does suggest that alternative policies less dependent upon prohibitionist methods are likely to prove more effective.

Legalization also implies a set of policy objectives at odds with the government's proclaimed objectives of fighting a war against drugs and creating a drug-free society. Any drug control strategy, I and others have argued, should seek to minimize both the negative consequences of drug use and the negative consequences of the policies themselves. This is as true of public policies with respect to alcohol, tobacco, and caffeine as it is of policies directed at limiting the misuse of cannabis, cocaine, amphetamine, opiates, hallucinogens, and all other drugs. It is imperative, for instance, that any drug control policy distinguish among casual drug use that results in little or no harm to anyone, drug misuse that causes harm primarily to the consumer, and drug misuse that results in palpable harm to others, and then focus primarily on the last of these, secondarily on preventing the misuse of drugs, and little if at all on casual drug use. It is also imperative that any drug control policy be assessed not only in terms of its success in reducing drug abuse but also in terms of its direct and indirect costs.

Implicit in the legalization critique of American drug control policies are in fact two different types of arguments. At one level, it points out the ways in which drug prohibition per se is responsible for many drug-related problems. By criminalizing the production, distribution, and use of particular drugs, drug prohibition fundamentally transforms the nature of the drug markets, the ways in which people consume drugs, the lenses through which much of society views the drug problem, and the range of policies deemed appropriate for dealing with drug abuse. On another level, however, the critique advances a far more modest claim, which is that there are better and worse types of drug prohibition, with the Dutch "harm reduction" approach epitomizing the former and the American "war on drugs" the latter. Indeed, for many of those characterized as advocates of drug legalization, the Dutch model offers an alternative that is preferable not only to current US policies but also to the extreme libertarian model. The ideal set of drug control policies, from this perspective, can be found somewhere between the Dutch example and the libertarian model.

The harm reduction (or harm minimization) approach emerged in the Netherlands and Great Britain during the 1970s and early 1980s. It has since become increasingly influential both in those countries and in other parts of Europe and Australia as public health and other officials have recognized the need for more innovative and less punitive policies to stem the transmission of the HIV virus by illicit drug users.[5] Harm reduction policies seek to minimize the harms that result from illicit drug use. Rather than attempt to wean all illicit drug addicts off drugs by punitive means, harm reduction policies begin with the acknowledgement that some users cannot be persuaded to quit. These policies then seek to reduce the likelihood that they will contract or spread diseases such as hepatitis and AIDS, overdose on drugs of unknown purity and potency, or otherwise harm themselves or others. Proponents of harm reduction policies typically favor an assortment of drug treatment programs including the use of methadone and other maintenance programs. They insist on the need for needle exchange programs. They recommend public health and community outreach efforts to maintain contact between health service providers and illicit drug users. And they demand that drug policies acknowledge, both in law and policy, the human rights of drug users. Also implicit in most harm reduction approaches is the notion of "normalization," which posits that the harms associated with illicit drug use are best minimized by integrating drug users into normal society rather than isolating them in separate clinics, programs, markets, and neighborhoods.[6]

The relationship between the harm reduction approach and the notion of drug legalization remains ambiguous. Some proponents of the harm reduction approach vigorously oppose any broader trend toward disassembling the drug prohibition system. They are quick to point out that much of the opposition they have encountered stems from fears and perceptions that the harm reduction approach represents no more than a stepping stone to legalization. Others insist that a harm reduction approach taken to its logical and sensible conclusion would more closely resemble a legal regulatory regime than the current prohibition system. Any harm reduction approach, they argue, must reduce not just the harms to users but also the many other negative consequences of drug prohibition: the violence that accompanies illicit drug markets; the corruption of public officials; the de facto subsidy of organized crime; the incarceration of hundreds of thousands of people; the deprivation of individual liberties; and so on. All agree, however, that modest efforts to reduce the negative consequences of status quo policies are better than no efforts whatsoever.

LEGALIZERS, PROHIBITIONISTS, AND THE COMMON GROUND

The basic analysis advanced by most "legalizers" is remarkably similar to that advanced by those who have appeared as the most sensible, progressive, and nonideological among the prohibitionists. Both generally agree on the basic diagnosis of American drug prohibition, on the need to assess drug policy options in terms of their costs and benefits, and on the set of objectives noted above. The "progressive prohibitionists" largely acknowledge that casual drug use is not a problem in and of itself, and the legalizers grant that some policies designed to reduce overall levels of drug use may be effective in reducing the overall negative consequences of use. There is a shared recognition that many dimensions of the American war on drugs represent a form of overkill, that more modest criminal justice measures can accomplish the same objectives as successfully as the harsher measures, and that a more vigorous adherence to public health precepts and objectives will result in a superior mix of drug control policies. Both further agree that a dramatic expansion in the availability of drugs in society will likely increase the cumulative consumption of drugs. And both agree that it is important to draw distinctions among different drugs, and among different formulations of the same drugs, in designing drug control policies. Stated otherwise, few in either camp believe that marijuana, or coca tea, should be treated the same as crack cocaine.

This common ground is fundamentally at odds with the views expressed by the more conservative and reactionary prohibitionists. Articulated most vigorously by President Bush's first Drug Czar, William Bennett, this perspective has demonstrated no interest whatsoever in analyses of costs and benefits or in the need to minimize the negative consequences of drug control policies. Casual use of illicit drugs has been depicted as an immoral form of activity as well as a dangerous source of contagion requiring the treatment of users.[7] Social science research and public health precepts are of value only insofar as they conform with their ideologically based assumptions and policies. There is, in short, no room for dispassionate dialogue concerning any policy alternatives that do not appear tougher than what has been tried before.[8] Combining a penchant for punitive sanctions with a view of drug use best described as "pharmacological Calvinism,"[9] the reactionary prohibitionists have insisted that the only legitimate objective of drug control policy must be the elimination of illicit drug use.

The common ground is also at odds, albeit not quite so fundamentally, with the conservative libertarian perspective on drug control.[10] For those libertarians who believe as an absolute matter of principle in the sanctity of individual sovereignty over property and the freedom of contract, no governmental controls on the commerce in drugs are acceptable no matter what the consequences. Other libertarians are more utilitarian in their thinking, placing their faith in the free market and assuming that the dual policy objectives would best be accomplished in the absence of governmental interventions. Less committed libertarians start from the same assumptions about the magic of the free market but acknowledge that modest governmental controls, particularly truth-in-advertising and labelling requirements, may be necessary to correct for the excesses and abuses that the free market invites. All of these libertarians tend to support the more civil libertarian commitments to individual privacy and freedom in the choice of one's lifestyle—although they insist that freedom of contract includes the freedom of employers to insist upon drug testing as a condition of employment. Civil libertarians, by contrast, tend to regard the freedom of contract with less deference than the right to privacy. They are more apt to speak of a right to consume drugs,[11] and are more likely to integrate considerations of social justice and public health into their principles and policy calculations.

Putting aside the perspectives of the reactionary prohibitionists and the hardcore libertarians, there are two principal differences among the progressive legalizers and the progressive prohibitionists. The first reflects disagreements as to the weight that should be accorded to such values as individual liberty, privacy, and tolerance in calculating the costs and benefits of different drug control policies.[12] Most legalizers weigh these values heavily, with the more committed civil libertarians regarding them as absolutes that cannot be compromised and other progressive legalizers perceiving them as highly important but not inherently immune to some restraints. At the very least, most legalizers insist, the possession of modest amounts of drugs for personal consumption should not be the subject of criminal laws. The progressive prohibitionists are sympathetic to such values but accord them much less weight, both because they perceive them as undermining efforts to reduce drug abuse and because they are more willing to defer to majoritarian opinion in defining and weighting them. Confronted with potential trade-offs between levels of drug abuse and levels of coercion directed at drug users and sellers, most legalizers are willing to concede modest increases in drug abuse levels in return for reductions in the numbers of those punished for using and selling drugs. Progressive prohibitionists, by contrast, are far more willing to limit individual liberty to the extent they perceive a potential gain in public health.

The second major difference of opinion involves the assessment of the vulnerability of the American population to the substantial increases in drug availability that would follow from any of the more far reaching drug legalization schemes. Where most prohibitionists can envision the possibility of a fiftyfold increase in the number of people dependent upon cocaine, and conclude that the future of the nation might well be at stake if cocaine were made as available as alcohol, most legalizers regard such estimates and predictions as the unsubstantiated folly of doomsayers.[13] Both agree that substantial research is required to better estimate this vulnerability, but the wide disparities are primarily a reflection of visceral fears, beliefs, and instincts regarding individual and collective human nature in the context of American society. Whereas most legalizers perceive, both instinctually and intellectually, ample evidence of a fundamental societal resilience, most progressive prohibitionists share with their more reactionary allies a fundamental pessimism regarding the susceptibility of American society to a dramatic liberalization of drug availability.

The roots of this viscerally based debate can be found in a related difference of opinions regarding the balance of power between psychoactive drugs and the human will. Prohibitionists typically see the balance favoring the former, with its potential to disrupt and destroy the lives of consumers. Legalizers, by contrast, emphasize the latter, with its assumption that the balance of basic human desires in most people effectively limits the destructive potential of drugs. For most prohibitionists, the relevant evidence includes the worst case examples of drug addiction and other abuse, the experiments on captive rats, monkeys, and other nonhuman animals to determine the addictive liability of different drugs, and the biological evidence of withdrawal symptoms in human beings following sustained consumption of particular drugs. Most legalizers, by contrast, focus on the less dramatic but more abundant evidence of casual and controlled drug use, insist that the "set and setting" of drug use are at least as important as the drug itself in determining whether a person becomes a drug abuser, and see the animal studies and biological evidence as less significant than the abundant historical, cross-cultural, and contemporaneous evidence of individual and societal resilience vis-à-vis all psychoactive drugs. ("Set is a person's expectations of what a drug will do to him, considered in the context of his whole personality. Setting is the environment, both physical and social, in which a drug is taken.")[14] Many prohibitionists seem to see some psychoactive drugs as possessed of powers akin to those of the Sirens whose alluring voices no man could resist. Most legalizers, by contrast, perceive such a notion as absurd. They find more persuasive the substantial evidence that most people (including children), given sufficient information, are unlikely to use a drug in the first place, that most of those who do try a particular drug tend either to stop shortly thereafter or to use it in moderation, and that even most of those who become addicted to a drug or otherwise misuse it, ultimately moderate or stop their use.

These differences, however, still leave abundant room for common ground on how drug control policies can be reformed in the short term. For even though the progressive prohibitionists share with their more reactionary allies a deep seated fear of greater drug availability, they lack the reactionaries' political and moral commitments to repressive policies. And even though most legalizers feel substantial revulsion for the more punitive prohibitionist measures, they recognize both the inevitability of, and the need for, some criminal justice accompaniments to any regulatory regime. The public health model, with its emphasis on reducing morbidity and mortality, appears to provide something of an ideologically neutral set of guidelines and parameters for working out a preferable set of drug policies—although legalizers are wary of the totalitarian potential of a public health model taken to its logical extreme. Both legalizers and most progressive prohibitionists also perceive merit in the harm reduction policies developed by the Dutch as well as local authorities in England and Australia—even if they differ as to the extent to which those policies could be adapted to the American environment.

There is also a shared assumption, from which only the most libertarian of the legalizers dissent, that government does have an important role to play in shaping and improving the lives of its citizens. Where all sides differ is in their view of the appropriate means by which government should pursue this, with the progressive prohibitionists viewing criminal justice and other coercive mechanisms as perfectly acceptable and often efficient means and the progressive legalizers favoring less coercive measures ranging from education and voluntary treatment programs to broader provision of social services. There also is something of a consensus that the top priority of drug control programs should be to minimize the harm that drug users do to others, with the secondary priority involving the more traditional public health objectives of minimizing the harm that drug users, and especially children, do to themselves. But underlying even this consensus are differing assumptions regarding the appropriate reach of social control measures designed to detect and curtail the illicit use of drugs. Thus even among those who identify themselves as proponents of a "public health" approach to the drug problem, there are some who sympathize deeply with the legalizers but prefer to keep their more ideological, liberty-based, values out of their analyses, and others who see criminal justice sanctions and civil commitment laws as useful means with which to coerce drug users into treatment programs.[15]

The fact that legalizers and progressive prohibitionists have so much in common is significant for a number of reasons. First, it suggests that there is a basic framework of analysis, predicated upon systematic assessment of costs and benefits, that is regarded as intellectually legitimate by all serious analysts of drug control policy. The fact that the evaluation of the costs and benefits varies greatly depending upon one's ethical values and ideological assumptions does not negate this. Second, it suggests that the current framework and direction of drug prohibition policies in the United States are fundamentally at odds with any conceivable policy predicated upon either public health precepts or notions of harm reduction. Indeed, the only way to explain and justify many current policies is by reference to the fears, prejudices, and primitive moralisms of those who have transformed drug control policy into a modern version of an authoritarian crusade. Third, it suggests that the debates *among* the legalizers over the design and evaluation of alternative drug control policies may well be of interest to many who share neither all of the legalizers' values nor their visceral confidences.

THE DRUG POLICY SPECTRUM

It should be clear by this point that drug legalization and drug prohibition do not represent simply radical alternatives to one another and that there is no single version of either one. Virtually all drug control policies incorporate elements of both prohibition and legal availability. Alcohol, for instance, is regarded as a legal drug but it is illegal to sell it to anyone under the age of twenty-one, illegal to drive while under its influence, and illegal, in many states and localities, to consume in public or to sell or buy except from government-controlled or government-licensed outlets. Many of the same prohibitions increasingly apply to cigarettes and other tobacco products. Nicotine gum, which is substantially less harmful than smokeable tobacco, cannot even be purchased over-the-counter. Cocaine and most opiates are typically regarded as illegal drugs, but both are prescribed by doctors, the former for nasal and dental surgery as well as (in a few cases) treatment of pain, the latter as a prescribed treatment for pain or, in the case of methadone, as an authorized alternative to illicit heroin. The distinction between legal regulatory policies and prohibitionist policies becomes even more obscure when one surveys the broad spectrum of alcohol control policies that have been employed around the world during the past century; the same is true of opiate control policies and, to a lesser extent, public policies directed at the control of most other psychoactive drugs.

Nonetheless, one can distinguish between prohibition and legalization in at least two significant respects. The sharper distinction concerns whether or not a drug can be purchased over-the-counter, which is to say that it can be purchased legally by adults without first obtaining permission from a government agency or government-licensed agent such as a doctor. The more ambiguous, but equally important, distinction is between those policies that rely primarily on criminal sanctions to control the misuse of drugs and those that rely primarily on the informed choices of citizens as shaped by public health policies, regulatory structures, and honest drug education.

It can be useful to think about alternative drug control policies as arrayed along a spectrum, with the strictly prohibitionist and highly punitive at one end, the unregulated free market at the other end, and a wide array of regulatory policies in the middle. It requires minimal insight, moreover, to recognize that any drug control policy driven principally by public health considerations and stripped of the moralistic and authoritarian impulses that motivate contemporary policy would have little use for many of the more punitive measures in evidence today. The hard questions begin when values such as privacy, tolerance, and a presumption against imprisonment for most nonviolent drug-related activities are factored into the analysis of costs and benefits. They become even tougher to answer the further we venture along the policy spectrum into the relatively unknown territory of untested regulatory mechanisms and over-the-counter availability of drugs that currently can be purchased, if at all, only with a doctor's prescription.

Why venture into the unknown terrain of a truly nonprohibitionist drug policy given both the difficulties of evaluating the consequences of such a policy and the unlikelihood of it being favored by a majority of Americans within the foreseeable future? There are four reasons, each of which are developed below. First, only such a policy can dramatically reduce the many negative consequences of drug prohibition. Second, it helps us to address fundamental questions about the basic need for a drug prohibition system—in particular long unexamined assumptions about the differences between psychoactive substances and other consumer items as well as the vulnerability of the population to a broader availability of psychoactive drugs. Third, drug policy is one area in which libertarian assumptions regarding the magic of the free market may be more right than wrong. And fourth, the future may bring both new drugs as well as new ways of altering our states of consciousness that are not readily susceptible to governmental controls and that transform the ways in which Americans think about drugs and consciousness alteration.[16]

Thinking seriously and systematically about radical alternatives to current drug prohibition policies requires a degree of intellectual "stretching" that is relatively unusual in policy analysis generally and virtually unknown in the specific case of drug control policy analysis. This stretch is best accomplished by asking two complementary questions: How do we best maximize the benefits of the free market model and minimize its risks? And how do we best retain the advantages of drug prohibition while minimizing its direct and indirect costs? This stretch can be visualized by focusing on the extremes of the drug policy spectrum, with the free market at one end and contemporary American drug prohibition near the other end, and then trying to stretch each toward the other by applying notions of harm minimization to each.

The stretch from contemporary prohibition is, of course, the easier and more familiar one. It begins with a known quantity, the status quo, which is far easier to evaluate than theoretical alternatives—even if many causal relationships resist precise identification. The tendency of policy analysts and policymakers to focus on options that fall within or close to the realm of politically acceptable options means that far more thought and discussion have been devoted to the more modest revisions of current prohibition policies. Many of the initial steps that one can envision already have been taken in the Netherlands, England, Australia, and elsewhere. And even many of the steps that might be taken beyond what is currently happening abroad still require no radical changes in either the structure or the mechanisms of prohibition.

The further one stretches from the contemporary prohibition model, however, in terms of reducing criminal justice and other coercive controls on the distribution of drugs, the more difficult it becomes to evaluate the consequences. It is, for instance, not that difficult to estimate the consequences of making marijuana, heroin, and other strictly prohibited drugs available by prescription, or of legalizing the sale and possession of syringes and other drug paraphernalia, or of extending the limited decriminalization of marijuana possession enacted by eleven states during the 1970s to the entire country. There are powerful reasons to believe that each of these policy changes would substantially reduce the undesirable consequences of drug prohibition and present only modest risks in terms of public health. But it is quite another thing to estimate the consequences of making cocaine, amphetamine, morphine or heroin more readily available to registered addicts, and surely an even greater intellectual challenge to evaluate the consequences of making these drugs legally available over-the-counter. That challenge cannot be met, I suspect, by taking contemporary prohibition, and the patterns of drug use that have emerged under it, as the starting reference points.

EVALUATING THE "SUPERMARKET" MODEL

Starting from the alternative extreme of the policy spectrum, the free market, obliges us to focus on the question that lies at the heart of the debate between legalizers and prohibitionists of all stripes: What would be the consequences for American society of having virtually no drug control policy whatsoever? Imagine, for instance, that Congress passed a law granting the freedom of drug consumption and even production and distribution the same legal protections as the rights of freedom of speech, press, religion, and assembly. And imagine that "supermarkets" existed all around the country in which drugs of every variety could be purchased at prices reflecting nothing more than retailers' costs plus reasonable profit margins and sales taxes. This is, of course, the nightmare scenario portrayed by the opponents of legalization—even if it is not the policy favored by virtually any of those identified as proponents of legalization apart from the most hardcore libertarians.[17] But it also bears a close resemblance to the relatively free market in drugs found in late nineteenth-century America—a period characterized by a fairly high rate of opiate and other drug consumption but dramatically fewer drug-related problems than we see today.[18]

The great advantage of this model is that it eliminates virtually all of the direct and indirect costs of drug prohibition: the many billions of dollars spent each year on arresting, prosecuting, and incarcerating hundreds of thousands of Americans, the diversion of scarce governmental resources from dealing with other, more immediately harmful, criminal activities, the tens of billions of dollars earned each year by organized and unorganized criminals, much of the violence, corruption and other criminal activity associated with the illicit drug markets, the distortion of economic incentives for inner-city residents, the severe problems posed by adulterated and otherwise unregulated drugs, the inadequate prescription of drugs for the treatment of pain, the abundant infringements on Americans' civil liberties, and all the other costs detailed in the extant literature on drug prohibition and legalization.

The great disadvantage of the supermarket model is its invitation to substantial increases in both the amount and the diversity of psychoactive drug consumption. What needs to be determined as best as possible are the magnitude and nature of that increase and its consequences. Among the more explicit assumptions of the legalization analysis is that the vast majority of Americans do not need drug prohibition laws to prevent them from becoming drug abusers. By contrast, prohibitionists typically assume that most Americans, and at the very least a substantial minority, do in fact need such laws—that but for drug prohibition, tens of millions more Americans would surely become drug abusers. The supermarket model provides no immediate insights into which perspective is closer to the truth, but it does suggest two important approaches on analyzing the implications of a free market.

First, it is imperative that analysts broaden their horizons to examine not just potential changes in the consumption of drugs that are currently illicit but changes in the cumulative consumption of all psychoactive substances. Virtually all human beings consume psychoactive substances. Alcohol and caffeine are certainly the two most common in the United States today, followed by nicotine, marijuana, and a variety of the more popular prescription drugs used to alleviate feelings of depression and anxiety. With the notable exception of alcohol, which has retained its preeminent position throughout the history of American psychoactive drug consumption, all other drugs have witnessed substantial changes in their levels of consumption.

Some of these changes have been a result of changes in drug laws. Others have reflected the emergence of new drugs, or new formulations of familiar drugs, as well as changes in medical prescription practices, new marketing techniques, changing fads and fashions in recreational drug usage, and broader changes in popular culture as well as particular subcultures. The notion of a truly free market in drugs obliges us to consider what would happen if alcohol, nicotine, and caffeine no longer were artificially favored over other drugs by virtue of their legal status. One strong possibility is that other drugs—including some that are common in other societies, some that were once more popular in America than they are today, and some that have yet to be designed or discovered—would compete with and substitute for those drugs that are most familiar to Americans today.

Indeed, one of the silver linings on the black cloud of greater drug use under different legalization regimes is the prospect that less dangerous drugs would drive out the more dangerous ones. By most accounts, alcohol and tobacco represent two of the most dangerous drugs that have ever entered into common usage in human society. Between them, they present a high proportion of all of the harms associated with other drugs that have experienced widespread usage at one time or another. Tobacco, especially when consumed in the form of cigarettes, is both highly addictive and readily identified as a cause of cancers, cardiovascular diseases, and other ills. Alcohol can be highly addictive for some users; consumed in abundance, it can cause death by overdose in the short-term and cirrhosis of the liver and other diseases in the long-term. It also is strongly associated with violent behavior and accidental injuries in a great variety of societies. There is no reason to assume that their predominant position in the hierarchy of favored psychoactive substances will persist forever, and good reason to believe that the desirable functions they serve can be replaced by other substances that pose far fewer dangers to the health of consumers in both the short and long-term. The same may well be true of relatively less dangerous drugs, such as caffeine, which might well lose out in the competition to other psychoactive substances, such as low potency coca and amphetamine products, that may improve performance more effectively with even fewer negative side effects.

The possibility of dramatic substitution effects under a free market regime suggests that the most important issue in evaluating the consequences of such a model is neither the overall magnitude of drug consumption nor the number of drug users under such conditions, but rather the magnitude of the negative consequences that would result: the immediate effects of drug misuse on the health and behavior of the user; the debilitating effects of sustained misuse; and the deadly effects of sustained consumption. Each of these effects may also be of consequence for nonusers ranging from those who love or live with drug abusers to those who depend upon them in the workplace to those who encounter them on the roads. The evaluation of these consequences, and the assessment of which are more or less serious, inevitably involve ethical judgments. But is important to recognize that public policy can seek to shift patterns of drug use and even abuse in safer directions by favoring drugs, sets, and settings that cause less harm to users and others. It is, in short, possible for the undesirable effects of drug use to decrease significantly even as the amount and diversity of drug consumption increase substantially.

Indeed, if we really seek to be truly objective in our assessments, what needs to be calculated are not just the cumulative negative consequences but the positive ones as well.[19] Proponents of the public health perspective as well as substantial segments of the American population are reluctant to speak of the positive benefits of psychoactive drug use except to the extent they conform with conventional notions of physical health and medical treatment. Alcohol's benefits, for instance, are defined primarily in terms of their potential to reduce heart disease, and those of prescription drugs entirely in terms of their capacity to alleviate pain, depression, anxiety, and feelings that disrupt normal functioning. Yet most people use drugs because they enjoy the effects and many perceive a variety of personal benefits that are rarely measured by physical, medical, or social scientists. Some of these resemble the effects approved by medical and public health criteria, but they typically are not interpreted as such either because they involve an informal form of self-medication or because they confront the common value judgment that one should not have to use psychoactive drugs to be or feel a certain way. The moderate consumption of alcohol as a social lubricant, and of coffee and other caffeinated beverages as a mild stimulant to increase alertness, are probably the most easily accepted and widely acknowledged nonmedical benefits associated with nonprescribed psychoactive drug consumption. But it is also the case that millions of Americans justify their past use and/or explain their current use of marijuana, cocaine, hallucinogens, and a variety of other drugs in terms of the benefits that they have derived from their consumption of those substances. Such claims are easily belittled in a society that adopts the notion of "drug-free" as its motto, and are often dismissed by scientists who find such benefits particularly difficult to measure. Nonetheless, it seems inherently unreasonable to dismiss entirely the perceptions of consumers, especially when the negative consequences of their consumption are not apparent. We thus have no choice but to calculate the consequences of changes in drug consumption not just in negative terms but as a net calculation that incorporates both positive and negative consequences.

The second perspective suggested by the supermarket model is that the potential negative health consequences of a free market, or of any other substantial change in policy, are best assessed by considering the respective susceptibilities of different sectors of the population to such changes. I proceed from two assumptions: that it is possible to distinguish among sectors based upon their susceptibility to drug abuse and hence their vulnerability to changes in drug policy; and that close examination of both current and historical patterns of drug use and abuse, as well as other patterns of human behavior, provide important clues into the nature and degree of susceptibility under alternative regimes. Implicit in the second assumption is the recognition that Americans, and most other people, already live in a society in which powerful psychoactive substances are widely available to both adults and children. One need only consider the easy availability of alcohol, tobacco, and caffeine virtually throughout the country; the continued ease of obtaining marijuana and other illicit drugs in much of the country; the extensive presence of powerful psychoactive substances, generally prescribed by medical practitioners, in the medicine closets of American homes; and the entirely uncontrolled availability throughout the United States of many other psychoactive substances, ranging from gasoline and glue to the wide array of drugs available over-the-counter in pharmacies.

What conclusions can be drawn from an analysis of the cumulative consumption of psychoactive drugs in this country? First, virtually all Americans consume psychoactive substances—and even the small minority who appear to abstain entirely, such as the Mormons, seem to compensate by consuming substances that are not traditionally viewed as psychoactive, such as sugar and caffeinated soft drinks. Second, a substantial majority of Americans consume these substances only in moderation, suffering little or no harm as a result. Third, the drugs that prove most addictive to most Americans are those, such as cigarettes and caffeinated beverages, that can be easily integrated into everyday life with minimal hassle or disruption. Fourth, virtually all drugs, even heroin, cocaine, and other drugs most associated with destructive patterns of consumption, are consumed in moderation by most of those who use them. [20] Fifth, a substantial majority of those who enter into destructive patterns of drug consumption eventually pass on to either abstinence or moderate patterns of consumption.[21]

When we focus on those who appear most susceptible to destructive patterns of drug consumption, further conclusions are apparent. First, while certain types of drugs are more difficult to use in moderation than others, the principal determinants of destructive drug use patterns involve not the pharmacology of the drug but the set and setting in which the drug is consumed. That is why alcohol consumption among conquered aboriginal groups and cocaine consumption among some inner-city populations have more in common with one another than either does with patterns of alcohol or cocaine consumption among less vulnerable sectors of the population. Indeed, no set and setting is more conducive to extensive and severe drug abuse than the combination of poverty and maladjustment to a mainstream society. Second, those who engage in destructive patterns of consumption with one drug are the most likely to repeat that pattern with other drugs; conversely, those who demonstrate an ability to consume alcohol and common prescription drugs responsibly, or who have succeeded in either stopping or dramatically curtailing their consumption of tobacco, are much less likely to engage in destructive patterns of consumption with other drugs.

Consider the results of recent polls on drug use in the United States. Approximately one-third of Americans over the age of twelve claim that they have not used alcohol in the past year, and close to half report that they have not consumed any alcohol in the past month.[22] In a December 1990 Gallup poll, 43 percent of those polled described themselves as abstainers from alcohol—up from 29 percent in the years 1976–1978.[23] Among African-Americans, the proportion who claim to abstain from alcohol is 58 percent.[24] Of those Americans who did drink within the past month, only one in ten (or about 5 percent of the household population) reported that they had drunk heavily during that time.[25] Approximately 75 percent of all Americans over the age of twelve have smoked at least one cigarette; slightly less than 30 percent report that they smoked within the past month, of which half consume about a pack or more a day.[26] With respect to marijuana, about 33 percent of Americans have used it at least once, 11 percent in the past year, 6 percent in the past month, and about 1 percent on something resembling a daily basis.[27] There is reason to believe that there is substantial overlap not only between those who drink heavily and those who smoke heavily, but also between those two groups and those who use illicit drugs heavily—although detailed cross-tabulations of available surveys are required to reach more exact estimates. Indeed, one also finds substantial overlap with those who engage in compulsive gambling and other harmful activities. The principal exception to this substantial overlap may involve the misuse of tranquilizers and other prescription drugs, especially among women. Even if we assume that self-reports of alcohol and tobacco consumption tend to underreport actual consumption by 30–50 percent, we still must conclude that at least 70 percent of Americans are resistant to the sorts of temptations and risks posed by the easy availability of cigarettes, and that more than 90 percent either refrain from powerful drugs altogether or else consume them responsibly and in moderation. This conclusion strongly suggests that a very substantial majority of Americans are immune to any far reaching liberalizations in drug availability for the simple reason that they do not really need drug laws to prevent them from entering into destructive relationships with drugs.

The important question is thus not whether or not millions of Americans would change their patterns of drug consumption under a radically different drug control regime—since there is good reason to assume they would—but rather whether those patterns would be more (or less) destructive than their current patterns of drug consumption. Among the tens of millions of Americans who abstain from alcohol consumption, it seems reasonable to assume that they would have little interest in, and perhaps substantial moral reservations against, consuming other powerful psychoactive drugs. Among the even larger number of Americans who consume alcohol in moderation, despite the great potential for that drug to be consumed in a destructive fashion, it is also reasonable to assume that the same individual and societal restraints that protect them against alcohol's seductive powers would control their consumption of other substances. For the vast majority of Americans, therefore, the principal danger posed by a free market in drugs has little to do with drugs like crack cocaine, since so few Americans would be likely either to try it in the first place or, if they did try it, to continue to use it. (Public opinion polls consistently reveal that few Americans believe they would consume cocaine, heroin or even marijuana if those drugs were legally available.)[28]

The greatest danger of a free market in drugs, I suspect, is the possibility that a drug, assumed at first to be relatively safe, becomes popular among millions of Americans and then is revealed to be far more harmful than initially believed. This danger is one that has proven commonplace in the annals of pharmaceutical innovation, medical prescription practice, and inebriation, from morphine and cocaine during the nineteenth century to cigarettes, barbiturates, amphetamine, tranquilizers, and many nonpsychoactive drugs, including steroids, during the twentieth. It is one that has continued to frustrate the regulatory efforts of the Food and Drug Administration in recent decades, and that promises to persist into the future regardless of whether or not the drug laws change substantially. But it is fair to assume that the dangers would be greater if far more products were to become legally available.

The most common fear of legalization, however, is usually of a different sort, and it must be taken seriously. It is that there are millions of Americans for whom the drug prohibition system represents the principal bulwark between an abstemious relationship with drugs and a destructive one. Under a free market regime, it is feared, many of those who currently abstain from, or consume in moderation, alcohol and other powerful intoxicants would become drug abusers, and many of those who already have demonstrated either a potential for, or a pattern of, drug abuse would engage in even more destructive patterns of drug use. Underlying this fear are a variety of assumptions: that the only things which prevent many current users of illicit drugs from engaging in far more destructive patterns of drug use are the high price and lower availability of those drugs under the current prohibition regime; that at least some of the illicit drugs are more seductive than those that are currently legal and/or available;

that a free market regime would inevitably invite greater levels of drug experimentation, which in turn would lead to higher levels of use and abuse; that many people would be more likely to complement their current drug use with newly available drugs than to substitute those for their current preferences; and that the heightened societal tolerance for more varied psychoactive drug use that would likely accompany a free market regime would lend itself to higher levels of drug misuse.

Even if we assume that the vast majority of those who now consume psychoactive drugs safely would continue to do so under a free market regime, and further assume that a substantial proportion of those who currently misuse illicit drugs would be no worse and quite likely better off under a free market regime, the fact remains that there is a relatively small, but indeterminate, proportion of Americans for whom the drug prohibition system provides not just the image but the reality of security. Figuring out, with some measure of confidence, the magnitude and composition of this vulnerable population is among the most important intellectual challenges confronting those who take seriously the need to estimate the consequences of alternative regimes. And designing policies that minimize the magnitude of this at-risk group without resorting to criminal justice and other coercive measures is surely an even greater challenge.

Most of those who would suffer from the absence of the current drug prohibition regime can be found among those who currently smoke cigarettes and/or abuse alcohol. The first group includes both those adolescents and adults who have demonstrated a willingness or ability to disregard the well known consequences of cigarette smoking, as well as those adults who have demonstrated an inability to abandon a dangerous habit. The second group, which overlaps substantially with the first, includes those adolescents and adults who have demonstrated an inability to control a powerful psychoactive substance, i.e., alcohol, despite the existence of increasingly strong social controls. There are certainly others who neither smoke cigarettes nor abuse alcohol who would enter into destructive relationships with other drugs if they were more readily available, but there is (as I already have suggested) good reason to doubt that their numbers would prove substantial.

In trying to predict which drugs will prove most popular in the future, who will use them responsibly and who will do so destructively, it is important to keep in mind why people use drugs and why they use the drugs they do. The choice of drugs for most members of most societies can barely be described as a choice at all. Dominant cultures strongly favor some drugs over others, hence the preferred position of alcohol throughout much of the world, with different societies evidencing a preference for beer, wine or distilled liquors, or of coffee in most Islamic societies and quat in some, of kava in some South Pacific islands and coca in the Andes. Alcohol's dominant position no doubt stems as well from the fact that its simple means of production was easily discovered millennia ago by a wide diversity of societies, so that it was not merely readily available in most societies but also provided with substantial opportunity to entrench itself.[29] Tobacco's secondary position somewhat similarly can be attributed to its great success in sweeping the globe and becoming entrenched in a great variety of societies before the emergence of any international capacity for its suppression—although its powerful addictive qualities must also be given credit for ensuring that markets once penetrated remained markets thereafter. As for substances such as kava, betel nut, coca, cannabis, opium, and various hallucinogens, each has benefited, not unlike alcohol, from being an indigenous product.

To the extent that drug consumption patterns and preferences can really be described as a choice, it is fair to say that people choose those drugs that give them what they want. Most people can in fact be described as rational consumers even in their choice of psychoactive drugs. They use drugs because they seek or like their effects, whether those involve relief from pain, reduction of stress and anxiety, release from inhibitions, stimulation of the senses and the intellect, enhancement of physical or mental performance, or any of the many other psychoactive effects of drugs. Most people, moreover, tend to limit their consumption in order to minimize the negative consequences, whether those involve hangovers, heart disease or cancer. The evidence from a broad variety of cultures suggests that the single most important determinant of a drug's popularity is its capacity to be integrated into ordinary lives with minimal disruption.

It is important to recognize that the same notion of rational drug consumption applies to some extent even to those who are engaged in highly destructive patterns of consumption. For many hard core drug users in the inner cities and among aboriginal populations, their intensive involvement with powerful drugs provides a powerful source of relief from emotional and other psychological pain, some excuse for isolating themselves both from mainstream society and difficult personal responsibilities, and (particularly for those most engaged in the day to day hustling for the means to procure their expensive drugs) a source of self esteem and motivation to keep getting out of bed in the mornings despite the absence of any promising prospects in their lives. This is not to say, of course, that the destructive drug use patterns of those living on the edge of despair can be described as entirely rational. But it is to say that even hard core drug abusers tend to prefer drug consumption options that minimize the risks of death in both the long and the short-term; the growing evidence about the willingness of intravenous drug addicts to take modest steps to reduce the likelihood of contracting the HIV virus attests to this.[30] Relatively few hard core drug addicts can be described as truly committed to an early death. It is thus reasonable to assume that even most current and potential hard core drug users will, if given the choice, opt for drugs that are, at the very least, no more dangerous than those consumed today.

One can supplement the notion of rational drug consumption, which focuses on the individuals' preferences, with another notion also drawn from libertarian philosophy. It is that societies, like individuals, generate nonlegal social norms in the absence of governmental prohibitions and other restrictive laws. Societies, simply stated, are not entirely at the mercy of free markets, but retain the potential to create self-protective mechanisms designed to minimize the risks presented by such markets. Indeed, some libertarians argue, one of the more significant costs imposed by governmental prohibitions is the withering of societal norms that often operate more powerfully and effectively than governmental interventions. Evidence in support of this argument can be found in anthropological and sociological studies of traditional and modern cultures alike, wherever patterns of human intercourse are allowed to evolve in the absence of significant governmental prohibitions. Particularly reassuring in this regard are the many decriminalizations that one can point to throughout civilized human history that were opposed by those who feared for the civility and even the survival of society but that turned out to be far less destabilizing than was feared. Such fears impeded efforts to do away with restrictions on speech, press, religion and assembly, on relations between people of different classes and races, on sexual and familial relations, and on the availability of psychoactive drugs that are now integrated into modern society.[31] The same sorts of unjustified fears now stand in the way of efforts to do away with current drug prohibitions.

The arguments of the libertarians are both powerful and, at least with respect to the majority of society, quite convincing. They confront, however, three counterarguments that most Americans currently find compelling. The first is simply that drugs and drug consumption are fundamentally different than all other commodities and activities—so different that ordinary libertarian assumptions do not apply. The second, like the notion of rational drug consumption, derives from economic reasoning. It is the evidence that suggests that levels of consumption of desirable consumer items tend to increase as their availability increases and their price decreases. And the third is the epidemiological evidence suggesting that the negative consequences associated with the use of any drug in a society are a direct function of the overall level of use of that drug. Of these three arguments, the first represents the weakest in terms of logical analysis but the most powerful from an emotional and political viewpoint. It can be repudiated by reference to the many ways in which other commodities and activities generate the same sorts of behavior as do the consumption of drugs, be it the alteration of consciousness, the transformation of social behavior or the creation of dependent relationships.[32] But the belief in the unique power of psychoactive drugs is so entrenched in our society that even highly prominent liberal theorists, including those with strong libertarian inclinations, either avoid the subject altogether or else carve out awkward exceptions to their otherwise more coherent philosophies. The second and third arguments, by contrast, present far more powerful reasons to refrain from placing one's faith entirely in libertarian assumptions.

There are other reasons as well to put the purist libertarian assumptions and the supermarket model to the side. The more one speculates about the consequences of such a model, the more one realizes that all sorts of additional assumptions have to be made about the type of society that would favor such a model—and that these assumptions are even more speculative than anything we assume about the vulnerability of today's population to such a model. At the very least, the sets and settings that so powerfully shape the nature and consequences of drug use would inevitably differ dramatically from their contemporary formulations. Furthermore, as soon as one engages in the process of trying to think through the consequences of such a model, one encounters the inevitable tendency to begin framing restrictions on the supermarket. Whether one analogizes to alcohol and tobacco, or to the nineteenth-century model of widespread drug availability, one confronts the tendency both in the United States and elsewhere to impose restrictions on the distribution of psychoactive drugs.

THE "RIGHT OF ACCESS" MODEL

We thus return to the question: How can the risks and harms of the free market model be reduced without undermining the many benefits that such a model offers? And how far can the free market model be stretched without giving up its essential feature? That essential feature, it must be stressed, is the legal availability of drugs in the absence of any requirement that the permission of a government-sanctioned gatekeeper be obtained beforehand. It is that feature that distinguishes the legal status of alcohol, tobacco, caffeine, and aspirin from that of marijuana, cocaine, morphine, and Valium—and that accounts for the generally greater and easier availability of the legal drugs compared to the illegal drugs. Legal drugs are almost always available over-the-counter; illegal drugs are not. Government-sanctioned medical authorities and pharmacists, and sometimes additional barriers as well, stand between the illegal drug and the person who wishes to obtain it.

It is important to recognize that legal availability does not always connote easy availability, and that the restricted legal status of a drug does not always make it that difficult to obtain. Legal drugs may, for instance, be so expensive—either because of high costs of production or high taxes—that they are for all intents and purposes unavailable to many potential consumers. Distribution channels may be relatively undeveloped or otherwise circumscribed. And efforts by government to restrict severely the availability of a legal drug without depriving consumers entirely of the right to purchase it legally may prove successful. Powerful evidence in support of these propositions can be found in the alcohol control efforts of the United States, Australia, and much of Europe during the 1920s and 1930s. Whereas the former initially favored Prohibition, the latter opted instead for tough, but nonprohibitionist, regulatory regimes. The results were more substantial, and more lasting, declines in alcohol consumption and alcohol-related ills in Europe and Australia than in the United States.[33]

Illegal drugs, by contrast, can occasionally prove to be highly available. Medical practitioners often write prescriptions for mild tranquilizers, sedatives, and other psychoactive drugs in response to their clients' plaints. They may do so because they believe that such drugs are a proper and effective way of medicating their clients, or because they believe that a client's satisfaction with a visit to her doctor depends in part upon the doctor's willingness to end the visit by writing a prescription. And even apart from such channels, illegal drugs can prove readily available wherever substantial markets generate high levels of supply—as was the case with marijuana in much of the country during the 1970s and 1980s. The same holds true of more localized markets, in particular the inner-city markets for cocaine since the mid-1980s as well as for other drugs that have attained high levels of popularity in particular neighborhoods or cities. In cases such as these, illegal drugs may prove more available than many legal drugs, such as alcohol, for which the hours of sale are often restricted by government. In many highly restricted environments, moreover, such as prisons, jails, and mental institutions, illegal drugs are often more available than alcohol because their smaller bulk makes them easier to smuggle past guards and other barriers.

The foregoing analysis suggests that it is possible to construct legal drug control regimes in which certain drugs may be less available than is the case under prohibition regimes. When we stretch as far as possible from the free market extreme of the drug policy continuum, but seek at the same time to retain the basic feature of nongatekeeper accessibility, the model that emerges is one that might be called the "right of access" or "mail-order" model. It is based on the notion that adults should be entitled not merely to the right to possess small amounts of any drug for personal consumption but also to the right to obtain any drug from a reliable, legally regulated source responsible (and liable) for the quality of its products. In identifying such a right, I must stress, I do not mean to suggest that it is on a par with the more privacy-based right of possession and/or consumption, but merely that it provides a useful parameter—both ethically and conceptually—for designing alternative drug control policies. Unlike the supermarket model, the right of access model is one that can be superimposed on the current drug prohibition system.

If such a right of access were legally acknowledged by Congress or the Supreme Court—a prospect, I recognize, with scant political or jurisprudential potential in the foreseeable future—those desirous of minimizing the potential threat to public health might well advocate the notion of a mail order system. In order to ensure a right of access to all residents of the United States no matter where they might live, at least one mail order source would have to be available in the United States from which any adult could order a modest amount of any drug at a reasonable price reflecting production costs and taxes. Most states, cities, and other communities might well continue to prohibit the sale and public consumption of most drugs within their jurisdictions as they do now, but would be obliged to acknowledge the basic right of access by mail order as well as the basic right of possession and consumption. Some localities might also adopt, if they had not already done so, the various sorts of harm reduction policies that are advisable under any regime. One might also imagine many other local variations by different states and municipalities to accommodate the particular health, criminal justice, and moral concerns of each. But the option of ordering one's drugs by mail would allow any adult to opt out, in effect, of the local control system insofar as private consumption was concerned.

The right of access notion offers us, I think, a more valuable, modest, and realistic alternative extreme than the supermarket model from which to stretch toward the optimal policy. As a model, it retains in skeletal form the essence of a legalization regime, which is the elimination of any sort of gatekeeper—policeman, doctor, pharmacist, etc.—between the seller and consumer of drugs with the power to deny the latter access. It thus strikes at the heart of much of what is wrong with drug prohibition, in particular the creation of violent and powerful black market entrepreneurs, the harms that result from unregulated production of psychoactive drugs, and the many infringements on individual freedoms. But it also provides a skeletal framework that can be filled out with many of the sorts of antidrug abuse measures that we associate with both harm reduction approaches to illicit drug control policy and public health approaches to alcohol and tobacco control. It has the advantage of resembling actual models in other domains of public policy both today and in recent history, including the alcohol distribution system in Canada and Sweden during the early decades of this century as well in pre- and post-Prohibition United States, and the modification of FDA policy in recent years to allow individuals to import by mail small amounts of drugs that are legally available outside the United States but that have yet to be approved by the FDA for the treatment of AIDS or cancer.[34] Given the preference among critics of drug prohibition for a fairly high degree of "local option," it addresses the inevitable tensions among different state and local drug control policies, between those policies and federal policies, and even (albeit to a lesser extent) between domestic policies and international requirements. At the same time, it offers a paradigm for addressing and reconciling the tensions between individual rights and communitarian interests that lie at the heart of so many struggles over public policy in democratic societies.

This model is not, I must stress, a panacea, nor should it be misconstrued as a final proposal for an alternative drug control regime. It raises numerous questions such as how such a mail-order system would be established and maintained, who would run it and profit from it, who would oversee it, who would have access to its mailing lists and other information about consumers, how consumer privacy would be protected, how minors would be prevented from taking advantage of it, how new drugs would be made available, and so on. Most of these questions strike me as susceptible to fairly precise answers, in good part because there are so many close analogies to a mail-order system. More difficult to assess are the same sorts of questions raised by the supermarket model and all other alternative models, in particular those that focus on assessing changes in psychoactive drug consumption—although I assume that they are easier to answer with respect to a mail-order model since such a system is more readily integrated with the current prohibition model than is the case with the supermarket model.

One prominent difference between the right of access or mail-order model and the supermarket model is that the former fails to eliminate the black market. Just as some gun control laws rely on waiting periods between the time a person orders a firearm and the time he obtains possession, so a mail-order system imposes a sort of waiting period—presumably a minimum of one day. It is highly reasonable to assume that black markets would persist not only to supply minors—which is presently the case with most psychoactive substances, including alcohol and tobacco—but also to supply those who will not or cannot wait to obtain their drugs from the mail-order system, as well as those who want to obtain more at any one time than is allowed by law.

We typically assume that an important objective of legalizing drugs is to undercut the black markets and place them in the hands of either government or government-licensed and regulated distributors. This objective is tempered by the recognition that there are better and worse features of illicit markets, and that a preferable drug policy ideally would focus on eliminating the worst while tolerating the better features. It would, for instance, attempt to undermine the accumulation of power by organized criminals, reduce the violence that attends such markets and generally push large-scale production into the hands of regulated, tax paying, and collecting producers and distributors. But at the same time, it might well choose to ignore smaller scale illicit markets—what are often referred to less disparagingly as informal or unregulated markets—which are of value not just because they often prove more innovative and enterprising in designing and offering new products but also because they provide an important source of income for many people who face substantial disadvantages in their efforts to penetrate and succeed in the more established legitimate markets. This holds true, for instance, of both rural producers of marijuana and inner-city entrepreneurs engaged in the low-level distribution of crack and other drugs. Two probable advantages of the right of access model are that it would effectively undercut efforts by organized criminals to create highly profitable national distribution systems, since any adult could purchase the drugs by mail. At the same time, it would not eliminate many illicit small scale, localized production and distribution systems that meet local demands for immediate availability, rapid delivery, and specialized products. Local authorities could choose, in effect, either to suppress such black markets vigorously or to manage them through conventional vice control methods. But the scale of such markets would probably bear a closer resemblance to illicit prostitution rings in cities that sanction regulated prostitution than to contemporary illicit drug markets.

TRANSITION ISSUES

Few drug control regimes are static. Prohibitions, regulations, and decriminalizations tend to evolve as new drugs emerge, as drug use patterns shift, as other drug-related norms change, and as popular and elite perceptions of various drugs, drug consumers and drug problems shift. In contemplating alternatives to the current drug prohibition regime, we need to distinguish between transition phases, longer term consequences and equilibria, keeping in mind that there is no drug control regime that will suffice forever. The distinction is important with respect to issues of both drug consumption and black markets. It is safe to assume that illicit markets do not just shrivel up and die when confronted with competition from licit markets. Rather, illicit entrepreneurs may continue to compete with licit markets during the initial phase when licit producers and distributors are still gearing up, having the advantage of their previous investments in production and/or distribution as well as their expertise. The share of the market that is captured by legal producers and distributors in the long-term, however, probably would depend more on price, availability, competition, the intensity of continued law enforcement efforts to suppress the remaining black market, and changing tastes and fads among consumers. There are also important policy questions regarding the extent to which those involved in the illicit markets during prohibition should be allowed or encouraged to play a role in legal markets after prohibition.

Close examination of the aftermath of Prohibition in the United States, other postprohibition periods elsewhere, and other decriminalizations, such as of gambling, prostitution, pornography as well as of nonvice markets in countries experiencing significant deregulations (such as the former Soviet bloc countries) can provide important insights into how drug markets are likely to evolve.[35] The impact of decriminalization on those involved in illicit drug dealing, as well as on those who would have become involved in drug dealing but for decriminalization, is especially important when we focus on African-American and Latino youth in the urban ghettos. Clearly the dramatic drop in the price of currently illicit drugs following decriminalization would greatly reduce one of the most powerful incentives for engaging in drug dealing and other criminal activities. According to a recent report by the Justice Department's Bureau of Justice Statistics, 13 percent of all convicted jail inmates, and 19 percent of those convicted of drug trafficking offenses, said they had committed their offense to obtain money to buy illicit drugs.[36] Dramatic reductions in the size and profitability of the illicit markets would also remove the powerful financial and social incentives that have lured so many urban youth into drug dealing activities even before they began to consume illicit drugs.

Further insights into this question can be derived both from analyzing the response of bootleggers to the repeal of Prohibition and from observing how illicit drug dealers adapt when illicit drug markets decline, as seems to be the case today.[37] Illicit vice entrepreneurs seem to respond to decriminalizations and shrinkages in illicit markets in any of four ways. Some succeed in making the transition to legal entrepreneurship in the same line of work. Some seek to remain in the business illegally, whether by supplying products and services in competition with the legal market or by employing criminal means to take advantage of the legal markets. For instance, following Prohibition, some bootleggers continued to market their products by forging liquor tax stamps, by strongarming bartenders into continuing to carry their moonshine and illegally imported liquors, and by muscling their way into the distribution of legal alcohol. Some also fought to retain their markets among those who had developed a taste for corn whiskey before and during Prohibition. The third response of bootleggers and drug dealers is to abandon their pursuits and branch out instead into other criminal activities involving both vice opportunities and other sorts of crime. Indeed, one potential negative consequence of decriminalization is that many committed criminals would adapt to the loss of drug dealing revenues by switching their energies to crimes of theft, thereby negating to some extent the reductions in such crimes that would result from drug addicts no longer needing to raise substantial amounts of money to pay the inflated prices of illicit drugs. The fourth response—one that has been and would be attractive to many past, current, and potential drug dealers—is to forego criminal activities altogether. Relatively few criminal pursuits can compare in terms of paying so well, requiring so few skills, remaining fairly accessible to newcomers, and presenting attractive capitalist opportunities to poorly educated and integrated inner-city youth. During Prohibition, tens if not hundreds of thousands of Americans with no particular interest in leading lives of crime were drawn into the business of illegally producing and distributing alcohol; following its repeal, many if not most of them abandoned their criminal pursuits altogether. There is every reason to believe that drug decriminalization would have the same impact on many involved in the drug dealing business who would not have been tempted into criminal pursuits but for the peculiar attractions of that business. The challenge for researchers, of course, is to estimate the relative proportions of current and potential drug dealers who would respond in any of these four ways. The even broader challenge is to determine the sorts of public policies that would maximize the proportion that forego criminal activities altogether.

The need to distinguish between transition phases and longer term consequences and equilibria also applies to the impact of decriminalization on potential and current illicit drug users. The initial liberalization of availability is likely to spark high levels of curiosity, stimulated both by the media and by the mere fact of legal access, and substantial experimentation with different drugs—but it is reasonable to assume that this would moderate over the long-term. At the same time, the initial reluctance of many Americans to try newly available drugs to which they are unaccustomed may fade over time. Those who have grown up under a prohibition system, moreover, and have thus been influenced to one degree or another by the many assumptions that prohibition conveys about drug use, are likely to experience a legal regime differently than succeeding generations for whom it will represent the norm.

GATEKEEPERS, NORMS, AND INFORMATION SYSTEMS

There is also the question of how a liberalization of legal availability will affect both the doctor-patient relationship and the role of pharmacists. It would be useful to know, for example, what proportion of visits to doctors are motivated principally by the desire or need to obtain a prescription for a controlled substance. Between one-half and two-thirds of all consultations with doctors result in the writing of a prescription.[38] A legal drug regime would negate the need for visits motivated solely by the need to obtain a prescription, with mixed results. Some people would suffer as a result of not being obliged to consult with a doctor, but many others who now must waste time and money on unnecessary doctor visits would surely benefit. The problem of undermedication, and particularly undertreatment of pain, would almost surely be less of a problem than it is now. But some people would surely be more likely to use inappropriate drugs and to develop unhealthy dependencies on drugs that are now available only by nonrenewable prescription. Better insights into these issues can be gained by analyzing the available evidence about why people go to doctors as well as patterns of self-medication and doctor visitation in other times and places in which there have been fewer controls on the availability of drugs.[39]

The role of doctors and pharmacists as gatekeepers for prescription drugs is of course part and parcel of a broader question about the basic need for creating and maintaining a distinction between over-the-counter and prescription drugs. This question has been addressed most sharply by economists, although the literature on the broader implications of the distinction remains quite limited.[40] The notion of requiring prescriptions for drugs other than cocaine and opiates is, as Peter Temin wrote in his historical study of drug regulation in the United States, a relatively recent notion—one that was not consonant with the 1938 Federal Food, Drug, and Cosmetic Act but that emerged in spite of a legislative intent to the contrary.[41] Implicit in the notion was the belief that many Americans would not act rationally in their choice and use of drugs and thus needed to be shielded from their own irresponsibility by governmental controls. One result was a significant constriction in the provision of information about drugs to consumers. The supposition that a mandatory drug prescription system plays an essential role in protecting the health of consumers has yet to be systematically tested. One study that employed a cross-national comparative perspective concluded that the prescription requirement did not yield a net benefit in health effects.[42] Another, by Peter Temin, suggested certain criteria that could be used to determine when a drug should be restricted or made available over-the-counter.[43] These studies provide valuable insights, but they represent only a small step in the direction of determining the likely consequences of severely restricting or eliminating the mandatory prescription system.

I should stress that these issues are at least as important with respect to the urban ghettos as they are in thinking about middle class drug usage. Much illicit drug abuse in urban ghettos can fairly be described as a form of self-medication for depression and other psychological pain among people who tend not to seek out psychiatrists and other doctors for such ills. The drugs they use to hide and forget their pains—alcohol, illegal heroin and cocaine, and other "street" drugs—are often more dangerous but no more effective than those prescribed to middle class patients by their doctors. At the same time, urban ghettos are full of poor people who might well benefit from access to the same sorts of antidepressants and other drugs that middle class Americans obtain from their doctors but who fail to obtain them both because they eschew the illicit markets and because financial and cultural limitations preclude visits to doctors. Here it is worth pointing out the patent absurdity of the claim that drug legalization would devastate inner-city populations. Both legal and illegal drugs are already so widely available in inner cities that virtually any resident can obtain them far more quickly than in suburban neighborhoods. But a liberalization of drug availability would make more easily available drugs that are safer than those now sold in urban liquor stores, crack houses, and street markets. At the same time, it would substantially reduce the negative consequences of prohibition—all of which are felt most severely in the urban ghettos.

More broadly, there is good reason to think that a regime of legal availability would substantially, even radically, transform the ways in which Americans relate to psychoactive drugs. One might well imagine that pharmacological experts, certified perhaps by either government or professional agencies, would play an increasingly important role not so much as gatekeepers but as educators and consultants on the preferred uses of drugs for medicinal, psychotherapeutic, recreational, and other purposes. But even more importantly, nonlegal norms would undoubtedly emerge in the absence of current prohibitionist norms to shape the way people relate to drugs, the ways in which they use them, and the cautions they exercise. Here again, there is the question of determining which people are likely to prefer the least potent and least risky drugs and which are more likely to opt for the most potent, quickest acting, and so on. There is also the possibility that a world of widespread drug availability might be more likely to generate self-protective norms against all forms of drug taking. And it is fair to assume that far more people would assume greater responsibility for their relationship to drugs than is currently the case, since the gatekeeper role of doctors effectively transforms consumers into far more passive actors.

This in turn leads to the question of how information about psychoactive drugs could be better distributed to a population so that it is readily available and intelligible to typical consumers. The challenges here are fourfold. The first is to design an effective means of distinguishing among categories of drugs so that those who purchase either by mail or at retail outlets are properly informed of the risks and appropriate uses. This task could be performed by either a Food and Drug Administration (FDA) or a nongovernmental agency such as Consumer Reports, or both. The second is to design an information system separate from the distribution systems whereby consumers can obtain necessary information on their own at little or no cost. This might involve information distribution systems accessible by telephone or other easily accessed computer hookups. Current efforts by the FDA, and by consumer organizations such as those promoted by Ralph Nader, to ensure that consumers are provided with both more accurate and more accessible information may well provide something of a model in thinking about issues such as these. The third challenge is to create honest drug education programs that tell children the truth about drugs without stimulating premature desires to try them.[44] And the fourth is to design public health campaigns that effectively discourage drug misuse without resorting to lies, scare tactics, and the demonization of people who use drugs. The public service advertisements directed at discouraging tobacco consumption and drunken driving provide far better models in this respect than the "Fried Egg" ads, caricatures, and untruths promoted by the Partnership for a Drug-Free America.[45]

Most of what people know about drugs they have never used comes from the commercial media. It has repeatedly played a central role in transforming local fads and fashions into national and even international phenomena.[46] We can safely assume that it will play a crucial role in the distribution of information and the shaping of public perceptions about drugs, particularly those that are relatively unfamiliar to most Americans. One need only imagine what impact the news magazines' cover stories in late 1989 and early 1990 on the new antidepressant, Prozac, would have had if Prozac were available over-the-counter or by mail; indeed, it would be interesting to know what impact those stories actually did have on potential consumers.[47] How many people, for instance, visited doctors thereafter with the intention of obtaining prescriptions for Prozac, how many succeeded, and—even more difficult to say—how many benefited or suffered as a consequence? Conversely, how many people who might benefit from Prozac have not yet tried it solely because they are unaccustomed to visiting a doctor to obtain assistance in alleviating depression? Certainly there is good reason to fear the media's impact on drug consumption preferences under a legal regime given its historic and persistent incapacity to provide accurate and balanced information about psychoactive drugs.[48] On the other hand, the media occasionally has demonstrated its capacity to shape preferences in healthier and otherwise better directions. It is certainly a loose cannon insofar as our efforts to evaluate the future direction of drug use are concerned. But there is good reason to devote at least some effort to considering how the media has shaped drug consumption patterns in the past.

The issue of advertising is a difficult one. In 1986, the Supreme Court ruled in *Posadas de Puerto Rico Associates vs. Tourism Company of Puerto Rico* that strict restrictions on advertising casino gambling were constitutionally permissible.[49] There seems to be little question that comparable restrictions on advertising psychoactive drugs would also be regarded as legal.[50] The difficult issues thus involve balancing the costs and benefits of both specific types of advertising as well as the advertising of psychoactive products generally. There is good reason to fear, and to curtail, the mass promotion of psychoactive drugs that present the sorts of harm associated with alcohol and cigarettes.[51] There are also substantial incentives to avoid a revival of medical quackery and the mass marketing of patent medicines that once tricked millions of Americans into buying products that did them little good and occasionally much harm. On the other hand, advertising can play a valuable role in informing people of new and beneficial products, in luring consumers to switch from more dangerous to less dangerous drugs, and in promoting competition that saves consumers money.[52] This is true of both psychoactive and nonpsychoactive drugs as well as those used for both recreational and more traditional therapeutic purposes. The solution to the advertising dilemma—to the extent we are willing to put aside First Amendment concerns—may well lie in a combination of restrictions on the promotion of more harmful products with vigorous educational campaigns to discourage their consumption.

CONCLUSION

Predicting human behavior remains, and shall always remain, an imprecise art. Social science can provide modest insights into the consequences of incremental changes in regulatory structures on human behavior. But when we try to envision the consequences of more far reaching changes in such structures, our confidence in social science insights falters. The variables are too numerous, the changes in individual and societal consciousness too unpredictable, and the tools too paltry to pretend that we can really know the future. Here history offers a more powerful guide—with its potential to shed light on both the accretion of incremental changes and the suddenness of revolutionary change. But even its lessons are limited by unanswerable questions regarding the potential of the future to evolve in unprecedented ways. Ultimately our predictions are bounded by theories of human behavior, and particularly of human and societal vulnerability and resilience, that have more to do with our visceral fears and confidences than any objective readings of the evidence.

When we switch from predicting the future to trying to plan it, our preferences are determined not only by our calculations of their consequences but also by our choices among competing ethical values. Such choices may be made implicitly, as when we accept without question conventional ethical values, or explicitly. They establish the parameters beyond which policy options will not be considered. They influence our calculations of the costs and benefits of various options. And they guide us in deciding who should benefit and who may be harmed by choosing one option over another. There are no objective standards by which to choose among ethical values. One can only appeal to conscience, principle, and empathy.

The challenges of evaluating radical alternatives to our current drug prohibition system are formidable. But so are the challenges of predicting the consequences of persisting with our current policies. In 1960, few Americans had ever heard of LSD, and the notion that sixty million Americans would smoke marijuana during the next three decades would have seemed bizarre to most Americans. In 1970, few Americans gave much thought to cocaine, and most would not have believed that twenty-five million Americans would try it during the next two decades. By the late 1970s, many Americans believed that marijuana would be sold legally within a few years. In 1980, no one had ever heard of "crack" cocaine; the notion of an AIDS epidemic among injecting drug users seemed inconceivable; and the prospect of a quarter-million Americans in jail or prison by 1990 for violating drug prohibition laws seemed preposterous. Clearly, retention of our drug prohibition system provides no guarantees about future patterns of drug use or the scale of future drug problems. Legalization may present a wider array of possibilities, but its uncertainties are not dramatically greater than those of persisting with prohibition.

There are powerful reasons for taking seriously the alternatives to drug prohibition. The first is simply that drug prohibition has proven relatively ineffective, increasingly costly, and highly counterproductive in all sorts of ways that many Americans are only beginning to appreciate. Nowhere is this more true than in the urban ghettos, where the war on drugs has failed to reduce the availability of illicit drugs or the incidence of drug abuse and offers no prospect of doing so in the future. At the same time, these neighborhoods and their residents have suffered the negative consequences of drug prohibition more severely than any others. Not unlike Chicago under Al Capone, they must live with the violence and corruption generated by prohibition, the diversion of law enforcement resources, the distortion of economic and social incentives for their youth, the overdoses that result from unregulated drugs, the AIDS that spreads more rapidly because clean syringes are not legally or readily available, and the incarceration of unprecedented numbers of young men and women. Those who contend that legalization would mean writing off impoverished inner-city neighborhoods ignore the remarkable extent to which drug prohibition has both failed and devastated the urban ghettos. Drug legalization offers no panacea, particularly if it is not accompanied by more fundamental changes in the norms and leadership of urban societies. But there is no question that it can alleviate many urban ills at relatively little risk.

Second, there are good reasons to believe that a nonprohibitionist regime would not result in dramatic increases in drug abuse. Public opinion polls reveal that few Americans believe they would use drugs that are now illicit if they were legally available. Important implications, moreover, can be derived from the observation that we already live in a society in which all sorts of psychoactive substances are cheaply and readily available to both adults and children. Legalizaton would make more drugs more available than they are today, but it would not present a situation dramatically different from that which currently exists. The same sorts of norms and interests that prevent most Americans from misusing drugs today would persist. And even many of those who do misuse illicit drugs would be no worse off, and in many ways better off, under an alternative regime. Some Americans would suffer from the abolition of drug prohibition, but all the evidence suggests that their numbers would be modest. We possess, in short, substantial evidence of a fundamental societal resilience in the face of widespread drug availability.

Third, there are also good reasons to anticipate positive shifts in drug consumption patterns if we move in the direction of nonprohibitionist controls. The current drug control regime favors certain legal and illegal drugs over others that may well present fewer dangers to both consumers and society generally. Under a legalization regime, alcohol and tobacco would no longer be artificially favored by their legal status. Crack cocaine would no longer benefit from the perverse dynamics of the illicit market. And traffickers and consumers would no longer be obliged to favor more compact and potent drugs over bulkier but more benign substances simply because the former were less detectable. Both illicit drug abusers and responsible consumers, particularly among the poor, would have better access to drugs that are safer than those that are most available now. Drug legalization might thus result in more consumption of a wider array of substances than is currently the case but with dramatically fewer negative consequences.

Fourth, those who take seriously such values as tolerance, privacy, individual freedom, and individual responsibility have little choice but to seek out alternatives to the current system. These values are fundamentally at odds with a prohibition regime that criminalizes the possession of small amounts of any drug for personal consumption. They are seriously threatened, moreover, by a war on drugs that promotes notions of zero tolerance toward drug users, that pursues its objective of a drug-free society with few restraints, that encourages neighbors and family members to inform on one another, and that incarcerates hundreds of thousands of Americans for engaging in vice activities that were entirely legal less than a century ago.

In proposing a mail-order distribution system based on a right of access, I have tried to offer a model that strikes at the heart of what is most problematic about drug prohibition. I realize that such a model is easily mocked by those with little interest in thinking seriously about alternatives to drug prohibition. My intended audience are the progressive prohibitionists and legalizers of all stripes interested in developing the discourse about alternatives to drug prohibition. I believe the model offers an effective means of eliminating or reducing the worst consequences of drug prohibition. It represents the best compromise I can envision between individual rights and communitarian interests. It provides for both a skeletal framework at the federal level and substantial flexibility for local option at the state and local level. It allows for substantial latitude in implementing public health measures and campaigns designed to reduce drug abuse. And it offers a system that can be fairly easily superimposed on the current prohibition system.

The model does not, to be sure, represent a panacea. It raises as many questions as it answers. Like any other model, it has its vulnerabilities and it is susceptible to abuse by those determined to take advantage of it. Its potential effectiveness depends, moreover, on the extent to which it is filled out with sensible and humane drug control policies at state and local levels of government. But it does compare favorably, I believe, with both the American prohibition system and the supermarket model preferred by extreme libertarians. It presents greater risks than the conventional, prohibition-bound harm reduction model one finds in parts of Europe and Australia, but it also offers far more potential to transform drug consumption patterns in both the urban ghettos and the population at large in safer directions.

Intellectual ruminations about supermarket models, mail-order distribution systems, and a right of access to psychoactive drugs seem far removed from current political debates over drug control policy in the United States. There are, nonetheless, good reasons to develop the intellectual capital associated with the analysis of alternative drug control regimes. First, scholars are obliged to pursue their intellectual inquiries unencumbered by the blinders imposed by current prejudices and political realities. To limit the questions that one asks and the answers that one ventures to those sanctioned by officialdom is to forsake our moral and intellectual obligations to both our profession and our society. Future generations are ill served if today's scholars uniformly submit to the intellectual conservatism that so dominates social science and public policy analysis. Second, many of the assumptions that underlie both the current war on drugs and the prohibition system itself have not been systematically examined for a long time. Even those who desire no substantial revisions in drug control policies can benefit from such an appraisal. Third, no one knows what the future will bring. New drugs and new ways of altering one's state of consciousness will surely emerge. The challenges of regulating psychoactive drugs are certain to increase. And the pharmacological Calvinism that dominates contemporary American public opinion and policy analysis can only persist for so long.

Cost-benefit analysis can, and should, play an important role in the debate over the future of drug control policy, if only because it provides us with the closest thing to an objective framework of analysis for clarifying our objectives and assessing our options. Ultimately, however, the debate over drug policy is really a debate over competing moral visions of society. I see no merit, and much evil, in calls for zero tolerance and a drug-free society. I also see nothing immoral, I must admit, about the consumption of psychoactive drugs by those who do no harm to others and who fulfill the obligations they have assumed to others. The challenge, from my perspective, is one of designing and promoting a drug control policy that combines a healthy respect for individual freedom and responsibility with a strong sense of compassion. These values do not trump all others all of the time. But it is important that they be not forgotten or pushed to the side whenever the fearful specter of DRUGS is uttered.

ACKNOWLEDGMENTS

I am grateful to the members of the Princeton Working Group on the Future of Drug Use and Alternatives to Drug Prohibition for their participation in the project, and to the Smart Family Foundation for its financial support of the working group. I am also indebted to the Ford Foundation and the Robert C. Linnell Foundation for their research support. I am grateful for comments on previous drafts of this paper from Michael Aldrich, Virginia Berridge, John DiIulio, Ernest Drucker, David Hawks, Sylvia Law, Stanton Peele, Craig Reinarman, Sasha Shulgin, Kenneth Warner, and Alex Wodak.

ENDNOTES

[1]The relationship between the current debate over drug legalization and prior debates is analyzed in Ronald Bayer, "Introduction: The Great Policy Debate—What Means This Thing Called Decriminalization?," *Milbank Quarterly* 69 (3) (1991): 341–63.

[2]See the following articles by Ethan A. Nadelmann, "Drug Prohibition in the United States: Costs, Consequences and Alternatives," *Science* 245 (1 September 1989): 939–47; "U. S. Drug Policy: A Bad Export," *Foreign Policy* 70 (Spring 1988): 1–39; and "The Case for Legalization," *The Public Interest* 92 (Summer 1988): 3–31. Also see James Ostrowski, "The Moral and Practical Case for Drug Legalization," *Hofstra Law Review* 18 (3) (Spring 1990): 607–702; Richard Lawrence Miller, *The Case for Legalizing Drugs* (New York: Praeger, 1991); Arnold S. Trebach, *The Great Drug War* (New York: Macmillan, 1987); Steven Wisotsky, *Breaking the Impasse in the War on Drugs* (Westport, Conn.: Greenwood Press, 1986); and the collections of articles in Melvyn B. Krauss and Edward P. Lazear, eds., *Searching for Alternatives: Drug-Control Policy in the United States* (Stanford, Calif.: Hoover Institution Press, 1991); in David Boaz, ed., *The Crisis in Drug Prohibition* (Washington, D.C.: CATO Institute, 1990); in Ronald Hamowy, ed., *Dealing with Drugs: Consequences of Government Control* (Lexington, Mass.: Lexington Books, 1987); in Arnold S. Trebach and Kevin B. Zeese, eds., the three-volume *Drug Prohibition and the Conscience of Nations* (Washington, D.C.: Drug Policy Foundation, 1990), *The Great Issues of Drug Policy* (1990), and *New Frontiers in Drug Policy* (1991); and in Bruce K. Alexander, *Peaceful Measures: Canada's Way Out of the 'War on Drugs'* (University of Toronto Press, 1990).

[3]Recent efforts to analyze nonprohibitionist drug policy options include Doug Bandow, "Dealing with Legalization," *The American Prospect* 8 (Winter 1992): 82–91; and Chester Nelson Mitchell, *The Drug Solution* (Ottawa: Carleton University Press, 1990). A proposed research agenda can be found in Ethan Nadelmann, "Beyond Drug Prohibition: Evaluating the Alternatives," in Krauss and Lazear, eds., 241–50.

[4]See Franklin E. Zimring and Gordon Hawkins, *The Search for Rational Drug Control* (New York: Cambridge University Press, 1992), 82–110; and Mark A. R. Kleiman and Aaron J. Saiger, "Drug Legalization: The Importance of Asking the Right Question," *Hofstra Law Review* 18 (3) (Spring 1990): 527–66.

[5]See, generally, Pat O'Hare, Russell Newcombe, Alan Matthews, Ernst C. Buning, and Ernest Drucker, eds., *The Reduction of Drug Related Harm* (London: Routledge, 1991); Peter McDermott and Pat O'Hare, eds., *Reducing Drug-*

Related Harm: New Developments in Theory and Practice (London: Whurr Publishers, 1992); and Nick Heather, Alex Wodak, Ethan Nadelmann, and Pat O'Hare, eds., *Psychoactive Drugs and Harm Reduction: From Faith to Science* (London: Whurr Publishers, 1993). Also see John Strang and Gerry V. Stimson, eds., *AIDS and Drug Misuse: The Challenge for Policy and Practice in the 1990s* (New York: Routledge, 1990).

[6]See Govert Frank van de Wijngaart, "A Social History of Drug Use in the Netherlands: Policy Outcomes and Implications," *Journal of Drug Issues* 18 (1988): 481–95.

[7]See the first *National Drug Control Strategy* issued by the Office of National Drug Control Policy, Executive Office of the President, in September 1989 (Washington, D.C.: US Government Printing Office, 1989), 11.

[8]See Zimring and Hawkins, *The Search for Rational Drug Control,* 4–21, for a fine analysis of the report and its ideological assumptions.

[9]See Gerald L. Klerman,"Psychotropic Hedonism vs. Pharmacological Calvinism," *Hastings Center Report* 2 (4) (September 1972): 1–3.

[10]See Thomas Szasz, *Our Right to Drugs: The Case for a Free Market* (Greenwood Press, 1992); David Boaz, "The Consequences of Prohibition," in Boaz, ed., *The Crisis in Drug Prohibition*; and the speech delivered by Milton Friedman to the Fifth International Conference on Drug Policy Reform, Washington, D.C., 16 November 1991.

[11]See David A. J. Richards, *Sex, Drugs, Death, and the Law: An Essay on Human Rights and Overcriminalization* (Totowa, N.J.: Rowman and Littlefield, 1982), 157–214.

[12]See, generally, the collection of articles in Thomas H. Murray, Willard Gaylin, and Ruth Macklin, eds., *Feeling Good and Doing Better: Ethics and Nontherapeutic Drug Use* (Clifton, N.J.: Humana Press, 1984), in particular the concluding article by Ruth Macklin, "Drugs, Models, and Moral Principles," 187–213. Also see James B. Bakalar and Lester Grinspoon, *Drug Control in a Free Society* (New York: Cambridge University Press, 1984), and Douglas Husak, *Drugs and Rights* (New York: Cambridge University Press, 1992).

[13]As John Kaplan wrote in 1988, "It is true that if the number of those dependent upon cocaine merely doubled, we would arguably be well ahead of the game, considering the large costs imposed by treating those users as criminals. But what if there were a fiftyfold increase in the number of those dependent on cocaine? We simply cannot guarantee that such a situation would not come to pass; since we cannot do so, it is the height of irresponsibility to advocate risking the future of the nation." See John Kaplan, "Taking Drugs Seriously," *The Public Interest* 92 (Summer 1988): 32–50. Avram Goldstein and Harold Kalant assert more confidently: "There is no reason to doubt that the increased costs to society [of drug legalization] would rival those now attributable to alcohol." See Avram Goldstein and Harold Kalant, "Drug Policy: Striking the Right Balance," *Science* 249 (28 September 1990): 1513–21.

[14]See Andrew Weil, *The Natural Mind: An Investigation of Drugs and the Higher Consciousness* (Boston: Houghton Mifflin, 1972, revised edition 1986), 29. Weil credits Timothy Leary and Richard Alpert with first recognizing the importance

of these two variables. The significance of "set and setting" is examined at length in Norman E. Zinberg, *Drug, Set, and Setting: the Basis for Controlled Intoxicant Use* (New Haven, Conn.: Yale University Press, 1984).

[15]See, for instance, Lawrence O. Gostin, "Compulsory Treatment for Drug-Dependent Persons: Justifications for a Public Health Approach to Drug Dependency," *Milbank Quarterly* 69 (4) (1991): 561–93.

[16]See Nathan S. Kline, "The Future of Drugs and Drugs of the Future," *Journal of Social Issues* 27 (3) (1971): 73–87; Wayne O. Evans and Nathan S. Kline, eds., *Psychotropic Drugs in the Year 2000* (Springfield, Ill.: Charles C. Thomas, 1971); Alexander Shulgin and Ann Shulgin, *PIHKAL: A Chemical Love Story* (Berkeley, Calif.: Transform Press, 1991); Ronald K. Siegel, *Intoxication: Life in Pursuit of Artificial Paradise* (New York: E. P. Dutton, 1989), 298–317; and Henry B. Clark, *Altering Behavior: The Ethics of Controlled Experience* (Newbury Park, Calif.: SAGE Publications, 1987). A particularly bleak and pessimistic perspective is provided in Morton A. Kaplan, "2042: A Choice of Futures—A Nightmare," *The World & I* (January 1992): 108–115.

[17]Note that the "needle park" experiment in Zurich, Switzerland, from 1990 to 1992 shared little in common with the sort of "supermarket" model developed here. Production and distribution of drugs remained illegal, the place of sale was strictly limited to one small park, and the entire scheme was developed within a fairly strict prohibitionist context. Much the same is true of the "open air" illicit drug markets in many urban ghettos. See Arnold S. Trebach, "Lessons from Needle Park," *The Washington Post,* 17 March 1992.

[18]See David T. Courtwright, *Dark Paradise: Opiate Addiction in America before 1940* (Cambridge, Mass.: Harvard University Press, 1982); and see Ethan A. Nadelmann, "Historical Perspectives on Drug Prohibition and its Alternatives," *American Heritage* (forthcoming).

[19]See, for instance, Michael R. Aldrich, "Legalize the Lesser to Minimize the Greater: Modern Applications of Ancient Wisdom," *Journal of Drug Issues* 20 (1990): 543–53.

[20]Controlled consumption of heroin is examined in Zinberg, *Drug, Set and Setting.* Controlled consumption of cocaine is examined in Dan Waldorf, Craig Reinarman, and Sheila Murphy, *Cocaine Changes: the Experience of Using and Quitting* (Philadelphia: Temple University Press, 1991), and in Peter Cohen, *Cocaine Use in Amsterdam in Non Deviant Subcultures* (Amsterdam: Instituut voor Sociale Geografie, Universiteit van Amsterdam, 1989).

[21]See Stanton Peele, *Diseasing of America: Addiction Treatment Out of Control* (Lexington, Mass.: Lexington Books, 1989), who further observes that most drug abusers eventually quit or curtail their destructive behavior without resort to conventional treatment programs. Also see Charles E. Faupel, *Shooting Dope: Career Patterns of Hard-Core Heroin Users* (Gainesville: University of Florida Press, 1991).

[22]US Department of Justice, Bureau of Justice Statistics, *Sourcebook of Criminal Justice Statistics—1990* (Washington, D.C.: US Government Printing Office, 1991), 347; and US National Institute on Drug Abuse, *National Household Survey on Drug Abuse: Highlights 1988* (Washington, D.C.: Department of

Health and Human Services, Alcohol, Drug Abuse and Mental Health Administration, 1990), 8.

23*The Gallup Poll Monthly*, Nos. 288 and 303, reprinted in *Sourcebook of Criminal Justice Statistics—1990*, 347.

24Ibid.

25*National Household Survey on Drug Abuse: Highlights 1988*, 44.

26Ibid., 8, 45–50.

27Ibid., 17–22.

28In a nationwide poll commissioned by Richard Dennis and the Drug Policy Foundation, 4 percent of the 1401 respondents said that they would be "very likely" to try marijuana if it were legal, 6 percent said they would be "somewhat likely," 8 percent said "not very likely," and 81 percent said "not at all likely." Asked the same question about the legalization of cocaine, 2 percent said they would be "very likely" or "somewhat likely," 4 percent said "not very likely," and 93 percent said "not at all likely." Similarly, in the annual survey of American high school students conducted by the Monitoring the Future Project at the University of Michigan, 73 percent of respondents said they would not use marijuana even if it were legal, 11 percent said they would use it about as often as they do now, or less, 7 percent said they might try it, and only 3 percent said they would use it more often than at present. See Lloyd D. Johnston, Patrick O'Malley, and Jerald G. Bachman, *Drug Use Among American High School Seniors, College Students and Young Adults, 1975–1990* (Rockville, Md.: National Institute on Drug Abuse, 1991), 141–42.

29See Richard H. Blum & Associates, *Society and Drugs* (San Francisco: Jossey-Bass, 1969), 25–44.

30See National Research Council, National Academy of Sciences, *Evaluating AIDS Prevention Programs* (Washington, D.C.: National Academy Press, 1988); and the report by the National Commission on AIDS, *The Twin Epidemics of Substance Abuse and HIV* (Washington, D.C., 1991).

31See Thomas Szasz, *Ceremonial Chemistry: The Ritual Persecution of Drugs, Addicts, and Pushers* (Anchor Books, 1975).

32See Stanton Peele, *The Meaning of Addiction: Compulsive Experience and Its Interpretation* (Lexington, Mass.: Lexington Books, 1985); and John Booth Davies, *The Myth of Addiction* (Philadelphia, Pa.: Harwood Academic Publishers, 1992).

33The Australian policy is analyzed in Robin Room, "The Dialectic of Drinking in Australian Life: From the Rum Corps to the Wine Column," *Australian Drug and Alcohol Review* 7 (1988): 413–37. The British policy is assessed in Arthus Shadwell, *Drink in 1914–1922: A Lesson in Control* (London: Longmans, Green & Co., 1923). The impact of Prohibition on alcohol consumption and alcohol-related ills in the United States is assessed in John P. Morgan, "Prohibition is Perverse Policy: What Was True in 1933 Is True Now," in Krauss and Lazear, eds., *Searching for Alternatives*, 405–23; Mark Thornton, *The Economics of Prohibition* (Salt Lake City: University of Utah Press, 1992); and Jeffrey A. Miron and Jeffrey Zweibel, "Alcohol Consumption during Prohibition," *American Economic Review* 81 (2) (1991): 242–47. More generally, see Ethan A. Nadelmann, "Response to Letters," *Science* 246 (1989): 1102–1103; and Harry G. Levine and Craig Reinarman, "From Prohibition to Regulation: Lessons from Alcohol Policy for Drug Policy," *Milbank Quarterly* 69 (3) (1991): 461–94.

[34]Early twentieth-century models of alcohol control, many of which allowed adults to import alcoholic beverages into "dry" locales, are analyzed in Raymond B. Fosdick and Albert L. Scott, *Toward Liquor Control* (New York: Harper & Brothers, 1933); Leonard V. Harrison and Elizabeth Laine, *After Repeal: A Study of Liquor Control Administration* (New York: Harper & Brothers, 1936); and Reginald E. Hose, *Prohibition or Control? Canada's Experience with the Liquor Problem, 1921–1927* (New York: Longmans, Green & Co., 1928). The modification in F.D.A. policy is discussed in James H. Johnson, *How to Buy Almost Any Drug Legally Without a Prescription* (New York: Avon Books, 1990).

[35]See, for instance, David Dixon, *From Prohibition to Regulation: Bookmaking, Anti-Gambling, and the Law* (Oxford: Clarendon Press, 1991).

[36]US Department of Justice, Bureau of Justice Statistics, "Drugs and Jail Inmates, 1989" (August 1991), 1, 9.

[37]See Mark H. Haller, "Bootleggers as Businessmen: From City Slums to City Builders," in David E. Kyvig, ed., *Law, Alcohol, and Order: Perspectives on National Prohibition* (Westport, Conn.: Greenwood Press, 1985), 139–57.

[38]See D. M. Warburton, "Internal Pollution," *Journal of Biosocial Science* 10 (1978): 309–19; and Ruth Cooperstock, "Current Trends in Prescribed Psychotropic Drug Use," in *Research Advances in Alcohol and Drug Problems* 3 (1976): 297–316.

[39]Some of these issues are considered in John P. Morgan and Doreen V. Kagan, eds., *Society and Medication: Conflicting Signals for Prescribers and Patients* (Lexington, Mass.: Lexington Books, 1983).

[40]But also see Chester N. Mitchell, "Deregulating Mandatory Medical Prescription," *American Journal of Law and Medicine* 12 (2) (1986): 207–39.

[41]See Peter Temin, *Taking Your Medicine: Drug Regulation in the United States* (Cambridge, Mass.: Harvard University Press, 1980), and Peter Temin, "The Origin of Compulsory Drug Prescriptions," *Journal of Law and Economics* 22 (April 1979): 91–105.

[42]See Sam Peltzman, "The Health Effects of Mandatory Prescriptions," *Journal of Law and Economics* 30 (October 1987): 207–38, and Sam Peltzman, "By Prescription Only . . . or Occasionally?" *AEI Journal on Government and Society* (3/4) (1987): 23–28.

[43]Peter Temin, "Costs and Benefits in Switching Drugs from Rx to OTC," *Journal of Health Economics* 2 (1983): 187–205.

[44]See the excellent drug education text by Andrew Weil and Winifred Rosen, *Chocolate to Morphine: Understanding Mind-Active Drugs* (Boston: Houghton Mifflin, 1983). Also see David F. Duncan, "Drug Abuse Prevention in Post-Legalization America: What Could It Be Like?" *The Journal of Primary Prevention* 12 (4): 317–22; I. Clements, J. Cohen, and J. Kay, *Taking Drugs Seriously: A Manual of Harm Reduction Education on Drugs* (Liverpool: Healthwise, 1990); David F. Duncan and Robert S. Gold, *Drugs and the Whole Person* (New

York: Macmillan, 1985); and Ruth C. Engs, *Responsible Drug and Alcohol Use* (New York: Macmillan, 1979).

[45]The efficacy of antismoking campaigns is discussed in Kenneth E. Warner, "The Effects of the Anti-Smoking Campaign On Cigarette Consumption," *American Journal of Public Health* 67 (1977): 645–50; and, by the same author, "Effects of the Anti-Smoking Campaign: An Update," *American Journal of Public Health* 79 (1989): 144–51. Also see Martin Raw, Patti White, and Ann McNeill, *Clearing the Air: A Guide for Action on Tobacco* (London: British Medical Association, 1990). The Partnership's advertisements are evaluated favorably in the Committee on the Value of Advertising, *What We've Learned About Advertising from The Media-Advertising Partnership for A Drug-Free America* (New York: American Association of Advertising Agencies, 1990). More critical analysis is provided in Richard Blow, "How to Decode the Hidden Agenda of the Partnership's Madison Avenue Propagandists," *Washington City Paper* 11 (49) (6–12 December 1991): 29–35; Cynthia Cotts, "Hard Sell in the Drug War," *The Nation* 254 (9) (9 March 1992): 300–302; and Lynn Zimmer, "The Partnership for a Drug-Free America and the Politics of Fear," paper delivered to the Fifth International Conference on Drug Policy Reform, Washington, D.C., 15 November 1991.

[46]See "How to Launch a Nationwide Drug Menace," in Edward M. Brecher and the Editors of Consumer Reports, *Licit and Illicit Drugs* (Boston: Little, Brown and Co., 1972).

[47]See "The Promise of Prozac," *Newsweek,* 26 March 1990; Fran Schumer, "Bye-Bye, Blues: A New Wonder Drug for Depression," *New York,* 18 December 1989; and the more balanced "Beating Depression," *U.S. News & World Report,* 5 March 1990.

[48]See F. Earle Barcus and Susan M. Jankowski, "Drugs and the Mass Media," *Annals of the American Academy of Political and Social Science* 417 (1975): 86–100; Patrick T. MacDonald and Rhoda Estep, "Prime Time Drug Depictions," *Contemporary Drug Problems* 12 (1985): 419–37; William Braden, "LSD and the Press," in B. Aaronson and H. Osmond, eds., *Psychedelics* (New York: Doubleday, 1970); Jock Young, "Drugs and the Mass Media," *Drugs and Society* 1 (November 1971): 14–18; and Craig Reinarman and Harry G. Levine, "Crack in Context: Politics and Media in the Making of a Drug Scare," *Contemporary Drug Problems* 16 (1989): 535–77.

[49]478 U.S. 328, 92 L. Ed. 266, 106 S. Ct. 2968 (1986).

[50]See Sylvia A. Law, "Addiction, Autonomy and Advertising," *Iowa Law Review* 54 (1992); and Peter Hirsch, "Advertising and the First Amendment," in Trebach and Zeese, eds., *New Frontiers in Drug Policy,* 404–407.

[51]See Joe B. Tye, Kenneth E. Warner, and Stanton A. Glantz, "Tobacco Advertising and Consumption: Evidence of a Causal Relationship," *Journal of Public Health Policy* 8 (1987): 492–508. The debate over tobacco advertising is aired in *Advertising of Tobacco Products: Hearings before the Subcommittee on Health and the Environment of the Committee on Energy and Commerce,* House of Representatives, 99th Cong., 2nd Sess. (1986) (Serial No. 99–167). The debate over alcohol advertising is aired in *Alcohol Advertising: Hearing Before The Subcommittee on Children, Family, Drugs and Alcoholism of the Committee on*

Labor and Human Resources, United States Senate, 99th Cong., 1st Sess. (1985) (S. Hrg. 99–16), and *Beer and Wine Advertising: Impact of Electronic Media: Hearing Before the Subcommittee on Telecommunications, Consumer Protection, and Finance of the Committee on Energy and Commerce,* House of Representatives, 99th Cong., 1st Sess. (1985) (Serial No. 99–16).

[52]See Alison Masson and Paul H. Rubin, "Plugs for Drugs," *Regulation* (September/October 1986), 37–53, which argues for fewer restrictions on prescription drug advertising.

The Journal of Drug Issues 24(2), 179-225 1994

WOMEN AND DRUGS REVISITED: FEMALE PARTICIPATION IN THE COCAINE ECONOMY

Jeffrey Fagan

Recent changes in illicit drug use and drug markets, and simultaneous changes in the social and economic contexts where drugs are bought and sold, suggest the possibility of significant shifts in women's involvement in drugs. The interaction between rapidly changing social structures and drug markets provides an explanatory framework for women's participation in the cocaine economy of New York City in the late 1980s. Data on both legal and illegal behaviors and incomes were collected through interviews with N=311 women from two northern Manhattan neighborhoods with high concentrations of crack use and selling. Women were involved extensively in both drug selling and nondrug crimes as part of diverse income strategies. Drug incomes and expenses dominated the economic lives of women in the cocaine economy. Higher incomes from drug selling were inversely related to prostitution and legal work. Prostitution, property crimes and assaults increased with the frequency of crack and cocaine use. Although women remain disadvantaged in highly gendered street networks of drug users, some women have constructed careers in illegal work that have insulated them from the exploitation that characterizes heavy cocaine and crack use. Although prostitution is a common role for many women, changes in the status of women in drug markets are evident in the relatively high incomes some achieve from selling and their diverse roles in the cocaine economy.

Women historically have received little attention in research on drug and alcohol use. For many years, the belief that men vastly outnumbered women as users and dealers justified the omission of gender as a variable in drug research. When women were the focus of research, variation in paradigms for men and women led to vastly different pictures of drug use by gender. While research on men focused on their lives as drug users or sellers (e.g., Preble and Casey 1969; Waldorf 1973; Agar 1973), research on women focused on their deviance from gender roles, the public health threats of drug use during pregnancy, or their psychopathology (Colten and Marsh 1984). Although research on women's drug use increased in the 1970s, it applied theories and models developed from men's experiences with heroin to explain gender differences. These filters limited the

---

Jeffrey Fagan, Ph.D., is associate professor in the School of Criminal Justice of Rutgers University. His current research examines the involvement of women in drug selling, the impacts of criminal and civil sanctions for domestic violence, and the dynamics of crime and drug markets in economically distressed urban neighborhoods. He is editor of the *Journal of Research in Crime and Delinquency*. Address correspondence to Jeffrey Fagan, School of Criminal Justice, Rutgers University, 15 Washington Street, Newark, N.J., 07102.

relevance of knowledge when applied to women's lives (Daly and Chesney-Lind 1988; Simpson 1989).

Research that focused on the lives of women drug users increased following the heroin crises in the 1970s. The results challenged earlier notions about women and drugs. Female drug use was situated in the literatures on prostitution (Goldstein 1979), "street hustling" (Valentine 1978; Rosenbaum 1981; Miller 1986), and crime (Anglin and Hser 1987). Rosenbaum (1981) described how heroin use reduced women's options for income. Women sold drugs as part of a diversified income strategy, but they also sold to support their own or their lovers' habits. Prostitution became the most salient income source for many. Much of the research in this era focused on the role of domestic arrangements and crime partnerships with males in shaping women's involvement in drugs (see, for example, Rosenbaum 1981; Pettiway 1987; but see Adler 1985 for a different view).

Recent changes in illicit drug use and drug markets, and simultaneous changes in the social and economic contexts where drugs are bought and sold, suggest the possibility of significant shifts in women's involvement in drugs. Three factors in particular have changed the dynamics and contexts of drug use and selling for women. First, the increased availability of inexpensive cocaine products, especially cheap smokable cocaine, made possible serious drug use without the risks of injection or physiological addiction (Bourgois 1989; Hamid 1990; Waldorf, Reinarman, and Murphy 1991). Smoking cocaine also carried with it the risk of high-rate drug use and dependency (Siegel 1987; Reinarman, Waldorf, and Murphy 1989; Williams 1992). The expansion of cocaine markets and lower price of cocaine made possible new forms of drug selling for both men and women (Johnson, Hamid and Morales 1990; Fagan 1992; Baskin, Sommers and Fagan 1993). Easier access to cocaine accelerated the developmental progression from "gateway" use of alcohol and marijuana to serious drug use among both men and women, and may have contributed to more prevalent and frequent cocaine use in inner cities (Golub and Johnson 1993).

Second, dramatic structural shifts in the social and economic compositions of inner cities changed the social organization of drug use and selling (Johnson, Hamid, and Morales 1990; Fagan 1992; Fagan and Chin 1991; Hamid n.d.). The loss of millions of manufacturing jobs in large cities since the 1960s (Kasarda 1988) led to dramatic shifts in the gender/age composition of inner-city neighborhoods. The proportion of adult males to females declined sharply from 1960 to 1980, and the proportion of female-headed households increased dramatically (Wilson 1987; Wacquant and Wilson 1989).[1] Many of these households had incomes below the poverty line (Jencks and Peterson 1991), and participation in the growing informal economy in inner cities became part of the diverse network of income sources for poor women (Sassen-Koob 1989). The influences of "female old heads" on young women weakened as neighborhoods grew poorer and younger (Anderson 1990; Baskin et al. 1993). With the expansion of the drug economy and its opportunities for "crazy money" (Williams 1989), street-smart girls (and boys) rejected the old heads' lessons about life and the work ethic. Thus, changes in population composition and labor market access may have weakened the informal controls that regulated drug networks and the people who participate in them.

Third, the demand for cheap cocaine products in the 1980s exceeded the capacity of existing drug distribution systems, creating new opportunities for both men and women to buy and sell cocaine and other drugs (Johnson et al. 1990; Goldstein et al. 1991). The growing cocaine economy improved access to supplies, expanded entry-level roles in drug distribution, made possible entry into drug selling with a small capital investment, and created "controlled" selling territories with a guaranteed income (Hamid 1990; Williams 1989; Johnson et al. 1990). However, to the extent that the social organization of the informal economy mirrors the formal economy, changing drug markets may have created opportunities for drugs and income that retained many of the traditional gender distinctions that characterize both work and drug networks (Maher and Curtis 1993).

To assess these changes, this article examines women's participation in the cocaine economy of New York City in the late 1980s. The interaction between rapidly changing social structures and drug markets provides an explanatory framework for revisiting women's participation in drug markets. Changes in drug markets, the population makeup of inner cities, and the informal economic arrangements in inner cities suggest parallel changes in women's participation as buyers and sellers in the street-level drug economy now dominated by cocaine products (Curtis and Maher, n.d.; Simpson 1991; Johnson, Hamid, and Morales 1990a; Johnson et al. 1990; Fagan 1992; Williams 1989; Pettiway 1987; Hamid 1990; Baskin et al. 1993; Inciardi, Lockwood, and Pottieger 1993). These changes are likely to affect patterns of drug use and their relation to drug-selling, nondrug crimes, income and income-producing strategies, the structure of women's drug selling organizations, and the social networks of women drug users. These dimensions are examined for a sample of women active in the large and active cocaine economy of New York City.

Background

From opium use to crack, gender roles and expectations have shaped explanations of women's involvement in drugs for over a century. Early observers of opium use among Chinese immigrants in New York in the 1880s noticed that the only white customers in opium dens were female prostitutes (Sante 1991). Opium dens were the forerunners of the contemporary crack house, including distinctions among classes of users and suppliers. Lowest on the social scale of opium users were those who got high on *bunk yen*, the ambient fumes from people smoking the higher grade pills, or *li yuen*. Just up the scale from the *bunk yen* were people who smoked the scrapings from the opium bowl, called the *gee yen*. As opium dens began to spread outside Chinese neighborhoods, opium became popular among "cheap actors, race track touts, . . . *prostitutes and showgirls* (emphasis added, Sante 1991:147, citing Stephen Crane). Such portrayals of women's opium use ignored the considerable number of middle-class women who were widely involved in opiate and cocaine use in the late nineteenth and early twentieth centuries in the United States (Musto 1973; Courtwright 1982). Nevertheless, the problem of female drug use was studied and defined in this era from the large number of prostitutes using opium who entered prisons following "reform" efforts such as the Lexow Commission, and later on the passage of the Harrison Act in 1914.

Accounts of modern day crack houses describe similar scenes. Those without the wherewithal to buy rocks often are seen on their knees in crack houses picking up morsels from rocks or scraping the last of the residue from crack pipes (French

1993; Hamid 1990; Bourgois 1989; Williams 1992; Bourgois and Dunlap 1993). Women are more likely to occupy these lower rungs of the social world of crack use (Inciardi, Lockwood, and Pottieger 1993; Ratner 1993), in part because they are seen as uncontrolled drug users willing to trade sex for drugs, but also because they are thought to have little access to drug supplies (Williams 1992). French (1993) points out that prostitutes and women users held the lowest status in the social hierarchy of social street drug networks, with abstinent dealers at the highest rungs. Their absence from the ranks of dealers relegated women to lower statuses, and their reliance on sex — a commodity under their control — as a means of barter for drugs was equated with loss of sexual control. Thus, the history of women's drug use has been equated in the popular and scientific literature with sexual promiscuity and other forms of gender role deviance.

The problems of women and drugs continue today to be viewed through the lens of gender role deviance, where the risks to children and sexual promiscuity become the foci of research and law (Roberts 1991). Drug use among women has been viewed as double deviance: social deviance from normative behaviors and gender-role deviance from the expected female role of nurturer (Ettorre 1992). *Illicit* drug use by women further violates gender roles and carries differential risks of social exclusion and legal sanction. Women who used drugs were seen as abandoning their moral stewardship and maternal roles (Ettore 1992). Cocaine, heroin, and other addictive substances are the top of a hierarchy of drugs, and their use by women may be interpreted as a sign of loss of control or instability (Inciardi, Lockwood, and Pottieger 1993).[2] The closer supervision and social monitoring of women's activities guarantees that their deviance will result in greater conflicts with family and community (Hagan, Simpson, and Gillis 1987).

In part, the perception of women's illicit drug use as more deviant than men's comes from the consistently higher rate of men's drug use (Erickson and Murray 1989). And the higher up on the drug hierarchy, the greater the gender imbalance (Inciardi, Lockwood, and Pottieger 1993). Thus, women users are more easily and more often labeled as "deviant" and likely to suffer additional legal and social consequences. Gender-based sanctions include criminal prosecutions for child abuse targeted at pregnant drug users (but not their male partners), suspension of public assistance or loss of public housing, and termination of parental rights (Roberts 1991). The presence of children paradoxically serves as a barrier for many women seeking entry to residential treatment.

Research on women and drugs has tended to overlook sociocultural and contextual factors, preferring instead to focus on gender role contradictions and subcultural processes. Gender roles also are overlooked in research on the informal economy and street networks where much illicit drug activity takes place. The broader structure of drug markets also has not been considered as a variable influencing women and drugs. Yet much of the prior research has been situated in the contexts of specific drugs and social contexts. Accordingly, the social processes that shaped the lives of women in drug markets may be specific to particular times and structural conditions. We examine these contexts to determine how recent changes in drugs, drug markets and socioeconomic contexts might alter these social processes.

Narrowing Options and Street Networks

Most explanations of women's involvement in drug markets in the United States are situated in the particular time and place of the recent heroin era, the twenty-year period beginning in the early 1960s.[3] Rosenbaum's (1981) important study showed how involvement with heroin typically narrowed the options for income production and social interactions among women. Women heroin users also risked being labelled as emotionally unstable and sexually promiscuous (Colten and Marsh 1984; Stephens 1991; Erickson and Murray 1991), effectively cutting off their participation in conventional economic activities and social circles. They also risked conflicts with and exclusion from social institutions that provide guardianship over women (Baskin, Sommers, and Fagan 1993; Hagan 1989). The natural history of women users' social interactions was characterized by becoming socially inundated in hustling, scoring, and doing heroin (Rosenbaum 1981). One consequence was increasing involvement in street networks comprised of addicts, decreasing contacts with nonusers, and the development of a social identity based not on drug use but on the culture surrounding it (Waldorf 1973).[4] Stephens (1991) describes this a process of role engulfment, with increasing commitment to a street addict role and social identity.

These gender-based roles for women heroin users tended to persist throughout their drug use careers. They were reinforced by gender roles within networks of street drug users and by the physiological effects of injected opiates. For example, domestic arrangements often mediated women's initiation into heroin use (Stephens 1991; Blom and van den Berg 1989), but heroin itself quickly replaced the boyfriend/spouse arrangement as the focus of their relationship (Rosenbaum 1981). However, women were more likely to obtain drugs from men than buying them directly, share needles (usually with men), and use drugs with others (usually males) (Rosenbaum 1981). According to Stephens (1991), women became addicted more quickly once initiated, and tended to have larger habits (in dollars). Rosenbaum (1981) suggests that prostitution may provide enough income to make larger habits possible. Thus, for women, involvement in heroin use meant social immersion in street drug networks where available roles were highly gendered.

For example, File (1976) noted several roles for women heroin addicts in street drug networks that were stereotypically female: hustling and prostitution, legal work (supplemented by hustling), women dependent on men for money and drugs, a small number of drug sellers, and "bag followers." The latter were women attached domestically to drug dealers and were easily able to obtain their drugs this way. Several studies of female addicts show that they rarely were involved in violent crimes, robbery, or large-scale theft or burglary (Eldred and Washington 1976; Rosenbaum 1981; Miller 1986; Stephens 1991).

Drug selling traditionally also has been a highly gendered activity (Preble and Casey 1969; Johnson et al. 1985; Adler 1985; Williams 1989, 1992). Women were rarely active for long periods in street drug selling, and domestic arrangements often mediated women's participation in both drug use and selling (Rosenbaum 1981; Valentine 1978; Miller 1986; Hunt 1990). For example, prior to the growth of street-level cocaine markets, women sellers usually were limited to roles as "holders" or peripheral members of male-dominated dealing groups (Goldstein 1979). Research on women and heroin suggest that being cut off from boyfriends/husbands who supply the women's drug habits, forced women into drug dealing only until consistent access to drugs vis-a-vis a lover is restored (Adler 1985; Inciardi et al. 1993; Miller 1986; Rosenbaum 1981).

Accordingly, options within two aspects of daily life became truncated after regular heroin use: how to get money, and what social networks were available.

Gender played an important role in each of these dimensions of "street life." Although prostitution and other criminal activity often preceded involvement in heroin (and other street drugs), the heavy expenses of heroin use required a diverse array of income sources. These incomes came mainly through illegal activity (Anglin and Hser 1987; Valentine 1978; Miller 1986), since heavy involvement as a user reduced the options for women to engage in legal work (Hunt 1990; Rosenbaum 1981). As heavy drug use increased, dependence on illegal incomes increased. Therefore, women often doubled up in drug distribution and prostitution both to "make a living" as well as skim or buy drugs with their "profits" (Rosenbaum 1981; Miller 1986; Waterston 1993). As involvement with heroin increased, the gendered world of drug distribution made it difficult for women to make sufficient money from selling to supply their drug needs (Adler 1985; Hser, Anglin and McGlothlin 1987). Access to supplies and viable roles in selling were difficult for women (Johnson et al. 1985). Although dealing provided access to small supplies of drugs, it provided little money for other needs. It was a less attractive economic choice than hustling, fraud, theft or prostitution.

For heroin users, prostitution was a common alternative that may have been preferable because of the gendered nature of other criminal enterprises (Blom and van den Berg 1989). In crime partnerships with males, women often were consigned to roles as look-outs while their men did the heavy and sometimes violent work associated with criminal enterprise (Pettiway 1987). Women also played a passive role simply as holders and/or users of stolen property or drugs, or were asked to provide support services for criminally active male members of domestic and boyfriend networks (Rosenbaum 1981). They contributed income from such crimes as fraudulent check cashing, prostitution, shoplifting, and other gendered types of criminal involvement, as well as providing sex, food, and housekeeping (Adler 1985; Blom and van den Berg 1989; Miller 1986; Johnson et al. 1985; Steffensmeier 1983). These relationships were exploitive, however, where women's incomes often supported either crime partnerships with men or men's drug use. The gender disparities in this informal economy mirrored the disadvantage of women in the formal economy.

Prostitution provided an income source perhaps preferable to these other forms of "gendered" illicit work. Hunt (1990) suggested that women turn from drug dealing to prostitution because the latter is easier or more profitable. Women also may see prostitution as less dangerous than drug dealing, although the risks of victimization from customers and pimps are considerable (Goldstein 1979; Cohen 1980; Maher and Curtis 1993; Williams 1992). But involvement in prostitution also risks further narrowing of social networks. Abandoning crime partnerships and their social networks for higher incomes from prostitution leads to a reduced network of social contacts and support systems. Prostitution also may lead to breakup of domestic relationships with husbands, boyfriends or lovers, further narrowing their social networks. This marginalization also carries the risk of legal sanctions including the loss of children, and health risks including higher rates of drug use and HIV infection (Longshore et al. 1993; French 1993).

In sum, women's involvement with heroin often lead to increasingly narrower options for income and for social interactions. Women initiated heavy drug use through their participation in street hustles, deviant social networks, and crime partnerships with males. While hustling and other "gender-consistent" crimes supported drug use for both partners, drug use eventually replaced the relationship the domestic/boyfriend arrangement for many women. Deepening involvement with drugs shaped economic decisions, too, making prostitution a more profitable alternative. Even women who avoided prostitution and earned incomes from selling drugs or other hustles suffered the presumption of prostitution and social marginalization it brings (Rosenbaum 1981). To the extent that social networks mediated involvements with heroin (Biernacki 1986), the closing off of income sources and social contacts made it difficult for women to extricate themselves from these narrowing options.

Drug Eras and Changing Street Networks

By 1980, heroin use stabilized and even declined in inner cities. Heroin users became a small and aging group (see, for example: Boyle and Brunswick 1980; Goldstein et al. 1984; Johnson et al. 1990). There were only enough heroin initiates each year to replace those who died, were incarcerated, or discontinued its use (Kleiman 1992). Beginning in 1975, cocaine use rose in concert with the decline of heroin use (see, for example, Kozel and Adams 1985),[5] with the highest rates of cocaine powder use reported in the late 1970s and early 1980s (Kleiman 1992). Crack emerged in New York City in 1985, and in other urban areas shortly afterward (Belenko, Fagan, and Chin 1991).[6,7] In New York City, street drug markets expanded from the small number of heroin locations to a diversified network of cocaine distribution points that at times resembled festive bazaars (Zimmer 1987). As cocaine use supplanted heroin as the most widely used "serious" drug (Johnson et al. 1990; Kleiman 1992), the development of a cocaine economy among street drugs changed the contexts and dynamics of women's drug involvement. The unfolding of the cocaine HCL and crack eras brought changes in two dimensions that had shaped women's drug involvement in the past: the social contexts of drug use, and the drug itself.

Urban Change and Street Networks

The social and economic contexts of women's drug involvement changed extensively beginning in the 1970s.[8] Changing population composition destabilized social controls in poor urban neighborhoods. High rates of residential mobility followed the exodus of manufacturing jobs from cities. The exodus of middle-class residents eroded informal social control in poor neighborhoods as they moved to better housing elsewhere in the city or suburbs (see, for example, Anderson 1990 and Wilson 1987). Among those remaining in the increasingly poor inner cities, the ranks of unemployed adult males grew (Kasarda 1989; Tienda 1989b). As the relatively small population of heroin users aged out or desisted, new cocaine (powder, freebase and crack) initiation took place in a social context of increasing racial segregation, residential mobility, economic decline, and weakening social regulation.

Social controls for women and men were compromised as the guardianship of both institutions and "old heads" weakened. New female models emerged to compete with the declining influence of traditional old heads (Anderson 1990; Baskin et al. 1993). They displayed the "high life," buying fancy clothes, jewelry, drugs, and alcohol. Like its male counterpart, the "female old head" traditionally served as important community role models. These women believed in hard work, family life and "repeatedly and insistently told attentive boys and girls 'what was good for them'" (Anderson 1990:4). But as meaningful employment became increasingly scarce and drugs and crime became institutionalized in poor neighborhoods, both male and female "old heads" lost their prestige and authority.

The structural circumstances of women changed as well. Marriage rates declined (Mare and Winship 1991), and the percentage of female headed households (both with and without children) increased from 1970–80 (Jargowsky and Bane 1990; 1991). Stable employment rates among African-American women in the same period masked important differences between poor and non-poor African-American women. Employment for female African-American high school dropouts and unmarried mothers declined sharply, while employment and wages increased for married women (Corcoran and Parrott 1992). Thus, since skills became a critical marker of employment success, manufacturing job losses excluded unskilled African-American women from the workforce. The growth of the informal economy in New York City and other urban areas created both motivation and opportunity for unskilled women to participate in the legal and illegal informal enterprises (Sassen-Koob 1989). Marriage rates, unmarried mothers' employment rates, and the real value of welfare benefits declined simultaneously through the 1980s (Corcoran and Parrott 1992; Farley 1988). Accordingly, economic and social forces beginning in the 1970s led to higher, more concentrated, and persistent poverty with adverse effects specifically for women.

At the same time, the number and fortunes of African-American males in the twenty to thirty-five year age group declined (Wilson 1987). The ratio of males to females in poor neighborhoods dropped from 1970–80, and adolescents "coming up" in that time were as likely to be raised by a woman or within a female kinship network as by a household with an adult male (Ricketts and Sawhill 1988; Jencks 1991; Wacquant and Wilson 1989). Unemployment increased and wages decreased among African-American males from 1970–90 despite a labor shortage economy (Freeman 1991: Moss and Tilley,1991), weakening the social control functions of "old heads" and limiting the prospects for long-term economic stability and earnings of young men considering entry into the work force. At least part of the decline in marriage may be attributable to the decline in men's "marriage capital" from their declining economic fortunes and increased troubles with the law and drugs (Wilson 1987; Mare and Winship 1991; Kirschenman and Neckerman 1991; Sampson 1992).

The changing fortunes of young men and young women changed the social contexts of street networks of drug users. The declining status of young men may have diminished their "gatekeeper" and mediating roles in both conventional and street networks in poor neighborhoods. There were fewer males in poor neighborhoods, and those who remained or survived in poor inner city neighborhoods were less likely to have stable, legal long-term work. In neighborhoods with concentrations of African-American adolescents, young men were increasingly likely to be incarcerated or victims of homicide, weakening their position in street networks (Wilson 1991). Young women were less likely to be involved in domestic arrangements or crime partnerships with males,[9] and increasingly likely to be heads of households. At the same time, African-American women with low education or job skills were losing ground in wages and employment rates to other women (Corcoran and Parrott 1992), motivating their participation in the growing informal economy and/or a number of hustles to generate income. To the extent that these contextual changes altered the gender composition and statuses of males and females in street networks, the mediating influence of street networks on women's drug involvement was likely to be far weaker than among previous cohorts of heroin users.

Cocaine, Crack, and Drug Markets

The transition of street drug markets from heroin to cocaine and crack changed the social organization of drug use and selling (Johnson et al. 1990). Street-level drug selling in New York, for example, was a family-centered heroin and marijuana business until the 1980s, when new organizations developed to control distribution of cocaine (Curtis and Maher n.d.; Johnson et al. 1990). Coupled with the structural and contextual changes in street drug networks, changes in drugs and drug markets made possible new avenues and contexts for women to participate in drug use and selling.

First, the psychoactive and physiological effects of cocaine were quite different from heroin. Cocaine is a short-acting central nervous system stimulant.[10] Cocaine effects are relatively short lived, and the declining stimulation of pleasure centers leads to anxiety, edginess, and depression (Waldorf, Reinarman, and Murphy 1991). Users can ward off the effects of this "crash" by using more cocaine. Thus, cocaine sessions often entail binges of many hours (sleeping is obviated) of repeated use. The effects of smoking crack or cocaine freebase are more intense but similar. Reports from users suggested that smoking a rock of crack produced a brief (about twenty minutes) but intense high, followed by a "crash" and the rapid onset of depression with a compelling drive to get high again (Spitz and Rosecan 1987; Siegel 1987; Reinarman et al. 1989; Fagan and Chin 1991).

While heroin use involved a small number of consistent daily doses, cocaine and crack use were characterized by multiple purchases in relatively short periods of time. The psychoactive effects of heroin and methods of administration limited the volume of sales and the number of users. But cocaine was different in every way: a stimulant rather than a depressant, ingested in a variety of ways (nasally, smoked, or injected), and with a shorter half-life for the high. Moreover, cocaine HCL was portrayed for many years as a "safe" drug that was not addictive, did not interfere with other social activities, and whose use could be easily self-controlled (Siegel 1987; Waldorf, Reinarman, and Murphy 1991). The ability to use intense drugs without needles and their risk of HIV transmission, was an added appeal for some users (Fagan and Chin 1991). Accordingly, attractions of the drug itself made possible the entry of women in what they may have seen as safer forms of expensive and intense drug use.

Second, cocaine products became widely available as drug-selling points and organizations grew to meet the expanded demand (Zimmer 1987; Williams 1989). The cocaine HCL and crack markets were nurtured by repeat purchases by customers on lengthy sessions often lasting days. Demand for cocaine products was fueled by its short lasting effects, its relatively low unit cost ($10 to $20 for a vial with three rocks, or $10 for a small packet of powder), and its ease of use (no needles, only a pipe for smoking or tools for snorting). The interaction of the changing social circumstances of women in inner cities, the weakening of the dominance of males in street networks, and the expanded opportunities for cocaine use, made possible the initiation of women into serious drug use in ways far different from earlier drug eras.

Third, drug-selling became an attractive income option for young people with low education and job skills in a shrinking labor market. Young people in illicit enterprises began to talk about drug selling as "going to work" and the money earned as "getting paid" (Sullivan 1989; Padilla 1992). Young men and, increasingly women, had several employment options within drug markets: support roles (lookout, tout), manufacturing (cut, package, weigh), or direct street sales (Johnson et al. 1990; Goldstein et al. 1991). In contrast, the heroin markets from the 1970s were far smaller than the cocaine HCL and crack markets, both in total volume of sales and the average purchase amount and quantity (Johnson et al. 1990. Cocaine HCL and crack sales became institutionalized in New York City. In storefronts, from behind the counters in bodegas, on streetcorners, in crack or "freak" houses, and through several types of "fronts," drug selling was a common and visible feature of the neighborhoods (Hamid 1992a). Cocaine markets were relatively easy to enter, requiring a capital investment of only a few dollars to create a product for a seemingly endless demand (Fagan and Chin 1990, 1991). In the late 1980s, law enforcement officials characterized the crack industry as "capitalism gone mad" (*New York Times* 1989a, 1989b).

Accordingly, the expansion of drug markets may have simplified the entry of women into drug selling. For women users,whose sales provided money and drugs, drug selling was simplified by the expanded circles of users and the opportunities for selling. It was easy and cheap for women users to add cocaine and crack to the repertoire of drugs they used and traded socially. Their transition to drug selling may simply have extended their routine involvement in a variety of hustles such as fraud, larceny, and theft (Johnson et al. 1985; Hunt 1990; Murphy, Waldorf, and Reinarman 1991). For other women, drug selling may be an extension of illegal careers and an opportunity for increasing their crime incomes. Reuter and associates (1990) and Hunt (1990) suggest that the retail cocaine markets are unregulated, comprised of many individual entrepreneurs who work their own areas as they would a private business. Informal organizations formed along a freelance model where a small group of central players is surrounded by many short-term employees who engage in dealing intermittently (Hunt 1990). The decentralization and deregulation of drug selling removed many of the gender barriers to drug selling. However, to the extent that the informal economy mirrors the gender and stratification dynamics of the licit economy, women sellers were likely to continue to experience income differentials relative to males and more difficulty in reaching managerial positions or ownership of drug selling groups.

Finally, street-level sex markets have expanded in tandem with cocaine and especially crack markets. Chin and Fagan (1990) showed that both the prevalence and rates of prostitution increased for women following their initiation into crack use. Several studies (Hamid 1990; Bourgois 1989; Goldstein, Ouellett, and Fendrich 1992; French 1993; Inciardi et al. 1993) report a strong association between cocaine and crack use and extremely high rates of sexual intercourse and other sexual transactions.[11] Evidently, expanded sex markets surrounding active drug markets have attracted women to prostitution and concurrently, drug use. For others, high rate cocaine or crack use may have motivated their involvement in the expanded sex markets when other economic options were weak. Sex provides an opportunity for income that is less constricted than legal work, other crimes or drug selling, and may be especially appealing if opportunities in the informal economy are gendered and limited.

Yet while prostitution has traditionally been a part of income-producing activities for women users, the growth of cocaine and crack markets has brought disorganization to sex markets. Sex markets have become more chaotic, with price cutting and "viccing" (robbing customers) more common, and basic changes in the nature of sex work from vaginal intercourse to other acts (Ouellet et al. 1993; Maher and Curtis 1992). The expanded sex markets and the compulsive patterns of crack use also increased women's risks of victimization for money or sex. Disorganization in sex markets has eroded the traditional structures dominated by pimps on the street or madams in brothels. These have been replaced by drug dealers or operators of crack houses (Goldstein et al. 1992). Thus, if prostitution provides an avenue for cocaine use, it brings with it increased risks of violence and threats to health.

Hypotheses

The effects of structural changes on the composition of street networks, and changes in the social organization of drug use and selling, are likely to result in women's involvement in drug markets that differs extensively from earlier eras when heroin dominated street markets. These changes from earlier eras suggest several hypotheses about women's involvement in drug markets. First, women's drug-selling enterprises are likely to range from loosely organized groups of freelance operators to highly structured networks, including both mixed sex or single sex groups. The declining role of males in deviant street networks will result in some women occupying managerial and ownership positions in drug-dealing groups. Drug-dealing networks are more likely to have informal "familial" forms of social control and dealership, where turf is distributed by kin in much the same way as other scarce resources (Stack 1974). Second, the opportunities for income production through selling may be a protective factor in limiting women's involvement either in prostitution or more serious forms of street crime. That is, after controlling for drug use and other crimes, women involved in drug selling will have less income from prostitution than women who do not sell drugs. A similar relationship is likely for nondrug crimes: involvement in drug selling provides income that mitigates participation in the riskier businesses of robbery and other hustles. Finally, the disorganized cocaine crack markets will place women sellers at greater risk for victimization than women who avoid drug sales.

Methods

Samples

Interviews were conducted with 311 women from two northern Manhattan neighborhoods with high concentrations of crack use and selling: Washington Heights and Central Harlem.[12] The neighborhoods had experienced severe economic restructuring characteristic of the structural changes in urban centers nationally beginning in the 1960s. They also had active heroin markets in the 1970s and were flash points for the growth of cocaine and crack markets a decade later. Samples were recruited in each neighborhood from subpopulations with known concentrations of drug users and sellers: arrestees for drug possession and/or sales, a matched sample of residents of the study neighborhoods who were not under any formal social control, pretrial detainees, prison inmates, probationers and parolees, and participants in residential drug treatment programs.[13] Social and demographic characteristics of the sample are shown by neighborhood in Appendix A, classified by their involvement in independent or organized drug selling.[14]

Within each group, samples were constructed to represent different patterns of drug involvement: crack users or sellers, cocaine HCL users or sellers who were not involved with crack, heroin users or sellers, polydrug (primarily marijuana) users, and nonusers or sellers. Table 1 shows the proportion of the sample from each neighborhood in each of these sample strata. Overall, crack users or sellers comprised 62% of the sample. Cocaine and heroin users comprised 14% and 9.5%, respectively; the remainder were polydrug users.

Table 1
Distribution of Respondents by Legal Status and Self-Reported Primary Drug Involvement by Neighborhood

	Central Harlem	Washington Heights
N	153	158
Legal Status at Arrest (%)		
Not in legal or treatment systems	57.6	61.5
Arrested, not detained	11.2	9.1
In residential treatment	13.2	6.8
Detained, in jail or prison	12.2	15.2
On probation or parole	5.8	7.4
Primary Drug Involvement (%)		
Crack	61.6	62.5
Cocaine HCL	13.2	15.9
Heroin	11.6	7.4
Marijuana	9.9	9.3
Nonusers	3.7	4.9

Subject Recruitment

Arrestees were recruited from the Manhattan central booking facility. They were identified from special charge flags for crack and cocaine recorded by arresting officers on booking slips.[15] Referrals for interview were made by pretrial services interviewers during routine jail screening to determine eligibility for release on their own recognizance. Arrestees who made bail or were otherwise released were given cards that told them where and how to arrange for an interview. Detained arrestees were interviewed in the detention facility.

Street samples were recruited through chain referral or "snowball" sampling procedures (Biernacki and Waldorf 1981; Watters and Biernacki 1989), techniques appropriate for "hidden" populations whose population parameters are not well known, who have an uncertain probability of being represented in official records, and whose behaviors are not amenable to social surveys with the general population. These included non-crack drug arrestees; nonarrested neighborhood samples who were matched to the arrested samples on age, gender and ethnicity; and participants in two residential treatment programs in Manhattan. Several types of chain referral methods were used. Arrestees were asked to nominate a potential respondent who "is like you, from your neighborhood and about your age, but who has avoided arrest." Interviewers then sought out the nominees, or they were referred to the field office by friends. Chains also were developed among drug users and sellers who were known to the interviewers. Interviewers were members of a street research unit that maintained ethnographic contact and reconnaissance on drug scenes throughout the New York metropolitan area.[16]

Residential treatment clients were recruited from their programs based on nominations of crack and other drug users by administrators and clinical staff. Treatment residents who had been in the program for at least one month and met screening criteria for each drug user type were asked to participate in the study. Incarcerated drug offenders were identified from criminal history and drug-related information they provided at reception interviews, or from information in their arrest records that indicated cocaine HCL or crack charges.

A brief (ten item) screening interview was used to classify respondents' drug use or selling patterns and validate their reports. Respondents were classified by their primary drug involvement if they used (or sold) that drug on more than fifty occasions in their lifetime, and if they had not used (or sold) another substance more than that amount. Multiple drug users were classified according to the most frequent drug used or sold in the past year.

Procedures

Interviews were conducted in settings where they could not be overheard, and where the identity of the respondent was unknown to anyone in the immediate setting. Prison and detention interviews were conducted in empty classrooms, usually on weekends. Interviews with arrestees and street samples were conducted in a storefront location, libraries, coffee shops, or other neutral, public locales. Interviews lasted from one to two hours, with a short break after the first hour.

Respondents received $25 stipends plus $5 each for referrals of potential interviewees and location information for possible follow-up. Respondents also were given two subway tokens and a pack of cigarettes. Treatment respondents were not given the stipend; it was donated to the treatment program. The items were read aloud. Cards with the response sets were shown to respondents and the choices read aloud to minimize literacy problems. Interviews were conducted either in English or Spanish. In most instances, the interviewers and respondents were matched by gender and ethnicity.

Variables and Measures

Interview protocols included four domains of information: initiation into substance use or selling; lifetime and annual involvement with both substances and non-drug crimes; the social organization of substance use or selling; and, income sources and expenditures from both legitimate and illegal activities. A calendar was used to record respondents' month by month social status from 1984 to the interview: working or in school, treatment or detoxification programs, jails or prisons, or other institutions. For initiation, respondents were asked to describe processes of initiation into their primary drug: how, where and with whom did they initially use (or sell) the substance, how much money did they spend, and the time until the next use and regular use (if any). Their expectations and reactions to the substance were recorded through multiple response items.

Criminal career parameters were recorded through self-reports of lifetime estimates and annual frequencies of drug use, selling and non-drug crimes from 1984 to the present. Specific estimates were recorded for several types of drugs used or sold, as well as a list of twenty non-drug crimes. Items were worded in common language (e.g., "beat someone so badly they needed to see a doctor"). A categorical scale was used to record frequencies of specific behaviors, and mid-point means were used to calculate rates. This was chosen in lieu of self-reports of actual numbers of crimes, to minimize distortion from the skewed distribution of responses for the small percentage of high-rate users or offenders. The response set represented an exponential scale of frequency, with nine categories ranging from "one or two times" to "about 10,000."

To examine the social organization of drug use and selling, respondents were asked whether they had sold drugs as part of an organization, and to describe their organization using dimensions developed by Fagan (1989), Fagan and Chin (1990) and Johnson et al. (1990a) in studies of drug selling in street drug markets. Items asked for reports of their participation in specific roles in drug selling, roles that were evident in their selling organization, and social processes that existed within their group. For example, respondents were asked if their group had specific prohibitions against drug use or sanctions for rules violations. *Systemic violence* (Goldstein 1985) associated with drug dealing was operationally defined through eight items with specific types of violence. Respondents were asked whether they had experienced each of these violent events "regularly" in the course of their selling activity.

The economic lives of respondents were described through questions on income and expenditures. Monthly dollar amounts were reported using a categorical scale of dollar ranges, ranging from 1 (less than $100 per month) to 9 ($10,000 or more). This option was chosen over actual dollar reports to minimize distortion of dollar estimates and possible recall problems of long-term substance users.[17] Dollar estimates were recorded for both legitimate and illegitimate sources of income, and for expenditures both for living costs and for drugs.

The Study Neighborhoods

Table 2 shows the social structural changes in Washington Heights and Central Harlem in the decade preceding the crack crisis. By 1980, both neighborhoods reflected concentrations of the urban "underclass," regardless of whether the definitions are based on individual-level indicators of poverty (Jencks 1991) or location-based aggregate measures (Ricketts and Sawhill 1988; Jargowsky and Bane 1990). Although both neighborhoods contained then and now a disproportionate share of severely distressed households, the neighborhoods changed in markedly different ways from 1970–80.

Central Harlem in 1980 remained a homogeneously African-American community, but it became far poorer during the preceding decade. The population declined by one-third during the 1970s, while the percentage of families with incomes below poverty levels grew to over one in three. When adjusted for inflation, median income for families decreased by over 20% and nearly 50% for unrelated individuals in households. More than one in five families (22.5%) were receiving public assistance by 1980.[18] In nearly all of the twenty-nine census tracts, more than 20% of the population had incomes below poverty in 1980. Using a more conservative "underclass" threshold of 40% below poverty (Jargowsky and Bane 1988), nine census tracts were classified as underclass areas by 1980.

The percentage of married couples also declined significantly in this period, while the percentage of non-couple households increased sharply. By 1985, over 80% of all births were out of wedlock in Central Harlem, compared to 46.3% in Washington Heights (New York City Department of City Planning 1991). Infant mortality in Central Harlem was 21.1 per 1,000 births, a rate 250 times higher than Washington Heights. These trends suggest the flight from Central Harlem of working- and middle-class African-American families whose incomes were above poverty levels. The exodus of non-poor African-American families has been noted by Wilson (1987) and others as a critical antecedent of the formation of persistent and concentrated poverty.

Table 2
Neighborhood Social Structural and Economic Profiles, 1970–80

	Washington Heights			Central Harlem		
	1970	1980	% Change	1970	1980	% Change
Population	180,710	179,941	-0.4	159,336	105,794	-33.6
Age						
1–4	6.3	9.5	3.2	7.6	6.8	-1.1
5–17	15.9	15.7	-0.2	21.8	16.7	-5.1
18–24	10.3	12.4	2.1	9.9	10.8	0.9
25–44	25.0	28.8	3.8	25.7	24.6	-1.1
45–64	42.5	33.6	-8.9	35.0	41.1	6.1
Family Composition						
Husband-Wife[a]	76.8	59.5	-17.3	56.7	40.6	-16.1
Other w/o children	13.6	18.2	4.6	15.8	27.8	12.0
Other w/children	9.6	22.3	12.7	27.5	31.6	4.1
Ethnicity						
White	73.6	27.7	-45.9	2.0	0.6	-1.4
African-American	14.3	15.4	1.1	94.6	94.1	0.5
Other	1.8	1.8	0	0.3	0.5	-0.2
Hispanic	b	54.2	—	b	4.4	—
Puerto Rican	9.2	c	—	3.1	c	—
Asian	b	1.8	—	b	0.2	—
American Indian	b	0.2	—	b	0.2	—
Spanish Language[d]	30.7	54.2	23.5	5.0	4.4	-0.6
Foreign-Born	36.6	48.0	11.4	3.2	6.5	3.3
Education Completed[e]						
Not HS graduate	55.0	51.3	-3.7	67.8	57.2	-10.6
HS graduate	27.5	25.3	-2.2	24.7	28.8	4.1
Some college	7.7	10.6	2.9	4.6	8.8	4.2
College graduate	9.8	12.8	3.0	2.9	5.2	2.3
Income - Families[f]						
Below $10,000	60.0	39.7	-20.3	79.0	65.6	-3.4
% below poverty	9.0	23.9	14.9	22.9	34.5	11.6
Median	$8,879	$12,477	40.5	$6,137	$9,185	49.7
Adjusted Median[g]	$16,614	$12,477	-24.9	$11,483	$9,185	-20.0
Income - Unrelated Individuals						
% below poverty	26.4	N/A	—	34.5	N/A	—
Median	$6,882	$6,180	-10.2	$5,499	$3,813	-30.7

a. With or without children.
b. Included in OTHER in 1970.
c. Included in Hispanic in 1980.
d. Of any race in 1970.
e. Persons over 24 years of age.
f. Income for 1969, 1979.
g. 1970 median income converted to 1980 levels using the GNP Implicit Price Deflator for Personal Consumption Expenditures for the U.S., 1970–79 (U.S. Bureau of Labor Statistics, Tuesday Spot Market Price Indexes and Prices).

In Washington Heights, the white population of the neighborhood declined precipitously from 1970–80: nearly three in four residents in 1970 were white, compared to 27.7% in 1980.[19] Departing white residents were replaced by Hispanics, who accounted for over half the 1980 population. The growth in the Spanish-speaking population from 1970–80 (23.5%) and foreign born residents (12.0%) suggest that the neighborhood has become a context of reception for immigrant Hispanic families. The percentage of married couples declined by 17.1%, while single-parent households with children grew (12.7%). This occurred simultaneously with the increase in family poverty.

Family income in 1980 was below poverty for nearly one in four families, an increase of almost 15% since 1970. Median incomes in 1970, adjusted for inflation during the decade, were nearly 25% lower in 1980 for families, and about 15% for individuals. More than 20% of the population had incomes below poverty in 1980 in over half (*N*=17) of the thirty populated census tracts in the area. One in six residents received public assistance in 1980.

Table 3
Concentration of Poverty Within Neighborhood Census Tracts, 1970–80
(Number And Percent Of Tracts, Percent Change)

	1970		1980		% Change
	N	%	*N*	%	1970–80[a]
Central Harlem					
No. of census tracts	70	(100)	71	(100)	
20% poverty	31	(44)	49	(69)	56.8
40% povert	3	(4)	23	(32)	800.0
Underclass	4	(6)	9	(13)	116.7
Washington Heights					
No. of census tracts	107	(100)	111	(100)[b]	
20% poverty	30	(28)	61	(55)	96.4
40% poverty	2	(2)	21	(19)	850.0
Underclass	0	(0)	8	(7)	700.0[c]
New York City					
No. census tracts	2,156	(100)	2,203	(100)	
20% poverty	457	(21)	791	(36)	71.4
40% poverty	73	(3)	311	(14)	366.7
Underclass	27	(1)	140	(6)	500.0

Source: J. Kasarda, *Urban Underclass Database*. Chapel Hill: Univ. of North Carolina, 1992.

a. Percent changes computed on yearly percentage, not counts of census tracts.

b. Nine tracts had no population and were removed from the analysis

c. Percent change is infinite.

Table 3 provides another look at the growing concentration of poverty in these neighborhoods in the decade from 1970–80. We compared the number of census tracts in each neighborhood that met each of three poverty definitions: at least 20% of the population below poverty, at least 40% of the population below poverty, and tracts defined as "underclass" using an aggregate, location-based definition from Ricketts and Sawhill (1988). For all three measures, the concentration of poverty increased sharply during the 1970s in both neighborhoods. For the most restrictive category, "underclass" census tracts, the percentage of tracts in poverty more than doubled (to nine tracts) in Central Harlem and increased from zero to eight tracts in Washington Heights. Evidently, the rate of change was comparable for the two neighborhoods. However, the percentage of tracts in poverty in 1980 suggests that poverty was more concentrated in Central Harlem. For all three measures, the percentage of census tracts with high poverty concentrations was greater for that neighborhood.

The contrasts in these neighborhoods show two faces of poverty. While Central Harlem is a severely distressed area, Washington Heights is changing rapidly in its composition. Central Harlem remains homogeneously poor, with a declining population of families. As a context of entry for Spanish-speaking immigrants, Washington Heights shares many of the challenges of immigrant communities in New York and other cities. African-Americans, other non-American blacks, and Latinos have replaced non-Hispanic whites at the same time that the employment base has been transformed from a manufacturing to a service economy (Kasarda 1991) requiring skill levels generally not attained by inner-city residents. This has left large proportions of minority immigrants (or migrants from other parts of the United States) to live either in poverty or on public support, survive in unstable low-wage jobs or both licit and illicit activities within the informal economy, or to use entrepreneurial skills to develop small businesses.

Results

Drug and Crime Activity

Table 4 shows the zero-order correlations for the annualized frequency of drug use with drug selling and eight nondrug crimes.[20] Among the illicit drugs, correlations between use and sale of each specific drug were significant. That is, correlations between cocaine use and selling, crack use and selling, heroin use and selling, and marijuana use and selling were significant. However, there were inconsistent patterns of drug use and selling across drug types. Cocaine HCL use was associated with heroin sales, and crack use was correlated only with marijuana sales. These patterns suggest that drug use and selling among women occur within distinct social worlds of specific drugs. Women seem to use the drugs they sell, but polydrug use patterns are inconsistent. Drug use and sales appear to be reciprocal patterns, where access to specific drugs may facilitate immersion in a drug-specific social network.

There also were varied patterns of drug use and non-drug crimes. The correlations were less that .25, suggesting overall weak associations even when significant. Crack use was significantly correlated with six of the eight crime types. Fighting and assault were weakly associated with drug use, suggesting weak links between drug use and violence among this population. Robbery, shoplifting, and prostitution were correlated with most drug use, suggesting that income-producing hustles and crimes increased with the frequency of drug use. These patterns suggest that women are involved in a variety of illegal hustles and crimes with little evidence of specialization or concentration of any income-producing activities. However, the consistent associations of crack and nondrug crimes suggest that cocaine smoking intensifies drug-crime relationships perhaps even more extensively than heroin use.

Table 4
Zero-Order Correlation Matrix And Two-Tailed Probabilities For Annualized Frequency Of Drug Use By Drug Selling And Nondrug Crimes

		Drug Used				
Drug Sold		Cocaine HCL	Heroin	Marijuana	Alcohol	Crack
Cocaine HCL	*r*	.263	.120	.075	.110	.065
	p	.000	.035	.187	.052	.252
Heroin	*r*	.128	.200	-.023	.227	.078
	p	.024	.000	.687	.000	.172
Marijuana	*r*	.038	.027	.269	-.061	.121
	p	.502	.633	.000	.284	.033
Other	*r*	.044	-.051	.044	-.026	.030
	p	.436	.368	.436	.650	.594
Crack	*r*	.083	-.076	.227	-.057	.279
	p	.143	.180	.000	.320	.000
Nondrug Crimes						
Fencing	*r*	.147	.037	-.0001	-.005	.131
	p	.009	.521	.998	.931	.021
Robbery	*r*	.104	.140	.002	.019	.156
	p	.068	.014	.974	.735	.006
Burglary	*r*	-.047	.090	.094	.050	.086
	p	.407	.112	.098	.382	.130
Aggravated	*r*	.089	.060	.022	.049	.092
assault	*p*	.119	.294	.694	.387	.106
Shoplifting	*r*	.160	.198	.099	.175	.210
	p	.005	.000	.080	.002	.000
Theft	*r*	.080	.125	.021	.081	.183
	p	.159	.028	.715	.154	.001
Fighting	*r*	.115	.032	.113	.039	.224
	p	.042	.577	.047	.495	.000
Prostitution	*r*	.166	.197	-.053	.133	.208
	p	.003	.000	.355	.019	.000

Note: N=311.

Drug Use and Selling

Table 5 shows the prevalence and average annual frequencies of drug use and selling for the three-year period for the total sample. To clarify the role of drug

Table 5
Prevalence and Average Annual Rates of Drug Use and Drug Selling, by Type of Drug Selling, 1986-88

		Type of Drug Seller					
		Non Seller[a]	Independent Seller	Group Seller	Total Sample	Chi-Square	F-value
N		209	56	46	311		
Drug Use							
Alcohol	%	71.3	83.9	84.8	75.6	6.3 *	
	λ	240.1	401.6	313.0	284.5		2.62
Cocaine HCL	%	60.8	78.6	78.3	66.6	9.6 **	
	λ	368.4	578.6	492.2	432.6		1.99
Heroin	%	28.2	28.6	23.9	27.0	0.4	
	λ	444.9	588.6	532.5	482.9		0.38
Marijuana	%	63.2	76.8	73.9	67.2	4.8	
	λ	244.9	483.4	536.1	341.4		5.39 ***
Crack	%	67.0	78.6	73.9	70.1	3.2	
	λ	568.9	808.4	905.3	669.7		4.33 **
Drug Selling							
Cocaine HCL	%	1.9	42.9	41.3	15.1	86.6 ***	
	λ	5.4	611.3	554.5	536.8		1.52
Heroin	%	1.0	17.9	13.0	5.8	28.3 ***	
	λ	3.0	570.7	777.5	576.5		1.41
Marijuana	%	1.4	28.6	26.1	10.0	51.9 ***	
	λ	1.7	308.3	342.1	291.8		0.48
Crack	%	1.4	60.7	80.4	23.8	181.1 **	
	λ	2.7	722.9	715.9	690.2		1.76
Others	%	1.0	35.7	47.8	13.8	98.39***	
	λ	1.0	158.4	205.8	179.0		0.14

[a] Less than fifty sales during the three year period (1986–88).
* = $p < .05$ ** = $p < .01$ *** = $p < .001$

selling in drug-crime relationships, the results also were disaggregated by involvement in drug selling. The sample was classified either as non-sellers,[21] "independent sellers" who were not part of a drug selling organization, or members of organized drug selling groups. For each drug, the percent involved at least once is reported. The annual frequencies were computed only for active participants during the three-year interval.

More than one in three women (36 %) were involved in drug selling, although at widely varying rates. About one in five (20.1 %) sold drugs independently, and one in five (15.9 %) were part of drug selling organizations. Crack was the most widely sold drug: 23.8% of the sample reported selling crack during the three-year period; over 80% of the group sellers sold crack, and 60% of the independent sellers. Crack also was the most frequently sold drug. Cocaine HCL was sold by 15.1% and marijuana by 10%. A variety of other drugs, mostly illegally obtained prescription drugs, were sold by 13.8%.

Drug and Alcohol Use. Alcohol was the most widely used intoxicant, but not the one used most often. Over three in four women reported alcohol use during the three-year interval. Among illicit drugs, participation rates varied from 27.0% for heroin to 70.1% for crack. There were small differences in participation rates for cocaine HCL, crack and marijuana use, with about two in three women reporting one or more uses. All four illicit substances were used at an annual rate equivalent to daily use or greater. Rates of crack use were far higher than use of other drugs.

For each illegal drug, sellers reported higher rates of use than non-sellers. With the exception of crack, drug sales made possible serious drug use. It is unclear, however, whether sales were instrumental to obtain money for personal drug use, or whether sales created sufficient incomes to afford high-rate use. For alcohol and cocaine HCL, participation rates were significantly higher for drug sellers, but the frequency of use among active users did not vary. For marijuana and crack, the frequency of use was significantly higher among drug sellers but not the participation rate. The highest rates of any drug use were for crack use by women who also sold drugs, but women who did not sell drugs also had very high rates of crack use. The patterns suggest initially that there are two social domains of crack use, one involving use supported by selling and another where use is supported by hustles other than selling.

Nondrug Crimes

Table 6 shows participation and annualized frequency rates for eight non-drug crimes. Once again, annualized frequency rates were computed only for participants in the specific crime type. The rates were disaggregated by involvement in drug selling.

Participation in non-drug crimes varied by type of crime. Shoplifting (including theft) was the most common crime: about one in four women (26.7%) reported shoplifting during the three-year period, and one in five (22.8%) reported thefts of items worth over $50. Shoplifting was the crime committed most often. Although felony assault was reported by few women (3.5%) and occurred infrequently (twice per year), fighting was reported by 17% and robbery by 10.9%. Both fighting and robbery occurred frequently.

Overall, the relationships between drug selling and nondrug crimes were inconsistent. Assaults were higher for sellers than nonsellers, and fighting was more frequent among group sellers. However, some of this violence may be unrelated to drug selling. Fagan and Chin (1990, 1991) analyzed these data and

Table 6
Prevalence and Average Annual Rates of Non-Drug Crimes, by Type of Drug Selling, 1986–88

		Type of Drug Seller					
		Non Seller	Independent Seller	Group Seller	Total Sample	Chi-Square	F-value
N		209	56	46	311		
Non-Drug Crime:							
Robbery	%	9.6	12.5	15.2	10.9	1.41	
	λ	118.1	92.8	71.0	103.2		0.40
Burglary	%	2.4	10.7	6.5	4.5	7.60 *	
	λ	86.9	1.2	18.3	35.4		35.44
Felony Assault	%	1.4	7.1	8.7	3.5	8.40 **	
	λ	1.7	2.0	2.5	2.1		0.64
Grand larceny	%	20.6	21.4	34.8	22.8	4.39	
	λ	97.9	43.0	18.3	70.7		0.70
Shoplifting	%	24.9	32.1	28.3	26.7	1.25	
	λ	126.3	60.8	230.6	128.4		1.28
Fighting	%	11.5	25.0	32.6	17.0	14.96***	
	λ	8.1	155.3	241.3	51.5		1.40
Prostitution	%	19.6	14.3	26.1	19.6	2.23	
	λ	55.3	84.1	45.7	57.2		0.20
Fencing	%	8.6	16.1	30.4	13.1	16.18****	
	λ	44.1	111.2	158.8	97.0		0.48

* = $p < .05$ ** = $p < .01$ *** = $p < .001$

showed that crack sellers were generally violent both within and outside the context of drug selling. They suggested that people skilled in violence were socially and self-selected into the hazardous world of drug selling. Shoplifting also was more frequent among group sellers, but not more prevalent. Evidently, women combine the higher incomes of drug selling with the less risky hustles of theft as part of their diverse income strategies. Fencing also was a high rate crime, again part of the varied income producing crimes that characterize street hustles (Valentine 1978; Miller 1986).

About one in five women (19.6%) were involved in prostitution. The average annual prostitution rates were comparable to rates of other income-producing crimes (grand larceny, shoplifting, fencing) and some nonincome crimes such as fighting. Few women *specialized* in prostitution (data not shown), instead engaging in several crimes simultaneously to generate income. The rates of prostitution were not appreciably higher than several other crimes, especially shoplifting. Accordingly, women in the cocaine and crack economies used prostitution to finance their drug use, but only as part of a diverse set of income-producing activities. There was no evidence of the patterns of hypersexuality and hyper-drug use that other researchers have found in crack scenes (see, for example, Inciardi et al. 1993). However, these measures did not include sex-for-drugs exchanges, and may underestimate their actual involvement in noncash forms of prostitution. Also, sample differences between this and other studies of women's involvement in crack and sex markets may explain differences in their findings.

The Social and Economic Contexts of Drug Use and Selling

The expansion of street-level drug selling accommodated the demand for cocaine products that grew in U.S. inner cities in the 1980s (Johnson, Hamid and Morales 1990a; Kleiman 1992). Reports of unlimited incomes and the relatively small capital investments to enter the business attracted both new and experienced drug sellers to the emerging crack markets. Independent sellers and new drug-selling organizations entered a market that was largely deregulated. The participation of women sellers was one of the new features of the cocaine and crack markets (Goldstein et al. 1991).

Both buyers and sellers in street-level crack markets were more likely to engage in and be victims of violence compared to other markets (Goldstein 1989; Hamid 1990; Fagan and Chin 1990; Johnson et al. 1990). Goldstein (1985) described the violence that is intrinsic to drug selling as "systemic violence." Systemic violence can be viewed as a regulatory process or a strategy for organizational maintenance in an economic activity that falls outside legal or formal economic control (Fagan and Chin 1990). Organizational and economic factors have been cited as sources of violence in drug markets. Groups with more articulated structures and organizational characteristics more often are involved in violence, both within and outside the context of drug selling. Violence also is used as a regulatory strategy to maintain selling territory and market share (Fagan and Chin 1990; Bourgois 1989). The lucrative drug trade also makes street-level sellers attractive targets for robbery and other hustles. Grievances and disputes in the drug trade, falling outside traditional means of dispute resolution, often are settled through violence. Violence also may be used within organizations to maintain discipline and efficiency (Padilla 1992; Mieczkowski 1986).

However, what is known about the internal workings of drug organizations is based mainly on research with males in drug-selling organizations where women are either excluded or marginalized. Accordingly, whether these features of male-dominated drug markets apply to the contexts of female drug-selling findings has not been examined for female sellers.

Organizational Characteristics of Drug Selling Groups

Table 7 compares the structures of drug-selling organizations in the two study neighborhoods. Overall, 36.0% participated in drug-selling, and about 15.9% participated in drug selling groups. Participation in drug-selling was greater in Washington Heights, but participation in selling organizations was comparable in the two neighborhoods. Drug-selling organizations in both neighborhoods seemed to be informal and loosely organized. Few group sellers reported that their organizations had names, rules, territories, well-articulated leadership structures, or that their organizations employed adolescents below sixteen years of age.[22] Most had been in existence for only a few months. Fewer than 5% said that their groups had existed for more than six months. The loose structures suggest that these are haphazard, ad hoc groups that reflect decentralized drug distribution networks rather than lasting groups that might evolve into incipient organized crime groups.

Table 7
Characteristics of Drug Selling Organizations by Study Neighborhood

	Central Harlem	Washington Heights	Total Sample
N	153	158	311
Percent Involved in Drug Selling	27.5	43.7	36.0
Percent Involved in Group Selling	15.0	16.5	15.9
Structural Characteristics of Selling Group			
"Does your crew have..."			
A name	5.2	1.9	3.5
A leadership structure	10.5	13.9	12.7
Rules and norms	9.2	13.3	11.4
Rules against drug use	7.2	7.0	7.5
Specific territory	9.8	8.9	9.6
Kids younger than 16 involved in selling	2.0	3.2	2.8

Like other businesses, cocaine selling is hierarchically organized with higher incomes concentrated among a small number of managers. The bulk of drug workers labor for hourly wages and, occasionally, drugs. They are drawn from the vast surplus of laborers who either lack the human capital to be successful in legal work, or who voluntarily leave low-paying and unpleasant jobs for what they perceive as the higher incomes of drug work (Bourgois 1989; Waterston 1993). Women sellers did manage to achieve roles in distribution that were different from the support roles that typified their involvement in heroin selling. The roles suggest an active involvement in selling that required handling money or drugs in direct selling transactions. Most (87.3%) were involved in direct sales either in curbside or indoor locations, a relatively rare role in the heroin markets of the 1970s (Johnson et al. 1985). Women involved in selling organizations had several different roles, often occupying more than one role at any one time. Some (41.0%) had management roles that involved "supervising" other sellers, distributing drugs for resale, or collecting money.

Few women were involved in important roles such as "scale boys" who weigh and distribute packages of cocaine powder for street sales. They were more likely to be "doormen" at crack spots or base or crack houses, lookouts, or "gofers" who run errands for scale boys and other direct dealers. None of the women in this sample were "owners" of drug groups, although the haphazard organizational structures compromised the concept of ownership or "queenpin." In part, the ethnic and family segmenation of the drug labor market makes it difficult for women to achieve higher ranks. The retail drug trade in Washington Heights, for example, is dominated by immigrants and first generation Americans from Latin American countries. They either are tied through kinship networks or know each other from their country of origin (Williams 1992; Waterston 1993). In these organizations, women are seen as ill-equipped to handle the violence that is necessary to maintain security and control. These excuses justify the assignment of women to menial and low-paying jobs such as line workers (baggers, for example) or other support roles that do not involve handling cash or drugs.

Accordingly, although women's roles in selling were different from previous eras, the diffusion of drug markets in the cocaine economy complicated any comparisons with heroin or other drug markets. Like the previous eras, however, women generally were at the lower ranks of the drug business. They are seen as vulnerable to manipuation, unable to handle the violence necessary to avert "take offs" (robberies), and untrustworthy in a world dominated by males with poor views of women (Williams 1992).

Violence and Drug Selling

Respondents were asked to report whether they were "regularly" involved in any of eight specific types of violent events.[23] An index of *systemic violence* was computed by summing positive responses to each of the eight items. The results are shown in Table 8.

Violence in drug selling was greater for women who were involved in selling groups. Group sellers more often reported "regular" participation in systemic violence than independent sellers or nonsellers for each of the eight items. The systemic violence scale score was over two times greater for group than independent sellers ($F=66.7$, $p < .001$). However, among sellers in groups, there was no significant association between the social organization of drug-selling groups and participation in systemic violence (data not shown).

Fights with buyers and sellers of bad drugs, and robberies of buyers and dealers were the most prevalent forms of systemic violence. Victimization was a more likely violence experience for group sellers than was commission of a violent act. Over half the group sellers, and nearly one in four women overall, were victims of crime in the course of drug transactions. To the extent that women are generally more likely to be victims than offenders in violent crimes, these findings suggest similar gendered processes within illicit drug markets.

Together with the results in Table 4, group sellers have generally higher rates of both nondrug crimes and systemic violence. This association suggests that, as with males, these two dimensions of violence tend to coincide and be part of a generalized pattern of violence among both male and female drug sellers (Fagan and Chin 1990; Fagan 1992). It appears that processes of both self- and social selection result in the participation of generally violent and criminally active people in drug selling. While drug selling may offer economic returns and other advantages in drug markets, the decision to participate in group selling seems to bring with it a high occupational risk of violent victimization. Victimization tends to be the most common experience of women sellers.

Table 8
Systemic Violence by Type of Drug Seller Type

	Seller Type				
	Nonseller	Independent	Group	Total	Chi-square
N	(209)	(56)	(46)	(311)	(p-value)
Systemic Violence (%)					
Fought with rival dealers	0.0	17.0	31.0	7.3	54.49***
Assaulted to collect drug debts	1.0	9.4	28.6	6.0	50.53***
Fought with dealers over bad drugs	2.9	15.1	33.3	9.3	41.03***
Robbed drug dealers	1.4	15.1	33.3	8.3	50.60***
Robbed drug buyers	1.0	13.2	34.1	7.6	56.20***
Disputes over drug paraphernalia	18.8	30.2	45.2	24.5	14.27***
Victim of robbery or assault while dealing	1.9	18.9	52.4	11.9	87.58***
Fought with buyers over drug quality	1.0	18.9	38.1	8.9	68.45***
Systemic Violence Index (mean)	0.3	1.3	2.7	1.0	F (p) 66.74***

Significance: * $p < .05$ ** = $p < .01$ *** = $p < .001$

Income and Expenses

For both users and sellers, income from drugs and crime often are a substantial part of a diversified financial support system (Anglin and Hser 1987; Pettiway 1987; Rosenbaum 1981; Hamid 1992). Women drug users may rely on nondrug crimes (hustles), prostitution, a variety of low-wage legal jobs, family relationships, or spouses/boyfriends for economic support (Inciardi et al. 1993; Hunt 1990; Murphy et al. 1990; Rosenbaum 1981; Valentine 1978). Depending on their position in the drug market and their level of distribution, women dealers may supplement their drug incomes from similarly varied sources (Miller 1986; Pettiway 1987). However, it has been difficult to gauge the share of their income that women in drug markets derive from these various sources. In general, these studies have avoided quantifying the economic activity of women in drug markets.

Table 9 shows the monthly income distribution by study neighborhood for sellers and nonsellers.[24] Drugs dominated the economic lives of women in this context, accounting for the majority of incomes and expenses.[25] Incomes for drug sellers were far greater than for nonsellers, with drug income accounting for over two-thirds of their total incomes. Income from drug-selling was higher for women in drug selling organizations, and higher overall for sellers in Washington Heights. The neighborhood has a diverse and less poor population, and its more active drug market is centrally located at the intersection of major highways in and out of the region surrounding New York City.

Table 9
Monthly Income Distribution (1988 Dollars, Percent Of Total Income)

		Central Harlem			Washington Heights		
		Non Sellers	Lone Sellers	Group Sellers	Non Sellers	Lone Sellers	Group Sellers
N		10	20	23	90	42	26
Total Monthy Income		$1,118	$2,245	$3,658	$2,248	$6,141	$5,648
Income source							
Drug business	$	133	1,375	2,798	86	4,080	4,696
	%	11.9	61.2	76.5	3.8	66.4	83.1
Legal work	$	230	141	182	470	439	196
	%	20.6	6.3	5.0	20.9	7.1	3.5
Public transfer	$	128	105	141	126	83	24
	%	11.4	4.7	3.9	5.6	1.4	.4
Gifts	$	74	58	57	155	96	140
	%	6.6	2.6	1.6	6.9	1.6	2.4
Robbery & burglary	$	67	56	30	183	384	180
	%	6.0	2.5	.8	8.1	6.3	3.3
Theft & other crimes	$	83	318	43	712	220	179
	%	7.5	14.2	1.1	31.8	3.6	3.2
Credits & loans	$	5	10	33	21	32	164
	%	.4	.4	.8	.9	.5	2.9
Selling personal items	$	22	15	153	46	42	6
	%	2.0	.6	4.2	2.0	.7	.1
Other	$	376	168	222	450	766	63
	%	33.6	7.5	6.1	20.0	12.4	1.1

Among drug sellers, earnings from drug selling far exceeded the earnings from all other sources. Incomes from legal sources were low, including licit work and public transfers (e.g., AFDC, SSI, unemployment insurance). The income distribution is similar to estimates from research on crack sellers in Washington, D.C. (Reuter, MacCoun and Murphy 1990), about $30 per hour of street time (MacCoun and Reuter 1992). The relatively high incomes from drug selling may have made legal work seem unattractive, and raise questions as to why they bother to work at all.

The low levels of legal work income suggests that most women had relatively little attachment to licit work, whether from formal (salaried) work or off-book but legal economic activities. For women who sold casually, legal work was part of their diverse income strategies to buy drugs. But for other women, shifts in and out of legal work were part of their episodic efforts to stop using crack. Women with higher drug incomes were less likely to be involved in legal work. Other analyses of these data (Fagan 1992) suggest, however that the skill and education level of participants in the cocaine economy was low. Rather than being drawn from licit work to drug selling, people who chose to sell drugs had few skills that were attractive to putative employers in a service or skilled labor economy. Legal work was a weak choice, and drug selling seemed to be an appropriate match for this surplus labor pool.

For nonsellers and independent sellers, incomes were derived from varied sources, and reflected a combination of work, nonviolent crimes and hustling. Women who made more from drug selling tended to rely less on income from other crimes or legal work (see Dunlap, Johnson and Manwar n.d.). However, nondrug crime was not a major income source for any of the women. Prostitution income was included in the "other" category, and was generally higher than income from either legal work or nondrug crimes. In Central Harlem, this residual category accounted for most of their income. Among independent sellers in Washington Heights, "other" income accounted for a substantial portion (12.4%) of their income and supplemented their drug income. Accordingly, participation in drug selling reduced but did not insulate women from prostitution or other income-producing activities. Instead, they seemed to pursue a variety of income sources while earning substantial incomes from the drug business.

Drugs also accounted for over 60% of monthly expenses (data not shown). For sellers, this may include the costs of products to sell, as well as drugs for personal consumption. Drug selling was profitable: drug incomes exceeded drug expenses among the active sellers. Again, however, drug selling may have facilitated drug use, or may have provided an income source to meet the needs of heavy drug use. But the distinction may not be a meaningful one. The highly disciplined drug seller who avoided drug use seems to be rare and elusive, and a pattern of drug use and selling are part of the social processes of drug use within these neighborhoods and among these sellers.

The Effects of Drug Involvement on Crime, Drug Selling and Incomes

Several competing forces may influence drug-crime relationships among women in complex cocaine and crack markets. Income from drug selling may be sufficiently high to discourage or "protect" some women from involvement in prostitution. Drug use may motivate others to participate in that market, and also to engage in "economic compulsive" crimes (Goldstein 1985) for money to buy drugs. Participation in drug selling may expose women to the systemic violence that is intrinsic to drug markets, and influence their participation in assaults and robberies. Beliefs in the potential for high incomes from drug selling may motivate women to abandon licit work in favor of the illegal work of drug selling.

These relationships can be examined from two perspectives: the influence of incomes and drug use on crime frequency, and the influence of illegal work and crime on income patterns. Tobit models were constructed to examine these relationships.

Rates of Drug and Non-Drug Behaviors

Table 10 shows the results of tobit regressions on the annual rates of four crime types. Tobit models were preferred to accommodate left-hand censoring of nonparticipants in each crime type (Greene 1990; Roncek 1992). Log transformations adjusted for the highly skewed distributions for drug use, drug selling, and total income. In addition to drug use and selling variables, predictors included socioeconomic variables and income variables. Income variables included total income and the percentage derived from specific legal or illegal sources. A dummy variable for group drug selling was included to reflect the higher assault and robbery rates of drug selling in that context. The four models reflect the strong influence of crack use on crime participation and income-producing activities.

Higher income from drug selling reduced the likelihood of prostitution, while more frequent crack use increased prostitution rates. The availability of drug incomes seems to be a protective factor in helping women avoid the dangers and exploitation of prostitution. But higher rates of crack use apparently motivate women to participate in the secondary sex economy as an income source for drug use. Yet there are several complex meanings to sex exchanges in the context of crack and cocaine use. Respondents tended to interpret the items on prostitution narrowly as sex-for-money exchanges with strangers, either on the "stroll" or in crack houses. They often did not view sex-for-drug exchanges as prostitution, but as a routine part of using crack. Sex during crack use often was part of the ritual of crack use, where sexual activity and crack or base smoking were shared and mutually consensual pleasures (see, for example, Williams 1992). At times, women contributed drugs to these scenes, and at other times they contributed sex as equal partners with males. Still other times, women initiated a sex-for-drugs trade but managed to avoid actually having sex.[26] The economic complexity of these exchanges suggests the need for deconstructing the term "prostitution" and careful attention to the instrumental nature of transactions involving drugs and sex.

The negative coefficient for licit work suggests that prostitution and drug use may close off options for legal work, place women in a social context incompatible with the day to day demands of legal work, or simply reduce the utility of legal work. The returns from legal work also are low, making prostitution a better income option that requires fewer social "excursions" outside of women's street networks. Younger and Hispanic women also were more likely to engage in higher rates of prostitution.

More frequent crack sales, but not crack use, increased the likelihood of higher assault rates. This suggests that, for women, the systemic violence that accompanies drug selling is especially salient for the crack market. Higher rates of crack use increased the likelihood of income-producing crimes including robbery, burglary, and theft. Theft rates also were influenced by heroin use, while robbery rates reflected a greater income share from property crimes. These trends suggest that drug use generally, and especially crack, motivate higher rates of instrumental crimes for money. Since expenses for drugs dominated the economic lives of most women in the sample, these crimes seem to provide money to buy drugs. For women involved in prostitution, trading sex for drugs provides the service equivalent of crime income.

Table 10
Tobit Models for Frequency of Crime

	Prostitution		Assault		Robbery/ Burglary		Larceny/ Shoplifting	
	β	S. E.	β	S. E.	β	S. E.	β	S. E
Constant	3.70	1.98	1.88	1.13*	-7.09	2.37**	-6.03	1.65***
Demographics								
White	2.17	1.29	-0.34	0.81	-2.18	1.95	0.49	1.06
Hispanic	3.51	1.31**	-0.10	0.81	1.31	1.45	-0.37	1.18
Puerto Rican	1.06	0.98	-0.72	0.57	0.84	1.04	1.27	0.78
Age	-0.17	0.06**	-0.03	0.03	-0.07	0.07	0.09	0.05*
High school education	-0.41	0.86	-0.67	0.50	0.10	0.93	-0.50	0.70
Some college	-1.27	1.28	0.05	0.62	-0.87	1.33	-1.52	0.70
Group Seller	0.09	1.41	-0.15	0.65	1.19	1.33	-0.85	1.10
Frequency of Drug Sales (logged)								
Crack	0.03	0.27	0.41	0.12***	-0.06	0.23	-0.19	0.20
Coke	0.06	0.32	0.01	0.16	0.03	0.31	0.01	0.12
Heroin	0.41	0.45	0.12	0.19	-0.32	0.43	-0.06	0.31
Marijuana	0.07	0.19	0.05	0.18	0.22	0.32	0.30	0.28
Frequency of Drug Use (logged)								
Crack	0.48	0.15***	0.15	0.09	0.57	0.19***	0.51	0.12***
Coke	0.17	0.16	0.09	0.08	-0.14	0.17	0.09	0.12
Heroin	0.27	0.18	0.08	0.10	0.42	0.19*	0.32	0.13**
Marijuana	-0.15	0.16	-0.03	0.09	0.05	0.18	0.15	0.12
Total Income ($)	-0.00	0.00	-0.00	0.00	0.00	0.00	-0.00	0.00
Percent of total income from								
Drug sales	-0.04	0.01***	0.01	0.00	0.01	0.01	-0.00	0.01
Property crimes	0.05	0.02	-0.02	0.03	0.16	0.01***	0.06	0.03
Public support	-0.02	0.01	0.00	0.00	-0.02	0.02	-0.01	0.01
Licit work	-0.04	0.01***	-0.01	0.01	-0.02	0.02	-0.01	0.00
σ	4.99	0.39***	2.26	0.25***	3.9	0.53***	4.04	0.30***
% Participation		37.9		17.7		13.8		36.0
Lambda		109		50		93		126
Restricted log-likelihood		-673.7		-352.02		-453.26		-619.73
Log-Likelihood		-407.9		-182.40		-161.45		-384.55

Notes: Dummy variables where entered for race with African-Americans as the excluded category, and for education with less than high school graduate as the excluded category.
* = $p < .05$ ** = $p < .01$ *** = $p < .001$

Legal and Illegal Incomes

Table 11 shows the results of tobit models to examine factors influencing legal and illegal incomes. Tobit regressions were used to accommodate censoring on the income variables. Log transformations were adjusted for the highly skewed distributions for drug selling and crimes. Drug expenses were included as a predictor to test the extent to which personal consumption was influencing drug selling. Prostitution activity was included as a predictor to determine the extent to which incomes were influenced by co-production of sex and drug use.

Table 11
Tobit Models for Income From Legal and Illegal Work

	Total Income		Drug Selling		Licit Work		Property Crime	
	β	S. E.	β	S. E.	β	S. E.	β	S. E.
Constant	5.86	0.28***	-2.75	1.18*	-5.46	1.48***	-4.96	2.28**
Demographics								
White	0.36	0.20	0.37	0.80	1.39	0.83	-0.95	1.63
Hispanic	0.02	0.22	-0.44	0.93	0.09	0.96	-3.94	2.10
Puerto Rican	0.04	0.15	-0.98	0.63	-1.33	0.73	-1.08	1.18
Age	0.02	0.00***	0.09	0.03**	0.03	0.04	0.05	0.07
High school	0.09	0.13	-1.20	0.57*	0.18	0.66	-0.98	1.07
Some college	0.22	0.18	-1.43	0.72*	0.88	0.78	-1.78	1.52
Labor force	0.01	0.01	-0.01	0.03	0.09	0.03***	0.10	0.06
Group seller	-0.13	0.20	0.15	0.63	0.65	0.88	2.39	1.54
Drug Selling (logged)								
Crack	0.04	0.04	0.35	0.12**	0.16	0.16	-0.13	0.30
Cocaine HCL	0.08	0.05	0.62	0.15***	0.29	0.19	-0.07	0.36
Heroin	-0.07	0.06	-0.12	0.19	-0.22	0.27	0.01	0.45
Marijuana	-0.08	0.06	0.13	0.18	0.23	0.22	0.38	0.39
Prostitution (logged)	0.03	0.03	-0.24	0.12*	-0.12	0.14	0.15	0.20
Total Drug Expenses	0.03	0.01***	-0.05	0.04	0.00	0.05	0.35	0.08***
Percentage of total income from...								
Drug sales	0.02	0.00***	0.10	0.00***	0.01	0.00	-0.03	0.02*
Non drug crimes	0.02	0.00**	-0.01	0.03	0.04	0.04	0.20	0.05***
Public support	-0.01	0.00***	-0.04	0.01**	-0.00	0.01	-0.04	0.02*
Licit work	-0.00	0.00	-0.01	0.01	0.12	0.01***	-0.09	0.02***
σ	0.94	0.04	2.82	0.22***	3.17	0.26***	5.72	0.52***
Restricted Log-likelihood		-461.52		-2113.75		-2107.56		-2100.80
Log-likelihood		-375.17		-300.31		-291.04		-347.92

Note: Dummy variables where entered for race with African-Americans as the excluded category, and for education with the less than a high school education as the excluded category.

* = $p < .05$ ** $p < .01$ *** $p < .001$

The models illustrate the economic impact of drug use and selling on incomes. Incomes generally were influenced by higher shares of total income from illicit sources, including drug selling and other crimes. The significant coefficient for drug expenses in the model for total income may be interpreted either as money spent for total consumption, or money spent for drugs for resale. But since total incomes were likely to be higher when drug incomes were higher, we may assume that drug purchases were part of the business.[27] Drug selling activity *per se* did not influence total income, but the income share from drug selling was significant. Thus, independent of their involvement in drug selling, women's incomes were higher when those incomes were dominated by illegal sources and especially drug incomes. When contrasted with the trends for illegal income, the nonsignificant coefficients for labor force participation and licit work income suggests that crime indeed pays. Legal income from irregular hourly jobs (waitressing, delivery work, clerical work) offer low wages that only marginally meet the demands of women with family responsibilities and who aspire to the material aspects of conventional lifestyles. Bourgois (1989) describes also how nonwhites experienced constant racial humiliations and harassment in legal work, adding to their incentives to abandon legal work to sell drugs.

Drug selling income predictably reflected the level of effort devoted to drug sales. Once again, drug selling seems to be a protective factor in avoiding prostitution. The significant negative coefficient for prostitution could be interpreted in several ways. Higher drug incomes may supply sufficient incomes and obviate other income sources for either cash or drugs. Drug selling usually has been a minor income source for prostitutes (Goldstein 1979; Valentine 1978). Also, the social context of drug *selling* may be separate and distinct from the drug *use* contexts (especially crack scenes) in which women trade sex for drugs and cash.

The model for licit work income suggests that there is no apparent tradeoff between illicit and licit sources of income. We might have expected drug sales and income to require greater attention to illegal work at the sacrifice of legal work. But the coefficients for illegal work were not significant. Thus, licit incomes from legal work were not incompatible with illegal activities. Incomes from property crimes (robbery, burglary, theft, fencing) were influenced by total drug expenses. This pattern was evident especially for property crime: higher amounts spent on drugs were more likely to reflect higher property crime incomes. Temporal order questions remain, however, and it is uncertain whether crime income is part of "economic compulsive" crimes. The significant negative coefficient for drug *sales* income on property crime suggests that in fact property crime income may be motivated by drug use patterns. Table 11 also shows that property crime income competes with licit income: as licit work income declines, higher property crime incomes are more likely.

Overall, the models show that drug use and selling exert strong influences on income, and that income strategies often shape women's involvement in other crimes. There is no evidence of tradeoffs between licit and illicit activities, but there appears to be tradeoffs between drug selling and other types of crime. Patterns of income, drug use and drug selling suggests that there may be two distinct patterns or strategies of economic life for women in drug markets. One strategy reflects the social processes evident in earlier drug eras, where women users of heavy drugs relied increasingly on prostitution for incomes to support drug use. Other women also relied on property crimes for income, and the model for property crime income suggests that they generally were not involved extensively in prostitution. A different pattern is evident for drug sellers, whose incomes often are quite high. Their selling incomes seems to mitigate their involvement in other hustles or prostitution, while providing sufficient income to support heavy drug use. Women who show toughness or power ("heart," according to Waterston [1993] or "juice," as described by Williams [1992]) seem also to avoid prostitution while obtaining a steady flow of drugs. They often sell drugs or barter services for drugs. While protecting them from immersion in gendered work, including prostitution and the risks of HIV infection or economic exploitation in a declining sex market, drug selling also exposes women sellers to risks of violence that are more lethal and whose legal consequences are far more severe.

Conclusions

Women's involvement in the cocaine economy of the 1980s has retained many of the features of the heroin markets of the 1960s and 1970s. Like women heroin users two decades earlier, cocaine powder and crack users rely on diverse income-producing strategies to support expensive or heavy drug use. Women sellers hold positions within drug-selling organizations that are skewed toward lower status roles and away from management-ownership status. But women's experiences in contemporary drug markets have also diversified in important ways. Although women remain disadvantaged in highly gendered street networks, some women have constructed careers in illegal work that have insulated them from the exploitation and destructive behaviors that characterize heavy cocaine and crack use. Signs of the changing status of women in drug markets are evident in the relatively high incomes some achieve, and the relatively insignificant role of prostitution in generating income.

Women continue to pursue diverse strategies for producing income. In the past, the worlds of drug dealing, drug use, prostitution, theft, and other hustles composed the "life" of people within active street networks (French 1993). Illegal businesses providing goods and services historically formed the heart of the economy of the "life." While women were consigned secondary, gender-specific roles in these businesses in the past, the size and seemingly frantic activity of the current drug markets has made possible for women new ways to participate in street networks. Their involvement in drug selling at high income levels defies the gendered norms and roles of the past, where drug dealing was an incidental income source often mediated by domestic partnerships. If the highest status in street networks is accorded to people who sell cocaine or heroin (Agar 1973; Preble and Casey 1969), the expansion of drug markets in the cocaine economy has provided new ways for women to escape their limited roles, statuses and incomes in previous eras. It also provides an outlet for women to achieve conventional goals for family through illegal work.

The expanded role of women in drug selling provides them with income options that also protect them from the exploitation and health risks of prostitution. Women sellers seem to avoid or reduce their dependence on prostitution as an income source, minimizing both their exposure to HIV and to the violence and victimization intrinsic to prostitution (Goldstein, Ouellet, and Fendrich 1992; Ouellet et al. 1993). Involvement in drug selling, however, continues to carry with it risks for violence (Fagan and Chin 1990) and a variety of legal sanctions more serious than the penalties for prostitution. Thus, women in the cocaine economy face Hobbesian choices regarding incomes and careers in illegal work. While achieving gender parity in the occupational hazards of drug selling, women drug sellers avoid the disproportionate risks to women of HIV infection from prostitution or drugs-for-sex transactions.

The emergence of women sellers earning high incomes and avoiding prostitution suggests a new dimension to women's drug involvement. The story of Rachel (Dunlap, Johnson, and Manwar 1993) illustrates how entrepreneurial skills can insulate women from many of the risks women face in street drug selling: sexual and other physical victimization, arrest, and heavy drug use. Nevertheless, the highly gendered social networks of earlier eras still persist in the cocaine economy. Like heroin addiction, crack use seems to result in immersion in a social world where options become narrower and exploitation more likely (Maher and Curtis 1993; French 1993). The narrowing options seem to reflect both the social contexts where crack is used and the effects of the drug itself. Similar to heroin use in past eras, heavy crack use seems to close off social exits from drug use or hustling. One user said that the intense pleasure from smoking crack, and the reinforcement when it is repeated, made it impossible "to make any space between [himself] and the world where [he] smoked it." Reinarman and associates (1989) described the isolation that accompanies obsessive crack use, the suspicions toward friends and family members, the withdrawal from social interactions, the rejection of activities that do not lead to refilling the pipe, and the cashing in of limited economic and social assets in pursuit of an elusive but mythically powerful high.

In the social context of crack use, it is not surprising that prostitution continues to be an important part of the "life," and an important income source for women who use crack. For many crack users, initiation often led to deeper immersion in the social scenes and behaviors that limited their participation in both street or conventional social networks. Although some walked away from it after experimentation or maintained limits on their use of crack, others immersed themselves in crack use and reconstructed their social and economic lives to accommodate their frequent crack use.

Drug selling and its dangers also may not have been an acceptable choice for many women crack users. Women were infrequent participants in the cocaine powder selling scenes described by Adler (1985). Bourgois (1989) reported that few women held selling positions in crack markets; women in selling groups rarely held positions for longer than six months. The crews described by Williams (1989) also were dominated by men. Not unlike other drug scenes, crack use and selling is a coercive context, marked by high levels of violence where men hold both physical and economic power. Bourgois (1989) describes the gratuitous physical and verbal abuse and sexual exploitation of low-level women sellers. Accordingly, many women decided to decline work in drug selling and instead pursue income in the chaotic and sometimes violent sex markets surrounding crack markets. Sacrificing perhaps higher income but avoiding risk of physical injury, prostitution affords at least a minimum of control not possible in the violent world of drug selling. Consigned by traditional gender inequalities to lower wage earning positions in the formal and informal economies, women logically used their bodies as the primary power and income-generating resource available to them.

The initial hypotheses stated that changes in the social structural makeup of urban neighborhoods, the gender composition of street networks, and the psychopharmacological effects of illicit drugs are important considerations in understanding women's involvement in drug markets. Changes in these dimensions seem to have led to two social worlds among women in drug markets. In one world, women continue to experience the longstanding patterns of hustling in a variety of income-producing strategies, with options steadily narrowing around prostitution and related sex-for-drugs hustles. Gender roles still weigh significantly in this social world. In another social context, the incomes produced by drug selling offer protection from the health risks and exploitation of prostitution. Still, drug selling carries its own health risks from violence. Also, the high drug use rates of women sellers suggest that problematic behaviors may result within this otherwise "protected" world. The importance of domestic partnerships and other gendered relationships is less certain here, but nevertheless a part of the social interactions of drug selling.

Continued research on women's involvement in drug markets may reveal additional income-producing strategies that involve hustles in the worlds of legal work, or involvement in other forms of income-producing crimes. The natural history of male drug users' illegal careers suggests a number of transitions and changes over time as drug users move into and away from drug use (Biernacki 1986; Waldorf et al. 1992). We may expect similar patterns for women as they fashion together lifestyles from a variety of hustles, more serious crimes, drug selling, and other work in the licit or illicit economies. But the changing gender composition of inner cities that host active drug markets suggest that partnerships with males will be a declining part of these social and economic worlds. Future efforts to understand the social contexts of women's involvement in drug markets requires that research continue to examine women's experiences and focus on their actions within the contexts that shape their options.

Finally, the use of money as a measure of participation in drug and other illegal activities provides an empirical dimension not readily available through other behavioral measures. Drug selling and prostitution are forms of income production requiring complex economic decisions with income satisficing motivations. Decisions to participate in or desist from behaviors reflect the instrumental goals of earning money to achieve other ends such as buying drugs or items for personal consumption. Drug researchers have long known that crimes vary with the extent of addiction, nearly desisting during periods of nonaddiction. We might assume that the extent of income-producing crime will vary with the frequency and amount of drug use. Once drug needs are met, illegal behaviors may desist. In this study, the ability to earn money from drug selling affords protection from prostitution. Accordingly, analyses using incomes provide tests of hypotheses that reflect the economic dimensions of deviant careers. Income should be used where appropriate as part of a strategy of multiple measurement of drug involvement.

ACKNOWLEDGMENTS

This research was supported in part by Grant 1 R01 DA 06615-01 from the National Institute of Drug Abuse, and Grant 87-IJ-CX-0064 from the National Institute of Justice. Ko-lin Chin, Bruce Johnson, Eloise Dunlap and Chris Maxwell made important contributions to the research.

NOTES

1. These jobs were important points of entry into labor market participation for working-class men and women. Blue collar employment provided the basis among minorities in poor neighborhoods for the expectati on of social mobility and steady if not spectacular wages over the work career (Farley and Allen 1987).

2. For males, drug use at this end of the hierarchy is more easily forgiven as a temporary transgression that is consistent with gender role performance, such as risk-taking and challenges to conventional authority (see Robbins 1989, for example).

3. See, for example, Clayton and Voss (1981); Hunt and Chambers (1976); Inciardi (1979).

4. Several studies have discussed the street networks of addicts and the interactions that make up their social worlds. For descriptions of the rewards of the street addict life, see Waldorf (1973), Preble and Casey (1969), Agar (1973), Johnson et al. (1985), Hanson et al. (1985), Rosenbaum (1981), and Stephens (1991). These works describe a tightly knit world whose rituals and rules revolve around getting and using drugs. There is a hierarchy of statuses based on conning ability and drug use patterns, distinct language, and extensive knowledge of drugs and drug effects (Stephens 1991). The rules, norms, roles and values are maintained through group processes that regulate the legal and nonlegal behaviors of people in the networks (Zinberg 1984).

5. Kleiman (1992:288), interpreting NIDA Household Survey data from 1982–90, claims that over twenty million Americans have used cocaine (in powder, freebase, or its crack forms) at least once, "several million use it at least occasionally, and between two and three million do so weekly or more."

It would be a mistake to assume that among either males or females, cocaine use replaced heroin. Although many heroin users also used cocaine, often "speedballing" them together via injection, newer and younger cocaine initiates beginning in the late 1970s began cocaine use following progressions through alcohol and marijuana but not heroin (Kandel, Yamaguchi, and Chen 1992; Fagan and Chin 1991). Cocaine in this period was used primarily through snorting cocaine powder (cocaine hydrochloride, or cocaine HCL) (Siegel 1987). After peaking in 1979 nationally, the prevalence of cocaine use quickly throughout the next decade (Office on National Drug Control Policy 1989). But the declines through 1985 were far slower among two populations: "high rate" cocaine users, and poor and minority groups in inner cities (Johnson et al. 1990). Crack emerged in New York's poorest neighborhoods in 1985, and in similar areas in other cities within a few years.

6. At first, crack was sold in street drug markets in cities in or near cocaine importation points. See Inciardi (1993) regarding Miami and Klein, Maxson and Cunningham (1986) regarding Los Angeles. How quickly it spread to other cities is a matter of debate. For example, Ouellet and associates (1993) found few persons with street reputations for smoking crack prior to 1990, but they came into contact with crack users as their ethnographic work progressed.

7. Most cocaine users had been aware of the intensified high experienced from smoking freebase cocaine (Siegel 1982; Waldorf, Reinarman, and Murphy 1991). However, quantities of cocaine sufficient for "basing" had been beyond the economic means of most drug users. Crack became widely available in small quantities at low unit costs ($10 for three small rocks). Compared to the manufacture of freebase cocaine, the crack production process was cheaper, simpler, safer, and more efficient. Distribution points proliferated, including both street markets and indoor locations in the city's poorest neighborhoods (Fagan and Chin 1990; Johnson et al. 1990). Crack houses sprang up as modern day opium dens (Hamid 1990; Bourgois 1989; Williams 1992), providing a controlled environment for crack use where supplies were limited only by the user's cash or ability to barter. Similar to its more expensive freebase form, crack cocaine posed considerable risk for compulsive use (Gawin and Kleber 1988; Siegel 1987; Spitz and Rosecan 1987). The intense crack high lasted a relatively short time (less than twenty minutes) and was followed by a sharp depression that led to a strong desire to get high again (Reinarman, Waldorf, and Murphy 1989). Many users reported

constantly "chasing" the initial euphoric high by continuing to smoke crack.

8. Since the early 1970s, neighborhoods and cities evidenced increasing social disorganization and isolation (Fernandez and Harris 1992; Tienda 1989a; Skogan 1990), intensifying racial segregation (Massey and Eggers 1990), rapid changes in population composition (Wilson 1991), and growing concentrations of poverty (Jargowsky and Bane 1991; Wacquant and Wilson 1989). Also, opportunities in the informal economy of barter, off-book labor, and unlicensed vending replaced the disappearing manufacturing economy during this period (Sassen 1991).

9. See, for example, Lauderback and colleagues (1992) regarding the development of female gangs in San Francisco, Campbell (1984) on female gangs in New York, and Moore (1993) on "cholas" in East Los Angeles who maintained organizations and social identities separate from their male counterparts. See, also, Pettiway (1987) and Sommers and Baskin (1993) on the declining significance of domestic arrangements and male-female crime partnerships. Campbell argues that female gangs regulate their own organizations and reject attempts by male gang leaders to interfere in their operations.

10. Cocaine blocks the reabsorption of dopamine, a neurotransmitter chemical, into the neurons that release it. It thereby temporarily accelerates perception and thoughts. Cocaine is powerfully reinforcing, and both animal and human subjects who find that a given behavior will lead to a dose of cocaine will increase the frequency of that behavior (Gawin 1991).

11. These studies describe women users who are willing to engage in any form of sexual activity, under any circumstances, and often for small sums of money or drugs. They are derisively called "tossups," "strawberries," "skeezers," and other degrading names.

12. See Belenko, Fagan, and Chin (1991) for analysis of arrest patterns for crack offenses in the two neighborhoods.

13. Although it is difficult to compare this sample to the general populations of the neighborhoods, it is representative of drug arrestees in New York City during the peak years of the crack crisis (Johnson et al. 1990; Dunlap et al. 1990).

14. Comparisons of the study samples with general neighborhood populations are complicated by significant undercounting in census data in each neighborhood (Hamid 1992a) and the high rate of legal and illegal immigration in Washington Heights through the 1980s (New York City Department of City Planning 1992). Accordingly, generalizations of the results to populations involved in drug markets in each neighborhood are appropriate. However, we should be cautious in broadening these findings to the general neighborhood populations of northern Manhattan.

15. The arrest flags have been used by the New York City Police Department since 1984 to identify first cocaine HCL arrestees in Operation Pressure Point (Zimmer 1987), and then crack offenders since 1986. The flags are used administratively to document arrests of special interest to the department. They were necessary to identify crack offenders since drug charge categories (P.L. 220) do not distinguish various types of controlled substances. See Belenko and associates 1991, for more details.

16. They often sought out potential respondents for each category in known "copping" locations in each neighborhood. See Dunlap and associates 1989, for details on subject recruitment, management of referral chains, interview procedures and techniques for minimizing validity threats from the interview conditions and test effects.

17. However, the use of these categories may risk upward response bias. Respondents may feel that the existence of the larger categories suggests that someone is making that much money. In a domain where one's illicit income can serve as a status marker, this might promote exaggeration.

18. Public assistance includes AFDC and Home Relief (New York City Human Resources Administration).

19. However, census data for 1970 failed to accurately distinguish whites from Hispanics.

20. Annual offending rates were calculated for each crime after adjusting for time on the street. Using monthly calendars, percentages of the year not at risk (on the street) were computed and the rates adjusted accordingly.

21. Women who sold drugs fewer than fifty times during the past three-years were classified as nonsellers. This threshold distinguished casual sellers, whose transactions were part of the normative process of drug exchanges in social networks of drug users (Fagan and Chin 1991; Waldorf et al. 1992), from regular sellers who were motivated by economic gain.

22. Adolescents are used to carry drugs and money while avoiding the risk of adult prosecution in New York State, where sixteen years is the age of majority for criminal court.

23. Confidentiality procedures precluded asking about specific organizations, so comparisons of responses from different members of the same organizations was not possible.

24. Some nonsellers reported small incomes from drug selling since they also were infrequent sellers.

25. Data for expenses showed that over 61.3% of total expenses were for purchases of drugs. However, since dealing and using were combined for *most* sellers, it was impossible to separate the reasons for drug purchases into drugs for use versus drugs for resale. Food, shelter, clothing and family/child care accounted for 30% of income. Respondents could not account for the balance. Excess incomes were dispersed through family and social networks. Older matriarchs of intergenerational families often are the recipients of special largesse, in recognition of past support and for preservation of a home location for family logistics (Dunlap 1992). Money also is given away in gifts to loved ones and personal consumption of jewelry or other luxury items (Hamid 1992b).

26. Both Williams (1992) and Hamid (1992b) describe how men would share drugs with women in return for sex, but the women fed drugs to the men before sex so that the men would become impotent or otherwise sexually dysfunctional. Women would avoid any sexual contact in these instances, and reported some pleasure in having duped the men.

27. Drug consumption also may increase when drug incomes increase, since more money is available for drug use and access to drugs increases. However, drug use interferes with efficient drug selling and tends to limit income (Murphy, Waldorf, and Reinarman 1991; Fagan 1992).

REFERENCES

Adler, P.
1985 *Wheeling and dealing: An ethnography of an upper-level dealing and smuggling community.* New York: Columbia Univ. Press.

Agar, M.
1973 *Ripping and running: A formal ethnography of urban heroin addicts.* New York: Seminar Press.

Anderson, E.
1990 *Streetwise.* Chicago: Univ. of Chicago Press.

Anglin, M. D. and Y. Hser
1987 Addicted women and crime. *Criminology* 25: 359–97.

Baskin, D., I. Sommers, and J. Fagan
1993 The political economy of female violent street crime. *Fordham Urban Law Journal* 20: 401–7.

Belenko, S.A., J. Fagan, and K. Chin
1991 Criminal justice responses to crack. *Journal of Research in Crime and Delinquency* 28:55–74.

Biernacki, P.
1986 *Pathways from addiction*. Philadelphia: Temple Univ. Press.

Biernacki, P. and Waldorf, D.
1981 Snowball sampling: Problems and techniques of chain referral sampling. *Sociological Methods and Research* 10: 141–63.

Blom, M. and T. van den Berg
1989 A typology of the life and work styles of "heroin-prostitutes." In *Growing up good: Policing the behavior of girls in Europe,* ed. M. Cain. London: Sage.

Bourgois, P.
1989 In search of Horatio Alger: Culture and ideology in the crack economy. *Contemporary Drug Problems* 16: 619–50.

Bourgois, P. and E. Dunlap,
1993 Exorcising sex-for-crack: An ethnographic perspective from Harlem. In *Crack pipe as pimp: An ethnographic investigation of sex-for-crack exchanges,* ed. M. S. Ratner. New York: Lexington Books.

Boyle, J. and A. Brunswick
1980 What happened in Harlem? Analysis of a decline in heroin use among a generation unit of urban black youth. *Journal of Drug Issues* 10: 109–30.

Campbell, A.
1984 *The girls in the gang*. New York, Blackwell.

Chin, K. and J. Fagan
1990 The impact of initiation into crack on crime and drug use. Presented at the annual meeting of the American Society of Criminology, November, Baltimore, Md.

Cohen, B.
1980 *Deviant street networks: Prostitutes in New York*. Lexington, Mass.: Lexington Books.

Colten, M. E. and J. E. Marsh
1984 A sex roles perspective on drug and alcohol use by women. In *Sex roles and psychopathology*, ed. C. S. Widom. New York: Plenum Press.

Corcoran, M. and S. Parrott
1992 Black women's economic progress. Paper presented at the Research Conference on the Urban Underclass: Perspectives from the Social Sciences. June, Ann Arbor, Michigan.

Courtwright, D. T.
1982 *Dark paradise: Opiate addiction in America before 1940.* Cambridge Mass.: Harvard University Press.

Curtis, R. A. and Maher, L.
1993 Highly structured crack markets in the southside of Williamsburg, Brooklyn. In *The ecology of crime and drug use in inner cities*, ed. J. Fagan. New York: Social Science Research Council. In press.

Daly, K., and M. Chesney-Lind
1988 Feminism and criminology. *Justice Quarterly* 5:497–538.

Dunlap, E.
1992 The impact of drugs on family life and kin networks in the inner-city African-American single parent household. In *Drugs, crime and social isolation: barriers to urban opportunity*, ed. A. Harrell and G. Peterson. Washington D.C.: The Urban Institute Press.

Dunlap, E., B. D. Johnson, and A. Manwar
n.d. A successful female crack dealer: Case study of a deviant career. *Deviant Behavior*. In press.

Dunlap, E., B.D. Johnson, H. Sanabria, E. Holliday, V. Lipsi, M. Barnett, W. Hopkins, I. Sobel, D. Randolph, and K. Chin
1990 Studying crack users and their criminal careers: The scientific and artistic aspects of locating hard-to-reach subjects and interviewing them about sensitive subjects. *Contemporary Drug Problems* 17(1):31–78.

Eldred, C.A., and M.N. Washington
1976 Interpersonal relationships in heroin use by men and women and their role in treatment outcome. *International Journal of the Addictions* 11:117–30.

Erickson, P. and G. Murray
1989 Sex differences in cocaine use and experiences: A double standard revived? *American Journal of Drug and Alcohol Abuse* 15:135–52.

Ettorre, E.
1992 *Women and substance use*. New Brunswick, N.J.: Rutgers Univ. Press.

Fagan, J.
1992 Drug selling and licit income in distressed neighborhoods: The economic lives of drug users and drug sellers. In *Drugs, crime and social isolation: Barriers to urban opportunity*, ed. A. Harrell and G. Peterson. Washington D.C.: The Urban Institute Press.

Fagan, J. and K. Chin
1990 Violence as regulation and social control in the distribution of crack. In *Drugs and violence*, ed. M. de la Rosa, E. Lambert, and B. Gropper. National Institute on Drug Abuse Research Monograph no. 103. DHHS Pub. No. (ADM)90-1721. Rockville, Md.

Fagan, J. and K. Chin
1991 Social processes of initiation into crack use and dealing. *Journal of Drug Issues* 21 (2): 313–43.

Farley, R.
1987 Disproportionate black and Hispanic unemployment in U.S. metropolitan areas. *American Journal of Economics and Sociology*. 46:129–50.

Farley, R.
1988 After the starting line: Blacks and women in an uphill race. *Demography* 25:447–95.

Farley, R. and W. R. Allen
1987 *The Color Line and the Quality of Life in America*. New York: Russell Sage Foundation.

Fernandez, R. and Harris, D.
1992 Social isolation and the underclass. In *Drugs, crime and social isolation: Barriers to urban opportunity*, ed. A. Harrell and G. Peterson. Washington, D.C.: The Urban Institute Press.

File, K. N.
1976 Sex roles and street roles. *International Journal of the Addictions* 11:263–8.

Freeman, R.
1991 Employment and earnings of disadvantaged young men in a labor shortage economy. In *The urban underclass*, ed. C. Jencks and P. E. Peterson. Washington, D.C.: The Brookings Institution.

French, J.
1993 Pipe dreams: Crack and the life in Philadelphia and Newark. In *Crack pipe as pimp: An ethnographic investigation of sex-for-crack exchanges*, ed. M. S. Ratner. New York: Lexington Books.

Gawin, F. H.
1991 Cocaine addiction: Psychology and neurophysiology. *Science* 251:1580–86.

Gawin, F. H. and H. D. Kleber
1988 Evolving conceptualizations of cocaine dependence. *The Yale Journal of Biology and Medicine* 61: 121–36.

Goldstein, P. J.
1979 *Prostitution and drugs*. Lexington, Mass.: Lexington

Goldstein, P. J.
1985 The drugs-violence nexus: a tri-partite conceptual framework. *Journal of Drug Issues* 15: 493–506.

Goldstein, P. J., D. Lipton, E. Preble, I. Sobel, T. Miller, W. Abbott, W. Paige, and F. Soto
1984 The marketing of street heroin in New York City. *Journal of Drug Issues* 14: 553–66.

Goldstein, P. J., B. Spunt, P. Belluci, and T. Miller
1991 Volume of cocaine use and violence: A comparison between men and women. *Journal of Drug Issues* 21: 345–67.

Goldstein, P. J., L. J. Ouellet, and M. Fendrich
1992 From bag brides to skeezers: An historical perspective on sex-for-drugs behavior. *Journal of Psychoactive Drugs* 24:349–61.

Golub, A. and B. D. Johnson
1993 Cohort differences in drug use pathways to crack among current crack users in New York City. Unpublished. New York: National Development and Research Institutes.

Greene, W. H.
1990 *Econometric analysis*. New York: MacMillan Publishing Company.

Hagan, J.
1989 *Structural criminology*. New Brunswick, N.J.: Rutgers Univ. Press.

Hagan, J. J., Simpson, and A. R. Gillis
1987 Class in the household: A power-control theory of gender and delinquency. *American Journal of Sociology* 92: 788–816.

Hamid, A.
1990a The political economy of crack-related violence. *Contemporary Drug Problems* 17 (1): 31–78.

Hamid, A.
1992a Ethnographic follow-up of a predominantly African-American population in a sample area in Central Harlem, New York City: Behavioral Causes of the undercount of the 1990 census. Washington, D.C.: Bureau of the Census/Center for Survey Methods Research, U.S. Department of Commerce.

Hamid, A.
1992b Drugs and patterns of opportunity in the inner city: The case of middle-aged, middle-income cocaine smokers. In *Drugs, crime and social isolation: Barriers to urban opportunity*, ed. A. Harrell and G. Peterson. Washington, D.C.: The Urban Institute Press.

Hamid, A.
1992c The developmental cycle of a drug epidemic: The cocaine smoking epidemic of 1981–91. *Journal of Psychoactive Drugs* 24: 337–48.

Hamid, A.
n.d. *The political economy of drugs*. New York: Guilford Press. In press.

Hanson, B. , G. Beschner, J. M. Walters, and E. Bovelle
1985 *Life with heroin*. Lexington, Mass.: Lexington Books.

Hser, Y., M.D. Anglin, and W. H. McGlothlin
1987 Sex differences in addict careers. 1. Initiation of use. *American Journal of Drug and Alcohol Abuse* 13: 33–57

Hunt, D.
1990 Drugs and consensual crimes: Drug dealing and prostitution. In *Drugs and crime*, ed. M. Tonry and J. Q. Wilson. Chicago: Univ. of Chicago Press.

Hunt, L. G. and C. D. Chambers
1976 The heroin epidemics: A study of heroin use in the U.S., 1965–75. Holliswood, N.Y.: Spectrum Press.

Inciardi, J. A.
1979 Heroin use and street crime. *Crime and Delinquency* 25: 335–346.

Inciardi, J. A., D. Lockwood, and A. E. Pottieger
1993 *Women and crack cocaine*. New York: MacMillan.

Jargowsky, P. A., and M. J. Bane
1990 Ghetto poverty: Basic questions. In *Inner city poverty in the United States*, ed. L. Lynn and M. G. H. McGeary. Washington, D.C.: National Academy Press.

Jargowsky, P. A., and M. J. Bane
1991 Ghetto poverty in the United States: 1970-80. In *The urban underclass*, ed. C. Jencks and P. E. Peterson. Washington, D.C.: The Brookings Institution.

Jencks, C.
1991 Is the American underclass growing? In *The urban underclass*, ed. C. Jencks and P. E. Peterson. Washinton, D.C.: The Brookings Institution.

Johnson, B. D., A. Hamid, and E. Morales
1990a Emerging models of crack distribution. In *Drugs and Crime: A Reader,* ed. T. Mieczkowski . Boston: Allyn-Bacon.

Johnson, B. D., T. Williams, K. Dei, and H. Sanabria
1990b Drug abuse and the inner city: Impacts of hard drug use and sales on low income communities. In *Drugs and crime*, ed. J. Q. Wilson and M. Tonry. Chicago: Univ. of Chicago Press.

Kandel, D. B., K. Yamaguchi, and K. Chen
1992 Stages of progression in drug involvement from adolescence to adulthood: Further evidence of the gateway theory. *Journal of Studies on Alcohol* 53: 447–57.

Kasarda, J. D.
1988 Jobs, migration and emerging urban mismatches. In *Urban change and poverty*, ed. M. G.H. McGeary and L. E. Lynn. Washington, D.C.: National Academy Press.

Kasarda, J. D.
1989 Urban industrial transition and the underclass. *The Annals of the American Academy of Political and Social Science* 501:26–47.

Kirschenman, J. and K. M. Neckerman
1991 "We'd love to hire them, but . . . ": The meaning of race for employers. In *The urban underclass*, ed. C. Jencks and P. E. Peterson. Washington, D.C.: The Brookings Institution.

Kleiman, M. A. R.
1992 *Against excess: Drug policy for results.* New York: Basic Books.

Klein, M.W., C.L. Maxson, and L.C. Cunningham
1991 Crack, street gangs, and violence. *Criminology* 29:623–50.

Kozel, N. J. and E. H. Adams, eds.
1985 *Cocaine use in America: Epidemiological and clinical perspectives.* National Institute on Drug Abuse Research Monograph no. 61. DHHS Pub. No. (ADM)85-1414. Rockville, Md.

Johnson, B.D., P.J. Goldstein, E. Preble, J. Schmeidler, D. Lipton, B. Spunt, and T. Miller
1985 *Taking care of business: The economics of crime by heroin abusers.* Lexington, Mass.: Lexington Books.

Lauderback, D., J. Hansen, and D. Waldorf
1992 "Sisters are doin' it for themselves": A black female gang in San Francisco. *The Gang Journal* 1:57–92.

Longshore, D. M. D., Anglin, S. Hsieh, and K. Annon
1993 Sexual behaviors and cocaine preference among injection heroin users in Los Angeles. *Journal of Drug Issues* 23:363–74.

MacCoun, R. and P. Reuter
1992 Are the wages of sin $30 an hour? Economic aspects of street-level drug dealing. *Crime and Delinquency* 38: 477–91.

Maher, L. and R. Curtis
1993 Women on the edge of crime: Crack cocaine and the changing contexts of street level sex work in New York City. *Crime, Law and Social Change* 18: 221–58.

Mare, R. D., and C. Winship
1991 Socioeconomic change and the decline of marriage for blacks and whites. In *The urban underclass*, ed. C. Jencks and P. E. Peterson. Washington, D.C.: The Brookings Institution.

Massey, D.S. and M.L. Eggers
1990 The ecology of inequality: Minorities and the concentration of poverty, 1970–80. *American Journal of Sociology* 95:1153–88.

Mieczkowski, T.
1986 Geeking up and throwing down: Heroin street life in Detroit. *Criminology* 24: 645–66.

Miller, E.
1986 *Street woman.* Philadelphia: Temple Univ. Press.

Moore, J.
1993 *Going down to the barrio: Homeboys and homegirls in change.* Philadelphia: Temple Univ. Press.

Moss, P. and C. Tilly
1991 Why black men are doing worse in the labor market: A review of supply-side and demand-side explanations. Paper prepared for the Social Science Research Council, Committee on Research on the Urban Underclass, Subcommittee on Joblessness and the Underclass. New York: Social Science Research Council.

Murphy, S., D. Waldorf, and C. Reinarman
1991 Drifting into dealing: Becoming a cocaine seller. *Qualitative Sociology* 13: 321–343.

Musto, D.
1973 *An American disease: Origins of narcotic control.* New Haven: Yale Univ. Press.

New York City Department of City Planning
1991 Annual Report on Social Indicators.

New York Times
1989a Report from the field on an endless war, 12 March.

New York Times
1989b Selling milk, bread, and cocaine in New York, 30 March.

Office of National Drug Control Policy
1989 *National Drug Control Strategy.* Washington, D.C.: The White House.

Ouellet, L. J., W.W. Wiebel, A.D. Jimenez, and W.A. Johnson
1993 Crack cocaine and the transformation of prostitution in three Chicago neighborhoods. In *Crack pipe as pimp: An ethnographic investigation of sex-for-crack exchanges,* ed. M. S. Ratner. New York: Lexington Books.

Padilla, F.
1992 *The gang as an American enterprise.* New Brunswick, N.J.: Rutgers Univ. Press.

Pettiway, L.
1987 Participation in crime partnerships by female drug users: The effects of domestic arrangements, drug use, and criminal involvement. *Criminology* 25:741–766.

Preble, E. and J. J. Casey, Jr.
1969 Taking care of business: The heroin user's life on the street. *International Journal of the Addictions* 4:1–24.

Ratner, M.
1993 Sex, drugs, and public policy: Studying and understanding the sex-for-crack phenomenon. In *Crack pipe as pimp: An ethnographic investigation of sex-for-crack exchanges,* ed. M. S. Ratner. New York: Lexington Books.

Reinarman, C., D. Waldorf, and S. Murphy
1989 The call of the pipe: Freebasing and crack use as norm-bound episodic compulsion. Paper presented at the Annual Meeting of the American Society of Criminology, November, Reno.

Reuter, P., R. MacCoun, and P. Murphy
1990 Money from crime. Report R-3894. Santa Monica, Calif.: The Rand Corporation.

Ricketts, E. and I. Sawhill
1988 Defining and measuring the underclass. *Journal of Policy Analysis and Management* 7:316–25.

Robbins, C.
1989 Sex differences in psychosocial consequences of alcohol and drug abuse. *Journal of Health and Social Behavior* 30: 117–30.

Roberts, D. E.
1991 Punishing drug addicts who have babies: Women of color, equality, and right of privacy. *Harvard Law Review* 194: 1419–82.

Roncek, D.
1992 Learning more from Tobit coefficients: Extending a comparative analysis. *American Sociological Review* 57:503–7.

Rosenbaum, M.
1981 *Women and heroin*. New Brunswick, N.J.: Rutgers Univ. Press.

Sampson, R. J.
1992 Family management and child development: Insights from social disorganization theory. In *Facts, forecasts, and frameworks*, ed. J. McCord. New Brunswick, N.J.: Transaction Publishers.

Sante, L.
1991 *Low life*. New York: Farrar, Giroux and Straus.

Sassen, S.
1991 The informal economy. In *Dual city: Restructuring New York*, ed. J. H. Mollenkopf and M. Castells. New York: Russell Sage.

Sassen-Koob, S.
1989 New York City's informal economy. In *The informal economy: Studies in advanced and less developed countries*, ed. A. Portes, M. Castells, and L. A. Benton. Baltimore: Johns Hopkins Univ. Press.

Siegel, R. K.
1982 Cocaine freebase: A new smoking disorder. *Journal of Psychoactive Drugs* 14: 321–337.

Siegel, R. K.
1987 Cocaine smoking: Nature and extent of coca paste and cocaine freebase abuse. In *Cocaine: A clinician's handbook*, ed. A. M. Washton and M. Gold, New York: The Guilford Press.

Simpson, S. S.
1989 Feminist theory, crime and justice. *Criminology* 27: 607–31.

Simpson, S. S.
1991 Caste, class and violent crime: Explaining differences in female offending. *Criminology* 29: 115–35.

Skogan, W.
1990 *Disorder and decline: Crime and the spiral of decay in American neighborhoods.* New York: Free Press.

Sommers, I. and D. Baskin
1993 The situational context of female offending. *Journal of Research in Crime and Delinquency* 30: 136–62.

Spitz, H. I. and J. S. Rosecan
1987 Cocaine reconceptualized: Historical overview. In *Cocaine abuse: New directions in treatment and research,* ed. H. I. Spitz and J. S. Rosecan. New York: Brunner-Mazel.

Stack, C.
1974 *All our kin: Strategies for survival in a black community*, New York: Harper and Row.

Steffensmeier, D.
1983 Organization properties and sex-segregation in the underworld: Building a sociological theory of sex differences in crime. *Social Forces* 61: 1010–1032.

Stephens, R. C.
1991 *The street addict role: A theory of heroin addiction.* Albany: State Univ. of New York Press.

Sullivan, M.
1989 *Getting paid.* Ithaca, N.Y.: Cornell Univ. Press.

Tienda, M.
1989a Neighborhood effects and the formation of the underclass. Paper presented at the Annual Meeting of the American Sociological Association, August San Francisco.

Tienda, M.
1989b Puerto Ricans and the underclass debate. *The Annals of the American Academy of Political and Social Science* 501:105–119.

Valentine, B.
1978 *Hustling and other hard work: Life styles in the ghetto.* New York: Free Press.

Wacquant, L. D., and W. J. Wilson
1989 The costs of racial and class exclusion in the inner city. *The Annals of the American Academy of Political and Social Science* 501:8–25.

Waldorf, D.
1973 *Careers in dope*. Englewood Cliffs, N.J.: Prentice Hall.

Waldorf, D., C. Reinarman, and S. Murphy
1991 *Cocaine changes: The experiences of using and quitting*. Philadelphia: Temple Univ. Press.

Waterston, A.
1993 *Street addicts in the political economy*. Philadephia: Temple Univ. Press.

Watters, J. K, and P. Biernacki
1989 Targeted sampling: Options for the study of hidden populations. *Social Problems* 6: 416–30.

Williams, T.
1989 *Cocaine kids*. Reading, Mass.: Addison-Wesley.

Williams, T.
1992 *Crackhouse*. Reading, Mass.: Addison-Wesley.

Wilson, W. J.
1987 *The truly disadvantaged*. Chicago: Univ. of Chicago Press.

Wilson, W. J.
1991 Studying inner-city social dislocations: The challenge of public agenda research. *American Sociological Review* 56: 1–14.

Zimmer, R.
1987 Operation pressure point. An occasional paper of the Center for Crime and Justice, New York Univ. School of Law.

Zinberg, N.
1984 *Drug, set and setting*. New Haven, Conn.: Yale Univ. Press.

Appendix A
Sample Characteristics by Study Neighborhood

	Central Harlem	Washington Heights
N	153	158
Ethnicity***		
African-American	69.5	54.3
Non-American, African	1.5	3.4
White	6.0	8.5
Puerto Rican	17.0	23.4
Other Spanish speaking	5.8	10.0
Other	0.2	0.4
Age***		
Less than 19	10.9	10.7
19–26	25.2	40.7
27–35	41.2	34.4
Over 35	22.7	14.2
Employment Status***		
Working	24.6	29.0
Unable to work/OLF	21.2	19.3
Unemployed	54.2	51.7
Educational Attainment***		
8th grade or less	4.2	8.5
9–11	37.6	44.8
HS graduate or GED	39.8	30.1
Some college	15.3	14.3
College graduate	3.1	1.6
Living Arrangement***		
Alone	36.3	41.7
Spouse/Child	26.8	26.0
Friends	9.7	4.5
Group situation	6.0	9.3
Streets	3.8	0.5
Public facility	0.2	3.6
Children		
Have children	60.1	63.3
Pregnant	0.7	1.3
Live with Children	28.1	30.4

p (Chi-square): * $p = .05$ ** $p = .01$ *** $p = .001$

Peter Reuter

Hawks Ascendant: The Punitive Trend of American Drug Policy

DRUG POLICY HAS GENERATED TWO DEBATES. The more elevated one concerns the retention of our current prohibitions, the legalization debate. Though it has occasionally impinged on the rhetoric of political discussion, as in the attack against legalization in the introduction to the first *National Drug Strategy*, this debate remains largely a parlor sport for intellectuals, divorced from the policy-making process. The more consequential, albeit less lofty, debate has been that between what are usually called the supply-side advocates and the demand-side advocates. The supply-siders, with former National Drug Control Director William Bennett as their most articulate spokesman, seek continued expansion cf the nation's effort to imprison drug sellers and detect and punish (in various ways) drug users, while denying that they are slighting demand-side considerations.[1] The demand-side advocates, led by Senator Joseph Biden, while generally accepting the need for "vigorous enforcement," argue that current resource commitments to programs directly aimed at demand (prevention and treatment) are grossly underfunded and should be massively increased, even if this is at the expense of enforcement.[2]

Neither debate is satisfactory. The legalization debate is too focused on extremes, excluding the possibility of compromise. It is strident, with both sides casting aspersion on the values of the other. On the other hand, the debate between the supply and demand-siders is too narrow, allowing only minor programmatic tinkering.

Borrowing liberally from the classic essay of Nye, Allison, and Carnesale on approaches to preventing nuclear war,[3] I propose to

Peter Reuter is Co-Director of the Drug Policy Research Center, RAND Corporation, Washington, D.C.

combine the two debates on drug policy into a three-sided discussion among hawks (supply-side advocates), doves (legalizers), and owls (bold demand-side advocates) about the nature of the drug problem and the consequences of different approaches to controlling it.[4]

Drug policy debates have been conducted largely in terms of images. The hawks point to the immediacy of the problems in the streets (particularly the carnage surrounding drug distribution) and reasonably (though in intemperate tones) ask whether efforts at drug prevention or treatment offer any reasonable hope for controlling those markets and associated violence in the near future. They note the apparently low success rates of drug treatment programs; many programs show relapse rates of more than 60 percent.[5] Prevention programs aimed at seventh graders (the most commonly targeted grade) will reduce the number of adult drug addicts only with a five to ten year lag. Finally, they argue that effective prevention and treatment require intense enforcement, both to make drugs difficult to obtain (driving users into treatment) and to make drug use appear legally risky (reinforcing prevention messages).[6]

The doves' message is even clearer than that of the hawks. After defending themselves from the charge that they condone the use of drugs by asserting that society should strive to reduce use of all dangerous psychoactive drugs[7] including alcohol and cigarettes, they go on to argue that most of the current evils associated with drugs arise from the prohibitions and enforcement of those prohibitions. The violence, overdoses, and massive illegal incomes that are such a prominent part of our current concerns with psychoactive drugs are not consequences of the nature of the drugs themselves but rather of the conditions of use that society has created. Doves are strong on critiques of the current regime[8] but rather weak in describing their preferred alternatives. However, they are clear that criminal prohibitions should play no role in society's efforts to keep use of psychoactive drugs to a minimum.[9]

The current owls are less eloquent. They argue that drug enforcement has proven a failure. The intensification of enforcement throughout the 1980s failed to stem a massive growth in the nation's drug problems. Enforcement does not go to the root of the problem; with a loss of faith in source country control programs (such as crop eradication and crop substitution),[10] the root of the problem is now seen to be the initiation of new users in the United States and the failure to provide good quality treatment for addicts. Prevention and treatment receive a derisory share of what the nation spends to control its drug problems. Public treatment programs, faced with the most difficult clients, have far fewer resources to spend on those clients than do private treatment programs.[11] Success in reducing the nation's drug problem requires a change in spending priorities. *Sotto voce,* at most, they also suggest that intense drug enforcement increases crime and may exacerbate health problems related to drug use; however, they believe in the value of the criminal prohibition and significant enforcement against drug dealers.

This essay has two goals. The first is to describe the increasing success of the hawks. To an extraordinary degree, they have taken control of drug policy and given it a distinctively punitive hew. The second goal is the more difficult one, namely to suggest that the hawks may have gone too far. The punishment is expensive, not so much in money terms (though the sums are no longer trivial, even in an inflation-adjusted Everett Dircksen sense) as in terms of the human costs of locking up many people for relatively minor offenses and not locking up many others for more serious offenses. Intense enforcement also increases the harms caused by drug users to themselves and others. I believe that we might well be better off if we simply punished drug dealers less aggressively; I believe that matters would be still further improved if some of the money saved by reduced punishment were spent on better quality treatment of the drug dependent. But the emphasis should be on "believe"; I cannot claim to have shown the consequences of shifting to a less punitive regime. I hope, however, that the reader will be persuaded that the question of "excessive punitiveness" is worth considering.

This is clearly the essay of an owl[12] but of one that feels that his current representatives fail to present the position strongly enough. The concession that enforcement must be maintained at its current level importantly limits the domain of policy options, particularly at a time when federal drug control budgets have stopped growing in real terms and when the corresponding state and local budgets are likely to shrink. I shall suggest that more aggressive owlishness, derived from the European "harm reduction" movement, is appropriate.

The differences among the three positions (summarized very crudely in *Table 1,* borrowed again from Nye, Allison, and Carnesale) in part come from different views of what constitutes the drug problem and the sources of that problem. For hawks, the heart of the matter is the threat to youth and to American values; drug use means an abandoning of concern with others, and focusing on short-term pleasures for oneself. It is a lack of clarity about values in society and a failure to ensure that drug use is punished that leads to so many young people becoming regular users of psychoactives. The violence and health damage are merely the visible emblems of a more fundamental problem. The first *National Drug Control Strategy* says it eloquently: For "most drug users" use is the result of a "human flaw" that leads them to pursue "a hollow, degrading and deceptive pleasure." What is required is "a firm moral stand that using drugs is wrong and should be resisted." If values are the heart of the matter, then all institutions of society must join in the fight; the 1992 *Strategy* says "[T]he family, neighborhood, community, church, school and workplace must be very active in this effort. If they are not, they implicitly signal to young people that drug use is not to be taken seriously, at least not seriously enough to do anything about it."

Doves believe that individuals use psychoactive substances because they provide pleasure and that society should minimize the harm that results from the use of such substances without criminalizing the choice of a particular substance. Psychoactive drugs can harm individuals and society has a responsibility to inform adolescents about the consequences of choosing drugs and to help those who become dependent deal with the problem. But the criminal law makes those tasks more difficult as well as imposing direct costs on society.

Owls focus on the damage arising from heavy drug use by a relatively small number of those who become dependent. The health consequences are given considerable weight. Again, drug use is regarded as evil in and of itself but, in my preferred version, attention is given to the evils created by enforcement. Criminal law may be an important tool for minimizing the damage done by dangerous and attractive psychoactives in a world of imperfect decisionmakers but enforcement is a not a good in itself; indeed, one wants the lowest level of enforcement compatible with keeping initiation down and encouraging the dependent to seek treatment.[13] Drug control is also not the only goal, and higher drug use may be accepted in return for

TABLE 1. Drug War Strategies: Hawks, Owls, and Doves

Position	Nature of Drug Problem	Explanation for Drug Use	Policy Emphasis	Consequence of Failure
HAWKS	Amorality of Drug Users & Sellers	Selfishness, Lack of Clear Social Values	Tough Enforcement	Violence, Repression
OWLS	Addiction, Disease	Adverse Social Conditions	Prevention, Treatment, Prohibition	Continuation of Present Problems
DOVES	The Bad Effects of Prohibition	Pleasures from Drugs	Legalize, Inform	Large Increase in Drug Abuse

better performance with respect to some other social goal, such as reduced spread of HIV infection.

There is much truth in the descriptive statements of all three groups. Indeed, I suspect that they are all true. However, none of them provide much help in working out what our drug policy should be. No one can describe, even very roughly, the consequences of doubling the number of treatment slots available for addicts without insurance coverage for such treatment, or what would happen if we were to increase the number of drug arrests by 25 percent. Over five years, would these result in declines of 20 percent in the extent of heroin addiction or in drug related homicides? What else might occur as a consequence, positive or negative, of these actions? The doves may be correct that many of the current evils are the consequence of prohibition but they have little basis for suggesting the consequence of the removal of those prohibitions on either the extent of use or the way that users would behave in a legalized regime.[14]

The research minded reader at this stage may object that recent experiences ought to allow us to examine the effects of at least some policy variation. Cities differ in the extent of treatment availability and stringency of enforcement. Surely that should provide the basis for determining whether tougher enforcement reduces drug use. Unfortunately, the data available at the local level are so sparse and inconsistent that research on the consequences of local variation is still in its infancy.[15]

An alternative source of insight might be the experiences of other countries, at least other developed nations. Again the research effort in this area is barely nascent but I will briefly show that some Western European nations have adopted much less punitive approaches and have fared no worse than the United States in terms of controlling drug use and its related harms.

But whatever the shakiness of the arguments and evidence of the various positions, the simple truth is that the hawks have prevailed; indeed their ascendance still seems to be increasing. Thus the next section deals mainly with their position, describing the many dimensions of their success. The section entitled "Changing Patterns of Drug Use and Related Problems," summarizes what has happened to the drug problem since 1980, pointing to the mixed record of success of American drug policy. A later section presents what we can reasonably claim to know about "the consequences of toughness;" both good and bad. It also includes a brief survey of the experiences of Western Europe, to show what other approaches are possible. The concluding section begins with a short excursion into the political dynamics of the drug issue, explaining why the hawks almost always win, and then speculates about the likely future of US drug policy.

THE TRIUMPH OF THE HAWKS

Many have noted that American drug policy has traditionally been heavily dependent on criminal law when compared to most other Western societies. Particularly in the last decade, the hawks have been in soaring ascendance. Though they grumble about the lack of severity in punishment of drug users and dealers, they have managed to massively increase funding for such punishment, to expand the scope of efforts to detect drug users in many settings and to intensify the severity of penalties imposed on those convicted of selling or using drugs.

Budgets, Legislation, and Programs

Budget allocations help make the point. The federal budget for drug control has increased substantially over the last decade; in constant dollars it has risen from $1.5 billion in fiscal year 1980 to $6.7 billion in fiscal year 1990. Throughout that period it has been dominated by enforcement programs; the share going to such programs never fell below 70 percent and rose as high as 80 percent. The federal drug control budget in 1990 allocated only 29 percent of total expenditures to treatment and prevention.

Even this understates the extent of the hawks' budgetary dominance. State and local governments spend more in total than the federal government (even eliminating federal pass-throughs) but allocate a still smaller share to treatment and prevention programs. It is difficult to assemble a national drug control budget, since most state and local drug enforcement is carried out by nonspecialized law enforcement agencies and the allocation of their budgets to drug control has a very judgemental element. My own estimate is that in 1990, state and local governments spent roughly $18 billion on drug control and 80 percent of that went for enforcement.[16] This suggests a 1990 national drug control budget of $28 billion for all levels of government, with 75 percent going to enforcement.[17] Less than $5 billion went to treatment, compared to over $20 billion spent on enforcement of various kinds, mostly at the local level. Indeed, the treatment figure may have been only $3 billion, though there may be another $2 billion of private funding through health insurance.

Budget allocation is of course only one measure of the hawks' triumph. Legislatures throughout the country, with the US Congress very much in the vanguard, have dramatically increased the sentences for drug offenses, though prison overcrowding has undercut the effectiveness of these sentencing statutes. For example, in the 1988 Anti-Drug Abuse Control Act, Congress raised the mandatory sentence for selling 50 grams of crack to five years. The state of Michigan has imposed mandatory life imprisonment without parole for those convicted of selling 650 grams of cocaine. Congress has required that states impose various penalties, such as loss of drivers' licenses, for persons convicted of drug offenses, including simple possession of marijuana; federal highway funds are to be withheld from states that do not impose such penalties.

Drug testing programs have become almost ubiquitous in many institutional settings, with an emphasis on penalty rather than treatment for those who test positive. For example, many of the new Intensively Supervised Probation programs require frequent drug testing though providing few of their clients with access to drug treatment.[18] The federal government has imposed drug testing on much of its civilian work force, while perhaps half of large corporations test job applicants for drug use.

I include the recent decisions by the Drug Enforcement Administration (DEA) and by the Public Health Service (PHS) to disallow use of marijuana for medical purposes, even on an experimental basis, as reflecting the hawkishness of current policies. DEA is responsible for the scheduling of drugs; marijuana is currently classified as Schedule I (high abuse potential, no currently accepted medical use in treatment). A number of organizations initiated a suit in 1972 seeking to have the drug reclassified as Schedule II, allowing it to be prescribed. They claimed that marijuana can alleviate nausea associated with chemotherapy as well as relieve glaucoma; it now also appears that marijuana can improve the appetite of AIDS patients. The PHS has, for the last year, allowed "compassionate" approval of marijuana prescriptions, produced on the government's marijuana farm in Mississippi, for thirteen patients.

In March 1992, the head of DEA once again refused to reschedule marijuana and the PHS announced the end of the compassionate exemption program. Both agencies deny that they had any concern with the symbolic effect of allowing marijuana to be used for therapeutic purposes.[19] On the basis of conversations with various government officials and other observers, I disbelieve that claim, though I can offer no documentary backing for this. The official argument asserts that there is no credible evidence that marijuana, as opposed to synthetic drugs containing some of its active ingredients, has greater therapeutic value. In large part this reflects the lack of research on the topic. The PHS rejection flew in the face of a survey of oncologists that found a majority who believed that marijuana should be available on prescription.[20] Indeed, that survey found that almost half of the oncologists responding currently advised their patients to use marijuana, even though the drug was not legally available. The DEA Administrator's decision reversed a remarkably strongly worded decision by the administrative law judge that the Schedule I classification was "unreasonable, arbitrary and capricious." The head of the Public Health Service did suggest that it would send a "wrong signal" to hand out a drug that can cloud judgement with respect to automobile driving or sexual behavior.[21]

The rejection of experimentation with marijuana for therapeutic purposes has an earlier parallel in the rejection of heroin for treatment of pain. In many other nations, heroin is routinely provided for relief of pain in terminal cancer patients; here it remains on

Schedule I, not allowed for any medicinal use in treatment. There is a genuine controversy about whether other synthetic opiates might not be more effective in each of the possible circumstances that heroin is a candidate pain reliever. However, the evidence for the effectiveness of heroin is strong enough that it might be left to the individual physician to decide; leakage to the illicit market is likely to provide only a negligible supplement to existing supplies.

Marijuana's "signal" value has also been emphasized by the concerted effort to reverse the decriminalization statutes that were passed in thirteen states in the 1970s. William Bennett appeared before a number of state legislatures to argue for recriminalization and was successful in Alaska in 1990.

Increasing Punitiveness

One symbol of the hawks' success is that they have managed to sustain the belief that drug sellers and users are at low risk from law enforcement, a belief that has helped promote more stringent sentencing statutes. They have emphasized stories about arrested drug sellers returning to the streets more rapidly than the police who arrested them and not getting jailed until they have been convicted numerous times. The truth is more complicated. By contemporary American standards, drug selling has become quite risky and drug use may be very risky for certain classes of users.

All this depends on a great deal of speculative arithmetic, which is only summarized here.[22] Enforcement intensity is a function not simply of the total number of arrests or imprisonments for drug offenses but of the ratio of such figures to the number of drug offenses. It is hard to find good measures of the number of such offenses but if the rise in illicit drug episodes, in Drug Abuse Warning Network (DAWN), is taken as a surrogate, then it rose faster than arrests or imprisonments from 1980 to 1985 but not as rapidly from 1985 to 1990. Moreover, most drug arrests probably did not lead to serious penal sanction in the first period but in the second half of the 1980s aggressive arrest policies at last led to large increases in the number of incarcerations. Thus it is likely that the intensity of enforcement decreased, at least for cocaine offenses, in the first half of the 1980s but then rose in the second half of that decade.

So far I have not made much of differences among drugs. Law and policy appropriately make such distinctions, though not necessarily

TABLE 2. Disposition of California felony drug arrests, 1980, 1985, 1990

	1980	1985	1990
Felony Arrests	40,451	63,766	84,538
Disposed of Number			
Convicted	18,800	30,100	53,200
(percent of arrests)	(45)	(48)	(63)
Number to State			
Prisons	921	3,366	10,494
(percent of convicted)	(5)	(11)	(20)
Number to Jail	9,700	22,500	33,900
(percent of convicted)	(52)	(75)	(64)

Source: Unpublished tabulations, California Bureau of Criminal Statistics

in appropriate ways. Enforcement has been quite drug specific and the impacts differ by drugs. Most attention in this section will be given to cocaine but it is worth noting marijuana enforcement patterns as well. In contrast to cocaine, marijuana enforcement became more stringent throughout the decade as usage dropped.

Enforcement has increased massively in absolute terms. The number of state and local arrests for drug offenses increased rapidly, from 581,000 in 1980 to 1,090,000 in 1990. The composition of these arrests changed in an important way over the same period. Whereas the 1980 total was dominated by arrests for marijuana (70 percent) and possession (82 percent) offenses, in 1990 heroin/cocaine[23] arrests had come to exceed the number for marijuana (591,000 versus 391,000) and distribution arrests now accounted for a much larger share than in 1980 (27 percent versus 18 percent). In effect, the average seriousness of arrest offense has increased sharply.

Arrest is only the first step in the criminal justice process; it is conviction and sentence that provide the principal punishment, though arrest itself can lead to seizure of drugs and other assets. At the national level we cannot systematically trace through the disposition of arrests prior to 1986. We have to rely on fragments of data collected for a few states on an occasional basis to get a sense of how many drug offenders were imprisoned during the earlier years.

The best data cover felony drug arrests in California; *Table 2* shows the disposition of these arrests in 1980, 1985, and 1990.

The number of felony drug arrests disposed of increased by about 21,000 in each half of the decade. What changed dramatically was the disposition of those arrests. The percentage convicted rose, particularly after 1985, and the percentage of convictions resulting in prison sentence went up dramatically. The total number of persons sent to prison for drug offenses rose threefold between 1980 and 1985 and tripled again in the following five years; over the entire decade the figure rose from less than 1,000 to over 10,000. A focus simply on the number of drug arrests fails to capture the increasing stringency of enforcement.

Nationally the only available data on the sentencing for felony drug convictions cover 1986 and 1988.[24] In that two year period there was a very sharp increase (from 135,000 to 225,000, approximately a 70 percent rise) in the number of persons convicted of felony drug trafficking or possession charges.[25] The number receiving state prison sentences (i.e., more than twelve months) rose from 49,900 to 92,500, though there was a modest decline in their expected time served from twenty-two months to twenty months.[26] In 1988 drug offenses accounted for approximately one-third of all felony convictions in state courts.[27]

The most recent year for which available data permit rough estimates of prison and jail years meted out for drug felonies by state courts is 1988. About 90,000 persons were sentenced to prison, and another 65,000 were sentenced to local jails. The federal court system also imposes punishment on drug dealers. Though federal drug convictions constitute a small share of the total, the average time served for those incarcerated is much higher than for state sentenced offenders, reflecting mandatory penalties for many drug selling offenses of ten years or more and no parole. In 1988 federal courts generated an estimated 50,000 years of expected prison time for drug dealers, compared to only one-tenth that amount in 1980. That reflected increasing numbers of convictions, rising sentence length and, most significantly, a rise in the share of sentences that the inmate expected to serve; this last was the result of the imposition of sentencing guidelines and the abolition of federal parole. The total of federal and state incarceration figures for 1988 was about 200,000 cell years; this is perhaps ten times the 1980 figure.

The Penal Risks of the Drug Trade

One way to assess what this punishment represents is to consider the risks of arrest faced by users, and the risk of imprisonment faced by sellers, of cocaine and marijuana.

To calculate roughly the 1990 absolute risks per user year for the two drugs, we need estimates of the total number of current users. If there were 15 million marijuana users, a relatively generous figure based on the survey data,[28] then they faced an average risk of 2 percent of arrest in that year; though this seems low, note that in steady state that amounted to a one in five chance of being arrested in a ten year using career. For cocaine, with a much smaller user base (no more than perhaps 5 million, ignoring those who use less than once per month), the annual arrest risk was 6 percent. The risk in a ten year using career might then be as high as 60 percent.

These are, of course, very aggregate calculations. Not all users are at the same risk of apprehension. Those who use frequently might be expected to be at much higher risk because they engage in more of the risky transaction of purchase. But there are other characteristics that seem to be associated with risk of arrest for drug possession, in particular race and gender. In the District of Columbia, of those residents arrested for drug possession between 1985 and 1987, 96 percent were African-American; 82 percent were male. No reasonable estimate of the prevalence of drug use in different populations would suggest that this represented the share of African-Americans or males in the drug using population. These percentages probably reflect the fact that many possession arrests are failed sales arrests; a seller is caught with drugs but not in the act of selling and the seller population in exposed situations (i.e., selling on the street and in crack houses) seems to be predominantly male and (in the District of Columbia) African-American.

In summary, some user groups may be at very high risk of apprehension, others at quite modest risk. That is not a casual observation, since I shall suggest later that it appears that the big declines in drug use have occurred among the groups at low risk of arrest.

For sellers the arrest risks differed even more substantially for the two drugs. Using the same assumptions as Reuter and Kleiman[29] concerning the ratio of buyers to sellers for each drug, marijuana sellers may have faced not much more than a 10 percent probability of being arrested in the course of a year of selling; the comparable figure for cocaine might be as high as 40 percent.

I estimate that the total cell years in 1988 for marijuana sellers was about 40,000 and for cocaine sellers about 110,000. The ratio of marijuana to cocaine is surprising in light of the great concern attached to cocaine use. But the federal courts, which provide clearly separated figures for the different drugs, show a similar ratio. The cell year calculations are more speculative than those for arrests, but 110,000 cell years for a population of perhaps 350,000 cocaine dealers suggests that by 1988 that activity had indeed become a risky one. A study of drug dealers in Washington, D.C. in the late 1980s[30] estimated that street sellers of drugs faced about a 22 percent probability of imprisonment in the course of a year's selling and that, given expected time served, they spent one-third of their selling career in prison.

Does this make drug selling appropriately risky? One-third of one's time in prison strikes me as a lot. On the other hand, the risk per selling transaction is extraordinarily low; a seller who works two days per week at this trade may make 1,000 transactions in the course of a year. His imprisonment risk per transaction is only about 1 in 4,500; by that metric it is a great deal lower than the risks associated with other crimes, such as burglary and robbery. Another way of expressing the risk is that a dealer may spend a day imprisoned for each ten sales transactions.

In many ways these figures mirror the realities for property crimes. Most robberies and burglaries result in no arrest; yet those who engage frequently in robbery or burglary are likely to spend a significant portion of their criminal careers incarcerated. So it appears to be for those who are regular drug sellers, at least in exposed settings.

CHANGING PATTERNS OF DRUG USE AND RELATED PROBLEMS

By historic and international standards, use of illegal psychoactive drugs in the United States in the early 1990s is extraordinarily high.[31] Moreover, that drug use is associated with more severe and diverse problems than those associated with illegal drugs in other periods or societies. It is almost certain nevertheless that the prevalence of drug use has declined sharply from the dizzying heights of the early to mid-1980s and is likely to continue to decline. These two discordant facts present a dilemma in assessing the effectiveness of current policies. Should we focus on the high absolute levels, and conclude that these policies have failed, or on the declines and conclude that they are finally succeeding?

In any assessment it is important to note that the levels of drug use and drug problems (as well as their declines) are far from uniform across population groups. Drug abuse or dependence[32] is increasingly concentrated in inner-city populations and appears to be disproportionately a problem for the minority community, particularly inner-city, young, African-American males. Drug use apart, inner-city communities have been much more affected by the violence and disorder surrounding drug distribution. This skewing of adversities has had an important influence on the politics of drug policies. For most of the nation the drug problem is lessening but for many poorer communities there are few, if any, signs of relief; this exacerbates the growing sense of a division within society, the emergence of a hardening into "Two Nations."

The Prevalence of Drug Use

The broad population surveys, of the household population and of high school seniors, tell a consistent story.[33] Initiation into drug use (as measured, for example, by the percentage of successive cohorts of 18 year olds reporting use in past year) escalated rapidly in the late 1970s and early 1980s and then began to decline by 1986 or slightly earlier. The peaks were alarming; in 1978, 11 percent of high school seniors reported using marijuana on a daily basis in the previous month. Every number is now down sharply from its peak; for example, by 1991 less than 2 percent of seniors reported daily use in the previous month.

The declines, as reported in the surveys, have been surprisingly evenly spread across age/race/sex groups. The surveys also have shown a complex and changing relationship between education and drug use. In 1985 prevalence rates among males born between 1959 and 1964 were very similar for high school graduates and for dropouts; indeed the former showed slightly higher rates for both recent use (past thirty days) and past use (last twelve months). By 1990 the rates had fallen much more sharply for the high school graduates, particularly for past use. Differences in the declines for recent use were less marked, perhaps because this included more people who were habituated to drug use. The emerging negative correlation between education and cocaine use is consistent with the changes in cigarette use.[34]

The surveys provide mixed support for hypotheses about higher rates of drug use among African-Americans and Hispanics. The high school senior surveys consistently show sharply higher prevalence rates among whites.[35] However, the National Household Survey shows higher rates for African-Americans; in the age group 26–34 for example, in 1990, the percentage reporting some use of an illegal drug in previous month was 13.7 percent, compared to 9.5 percent for white respondents.[36]

The broad surveys can reasonably claim to provide a valid measure of trends in the extent of drug use among the general population, though they have serious weaknesses even in that role. Increased stigmatization of drug use reduces the willingness of respondents to report that they are actually users; however, that stigmatization also reduces the extent of use. Thus the surveys may exaggerate the downward trend in use but it is unlikely that they misrepresent the direction.

But no one doubts that the broad population surveys miss a great deal of the most important behavior, namely frequent drug use. There are at least three reasons for this. First, the surveys do not include some critical populations in their sampling frames (for example, the homeless[37] and prisoners) who are believed to have high rates of drug abuse. Moreover, the size of these noncovered populations has risen and their composition has changed; both populations now seem to include higher percentages with drug abuse problems than they did in 1980. Second, those who use drugs frequently, even if formally included in the sampling frame, are likely to be more difficult to reach because they behave more erratically. Third, the response rate for the survey has declined from 83 percent in 1985 to 79 percent to 1990; this nonresponse increase may well be related to increased disapproval of drug use and thus lower willingness to even participate in a survey.

Moreover, the credibility of the surveys as a good representation of the nation's drug problems was undermined in the late 1980s by the dramatic discrepancy between the most publicized findings of those surveys and public perception of the changing problem. While the surveys pointed to substantial declines in drug use, it was widely believed that the drug problem was getting a great deal worse. The surveys also pointed to quite modest numbers of persons with severe drug problems; for example, the number of persons using cocaine weekly or more frequently was estimated at less than 1 million, which seemed inconsistent with the severity of cocaine-related problems.

Two official indicators supported the popular beliefs. DAWN reported data on the involvement of drugs in Emergency Room (ER) cases and in Medical Examiners' (ME) reports on deaths. DAWN, in contrast to the survey data, showed dramatic increases in cocaine mentions throughout the 1980s; the total number rose more than tenfold between 1980 and 1988. Beginning in 1988, the Drug Use Forecasting (DUF) system collected data on the prevalence of recent drug use by arrestees in twenty major cities, relying on analysis of urine specimens. It found very high rates of drug use in the arrested population and produced estimates of the number of frequent users that were very much higher than those derived from the household survey. Moreover, both DAWN and DUF pointed to a concentration of problems in the inner city. DAWN which increasingly measures the extent of drug dependence,[38] also suggested that whatever is happening to drug use generally, the number of cocaine dependent persons rose substantially between 1980 and 1990.[39]

Dependence

Measurement of the extent of drug dependence or frequent use is casual, almost to the point of irresponsibility. Though it is often asserted that there are 500,000–750,000 heroin addicts in the United States, it is impossible to find any systematic estimates post-1980; the number has its origins in murky and questionable manipulation of little understood data series.[40] It is, however, reasonably well documented that heroin use increased rapidly during the period of about 1967 to 1973 and that the number of new initiates fell rapidly after that. However, if the correct figure is 750,000, then the United States, fifteen years after the end of the epidemic of heroin initiation, appears to have as high a rate of heroin dependence as any developed nation.[41]

The DAWN data suggest that the heroin addicted population is still dominated by the cohort of inner-city minorities who first became addicted around 1970, when they were in their late teens and early twenties. The population of DAWN heroin ER cases is about 50 percent Hispanic and African-American, and getting older;

whereas 32 percent were over thirty-five in 1983, that percentage had risen to 50 percent by 1989.[42] Data on admissions to publicly funded treatment programs also point to an aging population that is dominated by minorities. Most heroin addicts have been in drug treatment programs frequently but heroin addiction, at least in this population, shows similarity to alcoholism; it can be characterized as a chronic, lifetime, relapsing disorder. DUF shows older arrestees to be more likely to test positive for opiates (almost exclusively heroin) but also shows surprisingly high rates among youthful arrestees, suggesting perhaps a resurgence of heroin initiation among the criminally active.[43] The new initiation may occur primarily among those who are already regular cocaine users.

More attention has been given to measuring the prevalence of frequent cocaine use. Indeed, there has even been a short-lived but vigorous controversy about this, with William Bennett and Senator Biden conducting an undignified shouting match about the number on national television.[44] The household survey produces an estimate of less than one million persons using cocaine at least once a week; indeed, for 1990 the figure was only 662,000. Using data from urine tests of arrestees in major cities, analysts have produced estimates of over two million.[45]

The urinalysis data show extremely high rates of cocaine use among arrestees. In most cities, over 50 percent of those arrested test positive for cocaine; supplemental interviews also show quite high rates of self-reported dependence among those who test positive for cocaine or heroin. What makes these figures particularly alarming is that arrest is not a rare event for young males, particularly less educated youth in large cities. Tillman,[46] reporting on the 1956 birth cohort in California found that 34 percent of white males were arrested between the ages of 18 and 29; the figure for black males was 66 percent. The 1956 cohort came to maturity before the growth of the cocaine markets. For the 1967 cohort, Reuter, MacCoun, and Murphy found that in the District of Columbia, perhaps one-quarter of the males were charged with at least one criminal offense, mostly a felony, between ages 18 and 21.[47] For African-American males in the Washington, D.C. cohort, the rate was approximately one-third. A majority of those charged had at least one drug offense among those charges.

The DUF data have only been collected since about 1988, so they cannot be used to describe trends over the decade of the 1980s. However, in the District of Columbia, urinalysis data have been collected since 1984. Over the period 1984–1988, there was a dramatic increase in the percent testing positive for cocaine, with little decline in the percent testing positive for other drugs. There has been a substantial drop since the peak figure of 68 percent for cocaine in May 1988 but in late 1991 the percentage testing positive for cocaine was still about 50 percent, and had been at that level for a year. DUF figures show most cities to have lower rates than the peaks of 1988 and 1989 but the declines are modest. In Chicago the cocaine positives were down to 53 percent in the first quarter of 1991, compared to the peak of 64 percent in the fourth quarter of 1989.

In summary, these, and other data, suggest that the number of drug users has declined since the peak of the early to mid-1980s. However, there has been a much slighter, and later, decline in the numbers experiencing, and causing, significant problems related to their own frequent use of drugs. An increasing share of the drug abusing population is found among the inner-city poor, as the more educated became more concerned about the health consequences of drug use. The poorer users are criminally active; their criminal activity is exacerbated by this drug use. That has enormous consequences for the politics of drug policy.

Costs

It is all very well to have estimates of the numbers of drug users and abusers. What costs, social and economic, should we attach to these figures? How significant is this problem?

The federal government has sponsored a series of four estimates of the economic cost of drug abuse.[48] For 1985, the estimated economic cost was $44 billion, compared to $70 billion for alcohol abuse and $103 billion for mental illness. It is hard to know what to make of these numbers, even if taken at face value, but the simple truth is that they are essentially irrelevant for our purposes because they are dominated by what the government spends to control the problem and they miss major elements of the social costs associated with illicit drugs. Particularly troubling is the treatment of the cost of crime associated with drug abuse. This is estimated to be $13 billion, of which 90 percent is public expenditures on law enforcement; the loss of safety and amenity is treated as zero. Yet in terms of dollars that individuals would be willing to spend to have lower crime rates in their community, that cost might well be much larger than the figures cited above.[49]

Estimates of the number of drug users is probably not a good metric for scaling the drug problem. After all, as even William Bennett noted in the introduction to the first *National Drug Strategy*, most drug using careers are short, with only a few episodes involving drugs other than marijuana and are ended without requiring any treatment. Estimates that large numbers experiment with drugs or use drugs on an occasional basis does not mean that use of illicit drugs constitutes a major problem. Alternatively put, is there a credible base for the popular fears that briefly made drugs the leading social problem in 1988 and 1989?

Some drugs such as LSD and PCP can cause substantial and lasting damage to an individual who uses them just once; this, however, is an extremely rare event for cocaine, heroin or marijuana. It seems likely that the vast majority of those who use these latter drugs only a few times suffer little harm as a consequence. The external costs of their use in aggregate may be high, if for example they provide a substantial share of the total market for illicit drugs and that market generates violence and corruption, but the costs to the individuals look modest. Moreover, it seems likely that occasional users actually account for a small share of total consumption, so that it is also unlikely that they impose high external costs through their contribution to the violence and disorder surrounding markets.

It is appropriate then to focus on those who are drug abusers in order to obtain an understanding of the costs to individuals. The standard comparison of morbidity and mortality suggests that illicit drugs present only a moderately serious problem. Compared to alcohol or tobacco, the numbers of users, abusers, premature deaths, and disease associated with all illegal drugs together is small. Tobacco accounts for about 400,000 premature deaths annually, alcohol for about 100,000. It would be hard to sustain a figure of more than 20,000 premature deaths from the direct effects of illegal drugs; even if half of all homicides are drug related, the figure is still barely 30,000.[50] Nor are the figures for morbidity impressive. With a base of frequent users of no more than 3 million, the health effects are tiny compared to those associated with the 50 million regular cigarette smokers and the 10 million heavy drinkers. On the grounds of the health costs, it could scarcely be claimed that use of illicit psychoactives constitutes a social problem of the first order.

That is a highly aggregative argument. Whereas alcohol and cigarettes strike all socioeconomic groups, illegal drugs bear disproportionately, in terms both of morbidity and mortality, on lower socioeconomic status and minority populations. Thus it might be that for these populations, particularly in center cities, illicit drugs are indeed a major health issue. However, it appears that these populations are also disproportionately affected by alcohol and cigarette related morbidity and mortality, so that in relative terms illegal drugs may not be much more important.

Yet there are other, distinctive and important problems associated with illegal drugs. Alcohol is comparable to cocaine in its individual criminogenic consequences. Of those sentenced to jail terms in 1989, 29 percent reported being under the influence of alcohol (and not drugs) at the time of the offense, compared to 15 percent reporting being under the influence of drugs alone; another 12 percent reported being under the influence of both.[51] However, the high price of cocaine and the extensive illegal markets associated with it have engendered crime and violence that have sources other than the direct effect of the drugs themselves. For example, Goldstein found that the majority of drug related homicides in New York were the result of "systemic" violence (for example, disputes over territories or contractual disagreements) rather than of the psychoactive effect of the drug or the need to obtain money to purchase drugs.[52] In some cities it is claimed that half of all homicides are drug related, though the criteria used to make the classification are quite murky. Moreover, the earnings from drug markets are believed to have been important in increasing the lethality of guns used in urban crime. That lethality may have contributed to the rise in killings of innocent bystanders.

The spread of HIV through needle sharing and other drug related behaviors (such as the extreme promiscuity of crack users) is another hard-to-value consequence of drug use.[53] Over one-quarter of AIDS cases include intravenous drug use as a primary risk factor and that percentage is rising. Curiously, though, in most of Western Europe, a concern with AIDS has been a principal influence on drug policy; in the United States it has been treated as almost a separate policy arena.[54] In particular, it has not been given much attention in the debates with which this paper is concerned.

In the last few years, a great deal of attention has been given to the phenomenon of "crack babies," who are severely damaged by the cocaine use of their mothers during pregnancy. From an official high of 375,000 in the first *National Strategy,* the estimated number of babies annually affected by mother's drug use has fallen to 30,000 to 50,000. Moreover, it is no longer so clear that the damage suffered by most of these babies is very long-lasting. The problem is an emotionally very troubling one but may be rare in most populations.

Corruption is another cost associated with drug prohibition and its enforcement. Though there are spectacular and troubling instances of such corruption, such as that involving the homicide squad in the Miami Police Department in the mid-1980s and the more recent convictions of numerous deputies in the Los Angeles Sheriff's department, the revealed corruption seems fairly opportunistic and small scale, certainly when compared with that surrounding the enforcement of gambling laws in the 1940s and 1950s.[55]

It is difficult then to say much about the real social costs of drug use and abuse. Violence, AIDS, corruption, and crack babies are all important and distinctive consequences of drug use under current conditions. There is enough of each of them to make understandable the public panic of the late 1980s. They have all become familiar enough to make equally understandable the declining concern of the last two years. That latter effect has been hastened by the fact that the most visible effects are highly concentrated in inner-city communities.

Knowing the scale of the social costs generated by drugs is important for determining what society should be willing to sacrifice in order to attain the goal of reduced use and abuse. Our inability to provide meaningful measures, along with the visibility and drama of illegal drugs, facilitates the task of those who would have the nation become harshly punitive.

THE CONSEQUENCES OF TOUGHNESS

To what extent can it be shown that reductions in drug use have been accomplished by the general toughening of society's approach to drug control? What are other negative consequences of toughness?

Unfortunately, discussion of these issues must be highly speculative since there is little research on which to draw.

The punitive approach should reduce drug use and abuse by making drugs more expensive and/or less accessible. This will drive addicts into treatment and discourage adolescents from initiating use. Intense enforcement should also increase disapproval of drugs, which will lead current users to desist earlier. The available evidence suggests that intensified enforcement has had modest success in raising drug prices and has not reduced already limited access for the middle class. Disapproval of drug use has increased, and that may well have reduced initiation, but it is unlikely that this disapproval is a function of enforcement stringency.

It is even harder to determine the costs of heavy enforcement, in other than budgetary terms. Drug enforcement bears particularly heavily on the African-American population. Large numbers of young poorly educated males are being locked up for long periods in institutions that do little to rehabilitate them. Tough enforcement may also exacerbate various harms of drug use.

The latter brings us to the issue of harm reduction, the European term for the more pragmatic approach to drug problems that takes account of the fact that goals of drug control can conflict with other social goals. The concluding part of this section describes what that approach entails, how (and why) it has been implemented elsewhere, and its possible application in the United States.

Prices, Attitudes, and Prevalence

Price is determined by the interaction of supply and demand. If the demand for cocaine was declining in the second half of the 1980s, as suggested by the surveys, the rising numbers entering treatment and increasing imprisonment rates, then, absent tougher enforcement, prices might have been expected to fall during that period. In fact we observe a complex pattern, with retail cocaine prices declining until 1988 and then rising for the next two years.

The failure of cocaine prices to collapse may be evidence of the effectiveness of stringent enforcement. Certainly the margins for different actors in the trade remain high and, if 1988 District of Columbia data are any guide, provide substantial wage levels (approximately $30 per hour for low level participants in 1988). But the price increase that has been achieved is surprisingly modest; late 1990 prices were perhaps 25 percent above their 1988 nadir and close to their levels of 1986 in nominal dollars. This may reflect a growing correlation between selling and heavy use. Adult cocaine retailers are frequent users themselves; if a significant portion of their earnings from this activity go to support their own consumption, then enforcement risks will have less effect on prices.

Marijuana seems to represent more of a success for enforcement. Its price is sharply higher than ten years ago, even after adjusting for potency increases and inflation. Interdiction may well have played a role; Colombia, the low cost producer of marijuana, no longer services the US market, as a consequence of increasingly effective interdiction. The primary sources are Mexico and the United States itself, both of which are very high cost producers. Moreover, the price increase has occurred over a period during which all the indicators point to a substantial decline in demand, making even clearer the impact of enforcement.

There is only one measure of availability, which comes from the High School Senior Survey. Respondents are asked whether it would be "easy," "very easy," etc. to get a particular drug. In 1980, 48 percent said that it was easy or very easy for them to get cocaine; by 1990 the figure was 59 percent. It declined for the first time in 1991, perhaps reflecting the falling demand among the seniors; with markedly fewer buyers in this population, the market may work less smoothly. In any case, if availability is a measure of enforcement success, then it certainly has lagged the increasing toughness by a long time. Marijuana availability as measured in the same survey, has remained essentially unchanged since the survey began in 1975; each year 80 to 85 percent report that marijuana is readily available or available.

These data make it difficult to evaluate enforcement success. In the legal market, where cocaine is available as a local anesthetic, it sells for $4 per pure gram, compared to the $130 on the streets. It is not readily available for many segments of the population. Marijuana prices are high by historical and international standards; indeed high enough to perhaps encourage more use of other drugs, such as alcohol and cocaine. The question is whether less rigorous enforcement, with fewer dealers incarcerated, would much reduce price or increase availability.

A striking feature of the general population surveys over the 1980s was the changing attitude toward both the dangers and perceived popularity of drug use. Whereas in 1980, only 31 percent of high school seniors believed that using cocaine once or twice was very risky, that percentage had risen to 59 percent in 1990; for marijuana the figures were 15 percent in 1980 and 37 percent in 1990. The responses stressed health dangers rather than legal dangers.

Fewer respondents also saw drug use as the norm. Whereas in 1980, 76 percent disapproved of using cocaine once or twice, the 1990 figure was 92 percent. The most sophisticated analysis of the high school senior survey data has found that it is these attitudinal changes which best explain declining drug use.[56]

As mentioned earlier, the evidence suggests that drug use has declined more sharply among those who have graduated from high school than those who have not. At the same time, it appears that enforcement risks have increased more for the less educated. It may well be that the more educated have greater sensitivity to the threat of arrest but the evidence is against enforcement as the primary engine for reduced drug use.

Incapacitation

Toughness works through incapacitation of sellers and users, as well as through the effect of deterrence on prices. Locking up sellers should raise the price of drugs by removing those who were the most willing to be dealers. On the other hand, locking up users should lower the price. Even if they use drugs while in prison, they are likely to use less; urinalysis programs for prisoners show very low use rates generally. Thus incapacitation can have ambiguous effects on prices, depending on the composition of the imprisoned population.

We have already seen that an increasing number of drug sellers were locked up during the second half of the 1980s. There was an even larger rise in the number of drug users incarcerated.

Over the second half of the 1980s there was a dramatic increase in the number of prison and jail inmates, continuing a trend that goes back to the mid-1970s. Between the end of 1985 and the end of 1990, that figure increased from 750,000 (including federal, state, and local correctional facilities) to 1,200,000. The incarcerated population became richer in drug users over that time; in 1988 nearly one-third of those sent to state prison were convicted of drug

TABLE 3. Race characteristics of arrestees

	Percent Black		
	1980	1985	1990
All Offenses	24.5	26.6	28.9
Crime Index	32.8	33.7	34.4
Drug Abuse	23.6	30.0	40.7

Source: *Uniform Crime Reports.*

offenses, compared to only 23 percent in 1986. Moreover, the data from local urinalysis programs suggests that the percentage of those imprisoned on nondrug charges who were drug users also rose. Taking account of both the increasing population of prisoners and the rising share that were drug users, perhaps a total of 450,000 additional drug users were removed from the population that might be involved in regular use or selling of drugs.[57]

What are the effects of this increase? In the context of an estimated 2 to 3 million frequent drug users, that is a substantial change and may do much to explain the decline in various indicators, including both DAWN and DUF. That is, declines in the numbers of persons showing up in emergency rooms for drug related problems or in the percentage of arrestees testing positive for drugs may reflect not just declines in drug using behavior but also the incapacitation of large numbers of drug users. The gains then are contingent on continued incarceration, given the lack of effective treatment in most prison facilities.

Other Consequences

A standard charge against the war on drugs is that it is racist and has led to a serious erosion of civil liberties. It is certainly true that African-Americans make up an extraordinarily high proportion of those charged with drug offenses, even when compared to their proportion in criminal offenses generally or to their share of the population of frequent drug users. That does not imply racism on the part of police or courts but it does point to the possibility of selective enforcement.

Table 3 provides data on the high and growing fraction of drug arrestees who are categorized as Black in the Uniform Crime Reports.

That share has increased dramatically over the ten years from 1980 to 1990, from less than one-fourth to more than two-fifths. The percentage has risen much faster for drug offenses than for others, including the more serious (represented by "Crime Index" offenses).

The emphasis on crack seems to have exacerbated this tendency. For example, the Minnesota legislature in 1989 raised the maximum penalty for possession of 3 grams of crack to twenty years; the same quantity of cocaine powder involved a maximum of five years. As it turned out, 96.6 percent of those charged with crack possession were African-American; for powder cocaine the figure was about 20 percent. The Minnesota Supreme Court overturned the statute for that reason in 1991.[58]

The high and rising drug arrest rates for African-Americans represents another dilemma for drug policy. It is in poorer sections of large cities, with high percentages of young African-American males, that the problems of disorder and violence surrounding drug distribution are most acute. These are the communities that have the greatest need for active drug enforcement. Yet that enforcement, responsive to community concerns, results in the incarceration of alarmingly high percentages of young males from the same communities.

This brings us to another concern, namely that those who are locked up are unimportant figures in the drug trades and that their sentences are too severe for the crime, particularly when prisons are regarded as more likely to worsen an inmate's behavior than to rehabilitate him. The contention about the role of those locked up is almost irrefutable because of the highly pyramided nature of the drug trade. Cocaine enters this country in 100 kilogram lots and sells in 1 gram units; under reasonable assumptions about how many others a wholesale dealer is willing to transact with, there are about 1,000 retailers for each importer. Thus most of those who are locked up must be retailers and their support personnel. There simply aren't 100,000 significant figures in the cocaine trade; indeed, there probably aren't more than 10,000 whose removal would make the trade go somewhat slower.[59]

Those locked up receive long sentences now, particularly at the federal level. The expected time served for conviction on a drug trafficking offense in federal court is over six years. Though federal courts confront the highest level dealers, they also sentence numerous minor agents of these dealers, such as the Colombian sailors who transport cocaine from that country. The sentences received by these agents are not light. Indeed, a horrible irony of the existing federal sentencing guidelines is that the only mitigating circumstance for shortening of the mandatory sentences is effective cooperation with the prosecutor. Unimportant agents such as sailors have little to offer, whereas the principal figures in seller networks can, if they choose, provide valuable information.

At the state level the average sentences are not particularly long by contemporary US standards but as we saw above, about 90,000 persons received sentences of at least one year for drug offenses in 1988. At a time of overcrowded prisons, even one uncomfortable with the level of incarceration in the United States must ask whether the space could not be allocated more sensibly for more serious offenses.

One response to this is that those sentenced for drug offenses are also involved in more serious offenses; the drug selling is merely a marker for these other crimes. Little data are available on this matter. In the District of Columbia in a sample of drug dealers on probation in 1988, only 5 percent reported a violent offense in the previous six months. Indeed, drug selling in that sample looked very much like a substitute for other kinds of income generating (and sometimes violent) crimes.

The issue here is that of the seriousness of the offense. Legislatures have been impressed by claims that drugs cause great harm and have consequently demanded that the criminal justice system treat this as a serious offense. As always, it is a question of emphasis and allocation of resources but I confess that it is not clear to me that marijuana selling, or even possession with intent to distribute cocaine, should necessarily lead to lengthy incarceration, particularly at a time when punishment capacity is stretched so thin. That so many of those being locked up in state prisons and local jails for drug offenses are African-Americans makes it particularly important that we judge whether this incarceration is necessary.

Moreover, there are other harms that may be exacerbated by tough enforcement. Frequent harassment of street drug sellers increases the incentives to use violence for the maintenance of market share. More variability in the purity of heroin, resulting from occasional large seizures, may cause more overdoses. Stringent enforcement has raised marijuana potency, while head shop laws prevent marijuana users from using water pipes; marijuana is consumed in the most harmful possible manner.

The list of conjectured harms from intense enforcement can be extended. How significant each of them is and what they amount to in the aggregate is impossible to even guess at. I believe though that they are troubling enough that one needs to consider whether there is an alternative approach to drug control that takes them into account.

Harm Minimization and Aggressive Owls[60]

Illicit drug use has become a prominent issue in much of Western Europe in recent years. For example, a survey of popular perceptions of the principal public health problems of the nations of the European Community found that in almost all of them illicit drugs was one of the top three concerns, always ahead of alcohol.[61] In four countries it was identified as the leading health problem. Deaths from drug use, almost exclusively involving heroin, have increased rapidly in Germany, Italy, and Spain. Switzerland, the south of France, Italy, and Spain have HIV epidemics dominated by intravenous drug users.

Despite these concerns, the reality and rhetoric of drug policy in most of Western Europe is very different from that in the United States. The crime consequences of drug use are given far less attention, though property crime is often believed to be substantially raised by drug addiction. The health consequences dominate discussion in most of Europe, though that has led to only a moderate hatching of doves. Syringe exchange schemes, scarcely permitted even on a pilot basis here, have become common in Britain, the Netherlands, Italy, and the German cantons of Switzerland. Spain and the Netherlands, with very different social policies toward drug use generally, have given the criminal law a minor role in dealing with drug users.

The discussion of drug policy in Europe, outside of Scandinavia, is dominated by debate about harm minimization rather than minimizing the prevalence of drug use. Cannabis use, outside of Scandinavia, is almost entirely ignored. The emergence of AIDS has been the catalytic force. As the Advisory Council on the Misuse of Drugs in Great Britain said in a 1988 report, "HIV is a greater threat to public and individual health than drug misuse."[62] Policy measures that might increase the extent of drug use but lower the prevalence of HIV are likely to be endorsed under this hierarchy of values.

The policy view extends though to more than just AIDS related matters. If tough enforcement lessens the likelihood of drug addicts seeking treatment, then less stringent enforcement might be preferred. Some Europeans even talk about police making harm minimization choices in their tactics, for example using selective enforcement to focus on heroin injectors rather than heroin smokers, since smoking poses lower risk of both HIV and hepatitis B.

My colleagues and I conjecture that the difference in policy tone between Europe and the United States is importantly affected by the much lower prevalence of violence associated with drug distribution and use in Europe. That in turn may reflect simply the lower level of violence in European crime generally. Without that violence it is much easier to see health measures as the most appropriate response.

How successful have harm minimization policies been? Precisely because they are more concerned with reducing harms than drug use, they cannot be judged simply by the extent of drug use that they have engendered. The Dutch make a reasonable case that their very conscious adoption of the harm minimization approach has permitted their addicts to lead healthier and less crime ridden lives than their counterparts in the United States. However, the much more generous income support schemes available to prime age males in Holland may be more significant here than any facet of targeted drug policy.

Harm minimization is not a policy but a framework for making decisions which considers that drug policy, particularly related to application of the criminal law, has effects on other aspects of the quality of life. The one instance of the application of harm minimization in American drug policy is in the developing consensus that drug abusing pregnant women should not be subject to criminal prosecution for the risks that they pose to their babies.[63] The belief that such prosecutions would reduce the probability of use of prenatal care seems to have played an important role in this consensus.

However, most US owls currently do not take the harm minimization approach. Their acceptance of the need for vigorous enforcement, which precludes consideration of the negative consequences of that enforcement, has made their contribution to drug policy discussions of limited value so far. We now turn to the sources of their timidity.

THE POLITICAL DYNAMICS OF DRUG POLICY

The success of the hawks is in part a function of how the drug problem has been characterized in the United States. So long as crime is the dominant part of the public image of the problem, then law enforcement is plausibly the most appropriate response. Drugs are produced by evil syndicates (the Medellin cartel), sold by ruthless gangs who kill innocent bystanders and generate fabulous incomes for the sellers (media stories about inner-city kids earning $1,000 a day[64]) operating in settings that generate neighborhood fear and disorder (street corners and crack houses); so runs the standard version of the problem.

That growing association between crime and drug use in popular perception reflects the reality of changing patterns of drug use reported earlier. As young, poorly educated males become a larger part of the population that is heavily involved with drugs, so drugs and crime have truly become more strongly associated. In this sense we are reliving the experience of the early twentieth century United States with respect to opiates. Courtwright argues that the total number of opiate addicts declined through the first quarter of this century but that the decline was much more pronounced among the middle class, where the addiction was generally associated with medical treatment.[65] The recreational user/addict, typically less educated, and more frequently a criminally active young urban male, was less likely to drop out of opiate use as disapproval increased and more restrictions were placed on access to drugs. Thus opiate addiction came increasingly to be seen as a behavior leading to crime. That helped create a climate of opinion in which criminal prohibitions on use and strict penalties against sellers received broad support; the Harrison Act of 1914 attracted little controversy.

The media reporting of the "drug crisis" has undoubtedly helped here. An analysis of prime-time network news bulletins in 1988 found that illegal drugs were the second most frequently mentioned item. Most of those news stories dealt with the drama of crime associated with drugs; few of the stories concerned drug treatment or

TABLE 4. Preferences for different drug control programs

	Percent Favoring Program		
PROGRAM	White	Nonwhite	Total
Interdiction	19	42	34
Prosecution/Arrest	17	9	12
Education/Prevention	41	29	33
Treatment	23	21	22

Note: Responses to question: "Which program should receive the most money and effort in the fight against drugs?"

Source: *The District of Columbia 1990 Public Opinion Survey of Drug Abuse and Crime*

prevention. The standard media mention of the issue is drugs and crime, rather than addiction to psychoactive substances of varying legal status.

All this has made it difficult for owls or doves to win the debate. No member of Congress has had political problems as the result of pressing for tougher penalties or expanded enforcement. The risks in arguing for more lenient punishment of drug users or dealers are clearly very serious, in face of popular opinion inflamed to believe in the need for toughness. It is depressing to note that a 1986 "Sense of Congress" resolution demanding the additions to the federal drug control budget be split evenly between enforcement and demand-side programs has led only to a modest shift in the balance of funding, even as federal drug budgets have rapidly escalated.

There is not a lot of good survey research on public opinion with respect to drugs, in particular about what people perceive to constitute the drug problem. The most relevant research survey was carried out in the District of Columbia in 1990 and showed a lack of faith in local enforcement. Respondents were asked to rate four kinds of programs in terms of their importance for controlling drug abuse. *Table 4* presents the results for both whites and nonwhites.

Three features of these responses are striking. The first is the relatively greater faith in interdiction (stopping drugs from coming into the country) as compared to enforcement at the local level. That reverses what I take to be the growing consensus among those who analyze drug enforcement. The second is the modest support for treatment, though a majority of respondents in the survey did believe that drug treatment was the appropriate sentence for arrested drug users. Third, whites and nonwhites have notably different attitudes.

Nonwhites are more for enforcement than whites; 51 percent of nonwhites chose one of the two enforcement options, compared to 36 percent of whites. But the nonwhites more strongly prefer that enforcement take the form of interdiction rather than arrest and prosecution in their own community. A higher percentage of whites show faith in education and prevention. But demand-side programs do get strong support from both whites and nonwhites; overall a bare majority favor such programs. Thus there may be more of a base of public opinion to support less punitive approaches than is currently believed.

CONCLUSION

A particularly disturbing aspect of the current situation is the difficulty of dismantling the punitive apparatus that has been assembled since the mid-1980s. With declines in drug involvement among American youth likely to continue for some years, the justification for the draconian sentences at the federal level, with their personal and fiscal costs, will be even harder to sustain. The problem is increasingly that of the adult drug addicts who became dependent during the heroin epidemic of 1967–1973 or the cocaine epidemic of the 1980s.

Yet the political forces are not favorable to changing this bent in the near future. The doves are likely to be pushed back to the fringe status they held until 1987. Their appearance on center stage was fueled by the pervasive sense of despair in the late 1980s that the nation's drug problem was continuing to worsen despite tough and intrusive control. That sense of despair has lessened, reflecting at last the great decline in initiation into drug use among the vast middle class of the nation. Notwithstanding the rhetoric of liberals and conservatives alike that it is "everybody's problem," drugs now seem to be moving to another entry on the long list of ills that emanate from the inner city and poor minority populations in particular. Hawkishness may not have been the primary cause for the diminution of the problem but nonetheless the diminution occurred during the hawks' ascendancy, so that hawks find it easy to claim that "toughness worked." Those who argue that the problem also worsened during the earlier ascendancy of the hawks will find a small audience. Calls for major changes in policy, in particular for the legal availability of what have come to be seen as "devil drugs," no matter how stringent the associated regulation, will also have limited appeal.

Owls may do better than doves. The imagery of war ought to work in their favor; victory is often followed by a period of humanitarian outreach by the winning side, an effort to help the casualties of war. The continuing decline in initiation among America's youth will make ever clearer that the drug problem is mostly the dangerous behavior of a relatively small number of adults, caught in the cocaine epidemic of the 1980s. Maybe locking them up will start to look more expensive and less attractive than developing better quality health and social services aimed at reducing their drug use and at improving their social functioning. Owls, even if their message lacks the simplicity and clarity of the competing birds, may yet come to dominate the aviary.

ACKNOWLEDGMENTS

Writing of this paper was supported by grants from the Ford, Alfred P. Sloan, and Weingart Foundations. Norval Morris, Douglas Besharov, and Michael Tonry made many helpful suggestions. I am also grateful for comments from Michael Marmot. Ann Flanagan provided valuable research assistance.

ENDNOTES

[1]Punishing drug users should reduce demand; to that extent the "supply-sider" label has an element of exaggeration.

[2]This debate was given its most explicit formulation in the congressional debate on the 1988 Omnibus Anti-Drug Control Act.

[3]Joseph Nye, Graham Allison, and Albert Carnesale, "Analytic Conclusions: Hawks, Doves and Owls," in Allison, Nye, and Carnesale, eds., *Hawks, Doves and Owls: An Agenda for Avoiding Nuclear War* (New York: W.W. Norton, 1985), 206–22.

[4]Nye et al.'s tripartite division added owls to the conventional hawks and doves. Whereas hawks believed that war could be avoided only if both sides have enough weapons to impose unacceptable damage on the other and doves believed that disarmament was essential to prevention of nuclear war, owls believed in confidence building measures and other elements of process, rather than the scale and comparability of nuclear arsenals as the key to peace.

[5]The most appropriate measurement of treatment success is a vexed issue. Does one include the large number of persons who drop out early in a particular program,

perhaps because they decide that other programs are more suitable? What constitutes success: abstinence or improved social functioning? The authoritative review is Dean Gerstein and Hendrick Harwood, eds., *Treating Drug Problems* (Washington, D.C.: National Academy Press, 1990).

[6]The argument is made most explicitly in reports of the Office of National Drug Control Policy. See *National Drug Strategy* (1989 and 1990) and *White Paper on Drug Treatment,* 1990.

[7]I shall not deal with the fringe dove movement that emphasizes the positive effects of psychoactive drugs. Thomas Szaz is probably the leading intellectual evangelist of this group; see Thomas Szaz, *Ceremonial Chemistry: The Ritual Persecution of Drugs, Addicts and Pushers* (Garden City, N.Y.: Anchor Books, 1974).

[8]Ethan Nadelmann, "America's Drug Problem," *Bulletin of the American Academy of Arts and Sciences* XLV (3) (December 1991): 24–40.

[9]Most acknowledge an exception for children; criminal prohibitions for the sale to children is a staple of dove advocacy.

[10]Recent statements of this pessimism include Peter Andreas, Eva Bertram, Morris Blachman, and Kenneth Sharpe, "Dead-End Drug Wars," *Foreign Policy* (85) (Winter 1991–1992); and *The Andean Initiative: Squeezing a Balloon,* Report prepared by the staff of the House Judiciary Committee's Subcommittee on Crime and Criminal Justice, 24 February 1992.

[11]Gerstein and Harwood, *Treating Drug Problems.*

[12]Some colleagues have argued that the imagery is loaded; after all, owls are generally thought of as wise. My own image of owls is more mixed, being derived from childhood readings of Winnie-the-Pooh, in which Owl is indeed learned (he can misspell long words) but unrealistic and self-deluded. The owls of Nye, Allison, and Carnesale exhibit some of the latter qualities.

[13]The most refined discussion of these matters is Mark Kleiman, *Against Excess: Drug Policy for Results* (New York: Basic Books, 1992).

[14]A point made by James Q. Wilson, "Drugs and Crime," in Michael Tonry and James Q. Wilson, eds., *Drugs and Crime* (Chicago: University of Chicago Press, 1990).

[15]For example, there are few cities or metropolitan areas with data on the prevalence of drug use in the general population, so that it is impossible to model the effect of policy variables on the extent of drug use. Other proxies, such as the number of deaths related to drug use, turn out to be unsatisfactory for this purpose.

[16]To estimate the share of criminal justice expenditures accounted for by drug enforcement, I separated police, courts, and corrections. The share of police expenditures on the drug "account" was measured by the ratio of drug selling arrests to Part I arrests plus drug selling arrests. For courts it was the ratio of drug felony convictions to all felony convictions. Finally, for prisons I used the share of all commitments to prison that were for drug offenses. These are all crude estimates. The only systematic effort to measure state and local expenditures on drug enforcement by police, Gerald Godshaw, Ross Pancoast, and Russell Koppel, *Anti-Drug Law Enforcement Efforts and Their Impact* (Bala Cynwyd,

Pa.: Wharton Econometric Forecasting Associates, 1987), showed an even higher share of the police expenditures going to that effort in 1985 and 1986.

[17]It is striking just how state and local governments have succeeded in keeping the public debate focused on the federal budget allocation. State and local expenditures on treatment and prevention have been growing very slowly compared to those of the federal government, even though these services are delivered almost exclusively by the lower levels of government.

[18]See Joan Petersilia, Joyce Peterson, and Susan Turner, *Intensive Probation and Parole: Research Findings and Policy Implications* (Santa Monica, Calif.: RAND Corporation, 1992).

[19]*New York Times*, 22 March 1992.

[20]Richard Doblin and Mark Kleiman, "Marijuana as an Antiemetic Medicine: A Survey of Oncologists' Experiences and Attitudes," *Journal of Clinical Oncology* 9 (July 1991).

[21]"Out of Joint," *New Republic*, 15 & 22 July 1991.

[22]A more detailed account is given in Reuter, "On the Consequences of Toughness," in Krauss, Melvyn, and Edward Lazear, eds., *Drug Policy in America: The Search for Alternatives* (Stanford, Calif.: Hoover Institution Press, 1991).

[23]The Uniform Crime Reports system of the FBI combines heroin and cocaine arrests into a single category. It is generally believed that the increase in this category throughout the 1980s was dominated by an increase in cocaine related arrests.

[24]Bureau of Justice Statistics, *Felony Sentences in State Courts* (Washington, D.C.: 1989, 1990).

[25]Since these possession charges were prosecuted as felonies, they are presumably possession with intent to distribute rather than simple possession offenses, which in most states are misdemeanors only.

[26]The declining average time served probably reflects two phenomena. The first is simply prison overcrowding, which has led to a reduction in the share of sentence actually served. The second is that the rapid increase in the number of drug offenders receiving prison sentences means that some are now being imprisoned for less severe offenses.

[27]All of these dispositional data, both national and Californian, bear on felonies, primarily related to distribution and/or manufacture. There are literally no published data concerning the sentences received by those arrested on simple possession charges.

[28]The household survey produces an estimate of ten million current users (i.e. reporting at least one use within the prior thirty days) in 1990. Allowing for one-third underreporting gives a total of fifteen million.

[29]Peter Reuter and Mark Kleiman, "Risks and Prices: An Economic Analysis of Drug Enforcement," in Norval Morris and Michael Tonry, eds., *Crime and Justice: A Review of Research* 7 (Chicago: University of Chicago Press, 1986).

[30]Peter Reuter Robert MacCoun, and Patrick Murphy, *Money From Crime: A Study of the Economics of Drug Dealing in Washington, D.C.*, RAND: R-3894-RF (Santa Monica, Calif.: June 1990).

[31]Mark Kleiman sensibly notes that this kind of statement ignores the prevalence of alcohol use. It may well be that the average hours of intoxication per citizen is no higher in the United States than in nations, such as France, where alcohol is more widely abused. Without denying the relevance of that measure, there are distinctive problems arising from use of illegal substances and it is worth considering differences among societies in the extent of that use.

[32]The federal government defines the use of an illicit drug as drug "abuse." Both medicine and ordinary language make a distinction between use and abuse or dependence. Though the latter two terms have different origins and formal definitions, they will be used interchangeably here to reflect levels and patterns of drug consumption that create health and/or behavioral problems to the user. None of the existing data systems allows for accurate measurement of the prevalence of one rather than the other.

[33]During the 1980s, the National Institute on Drug Abuse funded three surveys of drug use in the household population; that survey has been conducted annually since 1990. Each year since 1975 the University of Michigan has surveyed a sample of approximately 16,000 high school seniors.

[34]"Thirty years ago smoking was not associated with social class. It is now. In 1980, a quarter of professional men smoked, a third of white collar men and almost half of blue collar men..." Thomas Schelling, "Addictive Drugs: The Cigarette Experience," *Science* 255 (24 January 1992): 430–31.

[35]Nor is this simply explained by higher drop out rates among African-Americans, which would suggest that the high school senior population was a more select group within their age cohort when compared to the white seniors. Drop-out rates in recent years have been almost equal for the two populations.

[36]That difference is particularly striking since the percentage of incarcerated males aged 26–34 is much higher for African-Americans than for the rest of the population. The incarcerated males are much more likely to be drug users than the nonincarcerated; if the two ethnic groups have the same prevalence rate overall, the nonincarcerated African-American rate should be lower than the white race. Note that these are all unadjusted rates; the differences should not be ascribed to ethnicity but may be a function of urbanness, education, employment rates, etc.

[37]In 1991, the survey for the first time included homeless in shelters.

[38]The DAWN reports include data on the patient's motive for using the drug. In 1983, 42 percent reported that they took cocaine for its psychic effects (i.e. for pleasure) and 47 percent reported dependence. By 1989, 63 percent of those episodes involving cocaine were classified as drug dependence and for only 28 percent was "psychic effects" the motive for taking the drug.

[39]The number of DAWN cocaine mentions flattened out in 1988 and then fell by about 25 percent between the second and third quarters of 1989. The numbers then rose over the following two years, close to their prior peak. Little effort has been made to understand these changes, which may be affected by shifts in emergency room policies during an urban health care financing crisis, or by alterations in the behavior of addicts rather than by their numbers.

[40]For a severe criticism of those estimates, see Reuter, "The (Continued) Vitality of Mythical Numbers," *The Public Interest* (Spring 1984). A recent review of the literature leaves me with little reason to change that critique.

[41]Italy may have a higher rate; there are sharply conflicting estimates of the total number of addicts. If one trusts numbers of unknown provenance from distant lands, it is possible that Pakistan and Thailand have higher rates of heroin addiction. See the State Department's annual *International Control Strategy Report.*

[42]The figures on age composition refer to unweighted data, which are only available through 1989. For purposes of describing long-term trends, the new weighted data are not appropriate.

[43]The evidence for a new heroin epidemic is presented in BOTEC Analysis Corporation, *Heroin Situation Assessment*, a Working Paper prepared for the Office of National Drug Control Policy, 10 January 1992.

[44]See the MacNeil/Lehrer NewsHour, September 1990; debate between ONDCP Director, William Bennett, and Senator Joseph Biden.

[45]Eric Wish, "U.S. Drug Policy in the 1990s: Insights from New Data on Arrestees," *International Journal of Addictions* 25 (3A) (1990–1991): 377–409. See also Senate Judiciary Committee, *Hard-Core Cocaine Addicts: Measuring and Fighting the Epidemic* (Washington, D.C.: 1990).

[46]Robert Tillman, "The Size of the 'Criminal Population': The Prevalence and Incidence of Arrests," *Criminology* 25 (3) (Fall 1987).

[47]Reuter, MacCoun, and Murphy, *Money from Crime.*

[48]The most recent is Dorothy Rice, Sander Kelman, Leonard Miller, and Sarah Dunmeyer, *Economic Costs of Alcohol Abuse, Drug Abuse and Mental Illness, 1985* (Rockville, Md.: Alcohol, Mental Health and Drug Abuse Administration, 1990).

[49]To get a sense of this, the reader should consider what would happen to the value of her house if the crime rate in the surrounding area reached a figure comparable to that on Capitol Hill in Washington, D.C.

[50]A better measure is Years of Life Lost (YLL) which takes account of how premature a death is; for example, the average YLL is higher for alcohol than cigarettes, since lung cancer typically strikes its victims in late middle age, while many alcoholics die in early middle age. DAWN data suggest a much higher average YLL (i.e. earlier age of death) for illicit drugs but even that would not raise the significance of illegal drugs to that of either alcohol or tobacco.

[51]Bureau of Justice Statistics, *Profile of Jail Inmates, 1989* (April 1991).

[52]Paul Goldstein, H.H. Brownstein, P.J. Ryan, and P.A. Belluci, "Crack and Homicide in New York, 1988," *Contemporary Drug Problems* (1990).

[53]Medical costs for treatment and lost wages capture only the direct costs; the increased fear associated with sexual intercourse is an instance of those indirect consequences that seem both difficult to value and potentially very important.

[54]See the recent complaints by the National Commission on AIDS about lack of drug treatment capacity, *The Twin Epidemics of Substance Use and HIV* (1991), 7–10.

[55]This is discussed in more detail in Reuter, "Police Regulation of Illegal Gambling: Frustrations of Symbolic Enforcement," *Annals of the American Academy of Political Science* (July 1984).

[56]Jerald G. Bachman, Lloyd D. Johnston, and Patrick M. O'Malley, "Explaining the Recent Decline in Cocaine Use Among Young Adults: Further Evidence that Perceived Risks and Disapproval Lead to Reduced Drug Use," *Journal of Health and Social Behavior* 31 (June 1990).

[57]If 45 percent of the 1985 incarcerated population were drug users and the figure for 1990 were 65 percent, then the total number of drug users locked up rose from about 350,000 to 800,000. Both percentages seem fairly conservative.

[58]*Washington Post*, 14 December 1991, A10.

[59]This is not to say that the more senior figures are at low risk. Indeed, it seems unlikely that one could operate as long as five years in most American cities in the high levels of the drug market without facing substantial risk of long term imprisonment.

[60]This section draws on ongoing work being done in collaboration with James P. Kahan and Robert MacCoun.

[61]Public Opinion in the European Community, *Eurobarometer,* December 1989.

[62]The Advisory Council on the Misuse of Drugs, *Report: AIDS and Drug Misuse* (London: HMSO).

[63]I owe this example to Douglas Besharov.

[64]See for example the alarmist cover story in *Time*, 9 May 1988, 21–33.

[65]David Courtwright, *Dark Paradise: Opiate Addiction in America Before 1940* (Cambridge: Harvard University Press, 1982).

Crime, Law and Social Change **19**: 1–15, 1993.

Don't be your own best customer – Drug use of San Francisco gang drug sellers

DAN WALDORF
Home Boy Study, Institute for Scientific Analysis, 2719 Encinal Avenue No. A, Alameda, CA 94501, USA

Abstract. In general, it is believed that most retail drug sellers, those who sell small amounts, use the drugs they sell and that drug sales is undertaken not only for the purpose of making money but to get the drugs they desire or need. In a few instances there have been accounts of groups who rationalized drug sales to maximize profits and as a result did not use the drugs they sold, but the literature on the topic of the drug use of sellers has been sketchy. This paper will report preliminary findings of a survey of 300 gang members in San Francisco about the drug use of gang drug sellers. These findings reveal that the majority of gang crack sellers, who are usually African-American, do *not* use crack themselves while the majority of marijuana, powder cocaine and heroin sellers do use the drugs they sell. In general, African-American gangs that sell crack in San Francisco have rules about the use of crack by sellers and believe that it is highly addictive drug that is bad for business and is contrary to a gang principle of "being down" for the "hood" and other gang members.

Introduction

Historically, it was believed that most retail illicit drug sellers, people who sold small quantities, were drug users who sold drugs because of a desire or need for supplies and that most low-level sellers were also users of the drugs they sold. Smugglers and high level dealers, most notably organized crime groups such as the Mafia and Columbian cocaine cartels, were believed not to use the drugs they sold. This notion about retail sellers continued until 1986 when Mieczkowski[1] reported that retail drug sales for a group of fifteen adolescent heroin sellers in Detroit had become rationalized and that the group in an effort to maximize profit rejected heroin use. Simultaneously, street and "rock house" sales of rock cocaine or crack made a dramatic appearance in several cities – first in Miami, New York City and Los Angeles and eventually into the West and Midwest – and there were continuing reports that crack sellers had become highly organized and that many did not use the drug they sold. Since that time several researchers have endeavored to explore the notion with varying results and somewhat sketchy findings. In this paper we will report preliminary data of a study of drug sales of San Francisco gang members which should clarify some the issues for gang sellers in that city.

Review of the literature

In general, the literature on drug sales is sparse with most studies being small scale ethnographies with occasional larger social surveys. In one of the early social surveys of 204 marijuana users that dealt with sales, Eric Goode[2] found that marijuana sales was linked to frequency of use. This finding was supported by a larger study of 3,500 college students made by Johnson[3] who found that: students sold marijuana as they became regular users, no other factors affected the relationship of using and selling marijuana, and that marijuana sales was usually a prerequisite for sales of "hard" drugs. Both of these studies were buttressed by Carey's[4] earlier field observations of street sellers and Mandel's[5] marijuana sellers from the same field study conducted in Berkeley, California. More recently, Carpenter and her associates[6] found that adolescent sellers (primarily marijuana sellers) were regular users of the drugs they sold and summarized her findings by stating, "Virtually all youths who sold a substance were users of that substance . . ."

Cocaine hydrochloride sellers seemed to demonstrate a similar pattern of using the products they sold. Patricia Adler[7] in her extended field study of cocaine and marijuana smugglers found considerable use of both drugs by the smugglers of her study. And Waldorf et al.[8,9] in a study of 80 ex-cocaine sellers (53 who were wholesalers and 27 retailers) found only one who did not use his product and he was a pound and kilo dealer who was generally allergic to the drug. All of the retailers had used cocaine and many had experienced severe problems with the drug.

Retail heroin sellers have historically been considered to be users as well as sellers from the early descriptions by Preble and Casey.[10] Waldorf,[11] Walters,[12] Redlinger,[13] Hughes[14] and Moore.[15] I should add that the last study by Moore was a study of Chicano gangs in East Los Angeles and will have some relevance to our findings because we will be reporting about Latino gang members also. Johnson and his associates[16] in a study of the economic life of heroin users in Manhattan reiterated this notion in 1988 with the statement that "virtually all sellers [heroin] are users of drugs".

Mieczkowski[1] was the first to find exception to the rule for heroin sellers in an in-depth ethnography of a group of 15 adolescent sellers in Detroit known as Young Boys Inc. Of the 15 youth interviewed and observed most had used heroin previously, but only one was using the drug at the time of the interview. That is not to say that they did not use other drugs because they used marijuana and cocaine "recreationally". This study was later supported by other studies; Chin[17] who reported that Chinese gang members he studied who sold heroin did not use it and Vigil[18] who found that East Los Angeles gang members rejected heroin use because they believed that heroin addicts could not be loyal to the gang and their addiction at the same time.

With the advent of wide spread street sales of rock or crack cocaine beginning in the 1980s there have been journalistic[19] accounts and discussion about the increased incidence of street sellers who do not use the drug themselves. Johnson and members of the New York Street Studies Unit[20] were the first researchers to actually chronicle the existence of non-using crack distributors but considered them to be small in numbers. They described three types of non-using crack sellers – wholesale dealers and organizers of crack distribution groups, unemployed young adults who work for organizations as part-time paid employees, and lastly ex-crack users who sell but do not use the drug. Skolonick and his associates[21] noted similar non-users among gang members from Northern and Southern California in correction institutions. Skolonick's findings about gang members was reiterated by Reuter[22] in a review article that did not present new data.

To date the most detailed research on the crack use of crack sellers comes from two studies – a small scale ethnography of a crack selling group made by Williams[23] and a large survey of crack users and sellers from two Manhattan neighborhoods by Fagan and Chin.[24] Williams seems to present conflicting data; on the one hand he states that "... most dealers disdain the use of crack, so cash payments is now more common." But then in his description of the crack distribution network he studied all but the one of the eight members were using powder cocaine and many were having problems because of their use.

Fagan and Chin conducted interviews with 597 crack users and sellers from two Manhattan neighborhoods that has experienced extensive crack use and sales (Washington Heights and West Harlem) both in correction facilities and on the street. They concluded that:

> Despite the high proportion of sellers that reported prohibitions against use while selling, many sellers also used drugs. Evidently these prohibitions did not extend to personal recreational use, or they were ineffective ... The provocative image of the well-disciplined dealer, whose motivations are exclusively financial and who abstains from drug use to maximize his or her dealing skills, has no grounding in these data. Drug sellers also are drug users, and their efforts as dealers and behavior as users apparently overlap extensively.

Lastly, a survey of 387 inner city, male, high school students (ninth and tenth grades) by Althschuler and Brounstein[25] reported that 13% had sold drugs in the past year and half reported that they did not use drugs themselves. There was no specific details about specific drug sales or drugs used in the report.

In general, this literature review served as background for our study of drug sales among gang members in San Francisco. Prior to the study we were rather skeptical about the possibility that large numbers of retail drug sellers would not use the drugs they sold. This skepticism was based not only on the literature review but also on a previous study of heroin users and sellers[11] and two studies of cocaine sellers[26,27,8,9] and so we endeavored to gather extensive data to explore the idea at some length.

Methods

Data for the study consists of face-to-face interviews with 300 gang members from an on-going study of gangs in San Francisco. Interviews were conducted in two stages with a initial pre-coded schedule of questions followed by an in-depth, tape recorded section from an interview guide so that the study has both quantitative and qualitative data. Interviews were conducted by trained Black, Latino and Chinese interviewers and the interviews took from two to three hours to complete. Each respondent was paid $ 50 for their participation in the study.

Respondents were located by means of snowball sampling techniques.[28,29] Black respondents were recruited by two Black interviewers who had direct knowledge of gang members prior to the study and they developed networks of interviews without contacts with social agencies. Initial contacts with Latino respondents were developed from local social agencies that work with gang members, but have changed over time so that most respondents are located primarily by other gang members at the present time. Asian gang members were the most difficult to locate and recruit and most were located via social agencies. We should add that we have not utilized referrals from criminal justice or drug treatment agencies and do not plan to do so.

No efforts were made to locate White gangs during the first year of the study so that they are not represented in the data. We plan to begin locating and interviewing White, Samoan and Filipino gangs during the second year.

The original plan for the study was to identify all known gangs in San Francisco and interview 10 members from each gang (5 members under 20 years and five over 20 years). We gathered some initial information about crack selling gangs from the San Francisco Police Crack Gang Task Force in the form of names of gangs and street locations, but have learned that there are many more gangs than they identified.

During the first year of the study we located and interviewed 334 gang members from 77 different gangs and expect to interview at least 200 or 300 more in the remaining two years of the study. Data are available for 300 respondents at the present time from 74 different gangs.

Very briefly, the socio-demographics of the sample are as follows. The median age of the respondents is 22 years with a range of 14–40 years. More than half (57.5%) are Black and more than a quarter (28.7%) are Latino. A large number of the respondents were school drop outs as the median grade last attended was grade 11. Blacks generally stayed in school longer than Latinos did.

Patterns of drug use by gang members

There are obvious and recurring patterns of drug use for the two major ethnic groups studied thus far. Black gang members tend to avoid injectable drugs (heroin, cocaine and methamphetamines) and psychedelics; they concentrate on alcohol and marijuana and a only small percentages use cocaine and crack. Latino gang members use a broader range of drugs – alcohol, marijuana, heroin, cocaine and P.C.P. (known by the Spanish term "maton" or killer) and seldom use crack as they consider it a Black drug. There are many more injectors among their ranks, but injectors are usually older members.

Gang drug sales locales

Information of drug sales was explored in both the pre-coded quantitative and qualitative sections of the interview. These data along with field observations made of areas where gangs hang out and coping areas indicate that drug sales occurs at six possible locations – on the streets, in bars, in parks, in houses and apartments, in rock houses and shooting galleries. Rock houses in San Francisco are not as widespread as they are said to be in Los Angeles or other cities and gang members do not have extensive contacts with these types of venues. Crack use and sales also occurs in some shooting galleries[30] frequented by injectors (heroin, methamphetamines, cocaine), but again the majority of gang members do not frequent these establishments. The predominate locale for sales among gang members are streets, parks and houses or apartments.

Street sales generally consists of two styles – one a Black style and the other a Latino style. Black street sellers are usually located near selected housing projects and/or "mom and pop" food stores in Black communities. Very often a number of sellers will take over a street completely and approach all who come into the area either by foot or car. Transactions are easily observed at these locations as the sellers are both brazen and aggressive. There seem to be only rudimentary organization for such sellers as most are free-lance sellers who either buy supplies or are fronted small amounts and there are only a few groups that utilize elaborate divisions of labor as described by other studies of New York sellers.[31] Street sellers work out simple arrangements with other sellers and customers by cooperating to take turns selling to arriving customers or referring established customers to specific sellers. Sellers generally control those who are allowed to sell and one usually has to be a long standing member of the "hood" (neighborhood) and belong to the group. Outsiders who attempt to sell in the area are usually run off with dispatch. Arrangements among sellers are worked out amicably with little competition or violence. The majority of Black street sellers sell both crack (in rocks selling for $5, $10 up to $50) and marijuana (in $10 bags). Black gang members usually do not sell heroin or powder cocaine and those drugs are usually sold at different locations that are frequented by injectors.

Latino gang street sellers are generally less brazen and obvious than Black sellers. Very often they will circulate on a street where there is a mix of people and a wide range of activities (people frequenting shops, restaurants, etc.). Drug sales is only one of many activities occurring on the streets. Strangers are usually not approached, but sellers will wait until a know buyer approaches them and then go into a restaurant or store to conduct the transaction. Neither money nor drugs are exchanged in obvious manners in the streets. The drugs sold are different also – marijuana, powder cocaine and heroin rather than crack. In general, many more transactions occur in private than openly as in Black coping areas.

We should add that small numbers of sellers are now using telephone beepers and voice mail systems to take orders and deliver drugs but these methods are not widespread.

Drug sales and other hustles

In order to explore the extent of drug sales we asked a number of questions about sources for money and different types of hustling activities (Table 1). The first questions were about sources for money – the primary sources and the sources for money last week. Answers to both questions revealed that a minority (12.7% and 9.3%, respectively) cited jobs as sources for money and a majority (78.3% and 80.7%) cited "hustles" as sources for money.

Later on in the interview after we established rapport with the respondent we asked each to elaborate on possible hustles by asking a pre-coded question

Table 1. Sources for money – primary and last week – percent answering.

Sources	Primary source		Source last week	
	N	%	N	%
Job	38	12.7	28	9.3
Family	23	7.7	25	8.3
Hustles	235	78.3	242	80.7
Friends	3	1.0	5	1.7
Job, family & hustle	1	0.3	–	

Table 2. Types of hustles by ethnicity – percent answering "Yes".

Ethnicity	Type of hustles									
	Drug sales		Extortion		Burglary		Theft		Total	
	N	%	N	%	N	%	N	%	N	%
Black	170	98.3	2	1.1	10	5.8	10	5.8	173	57.6
Latino	56	65.1	3	3.5	47	54.6	48	55.8	86	28.7
Asian	12	46.1	7	26.9	10	38.5	15	57.7	26	86.7
Other	10	66.6	1	6.7	5	33.3	5	33.3	15	5.0

about the type of hustles they participated in. The codes were for the most common hustles – drug sales, extortion, burglary and theft – and there were considerable differences among the ethnic groups (Table 2). Black gang members reported almost universal participation in drug sales and only minor participation in burglary and theft. Latinos reported drug sales, theft and burglary in that order. Asians reported a broader range of activities than any other group.

As might be expected given the various ethnic differences in drugs used there were also differences in the kinds of drugs that were sold by the different groups. Black gang members reported predominant sales of crack (96.0%) and marijuana (71.7%) and only small numbers reported sales of heroin and cocaine. Latinos reported selling marijuana, cocaine and heroin and only a small number (4) reported crack sales (Table 3).

Drug sales was not a short term activity as the median period that respondents reported drug sales was 4 years; the range was from 1 month to 12 years.

Table 3. Drugs sold by ethnicity – percent reporting.

Drugs sold	Ethnicity							
	Black		Latino		Asian		Other	
	N	%	N	%	N	%	N	%
Marijuana	124	71.7	41	47.7	5	19.2	9	60.0
Crack	166	96.0	4	4.7	5	19.2	6	40.0
Powder cocaine	7	4.0	39	45.3	5	19.2	4	26.6
Heroin	6	3.5	37	43.0	–		2	13.3
Other drugs	1	5.6	6	33.3	5	27.8	6	33.3
Total	173*		86		26		15	

* These totals are for the total number of various ethnic groups and will not equal the totals because most respondents reported more than one drug sold.

Twenty-four gang members reported that they had been selling drugs for 10 years or more.

Drug use by drug sellers

In order to establish the use of drugs that were being sold we asked each respondent a series of questions about drug use for three time periods – over their lifetime, during the previous month, and during the previous week. For the first analysis we have used reports about drug use for the last two time periods – the previous week and previous month. This analysis presented some rather dramatic findings. Large percentages of maijuana (88.8.2%), cocaine (64.3%) and heroin (80.0%) sellers reported that they used the drugs they sold during the previous month while only 18.2% of the crack sellers reported that they used crack. So more than four out of every five (81.8%) of the crack sellers reported that they did not use crack during the previous month. This is

Table 4. Use of drugs sold during the previous month by types of drugs sold – percent reporting.

Drugs sold	Use of drugs during the previous month			
	Yes, uses drug		No, does not use	
	N	%	N	%
Marijuana	158	88.8	20	11.2
Crack	33	18.2	148	81.8
Powder cocaine	36	64.3	20	35.7
Heroin	36	80.0	9	20.0
Other drugs	9	56.3	7	43.7

Table 5. Ever used drug sold by type of drugs sold – percent reporting.

Drugs sold	Ever used drugs sold			
	Yes		No, never used	
	N	%	N	%
Marijuana	174	97.7	4	2.3
Crack	70	38.7	111	61.3
Powder cocaine	51	91.1	5	8.9
Heroin	41	91.1	4	8.9
Other drugs	13	81.3	3	18.7

not to say that the majority of crack sellers do not use drugs because they do; they use alcohol and marijuana regularly but do not use crack (Table 4).

When the lifetime history of drug use is considered as in Table 5 we found that the percentages of crack sellers who report using crack increases, but only by 20% (to 38.7%) and that the differences between the other type of drug sellers are still dramatic. More than 9 out of 10 of marijuana, powder cocaine and heroin sellers reported that they used the drugs they sold while only little more than a third of the crack sellers made such reports. It should also be noted that many of the additional 37 respondents who reported crack use in Table 5 reported using the drugs only once or twice (Table 5).

Reasons for not using crack

In the qualitative section of the interview we asked all respondents about rules of behavior of gangs in two questions – specific rules regarding crack use and general gang rules of behavior. The answers to the crack specific question indicate that many of the Black gangs have developed an ethos that crack use is "bad business" and is dangerous because it is "addictive". Answers to questions about general gang rules indicate that crack use is contrary to a general concept of the gang, namely "being down" for other gang members.

Bad for business

The notion that crack use is bad for business was expressed in several ways: that the group does not want crack using sellers to drive away customers by selling them "bad dope" or "gaffle",* that sellers cannot make money if they use the drug, that users will loss control and not be serious sellers. The first of these business reasons are illustrated by a 23 year old, Black member of the B.C.:

> *I:* Does the group have rules about crack use?
> *R:* Well you can't use crack.
> *I:* So if you use crack you can't sell in B.C.?
> *R:* No we don't allow gafflers, mother fuckers what come through with bullshit as rocks and run our customers off. We don't allow that. Somebody comes back and shoot [us] up for getting beat. We do business we are going to do it right. We ain't going to sell nobody bullshit. We don't allow no dope feens trying to gaffle our customers. We try to keep everybody happy and together. (Case #159)

This quotation indicates that gang sellers from this group (B.C.) want to maintain their sales markets by assuring customers that they will not be sold

* Gaffle is term used by San Francisco drug users and sellers to indicate phony rock cocaine and gafflers are people who sell it.

phony drugs by a seller who will "gaffle" customers. Gafflers, people who sell phony crack, are also seen as potentially dangerous sellers as buyers who are cheated or "burnt" may return to get their money back or retaliate.

Being "high and tweaking out" is not considered to be good selling demeanor as the seller cannot be as vigilant as he should be, may not be good for fronted drugs and cannot keep the money straight. These reasons are illustrated by two accounts:

> *R:* No, we can't be high out there on the street, we might tweak out and run off with the money and stuff. (Case # 38)
> *R:* You got to handle your business while you are out there. You can't be high or tweaking. (Case # 112)

Many of the groups and individuals within them have learned that crack use is an anathema to sales from past experience as this Home Boy explains:

> *I:* How about rules about homeboys of yours that are into crack?
> *R:* Yeah, we do [have rules]. You know, because we're really down on crack because now it's, you know, we've seen a lot of good homeboys go down to that. And we've seen a lot of homeboys enter rehab or wind up goin' to the joint behind it. So, more or less, we banned it because we've seen more people out of the abuses of heroin and whatever, dope, booze, whatever – crack has done the most damage, I think. To be honest with you. (Case # 116)

Their experience has told them that crack use can be very compulsive and that users can become unreliable, untrustworthy; that users become in short "dope feens". This 15 year old, Black youth was a member of gang known as Hollister the Hardway and elaborated:

> *I:* Does your group have rules about crack use?
> *R:* Yes, we don't like dope feens . . .
> *I:* Does anybody in your group use crack that you know of?
> *R:* No. (Case # 35)

Crack use and "being down"

Business and addictive considerations are not the only ones held by gang members. Indeed crack use can be considered to be a threat to one of the guiding principles of many San Francisco gangs, the notion of "being down". Being down is a term that was expressed by a number of Black and Latino gangs that reflects gang values: to standby other members, to be there when they are needed, to be tough and courageous. Some Latino gang members also use the Spanish term "un paro" to express similar values of "being there when you are needed", "that I am there for you and you are there for me". Being down is a regular theme for many gangs as it was expressed in the following quotations:

> *I:* What does being a Home Boy mean to you personally?
> *R:* It means I am down for him and he down for me and my partners and my buddies. Just like any social group that is the way we are. (Case # 20)

> *I:* What does being a Home Boy mean to you personally?
> *R:* Someone that is going to go down for me if any thing jump.
> *I:* When you say, 'if anything jump' what do you mean?
> *R:* Whatever, if we have to beat someone up for selling dope, [if] we get cracked together and we have to go to jail he ain't going to snitch on me. (Case # 126)

> *R:* I'm down with my boys. Whatever goes down, I'm there with them. (Case # 125)

More specific to drug sales one respondent spoke at some length about selling drugs and "being down".

> If you are going to sell dope here you got to be with us . . . You come you make your money. I wouldn't just sit and allow you to come sell dope on our spot and then I get into a fight one day and you don't back me up. I am not going to allow you to keep selling dope there. I am going to like spread it around. I would say that I got jumped and this dude watched me and now he wants to talk like he is my Home Boy. Then everybody else going to . . . If he ain't a real Home Boy we would probably get into his ass or something like that. But if he had been around there for a long time, we ain't just going to start to whip his ass. He ain't going to have no respect. He ain't going to have no back up. We just can't whip nobody's ass and especially if they are from our hood. (Case # 161)

All four of the above quotes suggest that mutual support is important component of the notion of "being down". And to be a member of the gang or the group one has to identify with the group, be there when other members may need them and be courageous as regards situations that might arise – other individuals or gangs coming onto their turf and the police attempting to make sales arrests. People who run when another gang comes onto their turf are *not* considered to "be down" because they are not courageous and do not standby other members when they are needed.

Protection from other people coming onto gang turf or to sell drugs on the turf is also integral to the notion of "being down". Very often this may be in the face of considerable numbers or invaders who have and use weapons:

> *I:* What does being a Home Boy mean to you personally?
> *R:* Somebody who identifies with the group. You got to come up and if somebody goes down you are right there with them. You try to help him out as much as you can. You don't turn back at all. If there are two of you and twenty other mother fuckers, you are down until you are down. (Case # 184)

Often leaders endeavor to express the epitome of "being down". Indeed for some individuals and groups "being down" refers to personal toughness. In the case of Latino gangs it can be people who are "the craziest" who have no qualms about violence and instigate others to commit violent acts against other gangs.

Exceptions to rules

Of course not all gangs have rules about using crack or the drugs they sell and not all members abide by the rules of the group. In general, Latino gangs do not have rules about using the drugs one sells and no particular rules about crack as many of them believe that crack is a drug that Black people use. Some Black groups are more lenient than others about crack use. For example here is account of a Black seller who also uses crack in a gang that give its members considerable lassitude:

> *I:* Are there any rules in the group?
> *R:* . . . No stealing and no scandalous moves, which you could consider stealing. In that circle stealing and scandalous moves covers a wide range. You could dibble dabble [use drugs] here out of the business work and you can burn a customer, you could sell bunk. All that would make you a negative.
> *I:* I understand in your group the drug they use the most would be crack, wouldn't that be detrimental to the business. If you are a user wouldn't that make you your own best customer?
> *R:* In a sense it does. But for instance in my case during working hours I don't use crack.
> *I:* So you are not addicted to it?
> *R:* No.
> *I:* But you use?
> *R:* On my free time. On my own time and it is not from the business. It is personal.
> *I:* Well wouldn't part of the money you are making out there go to personal use the majority of the money?
> *R:* Well here is how we do it. What you do with your percentage basically we look at it as you can do what you like. We prefer that you just didn't go out and buy crack all over the city. You are going to blow it.
> *I:* . . . What makes them different from the average junkie on the corner?
> *R:* Okay not all of us are on crack for one. Like I am a firm believer okay, I use the stuff. But I am drawing the line personally because I don't want to be "X"ed from the group, sliding out of door backwards. There is a line drawn and everybody is watching. Then we be saying, "Hey blood we been checking you out and you have been using a lot of crack and what is happening?" Okay you can get by with a story once or twice but after that if you have the same pattern first you won't be included like in the business deal. When it is supposed to be your turn to make the move for some business you will be told "how long, sit here and just kick back." They will give you a rock of crack and let you sit in the corner and everybody else handles business. Before you know it you will be slipping further and further out. So you won't be part

of the part. It will be smoothly; it is not just dropped on you. You won't be just tossed out. Here man here is a few dollars and a rock or two. Now if you are smart you will take that and you will get back on your feet and won't let it happen again. But if you aren't that is where you will be. (Case # 300)

Some individuals believe that if they can control their drug use and "take care of business" then they can use the drug as well as sell. Both positions are expressed in the following accounts:

I: Okay. Does the group have rules about such sales?
R: Right. You have a certain quota to make and without that quota, you have a penalty on what you receive.
I: Okay, what kind of penalty?
R: Well, they hold back on your money or you do not receive your drugs. Or more less to say, you're put on a suspension. (Case # 102)

I: Do you have rules about crack use?
R: Nah, it varies. As long as you don't blow your product. You cannot be your own best customer. (Case # 49)

Some groups are less adamant about rules about crack use than others; indeed some express very laissez faire attitudes. Within such groups if a person keeps his use in control and does not "mess up the money" then they are allowed to use in controlled ways. Taking care to meet financial responsibilities as a seller and to control crack use so that it does not undermine the individual's behavior are more important to some groups than firm rules against all crack use.

Summary

Preliminary results from a study of 300 gang members in San Francisco show that many Black gangs that sell rock cocaine on the streets endeavor to control the rock use of its members. Drugs are used, but they are usually alcohol and marijuana. Most groups have explicit rules about the use of crack based upon the beliefs that crack use by sellers is bad for business, is contrary to the interests of the gangs and that sellers should not be their own best customers. These rules appear to be based on a rational decision to maximize individual's profits for sales and avoid problems (both economic and personal) that may result from abuse of the drug. The ethos is not, however, universal for all illicit drugs as most of the very same sellers use marijuana which is often sold in conjunction with crack.

Latin groups do not have similar rules about the use of drugs that are sold. Indeed, a majority of Latino gang members use the drugs they sell, but they do not sell crack as it is believed to be a Black drug.

References

Inciardi, James A., "Beyond Cocaine: Basuco, Crack and Other Coca Products," *Contemporary Drug Problems,* 1987 (14), 460–492.

Reinarman, Craig and Harry J. Levine, "The Crack Attack: Politics and Media in America's Latest Drug Scare," in Joel Best (ed.), *Images and Issues: Current Perspectives on Social Problems* (New York: Adeline de Gruyer, 1989).

Cited references

1. Mieczkowski, Thomas, "Geeking Up and Throwing Down – Heroin Street Life in Detroit," *Criminology,* 1986 (24), 645–666.
2. Goode, Eric, *The Marijuana Smokers* (New York: Basic Books, 1970).
3. Johnson, Bruce D., *Marijuana Users and Drug Subcultures* (New York: John Wiley & Sons, 1973).
4. Carey, James T., *The College Drug Scene* (Englewood Cliffs: Prentice-Hall, 1968).
5. Mandel, Jerry, "Myths and Realities of Marijuana Pushing," in J.L. Simmons (ed.), *Marijuana: Myths and Realities* (North Hollywood, CA: Brandon House Books, 1967).
6. Carpenter, Cheryl, Barry Glassner, Bruce D. Johnson and Julia Loughlin, *Kids, Drugs and Crime* (Lexington, Mass: Lexington Books, D.C. Heath, 1988).
7. Adler, Patricia, *Wheeling and Dealing: An Ethnography of and Upper-Level Drug Dealing Community* (New York: Columbia University Press, 1985).
8. Waldorf, Dan, Sheigla Murphy and David Lauderback, "Cocaine Sellers: Self-reported Reasons for Stopping Cocaine Sales." Paper Presented at the 1989 Annual Meeting of the American Society of Criminology in Reno, Nevada, November 8–12, 1989.
9. Waldorf, Dan and Sheigla Murphy, "Perceived Risks and Criminal Justice Pressures on Cocaine Sellers." Paper Presented at the Annual Meetings of the American Society of Criminology, November 9–12, 1988.
10. Preble, Edward and J. Casey, "Taking Care of Business: the Heroin Users' Life on the Streets," *International Journal of the Addictions,* 1969 (4:1).
11. Waldorf, Dan, *Careers in Dope* (Englewood Cliffs, NJ: Prentice Hall, 1973).
12. Walters, James, "A Heroin Copping Community: Economics of Residency," *Quarterly Journal of Probation, Parole and Corrections,* 1973 (30).
13. Redlinger, Lawrence John, "Marketing and Distributing Heroin – Some Sociological Observations," *Journal of Psychedelic Drugs,* 1975 (3).
14. Hughes, Patrick, *Behind the Wall of Respect: Community Experiments in Heroin Addiction Control* (Chicago: University of Chicago Press, 1977).
15. Moore, Joan W., Robert Garcia, Carlos Garcia, Luis Cerda and Frank Valencia, *Homeboys: Gangs, Drugs and Prison in the Barrios of Los Angeles* (Philadelphia: Temple University Press, 1978).
16. Johnson, Bruce D., Mitchell A. Kaplan and James Schmeider, "Days of Drug Distribution: Which Drugs? How Many Transactions? With What Returns? Paper Presented at the Meetings of the American Society of Criminology, Chicago, IL, November 11, 1988.
17. Chin, Ko-lin, "Chinese Triad Societies, Tongs, Organized Crime and Street Gangs in Asia and the United States." Unpublished Ph.D. Dissertation, University of Pennsylvania, 1986.
18. Vigil, James Diego, *Barrio Gangs: Street Life and Identity in Southern California* (Austin, TX: University of Texas Press, 1988).
19. Cooper, B.M., "Motor City Breakdown," *Village Voice,* December 1, 1987, 23–35.

20. Johnson, Bruce D. and Terry Williams, "Economics of Dealing in a Non-monetary Labor Market." Paper Presented at the 15th International Institute on the Prevention and Treatment of Drug Dependence, International Council on Alcohol and Addictions; Amsterdam, The Netherlands; April 8, 1986.
21. Skolonick, Jerome K., Theodore Correl, Elizabeth Navarro and Roger Rabb, "The Social Structure of Street Drug Dealing," *BCS Forum* (Sacramento, CA: Office the State Attorney General, 1988).
22. Reuter, Peter, "Youth Gangs and Drug Distribution: A Preliminary Enquiry," (Washington, D.C.: Rand Corporation, 1989).
23. William, Terry, *The Cocaine Kids* (New York: Addison-Wesley, 1989).
24. Fagan, Jeffrey and Ko-lin Chin, "Violence as Regulation and Social Control in the Distribution of Crack," in Mario de la Rosa, Bernard Gropper and Elizabeth Lambert (eds.). *Drugs and Violence,* National Institute of Drug Abuse Research Monograph. (Rockville, MD: U.S. Department of Health and Human Services, 1990).
25. Altschuler, David M. and Paul J. Brounstein, "Patterns of Drug Use, Drug Trafficking, and Other Delinquency among Inner City Adolescents in Washington, D.C." Paper Presented at the Annual Meeting of the American Society of Criminology, Reno, Nevada; November, 1989.
26. Waldorf, Dan, Sheigla Murphy, Craig Reinarman and Bridget Joyce, "Doing Coke: An Ethnography of Cocaine Users and Sellers" (Washington, D.C.: Drug Abuse Council, Inc., 1977).
27. Murphy, Sheigla, Dan Waldorf and Craig Reinarman, "Drifting into Dealing: Becoming a Cocaine Seller," *Qualitative Sociology,* 1990 (13:4).
28. Biernacki, Patrick and Dan Waldorf, "Snowball Sampling, Problems and Techniques of Chain Referral Sampling," *Sociological Methods & Research,* 1981 (10:2), 141–163.
29. Watters, John and Patrick Biernacki, "Targeted Sampling: Options For the Study of Hidden Populations," *Social Problems,* 1989 (6:4), 416–430.
30. Murphy, Sheigla and Dan Waldorf, "Kickin' Down to the Street Doc: Shooting Galleries in the San Francisco Bay Area," *Contemporary Drug Problems,* 1991 (Spring).
31. Johnson, Bruce D., Ansley Hamid and Edmundo Morales, "Critical Dimensions of Crack Distribution." Paper Presented at the Meetings of the American Society of Criminology, Montreal, Canada; November 12, 1987.

STUDYING DRUGS IN RURAL AREAS: NOTES FROM THE FIELD

RALPH A. WEISHEIT

Most research on drug use and the drug industry in the United States has been done in urban areas. On a practical level, the neglect of rural areas is important because these areas (a) have problems with drug use, (b) are important in the transshipment of drugs across the country, and (c) are increasingly the sites for the production of synthetic drugs and marijuana. From a methodological and theoretical standpoint, the study of variability is the essence of the scientific approach. By excluding substantial rural-urban differences, the study of the drug industry is seriously handicapped. Research in rural areas presents a unique set of problems, however. This study examines research issues in the study of drugs in rural areas, drawing on the author's experiences in studying domestic marijuana production.

Since the 1960s, a number of researchers have studied the drug problem. Much of this research has focused on either middle-class marijuana users or on hard core addicts, people who have lost control of their drug use and of their lives. The former group has been the subject of numerous surveys and the latter has frequently been the subject of field research. Although survey research is more cost-effective than field research, many of the most fundamental issues regarding drugs do not lend themselves to the use of surveys. Respondents are often difficult to locate, the subject is one for which they may be reluctant to commit their behaviors to writing, and the interest is often in dynamic processes and interactions (e.g., Faupel 1991). Most importantly, surveys are ill suited for "fishing expeditions" into areas about which almost nothing is known. Without a basic understanding of the issues and the people involved, it is impossible to know what survey questions make the most sense and for whom they should be written.

An earlier version of this article was presented to the annual meeting of the American Society of Criminology in San Francisco, CA, November 1991. Data for this study were collected under a grant from the National Institute of Justice (NIJ Grant #88-IJ-CX-0016). The opinions expressed here are those of the author and do not necessarily represent those of the National Institute of Justice. A special thanks to Patrecia Mott and Anna Wells for their assistance in this research.

JOURNAL OF RESEARCH IN CRIME AND DELINQUENCY, Vol. 30 No. 2, May 1993 213-232

For these reasons, field research has often been used to develop an understanding of the dynamics of drug use and drug dealing. These studies have proven fruitful in describing the "drug scene" and have led to a richer understanding of the culture of drug use and drug dealing. Unfortunately, these studies all share a common weakness—with a few exceptions they are based on observations made in urban settings. The culture of drugs in rural areas has been largely unexplored.

Some have argued that most social research on rural populations has been dominated by survey research methods (Harper 1991), an allegation supported by a perusal of studies examining rural crime, which rely almost exclusively on either official data or survey research (e.g., Hagan 1977; Golden 1981; Austin 1981a, 1981b; Feld 1991; Smith and Huff, 1982; Laub 1983a, 1983b; Myers and Talarico 1986; Kowalski and Duffield 1990; Beleya and Zingraff 1988). Using such standardized data sources assumes that errors or problems related to the methodology are consistent across urban and rural areas, or that any inconsistencies will be readily apparent in the data.

Between 1988 and 1990 I was engaged in a study of commercial marijuana cultivators that involved locating and interviewing arrested growers, law enforcement officers, and others familiar with the domestic marijuana industry. Most commercial marijuana growing takes place in rural areas and it quickly became apparent that many of the techniques used in studies of the urban drug problem were either inappropriate in rural settings or had to be substantially modified.

This discussion focuses on the problems of studying drugs in rural areas by using research on commercial marijuana growers to illustrate several key points. In addition, the case of commercial marijuana growers can be used to suggest why rural drug problems receive such scant attention. Before that, however, it will be useful to briefly outline the nature of the commercial marijuana industry.

THE DOMESTIC MARIJUANA INDUSTRY

There is considerable evidence that domestic marijuana cultivation is widespread. In 1982, when the government first began keeping national records, it was estimated that U.S. domestic marijuana production was approximately 2,000 metric tons. By 1989, estimated production was 5,500 metric tons, a 175% increase (National Narcotics Intelligence Consumers Committee 1989). Similarly, the number of cultivated plants eradicated rose from 3,793,943 plants in 1983 to 7,328,769 plants in 1990 (Drug Enforcement

Administration 1990). In 1990 domestic marijuana was reported in every state, and the rise of indoor cultivation made it possible to grow year-round in any climate.

In 1986 the federal government estimated there were between 90,000 and 150,000 commercial marijuana growers in the United States, and over 1 million people who grew for personal use (cited in Gettman 1987). The National Organization for the Reform of Marijuana Laws (NORML) calculated the number of growers by combining crop production estimates with a projection of the amount that typical growers produce in a year (5 pounds for personal use growers and 13 pounds for commercial growers). Using this approach, NORML estimated there were approximately 250,000 commercial growers and over 2 million personal use growers (Gettman 1987).

By the late 1980s it was estimated that between 25% and 50% of the marijuana consumed in the United States was produced here (Slaughter 1988; Gettman 1987), and that the cash value of the domestic marijuana crop was as high as $60 billion a year, easily making it the largest cash crop in the United States (Weisheit 1992). The domestic marijuana industry may also be producing marijuana for export. In 1983 and 1984, for example, when the U.S. industry was just being recognized, it was estimated that 10% of Canada's marijuana supply came from the United States (Stamler, Fahlman, and Vigeant 1985).

Finally, the potency and value of domestic marijuana rose dramatically during the 1980s. THC (tetrahydrocannabinol), the active ingredient in marijuana, rose from 1.5% of purchased marijuana in 1970 to an average of 7% in 1989, with a high of 18.3% recorded for a 1986 sample. At the same time, the value of marijuana has risen sharply from $30 an ounce in the early 70s, to as much as $600 an ounce in 1990—with prices still rising. Thus domestic marijuana is becoming more potent over time and the economic incentives for growing have increased.

THE STUDY

Although these production estimates are useful starting points, they tell nothing about the kinds of people involved or the motivations for entering the business. To remedy this, a study was conducted in which 32 commercial marijuana growers from Illinois were interviewed, as were 20 Illinois officials, 13 officials from 5 other states, and over a dozen others from around the country who had some familiarity with marijuana growers. Important for this study is that marijuana cultivation is not simply more characteristic of rural areas, but is particularly concentrated in the rural Midwest. In 1990, 7 of the top 10 cultivation states were located in the midwest, including Illinois which ranked eighth (Drug Enforcement Administration 1990). Most interviews were face-to-face, although some officials and others familiar with growing were interviewed by telephone when time or distance precluded more personal contact. The focus of this discussion is on methodological issues. Details about the procedures and about the business of marijuana cultivation can be found elsewhere (Weisheit 1992, 1991a, 1991b).

WHY HAS THE INDUSTRY BEEN NEGLECTED?

Given its size and the increased attention of law enforcement, it may seem surprising that the domestic marijuana industry has received so little attention. During the course of this study three factors emerged that would account for this. These are (a) the rural setting in which marijuana growing takes place, (b) the nature of the marijuana industry, and (c) marijuana's place in the war on drugs. Although all three are important, the focus in this discussion is on the rural setting. The two remaining points are discussed elsewhere (Weisheit 1992).

Drugs in Rural Communities

Neglecting marijuana cultivation in rural areas cannot be explained solely as a result of the absence of drugs in rural communities. Surveys find that the rate of marijuana use in rural areas has rapidly approached that in urban areas. In addition, rural areas are increasingly used to produce synthetic drugs, such as methamphetamine (Baker et al. 1989; Weingarten 1989). Rural areas are also essential in the movement of imported drugs (e.g., heroin, cocaine) across the country (Weingarten and Coats 1989). Rural Kentucky, for example, is not only a major producer of marijuana, but has also been an important transshipment point for cocaine (Potter and Gaines 1990). And, just as drug-producing countries eventually develop problems with drug consumption (Inciardi 1986), rural transshipment points are also likely to develop problems associated with drug use. During interviews conducted for this study, for example, it was reported that some marijuana growers in Kentucky were using the profits from their operations to support cocaine habits.

A Question of Geography

The rural setting in which most large marijuana fields are found presents challenges regarding both geography and culture. Regarding geography, the media, special police drug units, and researchers are all more often centered in urban areas and have focused on drug issues in the urban environment. To urban observers of the drug scene, the domestic marijuana industry has been largely invisible.

The wide geographic dispersion of marijuana producers continues to limit research and media attention on the issue, and was a major limitation for law enforcement until the mid-1980s. Before then, marijuana detection and eradication was almost exclusively a local responsibility, usually headed by rural county sheriffs who are among the most underfunded and understaffed of law enforcement agencies. During the 1980s, the federal government became more involved in eradicating domestic marijuana. At the same time, there have been increased cooperative efforts across jurisdictions, such as the formation of task forces that include county sheriffs and the state police (Schlegel and McGarrell 1991). Despite the increased attention to rural drug enforcement, there are still comparatively more drug arrests in urban areas. Castellano and Uchida (1990) estimate the rate of drug arrests in urban areas is nearly four times that in rural counties. They also argue that because most drug enforcement is proactive, variations in arrest rates among jurisdictions are more the result of differences in enforcement efforts than of differences in consumption patterns.

For the media, rural drug cases are simply too scattered and are located in areas too remote for quick coverage. For researchers, the fact that marijuana cultivation cases are widely dispersed has meant that studying the problem is very labor intensive. In this study, for example, it was common for a single interview to require 2-3 hours of travel each way. By comparison the logistics of interviewing drug dealers and users in a single neighborhood or section of a city are simple.

Urban Ethnocentrism

Drugs in rural areas have also been ignored because of an urban bias among researchers, the media, and federal enforcement agencies. The urban bias in much social science research can be seen by walking through any library of a research university. Although there are hundreds of books on urban studies, there are relatively few on rural life and culture. Researchers who focus on rural environments have a smaller base of published research experiences from which to work.

Similarly, although a number of researchers have emphasized the role of poverty and urban decay as factors in urban drug trafficking, it has been all but ignored in rural areas. But poverty is not just an urban phenomenon. Weinberg (1987) has noted that "only 6 of 159 high-poverty counties in 1979 contained a city of 25,000 population" (p. 401). And, in 1986, the poverty rate in rural areas was 50% higher than in urban areas (Garkovich 1991). Despite this, the role of poverty in the development and spread of rural drug problems has never been addressed.

For the national media, an urban bias is partly a result of where stations are located, partly a result of the urban backgrounds of news personnel, and partly a result of "playing" to such large markets as New York, Chicago, and Los Angeles by taking urban problems and portraying them as national (Epstein 1973). This happened in the 1980s when the national media portrayed crack cocaine as a problem which had permeated "main street U.S.A." when in reality there was little evidence that it was widespread outside a few large urban areas, and did not penetrate rural areas until several years later. Conversely, rural drug problems are more likely to be seen as isolated problems of little national interest. Because marijuana cultivation is primarily rural, stories about it are more likely to be seen as curiosities that are primarily of local interest.

A similar attitude has been noted by Levin and Fox (1985) in the attention given serial killers. Ed Gein, for example, used the skin and body parts of his victims to make belts, household decorations, masks, and to upholster furniture. Despite the sensational and gruesome nature of the crime, his killings were given relatively little national attention. Levin and Fox suggest that because his crimes took place in the small town of Plainfield, Wisconsin they were little noted by the national press: "Outside of Wisconsin, few people had heard of Edward Gein . . . what happens in Plainfield is not nearly as important, at least to the national media, as what happens in a large city like Chicago or New York." (Levin and Fox 1985, p. 5). It would be a mistake, however, to attribute the neglect of rural drug issues to simple remoteness or low population density. Equally important is the culture of rural communities.

HOW RURAL CULTURE SHAPES THE RESEARCH PROCESS

Aside from geography and urban ethnocentrism, studies of drugs in rural areas must contend with rural culture. Rural culture affects the research process in several ways. First, rural communities are often closed to outsiders. Second, rural citizens may be particularly reluctant to tell outsiders about local deviants. Third, social interactions in rural areas may be less formal and legalistic. Finally, situations that have largely taken-for-granted definitions in urban areas may have very different meanings in rural areas.

Closed to Outsiders

An example of the self-imposed isolationism of rural areas is given in Kessler's description of the problems in establishing a legal services program in a rural community (Kessler 1990):

> The norms of cooperation, trust and courtesy shared by members of the local bar apply exclusively to attorneys with strong local roots. In general, the legal community is unreceptive to lawyers from outside the county using their local court. Further, members of the local legal community are suspicious of, if not openly hostile to, lawyers born and raised outside the county opening a practice within the county. The attitudes of the legal community to outsiders are illustrated in the comments of one veteran local attorney: "If you're part of the community, practicing law here can be great. But it's not particularly pleasant for out-of-county people. There's a very tight knit organization over here that doesn't particularly care for the outsider." (pp. 274-75)

Urban drug researchers may find it very difficult to penetrate and understand the rural culture in many parts of the United States. The current study provides an illustration of the problem of access. A local sheriff was reluctant to be interviewed about growers in his area, agreeing only after a state trooper with whom he had worked had recommended him. The sheriff began the interview by vaguely describing a large case and casually throwing out questions to "test" the researcher. For example: "The grower was a sorghum farmer—but being from the city you wouldn't know what that is. Would you?" As it turned out I grew up in a rural community and knew something of sorghum farming. Having passed his "test" by answering a series of similar questions, the tone of the interview changed to openness and cooperation. The interview lasted for several hours and was very informative. I left with the clear impression that his concern was that a stranger would be insensitive to local concerns and would paint an inaccurate (and unflattering) picture of the community. It was also my impression that a researcher with little knowledge of rural life would not have gotten very far in the interview, finding the sheriff polite but not very talkative.

In smaller communities strangers are not trusted. One grower was asked how difficult it would be to obtain the seeds and knowledge to get started in his community. He responded:

> Well, probably a little harder out here in the sticks than it would be in town—you know, in the city. Out here everybody knows everybody. You know if somebody like you showed up and started hanging out at the bar or something,

> and started asking people to sell you a bag of reefer, you'd soon get your ass trashed. That's what would happen.

In rural areas, outsiders are subject to particular scrutiny. Reservations about turning in local growers are not in play when the growers are clearly outsiders. One Minnesota case, for example, came to police attention because the new tenants of a local farm seemed to know nothing about farming and their behavior did not fit into that of the local area:

> "You could tell they weren't much as farmers. One of the first things they did was to plow under their best alfalfa. That was in late May, just after they moved in," said a neighbor. "We just kind of waited to see what they would do next."
>
> "They put up no trespassing signs—five of them right in a row that said 'Keep Out.' That's just not the way we do things up here," said another neighbor. (Karlson, 1987, p. 3)

Aside from preserving the community's good name, keeping things in is also a product of strong informal networks in rural areas. These informal networks mean that citizens are likely to know both the offender and the offender's family. Even if there is little sympathy for the offender, rural residents may be reluctant to discuss these cases with outsiders, out of concern for the feelings and reputation of the offender's family. Further, if the offender is even a distant relative, the citizens risk damage to their own reputations because of the considerable attention rural citizens pay to kinship networks.

Suspicion of Government

Although wary of outsiders in general, those in rural areas are often particularly suspicious of government agencies. Local government bodies are kept in check. For example, many of these rural communities actively reject such local government restrictions as zoning. Representatives of state and federal agencies are seen as too distant from the people to truly understand their problems, and unlikely to promote local interests.

One local sheriff spoke about serving on a state-wide commission, and of his experiences trying to communicate local problems to outsiders.

> I served on a commission. There were 22 people on this commission and it was aimed at the production of marijuana. I brought it up that we needed more conservation officers in this area, not only for marijuana but for deer poaching, because we have so many deer. There was no one on that commission but

> myself who was from southern Illinois. Everybody else was from Chicago and places far away. Their immediate solution was to buy two airplanes. I just sat there and laughed at them. You know, when you fly over my county what you see are the tops of about 10 million trees. You cannot find marijuana from the air in my county. They couldn't understand that, so I resigned. What they needed was more people on the ground. You have to have more people on the ground, that's all there is to it.

This same sheriff, whose office was chronically understaffed, was asked about using the DEA to assist in marijuana raids.

> I did call the feds in a couple of times. Then I quit. I have no confidence in them. In the first place, they are egomaniacs. They think they are really something on a stick. They come into an area like this, of which they know nothing. They don't know the history of it, the people, the terrain. They can mess up an investigation faster than you can shake a stick at it. I had two unfortunate experiences. One was with this 2½ million dollar patch we had. I could see it was quite an important thing; I mean we really needed to catch somebody. So I called in the DEA. You would have thought they were a SWAT team. They came in with all this fancy stuff. You can't imagine the equipment and stuff they had with them. I'm sure, just by the way they approached the plot, they scared the people off. And eventually, all we did was pull all the plants and burn them. I decided after that we would handle it ourselves, because we knew more about the territory than any of them did.

Similar concerns have been voiced by local sheriffs elsewhere. In California, for example, a contingent of 200 army soldiers, National Guardsmen, and federal agents spent 2 weeks clearing out growing operations in the King Range National Conservation Area in northern California. As a result of their efforts 1,200 plants were destroyed, but not everyone was satisfied.

> "This is so frustrating when the federal government comes in and spends enough money that would keep my operation going for three or four years," said Sheriff David Renner of Humboldt County. His team of five deputies, cooperating with the state's seven-year-old Campaign Against Marijuana Planting, destroyed over 3,000 plants in one day this week.
>
> "If the feds have the money for this kind of operation," Sheriff Renner said, "they ought to give it to local law enforcement that is more effective and is truly responsible to local citizens. Their results speak for themselves and they are not good." (Bishop 1990)

The belief that state and local governments are insensitive to local needs, along with a strong sense of autonomy that characterizes so many rural areas may explain why proponents of rural development warn against public policies dictated by a strong central government (Littrell and Littrell 1991; Seroka and Subramaniam 1991). Rural residents are generally less supportive than urban residents of government programs that provide welfare, housing, unemployment benefits, higher education, and Medicaid (Swanson, Cohen, and Swanson 1979).

However, hesitations to accept the help of state and local authorities should not be confused with a tolerance of crime. To the contrary, rural areas are often less tolerant of deviance (Wilson 1991). Paternoster (1983), for example, reports that rural prosecutors may be *more* likely to seek the death penalty. Further, when rural justice systems are more lenient, it is less a reflection of tolerance than of the simultaneous operation of *informal* sanctions (Feld 1991).

Keeping Things In

Rural areas are not only known for shutting others out, but for keeping things in. There is often a concern that the misbehavior of community members will give the community a bad name.

It was originally planned that community members would be interviewed about the effects of the arrest on the local area, and to determine the level of local sympathy for growers. This turned out to be extremely difficult. After repeated failed efforts, and a few disappointing interviews, the effort was stopped. These problems manifested themselves in several ways. In smaller communities, concern with community image was compounded by a hesitation to speak with outsiders and a concern that the grower or his family would be further embarrassed and hurt by any discussion of the case.

The caution shown by these residents is in many ways understandable. Even with assurances of confidentiality, residents and officials from these rural areas did not know the researcher personally and had no way of knowing that their comments would not come back to somehow damage the reputation of the community. On the positive side, difficulties in obtaining the cooperation of citizens illustrated the power of community in these areas and this, in turn, may have important implications for policies designed to regulate marijuana growing. Of course, a distrust of outsiders is not unique to rural communities, but seems especially pronounced there. Further, in rural areas where the pool of interview subjects is small from the start, the impact on research can be substantial.

Secrecy among growers was a common theme across the six states in the study. Although secrecy is an excellent means of self-defense against marijuana thieves and against information being leaked to the police, secrecy is also consistent with rural culture. Kentucky stands as an extreme example. The level of secrecy among growers in Kentucky was particularly strong when dealing with people outside of the local community. For example, at the time officials were interviewed, there had been indictments against 70 people linked to Kentucky's "cornbread mafia." Although each was facing 15 to 20 years in prison, none was willing to provide the names of others connected to the organization. In these cases all of the criminal investigations were conducted by state and federal police with little cooperation from local authorities. An official from another state observed:

> People in rural areas tend to be pretty conservative generally and don't want government coming in, or an outsider coming in, or foreigners coming in. They want the status quo and that's it. And when they develop a cancer from within they don't want it going out. They don't want people telling about it and they don't want people rocking the boat. They are the same people who will ostracize members of their society who get caught doing this [marijuana growing].

When cases were originally being located, six sheriffs reported having cases but were unwilling to provide names. And, although all agencies are supposed to report marijuana seizures to the State Police, at least 14 of the 74 cases originally identified through our searches were not in the State Police files. It appears they were handled locally without a report of the cases being forwarded to the state.

The secrecy that surrounds commercial marijuana growing, combined with the fact that it largely occurs in rural settings, means that some of the techniques used to study urban drug use and urban drug networks would be less useful for studying this group. For example, in their study of daily marijuana users, Hendin, Haas, Singer, Ellner, and Ulman (1987) located subjects by using newspaper advertisements. Such an approach would not be practical in sparsely populated rural settings in which growers are secretive, widely dispersed, and for whom anonymity would be harder to assure.

In addition to growers and law enforcement officials, the initial study had proposed short interviews with several citizens from each community in which a grower had been arrested. The intent was to supplement grower reports about community response, to determine how rural communities support or reject long-time members arrested for growing marijuana. This proved to be the most difficult task of the project and it was fortunate that the research did not hinge on successful interviews with community members. There were several problems in locating and interviewing community members. The most serious problem was the general unwillingness of citizens in rural communities to talk about the misfortune or misbehavior of fellow community members. In one community, frustration with finding citizens to interview led to a decision to first interview a police officer who was well known and respected in the community. More than 2 months of repeated efforts failed to produce an interview with the officer. He was willing to be interviewed about police procedure and technical details of the case, but was uncomfortable talking about the community response to the arrest and the way in which citizens changed their views of the offender following the arrest. Requests to the officer's supervisor generated a similar response. In another community, the local sheriff said a farmer had been arrested for growing marijuana in the county, but that he (the sheriff) and the local prosecutor had discussed the matter and decided they would not discuss the case, or even give the name of the farmer.

In still another instance a sheriff's deputy was asked about a case for which the researcher had only sketchy information. The deputy replied that his job would be in jeopardy if he discussed the case or even gave the names of the arrested growers, two established members of the community.

The reluctance of citizens to talk about the criminal activities of their rural neighbors is not unique to the study of marijuana growers. In his oral history of homicides in rural Kentucky, Montell (1986) describes the problems of getting citizens to talk about rural homicides, even as much as 60 years after the event. His work also illustrates the importance of informal networks for gaining entry to these groups.

The Informal Nature of Rural Life

Interactions in rural areas are less often formal and legalistic than in urban areas. For example, during the course of the study, several growers expressed annoyance at the manner in which they were arrested. This was particularly true when the arrest was conducted with a team of officers (often drawing in officers from the state police) in a conventional military-style rush of the house. These growers often knew the local sheriff (as did most people in the area) and could not understand why he did not simply call on the phone and ask them to turn themselves in. (There were several cases in which the sheriff did just that!) The complaint of these growers was *not* with the fact of their arrest, but with the formal manner in which it was done.

The best police officers knew the area and the people and were sensitive to this issue. One officer, who grew up in a rural area, illustrated this with an example:

> You can't act overly high and mighty with them, you won't get any cooperation. In the big cities, that's what you do, you come on strong, "I'm the boss." That's often a very effective method there, but not out here in the rural areas. . . . This summer I went down and there was a guy with maybe 200 plants spread out over a small farm. I was fairly confident it was there and I pull up in his driveway. He was unloading wood. I'm in the pickup truck, and obviously he knows who I am. I walked up and told him what I was doing there. I said, "I've come to get your marijuana and we're going to be doing an open field search. We're not going to be going through your barns or anything right now. You've got some marijuana out there and I've just come up here to tell you what I'm doing." I helped him unload his wood and then I said, "I'm going down by the pond and look at this marijuana. I'll be back in a minute." I went down, looked at it and came back up. I said, "Well, your marijuana is down there," and then I went ahead and helped him unload some more wood and talked about it. He went to jail with no problem. I think this was the kind of guy who would have liked to have fought you. But because of the way I handled it, he wasn't going to fight anybody. Because, I didn't go in there and say, "You're a marijuana grower and you're worthless." A lot of times if you're dealing with people in these rural areas, they don't have a problem with you coming in and arresting them. They just want to be treated like human beings.

What the officer accepted as a perfectly natural response was a good illustration of community policing, to which so many urban departments now aspire. The example also illustrates how effective community policing is much more than simply implementing foot patrol or other strategies that increase the visibility of police. For researchers, treating subjects with respect and gaining entrance to the research setting through informal channels is important for any type of field research on deviance, but for studying illegal behavior in rural areas it is essential.

The relatively informal nature of interactions in rural areas is also reflected in a stronger system of informal social control. Several studies have found that the justice system in rural areas is less bureaucratic than in urban areas. Austin (1981a), for example, found that social background factors were more important in rural criminal courts, whereas urban courts were more legalistic and formal. In his analysis of juvenile justice in Minnesota, Feld (1991, pp. 206-7) observed:

> Urban courts operate in communities with more disrupted families, more racially heterogeneous populations and less residential stability, all of which provide fewer mechanisms for informal social control. . . . Accordingly, urban counties place greater emphasis on formal, rather than informal, mechanisms of social control.

In the current study, informal social control was reflected in interviews in which arrested growers were asked to name the worst consequence of their arrest. For many growers, the toughest part of their arrest and punishment was not their fine or imprisonment, but the damage to their reputation and the shame brought to their families:

> Being put down for a federal conviction really puts you down into a deep hole. I've had to scratch, and claw, and dig, and try to repair what's left of the family name. And it's made me a lot hungrier for success than before my conviction. So, I have to prove to all these people that I'm not a piece-of-dirt-lowlife, I am a good person, good man, and an excellent manager. And as soon as I get up to success, then I'd have proved them wrong.

> Probably the publicity and the personal effect of it; it still hangs over my head. I'm getting over the money part of it; I mean, everybody gets over the money. For a while I wouldn't even go to town because I just didn't even want to be in town, people looking at you and staring at you. I don't like for people to think that I'm a criminal. For a long time, I wouldn't even go into the local IGA store, it's that type of community. If they were to go to New York and see the homeless people and these kids 12 years old doing crack and people shooting at another one, why they wouldn't believe it. So I just figured, well, I'll just have to go with the flow. So I'm a criminal, and they'll just have to think whatever they think. But it took me a while to get used to that pattern of people thinking you're that bad.

> The fact that I had a good reputation; I worked all my life for this reputation and my standing in the community, and then to just be laughed at. And, I am so disappointed at our legal system; it is such a joke.

> Probably the things that the prosecutor said bothered me. . . . The courtroom was full that day, and a lot of people from our neighborhood were there, a lot of people from the town were there. . . . It was the first time that anybody had ever said things like that. There's one person standing up there in front of everybody saying all that bad stuff about you . . . well, that hurt.

Despite the embarrassment, few had moved from their communities or planned to in the future. Many emphasized the importance of working hard to reestablish their good name.

> Well, letting down my friends has probably been the worst. But financially it's been the most devastating in that area. It about wrecks your business. In a big city, it probably wouldn't have made a difference. But in a small town, with professional people where you deal one on one with the same people all the

> time, it has a big effect. A lot of people say, "You should move out of here, this is a Peyton Place, and people will never forget." That's my goal; I may move away eventually, but I'm bound and determined to get my reputation back.

This informal control raised problems with setting up interviews with members of the grower's community. Several growers, particularly those with no prior arrests, were concerned that community interviews would rekindle public animosity and compel them to relive the public embarrassment of their arrest. Considering the reluctance of citizens to cooperate and the potential harm to growers who had agreed to take part in the study, it was decided to give citizen interviews a low priority.

The Role of Guns

The rural environment in which marijuana growing takes place also compels the researcher to rethink definitions that are taken for granted in urban areas. Perhaps the clearest example of this is the possession of weapons by marijuana growers. In urban settings (and in the law), the presence of weapons is synonymous with violence or violent intentions.

In the present study there was simultaneously an absence of violence and a presence of weapons, and this can partly be accounted for by the rural setting in which growing takes place. It is the issue of weapons where the definition of violence used by the law and that used by growers differed. In urban areas, firearms are carried with one main target in mind, other people. Of the growers who did not have guns in their houses at the time of the arrest, most lived in larger communities. In rural areas, however, guns have a very different meaning and a variety of other applications. They are commonly carried when traveling in remote areas for the purpose of shooting varmints, hunting, and general target practice. State and federal laws regarding carrying firearms during the commission of a crime (such as cultivating marijuana) are generally based on an urban definition of the function of personal weapons. Growers who carried weapons into the field for sport sometimes faced additional weapons charges, and everyone with felony charges faced the loss of their firearm registration cards after their conviction.

> Q: You said you had a gun just for sport?
> A: We would always go out and shoot by the creek [near the patch]. We had a couple of cows down there, and some hogs.
> Q: So you weren't carrying the gun for self-defense?
> A: No. They asked me that too. I said, "Hell, I spent a year in Vietnam. I carried an M16 and a grenade launcher there. Why would I carry a 25 automatic pistol

> in a tight pair of jeans if I was going to protect myself? I would have carried it in my hand." So, they don't use common sense.

Several growers lamented that their arrest forced them to give up hunting rifles they had used for sport. Despite their fondness of guns for recreational purposes, some growers tried to avoid trouble by making certain they were unarmed when they tended their crops. Others made it clear that the possibility of violence gave them pause about their growing activities.

> Q: Were you concerned about the possibility of violence from people who would steal your crop or from the police?
> A: No. Because we never carried weapons when we went down there.
> Q: You didn't feel the need to protect yourself?
> A: No. It wasn't worth it. I mean it was worth a lot of money but it wasn't worth shooting somebody over it.

> Yeah, I was [concerned], because the guy on that farm had an old junk car parked there. He said if anybody tried to rip him off, he'd take that car and he'd crash their cars. That's all he had it for, like a demolition car. If anybody came in there, and I was worried about somebody getting hurt, and I think he had a firearm, too, cause I saw him out shooting something one time. That I didn't go for, that's one of the reasons why I got out of it [commercial growing].

Overall, there was little evidence of violence in the cases examined for this study, or that guns were owned with the intention of using them against people. There was no indication that people prone to violence were drawn to marijuana growing. To the contrary there was a striking absence of violence considering the dollar amounts involved and the ease with which violence could have been adopted. Not all growers were concerned with violence, but such feelings were common. Most importantly, owning weapons in rural areas has a very different meaning from owning them in urban settings, particularly when the weapons are hunting rifles and small bore pistols.

None of the preceding discussion is to suggest that rural culture is a completely homogeneous entity. What has been presented is a caricature of rural culture and its effects on the research process. Of course, there are wide variations in rural culture, as there are in urban cultures. In the course of the study it was clear that some of the features of rural culture described here were more pronounced in some portions of the state than others, and that some interstate variations existed. Southern Illinois is closer to the pure case of rural culture than is central or northern Illinois. Not surprisingly, then, the researcher found access to interview subjects much more difficult in the south. For example, when comparing interviewed growers with those who refused, the two groups were similar in a variety of ways (age, sex, number of plants seized, and disposition of case). Consenters and refusers differed, however, by region of the state. In the southern part of the state, refusals outnumbered consents by two to one, and in the remainder of the state consents outnumbered refusals by two to one. To acknowledge variations in rural culture, however, is not to deny that it is distinct when juxtaposed against that of urban areas.

DISCUSSION

The study of drugs in rural areas has important theoretical and practical applications. At a theoretical level, a study of variation is the essence of social science research. A fuller understanding of the differences between urban and rural drug cultures is an important step toward understanding the drug problem more generally. The issue is not simply one of rural-urban differences, but of a general lack of sensitivity to local cultures (Weisheit, Klofas, and Wells 1992). Just as rural-urban differences have been ignored, so have differences *among* urban areas. For example, Drug Use Forecasting (DUF) data from over 22 U.S. cities report on the percentage of recent arrestees who test positive for drugs. Although overall over half of arrestees test positive, the range is substantial. In 1990, for example, the percentages ranged from 75% drug positive in Manhattan, New York, to only 23% positive in Omaha, Nebraska (National Institute of Justice 1991). Similarly, variability has been observed for crack cocaine arrests. Crack was being widely reported in New York City as early as 1986, and by 1988 the city was reporting as many as 3,200 arrests per month for crack cocaine (Belenko 1990; Inciardi 1992). In contrast, crack did not take hold in Chicago until much later. In fact, in 1989, crack cocaine made up only 1% of drug arrests in Chicago and was so rare that many police officers did not know what it looked like (Blau 1990).

These wide variations should be the foundation for research, but they are not, often dismissed as simple random error. This is not, however, merely an artifact of sampling or of the methodology used—indeed the ethnographic studies of urban drug dealing should be ideally suited for making comparisons of contexts. The failure is not in the methodology employed, but in the failure to think in terms of variability. Too often the focus of contemporary research is on generalizability and on the use of averages which, by their nature, factor out variability.

At a practical level, the study of drugs in rural areas is important for four reasons. First, a substantial number of people live in rural areas. Second, rural areas are important transshipment points for drugs moving across the country. Third, rural areas have played a larger and larger role in the production of synthetic drugs and marijuana. Finally, by ignoring drugs in rural areas, rural communities have been ill prepared to deal with the fallout from drugs. Rural areas, for example, have been much slower in responding to the problem of AIDS (Navarro 1992).

Because so little ethnographic research has been done on rural deviance, this discussion can only outline the issues in broad terms. It is clear, however, that rural and urban cultures differ in a variety of ways that have important implications for ethnographic research.

REFERENCES

Austin, Thomas L. 1981a. "The Influence of Court Location on Type of Criminal Sentence: The Rural-Urban Factor." *Journal of Criminal Justice* 9:305-16.

———. 1981b. "Criminal Sentencing in Urban, Suburban, and Rural Counties." *Criminal Justice Review* 6:31-37.

Baker, James N., Patricia King, Andrew Nurr, and Nonny Abbott. 1989. "The Newest Drug War: In Rural America, Crack and 'Crank' Are Now Hot Commodities in the Backwoods." *Newsweek*, April 3, pp. 20-22.

Belenko, Steven. 1990. "The Impact of Drug Offenders on the Criminal Justice System." In *Drugs, Crime and the Criminal Justice System*, edited by Ralph A. Weisheit. Cincinnati, OH: Anderson.

Belyea, Michale J. and Matthew T. Zingraff. 1988. "Fear of Crime and Residential Location." *Rural Sociology* 53:473-86.

Bishop, K. 1990. "Military Takes Part in Drug Sweep and Reaps Criticism and a Lawsuit." *New York Times*, August 10, p. A11.

Blau, Robert. 1990. "Crack Starts to Gain Chicago Foothold." *Chicago Tribune*, pp. 20, 23.

Castellano, Thomas C. and Craig D. Uchida. 1990. "Local Drug Enforcement, Prosecutors and Case Attrition: Theoretical Perspectives for the Drug War." *American Journal of Police* 9: 133-62.

Drug Enforcement Administration. 1990. *1990 Domestic Cannabis Eradication/Suppression Program*. Washington, DC: U.S. Government Printing Office.

Epstein, Edward J. 1973. *News From Nowhere: Television and the News*. New York: Vintage Books.

Faupel, Charles E. 1991. *Shooting Dope: Career Patterns of Hard-Core Heroin Users*. Gainesville: University of Florida Press.

Feld, Barry C. 1991. "Justice by Geography: Urban, Suburban, and Rural Variations in Juvenile Justice Administration." *Journal of Criminal Law and Criminology* 82:156-210.

Garkovich, Lorraine. 1991. "Governing the Countryside: Linking Politics and Administrative Resources." In *The Future of Rural America: Anticipating Policies for Constructive Change*, edited by Kenneth E. Pigg. Boulder, CO: Westview.

Gettman, Jon B. 1987. *Marijuana in America—1986*. Washington, DC: National Organization for the Reform of Marijuana Laws.

Golden, Kathryn. 1981. "Rural Courts: An Illinois Study." *Criminal Justice Review* 6:38-42.

Hagan, John. 1977. "Criminal Justice in Rural and Urban Communities: A Study of the Bureaucratization of Justice." *Social Forces* 55:597-612.

Harper, Douglas. 1991. "On 'Methodological Monism' in Rural Sociology." *Rural Sociology* 56:70-88.

Hendin, H., A. P. Haas, P. Singer, M. Ellner, and R. Ulman. 1987. *Living High: Daily Marijuana Use Among Adults*. New York: Human Sciences Press.

Inciardi, James A. 1986. *The War on Drugs: Heroin, Cocaine, Crime, and Public Policy*. Palo Alto, CA: Mayfield.

———. 1992. *The War on Drugs II*. Palo Alto, CA: Mayfield.

Karlson, Karl. 1987. "Strangers Were Too Strange: New Neighbors' Odd Habits Lead to Huge Drug Bust." *The Chicago Tribune*, October 28, p. 3.

Kessler, M. 1990. "Expanding Legal Services Programs to Rural America: A Case Study of Program Creation and Operations." *Judicature* 73:273-80.

Kowalski, Gregory S. and Don Duffield. 1990. "The Impact of the Rural Population Component on Homicide Rates in the United States: A County-Level Analysis." *Rural Sociology* 55:76-90.

Laub, John H. 1983a. "Patterns of Offending in Urban and Rural Areas." *Journal of Criminal Justice* 11:129-42.

———. 1983b. "Urbanism, Race, and Crime." *Journal of Research in Crime and Delinquency* 20:183-98.

Levin, Jack and James Alan Fox. 1985. *Mass Murder: America's Growing Menace*. New York: Plenum.

Littrell, Donald W. and Doris P. Littrell. 1991. "Civic Education, Rural Development, and the Land Grant Institutions." In *The Future of Rural America: Anticipating Policies for Constructive Change*, edited by Kenneth E. Pigg. Boulder, CO: Westview.

Montell, W. L. 1986. *Killings: Folk Justice in the Upper South*. Lexington: University of Kentucky Press.

Myers, Martha A. and Susette M. Talarico. 1986. "Urban Justice, Rural Injustice: Urbanization and Its Effect on Sentencing." *Criminology* 24:367-91.

National Institute of Justice. 1991. *DUF, Drug Use Forecasting, Fourth Quarter, 1990*. Washington, DC: U.S. Department of Justice.

National Narcotics Intelligence Consumers Committee. 1989. *The NNICC Report 1989: The Supply of Illicit Drugs to the United States From Foreign and Domestic Sources in 1989*.

Navarro, Mireya. 1992. "Outside Urban Centers, AIDS is Still a Stranger." *New York Times*, February 25, p. B12.

Paternoster, Raymond. 1983. "Race of Victim and Location of Crime: The Decision to Seek the Death Penalty in South Carolina." *Journal of Criminal Law and Criminology* 74:754-85.

Potter, Gary and Larry Gaines. 1990. "Organizing Crime in 'Copperhead County': An Ethnographic Look at Rural Crime Networks." Paper presented at the meeting of the Southern Sociological Association, Louisville, Kentucky.

Schlegel, Kip and Edmund McGarrell. 1991. "An Examination of Arrest Practices in Regions Served by Multijurisdictional Drug Task Forces." *Crime & Delinquency* 37:408-26.

Seroka, Jim and Seshan Subramaniam. 1991. "Governing the Countryside: Linking Politics and Administrative Resources." In *The Future of Rural America: Anticipating Policies for Constructive Change*, edited by Kenneth E. Pigg. Boulder, CO: Westview.

Slaughter, John B. 1988. "Marijuana Prohibition in the United States: History and Analysis of a Failed Policy." *Columbia Journal of Law and Social Problems* 51:417-74.

Smith, Brent L. and C. Ronald Huff. 1982. "Crime in the Country: The Vulnerability and Victimization of Rural Citizens." *Journal of Criminal Justice* 10:271-82.

Stamler, R. T., R. C. Fahlman, and H. Vigeant. 1985. "Illicit Traffic and Abuse of Cannabis in Canada." *Bulletin on Narcotics* 37:37-49.

Swanson, Bert E., Richard A. Cohen, and Edith P. Swanson. 1979. *Small Towns and Small Towners: A Framework for Survival and Growth.* Beverly Hills, CA: Sage.

Weinberg, D. 1987. "Rural Pockets of Poverty." *Rural Sociology* 52:398-408.

Weingarten, Paul. 1989. "Profits, Perils Higher for Today's Bootleggers." *The Chicago Tribune*, September 14, pp. 1, 8.

Weingarten, Paul and James Coates. 1989. "Drugs Blaze New Paths: Interstates, Backroads Join Courier System." *The Chicago Tribune*, September 12, pp. 1, 8.

Weisheit, Ralph A. 1991a. "Drug Use Among Domestic Marijuana Growers." *Contemporary Drug Problems* 18:191-217.

———. 1991b. "The Intangible Rewards From Crime: The Case of Domestic Marijuana Growers." *Crime & Delinquency* 37:506-27.

———. 1992. *Domestic Marijuana: A Neglected Industry.* Westport, CT: Greenwood.

Weisheit, Ralph A., John M. Klofas, and L. Edward Wells. 1992. "Studying Criminal Justice in Context: The Theoretical and Methodological Implications of Local Variation." Paper presented at the meeting of the American Society of Criminology, New Orleans, LA, November.

Wilson, Thomas C. 1991. "Urbanism, Migration, and Tolerance: A Reassessment." *American Sociological Review* 56:117-23.

Acknowledgments

Beckett, Katherine. "Setting the Public Agenda: 'Street Crime' and Drug Use in American Politics." *Social Problems* 41 (1994): 425–47. Reprinted with the permission of the University of California Press. Copyright (1994) by the Society for the Study of Social Problems.

Clear, Todd R., Val B. Clear, and Anthony A. Braga. "Correctional Alternatives for Drug Offenders in an Era of Overcrowding." *Prison Journal* 73 (1993): 178–98. Reprinted with the permission of Sage Publications Inc.

Dunlap, Eloise and Bruce D. Johnson. "The Setting for the Crack Era: Macro Forces, Micro Consequences (1960–1992)." *Journal of Psychoactive Drugs* 24 (1992): 307–21. Reprinted with the permission of Haight-Asbury Publications.

Ernett, Susan T., Nancy S. Tobler, Christopher L. Ringwalt, and Robert L. Flewelling. "How Effective Is Drug Abuse Resistance Education? A Meta-Analysis of Project DARE Outcome Evaluations." *American Journal of Public Health* 84 (1994): 1394–1401. Reprinted with the permission of the American Public Health Association.

Falkin, Gregory P., Michael Prendergast, and M. Douglas Anglin. "Drug Treatment in the Criminal Justice System." *Federal Probation* 58 (1994): 31–36. Reprinted with the permission of the Administrative Office of the U.S. Courts.

Fendrich, Michael and Yanchun Xu. "The Validity of Drug Use Reports from Juvenile Arrestees." *International Journal of the Addictions* 29 (1994): 971–85. Reprinted with the permission of Marcel Dekker, Inc.

Filippone, Robert. "The Medellin Cartel: Why We Can't Win the Drug War." *Studies in Conflict and Terrorism* 17 (1994): 323–44. Reprinted with the permission of Taylor and Francis.

Halsted, James B. "The Anti-Drug Policies of the 1980s: Have They Increased the Likelihood for Both Wrongful Convictions and Sentencing Disparities?" *Criminal Justice Policy Review* 6 (1992): 207–28. Reprinted with the permission of the Indiana University of Pennsylvania.

Inciardi, James A., Duane C. McBride, H. Virginia McCoy, and Dale D. Chitwood. "Recent Research on the Crack/Cocaine/Crime Connection." *Studies on Crime and Crime Prevention* 3 (1994): 63–82. Reprinted with the permission of Scandinavian University Press.

Jenkins, Philip. "'The Ice Age' The Social Construction of a Drug Panic." *Justice Quarterly* 11 (1994): 7–31. Reprinted with the permission of the Academy of Criminal Justice Sciences.

Kleinman, Mark A.R. "Neither Prohibition Nor Legalization: Grudging Toleration in Drug Control Policy." *Daedalus* 121, No. 3 *Political Pharmacology: Thinking About Drugs* (1992): 53–83. Reprinted by permission of *Daedalus*, Journal of the American Academy of Arts and Sciences.

Levine, Michael. "I Volunteer to Kidnap Oliver North." *Crime, Law and Social Change* 20 (1993): 1–12. Reprinted with the permission of Kluwer Academic Publishers.

McBride, Duane C. and Clyde B. McCoy. "The Drugs-Crime Relationship: An Analytical Framework." *Prison Journal* 73 (1993): 257–78. Reprinted with the permission of Sage Publications Inc.

Miller, J. Mitchell and Lance H. Selva. "Drug Enforcement's Double-Edged Sword: An Assessment of Asset Forfeiture Programs." *Justice Quarterly* 11 (1994): 313–35. Reprinted with the permission of the Academy of Criminal Justice Sciences.

Nadelmann, Ethan A. "Thinking Seriously About Alternatives to Drug Prohibition." *Daedalus* 121, No. 3 *Political Pharmacology: Thinking About Drugs* (1992): 85–132. Reprinted by permission of *Daedalus*, Journal of the American Academy of Arts and Sciences.

Fagan, Jeffrey. "Women and Drugs Revisited: Female Participation in the Cocaine Economy." *Journal of Drug Issues* 24 (1994): 179–226. Reprinted with the permission of Journal of Drug Issues, Inc.

Reuter, Peter. "Hawks Ascendant: The Punitive Trend of American Drug Policy." *Daedalus* 121, No. 3 *Political Pharmacology: Thinking About Drugs* (1992): 15–52. Reprinted by permission of *Daedalus*, Journal of the American Academy of Arts and Sciences.

Waldorf, Dan. "Don't Be Your Own Best Customer—Drug Use of San Francisco Gang Drug Sellers." *Crime, Law and Social Change* 19 (1993): 1–15. Reprinted with the permission of Kluwer Academic Publishers.

Weisheit, Ralph A. "Studying Drugs in Rural Areas: Notes from the Field." *Journal of Research in Crime and Delinquency* 30 (1993): 213–32. Reprinted with the permission of Sage Publications Inc.